Loss Models
From Data to Decisions
Second Edition

Loss Models
From Data to Decisions
Second Edition

Stuart A. Klugman
Drake University

Harry H. Panjer
University of Waterloo

Gordon E. Willmot
University of Waterloo

A JOHN WILEY & SONS, INC., PUBLICATION

For general information on our other products and services please contact our Customer Care Department within the U.S. at 877-762-2974, outside the U.S. at 317-572-3993 or fax 317-572-4002.

Wiley also publishes its books in a variety of electronic formats. Some content that appears in print, however, may not be available in electronic format.

Library of Congress Cataloging-in-Publication Data:

Klugman, Stuart A., 1949–
    Loss models : from data to decisions / Stuart A. Klugman, Harry H. Panjer, Gordon E. Willmot.—2nd ed.
      p. cm.
    Includes bibliographical references and index.
    ISBN 0-471-21577-5 (cloth)
      1. Insurance—Statistical methods.   2.Insurance—Mathematical models.   I. Panjer, Harry H., 1946–. II. Willmot, Gordon E., 1957–. III. Title.

HG8781.K583 2004
368'.01—dc22   2004048066

Printed in the United States of America.

10 9 8 7 6 5

Contents

Preface   *xvii*

Acknowledgments   *xxi*

Part I   Introduction

1   Modeling   *3*
    1.1   The model-based approach   *3*
       1.1.1   The modeling process   *3*
       1.1.2   The modeling advantage   *5*
    1.2   Organization of this book   *6*

Part II   Actuarial models

2   Random variables   *11*
    2.1   Introduction   *11*
    2.2   Key functions and four models   *13*
       2.2.1   Exercises   *23*

3 Basic distributional quantities   25
   3.1 Moments   25
        3.1.1 Exercises   33
   3.2 Percentiles   34
        3.2.1 Exercises   35
   3.3 Generating functions and sums of random
        variables   36
        3.3.1 Exercises   37

4 Classifying and creating distributions   39
   4.1 Introduction   39
   4.2 The role of parameters   40
        4.2.1 Parametric and scale distributions   41
        4.2.2 Parametric distribution families   42
        4.2.3 Finite mixture distributions   43
        4.2.4 Data-dependent distributions   45
        4.2.5 Exercises   46
   4.3 Tail weight   48
        4.3.1 Existence of moments   48
        4.3.2 Limiting ratios   50
        4.3.3 Hazard rate and mean residual life
               patterns   50
        4.3.4 Exercises   54
   4.4 Creating new distributions   56
        4.4.1 Introduction   56
        4.4.2 Multiplication by a constant   56
        4.4.3 Raising to a power   57
        4.4.4 Exponentiation   58
        4.4.5 Mixing   59
        4.4.6 Frailty models   62
        4.4.7 Splicing   64
        4.4.8 Exercises   65
   4.5 Selected distributions and their relationships   69
        4.5.1 Introduction   69
        4.5.2 Two parametric families   69
        4.5.3 Limiting distributions   70
        4.5.4 Exercises   72
   4.6 Discrete distributions   72
        4.6.1 Introduction   72

4.6.2   The Poisson distribution   73
4.6.3   The negative binomial distribution   76
4.6.4   The binomial distribution   79
4.6.5   The $(a, b, 0)$ class   81
4.6.6   Truncation and modification at zero   83
4.6.7   Compound frequency models   88
4.6.8   Further properties of the compound
         Poisson class   95
4.6.9   Mixed frequency models   101
4.6.10   Poisson mixtures   103
4.6.11   Effect of exposure on frequency   108
4.6.12   An inventory of discrete distributions   109
4.6.13   Exercises   109

5   Frequency and severity with coverage modifications   115
    5.1   Introduction   115
    5.2   Deductibles   115
          5.2.1   Exercises   120
    5.3   The loss elimination ratio and the effect of
          inflation for ordinary deductibles   121
          5.3.1   Exercises   123
    5.4   Policy limits   124
          5.4.1   Exercises   126
    5.5   Coinsurance, deductibles, and limits   126
          5.5.1   Exercises   128
    5.6   The impact of deductibles on claim frequency   129
          5.6.1   Exercises   133

6   Aggregate loss models   135
    6.1   Introduction   135
          6.1.1   Exercise   138
    6.2   Model choices   139
          6.2.1   Exercises   140
    6.3   The compound model for aggregate claims   140
          6.3.1   Exercises   148
    6.4   Analytic results   153
          6.4.1   Exercises   156
    6.5   Computing the aggregate claims distribution   159

6.6   The recursive method   161
   6.6.1   Applications to compound frequency
       models   162
   6.6.2   Underflow/overflow problems   165
   6.6.3   Numerical stability   166
   6.6.4   Continuous severity   166
   6.6.5   Constructing arithmetic distributions   167
   6.6.6   Exercises   170
6.7   The impact of individual policy modifications on
   aggregate payments   174
   6.7.1   Exercises   177
6.8   Calculations with approximate distributions   178
   6.8.1   Arithmetic distributions   178
   6.8.2   Empirical distributions   181
   6.8.3   Piecewise linear cdf   182
   6.8.4   Exercises   184
6.9   Inversion methods   184
   6.9.1   Fast Fourier transform   185
   6.9.2   Direct numerical inversion   188
   6.9.3   Exercise   190
6.10   Comparison of methods   190
6.11   The individual risk model   192
   6.11.1   Parametric approximation   192
   6.11.2   Exact calculation of the aggregate
       distribution   195
   6.11.3   Compound Poisson approximation   201
   6.11.4   Exercises   205

7   Discrete-time ruin models   209
7.1   Introduction   209
7.2   Process models for insurance   210
   7.2.1   Processes   210
   7.2.2   An insurance model   212
   7.2.3   Ruin   213
7.3   Discrete, finite-time ruin probabilities   215
   7.3.1   The discrete-time process   215
   7.3.2   Evaluating the probability of ruin   216
   7.3.3   Exercises   222

8   *Continuous-time ruin models*   *223*

   8.1   *Introduction*   *223*

      8.1.1   *The Poisson process*   *223*

      8.1.2   *The continuous-time problem*   *225*

   8.2   *The adjustment coefficient and Lundberg's*
      inequality   *225*

      8.2.1   *The adjustment coefficient*   *226*

      8.2.2   *Lundberg's inequality*   *230*

      8.2.3   *Exercises*   *232*

   8.3   *An integrodifferential equation*   *234*

      8.3.1   *Exercises*   *239*

   8.4   *The maximum aggregate loss*   *239*

      8.4.1   *Exercises*   *242*

   8.5   *Cramer's asymptotic ruin formula and Tijms'*
      approximation   *244*

      8.5.1   *Exercises*   *250*

   8.6   *The Brownian motion risk process*   *252*

   8.7   *Brownian motion and the probability of ruin*   *256*

Part III   Construction of empirical models

9   *Review of mathematical statistics*   *265*

   9.1   *Introduction*   *265*

   9.2   *Point estimation*   *266*

      9.2.1   *Introduction*   *266*

      9.2.2   *Measures of quality*   *267*

      9.2.3   *Exercises*   *273*

   9.3   *Interval estimation*   *275*

      9.3.1   *Exercise*   *277*

   9.4   *Tests of hypotheses*   *277*

      9.4.1   *Exercise*   *281*

10 *Estimation for complete data*   *283*

   10.1   *Introduction*   *283*

   10.2   *The empirical distribution for complete,*
      individual data   *288*

      10.2.1   *Exercises*   *291*

10.3 Empirical distributions for grouped data   292
      10.3.1 Exercises   295

11 Estimation for modified data   297
   11.1 Point estimation   297
         11.1.1 Exercises   304
   11.2 Means, variances, and interval estimation   305
         11.2.1 Exercises   315
   11.3 Kernel density models   316
         11.3.1 Exercises   321
   11.4 Approximations for large data sets   322
         11.4.1 Introduction   322
         11.4.2 Kaplan–Meier type approximations   323
         11.4.3 Multiple-decrement tables   324
         11.4.4 Exercises   325

Part IV   Parametric statistical methods

12 Parameter estimation   331
   12.1 Method of moments and percentile matching   331
         12.1.1 Exercises   335
   12.2 Maximum likelihood estimation   337
         12.2.1 Introduction   337
         12.2.2 Complete, individual data   340
         12.2.3 Complete, grouped data   341
         12.2.4 Truncated or censored data   341
         12.2.5 Exercises   345
   12.3 Variance and interval estimation   351
         12.3.1 Exercises   358
   12.4 Bayesian estimation   360
         12.4.1 Definitions and Bayes' theorem   360
         12.4.2 Inference and prediction   364
         12.4.3 Conjugate prior distributions and the
                 linear exponential family   371
         12.4.4 Computational issues   374
         12.4.5 Exercises   377
   12.5 Estimation for discrete distributions   383
         12.5.1 Poisson   383

12.5.2 Negative binomial 386

12.5.3 Binomial 389

12.5.4 The $(a, b, 1)$ class 392

12.5.5 Compound models 396

12.5.6 Effect of exposure on maximum likelihood estimation 398

12.5.7 Exercises 399

12.6 Bivariate models 402

12.6.1 Introduction 402

12.6.2 Copulas 403

12.6.3 Exercise 405

12.7 Models with covariates 405

12.7.1 Introduction 405

12.7.2 Proportional hazards models 407

12.7.3 The generalized linear and accelerated failure time models 413

12.7.4 Exercises 416

13 Model selection 419

13.1 Introduction 419

13.2 Representations of the data and model 420

13.3 Graphical comparison of the density and distribution functions 421

13.3.1 Exercises 426

13.4 Hypothesis tests 427

13.4.1 Kolmogorov–Smirnov test 428

13.4.2 Anderson–Darling test 430

13.4.3 Chi-square goodness-of-fit test 432

13.4.4 Likelihood ratio test 436

13.4.5 Exercises 438

13.5 Selecting a model 440

13.5.1 Introduction 440

13.5.2 Judgment-based approaches 441

13.5.3 Score-based approaches 442

13.5.4 Exercises 449

14 Five examples 455

14.1 Introduction 455

14.2 Time to death 455

14.2.1 The data   455
14.2.2 Some calculations   457
14.2.3 Exercise   459
14.3 Time from incidence to report   459
14.3.1 The problem and some data   460
14.3.2 Analysis   460
14.4 Payment amount   461
14.4.1 The data   462
14.4.2 The first model   463
14.4.3 The second model   465
14.5 An aggregate loss example   466
14.6 Another aggregate loss example   471
14.6.1 Distribution for a single policy   471
14.6.2 One hundred policies—excess of loss   471
14.6.3 One hundred policies—aggregate stop-loss   473
14.6.4 Numerical convolutions   474
14.7 Comprehensive exercises   476

Part V   Adjusted estimates and simulation

15 Interpolation and smoothing   483
15.1 Introduction   483
15.2 Polynomial interpolation and smoothing   485
15.2.1 Exercises   488
15.3 Cubic spline interpolation   489
15.3.1 Construction of cubic splines   491
15.3.2 Exercises   499
15.4 Approximating functions with splines   500
15.4.1 Exercise   504
15.5 Extrapolating with splines   504
15.5.1 Exercise   505
15.6 Smoothing splines   505
15.6.1 Exercise   514

16 Credibility   515
16.1 Introduction   515
16.2 Statistical concepts   517

16.2.1 Conditional distributions 518
16.2.2 Conditional expectation 520
16.2.3 Nonparametric unbiased estimators 523
16.2.4 Exercises 529
16.3 Limited fluctuation credibility theory 530
16.3.1 Full credibility 532
16.3.2 Partial credibility 535
16.3.3 Problems with the approach 539
16.3.4 Notes and References 539
16.3.5 Exercises 539
16.4 Greatest accuracy credibility theory 542
16.4.1 Introduction 542
16.4.2 The Bayesian methodology 545
16.4.3 The credibility premium 553
16.4.4 The Buhlmann model 557
16.4.5 The Buhlmann–Straub model 560
16.4.6 Exact credibility 566
16.4.7 Linear versus Bayesian versus no
credibility 569
16.4.8 Notes and References 577
16.4.9 Exercises 578
16.5 Empirical Bayes parameter estimation 589
16.5.1 Nonparametric estimation 592
16.5.2 Semiparametric estimation 600
16.5.3 Parametric estimation 602
16.5.4 Notes and References 607
16.5.5 Exercises 607

17 Simulation 611
17.1 Basics of simulation 611
17.1.1 The simulation approach 612
17.1.2 Exercises 617
17.2 Examples of simulation in actuarial modeling 618
17.2.1 Aggregate loss calculations 618
17.2.2 Examples of lack of independence or
identical distributions 619
17.2.3 Simulation analysis of the two examples 620
17.2.4 Statistical analyses 622
17.2.5 Exercises 625

Appendix A An inventory of continuous distributions   627
   A.1   Introduction   627
   A.2   Transformed beta family   631
      A.2.1   Four-parameter distribution   631
      A.2.2   Three-parameter distributions   631
      A.2.3   Two-parameter distributions   633
   A.3   Transformed gamma family   635
      A.3.1   Three-parameter distributions   635
      A.3.2   Two-parameter distributions   636
      A.3.3   One-parameter distributions   638
   A.4   Other distributions   638
   A.5   Distributions with finite support   640

Appendix B An inventory of discrete distributions   643
   B.1   Introduction   643
   B.2   The $(a, b, 0)$ class   644
   B.3   The $(a, b, 1)$ class   645
      B.3.1   The zero-truncated subclass   645
      B.3.2   The zero-modified subclass   647
   B.4   The compound class   648
      B.4.1   Some compound distributions   648
   B.5   A hierarchy of discrete distributions   650

Appendix C Frequency and severity relationships   651

Appendix D The recursive formula   653

Appendix E Discretization of the severity distribution   655
   E.1   The method of rounding   655
   E.2   Mean preserving   656
   E.3   Undiscretization of a discretized distribution   657

Appendix F Numerical optimization and solution of systems
   of equations   659
   F.1   Maximization using Solver   660
   F.2   The simplex method   664
   F.3   Using Excel® to solve equations   665

References   671

Index   681

Preface

The preface to the first edition of this text explained our mission as follows:

This textbook is organized around the principle that much of actuarial science consists of the construction and analysis of mathematical models which describe the process by which funds flow into and out of an insurance system. An analysis of the entire system is beyond the scope of a single text, so we have concentrated our efforts on the loss process, that is, the outflow of cash due to the payment of benefits.

We have not assumed that the reader has any substantial knowledge of insurance systems. Insurance terms are defined when they are first used. In fact, most of the material could be disassociated from the insurance process altogether, and this book could be just another applied statistics text. What we have done is kept the examples focused on insurance, presented the material in the language and context of insurance, and tried to avoid getting into statistical methods that would have little use in actuarial practice.

In particular, the first edition of this text was published in 1998 to achieve three goals:

1. Update the distribution fitting material from *Loss Distributions* [59] by Robert Hogg and Stuart Klugman, published in 1984.

2. Update material on discrete distributions and collective risk model calculations from *Insurance Risk Models* [106] by Harry Panjer and Gordon Willmot, published in 1992.

3. Integrate the material the three authors had developed for the Society of Actuaries' Intensive Seminar 152, Applied Risk Theory.

Shortly after publication, the Casualty Actuarial Society and the Society of Actuaries altered their examination syllabus to include our first edition. The good news was that the first edition was selected as source material for the new third and fourth examinations. The bad news was that the subject matter was split between the examinations in a manner that was not compatible with the organization of the text. By itself, that is sufficient reason to produce a revision. But there are others.

1. The first edition was written with an assumption that readers would be familiar with the subject of mathermatical statistics. This had been part of the actuarial examination process at the time the book was written but was subsequently removed. Some background material on mathematical statistics is now presented in Chapter 9.

2. For a long time, actuarial education has included the subject of survival models. This is the study of determining probability models for time to death, failure, or disability. It is not much different from the study of determining probability models for the amount or number of claims. This edition integrates that subject and in doing so adds an emphasis on building empirical models. This is covered in Chapters 10 and 11.

3. There were two items that had been removed from the actuarial syllabus over the years that we wanted to see returned, at least in brief. One is graduation, the smoothing of and interpolation of sequences of numbers. This is covered in Chapter 15. The other is the adjustment of estimation formulas when dealing with the large amounts of data in mortality studies. This is covered in Section 11.4.

4. While simulation was briefly covered in the first edition, the material has been slightly expanded and now appears in Chapter 17.

With regard to continuing material, besides the rearrangment of the material on models and modeling, other substantive changes are a significant rewrite of the ruin theory material (Chapters 7 and 8), and a better explanation of the limited fluctuation credibility formulas (Chapter 16).

While we have attempted to integrate the material into a single, logical development of actuarial model building, various sections stand alone, thus the division of the text into various parts.

Since the publication of the first edition, computational power continues to increase. For that edition, specialized DOS programs were made available for obtaining maximum likelihood estimates and performing aggregate loss calculations. Those programs continue to be available at the Wiley ftp site:

ftp://ftp.wiley.com/public/sci_tech_med/loss_models/

In addition, files containing the data for examples and exercises are also available. However, it is more likely that users will be calculating using a spreadsheet program such as Microsoft Excel®.[1] At various places in the text we indicate how Excel® commands may help. This is not an endorsement by the authors, but rather a recognition of the pervasiveness of this tool.

As in the first edition, many of the exercises are taken from examinations of the Casualty Actuarial Society and the Society of Actuaries. They have been reworded to fit the terminology and notation of this text and the five answer choices from the original questions are not provided. Such exercises are indicated with an asterisk (*). Of course, these questions may not be representative of those asked on examinations given in the future.

Finally, a word about our cover picture. In the summer of 1993 the Des Moines and Raccoon Rivers flooded, putting sections of Des Moines, Iowa under water. At the left center of the picture is the Des Moines Water Works. Contamination knocked out the water supply for 12 days. While living through adverse events can be interesting, it is not necessary to do so to build probability models for their occurrence, timing, and severity. Our thanks to Melissa Sharer of the Des Moines Water Works for providing the picture.

S. A. KLUGMAN
H. H. PANJER
G. E. WILLMOT

Des Moines, Iowa
Waterloo, Ontario

---

[1] Microsoft® and Excel® are either registered trademarks or trademarks of Microsoft Corporation in the United States and/or other countries.

Acknowledgments

Stuart Klugman:

While producing a second edition is not as daunting or grueling a task as creating the first edition, there was still a lot to be done and several people who helped make it possible. While many individuals provided corrections and suggestions to improve the first edition, Elias Shiu and Don Minassian were especially prolific in pointing out our shortcomings. Clive Keatinge provided many corrections to this text prior to publication. When the actuarial societies determined that the presentation needed to be altered to conform with the allocation of material to the two examinations, a committee was convened under the leadership of Clive Keatinge. This group laid out the plan that is reflected in the presentation in Chapters 2–5 and 9–13. We have added a few subjects to make the presentation more complete but have relied on the committee's expertise to set the agenda for these chapters.

Special thanks to my coauthors for meeting the deadline.

I am revising this acknowledgement shortly after my wife Marie died from a long struggle with multiple diseases. Both when healthy and throughout her illness she was an inspiration to me and all who knew her. The final draft was submitted to the publisher on time not because I was excited to be working but because meeting commitments and keeping promises was something she valued.

Harry Panjer:
Revising and editing a book is not much fun. However, in doing this second edition, we did have some fun in adding a lot of new material. Each coauthor made major contributions to several chapters of completely new material. I particularly enjoyed drafting the chapter on spline interpolation and smoothing which provides a modern treatment of the classical actuarial problem of graduation. I am indebted to Stuart Klugman and students at Drake University who field-tested this material and discovered several errors (thus saving me potential future embarrassment).

Stuart Klugman provided the visionary, spiritual, and practical leadership for this project. I am also indebted to Gordon Willmot who led the proofreading team at the University of Waterloo. Whatever errors remain are a tiny fraction of the total from the first draft. They did a fantastic job. And finally, thanks to my wife Joanne Coyle who tolerated my many weekends and evenings at the office. Our sons Lucas D. and Lucas R., who saw the first edition being written, have grown up and moved away since then. They will only discover this second edition when someone points out to them that they are mentioned in this acknowledgement.

Gordon Willmot:
The second edition has involved relatively substantial reorganization and updating. Many of these changes are a reflection of the somewhat novel nature of the combination of topics that are presented in order to attempt to provide an integrated approach to the use of data to calibrate models and the subsequent use of these models for pricing and related purposes. As such, the present treatment has undoubtedly benefitted from the input of many individuals who are clearly too numerous to mention. Special thanks, however, do go to Catherine Donnelly, Steve Drekic, Mary Lou Dufton, Jessica Ling-Wai Lam, and Claire Xiao-Dan Yang for their invaluable assistance on this second edition.

I also wish to express my sincere gratitude to my coauthors, and in particular to Stuart Klugman for spearheading this project, keeping us on track while leading by example, and for his nearly infinite patience in dealing with all related issues in spite of difficult circumstances. I also wish to again express my thanks to my wife Deborah and my daughters Rachel, Lauren, and Kristen for both the implicit and explicit sacrifices that they have made in order that I devote time and energy to this work.

S.A.K., H.H.P., G.E.W.

Part I

Introduction

1

Modeling

1.1 THE MODEL-BASED APPROACH

The model-based approach should be considered in the context of the objectives of any given problem. Many problems in actuarial science involve the building of a mathematical model that can be used to forecast or predict insurance costs in the future.

A model is a simplified mathematical description which is constructed based on the knowledge and experience of the actuary combined with data from the past. The data guide the actuary in selecting the form of the model as well as in calibrating unknown quantities, usually called **parameters**. The model provides a balance between simplicity and conformity to the available data.

The simplicity is measured in terms of such things as the number of unknown parameters (the fewer the simpler); the conformity to data is measured in terms of the discrepancy between the data and the model. Model selection is based on a balance between the two criteria, namely, fit and simplicity.

1.1.1 The modeling process

The modeling process is illustrated in Figure 1.1, which describes six stages.

Loss Models: From Data to Decisions, Second Edition.
By Stuart A. Klugman, Harry H. Panjer, and Gordon E. Willmot
ISBN 0-471-21577-5   Copyright © 2004 John Wiley & Sons, Inc.

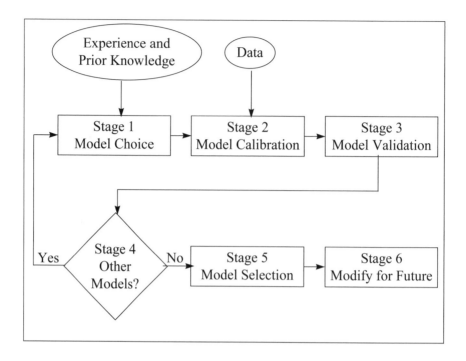

Fig. 1.1 The modeling process.

Stage 1 One or more models are selected based on the analyst's prior knowledge and experience and possibly on the nature and form of available
data. For example, in studies of mortality, models may contain covariate
information such as age, sex, duration, policy type, medical information,
and lifestyle variables. In studies of the size of insurance loss, a statistical distribution (e.g., lognormal, gamma, or Weibull) may be chosen.

Stage 2 The model is calibrated based on available data. In mortality studies, these data may be information on a set of life insurance policies. In
studies of property claims, the data may be information about each of
a set of actual insurance losses paid under a set of property insurance
policies.

Stage 3 The fitted model is validated to determine if it adequately conforms
to the data. Various diagnostic tests can be used. These may be well-
known statistical tests, such as the chi-square goodness-of-fit test or the
Kolmogorov–Smirnov test, or may be more qualitative in nature. The
choice of test may relate directly to the ultimate purpose of the modeling
exercise. In insurance-related studies, the fitted model is often required
to replicate in total the losses actually experienced in the data. In
insurance practice this is often referred to as **unbiasedness** of a model.

Stage 4 An opportunity is provided to consider other possible models. This is particularly useful if Stage 3 revealed that all models were inadequate. It is also possible that more than one valid model will be under consideration at this stage.

Stage 5 All valid models considered in Stages 1–4 are compared using some criteria to select between them. This may be done by using the test results previously obtained or may be done by using another criterion. Once a winner is selected, the losers may be retained for sensitivity analyses.

Stage 6 Finally, the selected model is adapted for application to the future. This could involve adjustment of parameters to reflect anticipated inflation from the time the data were collected to the period of time to which the model will be applied.

As new data are collected or the environment changes, the six stages will need to be repeated to improve the model.

1.1.2   The modeling advantage

Determination of the advantages of using models requires us to consider the alternative, decision making based strictly upon empirical evidence. The empirical approach assumes that the future can be expected to be exactly like a sample from the past, perhaps adjusted for trends such as inflation. Consider the following illustration.

Example 1.1 *A portfolio of group life insurance certificates consists of* 1,000 *employees of various ages and death benefits. Over the past five years,* 14 *employees died and received a total of* 580,000 *in benefits (adjusted for inflation because the plan relates benefits to salary). Determine the empirical estimate of next year's expected benefit payment.*

The empirical estimate for next year is then 116,000 (one-fifth of the total), which would need to be further adjusted for benefit increases. The danger, of course, is that it is unlikely that the experience of the past five years accurately reflects the future of this portfolio as there can be considerable fluctuation in such short-term results.   □

It seems much more reasonable to build a model, in this case a mortality table. This table would be based on the experience of many lives, not just the 1,000 in our group. With this model we not only can estimate the expected payment for next year, but we can also measure the risk involved by calculating the standard deviation of payments or perhaps various percentiles from the distribution of payments. This is precisely the problem covered in great detail in *Actuarial Mathematics* [16].

This approach was codified by the Society of Actuaries Committee on Actuarial Principles. In the publication "Principles of Actuarial Science" [123], p. 571, Principle 3.1 states that "Actuarial risks can be stochastically modeled based on assumptions regarding the probabilities that will apply to the actuarial risk variables in the future, including assumptions regarding the future environment." The actuarial risk variables referred to are occurrence, timing, and severity—that is, the chances of a claim event, the time at which the event occurs if it does, and the cost of settling the claim.

1.2 ORGANIZATION OF THIS BOOK

This text takes the reader through the modeling process, but not in the order presented in the previous section. There is a difference between how models are best applied and how they are best learned. In this text we first learn about the models and how to use them. This is followed by instruction in how to determine which model to use. The reason is that it is difficult to select models in a vacuum. Unless the analyst has a thorough knowledge of the set of available models, it is difficult to narrow the choice to the ones worth considering. With that in mind, the organization of the text is as follows:

1. Review of probability—Almost by definition, contingent events imply probability models. Chapters 2 and 3 review random variables and some of the basic calculations that may be done with such models, including moments and percentiles.

2. Understanding probability distributions—In order to select a probability model, the analyst should possess a reasonably large collection of such models. In addition, in order to make a good a priori model choice, characteristics of these models should be available. In Chapter 4 a variety of distributional models are introduced and their characteristics explored. This includes both continuous and discrete distributions.

3. Coverage modifications—Insurance contracts often do not provide full payment. For example, there may be a deductible (the insurance policy does not pay the first $250, for example) or a limit (the insurance policy does not pay more than $10,000 for any one loss event, for example). Such modifications alter the probability distribution and affect related calculations such as moments. Chapter 5 shows how this is done.

4. Aggregate losses and ruin—To this point the models are either for the amount of a single payment or for the number of payments. Of interest when modeling a portfolio, line of business, or entire company is the total amount paid. A model that combines the probabilities concerning the number of payments and the amounts of each payment is called an aggregate loss model. Calculations for such models are covered in

Chapter 6. Usually, the payments arrive sequentially through time. It is possible, if the payments turn out to be large, that at some point the entity will run out of money. This state of affairs is called ruin. In Chapters 7 and 8 models are established that allow for the calculation of the probability this will happen.

5. Review of mathematical statistics—Because most of the models being considered are probability models, techniques of mathematical statistics are needed to estimate model specifications and make choices. While Chapter 9 is not a replacement for a thorough text or course in mathematical statistics, it does contain the essential items needed later in this text.

6. Construction of empirical models—Sometimes it is appropriate to work with the empirical distribution of the data. It may be because the volume of data is sufficient or because a good portrait of the data is needed. Chapters 10 and 11 cover this for the simple case of straightforward data, adjustments for truncated and censored data, and modifications suitable for large data sets, particularly those encountered in mortality studies.

7. Construction of parametric models—Often it is valuable to smooth the data and thus represent the population by a probability distribution. Chapter 12 provides methods for parameter estimation for the models introduced earlier. Model selection is covered in Chapter 13.

8. Chapter 14 contains examples that summarize and integrate the topics discussed to this point.

9. Adjustment of estimates—At times, further adjustment of the results is needed. Two such adjustments are covered in this text. The first is interpolation and smoothing (also called graduation) and is covered in Chapter 15, where the emphasis is on cubic splines. There are situations, such as time to death, where no simple probability distribution is known to describe the observations. An empirical approach is likely to produce results that are not as smooth as the population is known to be. Graduation methods can provide the needed adjustment. A second situation occurs when there are one or more estimates based on a small number of observations. Accuracy could be improved by adding other, related observations, but care must be taken if the additional data are from a different population. Credibility methods, covered in Chapter 16, provide a mechanism for making the appropriate adjustment when additional data are to be included.

10. Simulation—When analytical results are difficult to obtain, simulation (use of random numbers) may provide the needed answer. A brief introduction to this technique is provided in Chapter 17.

Part II

Actuarial models

2

Random variables

2.1 INTRODUCTION

An actuarial model is an attempt to represent an uncertain stream of future payments. The uncertainty may be with respect to any or all of occurrence (is there a payment?), timing (when is the payment made?), and severity (how much is paid?). Because the most useful means of representing uncertainty is through probability, we concentrate on probability models. In all cases, the relevant probability distributions are assumed to be known. Determining appropriate distributions is covered in Chapters 10–13. In this part, the following aspects of actuarial probability models will be covered:

1. Definition of random variable, important functions, and some examples.

2. Basic calculations from probability models.

3. Specific probability distributions and their properties.

4. More advanced calculations using severity models.

5. Models incorporating the possibility of a random number of payments each of random amount.

6. Models that track a company's surplus through time.

Loss Models: From Data to Decisions, Second Edition.
By Stuart A. Klugman, Harry H. Panjer, and Gordon E. Willmot
ISBN 0-471-21577-5   Copyright © 2004 John Wiley & Sons, Inc.

There are two important models that are absent from this text. The first is a model for investment earnings in future years. While such techniques are within the scope of this text, the additional finance background needed to motivate these models would detract from the primary purpose of this text. The second is a model that combines the earning of interest (whether random or not) with the timing of the payment. While simple models of this type may show up in examples, thorough coverage of the use of these models for life insurance and annuities is sufficiently specialized to require a separate text, such as [16].

The commonality we seek here is that all models for random phenomena have similar elements. For each, there is a set of possible outcomes. The particular outcome that occurs will determine the success of our enterprise. Attaching probabilities to the various outcomes allows us to quantify our expectations and the risk of not meeting them. In this spirit, the underlying random variable will almost always be denoted X or Y. The context will provide a name and some likely characteristics. Of course, there are actuarial models that do not look like those covered here. For example, in life insurance a *model office* is a list of cells containing policy type, age range, gender, and so on.

To expand on this concept, consider the following definitions from the latest working draft of "Joint Principles of Actuarial Science"[1]:

> *Phenomena* are occurrences that can be observed. An *experiment* is an observation of a given phenomenon under specified conditions. The result of an experiment is called an *outcome*; an *event* is a set of one or more possible outcomes. A stochastic phenomenon is a phenomenon for which an associated experiment has more than one possible outcome. An event associated with a *stochastic phenomenon* is said to be *contingent*. *Probability* is a measure of the likelihood of the occurrence of an event. It is measured on a scale of increasing likelihood from zero to one. A *random variable* is a function that assigns a numerical value to every possible outcome.

The following list contains a number of random variables encountered in actuarial work:

1. The age at death of a randomly selected birth. (**Model 1**)

2. The time to death from when insurance was purchased for a randomly selected insured life.

3. The time from occurrence of a disabling event to recovery or death for a randomly selected workers compensation claimant.

---

[1] This document is a work in progress of a joint committee from the Casualty Actuarial Society and the Society of Actuaries. Key principles are that models exist that represent actuarial phenomena and that given sufficient data it is possible to calibrate models.

4. The time from the incidence of a randomly selected claim to its being reported to the insurer.

5. The time from the reporting of a randomly selected claim to its settlement.

6. The number of dollars paid on a randomly selected life insurance claim.

7. The number of dollars paid on a randomly selected automobile bodily injury claim. (**Model 2**)

8. The number of automobile bodily injury claims in one year from a randomly selected insured automobile. (**Model 3**)

9. The total dollars in medical malpractice claims paid in one year owing to events at a randomly selected hospital. (**Model 4**)

10. The time to default or prepayment on a randomly selected insured home loan that terminates early.

11. The amount of money paid at maturity on a randomly selected high-yield bond.

Because all of these phenomena can be expressed as random variables, the machinery of probability and mathematical statistics is at our disposal both to create and to analyze models for them. The following paragraphs discuss the five key functions used in describing a random variable. They will be illustrated with four ongoing models as identified in the list above plus two more to be introduced later.

2.2   KEY FUNCTIONS AND FOUR MODELS

Definition 2.1 *The **cumulative distribution function**, also called the **distribution function** and usually denoted $F_X(x)$ or $F(x)$,[2] for a random variable X is the probability that X is less than or equal to a given number. That is, $F_X(x) = \Pr(X \le x)$. The abbreviation **cdf** is often used.*

The distribution function must satisfy a number of requirements[3]:

- $0 \le F(x) \le 1$ for all x.

---

[2] When denoting functions associated with random variables, it is common to identify the random variable through a subscript on the function. Here, subscripts will be used only when needed to distinguish one random variable from another. In addition, for the six models to be introduced shortly, rather than write the distribution function for random variable 2 as $F_{X_2}(x)$, it will simply be denoted $F_2(x)$.

[3] The first point follows from the last three.

- $F(x)$ is nondecreasing.

- $F(x)$ is right-continuous.[4]

- $\lim_{x \to -\infty} F(x) = 0$ and $\lim_{x \to \infty} F(x) = 1$.

Because it need not be left-continuous, it is possible for the distribution function to jump. When it jumps, the value is assigned to the top of the jump.

Here are possible distribution functions for each of the four models.

Model 1[5] This random variable could serve as a model for the age at death. All ages between 0 and 100 are possible. While experience suggests that there is an upper bound for human lifetime, models with no upper limit may be useful if they assign extremely low probabilities to extreme ages. This allows the modeler to avoid setting a specific maximum age.

$$F_1(x) = \begin{cases} 0, & x < 0, \\ 0.01x, & 0 \le x < 100, \\ 1, & x \ge 100. \end{cases}$$ □

Model 2 This random variable could serve as a model for the number of dollars paid on an automobile insurance claim. All positive values are possible. As with mortality, there is more than likely an upper limit (all the money in the world comes to mind), but this model illustrates that in modeling, correspondence to reality need not be perfect.

$$F_2(x) = \begin{cases} 0, & x < 0, \\ 1 - \left(\dfrac{2000}{x + 2000}\right)^3, & x \ge 0. \end{cases}$$ □

Example 2.2 *Draw graphs of the distribution function for Models 1 and 2 (graphs for the other models are requested in Exercise 2.2).*

The graphs appear in Figures 2.1 and 2.2. □

Model 3 This random variable could serve as a model for the number of claims on one policy in one year. Probability is concentrated at the five points (0,1,2,3,4) and the probability at each is given by the size of the jump in the distribution function. While this model places a maximum on the number of claims, models with no limit (such as the Poisson distribution) could also be used.

---

[4]Right-continuous means that at any point x_0 the limiting value of $F(x)$ as x approaches x_0 from the right is equal to $F(x_0)$. This need not be true as x approaches x_0 from the left.
[5]The six models (four introduced here and two later) will be identified by the numbers 1-6. Other examples will use the traditional numbering scheme as used for Definitions, etc.

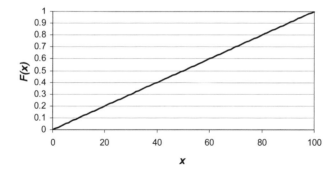

Fig. 2.1 Distribution function for Model 1.

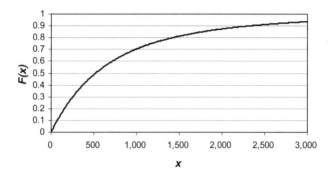

Fig. 2.2 Distribution function for Model 2.

$$
F_3(x) = \begin{cases}
0, & x < 0, \\
0.5, & 0 \le x < 1, \\
0.75, & 1 \le x < 2, \\
0.87, & 2 \le x < 3, \\
0.95, & 3 \le x < 4, \\
1, & x \ge 4.
\end{cases}
$$

$\square$

Model 4 This random variable could serve as a model for the total dollars paid on a malpractice policy in one year. Most of the probability is at zero (0.7) because in most years nothing is paid. The remaining 0.3 of probability is distributed over positive values.

$$F_4(x) = \begin{cases} 0, & x < 0, \\ 1 - 0.3e^{-0.00001x}, & x \geq 0. \end{cases} \qquad \square$$

Definition 2.3 *The **support** of a random variable is the set of numbers that are possible values of the random variable.*

Definition 2.4 *A random variable is called **discrete** if the support contains at most a countable number of values. It is called **continuous** if the distribution function is continuous and is differentiable everywhere with the possible exception of a countable number of values. It is called **mixed** if it is not discrete and is continuous everywhere with the exception of at least one value and at most a countable number of values.*

These three definitions do not exhaust all possible random variables but will cover all cases encountered in this text. The distribution function for a discrete variable will be constant except for jumps at the values with positive probability. A mixed distribution will have at least one jump. Requiring continuous variables to be differentiable allows the variable to have a density function (defined later) at almost all values.

Example 2.5 *For each of the four models, determine the support and indicate which type of random variable it is.*

The distribution function for Model 1 is continuous and is differentiable except at 0 and 100 and therefore is a continuous distribution. The support is values from 0 to 100 with it not being clear if 0 or 100 are included. The distribution function for Model 2 is continuous and is differentiable except at 0 and therefore is a continuous distribution. The support is all positive numbers and perhaps 0. The random variable for Model 3 places probability only at 0, 1, 2, 3, and 4 (the support) and thus is discrete. The distribution function for Model 4 is continuous except at 0, where it jumps. It is a mixed distribution with support on nonnegative numbers. $\qquad \square$

These four models illustrate the most commonly encountered forms of the distribution function. For the remainder of this text, values of functions like the distribution function will be presented only for values in the range of the support of the random variable.

Definition 2.6 *The **survival function**, usually denoted $S_X(x)$ or $S(x)$, for a random variable X is the probability that X is greater than a given number. That is, $S_X(x) = \Pr(X > x) = 1 - F_X(x)$.*

As a result:

- $0 \leq S(x) \leq 1$ for all x.

- $S(x)$ is nonincreasing.

- $S(x)$ is right-continuous.

- $\lim_{x \to -\infty} S(x) = 1$ and $\lim_{x \to \infty} S(x) = 0$.

Because the survival function need not be left-continuous, it is possible for it to jump (down). When it jumps, the value is assigned to the bottom of the jump.

Because the survival function is the complement of the distribution function, knowledge of one implies knowledge of the other. Historically, when the random variable is measuring time, the survival function is presented, while when it is measuring dollars, the distribution function is presented.

Example 2.7 *For completeness, here are the survival functions for the four models.*

$$S_1(x) = 1 - 0.01x, \; 0 \le x < 100,$$

$$S_2(x) = \left(\frac{2,000}{x + 2,000} \right)^3, \; x \ge 0,$$

$$S_3(x) = \begin{cases} 0.5, & 0 \le x < 1, \\ 0.25, & 1 \le x < 2,, \\ 0.13, & 2 \le x < 3 \\ 0.05, & 3 \le x < 4,, \\ 0, & x \ge 4 \end{cases}$$

$$S_4(x) = 0.3e^{-0.00001x}, \; x \ge 0. \qquad \square$$

Example 2.8 *Graph the survival function for Models 1 and 2.*

The graphs appear in Figures 2.3 and 2.4. $\qquad \square$

Either the distribution or survival function can be used to determine probabilities. Let $F(b-) = \lim_{x \nearrow b} F(x)$ and let $S(b-)$ be similarly defined. That is, we want the limit as x approaches b from below. We have $\Pr(a < X \le b) = F(b) - F(a) = S(a) - S(b)$ and $\Pr(X = b) = F(b) - F(b-) = S(b-) - S(b)$. When the distribution function is continuous at x, $\Pr(X = x) = 0$; otherwise the probability is the size of the jump. The next two functions are more directly related to the probabilities. The first is for continuous distributions, the second for discrete distributions.

Definition 2.9 *The **probability density function**, also called the **density function**, usually denoted $f_X(x)$ or $f(x)$, is the derivative of the distribution function or, equivalently, the negative of the derivative of the survival function.*

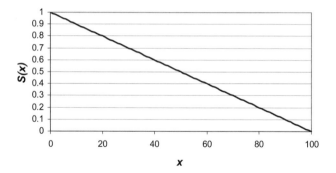

Fig. 2.3   Survival function for Model 1.

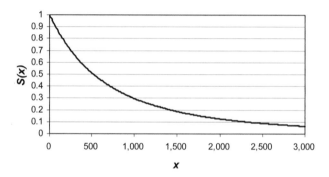

Fig. 2.4   Survival function for Model 2.

That is, $f(x) = F'(x) = -S'(x)$. The density function is defined only at those points where the derivative exists. The abbreviation **pdf** *is often used.*

While the density function does not directly provide probabilities, it does provide relevant information. Values of the random variable in regions with higher density values are more likely to occur than those in regions with lower values. Probabilities for intervals and the distribution and survival functions can be recovered by integration. That is, when the density function is defined over the relevant interval, $\Pr(a < X \le b) = \int_a^b f(x)dx$, $F(b) = \int_{-\infty}^b f(x)dx$, and $S(b) = \int_b^\infty f(x)dx$.

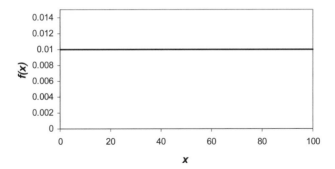

Fig. 2.5 Density function for Model 1.

Example 2.10 *For our models,*

$$f_1(x) = 0.01, \quad 0 < x < 100,$$
$$f_2(x) = \frac{3(2{,}000)^3}{(x + 2{,}000)^4}, \quad x > 0,$$
$$f_3(x) \text{ is not defined,}$$
$$f_4(x) = 0.000003e^{-0.00001x}, \quad x > 0.$$

It should be noted that for Model 4 the density function does not completely describe the probability distribution. As a mixed distribution, there is also discrete probability at 0. □

Example 2.11 *Graph the density function for Models 1 and 2.*

The graphs appear in Figures 2.5 and 2.6. □

Definition 2.12 *The **probability function,** also called the **probability mass function,** usually denoted $p_X(x)$ or $p(x)$, describes the probability at a distinct point when it is not 0. The formal definition is $p_X(x) = \Pr(X = x)$.*

For discrete random variables, the distribution and survival functions can be recovered as $F(x) = \sum_{y \le x} p(y)$ and $S(x) = \sum_{y > x} p(y)$.

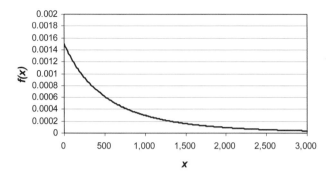

Fig. 2.6 Density function for Model 2.

Example 2.13 *For our models,*

$$p_1(x) \text{ is not defined,}$$
$$p_2(x) \text{ is not defined,}$$
$$p_3(x) = \begin{cases} 0.50, & x = 0, \\ 0.25, & x = 1, \\ 0.12, & x = 2, \\ 0.08, & x = 3, \\ 0.05, & x = 4, \end{cases}$$
$$p_4(0) = 0.7.$$

It is again noted that the distribution in Model 4 is mixed, so the above describes only the discrete portion of that distribution. There is no easy way to present probabilities/densities for a mixed distribution. On the other hand, they tend to be more revealing of the mixed nature of the distribution. For Model 4 we would present the probability density function as

$$f_4(x) = \begin{cases} 0.7, & x = 0, \\ 0.000003e^{-0.00001x}, & x > 0, \end{cases}$$

realizing that, technically, it is not a probability density function at all. When the density function is assigned a value at a specific point, as opposed to being defined on an interval, it is understood to be a discrete probability mass. □

Definition 2.14 *The **hazard rate**, also known as the **force of mortality** and the **failure rate** and usually denoted $h_X(x)$ or $h(x)$, is the ratio of the density and survival functions when the density function is defined. That is, $h_X(x) = f_X(x)/S_X(x)$.*

When called the force of mortality, the hazard rate is often denoted $\mu(x)$, and when called the failure rate, it is often denoted $\lambda(x)$. Regardless, it may be interpreted as the probability density at x given that the argument will be at least x. We also have $h_X(x) = -S'(x)/S(x) = -d\ln S(x)/dx$. The survival function can be recovered from $S(b) = e^{-\int_0^b h(x)dx}$. Though not necessary, this formula implies that the support is on nonnegative numbers. In mortality terms, the force of mortality is the annualized probability[6] that a person age x will die in the next instant, expressed as a death rate per year. In this text we will always use $h(x)$ to denote the hazard rate, although one of the alternative names may be used.

Example 2.15 *For our models,*

$$h_1(x) = \frac{0.01}{1 - 0.01x}, \quad 0 < x < 100,$$

$$h_2(x) = \frac{3}{x + 2,000}, \quad x > 0,$$

$$h_3(x) \text{ is not defined,}$$

$$h_4(x) = 0.00001, \quad x > 0.$$

Once again, note that for the mixed distribution the hazard rate is only defined over part of the random variable's support. This is different from the problem above where both a probability density function and a probability function are involved. Where there is a discrete probability mass, the hazard rate is not defined.   ☐

Example 2.16 *Graph the hazard rate function for Models 1 and 2.*

The graphs appear in Figures 2.7 and 2.8.   ☐

The following model illustrates a situation in which there is a point where the density and hazard rate functions are not defined.

Model 5 An alternative to the simple lifetime distribution in Model 1 is given below. Note that it is piecewise linear and the derivative at 50 is not defined. Therefore, neither the density function nor the hazard rate function is defined at 50. Unlike the mixed model of Model 4, there is no discrete probability mass at this point. Because the probability of 50 occurring is zero, the density or hazard rate at 50 could be arbitrarily defined with no effect on subsequent

---

[6] Note that the force of mortality is not a probability (in particular, it can be greater than 1) although it does no harm to visualize it as a probability.

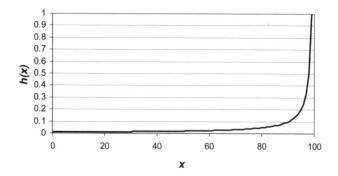

Fig. 2.7 Hazard rate function for Model 1.

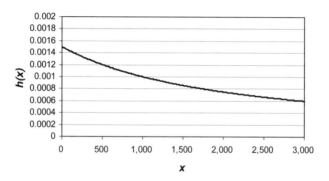

Fig. 2.8 Hazard rate function for Model 2.

calculations. In this text such values will be arbitrarily defined so that the function is right continuous.[7] See the solution to Exercise 2.1 for an example.

$$S_5(x) = \begin{cases} 1 - 0.01x, & 0 \le x < 50, \\ 1.5 - 0.02x, & 50 \le x < 75. \end{cases}$$

□

---

[7]By arbitrarily defining the value of the density or hazard rate function at such a point, it is clear that using either of them to obtain the survival function will work. If there is discrete probability at this point (in which case these functions are left undefined), then the density and hazard functions are not sufficient to completely describe the probability distribution.

A variety of commonly used continuous distributions are presented in Appendix A and many discrete distributions are presented in Appendix B. An interesting feature of a random variable is the value that is most likely to occur.

Definition 2.17 *The **mode** of a random variable is the most likely value. For a discrete variable it is the value with the largest probability. For a continuous variable it is the value for which the density function is largest. If there are local maxima, these points are also considered to be modes.*

Example 2.18 *Where possible, determine the mode for Models 1–5.*

For Model 1, the density function is constant. All values from 0 to 100 could be the mode, or equivalently, it could be said that there is no mode. For Model 2, the density function is strictly decreasing and so the mode is at 0. For Model 3, the probability is highest at 0. As a mixed distribution, it is not possible to define a mode for Model 4. Model 5 has a density that is constant over two intervals, with higher values from 50 to 75. These values are all modes. □

2.2.1 Exercises

2.1 Determine the distribution, density, and hazard rate functions for Model 5.

2.2 Construct graphs of the distribution function for Models 3–5. Also graph the density or probability function as appropriate and the hazard rate function, where it exists.

2.3 (*) A random variable X has density function $f(x) = 4x(1 + x^2)^{-3}$, $x > 0$. Determine the mode of X.

2.4 (*) A nonnegative random variable has a hazard rate function of $h(x) = A + e^{2x}$, $x \geq 0$. You are also given $S(0.4) = 0.5$. Determine the value of A.

2.5 (*) X has a Pareto distribution with parameters $\alpha = 2$ and $\theta = 10{,}000$. Y has a Burr distribution with parameters $\alpha = 2$, $\gamma = 2$, and $\theta = \sqrt{20{,}000}$. Let r be the ratio of $\Pr(X > d)$ to $\Pr(Y > d)$. Determine $\lim_{d \to \infty} r$.

3

Basic distributional quantities

3.1 MOMENTS

There are a variety of interesting calculations that can be done from the models described in the previous chapter. Examples are the average amount paid on a claim that is subject to a deductible or policy limit or the average remaining lifetime of a person age 40.

Definition 3.1 *The k**th raw moment** of a random variable is the expected (average) value of the kth power of the variable, provided it exists. It is denoted by* $\mathrm{E}(X^k)$ *or by* μ'_k. *The first raw moment is called the **mean** of the random variable and is usually denoted by* μ.

Note that μ is not related to $\mu(x)$, the force of mortality as mentioned on page 21. For random variables that take on only nonnegative values [that is, $\Pr(X \geq 0) = 1$], k may be any real number. When presenting formulas for calculating this quantity, a distinction between continuous and discrete variables needs to be made. Formulas will be presented for random variables that are either everywhere continuous or everywhere discrete. For mixed models, evaluate the formula by integrating with respect to its density function wherever the random variable is continuous and by summing with respect to its probability function wherever the random variable is discrete and adding

Loss Models: From Data to Decisions, Second Edition.
By Stuart A. Klugman, Harry H. Panjer, and Gordon E. Willmot
ISBN 0-471-21577-5   Copyright © 2004 John Wiley & Sons, Inc.

the results. The formula for the kth raw moment is

$$\mu'_k = \mathrm{E}(X^k) \quad = \quad \int_{-\infty}^{\infty} x^k f(x)dx \text{ if the random variable is continuous}$$

$$= \quad \sum_j x_j^k p(x_j) \text{ if the random variable is discrete,} \qquad (3.1)$$

where the sum is to be taken over all x_j with positive probability. Finally, note that it is possible that the integral or sum will not converge, in which case the moment is said not to exist.

Example 3.2 *Determine the first two raw moments for each of the five models.*

The subscripts on the random variable X indicate which model is being used.

$$\mathrm{E}(X_1) \quad = \quad \int_0^{100} x(0.01)dx = 50,$$

$$\mathrm{E}(X_1^2) \quad = \quad \int_0^{100} x^2(0.01)dx = 3{,}333.33,$$

$$\mathrm{E}(X_2) \quad = \quad \int_0^{\infty} x\frac{3(2{,}000)^3}{(x+2{,}000)^4}dx = 1{,}000,$$

$$\mathrm{E}(X_2^2) \quad = \quad \int_0^{\infty} x^2\frac{3(2{,}000)^3}{(x+2{,}000)^4}dx = 4{,}000{,}000,$$

$$\mathrm{E}(X_3) \quad = \quad 0(0.5) + 1(0.25) + 2(0.12) + 3(0.08) + 4(0.05) = 0.93,$$

$$\mathrm{E}(X_3^2) \quad = \quad 0(0.5) + 1(0.25) + 4(0.12) + 9(0.08) + 16(0.05) = 2.25,$$

$$\mathrm{E}(X_4) \quad = \quad 0(0.7) + \int_0^{\infty} x(0.000003)e^{-0.00001x}dx = 30{,}000,$$

$$\mathrm{E}(X_4^2) \quad = \quad 0^2(0.7) + \int_0^{\infty} x^2(0.000003)e^{-0.00001x}dx = 6{,}000{,}000{,}000,$$

$$\mathrm{E}(X_5) \quad = \quad \int_0^{50} x(0.01)dx + \int_{50}^{75} x(0.02)dx = 43.75,$$

$$\mathrm{E}(X_5^2) \quad = \quad \int_0^{50} x^2(0.01)dx + \int_{50}^{75} x^2(0.02)dx = 2{,}395.83. \qquad \square$$

Before proceeding further, an additional model will be introduced. This one looks similar to Model 3, but with one key difference. It is discrete, but with the added requirement that all of the probabilities must be integral multiples of some number. In addition, the model must be related to sample data in a particular way.

Definition 3.3 *The **empirical model** is a discrete distribution based on a sample of size n which assigns probability $1/n$ to each data point.*

Model 6 Consider a sample of size 8 in which the observed data points were 3, 5, 6, 6, 6, 7, 7, and 10. The empirical model then has probability function

$$p_6(x) = \begin{cases} 0.125, & x = 3, \\ 0.125, & x = 5, \\ 0.375, & x = 6, \\ 0.25, & x = 7, \\ 0.125, & x = 10. \end{cases} \qquad \square$$

Alert readers will note that many discrete models with finite support look like empirical models. Model 3 could have been the empirical model for a sample of size 100 that contained 50 zeros, 25 ones, 12 twos, 8 threes, and 5 fours. Regardless, we will use the term empirical model only when there is an actual sample behind it. The two moments for Model 6 are

$$\mathrm{E}(X_6) = 6.25, \quad \mathrm{E}(X_6^2) = 42.5$$

using the same approach as in Model 3. It should be noted that the mean of this random variable is equal to the sample arithmetic average (also called the sample mean).

Definition 3.4 *The **kth central moment** of a random variable is the expected value of the kth power of the deviation of the variable from its mean. It is denoted by $\mathrm{E}[(X - \mu)^k]$ or by μ_k. The second central moment is usually called the **variance** and denoted σ^2 and its square root, σ, is called the **standard deviation**. The ratio of the standard deviation to the mean is called the **coefficient of variation**. The ratio of the third central moment to the cube of the standard deviation, $\gamma_1 = \mu_3/\sigma^3$, is called the **skewness**. The ratio of the fourth central moment to the fourth power of the standard deviation, $\gamma_2 = \mu_4/\sigma^4$, is called the **kurtosis**.*[1]

The continuous and discrete formulas for calculating central moments are

$$\begin{aligned} \mu_k & = \mathrm{E}[(X - \mu)^k] \\ & = \int_{-\infty}^{\infty} (x - \mu)^k f(x)dx \text{ if the random variable is continuous} \\ & = \sum_j (x_j - \mu)^k p(x_j) \text{ if the random variable is discrete.} \quad (3.2) \end{aligned}$$

---

[1] It would be more accurate to call these items the "coefficient of skewness" and "coefficient of kurtosis" because there are other quantities that also measure asymmetry and flatness. The simpler expressions will be used in this text.

In reality, the integral need be taken only over those x values where $f(x)$ is positive. The standard deviation is a measure of how much the probability is spread out over the random variable's possible values. It is measured in the same units as the random variable itself. The coefficient of variation measures the spread relative to the mean. The skewness is a measure of asymmetry. A symmetric distribution has a skewness of zero, while a positive skewness indicates that probabilities to the right tend to be assigned to values further from the mean than those to the left. The kurtosis measures flatness of the distribution relative to a normal distribution (which has a kurtosis of 3). Kurtosis values above 3 indicate that (keeping the standard deviation constant), relative to a normal distribution, more probability tends to be at points away from the mean than at points near the mean. The coefficients of variation, skewness, and kurtosis are all dimensionless.

There is a link between raw and central moments. The following equation indicates the connection between second moments. The development uses the continuous version from (3.1) and (3.2), but the result applies to all random variables.

$$\mu_2 = \int_{-\infty}^{\infty} (x-\mu)^2 f(x)dx = \int_{-\infty}^{\infty} (x^2 - 2x\mu + \mu^2)f(x)dx$$
$$= \mathrm{E}(X^2) - 2\mu\mathrm{E}(X) + \mu^2 = \mu_2' - \mu^2. \tag{3.3}$$

Example 3.5 *The density function of the gamma distribution appears to be positively skewed. Demonstrate that this is true and illustrate with graphs.*

From Appendix A, the first three raw moments of the gamma distribution are $\alpha\theta$, $\alpha(\alpha+1)\theta^2$, and $\alpha(\alpha+1)(\alpha+2)\theta^3$. From (3.3) the variance is $\alpha\theta^2$ and from the solution to Exercise 3.1 the third central moment is $2\alpha\theta^3$. Therefore, the skewness is $2\alpha^{-1/2}$. Because α must be positive, the skewness is always positive. Also, as α decreases, the skewness increases.

Consider the following two gamma distributions. One has parameters $\alpha = 0.5$ and $\theta = 100$ while the other has $\alpha = 5$ and $\theta = 10$. These have the same mean, but their skewness coefficients are 2.83 and 0.89, respectively. Figure 3.1 demonstrates the difference. □

Note that when calculating the standard deviation for Model 6 in Exercise 3.2 the result is the sample standard deviation using n (as opposed to the more commonly used $n-1$) in the denominator. Finally, it should be noted that when calculating moments it is possible that the integral or sum will not exist (as is the case for the third and fourth moments for Model 2). For the models we typically encounter, the integrand and summand are nonnegative and so failure to exist implies that the required limit that gives the integral or sum is infinity. See Example 4.15 for an illustration.

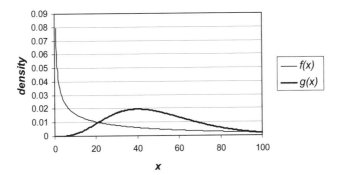

Fig. 3.1 Densities of $f(x) \sim \mathrm{gamma}(0.5, 100)$ and $g(x) \sim \mathrm{gamma}(5, 10)$.

Definition 3.6 *For a given value of d with* $\Pr(X > d) > 0$, *the **excess loss variable** is* $Y = X - d$ *given that* $X > d$. *Its expected value,*

$$e_X(d) = e(d) = \mathrm{E}(Y) = \mathrm{E}(X - d | X > d),$$

*is called the **mean excess loss function.** Other names for this expectation are **mean residual life function** and **complete expectation of life.** When the latter terminology is used, the commonly used symbol is* $\overset{\circ}{e}_d$.

This variable could also be called a **left truncated and shifted variable**. It is left truncated because observations below d are discarded. It is shifted because d is subtracted from the remaining values. When X is a payment variable, the mean excess loss is the expected amount paid given that there has been a payment in excess of a deductible of d. When X is the age at death, the mean excess loss is the expected remaining time until death given that the person is alive at age d. The kth moment of the excess loss variable is determined from

$$
\begin{aligned}
e_X^k(d) &= \frac{\int_d^\infty (x - d)^k f(x)\,dx}{1 - F(d)} \text{ if the variable is continuous} \\
&= \frac{\sum_{x_j > d}(x_j - d)^k p(x_j)}{1 - F(d)} \text{ if the variable is discrete.} \quad (3.4)
\end{aligned}
$$

Here, $e_X^k(d)$ is defined only if the integral or sum converges. There is a particularly convenient formula for calculating the first moment. The development is given below for the continuous version, but the result holds for all random variables. The second line is based on an integration by parts where the antiderivative of $f(x)$ is taken as $-S(x)$.

$$e_X(d) = \frac{\int_d^\infty (x-d)f(x)dx}{1-F(d)}$$

$$= \frac{-(x-d)S(x)\big|_d^\infty + \int_d^\infty S(x)dx}{S(d)}$$

$$= \frac{\int_d^\infty S(x)dx}{S(d)}. \tag{3.5}$$

Definition 3.7 *The **left censored and shifted variable** is*

$$Y = (X-d)_+ = \begin{cases} 0, & X < d, \\ X - d, & X \geq d. \end{cases}$$

It is left censored because values below d are not ignored but are set equal to 0. There is no standard name or symbol for the moments of this variable. For dollar events, the distinction between the excess loss variable and the left censored and shifted variable is one of *per payment* versus *per loss*. In the former situation, the variable exists only when a payment is made. The latter variable takes on the value 0 whenever a loss produces no payment. The moments can be calculated from

$$E[(X-d)_+^k] = \int_d^\infty (x-d)^k f(x)dx \text{ if the variable is continuous,}$$

$$= \sum_{x_j > d} (x_j - d)^k p(x_j) \text{ if the variable is discrete.} \tag{3.6}$$

It should be noted that

$$E[(X-d)_+^k] = e^k(d)[1 - F(d)]. \tag{3.7}$$

Example 3.8 *Construct graphs to illustrate the difference between the excess loss variable and the left censored and shifted variable.*

The two graphs in Figures 3.2 and 3.3 plot the modified variable Y as a function of the unmodified variable X. The only difference is that for X values below 100 the variable is undefined while for the left censored and shifted variable it is set equal to zero. $\square$

The next definition provides a complementary function to the excess loss.

Definition 3.9 *The **limited loss variable** is*

$$Y = X \wedge u = \begin{cases} X, & X < u, \\ u, & X \geq u. \end{cases}$$

*Its expected value, $E[X \wedge u]$, is called the **limited expected value**.*

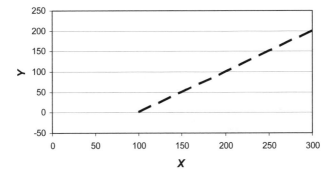

Fig. 3.2   Excess loss variable.

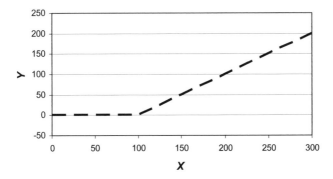

Fig. 3.3   Left censored and shifted variable.

This variable could also be called the **right censored variable**. It is right censored because values above u are set equal to u. An insurance phenomenon that relates to this variable is the existence of a policy limit that sets a maximum on the benefit to be paid. Note that $(X - d)_+ + (X \wedge d) = X$. That is, buying one policy with a limit of d and another with a deductible of d is equivalent to buying full coverage. This is illustrated in Figure 3.4.

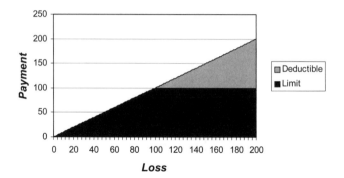

Fig. 3.4   Limit of 100 plus deductible of 100 equals full coverage.

The most direct formulas for the kth moment of the limited loss variable are

$$E[(X \wedge u)^k] = \int_{-\infty}^{u} x^k f(x)dx + u^k[1 - F(u)]$$

if the random variable is continuous

$$= \sum_{x_j \leq u} x_j^k p(x_j) + u^k[1 - F(u)]$$

if the random variable is discrete.   (3.8)

Another interesting formula is derived as follows:

$$E[(X \wedge u)^k] = \int_{-\infty}^{0} x^k f(x)dx + \int_{0}^{u} x^k f(x)dx + u^k[1 - F(u)]$$

$$= x^k F(x)\big|_{-\infty}^{0} - \int_{-\infty}^{0} kx^{k-1}F(x)dx$$

$$\quad - x^k S(x)\big|_{0}^{u} + \int_{0}^{u} kx^{k-1}S(x)dx + u^k S(u)$$

$$= -\int_{-\infty}^{0} kx^{k-1}F(x)dx + \int_{0}^{u} kx^{k-1}S(x)dx,   (3.9)$$

where the second line uses integration by parts. For $k = 1$, we have

$$E(X \wedge u) = -\int_{-\infty}^{0} F(x)dx + \int_{0}^{u} S(x)dx.$$

The corresponding formula for discrete random variables is not particularly interesting. The limited expected value also represents the expected dollar saving per incident when a deductible is imposed. The kth limited moment of many common continuous distributions is presented in Appendix A. Exercise 3.8 asks you to develop a relationship between the three first moments introduced previously.

3.1.1   Exercises

3.1 Develop formulas similar to (3.3) for μ_3 and μ_4.

3.2 Calculate the standard deviation, skewness, and kurtosis for each of the six models. It may help to note that Model 2 is a Pareto distribution and the density function in the continuous part of Model 4 is an exponential distribution. Formulas that may help with calculations for these models appear in Appendix A.

3.3 (*) A random variable has a mean and a coefficient of variation of 2. The third raw moment is 136. Determine the skewness.

3.4 (*) Determine the skewness of a gamma distribution that has a coefficient of variation of 1.

3.5 Determine the mean excess loss function for Models 1–4. Compare the functions for Models 1, 2, and 4.

3.6 (*) For two random variables, X and Y, $e_Y(30) = e_X(30) + 4$. Let X have a uniform distribution on the interval from 0 to 100 and let Y have a uniform distribution on the interval from 0 to w. Determine w.

3.7 (*) A random variable has density function $f(x) = \lambda^{-1}e^{-x/\lambda}$, $x, \lambda > 0$. Determine $e(\lambda)$, the mean residual life function evaluated at λ.

3.8 Show that the following relationship holds:

$$E(X) = e(d)S(d) + E(X \wedge d). \qquad (3.10)$$

3.9 Determine the limited expected value function for Models 1–4. Do this using both (3.8) and (3.10). For Models 1 and 2 also obtain the function using (3.9).

3.10 (*) Which of the following statements are true?

  (a) The mean residual life function for an empirical distribution is continuous.

  (b) The mean residual life function for an exponential distribution is constant.

  (c) If it exists, the mean residual life function for a Pareto distribution is decreasing.

3.11 (*) Losses have a Pareto distribution with $\alpha = 0.5$ and $\theta = 10{,}000$. Determine the mean residual life at 10,000.

3.12 Define a right truncated variable and provide a formula for its kth moment.

3.13 (*) The severity distribution of individual claims has pdf

$$f(x) = 2.5x^{-3.5}, \ x \geq 1.$$

Determine the coefficient of variation.

3.14 (*) Claim sizes are for 100, 200, 300, 400, or 500. The true probabilities for these values are 0.05, 0.20, 0.50, 0.20, and 0.05, respectively. Determine the skewness and kurtosis for this distribution.

3.15 (*) Losses follow a Pareto distribution with $\alpha > 1$ and θ unspecified. Determine the ratio of the mean excess loss function at $x = 2\theta$ to the mean excess loss function at $x = \theta$.

3.2   PERCENTILES

One other value of interest that may be derived from the distribution function is the percentile function. It is the inverse of the distribution function, but because this quantity is not well defined, an arbitrary definition must be created.

Definition 3.10 *The **100pth percentile** of a random variable is any value π_p such that $F(\pi_p-) \leq p \leq F(\pi_p)$. The 50th percentile, $\pi_{0.5}$ is called the **median**.*

If the distribution function has a value of p for one and only one x value, then the percentile is uniquely defined. In addition, if the distribution function jumps from a value below p to a value above p, then the percentile is at the location of the jump. The only time the percentile is not uniquely defined is when the distribution function is constant at a value of p over a range of values. In that case, any value in that range can be used as the percentile.

Example 3.11 *Determine the 50th and 80th percentiles for Models 1 and 3.*

For Model 1, the pth percentile can be obtained from $p = F(\pi_p) = 0.01\pi_p$ and so $\pi_p = 100p$, and in particular, the requested percentiles are 50 and 80 (see Figure 3.5). For Model 3 the distribution function equals 0.5 for all $0 \leq x < 1$ and so all such values can be the 50th percentile. For the 80th percentile, note that at $x = 2$ the distribution function jumps from 0.75 to 0.87 and so $\pi_{0.8} = 2$ (see Figure 3.6). □

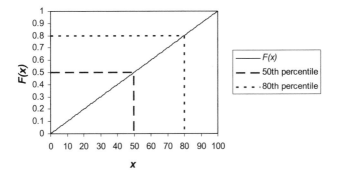

Fig. 3.5   Percentiles for Model 1.

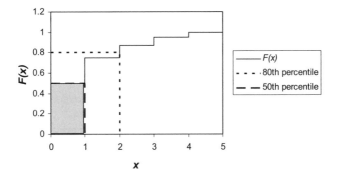

Fig. 3.6   Percentiles for Model 3.

3.2.1   Exercises

3.16 (*) The cdf of a random variable is $F(x) = 1 - x^{-2}$, $x \geq 1$. Determine the mean, median, and mode of this random variable.

3.17 Determine the 50th and 80th percentiles for Models 2, 4, 5, and 6.

3.18 (*) Losses have a Pareto distribution with parameters α and θ. The 10th percentile is $\theta - k$. The 90th percentile is $5\theta - 3k$. Determine the value of α.

3.19 (*) Losses have a Weibull distribution with parameters τ and θ. The 25th percentile is 1,000 and the 75th percentile is 100,000. Determine the value of τ.

3.3 GENERATING FUNCTIONS AND SUMS OF RANDOM VARIABLES

An insurance company rarely insures only one person. The total claims paid on all policies is the sum of all payments. Thus it is useful to be able to determine properties of $S_k = X_1 + \cdots + X_k$. The first result is a version of the central limit theorem.

Theorem 3.12 *For a random variable S_k as defined above, $E(S_k) = E(X_1) + \cdots + E(X_k)$. Also, if $X_1, \ldots, X_k$ are independent, $Var(S_k) = Var(X_1) + \cdots + Var(X_k)$. If the random variables $X_1, X_2, \ldots$ are independent and their first two moments meet certain conditions, $\lim_{k \to \infty} [S_k - E(S_k)]/\sqrt{Var(S_k)}$ has a normal distribution with mean 0 and variance 1.*

Obtaining the distribution or density function of S_k is usually very difficult. However, there are a few cases where it is simple. The key to this simplicity is the generating function.

Definition 3.13 *For a random variable X, the **moment generating function** (mgf) is $M_X(t) = E(e^{tX})$ for all t for which the expected value exists. The **probability generating function** (pgf) is $P_X(z) = E(z^X)$ for all z for which the expectation exists.*

Note that $M_X(t) = P_X(e^t)$ and $P_X(z) = M_X(\ln z)$. Often the mgf is used for continuous random variables and the pgf for discrete random variables. For us, the value of these functions is not so much that they generate moments or probabilities but that there is a one-to-one correspondence between a random variable's distribution function and its mgf and pgf (i.e., two random variables with different distribution functions cannot have the same mgf or pgf). The following result aids in working with sums of random variables.

Theorem 3.14 *Let $S_k = X_1 + \cdots + X_k$, where the random variables in the sum are independent. Then $M_{S_k}(t) = \prod_{j=1}^{k} M_{X_j}(t)$ and $P_{S_k}(z) = \prod_{j=1}^{k} P_{X_j}(z)$ provided all the component mgfs and pgfs exist.*

Proof: We use the fact that the expected product of independent random variables is the product of the individual expectations. Then,

$$
\begin{aligned}
M_{S_k}(t) &= E(e^{tS_k}) = E[e^{t(X_1 + \cdots + X_k)}] \\
&= \prod_{j=1}^{k} E(e^{tX_j}) = \prod_{j=1}^{k} M_{X_j}(t).
\end{aligned}
$$

A similar argument can be used for the pgf. □

Example 3.15 *Show that the sum of independent gamma random variables, each with same value of θ, has a gamma distribution.*

The moment generating function of a gamma variable is

$$
\begin{aligned}
\mathrm{E}(e^{tX}) &= \frac{\int_0^\infty e^{tx} x^{\alpha-1} e^{-x/\theta} dx}{\Gamma(\alpha)\theta^\alpha} \\
&= \frac{\int_0^\infty x^{\alpha-1} e^{-x(-t+1/\theta)} dx}{\Gamma(\alpha)\theta^\alpha} \\
&= \frac{\int_0^\infty y^{\alpha-1} (-t+1/\theta)^{-\alpha} e^{-y} dy}{\Gamma(\alpha)\theta^\alpha} \\
&= \frac{\Gamma(\alpha)(-t+1/\theta)^{-\alpha}}{\Gamma(\alpha)\theta^\alpha} = \left(\frac{1}{1-\theta t}\right)^\alpha, \quad t < 1/\theta.
\end{aligned}
$$

Now let X_j have a gamma distribution with parameters α_j and θ. Then the moment generating function of the sum is

$$
M_{S_k}(t) = \prod_{j=1}^{k} \left(\frac{1}{1-\theta t}\right)^{\alpha_j} = \left(\frac{1}{1-\theta t}\right)^{\alpha_1+\cdots+\alpha_k}
$$

which is the moment generating function of a gamma distribution with parameters $\alpha_1 + \cdots + \alpha_k$ and θ. □

Example 3.16 *Obtain the mgf and pgf for the Poisson distribution.*

The pgf is

$$
P_X(z) = \sum_{x=0}^{\infty} z^x \frac{\lambda^x e^{-\lambda}}{x!} = e^{-\lambda} \sum_{x=0}^{\infty} \frac{(z\lambda)^x}{x!} = e^{-\lambda} e^{z\lambda} = e^{\lambda(z-1)}.
$$

Then the mgf is $M_X(t) = P_X(e^t) = \exp[\lambda(e^t - 1)]$. □

3.3.1 Exercises

3.20 (*) A portfolio contains 16 independent risks, each with a gamma distribution with parameters $\alpha = 1$ and $\theta = 250$. Give an expression using the incomplete gamma function for the probability that the sum of the losses exceeds 6,000. Then approximate this probability using the central limit theorem.

3.21 (*) The severities of individual claims have the Pareto distribution with parameters $\alpha = 8/3$, and $\theta = 8,000$. Use the central limit theorem to approximate the probability that the sum of 100 independent claims will exceed 600,000.

3.22 (*) The severities of individual claims have the gamma distribution (see Appendix A) with parameters $\alpha = 5$ and $\theta = 1,000$. Use the central limit theorem to approximate the probability that the sum of 100 independent claims exceeds 525,000.

3.23 A sample of 1,000 health insurance contracts on adults produced a sample mean of 1,300 for the annual benefits paid with a standard deviation of 400. It is expected that 2,500 contracts will be issued next year. Use the central limit theorem to estimate the probability that benefit payments will be more than 101% of the expected amount.

3.24 Show that the mgf for the inverse Gaussian distribution with θ replaced by $\beta = \mu^2/\theta$ is given by

$$M(t) = \exp\left[\frac{\mu}{\beta}\left(1 - \sqrt{1 - 2\beta t}\right)\right], \ t < 1/(2\beta).$$

4

Classifying and creating distributions

4.1 INTRODUCTION

The set of all possible distribution functions is too large to comprehend. Therefore, when searching for a distribution function to use as a model for a random phenomenon, it can be helpful if the field can be narrowed. One division that has already been discussed is the separation into discrete, continuous, and mixed distributions. In most situations it will be obvious which of the three applies. Beyond this, we need more artificial distinctions. The next section describes a split based on the complexity of the model. The following section then looks at the shape of the distribution to distinguish one from another. After that, a few methods of creating additional distributions are introduced. This is followed by a listing of some commonly used continuous distributions. The final section is an extensive treatment of discrete distributions. By the end of this chapter, most of the distributions in Appendices A and B will have been introduced. While this chapter is more about differences from one distribution to another, these distributions have some common elements that are desirable for actuarial models. Among them are:

- The support is a subset of the nonnegative real numbers. Most actuarial phenomena are counts or are measurements of time or money and as such are rarely negative, although if the random variable of interest

Loss Models: From Data to Decisions, Second Edition.
By Stuart A. Klugman, Harry H. Panjer, and Gordon E. Willmot
ISBN 0-471-21577-5   Copyright © 2004 John Wiley & Sons, Inc.

is financial gain, negative outcomes are certainly possible. However, financial gain is often the result of the realization of several nonnegative variables, some measuring income and some measuring expenses.

- Some distributions are special cases of others. This allows the modeler to choose from models of varying complexity.

- They can have one or more modes and a mode may or may not be at zero.

4.2   THE ROLE OF PARAMETERS

This split has to do with how much information is needed to specify the model. The number of quantities (parameters) needed to do so gives some indication of how complex a model is, in the sense that many items are needed to describe it. Arguments for a simple model include the following:

- With few items required in its specification, it is more likely that each item can be determined more accurately.

- It is more likely to be stable across time and across settings. That is, if the model does well today, it (perhaps with small changes to reflect inflation or similar phenomena) will probably do well tomorrow and will also do well in other, similar, situations.

- Because data can often be irregular, a simple model may provide necessary smoothing.

Of course, complex models also have advantages.

- With many items required in its specification, it can more closely match reality.

- With many items required in its specification, it can more closely match irregularities in the data.

Another way to express the difference is that simpler models can be estimated more accurately, but the model itself may be too superficial. The principle of parsimony states that the simplest model that adequately reflects reality should be used. The definition of "adequately" will depend on the purpose for which the model is to be used.

In the following subsections, we will move from simpler models to more complex models. There is some difficulty in naming the various classifications because there is not universal agreement on the definitions. With the exception of parametric distributions, the other category names have been created by the authors. It should also be understood that these categories do not cover the universe of possible models nor will every model be easy to categorize. These should be considered as qualitative descriptions.

4.2.1   Parametric and scale distributions

These models are simple enough to be specified by a few key numbers.

Definition 4.1 *A **parametric distribution** is a set of distribution functions, each member of which is determined by specifying one or more values called **parameters**. The number of parameters is fixed and finite.*

The most familiar parametric distribution is the normal distribution with parameters μ and σ^2. When values for these two parameters are specified, the distribution function is completely known.

These are the simplest distributions in this subsection, because typically only a small number of values need to be specified. All of the individual distributions in Appendices A and B are parametric. Within this class, distributions with fewer parameters are simpler than those with more parameters.

For much of actuarial modeling work, it is especially convenient if the name of the distribution is unchanged when the random variable is multiplied by a constant. The most common uses for this phenomenon are to model the effect of inflation and to accommodate a change in the monetary unit.

Definition 4.2 *A parametric distribution is a **scale distribution** if, when a random variable from that set of distributions is multiplied by a positive constant, the resulting random variable is also in that set of distributions.*

Example 4.3 *Demonstrate that the exponential distribution is a scale distribution.*

According to Appendix A, the distribution function is $F_X(x) = 1 - e^{-x/\theta}$. Let $Y = cX$, where $c > 0$. Then,

$$
\begin{aligned}
F_Y(y) &= \Pr(Y \leq y), \\
&= \Pr(cX \leq y), \\
&= \Pr\left(X \leq \frac{y}{c}\right), \\
&= 1 - e^{-y/c\theta}.
\end{aligned}
$$

But this is an exponential distribution with parameter $c\theta$. $\square$

Definition 4.4 *For random variables with nonnegative support, a **scale parameter** is a parameter for a scale distribution that meets two conditions. First, when a member of the scale distribution is multiplied by a positive constant, the scale parameter is multiplied by the same constant. Second, when a member of the scale distribution is multiplied by a positive constant, all other parameters are unchanged.*

Example 4.5 *Demonstrate that the gamma distribution, as defined in Appendix A, has a scale parameter.*

Let X have the gamma distribution and $Y = cX$. Then, using the incomplete gamma notation in Appendix A,

$$
\begin{aligned}
F_Y(y) &= \Pr\left(X \le \frac{y}{c}\right) \\
&= \Gamma\left(\alpha; \frac{y}{c\theta}\right)
\end{aligned}
$$

indicating that Y has a gamma distribution with parameters α and $c\theta$. Therefore, the parameter θ is a scale parameter. $\square$

Many textbooks write the density function for the gamma distribution as

$$
f(x) = \frac{x^{\alpha-1}e^{-\beta x}\beta^{\alpha}}{\Gamma(\alpha)}.
$$

We have chosen to use the version of the density function that has a scale parameter. When the alternative version is multiplied by c, the parameters become α and β/c. As well, the mean is proportional to θ in our version, while it is proportional to $1/\beta$ in the alternative version. Our version makes it easier to get ballpark estimates of this parameter, although, for the alternative definition, one need only keep in mind that the parameter is inversely proportional to the mean.

It is often possible to recognize a scale parameter from looking at the distribution or density function. In particular, the distribution function would have x always appear as x/θ.

4.2.2   Parametric distribution families

A slightly more complex version of a parametric distribution is one in which the number of parameters is finite but not fixed in advance.

Definition 4.6 *A **parametric distribution family** is a set of parametric distributions that are related in some meaningful way.*

The most common type of parametric distribution family is described in the following example.

Example 4.7 *One type of parametric distribution family is based on a specified parametric distribution. Other members of the family are obtained by setting one or more parameters from the specified distribution equal to a preset value or to each other. Demonstrate that the transformed beta family as defined in Appendix A is a parametric distribution family.*

The transformed beta distribution has four parameters. Each of the other named distributions in the family is a transformed beta distribution with certain parameters set equal to 1 (for example, the Pareto distribution has $\gamma = \tau = 1$) or to each other (the paralogistic distribution has $\tau = 1$ and $\gamma = \alpha$). Note that the number of parameters (ranging from two to four) is not known in advance. There is a subtle difference in definitions. A modeler who uses the transformed beta distribution looks at all four parameters over their range of possible values. A modeler who uses the transformed beta family pays particular attention to the possibility of using special cases such as the Burr distribution. For example, if the former modeler collects some data and decides that $\tau = 1.01$, that will be the value to use. The latter modeler will note that $\tau = 1$ gives a Burr distribution and will likely use that model instead. □

4.2.3 Finite mixture distributions

By themselves, mixture distributions are no more complex, but later in this subsection we will find a way to increase the complexity level. One motivation for mixing is that the underlying phenomenon may actually be several phenomena that occur with unknown probabilities. For example, a randomly selected dental claim may be from a check-up, from a filling, from a repair (such as a crown), or from a surgical procedure. Because of the differing modes for these possibilities, a mixture model may work well.

Definition 4.8 *A random variable Y is a **k-point mixture**[1] of the random variables $X_1, X_2, \ldots, X_k$ if its cdf is given by*

$$F_Y(y) = a_1 F_{X_1}(y) + a_2 F_{X_2}(y) + \cdots + a_k F_{X_k}(y), \tag{4.1}$$

where all $a_j > 0$ and $a_1 + a_2 + \cdots + a_k = 1$.

This essentially assigns probability a_j to the outcome that Y is a realization of the random variable X_j. Note that, if we have 20 choices for a given random variable, a two-point mixture allows us to create over 200 new distributions.[2] This may be sufficient for most modeling situations. Nevertheless, these are still parametric distribution, though perhaps with many parameters.

Example 4.9 *For models involving general liability insurance, actuaries at the Insurance Services Office has had some success with a mixture of two*

---

[1] The words "mixed" and "mixture" have been used interchangeably to refer to the type of distribution described here as well as distributions that are partly discrete and partly continuous. This text will not attempt to resolve that confusion. The context will make clear which type of distribution is being considered.

[2] There are actually $\binom{20}{2} + 20 = 210$ choices. The extra 20 represent the cases where both distributions are of the same type but with different parameters.

Pareto distributions. They also found that five parameters were not necessary. The distribution they selected has cdf

$$F(x) = 1 - a \left(\frac{\theta_1}{\theta_1 + x} \right)^\alpha - (1 - a) \left(\frac{\theta_2}{\theta_2 + x} \right)^{\alpha+2}.$$

Note that the shape parameters in the two Pareto distributions differ by 2. The second distribution places more probability on smaller values. This might be a model for frequent, small claims while the first distribution covers large, but infrequent claims. This distribution has only four parameters, bringing some parsimony to the modeling process. □

Suppose we do not know how many distributions should be in the mixture. Then the value of k becomes a parameter, as indicated in the following definition.

Definition 4.10 *A **variable-component mixture distribution** has a distribution function that can be written as*

$$F(x) = \sum_{j=1}^{K} a_j F_j(x), \ \sum_{j=1}^{K} a_j = 1, \ a_j > 0, \ j = 1, \ldots, K, \ K = 1, 2, \ldots.$$

These models have been called *semiparametric* because in complexity they are between parametric models and nonparametric models (see the next subsection). This distinction becomes more important when model selection is discussed in Chapter 13. When the number of parameters is to be estimated from data, hypothesis tests to determine the appropriate number of parameters become more difficult. When all of the components have the same parametric distribution (but different parameters), the resulting distribution is called a "variable mixture of gs" distribution, where g stands for the name of the component distribution.

Example 4.11 *Determine the distribution, density, and hazard rate functions for the variable mixture of exponentials distribution.*

A combination of exponential distribution functions can be written

$$F(x) = 1 - a_1 e^{-x/\theta_1} - a_2 e^{-x/\theta_2} - \cdots - a_K e^{-x/\theta_K},$$
$$\sum_{j=1}^{K} a_j = 1, \ a_j, \theta_j > 0, \ j = 1, \ldots, K, \ K = 1, 2, \ldots.$$

and then the other functions are

$$f(x) = a_1 \theta_1^{-1} e^{-x/\theta_1} + a_2 \theta_2^{-1} e^{-x/\theta_2} + \cdots + a_K \theta_K^{-1} e^{-x/\theta_K},$$
$$h(x) = \frac{a_1 \theta_1^{-1} e^{-x/\theta_1} + a_2 \theta_2^{-1} e^{-x/\theta_2} + \cdots + a_K \theta_K^{-1} e^{-x/\theta_K}}{a_1 e^{-x/\theta_1} + a_2 e^{-x/\theta_2} + \cdots + a_K e^{-x/\theta_K}}.$$

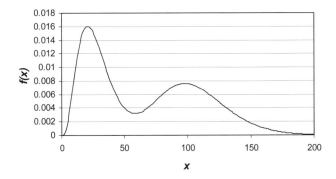

Fig. 4.1 Two-point mixture of gammas distribution.

The number of parameters is not fixed nor is it even limited. For example, when $K = 2$ there are three parameters $(a_1, \theta_1, \theta_2)$, noting that a_2 is not a parameter because once a_1 is set the value of a_2 is determined. However, when $K = 4$ there are seven parameters. ☐

Example 4.12 *Illustrate how a two-point mixture of gamma variables can create a bimodal distribution.*

Consider a fifty–fifty mixture of two gamma distributions. One has parameters $\alpha = 4$ and $\theta = 7$ (for a mode of 21) and the other has parameters $\alpha = 15$ and $\theta = 7$ (for a mode of 98). The density function is

$$f(x) = 0.5 \frac{x^3 e^{-x/7}}{3! 7^4} + 0.5 \frac{x^{14} e^{-x/7}}{14! 7^{15}}$$

and a graph appears in Figure 4.1. ☐

4.2.4 Data-dependent distributions

Models 1–5 and many of the examples rely on an associated phenomenon (the random variable) but not on observations of that phenomenon. For example, without having observed any dental claims, we could postulate a lognormal distribution with parameters $\mu = 5$ and $\sigma = 1$. Our model may be a poor description of dental claims, but that is a different matter. On the other hand, it is possible to construct models that require data. These models also have parameters but are often called nonparametric.

Definition 4.13 *A **data-dependent distribution** is at least as complex as the data or knowledge that produced it, and the number of "parameters" increases as the number of data points or amount of knowledge increases.*

Essentially, these models have as many (or more) "parameters" than observations in the data set. The empirical distribution as illustrated by Model 6 on page 27 is a data-dependent distribution. Each data point contributes probability $1/n$ to the probability function, so the n parameters are the n observations in the data set that produced the empirical distribution.

Another example of a data-dependent model is the kernel smoothing model, which is covered in more detail in Section 11.3. Rather than place a spike of probability $1/n$ at each data point, a continuous density function with area $1/n$ replaces the data point. This piece is centered at the data point so that this model follows the data, but not perfectly. It provides some smoothing versus the empirical distribution. A simple example is given below.

Example 4.14 *Construct a kernel smoothing model from Model 6 using the uniform kernel and a bandwidth of 2.*

The probability density function is

$$f(x) = \sum_{j=1}^{5} p_6(x_j) K_j(x),$$

$$K_j(x) = \begin{cases} 0, & |x - x_j| > 2, \\ 0.25, & |x - x_j| \leq 2, \end{cases}$$

where the sum is taken over the five points where the original model has positive probability. For example, the first term of the sum is the function

$$p_6(x_1) K_1(x) = \begin{cases} 0, & x < 1, \\ 0.03125, & 1 \leq x \leq 5, \\ 0, & x > 5. \end{cases}$$

The complete density function is the sum of five such functions, which are illustrated in Figure 4.2.   □

Note that both the kernel smoothing model and the empirical distribution can also be written as mixture distributions. The reason these models are classified separately is that the number of components relates to the sample size rather than to the phenomenon and its random variable.

4.2.5 Exercises

4.1 Demonstrate that the lognormal distribution as parameterized in Appendix A is a scale distribution but has no scale parameter. Display an alternative parametrization of this distribution that does have a scale parameter.

4.2 Which of Models 1–6 could be considered as members of a parametric distribution? For those that are, name or describe the distribution.

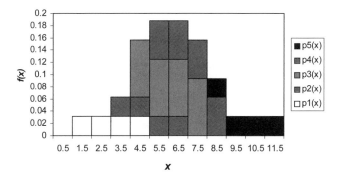

Fig. 4.2   Kernel density distribution.

4.3 (*) Claims have a Pareto distribution with $\alpha = 2$ and θ unknown. Claims the following year experience 6% uniform inflation. Let r be the ratio of the proportion of claims that will exceed d next year to the proportion of claims that exceed d this year. Determine the limit of r as d goes to infinity.

4.4 Determine the mean and second moment of the two-point mixture distribution in Example 4.9. The solution to this exercise provides general formulas for raw moments of a mixture distribution.

4.5 Determine expressions for the mean and variance of the mixture of gammas distribution.

4.6 Which of Models 1–6 could be considered to be from parametric distribution families? Which could be considered to be from variable-component mixture distributions?

4.7 (*) Seventy-five percent of claims have a normal distribution with a mean of 3,000 and a variance of 1,000,000. The remaining 25% have a normal distribution with a mean of 4,000 and a variance of 1,000,000. Determine the probability that a randomly selected claim exceeds 5,000.

4.8 (*) Let X has a Burr distribution with parameters $\alpha = 1$, $\gamma = 2$, and $\theta = \sqrt{1,000}$ and let Y has a Pareto distribution with parameters $\alpha = 1$ and $\theta = 1,000$. Let Z be a mixture of X and Y with equal weight on each component. Determine the median of Z. Let $W = 1.1Z$. Demonstrate that W is also a mixture of a Burr and a Pareto distribution and determine the parameters of W.

4.9 (*) Consider three random variables: X is a mixture of a uniform distribution on the interval 0 to 2 and a uniform distribution on the interval 0 to 3;

Y is the sum of two random variables, one is uniform on 0 to 2 and the other is uniform on 0 to 3; Z is a normal distribution that has been right censored at 1. Match these random variables with the following descriptions:

(a) Both the distribution and density functions are continuous.

(b) The distribution function is continuous but the density function is discontinuous.

(c) The distribution function is discontinuous.

4.10 Demonstrate that the model in Example 4.14 is a mixture of uniform distributions.

4.11 Show that the inverse Gaussian distribution as parameterized in Appendix A is a scale family but does not have a scale parameter.

4.12 Show that the Weibull distribution has a scale parameter.

4.3   TAIL WEIGHT

The *tail* of a distribution (more properly, the right tail) is that part that reveals probabilities about large values. It is of interest to actuaries because it is the occurrence (or lack thereof) of large values that is most influential on profits. Risky types of insurance such as medical malpractice feature more large claims (relative to the mean) than less risky insurances such as automobile physical damage. Random variables that tend to assign higher probabilities to large values are said to be heavy tailed. Tail weight can be a relative concept (model A has a heavier tail than model B) or an absolute concept (distributions with a certain property are classified as heavy tailed). When choosing models, tail weight can help narrow the choices or can confirm someone else's choice. For example, when someone models medical malpractice payments with a Pareto distribution, it seems reasonable as the Pareto distribution is regarded as having a heavy tail. Conversely, the light-tailed lognormal distribution may be a reasonable model for dental insurance payments. However, it should be noted that various measures of tail weight need not agree.

4.3.1   Existence of moments

Recall that in the continuous case the kth raw moment for a random variable that takes on only positive values (like most insurance payment variables) is given by $\int_0^\infty x^k f(x)dx$. Depending on the density function and the value of k, this integral may not exist. If the density function is too large for large values of x, then, when multiplied by the large number x^k, the values will be too large for the integral to converge. Thus, existence of all positive moments indicates a light right tail, while existence of only positive moments up to a certain value (or existence of no positive moments at all) indicates a heavy right tail.[3]

Example 4.15 *Demonstrate that for the gamma distribution all positive raw moments exist but for the Pareto distribution they do not.*

For the gamma distribution

$$
\begin{aligned}
\mu'_k &= \int_0^\infty x^k \frac{x^{\alpha-1}e^{-x/\theta}}{\Gamma(\alpha)\theta^\alpha}\,dx \\
&= \int_0^\infty (y\theta)^k \frac{(y\theta)^{\alpha-1}e^{-y}}{\Gamma(\alpha)\theta^\alpha}\theta\,dy, \text{ making the substitution } y = x/\theta \\
&= \frac{\theta^k}{\Gamma(\alpha)}\Gamma(\alpha+k) < \infty \text{ for all } k > 0.
\end{aligned}
$$

while for the Pareto distribution

$$
\begin{aligned}
\mu'_k &= \int_0^\infty x^k \frac{\alpha\theta^\alpha}{(x+\theta)^{\alpha+1}}\,dx \\
&= \int_\theta^\infty (y-\theta)^k \frac{\alpha\theta^\alpha}{y^{\alpha+1}}\,dy, \text{ making the substitution } y = x+\theta \\
&= \alpha\theta^\alpha \int_\theta^\infty \sum_{j=0}^k \binom{k}{j} y^{j-\alpha-1}(-\theta)^{k-j}\,dy \text{ for integer values of } k.
\end{aligned}
$$

The integral exists only if all of the exponents on y in the sum are less than -1. That is, $j - \alpha - 1 < -1$ for all j, or, equivalently, $k < \alpha$. Therefore, only some moments exist. □

By this reckoning, the Pareto distribution is said to have a heavier tail than the gamma distribution. A look at the moment formulas in Appendix

---

[3] In the same manner, existence of all negative moments indicates a light left tail. A feel for the left tail may aid in choosing an appropriate distributional model. The following statements apply to density functions that are monotonic and differentiable near zero.

In particular, $f(0)$ and the slope of the density function near zero are related to the existence of negative moments [that is, $E(X^k)$ where k is negative]. Suppose that negative moments exist only for $k > -r$. If $r < 1$, $f(x)$ goes to infinity as $x \to 0$. If $r = 1$, $f(0)$ is a nonnegative number. If $1 < r < 2$, $f(0) = 0$ and the slope goes to infinity as $x \to 0$. If $r = 2$, $f(0) = 0$ and the slope at 0 is a nonnegative number. If $r > 2$, $f(0) = 0$ and the slope at 0 is 0, so only a small portion of the distribution is near zero.

As an example, the Weibull distribution with $\tau = 0.2$ has been used for workers compensation insurance. The value of r is 0.2, which means that a lot of probability is near 0. Setting θ to produce a mean of 30,000 gives a 28% chance of a claim being less than 1 and a 1% chance of it exceeding 500,000. This may be a reasonable model for large losses (see Section 4.4.7 for a way to use part of a model). In contrast, the lognormal distribution that has the same mean and variance has less than 0.1% probability of being less than 1 and also about 1% probability of exceeding 500,000. The lognormal distribution has all negative moments and thus has $f(x)$ go to zero as x goes to zero.

A reveals which distributions have heavy tails and which do not, as indicated by the existence of moments.

4.3.2   Limiting ratios

An indication that one distribution has a heavier tail than another is that the ratio of the two survival functions should diverge to infinity (with the heavier tailed distribution in the numerator). This implies that the numerator distribution puts significantly more probability on large values. It is equivalent to examine the ratio of density functions. The limit will be the same, as can be seen by an application of L'Hôpital's rule:

$$\lim_{x \to \infty} \frac{S_1(x)}{S_2(x)} = \lim_{x \to \infty} \frac{S_1'(x)}{S_2'(x)} = \lim_{x \to \infty} \frac{-f_1(x)}{-f_2(x)}.$$

Example 4.16 *Demonstrate that the Pareto distribution has a heavier tail than the gamma distribution using the limit of the ratio of their density functions.*

To avoid confusion, the letters τ and λ will be used for the parameters of the gamma distribution instead of the customary α and θ. Then the required limit is

$$
\begin{aligned}
\lim_{x \to \infty} \frac{f_{\text{Pareto}}(x)}{f_{\text{gamma}}(x)} &= \lim_{x \to \infty} \frac{\alpha \theta^\alpha (x + \theta)^{-\alpha-1}}{x^{\tau-1} e^{-x/\lambda} \lambda^{-\tau} \Gamma(\tau)^{-1}} \\
&= c \lim_{x \to \infty} \frac{e^{x/\lambda}}{(x+\theta)^{\alpha+1} x^{\tau-1}} \\
&> c \lim_{x \to \infty} \frac{e^{x/\lambda}}{(x+\theta)^{\alpha+\tau}}
\end{aligned}
$$

and, either by application of L'Hôpital's rule or by remembering that exponentials go to infinity faster than polynomials, the limit is infinity. Figure 4.3 shows a portion of the density functions for a Pareto distribution with parameters $\alpha = 3$ and $\theta = 10$ and a gamma distribution with parameters $\alpha = \frac{1}{3}$ and $\theta = 15$. Both distributions have a mean of 5 and a variance of 75. The graph is consistent with the algebraic derivation. □

4.3.3   Hazard rate and mean residual life patterns

The nature of the hazard rate function also reveals information about the tail of the distribution. If the hazard rate function is decreasing, then at large values the chance of that value becomes small and the chance of larger values becomes greater. Thus the distribution will have a heavier tail. Conversely, if the hazard rate function is increasing, a lighter tail is expected.

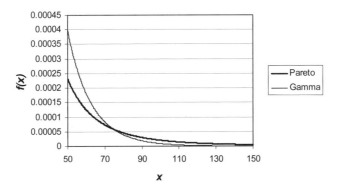

Fig. 4.3 Tails of gamma and Pareto distributions.

Example 4.17 *Compare the tails of the Pareto and gamma distributions by looking at their hazard rate functions.*

The hazard rate function for the Pareto distribution is

$$h(x) = \frac{f(x)}{S(x)} = \frac{\alpha\theta^\alpha(x+\theta)^{-\alpha-1}}{\theta^\alpha(x+\theta)^{-\alpha}} = \frac{\alpha}{x+\theta}$$

which is decreasing. For the gamma distribution we need to be a bit more clever because there is no closed form expression for $S(x)$. Observe that

$$\frac{1}{h(x)} = \frac{\int_x^\infty f(t)dt}{f(x)} = \frac{\int_0^\infty f(x+y)dy}{f(x)}$$

and so, if $f(x+y)/f(x)$ is an increasing function of x for any fixed y, then $1/h(x)$ will be increasing in x and so the random variable will have a decreasing hazard rate. Now, for the gamma distribution

$$\frac{f(x+y)}{f(x)} = \frac{(x+y)^{\alpha-1}e^{-(x+y)/\theta}}{x^{\alpha-1}e^{-x/\theta}} = \left(1+\frac{y}{x}\right)^{\alpha-1} e^{-y/\theta},$$

which is strictly increasing in x provided $\alpha < 1$ and strictly decreasing in x if $\alpha > 1$. By this measure, some gamma distributions have a heavy tail (those with $\alpha < 1$) and some have a light tail. Note that when $\alpha = 1$ we have the exponential distribution and a constant hazard rate. Also, even though $h(x)$ is complicated in the gamma case, we know what happens for large x. Because $f(x)$ and $S(x)$ both go to 0 as $x \to \infty$, L'Hôpital's rule yields

$$\lim_{x\to\infty} h(x) = \lim_{x\to\infty} \frac{f(x)}{S(x)} = -\lim_{x\to\infty}\frac{f'(x)}{f(x)} = -\lim_{x\to\infty}\left[\frac{d}{dx}\ln f(x)\right]$$

$$= -\lim_{x\to\infty}\frac{d}{dx}\left[(\alpha-1)\ln x - \frac{x}{\theta}\right] = \lim_{x\to\infty}\left(\frac{1}{\theta} - \frac{\alpha-1}{x}\right) = \frac{1}{\theta}.$$

That is, $h(x) \to 1/\theta$ as $x \to \infty$.   □

The mean residual life also gives information about tail weight. If the mean residual life function is increasing in d, then at large values the expected outcome is much larger and thus probability is moved to the right, indicating a heavier tail than a model where the mean residual life function is decreasing or is increasing at a slower rate. In fact, the mean residual life function and the hazard rate are closely related in several ways. First, note that

$$
\begin{aligned}
\frac{S(y+d)}{S(d)} &= \frac{\exp\left[-\int_0^{y+d} h(x)dx\right]}{\exp\left[-\int_0^d h(x)dx\right]} = \exp\left[-\int_d^{y+d} h(x)dx\right] \\
&= \exp\left[-\int_0^y h(d+t)dt\right].
\end{aligned}
$$

Therefore, if the hazard rate is decreasing, then for fixed y it follows that $\int_0^y h(d+t)dt$ is a decreasing function of d, and from the above $S(y+d)/S(d)$ is an increasing function of d. But from (3.5), the mean residual life function may be expressed as

$$
e(d) = \frac{\int_d^\infty S(x)dx}{S(d)} = \int_0^\infty \frac{S(y+d)}{S(d)}dy.
$$

Thus, if the hazard rate is a decreasing function, then the mean residual life function $e(d)$ is an increasing function of d because the same is true of $S(y+d)/S(d)$ for fixed y. Similarly, if the hazard rate is an increasing function, then the mean residual life function is a decreasing function. It is worth noting (and is perhaps counterintuitive), however, that the converse implication is not true. Exercise 4.16 gives an example of a distribution which has a decreasing mean residual life function, but the hazard rate is not increasing for all values. Nevertheless, the implications described above are generally consistent with the above discussions of heaviness of the tail.

There is a second relationship between the mean residual life function and the hazard rate. As $d \to \infty$, $S(d)$ and $\int_d^\infty S(x)dx$ go to 0. Thus, the limiting behavior of the mean residual life function as $d \to \infty$ may be ascertained via L'Hôpital's rule because (3.5) holds. We have

$$
\lim_{d\to\infty} e(d) = \lim_{d\to\infty} \frac{\int_d^\infty S(x)dx}{S(d)} = \lim_{d\to\infty} \frac{-S(d)}{-f(d)} = \lim_{d\to\infty} \frac{1}{h(d)}
$$

as long as the indicated limits exist. These limiting relationships are useful if $S(x)$ [and hence also $h(x)$ and $e(d)$] is complicated.

Example 4.18 *Examine the behavior of the mean residual life function of the gamma distribution.*

Because $e(d) = \int_d^\infty S(x)dx/S(d)$ and $S(x)$ is complicated, $e(d)$ is compli-cated. But $e(0) = \mathrm{E}(X) = \alpha\theta$ from Appendix A, and, using Example 4.17, we have

$$\lim_{x\to\infty} e(x) = \lim_{x\to\infty} \frac{1}{h(x)} = \frac{1}{\lim\limits_{x\to\infty} h(x)} = \theta.$$

Also, from Example 4.17, $h(x)$ is strictly decreasing in x for $\alpha < 1$ and strictly increasing in x for $\alpha > 1$, implying that $e(d)$ is strictly increasing from $e(0) = \alpha\theta$ to $e(\infty) = \theta$ for $\alpha < 1$ and strictly decreasing from $e(0) = \alpha\theta$ to $e(\infty) = \theta$ for $\alpha > 1$. For $\alpha = 1$, we have the exponential distribution for which $e(d) = \theta$. $\qquad\square$

Further insight into the mean residual lifetime and the heaviness of the tail may be obtained by introducing the so-called equilibrium distribution, which has important applications in connection with the continuous time ruin model of Chapter 8. For positive random variables with $S(0) = 1$, it follows from Definition 3.6 and (3.5) with $d = 0$ that $\mathrm{E}(X) = \int_0^\infty S(x)dx$, or equivalently $1 = \int_0^\infty [S(x)/\mathrm{E}(X)]dx$, so that

$$f_e(x) = \frac{S(x)}{\mathrm{E}(X)}, \quad x \geq 0, \tag{4.2}$$

is a probability density function. The corresponding survival function is

$$S_e(x) = \int_x^\infty f_e(t)dt = \frac{\int_x^\infty S(t)dt}{\mathrm{E}(X)}, \quad x \geq 0.$$

The hazard rate corresponding to the equilibrium distribution is

$$h_e(x) = \frac{f_e(x)}{S_e(x)} = \frac{S(x)}{\int_x^\infty S(t)dt} = \frac{1}{e(x)}$$

using (3.5). Thus, the reciprocal of the mean residual life function is itself a hazard rate, and this fact may be used to show that the mean residual life function uniquely characterizes the original distribution. We have

$$f_e(x) = h_e(x)S_e(x) = h_e(x)e^{-\int_0^x h_e(t)dt},$$

or equivalently

$$S(x) = \frac{e(0)}{e(x)} e^{-\int_0^x \left\{\frac{1}{e(t)}\right\}dt}$$

using $e(0) = \mathrm{E}(X)$.

The equilibrium distribution also provides further insight into the rela-tionship between the hazard rate, the mean residual life function, and heav-iness of the tail. Assuming that $S(0) = 1$, and thus $e(0) = \mathrm{E}(X)$, we have

$\int_x^\infty S(t)dt = e(0)S_e(x)$, and from (3.5), $\int_x^\infty S(t)dt = e(x)S(x)$. Equating these two expressions results in

$$\frac{e(x)}{e(0)} = \frac{S_e(x)}{S(x)}.$$

If the mean residual life function is increasing (implied if the hazard rate is decreasing), then $e(x) \geq e(0)$, which is obviously equivalent to $S_e(x) \geq S(x)$ from the above equality. This in turn implies that

$$\int_0^\infty S_e(x)dx \geq \int_0^\infty S(x)dx.$$

But $E(X) = \int_0^\infty S(x)dx$ from Definition 3.6 and (3.5) if $S(0) = 1$. Also, $\int_0^\infty S_e(x)dx = \int_0^\infty x f_e(x)dx$ since both sides represent the mean of the equilibrium distribution. This may be evaluated using (3.9) with $u = \infty, k = 2$, and $F(0) = 0$ to give the equilibrium mean, that is,

$$\int_0^\infty S_e(x)dx = \int_0^\infty x f_e(x)dx = \frac{1}{E(X)} \int_0^\infty x S(x)dx = \frac{E(X^2)}{2E(X)}.$$

The inequality may thus be expressed as

$$\frac{E(X^2)}{2E(X)} \geq E(X),$$

or using $\mathrm{Var}(X) = E(X^2) - \{E(X)\}^2$ as $\mathrm{Var}(X) \geq \{E(X)\}^2$. That is, the squared coefficient of variation, and hence the coefficient of variation itself, is at least 1 if $e(x) \geq e(0)$. Reversing the inequalities implies that the coefficient of variation is at most 1 if $e(x) \leq e(0)$, in turn implied if the mean residual life function is decreasing or the hazard rate is increasing. These values of the coefficient of variation are consistent with the comments made here about the heaviness of the tail.

4.3.4   Exercises

4.13 Using the methods in this section (except for the mean residual life), compare the tail weight of the Weibull and inverse Weibull distributions.

4.14 Arguments as in Example 4.16 place the lognormal distribution between the gamma and Pareto distributions with regard to tail weight. To reinforce this conclusion, consider a gamma distribution with parameters $\alpha = 0.2$, $\theta = 500$; a lognormal distribution with parameters $\mu = 3.709290$, $\sigma = 1.338566$; and a Pareto distribution with parameters $\alpha = 2.5$, $\theta = 150$. First demonstrate that all three distributions have the same mean and variance. Then numerically demonstrate that there is a value such that the gamma pdf is smaller than the lognormal and Pareto pdfs for all arguments above that value and that there is another value such that the lognormal pdf is smaller than the Pareto pdf for all arguments above that value.

4.15 Let Y be a random variable that has the equilibrium density from (4.2). That is, $f_Y(y) = f_e(y) = S_X(y)/\mathrm{E}(X)$ for some random variable X. Use integration by parts to show that

$$M_Y(t) = \frac{M_X(t) - 1}{t\mathrm{E}(X)}$$

whenever $M_X(t)$ exists.

4.16 You are given that the random variable X has probability density function $f(x) = (1 + 2x^2)e^{-2x}, x \geq 0$.

(a) Determine the survival function $S(x)$.

(b) Determine the hazard rate $h(x)$.

(c) Determine the survival function $S_e(x)$ of the equilibrium distribution.

(d) Determine the mean residual life function $e(x)$.

(e) Determine $\lim_{x \to \infty} h(x)$ and $\lim_{x \to \infty} e(x)$.

(f) Prove that $e(x)$ is strictly decreasing but $h(x)$ is not strictly increasing.

4.17 Assume that X has probability density function $f(x), x \geq 0$.

(a) Prove that

$$S_e(x) = \frac{\int_x^\infty (y - x)f(y)dy}{\mathrm{E}(X)}.$$

(b) Use (a) to show that

$$\int_x^\infty yf(y)dy = xS(x) + \mathrm{E}(X)S_e(x).$$

(c) Prove that (b) may be rewritten as

$$S(x) = \frac{\int_x^\infty yf(y)dy}{x + e(x)}$$

and that this in turn implies that

$$S(x) \leq \frac{\mathrm{E}(X)}{x + e(x)}.$$

(d) Use (c) to prove that, if $e(x) \geq e(0)$, then

$$S(x) \leq \frac{\mathrm{E}(X)}{x + \mathrm{E}(X)}$$

and that this in turn implies that the mean is at least as large as the (smallest) median.

(e) Prove that (b) may be rewritten as

$$S_e(x) = \frac{e(x)}{x + e(x)} \cdot \frac{\int_x^\infty y f(y) dy}{\mathrm{E}(X)}$$

and thus that

$$S_e(x) \leq \frac{e(x)}{x + e(x)}.$$

4.4 CREATING NEW DISTRIBUTIONS

4.4.1 Introduction

This section indicates how new parametric distributions can be created from existing ones. Many of the distributions in Appendix A were created this way.

4.4.2 Multiplication by a constant

This transformation is equivalent to applying inflation uniformly across all loss levels and is known as a change of scale. For example, if this year's losses are given by the random variable X, then uniform inflation of 5% indicates that next year's losses can be modeled with the random variable $Y = 1.05X$.

Theorem 4.19 *Let X be a continuous random variable with pdf $f_X(x)$ and cdf $F_X(x)$. Let $Y = \theta X$ with $\theta > 0$. Then*

$$F_Y(y) = F_X\left(\frac{y}{\theta}\right), \quad f_Y(y) = \frac{1}{\theta} f_X\left(\frac{y}{\theta}\right).$$

Proof:

$$
\begin{aligned}
F_Y(y) &= \Pr(Y \leq y) = \Pr(\theta X \leq y) = \Pr\left(X \leq \frac{y}{\theta}\right) = F_X\left(\frac{y}{\theta}\right) \\
f_Y(y) &= \frac{d}{dy} F_Y(y) = \frac{1}{\theta} f_X\left(\frac{y}{\theta}\right).
\end{aligned}
$$

$\square$

Corollary 4.20 *The parameter θ is a scale parameter for the random variable Y.*

The following example illustrates this process.

Example 4.21 *Let X have pdf $f(x) = e^{-x}$, $x > 0$. Determine the cdf and pdf of $Y = \theta X$.*

$$
\begin{aligned}
F_X(x) &= 1 - e^{-x}, \quad F_Y(y) = 1 - e^{-y/\theta}, \\
f_Y(y) &= \frac{1}{\theta} e^{-y/\theta}.
\end{aligned}
$$

We recognize this as the exponential distribution. $\qquad \square$

4.4.3 Raising to a power

Theorem 4.22 *Let X be a continuous random variable with pdf $f_X(x)$ and cdf $F_X(x)$ with $F_X(0) = 0$. Let $Y = X^{1/\tau}$. Then, if $\tau > 0$,*

$$
F_Y(y) = F_X(y^\tau), \quad f_Y(y) = \tau y^{\tau-1} f_X(y^\tau), \quad y > 0
$$

while, if $\tau < 0$,

$$
F_Y(y) = 1 - F_X(y^\tau), \quad f_Y(y) = -\tau y^{\tau-1} f_X(y^\tau). \tag{4.3}
$$

Proof: If $\tau > 0$

$$
F_Y(y) = \Pr(X \le y^\tau) = F_X(y^\tau),
$$

while if $\tau < 0$

$$
F_Y(y) = \Pr(X \ge y^\tau) = 1 - F_X(y^\tau).
$$

The pdf follows by differentiation. $\qquad \square$

It is more common to keep parameters positive and so, when τ is negative, create a new parameter $\tau^* = -\tau$. Then (4.3) becomes

$$
F_Y(y) = 1 - F_X(y^{-\tau^*}), \quad f_Y(y) = \tau^* y^{-\tau^*-1} f_X(y^{-\tau^*}).
$$

Drop the asterisk for future use of this positive parameter.

Definition 4.23 *When raising a distribution to a power, if $\tau > 0$ the resulting distribution is called **transformed**, if $\tau = -1$ it is called **inverse**, and if $\tau < 0$ (but is not -1) it is called **inverse transformed**. To create the distributions in Appendix A and to retain θ as a scale parameter, the base distribution should be raised to a power before being multiplied by θ.*

Example 4.24 *Suppose X has the exponential distribution. Determine the cdf of the inverse, transformed, and inverse transformed exponential distributions.*

The inverse exponential distribution with no scale parameter has cdf

$$
F(y) = 1 - [1 - e^{-1/y}] = e^{-1/y}.
$$

With the scale parameter added it is $F(y) = e^{-\theta/y}$.

The transformed exponential distribution with no scale parameter has cdf

$$F(y) = 1 - \exp(-y^\tau).$$

With the scale parameter added it is $F(y) = 1 - \exp[-(y/\theta)^\tau]$. This distribution is more commonly known as the **Weibull distribution**.

The inverse transformed exponential distribution with no scale parameter has cdf

$$F(y) = 1 - [1 - \exp(-y^{-\tau})] = \exp(-y^{-\tau}).$$

With the scale parameter added it is $F(y) = \exp[-(\theta/y)^\tau]$. This distribution is the **inverse Weibull**. $\square$

Another base distribution has pdf $f(x) = x^{\alpha-1}e^{-x}/\Gamma(\alpha)$. When a scale parameter is added, this becomes the **gamma distribution.** It has inverse and transformed versions that can be created using the results in this section. Unlike the distributions introduced to this point, this one does not have a closed form cdf. The best we can do is define notation for the function.

Definition 4.25 *The **incomplete gamma function** with parameter $\alpha > 0$ is denoted and defined by*

$$\Gamma(\alpha; x) = \frac{1}{\Gamma(\alpha)} \int_0^x t^{\alpha-1}e^{-t}\, dt$$

*while the **gamma function** is denoted and defined by*

$$\Gamma(\alpha) = \int_0^\infty t^{\alpha-1}e^{-t}\, dt.$$

In addition, $\Gamma(\alpha) = (\alpha - 1)\Gamma(\alpha - 1)$ and for positive integer values of n, $\Gamma(n) = (n - 1)!$. Appendix A provides details on numerical methods of evaluating these quantities. Furthermore, these functions are built into most spreadsheet programs and many statistical and numerical analysis programs.

4.4.4   Exponentiation

Theorem 4.26 *Let X be a continuous random variable with pdf $f_X(x)$ and cdf $F_X(x)$ with $f_X(x) > 0$ for all real x. Let $Y = \exp(X)$. Then, for $y > 0$,*

$$F_Y(y) = F_X(\ln y), \quad f_Y(y) = \frac{1}{y}f_X(\ln y).$$

Proof: $F_Y(y) = \Pr(e^X \le y) = \Pr(X \le \ln y) = F_X(\ln y)$. $\square$

Example 4.27 *Let X have the normal distribution with mean μ and variance σ^2. Determine the cdf and pdf of $Y = e^X$.*

$$F_Y(y) = \Phi\left(\frac{\ln y - \mu}{\sigma}\right)$$

$$f_Y(y) = \frac{1}{y\sigma}\phi\left(\frac{\ln y - \mu}{\sigma}\right) = \frac{1}{y\sigma\sqrt{2\pi}}\exp\left[-\frac{1}{2}\left(\frac{\ln y - \mu}{\sigma}\right)^2\right]. \qquad \square$$

We could try to add a scale parameter by creating $W = \theta Y$, but this adds no value, as is demonstrated in Exercise 4.22. This example created the **lognormal** distribution (the name has stuck even though "expnormal" would seem more descriptive).

4.4.5 Mixing

The concept of mixing can be extended from mixing a finite number of random variables to mixing an uncountable number. In the following theorem, the pdf $f_\Lambda(\lambda)$ plays the role of the discrete probabilities a_j in the k-point mixture.

Theorem 4.28 *Let X have pdf $f_{X|\Lambda}(x|\lambda)$ and cdf $F_{X|\Lambda}(x|\lambda)$, where λ is a parameter of X. While X may have other parameters, they are not relevant. Let λ be a realization of the random variable Λ with pdf $f_\Lambda(\lambda)$. Then the unconditional pdf of X is*

$$f_X(x) = \int f_{X|\Lambda}(x|\lambda)f_\Lambda(\lambda)\,d\lambda, \qquad (4.4)$$

*where the integral is taken over all values of λ with positive probability. The resulting distribution is a **mixture distribution**. The distribution function can be determined from*

$$
\begin{aligned}
F_X(x) &= \int_{-\infty}^x \int f_{X|\Lambda}(y|\lambda)f_\Lambda(\lambda)d\lambda\,dy \\
&= \int \int_{-\infty}^x f_{X|\Lambda}(y|\lambda)f_\Lambda(\lambda)dy\,d\lambda \\
&= \int F_{X|\Lambda}(x|\lambda)f_\Lambda(\lambda)d\lambda.
\end{aligned}
$$

Moments of the mixture distribution can be found from

$$\mathrm{E}(X^k) = \mathrm{E}[\mathrm{E}(X^k|\Lambda)]$$

and, in particular,

$$\mathrm{Var}(X) = \mathrm{E}[\mathrm{Var}(X|\Lambda)] + \mathrm{Var}[\mathrm{E}(X|\Lambda)].$$

Proof: The integrand is, by definition, the joint density of X and Λ. The integral is then the marginal density. For the expected value (assuming the order of integration can be reversed),

$$
\begin{aligned}
\mathrm{E}(X^k) &= \int\int x^k f_{X|\Lambda}(x|\lambda)f_\Lambda(\lambda)\,d\lambda\,dx \\
&= \int\left[\int x^k f_{X|\Lambda}(x|\lambda)dx\right]f_\Lambda(\lambda)d\lambda \\
&= \int \mathrm{E}(X^k|\lambda)f_\Lambda(\lambda)d\lambda \\
&= \mathrm{E}[\mathrm{E}(X^k|\Lambda)].
\end{aligned}
$$

For the variance,

$$
\begin{aligned}
\mathrm{Var}(X) &= \mathrm{E}(X^2) - [\mathrm{E}(X)]^2 \\
&= \mathrm{E}[\mathrm{E}(X^2|\Lambda)] - \{\mathrm{E}[\mathrm{E}(X|\Lambda)]\}^2 \\
&= \mathrm{E}\{\mathrm{Var}(X|\Lambda) + [\mathrm{E}(X|\Lambda)]^2\} - \{\mathrm{E}[\mathrm{E}(X|\Lambda)]\}^2 \\
&= \mathrm{E}[\mathrm{Var}(X|\Lambda)] + \mathrm{Var}[\mathrm{E}(X|\Lambda)]. \qquad \square
\end{aligned}
$$

Note that, if $f_\Lambda(\lambda)$ is discrete, the integrals must be replaced with sums. An alternative way to write the results is $f_X(x) = \mathrm{E}_\Lambda[f_{X|\Lambda}(x|\Lambda)]$ and $F_X(x) = \mathrm{E}_\Lambda[F_{X|\Lambda}(x|\Lambda)]$, where the subscript on E indicates that the random variable is Λ.

An interesting phenomenon is that mixture distributions tend to be heavy-tailed so this method is a good way to generate such a model. In particular, if $f_{X|\Lambda}(x|\lambda)$ has a decreasing hazard rate function for all λ, then the mixture distribution will also have a decreasing hazard rate function (see Ross [114], pp. 407–409 for details). The following example shows how a familiar heavy-tailed distribution may be obtained by mixing.

Example 4.29 *Let $X|\Lambda$ have an exponential distribution with parameter $1/\Lambda$. Let Λ have a gamma distribution. Determine the unconditional distribution of X.*

We have (note that the parameter θ in the gamma distribution has been replaced by its reciprocal)

$$
\begin{aligned}
f_X(x) &= \frac{\theta^\alpha}{\Gamma(\alpha)}\int_0^\infty \lambda e^{-\lambda x}\lambda^{\alpha-1}e^{-\theta\lambda}d\lambda \\
&= \frac{\theta^\alpha}{\Gamma(\alpha)}\int_0^\infty \lambda^\alpha e^{-\lambda(x+\theta)}d\lambda \\
&= \frac{\theta^\alpha}{\Gamma(\alpha)}\frac{\Gamma(\alpha+1)}{(x+\theta)^{\alpha+1}} \\
&= \frac{\alpha\theta^\alpha}{(x+\theta)^{\alpha+1}}.
\end{aligned}
$$

This is a Pareto distribution.   □

The following example provides an illustration useful in Chapter 16.

Example 4.30 *Suppose that, given* $\Theta = \theta$, *X is normally distributed with mean* θ *and variance* v, *so that*

$$f_{X|\Theta}(x|\theta) = \frac{1}{\sqrt{2\pi v}} \exp\left[-\frac{1}{2v}(x-\theta)^2\right], \quad -\infty < x < \infty,$$

and Θ *is itself normally distributed with mean* μ *and variance* a, *that is,*

$$f_\Theta(\theta) = \frac{1}{\sqrt{2\pi a}} \exp\left[-\frac{1}{2a}(\theta-\mu)^2\right], \quad -\infty < \theta < \infty.$$

Determine the marginal pdf of X.

The marginal pdf of X is

$$
\begin{aligned}
f_X(x) &= \int_{-\infty}^{\infty} \frac{1}{\sqrt{2\pi v}} \exp\left[-\frac{1}{2v}(x-\theta)^2\right] \frac{1}{\sqrt{2\pi a}} \exp\left[-\frac{1}{2a}(\theta-\mu)^2\right] d\theta \\
&= \frac{1}{2\pi\sqrt{va}} \int_{-\infty}^{\infty} \exp\left[-\frac{1}{2v}(x-\theta)^2 - \frac{1}{2a}(\theta-\mu)^2\right] d\theta.
\end{aligned}
$$

We leave as an exercise for the reader the verification of the algebraic identity

$$\frac{(x-\theta)^2}{v} + \frac{(\theta-\mu)^2}{a} = \frac{a+v}{va}\left(\theta - \frac{ax+v\mu}{a+v}\right)^2 + \frac{(x-\mu)^2}{a+v}$$

obtained by completion of the square in θ. Thus,

$$f_X(x) = \frac{\exp\left[-\dfrac{(x-\mu)^2}{2(a+v)}\right]}{\sqrt{2\pi(a+v)}} \int_{-\infty}^{\infty} \sqrt{\frac{a+v}{2\pi va}} \exp\left[-\frac{a+v}{2va}\left(\theta - \frac{ax+v\mu}{a+v}\right)^2\right] d\theta.$$

We recognize the integrand as the pdf (as a function of θ) of a normal distribution with mean $(ax + v\mu)/(a + v)$ and variance $(va)/(a + v)$. Thus the integral is 1 and so

$$f_X(x) = \frac{\exp\left[-\dfrac{(x-\mu)^2}{2(a+v)}\right]}{\sqrt{2\pi(a+v)}}, \quad -\infty < x < \infty;$$

that is, X is normal with mean μ and variance $a + v$.   □

The following example is taken from Hayne [50]. It illustrates how this type of mixture distribution can arise. In particular, continuous mixtures are often used to provide a model for parameter uncertainty. That is, the exact value of a parameter is not known, but a probability density function can be elucidated to describe possible values of that parameter.

Example 4.31 *In the valuation of warranties on automobiles it is important to recognize that the number of miles driven varies from driver to driver. It is also the case that for a particular driver the number of miles varies from year to year. Suppose the number of miles for a randomly selected driver has the inverse Weibull distribution but that the year-to-year variation in the scale parameter has the transformed gamma distribution with the same value for τ. Determine the distribution for the number of miles driven in a randomly selected year by a randomly selected driver.*

Using the parameterizations from Appendix A, the inverse Weibull for miles driven in a year has parameters Λ (in place of Θ) and τ while the transformed gamma distribution for the scale parameter Λ has parameters τ, θ, and α. The marginal density is

$$
\begin{aligned}
f(x) &= \int_0^\infty \frac{\tau\lambda^\tau}{x^{\tau+1}} e^{-(\lambda/x)^\tau} \frac{\tau\lambda^{\tau\alpha-1}}{\theta^{\tau\alpha}\Gamma(\alpha)} e^{-(\lambda/\theta)^\tau} d\lambda \\
&= \frac{\tau^2}{\theta^{\tau\alpha}\Gamma(\alpha)x^{\tau+1}} \int_0^\infty \lambda^{\tau+\tau\alpha-1} \exp[-\lambda^\tau(x^{-\tau}+\theta^{-\tau})] \, d\lambda \\
&= \frac{\tau^2}{\theta^{\tau\alpha}\Gamma(\alpha)x^{\tau+1}} \int_0^\infty [y^{1/\tau}(x^{-\tau}+\theta^{-\tau})^{-1/\tau}]^{\tau+\tau\alpha-1} e^{-y} \\
&\quad \times y^{\tau^{-1}-1} \tau^{-1}(x^{-\tau}+\theta^{-\tau})^{-1/\tau} \, dy \\
&= \frac{\tau}{\theta^{\tau\alpha}\Gamma(\alpha)x^{\tau+1}(x^{-\tau}+\theta^{-\tau})^{\alpha+1}} \int_0^\infty y^\alpha e^{-y} \, dy \\
&= \frac{\tau\Gamma(\alpha+1)}{\theta^{\tau\alpha}\Gamma(\alpha)x^{\tau+1}(x^{-\tau}+\theta^{-\tau})^{\alpha+1}} \\
&= \frac{\tau\alpha\theta^\tau x^{\tau\alpha-1}}{(x^\tau+\theta^\tau)^{\alpha+1}}.
\end{aligned}
$$

The third line is obtained by the transformation $y = \lambda^\tau(x^{-\tau}+\theta^{-\tau})$. The final line uses the fact that $\Gamma(\alpha+1) = \alpha\Gamma(\alpha)$. The result is an inverse Burr distribution. Note that this distribution applies to a particular driver. Another driver may have a different Weibull shape parameter τ and as well that driver's Weibull scale parameter Θ may have a different distribution and, in particular, a different mean. □

4.4.6   Frailty models

An important type of mixture distribution is a frailty model. Although the physical motivation for this particular type of mixture is originally from the analysis of lifetime distributions in survival analysis, the resulting mathematical convenience implies that the approach may also be viewed as a useful way to generate new distributions by mixing.

We begin by introducing a *frailty* random variable $\Lambda > 0$ and define the conditional hazard rate (given $\Lambda = \lambda$) of X to be $h_{X|\Lambda}(x|\lambda) = \lambda a(x)$, where $a(x)$ is a known function of x [that is, $a(x)$ is to be specified in a particular application]. The frailty is meant to quantify uncertainty associated with the hazard rate, which by the above specification of the conditional hazard rate acts in a multiplicative manner.

The conditional survival function of $X|\Lambda$ is therefore

$$S_{X|\Lambda}(x|\lambda) = e^{-\int_0^x h_{X|\Lambda}(t|\lambda)dt} = e^{-\lambda A(x)},$$

where $A(x) = \int_0^x a(t)dt$. In order to specify the mixture distribution (that is, the marginal distribution of X), we define the moment generating function of the frailty random variable Λ to be $M_\Lambda(t) = \mathrm{E}(e^{t\Lambda})$. Then, the marginal survival function is

$$S_X(x) = \mathrm{E}[e^{-\Lambda A(x)}] = M_\Lambda[-A(x)], \tag{4.5}$$

and obviously $F_X(x) = 1 - S_X(x)$.

The type of mixture to be used determines the choice of $a(x)$ and hence $A(x)$. The most important subclass of the frailty models is the class of exponential mixtures with $a(x) = 1$ and $A(x) = x$, so that $S_{X|\Lambda}(x|\lambda) = e^{-\lambda x}$, $x \geq 0$. Other useful mixtures include Weibull mixtures with $a(x) = \gamma x^{\gamma-1}$ and $A(x) = x^\gamma$.

Evaluation of the frailty distribution requires an expression for the moment generating function $M_\Lambda(t)$ of Λ. The most common choice is gamma frailty, but other choices such as inverse Gaussian frailty are also used.

Example 4.32 *Let Λ have a gamma distribution and let $X|\Lambda$ have a Weibull distribution with conditional survival function $S_{X|\Lambda}(x|\lambda) = e^{-\lambda x^\gamma}$. Determine the unconditional or marginal distribution of X.*

In this case it follows from Example 3.15 that the gamma moment generating function is $M_\Lambda(t) = (1 - \theta t)^{-\alpha}$, and from (4.5) it follows that X has survival function

$$S_X(x) = M_\Lambda(-x^\gamma) = (1 + \theta x^\gamma)^{-\alpha}.$$

This is a Burr distribution (see Appendix A) with the usual parameter θ replaced by $\theta^{-1/\gamma}$. Note that when $\gamma = 1$ this is an exponential mixture which is a Pareto distribution, considered previously in Example 4.29.   □

As mentioned earlier, mixing tends to create heavy-tailed distributions, and in particular a mixture of distributions which all have decreasing hazard rates also has a decreasing hazard rate. In Exercise 4.32 the reader is asked to prove this fact for frailty models. For further details on frailty models, see the book by Hougaard [63].

4.4.7   Splicing

Another method for creating a new distribution is by splicing. This approach is similar to mixing in that it might be believed that two or more separate processes are responsible for generating the losses. With mixing, the various processes operate on subsets of the population. Once the subset is identified, a simple loss model suffices. For splicing, the processes differ with regard to the loss amount. That is, one model governs the behavior of losses in some interval of possible losses while other models cover the other intervals. The following definition makes this precise.

Definition 4.33 *A **k-component spliced distribution** has a density function that can be expressed as follows:*

$$f_X(x) = \begin{cases} a_1 f_1(x), & c_0 < x < c_1, \\ a_2 f_2(x), & c_1 < x < c_2, \\ \vdots & \vdots \\ a_k f_k(x), & c_{k-1} < x < c_k. \end{cases}$$

For $j = 1, \ldots, k$, each $a_j > 0$ and each $f_j(x)$ must be a legitimate density function with all probability on the interval (c_{j-1}, c_j). Also, $a_1 + \cdots + a_k = 1$.

Example 4.34 *Demonstrate that Model 5 on Page 21 is a two-component spliced model.*

The density function is

$$f(x) = \begin{cases} 0.01, & 0 \le x < 50, \\ 0.02, & 50 \le x < 75 \end{cases}$$

and the spliced model is created by letting $f_1(x) = 0.02$, $0 \le x < 50$, which is a uniform distribution on the interval from 0 to 50, and $f_2(x) = 0.04$, $50 \le x < 75$, which is a uniform distribution on the interval from 50 to 75. The coefficients are then $a_1 = 0.5$ and $a_2 = 0.5$. □

It was not necessary to use density functions and coefficients, but this is one way to ensure that the result is a legitimate density function. When using parametric models, the motivation for splicing is that the tail behavior may be inconsistent with the behavior for small losses. For example, experience (based on knowledge beyond that available in the current, perhaps small, data set) may indicate that the tail follows the Pareto distribution, but there is a positive mode more in keeping with the lognormal or inverse Gaussian distributions. A second instance is when there is a large amount of data below some value but a limited amount of information elsewhere. We may want to use the empirical distribution (or a smoothed version of it) up to a certain point and a parametric model beyond that value. The definition given above is appropriate when the break points $c_0, \ldots, c_k$ are known in advance.

Another way to construct a spliced model is to use standard distributions over the range from c_0 to c_k. Let $g_j(x)$ be the jth such density function. Then, in Definition 4.33 replace $f_j(x)$ with $g_j(x)/[G(c_j) - G(c_{j-1})]$. This formulation makes it easier to have the break points become parameters that can be estimated.

Neither approach to splicing ensures that the resulting density function will be continuous (that is, the components will meet at the break points). Such a restriction could be added to the specification.

Example 4.35 *Create a two-component spliced model using an exponential distribution from 0 to c and a Pareto distribution (using γ in place of θ) from c to ∞.*

The basic format is

$$
f_X(x) = \begin{cases} a_1 \dfrac{\theta^{-1}e^{-x/\theta}}{1 - e^{-c/\theta}}, & 0 < x < c, \\ a_2 \dfrac{\alpha\gamma^\alpha(x+\gamma)^{-\alpha-1}}{\gamma^\alpha(c+\gamma)^{-\alpha}}, & c < x < \infty. \end{cases}
$$

However, we must force the density function to integrate to 1. All that is needed is to let $a_1 = v$ and $a_2 = 1 - v$. The spliced density function becomes

$$
f_X(x) = \begin{cases} v\dfrac{\theta^{-1}e^{-x/\theta}}{1 - e^{-c/\theta}}, & 0 < x < c, \\ (1-v)\dfrac{\alpha(c+\gamma)^\alpha}{(x+\gamma)^{\alpha+1}}, & c < x < \infty \end{cases}, \quad \theta, \alpha, \gamma, c > 0, \ 0 < v < 1.
$$

Figure 4.4 illustrates this density function using the values $c = 100$, $v = 0.6$, $\theta = 100$, $\gamma = 200$, and $\alpha = 4$. It is clear that this density is not continuous. □

4.4.8 Exercises

4.18 Let X have cdf $F_X(x) = 1 - (1 + x)^{-\alpha}$, $x, \alpha > 0$. Determine the pdf and cdf of $Y = \theta X$.

4.19 (*) One hundred observed claims in 1995 were arranged as follows: 42 were between 0 and 300, 3 were between 300 and 350, 5 were between 350 and 400, 5 were between 400 and 450, 0 were between 450 and 500, 5 were between 500 and 600, and the remaining 40 were above 600. For the next three years, all claims are inflated by 10% per year. Based on the empirical distribution from 1995, determine a range for the probability that a claim exceeds 500 in 1998 (there is not enough information to determine the probability exactly).

4.20 Let X have the Pareto distribution. Determine the cdf of the transformed, inverse, and inverse transformed distributions. Check Appendix A to determine if any of these distributions have special names.

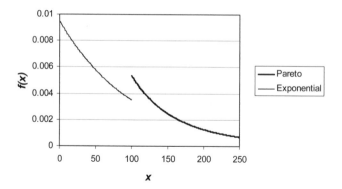

Fig. 4.4 Two-component spliced density.

4.21 Let X have the loglogistic distribution. Demonstrate that the inverse distribution also has the loglogistic distribution. Therefore there is no need to identify a separate inverse loglogistic distribution.

4.22 Let Y have the lognormal distribution with parameters μ and σ. Let $Z = \theta Y$. Show that Z also has the lognormal distribution and therefore the addition of a third parameter has not created a new distribution.

4.23 (*) Let X have a Pareto distribution with parameters α and θ. Let $Y = \ln(1 + X/\theta)$. Determine the name of the distribution of Y and its parameters.

4.24 In [132], Venter noted that if X has the transformed gamma distribution and its scale parameter θ has an inverse transformed gamma distribution (where the parameter τ is the same in both distributions) the resulting mixture has the transformed beta distribution. Demonstrate that this is true.

4.25 (*) Let N have a Poisson distribution with mean Λ. Let Λ have a gamma distribution with mean 1 and variance 2. Determine the unconditional probability that $N = 1$.

4.26 (*) Given a value of $\Theta = \theta$, the random variable X has an exponential distribution with hazard rate function $h(x) = \theta$, a constant. The random variable Θ has a uniform distribution on the interval $(1, 11)$. Determine $S_X(0.5)$ for the unconditional distribution.

4.27 (*) Let N have a Poisson distribution with mean Λ. Let Λ have a uniform distribution on the interval $(0, 5)$. Determine the unconditional probability that $N \geq 2$.

4.28 Determine the probability density function and the hazard rate of the frailty distribution.

4.29 Suppose that $X|\Lambda$ has the Weibull survival function $S_{X|\Lambda}(x|\lambda) = e^{-\lambda x^\gamma}$, $x \geq 0$, and Λ has an exponential distribution. Demonstrate that the unconditional distribution of X is loglogistic.

4.30 Consider the exponential–inverse Gaussian frailty model with $a(x) = \theta/(2\sqrt{1+\theta x})$, where $\theta > 0$.

(a) Verify that the conditional hazard rate $h_{X|\Lambda}(x|\lambda)$ of $X|\Lambda$ is indeed a valid hazard rate.

(b) Determine the conditional survival function $S_{X|\Lambda}(x|\lambda)$.

(c) If Λ has a gamma distribution with parameters $\theta = 1$ and α replaced by 2α, determine the marginal or unconditional survival function of X.

(d) Use (c) to argue that a given frailty model may arise from more than one combination of conditional distributions of $X|\Lambda$ and frailty distributions of Λ.

4.31 Suppose that X has survival function $S_X(x) = 1 - F_X(x)$ given by (4.5). Show that $S_1(x) = F_X(x)/[\mathrm{E}(\Lambda)A(x)]$ is again a survival function of the form given by (4.5), and identify the distribution of Λ associated with $S_1(x)$.

4.32 Fix $s \geq 0$, and define an "Esscher-transformed" frailty random variable Λ_s with probability density function (or discrete probability mass function in the discrete case) $f_{\Lambda_s}(\lambda) = e^{-s\lambda} f_\Lambda(\lambda)/M_\Lambda(-s)$, $\lambda \geq 0$.

(a) Show that Λ_s has moment generating function

$$M_{\Lambda_s}(t) = E(e^{t\Lambda_s}) = \frac{M_\Lambda(t-s)}{M_\Lambda(-s)}.$$

(b) Define the cumulant generating function of Λ to be

$$c_\Lambda(t) = \ln[M_\Lambda(t)],$$

and use (a) to prove that

$$c'_\Lambda(-s) = \mathrm{E}(\Lambda_s) \text{ and } c''_\Lambda(-s) = \mathrm{Var}(\Lambda_s).$$

(c) For the frailty model with survival function given by (4.5), prove that the associated hazard rate may be expressed as $h_X(x) = a(x)c'_\Lambda[-A(x)]$, where c_Λ is defined in (b).

(d) Use (c) to show that

$$h'_X(x) = a'(x)c'_\Lambda[-A(x)] - [a(x)]^2 c''_\Lambda[-A(x)].$$

(e) Prove using (d) that, if the conditional hazard rate $h_{X|\Lambda}(x|\lambda)$ is nonincreasing in x, then $h_X(x)$ is also nonincreasing in x.

4.33 Write the density function for a two-component spliced model in which the density function is proportional to a uniform density over the interval from 0 to 1,000 and is proportional to an exponential density function from 1,000 to ∞. Ensure that the resulting density function is continuous.

4.34 Let X have pdf $f(x) = \exp(-|x/\theta|)/2\theta$ for $-\infty < x < \infty$. Let $Y = e^X$. Determine the pdf and cdf of Y.

4.35 (*) Losses in 1993 follow the density function $f(x) = 3x^{-4}$, $x \geq 1$, where x is the loss in millions of dollars. Inflation of 10% impacts all claims uniformly from 1993 to 1994. Determine the cdf of losses for 1994 and use it to determine the probability that a 1994 loss exceeds 2,200,000.

4.36 Consider the inverse Gaussian random variable X with pdf (from Appendix A)

$$f(x) = \sqrt{\frac{\theta}{2\pi x^3}} \exp\left[-\frac{\theta}{2x}\left(\frac{x - \mu}{\mu}\right)^2\right], \quad x > 0,$$

where $\theta > 0$ and $\mu > 0$ are parameters.

(a) Derive the pdf of the reciprocal inverse Gaussian random variable $1/X$.

(b) Prove that the "joint" moment generating function of X and $1/X$ is given by

$$
\begin{aligned}
M(t_1, t_2) &= \mathrm{E}\left(e^{t_1 X + t_2 X^{-1}}\right) \\
&= \sqrt{\frac{\theta}{\theta - 2t_2}} \exp\left(\frac{\theta - \sqrt{(\theta - 2\mu^2 t_1)(\theta - 2t_2)}}{\mu}\right),
\end{aligned}
$$

where $t_1 < \theta/(2\mu^2)$ and $t_2 < \theta/2$.

(c) Use (b) to show that the moment generating function of X is

$$M_X(t) = \mathrm{E}\left(e^{tX}\right) = \exp\left[\frac{\theta}{\mu}\left(1 - \sqrt{1 - \frac{2\mu^2}{\theta}t}\right)\right], \quad t < \frac{\theta}{2\mu^2},$$

and that this agrees with the reparameterized result in Exercise 3.24.

(d) Use (b) to show that the reciprocal inverse Gaussian random variable $1/X$ has moment generating function

$$
\begin{aligned}
M_{1/X}(t) &= \mathrm{E}\left(e^{tX^{-1}}\right) \\
&= \sqrt{\frac{\theta}{\theta - 2t}} \exp\left[\frac{\theta}{\mu}\left(1 - \sqrt{1 - \frac{2}{\theta}t}\right)\right], \quad t < \frac{\theta}{2}.
\end{aligned}
$$

Hence prove that $1/X$ has the same distribution as $Z_1 + Z_2$, where Z_1 has a gamma distribution, Z_2 has an inverse Gaussian distribution, and Z_1 is independent of Z_2. Also, identify the gamma and inverse Gaussian parameters in this representation.

(e) Use (b) to show that

$$Z = \frac{1}{X}\left(\frac{X - \mu}{\mu}\right)^2$$

has a gamma distribution with parameters $\alpha = \frac{1}{2}$ and the usual parameter θ (in Appendix A) replaced by $2/\theta$.

4.5   SELECTED DISTRIBUTIONS AND THEIR RELATIONSHIPS

4.5.1   Introduction

There are many ways to organize distributions into groups. Families such as Pearson (12 types), Burr (12 types), Stoppa (5 types), and Dagum (11 types) are discussed in Chapter 2 of [73]. The same distribution can appear in more than one system, indicating that there are many relations among the distributions beyond those presented here. The systems presented in the next subsection are particularly useful for actuarial modeling because all the members have support on the positive real line and all tend to be skewed to the right. For a comprehensive set of continuous distributions, the two volumes by Johnson, Kotz, and Balakrishnan [67] and [68] are a valuable reference. In addition, there are entire books devoted to single distributions (such as Arnold [5] for the Pareto distribution).

4.5.2   Two parametric families

As noted when defining parametric families, many of the distributions presented in this section and in Appendix A are special cases of others. For example, a Weibull distribution with $\tau = 1$ and θ arbitrary is an exponential distribution. Through this process, many of our distributions can be organized into groupings, as illustrated in Figures 4.5 and 4.6. The transformed beta family includes two special cases of a different nature. The paralogistic and inverse paralogistic distributions are created by setting the two nonscale parameters of the Burr and inverse Burr distributions equal to each other rather than to a specified value.

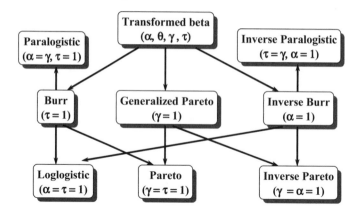

Fig. 4.5   Transformed beta family.

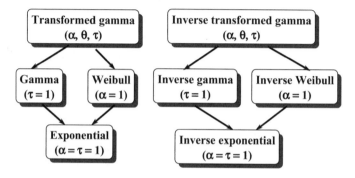

Fig. 4.6   Transformed/inverse transformed gamma family.

4.5.3   Limiting distributions

The classification in the preceding section involved distributions that are special cases of other distributions. Another way to relate distributions is to see what happens as parameters go to their limiting values of zero or infinity.

Example 4.36 *Show that the transformed gamma distribution is a limiting case of the transformed beta distribution as $\theta \to \infty$, $\alpha \to \infty$, and $\theta/\alpha^{1/\gamma} \to \xi$, a constant.*

The demonstration relies on two facts concerning limits:

$$\lim_{\alpha \to \infty} \frac{e^{-\alpha} \alpha^{\alpha-1/2}(2\pi)^{1/2}}{\Gamma(\alpha)} = 1 \tag{4.6}$$

and

$$\lim_{a \to \infty} \left(1 + \frac{x}{a}\right)^{a+b} = e^x. \tag{4.7}$$

The limit in (4.6) is known as Stirling's formula and provides an approximation for the gamma function. The limit in (4.7) is a standard result found in most calculus texts.

To ensure that the ratio $\theta/\alpha^{1/\gamma}$ goes to a constant, it is sufficient to force it to be constant as α and θ become larger and larger. This can be accomplished by substituting $\xi\alpha^{1/\gamma}$ for θ in the transformed beta pdf and then letting $\alpha \to \infty$. The first steps, which also include using Stirling's formula to replace two of the gamma function terms, are

$$
\begin{aligned}
f(x) &= \frac{\Gamma(\alpha+\tau)\gamma x^{\gamma\tau-1}}{\Gamma(\alpha)\Gamma(\tau)\theta^{\gamma\tau}(1+x^\gamma\theta^{-\gamma})^{\alpha+\tau}} \\[2mm]
&= \frac{e^{-\alpha-\tau}(\alpha+\tau)^{\alpha+\tau-1/2}(2\pi)^{1/2}\gamma x^{\gamma\tau-1}}{e^{-\alpha}\alpha^{\alpha-1/2}(2\pi)^{1/2}\Gamma(\tau)(\xi\alpha^{1/\gamma})^{\gamma\tau}(1+x^\gamma\xi^{-\gamma}\alpha^{-1})^{\alpha+\tau}} \\[2mm]
&= \frac{e^{-\tau}[(\alpha+\tau)/\alpha]^{\alpha+\tau-1/2}\gamma x^{\gamma\tau-1}}{\Gamma(\tau)\xi^{\gamma\tau}\left[1+(x/\xi)^\gamma/\alpha\right]^{\alpha+\tau}}.
\end{aligned}
$$

The two limits

$$
\lim_{\alpha\to\infty}\left(1+\frac{\tau}{\alpha}\right)^{\alpha+\tau-1/2} = e^\tau, \quad \lim_{\alpha\to\infty}\left[1+\frac{(x/\xi)^\gamma}{\alpha}\right]^{\alpha+\tau} = e^{(x/\xi)^\gamma}
$$

can be substituted to yield

$$
\lim_{\alpha\to\infty} f(x) = \frac{\gamma x^{\gamma\tau-1}e^{-(x/\xi)^\gamma}}{\Gamma(\tau)\xi^{\gamma\tau}}
$$

which is the pdf of the transformed gamma distribution.   □

With a similar argument, the inverse transformed gamma distribution is obtained by letting τ go to infinity instead of α (see Exercise 4.39).

Because the Burr distribution is a transformed beta distribution with $\tau = 1$, its limiting case is the transformed gamma with $\tau = 1$ (using the parameterization in the previous example), which is the Weibull distribution. Similarly, the inverse Burr has the inverse Weibull as a limiting case. Finally, letting $\tau = \gamma = 1$ shows that the limiting case for the Pareto distribution is the exponential (and similarly for their inverse distributions).

As a final illustration of a limiting case, consider the transformed gamma distribution as parameterized above. Let $\gamma^{-1}\sqrt{\xi^\gamma} \to \sigma$ and $\gamma^{-1}(\xi^\gamma\tau-1) \to \mu$. If this is done by letting $\tau \to \infty$ (so both γ and ξ must go to zero), the limiting distribution will be lognormal.

In Figure 4.7 some of the limiting and special case relationships are shown. Other interesting facts about the various distributions are also given.[4]

---

[4] Thanks to Dave Clark of American Re-Insurance Company for creating this picture.

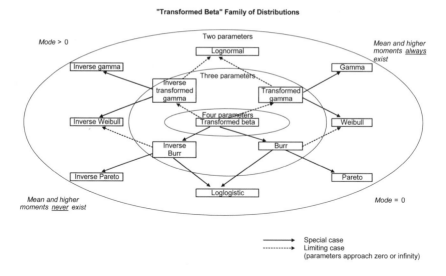

Fig. 4.7 Distributional relationships and characteristics.

4.5.4   Exercises

4.37 For a Pareto distribution, let both α and θ go to infinity with the ratio α/θ held constant. Show that the result is an exponential distribution.

4.38 Determine the limiting distribution of the generalized Pareto distribution as α and θ both go to infinity.

4.39 Show that as $\tau \to \infty$ in the transformed beta distribution the result is the inverse transformed gamma distribution.

4.6   DISCRETE DISTRIBUTIONS

4.6.1   Introduction

The purpose of this section is to introduce a large class of counting distributions. Counting distributions are discrete distributions with probabilities only on the nonnegative integers; that is, probabilities are defined only at the points $0, 1, 2, 3, 4, \ldots$. In an insurance context, counting distributions describe the number of events such as losses to the insured or claims to the insurance company. With an understanding of both the number of claims and the size of claims, one can have a deeper understanding of a variety of issues surrounding insurance than if one has only information about total losses. The description of total losses in terms of numbers and amounts separately also allows one to address issues of modification of an insurance contract. Another reason for separating numbers and amounts of claims is that models for the number of claims are fairly easy to obtain and experience has shown that the commonly used distributions really do model the propensity to generate losses.

We now formalize some of the notation that will be used for models for discrete phenomena. The **probability function** (pf) p_k denotes the probability that exactly k events (such as claims or losses) occur. Let N be a random variable representing the number of such events. Then

$$p_k = \Pr(N = k), \qquad k = 0, 1, 2, \dots.$$

As a reminder, the probability generating function (pgf) of a discrete random variable N with pf p_k is

$$P(z) = P_N(z) = \mathrm{E}\left(z^N\right) = \sum_{k=0}^{\infty} p_k z^k. \qquad (4.8)$$

As is true with the moment generating function, the pgf can be used to generate moments. In particular, $P'(1) = \mathrm{E}(N)$ and $P''(1) = \mathrm{E}[N(N - 1)]$ (see Exercise 4.42). To see that the pgf really does generate probabilities,

$$\begin{aligned}
P^{(m)}(z) &= \mathrm{E}\left(\frac{d^m}{dz^m} z^N\right) = \mathrm{E}[N(N - 1) \cdots (N - m + 1)z^{N-m}] \\
&= \sum_{k=m}^{\infty} k(k - 1) \cdots (k - m + 1)z^{k-m} p_k \\
P^{(m)}(0) &= m! p_m \text{ or } p_m = \frac{P^{(m)}(0)}{m!}.
\end{aligned}$$

4.6.2 The Poisson distribution

The pf for the Poisson distribution is

$$p_k = \frac{e^{-\lambda}\lambda^k}{k!}, \qquad k = 0, 1, 2, \dots.$$

The probability generating function from Example 3.16 is

$$P(z) = e^{\lambda(z-1)}, \qquad \lambda > 0.$$

The mean and variance can be computed from the probability generating function as follows:

$$\begin{aligned}
\mathrm{E}(N) &= P'(1) = \lambda \\
\mathrm{E}[N(N - 1)] &= P''(1) = \lambda^2 \\
\mathrm{Var}(N) &= \mathrm{E}[N(N - 1)] + \mathrm{E}(N) - [\mathrm{E}(N)]^2 \\
&= \lambda^2 + \lambda - \lambda^2 \\
&= \lambda.
\end{aligned}$$

For the Poisson distribution the variance is equal to the mean. The Poisson distribution can arise from a Poisson process (to be discussed in Chapter 8). The Poisson distribution and Poisson processes are also discussed in many textbooks in statistics and actuarial science, including Panjer and Willmot [106] and Ross [116].

The Poisson distribution has at least two additional useful properties. The first is given in the following theorem.

Theorem 4.37 *Let $N_1, \ldots, N_n$ be independent Poisson variables with parameters $\lambda_1, \ldots, \lambda_n$. Then $N = N_1 + \cdots + N_n$ has a Poisson distribution with parameter $\lambda_1 + \cdots + \lambda_n$.*

Proof: The pgf of the sum of independent random variables is the product of the individual pgfs. For the sum of Poisson random variables we have

$$
\begin{aligned}
P_N(z) &= \prod_{j=1}^{n} P_{N_j}(z) = \prod_{j=1}^{n} \exp[\lambda_j(z-1)] \\
&= \exp\left[\sum_{j=1}^{n} \lambda_j(z-1)\right] \\
&= e^{\lambda(z-1)},
\end{aligned}
$$

where $\lambda = \lambda_1 + \cdots + \lambda_n$. Just as is true with moment generating functions, the pgf is unique and therefore N must have a Poisson distribution with parameter λ. $\qquad\square$

The second property is particularly useful in modeling insurance risks. Suppose that the number of claims in a fixed time period, such as one year, follows a Poisson distribution. Further suppose that the claims can be classified into m distinct types. For example, claims could be classified by size, such as those below a fixed limit and those above the limit. It turns out that, if one is interested in studying the number of claims above the limit, that distribution is also Poisson but with a new Poisson parameter.

This is also useful when considering removing or adding a part of an insurance coverage. Suppose that the number of claims for a complicated medical benefit coverage follows a Poisson distribution. Consider the "types" of claims to be the different medical procedures or medical benefits under the plan. If one of the benefits is removed from the plan, again it turns out that the distribution of the number of claims under the revised plan will still have a Poisson distribution but with a new parameter.

In each of the cases mentioned in the previous paragraph, the number of claims of the different types will not only be Poisson distributed but also be independent of each other; that is, the distributions of the number of claims above the limit and the number below the limit will be independent. This is a somewhat surprising result. For example, suppose we currently sell a policy with a deductible of 50 and experience has indicated that a Poisson distribution with a certain parameter is a valid model for the number of payments. Further suppose we are also comfortable with the assumption that the number of losses in a period also has the Poisson distribution but we do not know the parameter. Without additional information, it is impossible to infer the value of the Poisson parameter should the deductible be lowered or removed entirely. We now formalize these ideas in the following theorem.

Theorem 4.38 *Suppose that the number of events N is a Poisson random variable with mean λ. Further suppose that each event can be classified into one of m types with probabilities $p_1, \ldots, p_m$ independent of all other events. Then the number of events $N_1, \ldots, N_m$ corresponding to event types $1, \ldots, m$ respectively, are mutually independent Poisson random variables with means $\lambda p_1, \ldots, \lambda p_m$, respectively.*

Proof: For fixed $N = n$, the conditional joint distribution of $(N_1, \ldots, N_m)$ is multinomial with parameters $(n, p_1, \ldots, p_m)$. Also, for fixed $N = n$, the conditional marginal distribution of N_j is binomial with parameters (n, p_j).

The joint pf of $(N_1, \ldots, N_m)$ is given by

$$
\begin{aligned}
\Pr(N_1 = n_1, \ldots, N_m = n_m) &= \Pr(N_1 = n_1, \ldots, N_m = n_m | N = n) \\
&\quad \times \Pr(N = n) \\
&= \frac{n!}{n_1! n_2! \cdots n_m!} p_1^{n_1} \cdots p_m^{n_m} \frac{e^{-\lambda} \lambda^n}{n!} \\
&= \prod_{j=1}^{m} e^{-\lambda p_j} \frac{(\lambda p_j)^{n_j}}{n_j!},
\end{aligned}
$$

where $n = n_1 + n_2 + \cdots + n_m$. Similarly, the marginal pf of N_j is determined below.

$$
\begin{aligned}
\Pr(N_j = n_j) &= \sum_{n=n_j}^{\infty} \Pr(N_j = n_j | N = n) \Pr(N = n) \\
&= \sum_{n=n_j}^{\infty} \binom{n}{n_j} p_j^{n_j} (1 - p_j)^{n-n_j} \frac{e^{-\lambda} \lambda^n}{n!} \\
&= e^{-\lambda} \frac{(\lambda p_j)^{n_j}}{n_j!} \sum_{n=n_j}^{\infty} \frac{[\lambda(1-p_j)]^{n-n_j}}{(n-n_j)!} \\
&= e^{-\lambda} \frac{(\lambda p_j)^{n_j}}{n_j!} e^{\lambda(1-p_j)} \\
&= e^{-\lambda p_j} \frac{(\lambda p_j)^{n_j}}{n_j!}.
\end{aligned}
$$

Hence the joint pf is the product of the marginal pfs, establishing mutual independence. □

Example 4.39 *In a study of medical insurance the expected number of claims per individual policy is 2.3 and the number of claims is Poisson distributed. You are considering removing one medical procedure from the coverage under this policy. Based on historical studies, this procedure accounts for approximately 10% of the claims. Determine the new frequency distribution.*

From Theorem 4.38, we know that the distribution of the number of claims expected under the revised insurance policy after removing the procedure from coverage is Poisson with mean $0.9(2.3) = 2.07$. In carrying out studies of the distribution of total claims, and hence the appropriate premium under the new policy, one also needs to study the change in the amounts of losses, the severity distribution, because the distribution of amounts of losses for the procedure which was removed may be different from the distribution of amounts when all procedures are covered. □

4.6.3   The negative binomial distribution

The negative binomial distribution has been used extensively as an alternative to the Poisson distribution. Like the Poisson distribution, it has positive probabilities on the nonnegative integers. Because it has two parameters, it has more flexibility in shape than the Poisson.

Definition 4.40 *The probability function of the **negative binomial distribution** is given by*

$$\Pr(N = k) = p_k = \binom{k+r-1}{k} \left(\frac{1}{1+\beta}\right)^r \left(\frac{\beta}{1+\beta}\right)^k,$$

$$k = 0, 1, 2, \ldots, \quad r > 0, \ \beta > 0. \qquad (4.9)$$

The binomial coefficient is to be evaluated as

$$\binom{x}{k} = \frac{x(x-1)\cdots(x-k+1)}{k!}.$$

While k must be an integer, x may be any real number. When $x > k-1$, it can also be written as

$$\binom{x}{k} = \frac{\Gamma(x+1)}{\Gamma(k+1)\Gamma(x-k+1)},$$

which may be useful because $\ln \Gamma(x)$ is available in many spreadsheets, programming languages, and mathematics packages.

It is not difficult to show that the probability generating function for the negative binomial distribution is

$$P(z) = [1 - \beta(z-1)]^{-r}.$$

From this it follows that the mean and variance of the negative binomial distribution are

$$\mathrm{E}(N) = r\beta \quad \text{and} \quad \mathrm{Var}(N) = r\beta(1+\beta).$$

Because β is positive, the variance of the negative binomial distribution exceeds the mean. This is in contrast to the Poisson distribution for which the variance is equal to the mean. This suggests that for a particular set of data, if the observed variance is larger than the observed mean, the negative binomial might be a better candidate than the Poisson distribution as a model to be used.

The negative binomial distribution is a generalization of the Poisson in at least two different ways, namely as a mixed Poisson distribution with a gamma mixing distribution (demonstrated later in this subsection) and as a compound Poisson distribution with a logarithmic secondary distribution (see Section 4.6.7). Another view of the Poisson distribution is presented in Chapter 8. There, among other assumptions, the rate at which claims occur is assumed constant over time. If the rate is linearly increasing with regard to the number of past claims, then the number of claims in any period will have the negative binomial distribution. See *Insurance Risk Models* [106, Theorem 3.6.1] for this derivation of the negative binomial distribution.

The **geometric distribution** is the special case of the negative binomial distribution when $r = 1$. The geometric distribution is, in some senses, the discrete analogue of the continuous exponential distribution. Both the geometric and exponential distributions have an exponentially decaying probability function and hence the memoryless property. The memoryless property can be interpreted in various contexts as follows. If the exponential distribution is a distribution of lifetimes, then the expected future lifetime is constant for any age. If the exponential distribution describes the size of insurance claims, then the memoryless property can be interpreted as follows: *Given that a claim exceeds a certain level d, the expected amount of the claim in excess of d is constant and so does not depend on d.* That is, if a deductible of d is imposed, the expected payment per claim will be unchanged, but of course the expected number of payments will decrease. If the geometric distribution describes the number of claims, then the memoryless property can be interpreted as follows: *Given that there are at least m claims, the probability distribution of the number of claims in excess of m does not depend on m.* Among continuous distributions, the exponential distribution is used to distinguish between *subexponential* distributions with heavy (or fat) tails and distributions with light (or thin) tails. Similarly for frequency distributions, distributions that decay in the tail slower than the geometric distribution are often considered to have long tails, whereas distributions that decay more rapidly than the geometric have short tails. The negative binomial distribution has a long tail (decays more slowly than the geometric distribution) when $r < 1$ and a lighter tail than the geometric distribution when $r > 1$.

As noted earlier, one way to create the negative binomial distribution is as a mixture of Poissons. Suppose that we know that a risk has a Poisson number of claims distribution when the risk parameter λ is known. Now treat λ as being the outcome of a random variable Λ. We will denote the pf of Λ by $u(\lambda)$, where Λ may be continuous or discrete, and denote the cdf by $U(\lambda)$. The idea that λ is the outcome of a random variable can be justified in several ways. First, we can think of the population of risks as being heterogeneous with respect to the risk parameter Λ. In practice this makes sense. Consider a block of insurance policies with the same premium, such as a group of automobile drivers in the same rating category. Such categories are usually broad ranges such as 0–7,500 miles per year, garaged in a rural area, commuting less than 50 miles per week, and so on. We know that not all drivers in the same rating category are the same even though they may "appear" to be the same from the point of view of the insurer and are charged the same premium. The parameter λ measures the expected number of accidents. If λ varies across the population of drivers, then we can think of the insured individual as a sample value drawn from the population of possible drivers. This means implicitly that λ is unknown to the insurer but follows some distribution, in this case $u(\lambda)$, over the population of drivers. The true value of λ is unobservable. All we observe are the number of accidents coming from the driver. There is now an additional degree of uncertainty, that is, uncertainty about the parameter.

This is the same mixing process that was discussed with regard to continuous distributions in Section 4.4.5. In some contexts this is referred to as *parameter uncertainty*. In the Bayesian context, the distribution of Λ is called a *prior distribution* and the parameters of its distribution are sometimes called *hyperparameters*. The role of the distribution $u(\cdot)$ is very important in credibility theory, the subject of Chapter 16. When the parameter λ is unknown, the probability that exactly k claims will arise can be written as the expected value of the same probability but conditional on $\Lambda = \lambda$ where the expectation is taken with respect to the distribution of Λ. From the law of total probability, we can write

$$
\begin{aligned}
p_k &= \Pr(N = k) \\
&= \mathrm{E}[\Pr(N = k | \Lambda)] \\
&= \int_0^\infty \Pr(N = k | \Lambda = \lambda) u(\lambda)\, d\lambda \\
&= \int_0^\infty \frac{e^{-\lambda} \lambda^k}{k!} u(\lambda)\, d\lambda.
\end{aligned}
$$

Now suppose Λ has a gamma distribution. Then

$$
p_k = \int_0^\infty \frac{e^{-\lambda} \lambda^k}{k!} \frac{\lambda^{\alpha-1} e^{-\frac{\lambda}{\theta}}}{\theta^\alpha \Gamma(\alpha)}\, d\lambda = \frac{1}{l!} \cdot \frac{1}{\theta^\alpha \Gamma(\alpha)} \int_0^\infty e^{-\lambda(1+\frac{1}{\theta})} \lambda^{k+\alpha-1}\, d\lambda.
$$

From the definition of the gamma distribution in Appendix A, this expression can be evaluated as

$$p_k = \frac{\Gamma(k+\alpha)}{k!\Gamma(\alpha)} \frac{\theta^k}{(1+\theta)^{k+\alpha}}$$

$$= \binom{k+\alpha-1}{k} \left(\frac{\theta}{1+\theta}\right)^k \left(\frac{1}{1+\theta}\right)^\alpha.$$

This formula is of the same form as (4.9), demonstrating that the mixed Poisson, with a gamma mixing distribution, is the same as a negative binomial distribution.

It is worth noting that the Poisson distribution is a limiting case of the negative binomial distribution. To see this, let r go to infinity and β go to zero while keeping their product constant. Let $\lambda = r\beta$ be that constant. Substituting $\beta = \lambda/r$ in the pgf leads to (using L'Hôpital's rule in lines 3 and 5)

$$\lim_{r\to\infty} \left[1 - \frac{\lambda(z-1)}{r}\right]^{-r} = \exp\left\{\lim_{r\to\infty} -r\ln\left[1 - \frac{\lambda(z-1)}{r}\right]\right\}$$

$$= \exp\left\{-\lim_{r\to\infty} \frac{\ln[1-\lambda(z-1)/r]}{r^{-1}}\right\}$$

$$= \exp\left\{\lim_{r\to\infty} \frac{[1-\lambda(z-1)/r]^{-1}\lambda(z-1)/r^2}{r^{-2}}\right\}$$

$$= \exp\left[\lim_{r\to\infty} \frac{r\lambda(z-1)}{r-\lambda(z-1)}\right]$$

$$= \exp\left\{\lim_{r\to\infty} [\lambda(z-1)]\right\}$$

$$= \exp[\lambda(z-1)]$$

which is the pgf of the Poisson distribution.

4.6.4   The binomial distribution

The binomial distribution is another counting distribution that arises naturally in claim number modeling. It possesses some properties different from the Poisson and the negative binomial that make it particularly useful. First, its variance is smaller than its mean. This makes it useful for data sets in which the observed sample variance is less than the sample mean. This contrasts with the negative binomial, where the variance exceeds the mean, and it also contrasts with the Poisson distribution, where the variance is equal to the mean.

Second, it describes a physical situation in which m risks are each subject to claim or loss. We can formalize this as follows. Consider m independent and identical risks each with probability q of making a claim. This might apply to a life insurance situation in which all the individuals under consideration are in the same mortality class; that is, they may all be male smokers at age 35 and duration 5 of an insurance policy. In that case, q is the probability that a person with those attributes will die in the next year. Then the number of claims for a single person follows a Bernoulli distribution, a distribution with probability $1 - q$ at 0 and probability q at 1. The probability generating function of the number of claims per individual is then given by

$$P(z) = (1 - q)z^0 + qz^1 = 1 + q(z - 1).$$

Now, if there are m such independent individuals, then the probability generating functions can be multiplied together to give the probability generating function of the total number of claims arising from the group of m individuals. That probability generating function is

$$P(z) = [1 + q(z - 1)]^m, \qquad 0 < q < 1.$$

Then from this it is easy to show that the probability of exactly k claims from the group is

$$p_k = \Pr(N = k) = \binom{m}{k} q^k (1 - q)^{m-k}, \quad k = 0, 1, \ldots, m,$$

the pf for a binomial distribution with parameters m and q. From this Bernoulli trial framework, it is clear that at most m events (claims) can occur. Hence, the distribution only has positive probabilities on the nonnegative integers up to and including m.

Consequently, an additional attribute of the binomial distribution that is sometimes useful is that it has finite support; that is, the range of values for which there exist positive probabilities has finite length. This may be useful, for instance, in modeling the number of individuals injured in an automobile accident or the number of family members covered under a health insurance policy. In each case it is reasonable to have an upper limit on the range of possible values. It is useful also in connection with situations where it is believed that it is unreasonable to assign positive probabilities beyond some point. For example, if one is modeling the number of accidents per automobile during a one-year period, it is probably physically impossible for there to be more than some number, say 12, of claims during the year given the time it would take to repair the automobile between accidents. If a model with probabilities that extend beyond 12 were used, those probabilities should be very small so that they have little impact on any decisions that are made. The mean and variance of the binomial distribution are given by

$$E(N) = mq, \quad \text{Var}(N) = mq(1 - q).$$

Table 4.1 Members of the $(a, b, 0)$ class

Distribution	a	b	p_0
Poisson	0	λ	$e^{-\lambda}$
Binomial	$-\dfrac{q}{1-q}$	$(m+1)\dfrac{q}{1-q}$	$(1-q)^m$
Negative binomial	$\dfrac{\beta}{1+\beta}$	$(r-1)\dfrac{\beta}{1+\beta}$	$(1+\beta)^{-r}$
Geometric	$\dfrac{\beta}{1+\beta}$	0	$(1+\beta)^{-1}$

4.6.5 The $(a, b, 0)$ class

The following definition characterizes the members of this class of distributions.

Definition 4.41 *Let p_k be the pf of a discrete random variable. It is a member of the* (**a**, **b**, **0**) *class of distributions, provided that there exists constants a and b such that*

$$\frac{p_k}{p_{k-1}} = a + \frac{b}{k}, \qquad k = 1, 2, 3, \ldots.$$

This recursion describes the relative size of successive probabilities in the counting distribution. The probability at zero, p_0, can be obtained from the recursive formula because the probabilities must add up to 1. This provides a boundary condition. The $(a, b, 0)$ class of distributions is a two-parameter class, the two parameters being a and b. By substituting in the probability function for each of the Poisson, binomial, and negative binomial distributions on the left-hand side of the recursion, it can be seen that each of these three distributions satisfies the recursion and that the values of a and b are as given in Table 4.1. In addition the table gives the value of p_0, the starting value for the recursion. Also in the table is the geometric distribution, the one-parameter special case $(r = 1)$ of the negative binomial distribution.

It can be shown (see Panjer and Willmot [106, Chapter 6]) that these are the only possible distributions satisfying this recursive formula.

The recursive formula can be rewritten as

$$k\frac{p_k}{p_{k-1}} = ak + b, \qquad k = 1, 2, 3, \ldots.$$

The expression on the left-hand side is a linear function in k. Note from Table 4.1 that the slope a of the straight line is 0 for the Poisson distribution, is negative for the binomial distribution, and is positive for the negative binomial distribution, including the geometric. This suggests a graphical way of indicating which of the three distributions might be selected for fitting. First,

Table 4.2   Accident profile

Number of accidents, k	Number of policies, n_k	$k\dfrac{n_k}{n_{k-1}}$
0	7,840	
1	1,317	0.17
2	239	0.36
3	42	0.53
4	14	1.33
5	4	1.43
6	4	6.00
7	1	1.75
8+	0	
Total	9,461	

one can plot

$$k\frac{\hat{p}_k}{\hat{p}_{k-1}} = k\frac{n_k}{n_{k-1}}$$

against k. The observed values should form approximately a straight line if one of these models is to be selected, and the value of the slope should be an indication of which of the models should be selected. Note that this cannot be done if any of the n_k are 0. Hence this procedure is less useful for a small number of observations.

Example 4.42 *Consider the accident data in Table 4.2, which is taken from Thyrion [128]. For the 9,461 automobile insurance policies studied, the number of accidents under the policy is recorded in the table. Also recorded in the table is the observed value of the quantity that should be linear.*

Figure 4.8 plots the value of the quantity of interest against k, the number of accidents. It can be seen from the graph that the quantity of interest looks approximately linear except for the point at $k = 6$. The reliability of the quantities as k increases diminishes because the number of observations becomes small and the variability of the results grows. This illustrates the weakness of this ad hoc procedure. Visually, all the points appear to have equal value. However, the points on the left are more reliable than the points on the right. From the graph, it can be seen that the slope is positive and the data appear approximately linear. This suggests the negative binomial distribution is an appropriate model. Whether or not the slope is significantly different from 0 is also not easily judged from the graph. By rescaling the vertical axis of the graph, the slope can be made to look steeper and hence the slope could be made to appear to be significantly different from 0. Graphically, it is difficult to distinguish between the Poisson and the negative binomial

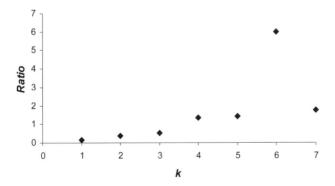

Fig. 4.8 Plot of the ratio kn_k/n_{k-1} against k.

distribution because the Poisson requires a slope of 0. However, we can say that the binomial distribution is probably not a good choice since there is no evidence of a negative slope. In this case it is advisable to fit both the Poisson and negative binomial distributions and conduct a more formal test to choose between them.

It is also possible to compare the appropriateness of the distributions by looking at the relationship of the variance to the mean. For this data set, the mean number of claims per policy is 0.2144. The variance is 0.2889. Because the variance exceeds the mean, the negative binomial should be considered as an alternative to the Poisson. Again this is a qualitative comment because we have, at this point, no formal way of determining whether the variance is sufficiently larger than the mean to warrant use of the negative binomial. In order to do some formal analysis, Table 4.3 gives the results of maximum likelihood estimation (to be discussed in Chapter 12) of the parameters of the Poisson and negative binomial distributions and the negative loglikelihood in each case. In Chapter 13 formal selection methods are presented. They would indicate that the negative binomial is superior to the Poisson as a model for this data set. However, those methods also indicate that the negative binomial is not a particularly good model, and thus some of the distributions yet to be introduced should be considered.

In subsequent subsections we will expand the class of the distributions beyond the three discussed in this section by constructing more general models related to the Poisson, binomial, and negative binomial distributions.

4.6.6   Truncation and modification at zero

At times, the distributions discussed previously do not adequately describe the characteristics of some data sets encountered in practice. This may be

Table 4.3 Poisson–negative binomial comparison

Distribution	Parameter estimates	−Loglikelihood
Poisson	$\hat{\lambda} = 0.2143537$	5,490.78
Negative binomial	$\hat{\beta} = 0.3055594$ $\hat{r} = 0.7015122$	5,348.04

because the tail of the negative binomial is not heavy enough or because the distributions in the $(a, b, 0)$ class cannot capture the shape of the data set in some other part of the distribution.

In this section, we address the problem of a poor fit at the left-hand end of the distribution, in particular the probability at zero.

For insurance count data, the probability at zero is the probability that no claims occur during the period under study. For applications in insurance where the probability of occurrence of a loss is low, the probability at zero has the largest value. Thus, it is important to pay special attention to the fit at this point.

There are also situations that naturally occur which generate unusually large probabilities at zero. Consider the case of group dental insurance. If, in a family, both husband and wife have coverage with their employer-sponsored plans and both group insurance contracts provide coverage for all family members, the claims will be made to the insurer of the plan which provides the better benefits, and no claims may be made under the other contract. Then, in conducting studies for a specific insurer, one may find a higher than expected number of individuals who made no claim.

Similarly, it is possible to have situations in which there is less than the expected number, or even zero, occurrences at zero. For example, if one is counting the number of claims from accidents resulting in a claim, the minimum observed value is 1.

An adjustment of the probability at zero is easily handled for the Poisson, binomial, and negative binomial distributions.

Definition 4.43 *Let p_k be the pf of a discrete random variable. It is a member of the* **(a,b,1)** *class of distributions provided that there exists constants a and b such that*

$$\frac{p_k}{p_{k-1}} = a + \frac{b}{k}, \qquad k = 2, 3, 4, \ldots .$$

Note that the only difference from the $(a, b, 0)$ class is that the recursion begins at p_1 rather than p_0. This forces the distribution from $k = 1$ to $k = \infty$ to have the same shape as the $(a, b, 0)$ class in the sense that the probabilities are the same up to a constant of proportionality because $\sum_{k=1}^{\infty} p_k$ can be set to any number in the interval $(0, 1]$. The remaining probability is at $k = 0$.

We will distinguish between the situations in which $p_0 = 0$ and those where $p_0 > 0$. The first subclass is called the **truncated** (more specifically, **zero-truncated**) distributions. The members are the zero-truncated Poisson, zero-truncated binomial, and zero-truncated negative binomial (and its special case, the zero-truncated geometric) distributions.

The second subclass will be referred to as the **zero-modified** distributions because the probability is modified from that for the $(a, b, 0)$ class. These distributions can be viewed as a mixture of an $(a, b, 0)$ distribution and a degenerate distribution with all the probability at zero. Alternatively, they can be called **truncated with zeros** distributions since the distribution can be viewed as a mixture of a truncated distribution and a degenerate distribution with all the probability at zero. We now show this more formally. Note that all zero-truncated distributions can be considered as zero-modified distributions, with the particular modification being to set $p_0 = 0$.

With three types of distributions, notation can become confusing. When writing about discrete distributions in general, we will continue to let $p_k = \Pr(N = k)$. When referring to a zero-truncated distribution, we will use p_k^T, and when referring to a zero-modified distribution, we will use p_k^M. Once again, it is possible for a zero-modified distribution to be a zero-truncated distribution.

Let $P(z) = \sum_{k=0}^{\infty} p_k z^k$ denote the pgf of a member of the $(a, b, 0)$ class. Let $P^M(z) = \sum_{k=0}^{\infty} p_k^M z^k$ denote the pgf of the corresponding member of the $(a, b, 1)$ class; that is,

$$p_k^M = c p_k, \qquad k = 1, 2, 3, \ldots,$$

and p_0^M is an arbitrary number. Then

$$
\begin{aligned}
P^M(z) &= p_0^M + \sum_{k=1}^{\infty} p_k^M z^k \\
&= p_0^M + c \sum_{k=1}^{\infty} p_k z^k \\
&= p_0^M + c[P(z) - p_0].
\end{aligned}
$$

Because $P^M(1) = P(1) = 1$,

$$1 = p_0^M + c(1 - p_0),$$

resulting in

$$c = \frac{1 - p_0^M}{1 - p_0} \text{ or } p_0^M = 1 - c(1 - p_0).$$

This relationship is necessary to ensure that the p_k^M sum to 1. We then have

$$
\begin{aligned}
P^M(z) &= p_0^M + \frac{1 - p_0^M}{1 - p_0}[P(z) - p_0] \\
&= \left(1 - \frac{1 - p_0^M}{1 - p_0}\right)1 + \frac{1 - p_0^M}{1 - p_0}P(z).
\end{aligned}
\tag{4.10}
$$

This is a weighted average of the pgfs of the degenerate distribution and the corresponding $(a, b, 0)$ member. Furthermore,

$$
p_k^M = \frac{1 - p_0^M}{1 - p_0}p_k, \qquad k = 1, 2, \dots .
\tag{4.11}
$$

Let $P^T(z)$ denote the pgf of the zero-truncated distribution corresponding to an $(a, b, 0)$ pgf $P(z)$. Then, by setting $p_0^M = 0$ in (4.10) and (4.11),

$$
P^T(z) = \frac{P(z) - p_0}{1 - p_0}
$$

and

$$
p_k^T = \frac{p_k}{1 - p_0}, \qquad k = 1, 2, \dots .
\tag{4.12}
$$

Then from (4.11)

$$
p_k^M = (1 - p_0^M)p_k^T, \qquad k = 1, 2, \dots ,
\tag{4.13}
$$

and

$$
P^M(z) = p_0^M(1) + (1 - p_0^M)P^T(z).
\tag{4.14}
$$

Then the zero-modified distribution is also the weighted average of a degenerate distribution and the zero-truncated member of the $(a, b, 0)$ class. The following example illustrates these relationships.

Example 4.44 *Consider a negative binomial random variable with parameters $\beta = 0.5$ and $r = 2.5$. Determine the first four probabilities for this random variable. Then determine the corresponding probabilities for the zero-truncated and zero-modified (with $p_0^M = 0.6$) versions.*

From Table 4.4 on Page 89 we have, for the negative binomial distribution,

$$
\begin{aligned}
p_0 &= (1 + 0.5)^{-2.5} = 0.362887, \\
a &= \frac{0.5}{1.5} = \frac{1}{3}, \\
b &= \frac{(2.5 - 1)(0.5)}{1.5} = \frac{1}{2}.
\end{aligned}
$$

The first three recursions are

$$
\begin{aligned}
p_1 &= 0.362887\left(\tfrac{1}{3} + \tfrac{1}{2}\tfrac{1}{1}\right) = 0.302406, \\
p_2 &= 0.302406\left(\tfrac{1}{3} + \tfrac{1}{2}\tfrac{1}{2}\right) = 0.176404, \\
p_3 &= 0.176404\left(\tfrac{1}{3} + \tfrac{1}{2}\tfrac{1}{3}\right) = 0.088202.
\end{aligned}
$$

For the zero-truncated random variable, $p_0^T = 0$ by definition. The recursions start with [from (4.12)] $p_1^T = 0.302406/(1 - 0.362887) = 0.474651$. Then

$$
\begin{aligned}
p_2^T &= 0.474651 \left(\tfrac{1}{3} + \tfrac{1}{2}\tfrac{1}{2} \right) = 0.276880, \\
p_3^T &= 0.276880 \left(\tfrac{1}{3} + \tfrac{1}{2}\tfrac{1}{3} \right) = 0.138440.
\end{aligned}
$$

If the original values were all available, then the zero-truncated probabilities could have all been obtained by multiplying the original values by $1/(1 - 0.362887) = 1.569580$.

For the zero-modified random variable, $p_0^M = 0.6$ arbitrarily. From (4.11), $p_1^M = (1 - 0.6)(0.302406)/(1 - 0.362887) = 0.189860$. Then

$$
\begin{aligned}
p_2^M &= 0.189860 \left(\tfrac{1}{3} + \tfrac{1}{2}\tfrac{1}{2} \right) = 0.110752, \\
p_3^M &= 0.110752 \left(\tfrac{1}{3} + \tfrac{1}{2}\tfrac{1}{3} \right) = 0.055376.
\end{aligned}
$$

In this case, each original negative binomial probability has been multiplied by $(1 - 0.6)/(1 - 0.362887) = 0.627832$. Also note that, for $j \geq 1$, $p_j^M = 0.4 p_j^T$. □

Although we have only discussed the zero-modified distributions of the $(a, b, 0)$ class, the $(a, b, 1)$ class admits additional distributions. The (a, b) parameter space can be expanded to admit an extension of the negative binomial distribution to include cases where $-1 < r < 0$. For the $(a, b, 0)$ class, $r > 0$ is required. By adding the additional region to the sample space, the "extended" truncated negative binomial (ETNB) distribution has parameter restrictions $\beta > 0$, $r > -1$, $r \neq 0$.

To show that the recursive equation

$$
p_k = p_{k-1} \left(a + \frac{b}{k} \right), \qquad k = 2, 3, \ldots, \tag{4.15}
$$

with $p_0 = 0$ defines a proper distribution, it is sufficient to show that for any value of p_1, the successive values of p_k obtained recursively are each positive and that $\sum_{k=1}^{\infty} p_k < \infty$. For the ETNB, this must be done for the parameter space

$$
\begin{aligned}
a &= \frac{\beta}{1 + \beta}, \qquad \beta > 0, \\
b &= (r - 1)\frac{\beta}{1 + \beta}, \qquad r > -1, r \neq 0
\end{aligned}
$$

(see Exercise 4.44).

When $r \to 0$, the limiting case of the ETNB is the logarithmic distribution with

$$
p_k^T = \frac{[\beta/(1 + \beta)]^k}{k \ln(1 + \beta)}, \qquad k = 1, 2, 3, \ldots \tag{4.16}
$$

(see Exercise 4.45). The pgf of the logarithmic distribution is

$$P^T(z) = 1 - \frac{\ln[1 - \beta(z - 1)]}{\ln(1 + \beta)} \tag{4.17}$$

(see Exercise 4.46). The zero-modified logarithmic distribution is created by assigning an arbitrary probability at zero and reducing the remaining probabilities.

It is also interesting that the special extreme case with $-1 < r < 0$ and $\beta \to \infty$ is a proper distribution, and is sometimes called the Sibuya distribution. It has pgf $P(z) = 1 - (1 - z)^{-r}$ and no moments exist (see Exercise 4.47). Distributions with no moments are not particularly interesting for modeling claim numbers (unless the right tail is subsequently modified) because then an infinite number of claims are expected. This might be difficult to price!

Example 4.45 *Determine the probabilities for an ETNB distribution with $r = -0.5$ and $\beta = 1$. Do this both for the truncated version and for the modified version with $p_0^M = 0.6$ set arbitrarily.*

We have $a = 1/(1+1) = 0.5$ and $b = (-0.5 - 1)(1)/(1+1) = -0.75$. From Appendix B we also have $p_1^T = -0.5(1)/[(1 + 1)^{0.5} - (1 + 1)] = 0.853553$. Subsequent values are

$$p_2^T = \left(0.5 - \frac{0.75}{2}\right)(0.853553) = 0.106694,$$

$$p_3^T = \left(0.5 - \frac{0.75}{3}\right)(0.106694) = 0.026674.$$

For the modified probabilities, the truncated probabilities need to be multiplied by 0.4 to produce $p_1^M = 0.341421$, $p_2^M = 0.042678$, and $p_3^M = 0.010670$.

A reasonable question is to ask if there is a "natural" member of the ETNB distribution, that is, one for which the recursion would begin with p_1 rather than p_2. For that to be the case, the natural value of p_0 would have to satisfy $p_1 = (0.5 - 0.75/1)p_0 = -0.25p_0$. This would force one of the two probabilities to be negative and so there is no acceptable solution. It is easy to show that this occurs for any $r < 0$.   □

There are no other members of the $(a, b, 1)$ class beyond the ones discussed above. A summary is given in Table 4.4.

4.6.7 Compound frequency models

A larger class of distributions can be created by the processes of compounding any two discrete distributions. The term *compounding* reflects the idea that the pgf of the new distribution $P(z)$ is written as

$$P(z) = P_N[P_M(z)], \tag{4.18}$$

Table 4.4   Members of the $(a, b, 1)$ class

Distribution[a]	p_0	a	b	Parameter space
Poisson	$e^{-\lambda}$	0	λ	$\lambda > 0$
ZT Poisson	0	0	λ	$\lambda > 0$
ZM Poisson	Arbitrary	0	λ	$\lambda > 0$
Binomial	$(1-q)^m$	$-\dfrac{q}{1-q}$	$(m+1)\dfrac{q}{1-q}$	$0 < q < 1$
ZT binomial	0	$-\dfrac{q}{1-q}$	$(m+1)\dfrac{q}{1-q}$	$0 < q < 1$
ZM binomial	Arbitrary	$-\dfrac{q}{1-q}$	$(m+1)\dfrac{q}{1-q}$	$0 < q < 1$
Negative binomial	$(1+\beta)^{-r}$	$\dfrac{\beta}{1+\beta}$	$(r-1)\dfrac{\beta}{1+\beta}$	$r > 0,\ \beta > 0$
ETNB	0	$\dfrac{\beta}{1+\beta}$	$(r-1)\dfrac{\beta}{1+\beta}$	$r > -1,^b\ \beta > 0$
ZM ETNB	Arbitrary	$\dfrac{\beta}{1+\beta}$	$(r-1)\dfrac{\beta}{1+\beta}$	$r > -1,^b\ \beta > 0$
Geometric	$(1+\beta)^{-1}$	$\dfrac{\beta}{1+\beta}$	0	$\beta > 0$
ZT geometric	0	$\dfrac{\beta}{1+\beta}$	0	$\beta > 0$
ZM geometric	Arbitrary	$\dfrac{\beta}{1+\beta}$	0	$\beta > 0$
Logarithmic	0	$\dfrac{\beta}{1+\beta}$	$-\dfrac{\beta}{1+\beta}$	$\beta > 0$
ZM logarithmic	Arbitrary	$\dfrac{\beta}{1+\beta}$	$-\dfrac{\beta}{1+\beta}$	$\beta > 0$

[a]ZT = zero truncated, ZM = zero modified.
[b]Excluding $r = 0$, which is the logarithmic distribution.

where $P_N(z)$ and $P_M(z)$ are called the *primary* and *secondary* distributions, respectively.

The compound distributions arise naturally as follows. Let N be a counting random variable with pgf $P_N(z)$. Let $M_1, M_2, \ldots$ be identically and independently distributed random variables with pgf $P_M(z)$. Assuming that the M_js do not depend on N, the pgf of the random sum $S = M_1 + M_2 + \cdots + M_N$ (where $N = 0$ implies that $S = 0$) is $P_S(z) = P_N[P_M(z)]$. This is shown as

$$P_S(z) = \sum_{k=0}^{\infty} \Pr(S = k)z^k = \sum_{k=0}^{\infty}\sum_{n=0}^{\infty} \Pr(S = k | N = n)\Pr(N = n)z^k$$

$$= \sum_{n=0}^{\infty} \Pr(N = n) \sum_{k=0}^{\infty} \Pr(M_1 + \cdots + M_n = k | N = n) z^k$$

$$= \sum_{n=0}^{\infty} \Pr(N = n)[P_M(z)]^n$$

$$= P_N[P_M(z)].$$

In insurance contexts, this distribution can arise naturally. If N represents the number of accidents arising in a portfolio of risks and $\{M_k; \ k = 1, 2, \ldots, N\}$ represents the number of claims (injuries, number of cars, etc.) from the accidents, then S represents the total number of claims from the portfolio. This kind of interpretation is not necessary to justify the use of a compound distribution. If a compound distribution fits data well, that may be enough justification itself. Also, there are other motivations for these distributions, as presented in Section 4.6.12.

Example 4.46 *Demonstrate that any zero-modified distribution is a compound distribution.*

Consider a primary Bernoulli distribution. It has pgf $P_N(z) = 1 - q + qz$. Then consider an arbitrary secondary distribution with pgf $P_M(z)$. Then, from (4.18) we obtain

$$P_S(z) = P_N[P_M(z)] = 1 - q + qP_M(z).$$

From (4.10) this is the pgf of a ZM distribution with

$$q = \frac{1 - p_0^M}{1 - p_0}.$$

That is, the ZM distribution has assigned arbitrary probability p_0^M at zero, while p_0 is the probability assigned at zero by the secondary distribution. □

Example 4.47 *Consider the case where both M and N have the Poisson distribution. Determine the pgf of this distribution.*

This distribution is called the Poisson–Poisson or Neyman Type A distribution. Let $P_N(z) = e^{\lambda_1(z-1)}$ and $P_M(z) = e^{\lambda_2(z-1)}$. Then

$$P_S(z) = e^{\lambda_1[e^{\lambda_2(z-1)}-1]}.$$

When λ_2 is a lot larger than λ_1—for example, $\lambda_1 = 0.1$ and $\lambda_2 = 10$—the resulting distribution will have two local modes. □

The probability of exactly k claims can be written as

$$
\begin{aligned}
\Pr(S = k) &= \sum_{n=0}^{\infty} \Pr(S = k | N = n) \Pr(N = n) \\
&= \sum_{n=0}^{\infty} \Pr(M_1 + \cdots + M_N = k | N = n) \Pr(N = n) \\
&= \sum_{n=0}^{\infty} \Pr(M_1 + \cdots + M_n = k) \Pr(N = n).
\end{aligned}
\tag{4.19}
$$

Letting $g_n = \Pr(S = n)$, $p_n = \Pr(N = n)$, and $f_n = \Pr(M = n)$, this is rewritten as

$$
g_k = \sum_{n=0}^{\infty} p_n f_k^{*n}
\tag{4.20}
$$

where f_k^{*n}, $k = 0, 1, \ldots$, is the "n-fold convolution" of the function f_k, $k = 0, 1, \ldots$, that is, the probability that the sum of n random variables which are each independent and identically distributed (i.i.d.) with probability function f_k will take on value k.

When $P_N(z)$ is chosen to be a member of the $(a, b, 0)$ class,

$$
p_k = \left(a + \frac{b}{k} \right) p_{k-1}, \qquad k = 1, 2, \ldots,
\tag{4.21}
$$

and a simple recursive formula can be used. This formula avoids the use of convolutions and thus reduces the computations considerably.

Theorem 4.48 *If the primary distribution is a member of the $(a, b, 0)$ class, the recursive formula is*

$$
g_k = \frac{1}{1 - a f_0} \sum_{j=1}^{k} \left(a + \frac{bj}{k} \right) f_j g_{k-j}, \qquad k = 1, 2, 3, \ldots .
\tag{4.22}
$$

Proof: From (4.21),

$$
n p_n = a(n-1) p_{n-1} + (a+b) p_{n-1}.
$$

Multiplying each side by $[P_M(z)]^{n-1} P_M'(z)$ and summing over n yields

$$
\begin{aligned}
\sum_{n=1}^{\infty} n p_n [P_M(z)]^{n-1} P_M'(z) &= a \sum_{n=1}^{\infty} (n-1) p_{n-1} [P_M(z)]^{n-1} P_M'(z) \\
&\quad + (a+b) \sum_{n=1}^{\infty} p_{n-1} [P_M(z)]^{n-1} P_M'(z).
\end{aligned}
$$

Because $P_S(z) = \sum_{n=0}^{\infty} p_n [P_M(z)]^n$, the previous equation is

$$P_S'(z) = a \sum_{n=0}^{\infty} n p_n [P_M(z)]^n P_M'(z) + (a+b) \sum_{n=0}^{\infty} p_n [P_M(z)]^n P_M'(z).$$

Therefore

$$P_S'(z) = a P_S'(z) P_M(z) + (a+b) P_S(z) P_M'(z).$$

Each side can be expanded in powers of z. The coefficients of z^{k-1} in such an expansion must be the same on both sides of the equation. Hence, for $k = 1, 2, \ldots$ we have

$$\begin{aligned}
k g_k &= a \sum_{j=0}^{k} (k-j) f_j g_{k-j} + (a+b) \sum_{j=0}^{k} j f_j g_{k-j} \\
&= a k f_0 g_k + a \sum_{j=1}^{k} (k-j) f_j g_{k-j} + (a+b) \sum_{j=1}^{k} j f_j g_{k-j} \\
&= a k f_0 g_k + a k \sum_{j=1}^{k} f_j g_{k-j} + b \sum_{j=1}^{k} j f_j g_{k-j}.
\end{aligned}$$

Therefore,

$$g_k = a f_0 g_k + \sum_{j=1}^{k} \left(a + \frac{bj}{k} \right) f_j g_{k-j}.$$

Rearrangement yields (4.22). □

In order to use (4.22), the starting value g_0 is required and is given in Theorem 4.51 below. If the primary distribution is a member of the $(a, b, 1)$ class, the proof must be modified to reflect the fact that the recursion for the primary distribution begins at $k = 2$. The result is the following.

Theorem 4.49 *If the primary distribution is a member of the $(a, b, 1)$ class, the recursive formula is*

$$g_k = \frac{[p_1 - (a+b)p_0]f_k + \sum_{j=1}^{k}(a+bj/k)f_j g_{k-j}}{1 - a f_0}, \qquad k = 1, 2, 3, \ldots . \quad (4.23)$$

Proof: It is similar to the proof of Theorem 4.48 and is left to the reader. □

Example 4.50 *Develop the recursive formula for the case where the primary distribution is Poisson.*

In this case $a = 0$ and $b = \lambda$, yielding the recursive form

$$g_k = \frac{\lambda}{k} \sum_{j=1}^{k} j f_j g_{k-j}.$$

The starting value is, from (4.18),

$$
\begin{aligned}
g_0 &= \Pr(S = 0) = P(0) \\
&= P_N[P_M(0)] = P_N(f_0) \\
&= e^{-\lambda(1-f_0)}.
\end{aligned}
\tag{4.24}
$$

Distributions of this type are called compound Poisson distributions. When the secondary distribution is specified, the compound distribution is called Poisson–X, where X is the name of the secondary distribution. □

The method used to obtain g_0 applies to any compound distribution.

Theorem 4.51 *For any compound distribution, $g_0 = P_N(f_0)$, where $P_N(z)$ is the pgf of the primary distribution and f_0 is the probability that the secondary distribution takes on the value zero.*

Proof: See the second line of (4.24) □

Note that the secondary distribution is not required to be in any special form. However, to keep the number of distributions manageable, secondary distributions will be selected from the $(a, b, 0)$ or the $(a, b, 1)$ class.

Example 4.52 *Calculate the probabilities for the Poisson–ETNB distribution where $\lambda = 3$ for the Poisson distribution and the ETNB distribution has $r = -0.5$ and $\beta = 1$.*

From Example 4.45 the secondary probabilities are $f_0 = 0$, $f_1 = 0.853553$, $f_2 = 0.106694$, and $f_3 = 0.026674$. From (4.24), $g_0 = \exp[-3(1 - 0)] = 0.049787$. For the Poisson primary distribution, $a = 0$ and $b = 3$. The recursive formula in (4.22) becomes

$$
g_k = \frac{\sum_{j=1}^{k}(3j/k)f_j g_{k-j}}{1 - 0(0)} = \sum_{j=1}^{k}\frac{3j}{k}f_j g_{k-j}.
$$

Then,

$$
g_1 = \frac{3(1)}{1}0.853553(0.049787) = 0.127488,
$$

$$
g_2 = \frac{3(1)}{2}0.853553(0.127488) + \frac{3(2)}{2}0.106694(0.049787) = 0.179163,
$$

$$
\begin{aligned}
g_3 &= \frac{3(1)}{3}0.853553(0.179163) + \frac{3(2)}{3}0.106694(0.127488) \\
&\quad + \frac{3(3)}{3}0.026674(0.049787) = 0.184114.
\end{aligned}
$$

□

Example 4.53 *Demonstrate that the Poisson–logarithmic distribution is a negative binomial distribution.*

The negative binomial distribution has pgf

$$P(z) = [1 - \beta(z - 1)]^{-r}.$$

Suppose $P_N(z)$ is Poisson(λ) and $P_M(z)$ is logarithmic(β); then

$$
\begin{aligned}
P_N[P_M(z)] &= \exp\{\lambda[P_M(z) - 1]\} \\
&= \exp\left\{\lambda\left[1 - \frac{\ln[1 - \beta(z - 1)]}{\ln(1 + \beta)} - 1\right]\right\} \\
&= \exp\left\{\frac{-\lambda}{\ln(1 + \beta)}\ln[1 - \beta(z - 1)]\right\} \\
&= [1 - \beta(z - 1)]^{-\lambda/\ln(1+\beta)} \\
&= [1 - \beta(z - 1)]^{-r},
\end{aligned}
$$

where $r = \lambda/\ln(1+\beta)$. This shows that the negative binomial distribution can be written as a compound Poisson distribution with a logarithmic secondary distribution.   □

The above example shows that the "Poisson–logarithmic" distribution does not create a new distribution beyond the $(a, b, 0)$ and $(a, b, 1)$ classes. As a result, this combination of distributions is not useful to us. Another combination which does not create a new distribution beyond the $(a, b, 1)$ class is the compound geometric distribution where both the primary and secondary distributions are geometric. The resulting distribution is a zero-modified geometric distribution, as shown in Exercise 4.51. The following theorem shows that certain other combinations are also of no use in expanding the class of distributions through compounding. Suppose $P_S(z) = P_N[P_M(z); \theta]$ as before. Now, $P_M(z)$ can always be written as

$$P_M(z) = f_0 + (1 - f_0)P_M^*(z) \qquad (4.25)$$

where $P_M^*(z)$ is the pgf of the conditional distribution over the positive range (in other words, the zero-truncated version).

Theorem 4.54 *Suppose the pgf $P_N(z; \theta)$ satisfies*

$$P_N(z; \theta) = B[\theta(z - 1)]$$

for some parameter θ and some function $B(z)$ which is independent of θ. That is, the parameter θ and the argument z only appear in the pgf as $\theta(z-1)$. There may be other parameters as well, and they may appear anywhere in the pgf. Then $P_S(z) = P_N[P_M(z); \theta]$ can be rewritten as

$$P_S(z) = P_N[P_M^T(z); \theta(1 - f_0)].$$

Proof:

$$
\begin{aligned}
P_S(z) &= P_N[P_M(z); \theta] \\
&= P_N[f_0 + (1 - f_0)P_M^T(z); \theta] \\
&= B\{\theta[f_0 + (1 - f_0)P_M^T(z) - 1]\} \\
&= B\{\theta(1 - f_0)[P_M^T(z) - 1]\} \\
&= P_N[P_M^T(z); \theta(1 - f_0)]. \qquad \square
\end{aligned}
$$

This shows that adding, deleting, or modifying the probability at zero in the secondary distribution does not add a new distribution because it is equivalent to modifying the parameter θ of the primary distribution. This means that, for example, a Poisson primary distribution with a Poisson, zero-truncated Poisson, or zero-modified Poisson secondary distribution will still lead to a Neyman Type A (Poisson–Poisson) distribution.

Example 4.55 *Determine the probabilities for a Poisson–zero-modified ETNB distribution where the parameters are $\lambda = 7.5$, $p_0^M = 0.6$, $r = -0.5$, and $\beta = 1$.*

From Example 4.45 the secondary probabilities are $f_0 = 0.6$, $f_1 = 0.341421$, $f_2 = 0.042678$, and $f_3 = 0.010670$. From (4.24), $g_0 = \exp[-7.5(1 - 0.6)] = 0.049787$. For the Poisson primary distribution, $a = 0$ and $b = 7.5$. The recursive formula in (4.22) becomes

$$
g_k = \frac{\sum_{j=1}^{k}(7.5j/k)f_j g_{k-j}}{1 - 0(0.6)} = \sum_{j=1}^{k} \frac{7.5j}{k} f_j g_{k-j}.
$$

Then,

$$
g_1 = \frac{7.5(1)}{1}0.341421(0.049787) = 0.127487,
$$

$$
g_2 = \frac{7.5(1)}{2}0.341421(0.127487) + \frac{7.5(2)}{2}0.042678(0.049787) = 0.179161,
$$

$$
g_3 = \frac{7.5(1)}{3}0.341421(0.179161) + \frac{7.5(2)}{3}0.042678(0.127487)
$$

$$
+ \frac{7.5(3)}{3}0.010670(0.049787) = 0.184112.
$$

Except for slight rounding differences, these probabilities are the same as those obtained in Example 4.52. $\qquad \square$

4.6.8   Further properties of the compound Poisson class

Of central importance within the class of compound frequency models is the class of compound Poisson frequency distributions. Physical motivation for this model arises from the fact that the Poisson distribution is often a good model to describe the number of claim-causing accidents, and the number of claims from an accident is often itself a random variable. This physical motivation is discussed in the previous subsection. However, there are numerous convenient mathematical properties enjoyed by the compound Poisson class. In particular, those involving recursive evaluation of the probabilities were also discussed in the previous subsection. In addition, there is a close connection between the compound Poisson distributions and the mixed Poisson frequency distributions which is discussed in more detail in Section 4.6.10. Here we consider some other properties of these distributions. The compound Poisson pgf may be expressed as

$$P(z) = \exp\{\lambda[Q(z) - 1]\}, \tag{4.26}$$

where $Q(z)$ is the pgf of the secondary distribution.

Example 4.56 *Obtain the pgf for the Poisson–ETNB distribution and show that it looks like the pgf of a Poisson–negative binomial distribution.*

The ETNB distribution has pgf

$$Q(z) = \frac{[1 - \beta(z - 1)]^{-r} - (1 + \beta)^{-r}}{1 - (1 + \beta)^{-r}}$$

for $\beta > 0$, $r > -1$, and $r \neq 0$. Then the Poisson–ETNB distribution has as the logarithm of its pgf

$$
\begin{aligned}
\ln P(z) &= \lambda \left\{ \frac{[1 - \beta(z - 1)]^{-r} - (1 + \beta)^{-r}}{1 - (1 + \beta)^{-r}} - 1 \right\} \\
&= \lambda \left\{ \frac{[1 - \beta(z - 1)]^{-r} - 1}{1 - (1 + \beta)^{-r}} \right\} \\
&= \mu \{ [1 - \beta(z - 1)]^{-r} - 1 \},
\end{aligned}
$$

where $\mu = \lambda/[1 - (1 + \beta)^{-r}]$. This defines a compound Poisson distribution with primary mean μ and secondary pgf $[1 - \beta(z - 1)]^{-r}$, which is the pgf of a negative binomial random variable, as long as r and hence μ are positive. This illustrates that the probability at zero in the secondary distribution has no impact on the compound Poisson form. Also, the above calculation demonstrates that the Poisson–ETNB pgf $P(z)$, with $\ln P(z) = \mu\{[1 - \beta(z - 1)]^{-r} - 1\}$, has parameter space $\{\beta > 0, r > -1, \mu r > 0\}$, a useful observation with respect to estimation and analysis of the parameters.   □

We can compare the skewness (third moment) of these distributions to develop an appreciation of the amount by which the skewness, and hence the tails of these distributions, can vary even when the mean and variance are fixed. From (4.26) (see Exercise 4.53) and Definition 3.4, the mean and second and third central moments of the compound Poisson distribution are

$$
\begin{aligned}
\mu_1' &= \mu = \lambda m_1', \\
\mu_2 &= \sigma^2 = \lambda m_2', \\
\mu_3 &= \lambda m_3',
\end{aligned}
\tag{4.27}
$$

where m_j' is the jth raw moment of the secondary distribution. The coefficient of skewness is

$$
\gamma_1 = \frac{\mu_3}{\sigma^3} = \frac{m_3'}{\lambda^{1/2}(m_2')^{3/2}}.
$$

For the Poisson–binomial distribution, with a bit of algebra (see Exercise 4.54) we obtain

$$
\begin{aligned}
\mu &= \lambda m q, \\
\sigma^2 &= \mu[1 + (m-1)q], \\
\mu_3 &= 3\sigma^2 - 2\mu + \frac{m-2}{m-1}\frac{(\sigma^2 - \mu)^2}{\mu}.
\end{aligned}
\tag{4.28}
$$

Carrying out similar exercises for the negative binomial, Polya–Aeppli, Neyman Type A, and Poisson–ETNB distributions yields

Negative binomial: $\quad \mu_3 = 3\sigma^2 - 2\mu + 2\dfrac{(\sigma^2 - \mu)^2}{\mu}$

Polya–Aeppli: $\quad \mu_3 = 3\sigma^2 - 2\mu + \dfrac{3}{2}\dfrac{(\sigma^2 - \mu)^2}{\mu}$

Neyman Type A: $\quad \mu_3 = 3\sigma^2 - 2\mu + \dfrac{(\sigma^2 - \mu)^2}{\mu}$

Poisson–ETNB: $\quad \mu_3 = 3\sigma^2 - 2\mu + \dfrac{r+2}{r+1}\dfrac{(\sigma^2 - \mu)^2}{\mu}$

For the Poisson–ETNB distribution, the range of r is $-1 < r < \infty$, $r \neq 0$. Note that as $r \to 0$ the secondary distribution is logarithmic, resulting in the negative binomial distribution.

Note that for fixed mean and variance the third moment only changes through the coefficient in the last term for each of the five distributions. For the Poisson distribution, $\mu_3 = \lambda = 3\sigma^2 - 2\mu$, and so the third term for each expression for μ_3 represents the change from the Poisson distribution. For the Poisson–binomial distribution, if $m = 1$, the distribution is Poisson because it is equivalent to a Poisson–zero-truncated binomial as truncation at zero leaves only probability at 1. Another view is that from (4.28) we have

$$
\begin{aligned}
\mu_3 &= 3\sigma^2 - 2\mu + \frac{m-2}{m-1}\frac{(m-1)^2 q^4 \lambda^2 m^2}{\lambda m q} \\
&= 3\sigma^2 - 2\mu + (m-2)(m-1)q^3 \lambda m,
\end{aligned}
$$

which reduces to the Poisson value for μ_3 when $m = 1$. Hence, it is necessary that $m \geq 2$ for non-Poisson distributions to be created. Then the coefficient satisfies

$$0 \leq \frac{m - 2}{m - 1} < 1.$$

For the Poisson–ETNB, because $r > -1$, the coefficient satisfies

$$1 < \frac{r + 2}{r + 1} < \infty,$$

noting that when $r = 0$ this refers to the negative binomial distribution. For the Neyman Type A distribution, the coefficient is exactly 1. Hence, these three distributions provide any desired degree of skewness greater than that of the Poisson distribution. Note that the Polya–Aeppli and the negative binomial distributions are special and limiting cases of the Poisson–ETNB with $r = 1$ and $r \to 0$, respectively.

Example 4.57 *The data in Table 4.5 are taken from Hossack et al. [62] and give the distribution of the number of claims on automobile insurance policies in Australia. Determine an appropriate frequency model based on the skewness results of this section.*

The mean, variance, and third central moment are 0.1254614, 0.1299599, and 0.1401737, respectively. For these numbers,

$$\frac{\mu_3 - 3\sigma^2 + 2\mu}{(\sigma^2 - \mu)^2/\mu} = 7.543865.$$

From among the Poisson–binomial, negative binomial, Polya–Aeppli, Neyman Type A, and Poisson–ETNB distributions, only the latter is appropriate. For this distribution, an estimate of r can be obtained from

$$7.543865 = \frac{r + 2}{r + 1}$$

resulting in $r = -0.8471851$. In Example 13.14 a more formal estimation and selection procedure will be applied, but the conclusion will be the same.   □

A very useful property of the compound Poisson class of probability distributions is the fact that it is closed under convolution. We have the following theorem.

Theorem 4.58 *Suppose that S_i has a compound Poisson distribution with Poisson parameter λ_i and secondary distribution $\{q_n(i); \; n = 0, 1, 2, \ldots\}$ for $i = 1, 2, 3, \ldots, k$. Suppose also that $S_1, S_2, \ldots, S_k$ are independent random variables. Then $S = S_1 + S_2 + \cdots + S_k$ also has a compound Poisson distribution with Poisson parameter $\lambda = \lambda_1 + \lambda_2 + \cdots + \lambda_k$ and secondary distribution $\{q_n; \; n = 0, 1, 2, \ldots\}$, where $q_n = [\lambda_1 q_n(1) + \lambda_2 q_n(2) + \cdots + \lambda_k q_n(k)]/\lambda$.*

Table 4.5 Hossack et al. data

No. of claims	Observed frequency
0	565,664
1	68,714
2	5,177
3	365
4	24
5	6
6+	0

Proof: Let $Q_i(z) = \sum_{n=0}^{\infty} q_n(i)z^n$ for $i = 1, 2, \ldots, k$. Then S_i has pgf $P_{S_i}(z) = \mathrm{E}(z^{S_i}) = \exp\{\lambda_i[Q_i(z) - 1]\}$. Because the S_is are independent, S has pgf

$$
\begin{aligned}
P_S(z) &= \prod_{i=1}^{k} P_{S_i}(z) \\
&= \prod_{i=1}^{k} \exp\{\lambda_i[Q_i(z) - 1]\} \\
&= \exp\left[\sum_{i=1}^{k} \lambda_i Q_i(z) - \sum_{i=1}^{k} \lambda_i\right] \\
&= \exp\{\lambda[Q(z) - 1]\}
\end{aligned}
$$

where $\lambda = \sum_{i=1}^{k} \lambda_i$ and $Q(z) = \sum_{i=1}^{k} \lambda_i Q_i(z)/\lambda$. The result follows by the uniqueness of the generating function.   □

One main advantage of this result is computational. If we are interested in the sum of independent compound Poisson random variables, then we do not need to compute the distribution of each compound Poisson random variable separately (i.e., recursively using Example 4.50) because Theorem 4.58 implies that a single application of the compound Poisson recursive formula in Example 4.50 will suffice. The following example illustrates this idea.

Example 4.59 *Suppose that $k = 2$ and S_1 has a compound Poisson distribution with $\lambda_1 = 2$ and secondary distribution $q_1(1) = 0.2, q_2(1) = 0.7$, and $q_3(1) = 0.1$. Also, S_2 (independent of S_1) has a compound Poisson distribution with $\lambda_2 = 3$ and secondary distribution $q_2(2) = 0.25, q_3(2) = 0.6$, and $q_4(2) = 0.15$. Determine the distribution of $S = S_1 + S_2$.*

We have $\lambda = \lambda_1 + \lambda_2 = 2 + 3 = 5$. Then

$$
\begin{aligned}
q_1 &= 0.4(0.2) + 0.6(0) = 0.08, \\
q_2 &= 0.4(0.7) + 0.6(0.25) = 0.43, \\
q_3 &= 0.4(0.1) + 0.6(0.6) = 0.40, \\
q_4 &= 0.4(0) + 0.6(0.15) = 0.09.
\end{aligned}
$$

Thus, S has a compound Poisson distribution with Poisson parameter $\lambda = 5$ and secondary distribution $q_1 = 0.08, q_2 = 0.43, q_3 = 0.40$, and $q_4 = 0.09$. Numerical values of the distribution of S may be obtained using the recursive formula

$$\Pr(S = x) = \frac{5}{x} \sum_{n=1}^{x} n q_n \Pr(S = x - n), \quad x = 1, 2, \ldots,$$

beginning with $\Pr(S = 0) = e^{-5}$.   □

In various situations the convolution of negative binomial distributions is of interest. The following example indicates how this distribution may be evaluated.

Example 4.60 (Convolutions of negative binomial distributions). *Suppose that N_i has a negative binomial distribution with parameters r_i and β_i for $i = 1, 2, \ldots, k$ and that $N_1, N_2, \ldots, N_k$ are independent. Determine the distribution of $N = N_1 + N_2 + \cdots + N_k$.*

The pgf of N_i is $P_{N_i}(z) = [1 - \beta_i(z - 1)]^{-r_i}$ and that of N is $P_N(z) = \prod_{i=1}^{k} P_{N_i}(z) = \prod_{i=1}^{k} [1 - \beta_i(z - 1)]^{-r_i}$. If $\beta_i = \beta$ for $i = 1, 2, \ldots, k$, then $P_N(z) = [1 - \beta(z - 1)]^{-(r_1 + r_2 + \cdots + r_k)}$, and N has a negative binomial distribution with parameters $r = r_1 + r_2 + \cdots + r_k$ and β.

If not all the β_is are identical, however, we may proceed as follows. From Example 4.53,

$$P_{N_i}(z) = [1 - \beta_i(z - 1)]^{-r_i} = e^{\lambda_i[Q_i(z) - 1]}$$

where $\lambda_i = r_i \ln(1 + \beta_i)$ and

$$Q_i(z) = 1 - \frac{\ln[1 - \beta_i(z - 1)]}{\ln(1 + \beta_i)} = \sum_{n=1}^{\infty} q_n(i) z^n$$

with

$$q_n(i) = \frac{[\beta_i/(1 + \beta_i)]^n}{n \ln(1 + \beta_i)}; \quad n = 1, 2, \ldots.$$

But Theorem 4.58 implies that $N = N_1 + N_2 + \cdots + N_k$ has a compound Poisson distribution with Poisson parameter

$$\lambda = \sum_{i=1}^{k} r_i \ln(1 + \beta_i)$$

and secondary distribution

$$
\begin{aligned}
q_n &= \sum_{i=1}^{k} \frac{\lambda_i}{\lambda} q_n(i) \\
&= \frac{\sum_{i=1}^{k} r_i [\beta_i/(1 + \beta_i)]^n}{n \sum_{i=1}^{k} r_i \ln(1 + \beta_i)}, \quad n = 1, 2, 3, \ldots.
\end{aligned}
$$

The distribution of N may be computed recursively using the formula

$$\Pr(N = n) = \frac{\lambda}{n} \sum_{k=1}^{n} k q_k \Pr(N = n - k), \ n = 1, 2, \ldots,$$

beginning with $\Pr(N = 0) = e^{-\lambda} = \prod_{i=1}^{k}(1 + \beta_i)^{-r_i}$ and with λ and q_n as given above. $\square$

It is not hard to see that Theorem 4.58 is a generalization of Theorem 4.37, which may be recovered with $q_1(i) = 1$ for $i = 1, 2, \ldots, k$. Similarly, the decomposition result of Theorem 4.38 may also be extended to compound Poisson random variables, where the decomposition is on the basis of the region of support of the secondary distribution. See Panjer and Willmot [106], Sec. 6.4 or Karlin and Taylor [72], Sec. 16.9 for further details.

4.6.9   Mixed frequency models

Many compound distributions can arise in a way that is very different from compounding. In this section, we examine mixture distributions by treating one or more parameters as being "random" in some sense. This section expands on the ideas discussed in Section 4.6.3 in connection with the gamma mixture of the Poisson distribution being negative binomial.

We assume that the parameter is distributed over the population under consideration (the *collective*) and that the sampling scheme that generates our data has two stages. First, a value of the parameter is selected. Then, given that parameter value, an observation is generated using that parameter value.

In automobile insurance, for example, classification schemes attempt to put individuals into (relatively) homogeneous groups for the purpose of pricing. Variables used to develop the classification scheme might include age, experience, a history of violations, accident history, and other variables. Because there will always be some residual variation in accident risk within each class, mixed distributions provide a framework for modeling this heterogeneity.

Let $P(z|\theta)$ denote the pgf of the number of events (e.g., claims) if the risk parameter is known to be θ. The parameter, θ, might be the Poisson mean, for example, in which case the measurement of risk is the expected number of events in a fixed time period.

Let $U(\theta) = \Pr(\Theta \leq \theta)$ be the cdf of Θ, where Θ is the risk parameter, which is viewed as a random variable. Then $U(\theta)$ represents the probability that, when a value of Θ is selected (e.g., a driver is included in our sample), the value of the risk parameter does not exceed θ. Let $u(\theta)$ be the pf or pdf of Θ. Then

$$P(z) = \int P(z|\theta)u(\theta) \, d\theta \text{ or } P(z) = \sum P(z|\theta_j)u(\theta_j) \qquad (4.29)$$

is the unconditional pgf of the number of events (where the formula selected depends on whether Θ is discrete or continuous[5]). The corresponding probabilities are denoted by

$$p_k = \int p_k(\theta)u(\theta)d\theta \quad \text{or} \quad p_k = \sum p_k(\theta_j)u(\theta_j). \tag{4.30}$$

The **mixing distribution** denoted by $U(\theta)$ may be of the discrete or continuous type or even a combination of discrete and continuous types. **Discrete mixtures** are mixtures of distributions when the mixing function is of the discrete type. Similarly for **continuous mixtures**. This phenomenon was introduced for continuous mixtures of severity distributions in Section 4.4.5 and for finite discrete mixtures in Section 4.2.3.

It should be noted that the mixing distribution is unobservable because the data are drawn from the mixed distribution.

Example 4.61 *Demonstrate that the zero-modified distributions may be created by using a two-point mixture.*

Suppose

$$P(z) = p \cdot 1 + (1 - p)P_2(z).$$

This is a (discrete) two-point mixture of a degenerate distribution that places all probability at zero and a distribution with pgf $P_2(z)$. From (4.25) this is also a compound Bernoulli distribution. □

Many mixed models can be constructed beginning with a simple distribution. Two examples are given here.

Example 4.62 *Determine the pf for a mixed binomial with a beta mixing distribution. This distribution is called binomial–beta, negative hypergeometric, or Polya–Eggenberger.*

The beta distribution has pdf

$$u(q) = \frac{\Gamma(a+b)}{\Gamma(a)\Gamma(b)}q^{a-1}(1-q)^{b-1}, \quad a > 0, b > 0.$$

---

[5]We could have written the more general $P(z) = \int P(z|\theta)\,dU(\theta)$, which would include situations where Θ has a distribution that is partly continuous and partly discrete.

Then the mixed distribution has probabilities

$$p_k = \int_0^1 \binom{m}{k} q^k (1-q)^{m-k} \frac{\Gamma(a+b)}{\Gamma(a)\Gamma(b)} q^{a-1}(1-q)^{b-1}\, dq$$

$$= \frac{\Gamma(a+b)\Gamma(m+1)\Gamma(a+k)\Gamma(b+m-k)}{\Gamma(a)\Gamma(b)\Gamma(k+1)\Gamma(m-k+1)\Gamma(a+b+m)}$$

$$= \frac{\binom{-a}{k}\binom{-b}{m-k}}{\binom{-a-b}{m}}, \quad k=0,1,2,\dots .$$

☐

Example 4.63 *Determine the pf for a mixed negative binomial distribution with mixing on the parameter* $p = (1+\beta)^{-1}$. *Let p have a beta distribution. The mixed distribution is called the generalized Waring.*

Arguing as in Example 4.62 we have

$$p_k = \frac{\Gamma(r+k)}{\Gamma(r)\Gamma(k+1)} \frac{\Gamma(a+b)}{\Gamma(a)\Gamma(b)} \int_0^1 p^{a+r-1}(1-p)^{b+k-1}\, dp$$

$$= \frac{\Gamma(r+k)}{\Gamma(r)\Gamma(k+1)} \frac{\Gamma(a+b)}{\Gamma(a)\Gamma(b)} \frac{\Gamma(a+r)\Gamma(b+k)}{\Gamma(a+r+b+k)}, \quad k=0,1,2,\dots .$$

When $b = 1$, this distribution is called the Waring distribution. When $r = b = 1$, it is termed the Yule distribution.   ☐

4.6.10   Poisson mixtures

If we let $p_k(\theta)$ in (4.30) have the Poisson distribution, this leads to a class of distributions with useful properties. A simple example of a Poisson mixture is the two-point mixture.

Example 4.64 *Suppose drivers can be classified as "good drivers" and "bad drivers," each group with its own Poisson distribution. Determine the pf for this model and fit it to the data from Example 12.56. This model and its application to the data set are from Tröbliger [130].*

From (4.30) the pf is

$$p_k = p \frac{e^{-\lambda_1}\lambda_1^k}{k!} + (1-p)\frac{e^{-\lambda_2}\lambda_2^k}{k!}.$$

The maximum likelihood estimates[6] were calculated by Tröbliger to be $\hat{p} = 0.94$, $\hat{\lambda}_1 = 0.11$ and $\hat{\lambda}_2 = 0.70$. This means that about 94% of drivers

---

[6]Maximum likelihood estimation is discussed in Section 12.2.

were "good" with a risk of $\lambda_1 = 0.11$ expected accidents per year and 6% were "bad" with a risk of $\lambda_2 = 0.70$ expected accidents per year. Note that it is not possible to return to the data set and identify which were the bad drivers.   □

This example illustrates two important points about finite mixtures. First, the model is probably oversimplified in the sense that risks (e.g., drivers) probably exhibit a continuum of risk levels rather than just two. The second point is that finite mixture models have a lot of parameters to be estimated. The simple two-point Poisson mixture above has three parameters. Increasing the number of distributions in the mixture to r will then involve $r-1$ mixing parameters in addition to the total number of parameters in the r component distributions. As a result of this, continuous mixtures are frequently preferred.

The class of mixed Poisson distributions has some interesting properties that will be developed here.

Let $P(z)$ be the pgf of a mixed Poisson distribution with arbitrary mixing distribution $U(\theta)$. Then (with formulas given for the continuous case), by introducing a scale parameter λ, we have

$$
\begin{aligned}
P(z) &= \int e^{\lambda\theta(z-1)} u(\theta)\, d\theta = \int \left[e^{\lambda(z-1)} \right]^{\theta} u(\theta)\, d\theta \\
&= E\left\{ \left[e^{\lambda(z-1)} \right]^{\theta} \right\} = M_\Theta\left[\lambda(z-1) \right], \qquad (4.31)
\end{aligned}
$$

where $M_\Theta(z)$ is the mgf of the mixing distribution.

Therefore, $P'(z) = \lambda M'_\Theta[\lambda(z-1)]$ and with $z=1$ we obtain $E(N) = \lambda E(\Theta)$, where N has the mixed Poisson distribution. Also, $P''(z) = \lambda^2 M''_\Theta[\lambda(z-1)]$, implying that $E[N(N-1)] = \lambda^2 E(\Theta^2)$ and therefore

$$
\begin{aligned}
\mathrm{Var}(N) &= E[N(N-1)] + E(N) - [E(N)]^2 \\
&= \lambda^2 E(\Theta^2) + E(N) - \lambda^2 [E(\Theta)]^2 \\
&= \lambda^2 \mathrm{Var}(\Theta) + E(N) \\
&> E(N)
\end{aligned}
$$

and thus for mixed Poisson distributions the variance is always greater than the mean.

Douglas [29] proves that for any mixed Poisson distribution the mixing distribution is unique. This means that two different mixing distributions cannot lead to the same mixed Poisson distribution. This allows us to identify the mixing distribution in some cases.

There is also an important connection between mixed Poisson distributions and compound Poisson distributions.

Definition 4.65 *A distribution is said to be **infinitely divisible** if for all values of $n = 1, 2, 3, \ldots$ its characteristic function $\varphi(z)$ can be written as*

$$
\varphi(z) = [\varphi_n(z)]^n,
$$

where $\varphi_n(z)$ is the characteristic function of some random variable.

In other words, taking the $(1/n)$th power of the characteristic function still results in a characteristic function. The characteristic function is defined as follows.

Definition 4.66 *The **characteristic function** of a random variable X is*

$$\varphi_X(z) = \mathrm{E}(e^{izX}) = \mathrm{E}(\cos zX + i \sin zX),$$

where $i = \sqrt{-1}$.

In Definition 4.65, "characteristic function" could have been replaced by "moment generating function" or "probability generating function," or some other transform. That is, if the definition is satisfied for one of these transforms, it will be satisfied for all others which exist for the particular random variable. We choose the characteristic function because it exists for all distributions while the moment generating function does not exist for some distributions with heavy tails. Because many earlier results involved probability generating functions, it is useful to note the relationship between it and the characteristic function.

Theorem 4.67 *If the probability generating function exists for a random variable X, then $P_X(z) = \varphi(-i \ln z)$ and $\varphi_X(z) = P(e^{iz})$.*

Proof:

$$P_X(z) = \mathrm{E}(z^X) = \mathrm{E}(e^{X \ln z}) = \mathrm{E}[e^{-i(i \ln z)X}] = \varphi_X(-i \ln z)$$

and

$$\varphi_X(z) = \mathrm{E}(e^{izX}) = \mathrm{E}[(e^{iz})^X] = P_X(e^{iz}). \qquad \square$$

The following distributions, among others, are infinitely divisible: normal, gamma, Poisson, negative binomial. The binomial distribution is not infinitely divisible because the exponent m in its pgf must take on integer values. Dividing m by $n = 1, 2, 3, \ldots$ will result in nonintegral values. In fact, no distributions with a finite range of support (the range over which positive probabilities exist) can be infinitely divisible. Now to the important result.

Theorem 4.68 *Suppose $P(z)$ is a mixed Poisson pgf with an infinitely divisible mixing distribution. Then $P(z)$ is also a compound Poisson pgf and may be expressed as*

$$P(z) = e^{\lambda[P_2(z)-1]},$$

where $P_2(z)$ is a pgf. If one adopts the convention that $P_2(0) = 0$, then $P_2(z)$ is unique.

A proof can be found in Feller [35], Ch. 12. If one chooses any infinitely divisible mixing distribution, the corresponding mixed Poisson distribution can be equivalently described as a compound Poisson distribution. For some distributions, this is a distinct advantage when carrying out numerical work because the recursive formula (4.22) can be used in evaluating the probabilities once the secondary distribution is identified. For most cases, this identification is easily carried out. A second advantage is that, because the same distribution can be motivated in two different ways, a specific explanation is not required in order to use it. Conversely, the fact that one of these models fits well does not imply that it is the result of mixing or compounding. For example, the fact that claims follow a negative binomial distribution does not imply that individuals have the Poisson distribution and the Poisson parameter has a gamma distribution.

Example 4.69 *Use the above results and (4.31) to demonstrate that a gamma mixture of Poisson variables is negative binomial.*

If the mixing distribution is gamma, it has the following moment generating function (as derived in Example 3.15 and where β plays the role of $1/\theta$):

$$M_\Theta(t) = \left(\frac{\beta}{\beta - t}\right)^\alpha, \quad \beta > 0, \ \alpha > 0, \ t < \beta.$$

It is clearly infinitely divisible because $[M_\Theta(t)]^{1/n}$ is the mgf of a gamma distribution with parameters α/n and β. Then the pgf of the mixed Poisson distribution is

$$P(z) = \left[\frac{\beta}{\beta - \lambda(z - 1)}\right]^\alpha = \left[1 - \frac{\lambda}{\beta}(z - 1)\right]^{-\alpha},$$

which is the form of the pgf of the negative binomial distribution where the negative binomial parameter r is equal to α and the parameter β is equal to λ/β. □

It was shown in Example 4.53 that a compound Poisson distribution with a logarithmic secondary distribution is a negative binomial distribution. Therefore the theorem holds true for this case. It is not difficult to see that, if $u(\theta)$ is the pf for any discrete random variable with pgf $P_\Theta(z)$, then the pgf of the mixed Poisson distribution is $P_\Theta\left[e^{\lambda(z-1)}\right]$, a compound distribution with a Poisson secondary distribution.

Example 4.70 *Demonstrate that the Neyman Type A distribution can be obtained by mixing.*

If in (4.31) the mixing distribution has pgf

$$P_\Theta(z) = e^{\mu(z-1)},$$

then the mixed Poisson distribution has pgf

$$P(z) = \exp\{\mu[e^{\lambda(z-1)} - 1]\},$$

the pgf of a compound Poisson with a Poisson secondary distribution, that is, the Neyman Type A distribution.   □

A further interesting result obtained by Holgate [60] is that, if a mixing distribution is absolutely continuous and unimodal, then the resulting mixed Poisson distribution is also unimodal. Multimodality can occur when discrete mixing functions are used. For example, the Neyman Type A distribution can have more than one mode. The reader should try this calculation for various combinations of the two parameters.

Most continuous distributions in this book involve a scale parameter. This means that scale changes to distributions do not cause a change in the form of the distribution, only in the value of its scale parameter. For the mixed Poisson distribution, with pgf (4.31), any change in λ is equivalent to a change in the scale parameter of the mixing distribution. Hence, it may be convenient to simply set $\lambda = 1$ where a mixing distribution with a scale parameter is used.

Example 4.71 *Show that a mixed Poisson with an inverse Gaussian mixing distribution is the same as a Poisson–ETNB distribution with $r = -0.5$.*

The inverse Gaussian distribution is described in Appendix A. It has pdf

$$f(x) = \left(\frac{\theta}{2\pi x^3}\right)^{1/2} \exp\left[-\frac{\theta}{2x}\left(\frac{x-\mu}{\mu}\right)^2\right], \quad x > 0,$$

which is conveniently rewritten as

$$f(x) = \frac{\mu}{(2\pi\beta x^3)^{1/2}} \exp\left[-\frac{(x-\mu)^2}{2\beta x}\right], \quad x > 0,$$

where $\beta = \mu^2/\theta$. The mgf of this distribution is (see Exercise 3.24)

$$M(t) = \exp\left\{-\frac{\mu}{\beta}[(1-2\beta t)^{1/2} - 1]\right\}.$$

Hence, the inverse Gaussian distribution is infinitely divisible ($[M(t)]^{1/n}$ is the mgf of an inverse Gaussian distribution with μ replaced by μ/n). From (4.31) with $\lambda = 1$, the pgf of the mixed distribution is

$$P(z) = \exp\left(-\frac{\mu}{\beta}\{[1 + 2\beta(1 - z)]^{1/2} - 1\}\right).$$

By setting

$$\lambda = \frac{\mu}{\beta}[(1 + 2\beta)^{1/2} - 1]$$

Table 4.6 Pairs of compound and mixed Poisson distributions

Name	Compound secondary distribution	Mixing distribution
Negative binomial	logarithmic	gamma
Neyman–A	Poisson	Poisson
Poisson–inverse Gaussian	ETNB $(r = -0.5)$	inverse Gaussian

and

$$P_2(z) = \frac{[1 - 2\beta(z - 1)]^{1/2} - (1 + 2\beta)^{1/2}}{1 - (1 + 2\beta)^{1/2}},$$

we see that

$$P(z) = \exp\{\lambda[P_2(z) - 1]\},$$

where $P_2(z)$ is the pgf of the extended truncated negative binomial distribution with $r = -\frac{1}{2}$.

Hence, the Poisson–inverse Gaussian distribution is a compound Poisson distribution with an ETNB $(r = -\frac{1}{2})$ secondary distribution. □

The relationships between mixed and compound Poisson distributions are given in Table 4.6.

In this chapter, we focused on distributions that are easily handled computationally. Although many other discrete distributions are available, we believe that those discussed form a sufficiently rich class for most problems.

4.6.11   Effect of exposure on frequency

Assume that the current portfolio consists of n entities, each of which could produce claims. Let N_j be the number of claims produced by the jth entity. Then $N = N_1 + \cdots + N_n$. If we assume that the N_j are independent and identically distributed, then

$$P_N(z) = [P_{N_1}(z)]^n.$$

Now suppose the portfolio is expected to expand to n^* entities with frequency N^*. Then

$$P_{N^*}(z) = [P_{N_1}(z)]^{n^*} = [P_N(z)]^{n^*/n}.$$

Thus, if N is infinitely divisible, the distribution of N^* will have the same form as that of N, but with modified parameters.

Example 4.72 *It has been determined from past studies that the number of workers compensation claims for a group of 300 employees in a certain occupation class has the negative binomial distribution with $\beta = 0.3$ and $r = 10$. Determine the frequency distribution for a group of 500 such individuals.*

The pgf of N^* is

$$\begin{aligned} P_{N^*}(z) &= [P_N(z)]^{500/300} = \{[1 - 0.3(z - 1)]^{-10}\}^{500/300} \\ &= [1 - 0.3(z - 1)]^{-16.67}, \end{aligned}$$

which is negative binomial with $\beta = 0.3$ and $r = 16.67$. $\qquad\square$

For the $(a, b, 0)$ class, all members except the binomial have this property. For the $(a, b, 1)$ class, none of the members do. For compound distributions, it is the primary distribution that must be infinitely divisible. In particular, compound Poisson and compound negative binomial (including the geometric) distributions will be preserved under an increase in exposure. Earlier, some reasons were given to support the use of zero-modified distributions. If exposure adjustments are anticipated, it may be better to choose a compound model, even if the fit is not quite as good. It should be noted that compound models have the ability to place large amounts of probability at zero.

4.6.12 An inventory of discrete distributions

We have introduced the simple $(a, b, 0)$ class, generalized to the $(a, b, 1)$ class, and then used compounding and mixing to create a larger class of distributions. Calculation of the probabilities of these distributions can be carried out by using simple recursive procedures. In this section we note that there are relationships among the various distributions similar to those of Section 4.5.2. The specific relationships are given in Table 4.7.

It is clear from earlier developments that members of the $(a, b, 0)$ class are special cases of members of the $(a, b, 1)$ class and that zero-truncated distributions are special cases of zero-modified distributions. The limiting cases are best discovered through the probability generating function, as was done on page 79 where the Poisson distribution is shown to be a limiting case of the negative binomial distribution.

We have not listed compound distributions where the primary distribution is one of the two parameter models such as the negative binomial or Poisson–inverse Gaussian. This was done because these distributions are often themselves compound Poisson distributions and, as such, are generalizations of distributions already presented. This collection forms a particularly rich set of distributions in terms of shape. However, many other distributions are also possible. Many others are discussed in Johnson, Kotz, and Kemp [69], Douglas [29], and Panjer and Willmot [106].

4.6.13 Exercises

4.40 For each of the data sets in Exercises 12.96 and 12.98 on page 400 calculate values similar to those in Table 4.2. For each, determine the most appropriate model from the $(a, b, 0)$ class.

Table 4.7   Relationships among discrete distributions

Distribution	Is a special case of	Is a limiting case of
Poisson	ZM Poisson	negative binomial
		Poisson–binomial
		Poisson–inv. Gaussian
		Polya–Aeppli[a]
		Neyman–A[b]
ZT Poisson	ZM Poisson	ZT negative binomial
ZM Poisson		ZM negative binomial
geometric	negative binomial,	geometric–Poisson
	ZM geometric	
ZT geometric	ZT negative binomial	
ZM geometric	ZM negative binomial	
logarithmic		ZT negative binomial
ZM logarithmic		ZM negative binomial
binomial	ZM binomial	
negative binomial	ZM negative binomial,	
	Poisson–ETNB	
Poisson–inverse Gaussian	Poisson–ETNB	
Polya–Aeppli	Poisson–ETNB	
Neyman–A		Poisson–ETNB

[a] Also called Poisson-geometric.
[b] Also called Poisson-Poisson.

4.41 Calculate $\Pr(N = 0)$, $\Pr(N = 1)$, and $\Pr(N = 2)$ for each of the following distributions.

    (a) Poisson($\lambda = 4$)

    (b) Geometric($\beta = 4$)

    (c) Negative binomial($r = 2, \beta = 2$)

    (d) Binomial($m = 8, q = 0.5$)

    (e) Logarithmic($\beta = 4$)

    (f) ETNB($r = -0.5, \beta = 4$)

    (g) Poisson–inverse Gaussian($\lambda = 2, \beta = 4$)

    (h) Zero-modified geometric($p_0^M = 0.5, \beta = 4$)

    (i) Poisson–Poisson(Neyman Type A)($\lambda_{primary} = 4, \lambda_{secondary} = 1$)

    (j) Poisson–ETNB($\lambda = 4, r = 2, \beta = 0.5$)

    (k) Poisson–zero-modified geometric distribution($\lambda = 8, p_0^M = 0.5, r = 2, \beta = 0.5$)

4.42 The **moment generating function** (mgf) for discrete variables is defined as

$$M_N(z) = \mathrm{E}\left(e^{zN}\right) = \sum_{k=0}^{\infty} p_k e^{zk}.$$

Demonstrate that $P_N(z) = M_N(\ln z)$. Use the fact that $\mathrm{E}(N^k) = M_N^{(k)}(0)$ to show that $P'(1) = \mathrm{E}(N)$ and $P''(1) = \mathrm{E}[N(N-1)]$.

4.43 Use your knowledge of the permissible ranges for the parameters of the Poisson, negative binomial, and binomial to determine all possible values of a and b for these members of the $(a, b, 0)$ class. Because these are the only members of the class, all other pairs must not lead to a legitimate probability distribution (nonnegative values that sum to 1). Show that the pair $a = -1$ and $b = 1.5$ (which is not on the list of possible values) does not lead to a legitimate distribution.

4.44 Show that for the negative binomial distribution with any $\beta > 0$ and $r > -1$, but $r \neq 0$, the successive values of p_k given by (4.15) are, for any p_1, positive and $\sum_{k=1}^{\infty} p_k < \infty$.

4.45 Show that when, in the zero-truncated negative binomial distribution, $r \to 0$ the pf is as given in (4.16).

4.46 Show that the pgf of the logarithmic distribution is as given in (4.17).

4.47 Show that for the Sibuya distribution, which is the ETNB distribution with $-1 < r < 0$ and $\beta \to \infty$, the mean does not exist (that is, the sum which defines the mean does not converge). Because this random variable takes on nonnegative values, this also shows that no other positive moments exist.

4.48 A frequency model that has not been mentioned to this point is the **zeta distribution**. It is a zero-truncated distribution with $p_k^T = k^{-(\rho+1)}/\zeta(\rho + 1)$, $k = 1, 2, \ldots, \rho > 0$. The denominator is the zeta function, which must be evaluated numerically as $\zeta(\rho + 1) = \sum_{k=1}^{\infty} k^{-(\rho+1)}$. The zero-modified zeta distribution can be formed in the usual way. More information can be found in Luong and Doray [88]. Verify that the zeta distribution is not a member of the $(a, b, 1)$ class.

4.49 Do all the members of the $(a, b, 0)$ class satisfy the condition of Theorem 4.54? For those that do, identify the parameter (or function of its parameters) that plays the role of θ in the theorem.

4.50 For $i = 1, \ldots, n$ let S_i have independent compound Poisson frequency distributions with Poisson parameter λ_i and a secondary distribution with pgf $P_2(z)$. Note that all n of the variables have the same secondary distribution. Determine the distribution of $S = S_1 + \cdots + S_n$.

4.51 Show that the following three distributions are identical: (1) geometric–geometric, (2) Bernoulli–geometric, (3) zero-modified geometric. That is, for any one of the distributions with arbitrary parameters, show that there is a member of the other two distribution types that has the same pf or pgf.

4.52 Show that the binomial–geometric and negative binomial–geometric (with negative binomial parameter r a positive integer) distributions are identical.

4.53 Show that, for any pgf, $P^{(k)}(1) = E[N(N-1)\cdots(N-k+1)]$ provided the expectation exists. Here $P^{(k)}(z)$ indicates the kth derivative. Use this result to confirm the three moments as given in (4.27).

4.54 Verify the three moments as given in (4.28).

4.55 Show that the negative binomial–Poisson compound distribution is the same as a mixed Poisson distribution with a negative binomial mixing distribution.

4.56 For $i = 1, \ldots, n$ let N_i have a mixed Poisson distribution with parameter λ. Let the mixing distribution for N_i have pgf $P_i(z)$. Show that $N = N_1 + \cdots + N_n$ has a mixed Poisson distribution and determine the pgf of the mixing distribution.

4.57 Let N have a Poisson distribution with (given that $\Theta = \theta$) parameter $\lambda\theta$. Let the distribution of the random variable Θ have a scale parameter. Show that the mixed distribution does not depend on the value of λ.

4.58 Let N have a Poisson distribution with (given that $\Theta = \theta$) parameter θ. Let the distribution of the random variable Θ have pdf $u(\theta) = \alpha^2(\alpha + 1)^{-1}(\theta + 1)e^{-\alpha\theta}$, $\theta > 0$. Determine the pf of the mixed distribution. Also, show that the mixed distribution is also a compound distribution.

4.59 For the discrete counting random variable N with probabilities $p_n = \Pr(N = n)$; $n = 0, 1, 2, \ldots$, let $a_n = \Pr(N > n) = \sum_{k=n+1}^{\infty} p_k$; $n = 0, 1, 2, \ldots$.

   (a) Demonstrate that $E(N) = \sum_{n=0}^{\infty} a_n$.
   (b) Demonstrate that $A(z) = \sum_{n=0}^{\infty} a_n z^n$ and $P(z) = \sum_{n=0}^{\infty} p_n z^n$ are related by $A(z) = [1 - P(z)]/(1 - z)$. What happens as $z \to 1$?
   (c) Suppose that N has the negative binomial distribution

$$p_n = \binom{n+r-1}{n}\left(\frac{1}{1+\beta}\right)^r\left(\frac{\beta}{1+\beta}\right)^n, \quad n = 0, 1, 2, \ldots,$$

   where r is a positive integer. Prove that

$$a_n = \beta\sum_{k=1}^{r}\binom{n+k-1}{n}\left(\frac{1}{1+\beta}\right)^k\left(\frac{\beta}{1+\beta}\right)^n, \quad n = 0, 1, 2, \ldots.$$

(d) Suppose that N has the Sibuya distribution with pgf $P(z) = 1 - (1 - z)^{-r}$, $-1 < r < 0$. Prove that

$$p_n = \frac{(-r)\Gamma(n+r)}{n!\Gamma(1+r)}, \quad n = 1, 2, 3, \ldots,$$

and that

$$a_n = \binom{n+r}{n}, \quad n = 0, 1, 2, \ldots.$$

(e) Suppose that N has the mixed Poisson distribution with

$$p_n = \int_0^\infty \frac{(\lambda\theta)^n e^{-\lambda\theta}}{n!} dU(\theta), \quad n = 0, 1, 2, \ldots,$$

where $U(\theta)$ is a cumulative distribution function. Prove that

$$a_n = \lambda \int_0^\infty \frac{(\lambda\theta)^n e^{-\lambda\theta}}{n!} [1 - U(\theta)]\, d\theta, \quad n = 0, 1, 2, \ldots.$$

4.60 Consider the mixed Poisson distribution

$$p_n = \Pr(N = n) = \int_0^1 \frac{(\lambda\theta)^n e^{-\lambda\theta}}{n!} U'(\theta)d\theta, \quad n = 0, 1, \ldots,$$

where $U(\theta) = 1 - (1 - \theta)^k$, $0 < \theta < 1$, $k = 1, 2, \ldots.$

(a) Prove that

$$p_n = k e^{-\lambda} \sum_{m=0}^\infty \frac{\lambda^{m+n}(m+k-1)!}{m!(m+k+n)!}, \quad n = 0, 1, \ldots.$$

(b) Using Exercise 4.59 prove that

$$\Pr(N > n) = e^{-\lambda} \sum_{m=0}^\infty \frac{\lambda^{m+n+1}(m+k)!}{m!(m+k+n+1)!}.$$

(c) When $k = 1$, prove that

$$p_n = \frac{1 - \sum_{m=0}^n \lambda^m e^{-\lambda}/m!}{\lambda}, \quad n = 0, 1, 2, \ldots.$$

4.61 Consider the mixed Poisson distribution

$$p_n = \int_0^\infty \frac{(\lambda\theta)^n e^{-\lambda\theta}}{n!} u(\theta)d\theta, \quad n = 0, 1, \ldots,$$

where the pdf $u(\theta)$ is that of the positive stable distribution (see, for example, Feller [36], pp. 448, 583) given by

$$u(\theta) = \frac{1}{\pi} \sum_{k=1}^{\infty} \frac{\Gamma(k\alpha + 1)}{k!}(-1)^{k-1}\theta^{-k\alpha-1} \sin(k\alpha\pi), \ \theta > 0,$$

where $0 < \alpha < 1$. The Laplace transform is $\int_0^{\infty} e^{-s\theta} u(\theta)d\theta = \exp(-s^{\alpha})$, $s \geq 0$. Prove that $\{p_n; \ n = 0, 1, \ldots\}$ is a compound Poisson distribution with Sibuya secondary distribution (this mixed Poisson distribution is sometimes called a discrete stable distribution).

4.62 Consider a mixed Poisson distribution with a reciprocal inverse Gaussian distribution as the mixing distribution.

(a) Use Exercise 4.36 to show that this distribution is the convolution of a negative binomial distribution and a Poisson–ETNB distribution with $r = -\frac{1}{2}$ (i.e., a Poisson–inverse Gaussian distribution).

(b) Show that the mixed Poisson distribution in (a) is a compound Poisson distribution and identify the secondary distribution.

5

Frequency and severity with coverage modifications

5.1 INTRODUCTION

We have seen a variety of examples that involve functions of random variables. In this chapter we relate those functions to insurance applications. Throughout this chapter we assume that all random variables have support on all or a subset of the nonnegative real numbers. At times in this chapter and later in the text we will need to distinguish between a random variable that measures the payment per loss (so zero is a possibility, taking place when there is a loss without a payment) and a variable that measures the payment per payment (the random variable is not defined when there is no payment). For notation, a per-loss variable will be denoted Y^L and a per-payment variable will be noted Y^P. When the distinction is not material (for example, setting a maximum payment does not create a difference), the superscript will be left off.

5.2 DEDUCTIBLES

Insurance policies are often sold with a per-loss deductible of d. When the loss, x, is at or below d, the insurance pays nothing. When the loss is above

Loss Models: From Data to Decisions, Second Edition.
By Stuart A. Klugman, Harry H. Panjer, and Gordon E. Willmot
ISBN 0-471-21577-5   Copyright © 2004 John Wiley & Sons, Inc.

d, the insurance pays $x - d$. In the language of Chapter 3 such a deductible can be defined as follows.

Definition 5.1 *An **ordinary deductible** modifies a random variable into either the excess loss or left censored and shifted variable (see Definition 3.6). The difference depends on whether the result of applying the deductible is to be per payment or per loss, respectively.*

This concept has already been introduced along with formulas for determining its moments. The per-payment variable is

$$Y^P = \begin{cases} \text{undefined}, & X \le d, \\ X - d, & X > d, \end{cases}$$

while the per-loss variable is

$$Y^L = \begin{cases} 0, & X \le d, \\ X - d, & X > d. \end{cases}$$

Note that the per-payment variable $Y^P = Y^L | Y^L > 0$. That is, the per-payment variable is the per-loss variable conditioned on the loss being positive. For the excess loss/per-payment variable, the density function is

$$f_{Y^P}(y) = \frac{f_X(y + d)}{S_X(d)}, \; y > 0, \tag{5.1}$$

noting that for a discrete distribution the density function need only be replaced by the probability function. Other key functions are

$$S_{Y^P}(y) = \frac{S_X(y + d)}{S_X(d)},$$

$$F_{Y^P}(y) = \frac{F_X(y + d) - F_X(d)}{1 - F_X(d)},$$

$$h_{Y^P}(y) = \frac{f_X(y + d)}{S_X(y + d)} = h_X(y + d).$$

Note that as a per-payment variable the excess loss variable places no probability at 0.

The left censored and shifted variable has discrete probability at zero of $F_X(d)$ representing the probability that a payment of zero is made because the loss did not exceed d. Above zero, the density function is

$$f_{Y^L}(y) = f_X(y + d), \; y > 0, \tag{5.2}$$

while the other key functions are[1] (for $y \geq 0$)

$$
\begin{aligned}
S_{YL}(y) &= S_X(y+d), \\
F_{YL}(y) &= F_X(y+d).
\end{aligned}
$$

It is important to recognize that when counting claims on a per payment, changing the deductible will change the frequency with which payments are made (while the frequency of losses will be unchanged). The nature of these changes will be discussed in Section 5.6.

Example 5.2 *Determine similar quantities for a Pareto distribution with $\alpha = 3$ and $\theta = 2000$ for an ordinary deductible of 500.*

Using the above formulas, for the excess loss variable,

$$
\begin{aligned}
f_{YP}(y) &= \frac{3(2,000)^3(2,000+y+500)^{-4}}{(2,000)^3(2,000+500)^{-3}} = \frac{3(2,500)^3}{(2,500+y)^4}, \\
S_{YP}(y) &= \left(\frac{2,500}{2,500+y}\right)^3, \\
F_{YP}(y) &= 1 - \left(\frac{2,500}{2,500+y}\right)^3, \\
h_{YP}(y) &= \frac{3}{2,500+y}.
\end{aligned}
$$

Note that this is a Pareto distribution with $\alpha = 3$ and $\theta = 2,500$. For the left censored and shifted variable,

$$
f_{YL}(y) = \begin{cases} 0.488, & y = 0, \\ \dfrac{3(2,000)^3}{(2,500+y)^4}, & y > 0, \end{cases} \qquad S_{YL}(y) = \begin{cases} 0.512, & y = 0, \\ \dfrac{(2,000)^3}{(2,500+y)^3}, & y > 0, \end{cases}
$$

$$
F_{YL}(y) = \begin{cases} 0.488, & y = 0, \\ 1 - \dfrac{(2,000)^3}{(2,500+y)^3}, & y > 0, \end{cases} \qquad h_{YL}(y) = \begin{cases} \text{undefined}, & y = 0, \\ \dfrac{3}{2,500+y}, & y > 0. \end{cases}
$$

Figure 5.1 contains a plot of the densities. The modified densities are created as follows. For the excess loss variable, take the portion of the original density from 500 and above. Then shift it to start at zero and multiply it by a constant so that the area under it is still 1. The left censored and shifted variable also takes the original density function above 500 and shifts it to the origin, but then leaves it alone. The remaining probability is concentrated at zero, rather than spread out. □

---

[1] The hazard rate function is not presented because it is not defined at zero, making it of limited value. Note that for the excess loss variable the hazard rate function is simply shifted.

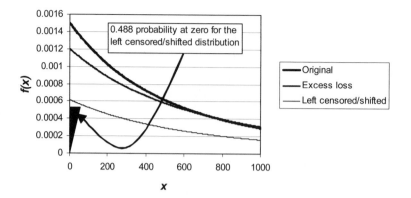

Fig. 5.1   Densities for Example 5.2.

An alternative to the ordinary deductible is the franchise deductible. This deductible differs from the ordinary deductible in that, when the loss exceeds the deductible, the loss is paid in full. One example is in disability insurance where, for example, if a disability lasts seven or fewer days, no benefits are paid. However, if the disability lasts more than seven days, daily benefits are paid retroactively to the onset of the disability.

Definition 5.3 *A **franchise deductible** modifies the ordinary deductible by adding the deductible when there is a positive amount paid.*

The terms *left censored and shifted* and *excess loss* are not used here. Because this modification is unique to insurance applications, we will use per-payment and per-loss terminology. The per-loss variable is

$$Y^L = \begin{cases} 0, & X \le d, \\ X, & X > d, \end{cases}$$

while the per-payment variable is

$$Y^P = \begin{cases} \text{undefined}, & X \le d, \\ X, & X > d. \end{cases}$$

Note that, as usual, the per-payment variable is a conditional random variable. The quantities derived above for the ordinary deductible are now

$$f_{Y^L}(y) = \begin{cases} F_X(d), & y = 0, \\ f_X(y), & y > d, \end{cases} \quad S_{Y^L}(y) = \begin{cases} S_X(d), & 0 \le y \le d, \\ S_X(y), & y > d, \end{cases}$$

$$F_{Y^L}(y) = \begin{cases} F_X(d), & 0 \le y \le d, \\ F_X(y), & y > d, \end{cases} \quad h_{Y^L}(y) = \begin{cases} 0, & 0 < y < d, \\ h_X(y), & y > d, \end{cases}$$

for the per loss variable and

$$f_{YP}(y) = \frac{f_X(y)}{S_X(d)}, \ y > d, \ S_{YP}(y) = \begin{cases} 1, & 0 \le y \le d, \\ \dfrac{S_X(y)}{S_X(d)}, & y > d, \end{cases}$$

$$F_{YP}(y) = \begin{cases} 0, & 0 \le y \le d, \\ \dfrac{F_X(y) - F_X(d)}{1 - F_X(d)}, & y > d, \end{cases}$$

$$h_{YP}(y) = \begin{cases} 0, & 0 < y < d, \\ h_X(y), & y > d \end{cases}$$

for the per-payment variable.

Example 5.4 *Repeat Example 5.2 for a franchise deductible.*

Using the above formulas for the per-payment variable, for $y > 500$,

$$f_{YP}(y) = \frac{3(2,000)^3(2,000 + y)^{-4}}{(2,000)^3(2,000 + 500)^{-3}} = \frac{3(2,500)^3}{(2,000 + y)^4},$$

$$S_{YP}(y) = \left(\frac{2,500}{2,000 + y}\right)^3,$$

$$F_{YP}(y) = 1 - \left(\frac{2,500}{2,000 + y}\right)^3,$$

$$h_{YP}(y) = \frac{3}{2,000 + y}.$$

For the per-loss variable,

$$f_{YL}(y) = \begin{cases} 0.488, & y = 0, \\ \dfrac{3(2,000)^3}{(2,000 + y)^4}, & y > 500, \end{cases}$$

$$S_{YL}(y) = \begin{cases} 0.512, & 0 \le y \le 500, \\ \dfrac{(2,000)^3}{(2,000 + y)^3}, & y > 500, \end{cases}$$

$$F_{YL}(y) = \begin{cases} 0.488, & 0 \le y \le 500, \\ 1 - \dfrac{(2,000)^3}{(2,000 + y)^3}, & y > 500, \end{cases}$$

$$h_{YL}(y) = \begin{cases} 0, & 0 < y < 500, \\ \dfrac{3}{2,000 + y}, & y > 500. \end{cases} \qquad \square$$

Expected costs for the two types of deductible may also be calculated.

Theorem 5.5 *For an ordinary deductible, the expected cost per loss is $E(X)-E(X \wedge d)$ and the expected cost per payment is $[E(X)-E(X \wedge d)]/[1-F(d)]$. For a franchise deductible the expected cost per loss is $E(X)-E(X \wedge d)+d[1-F(d)]$ and the expected cost per payment is $[E(X)-E(X \wedge d)]/[1-F(d)]+d$.*

Proof: For the per-loss expectation with an ordinary deductible, we have, from (3.7) and (3.10) that the expectation is $E(X)-E(X \wedge d)$. From (5.1) and (5.2) we see that, to change to a per-payment basis, division by $1-F(d)$ is required. The adjustments for the franchise deductible come from the fact that when there is a payment it will exceed that for the ordinary deductible by d.   □

Example 5.6 *Determine the four expectations for the Pareto distribution from Examples 5.2 and 5.4 using a deductible of 500.*

Expectations could be derived directly from the density functions obtained in Examples 5.2 and 5.4. Using Theorem 5.5 and recognizing that we have a Pareto distribution, we can also look up the required values (the formulas are in Appendix A). That is,

$$F(500) = 1 - \left(\frac{2,000}{2,000+500} \right)^3 = 0.488,$$

$$E(X \wedge 500) = \frac{2,000}{2} \left[1 - \left(\frac{2,000}{2,000+500} \right)^2 \right] = 360.$$

With $E(X) = 1,000$ we have, for the ordinary deductible, the expected cost per loss is $1,000 - 360 = 640$ while the expected cost per payment is $640/0.512 = 1,250$. For the franchise deductible the expectations are $640+500(1-0.488) = 896$ and $1,250 + 500 = 1,750$.   □

5.2.1   Exercises

5.1 Perform the calculations in Example 5.2 for the following distribution (which is Model 4 on page 15) using an ordinary deductible of 5,000.

$$F_4(x) = \begin{cases} 0, & x < 0, \\ 1 - 0.3e^{-0.00001x}, & x \geq 0. \end{cases}$$

5.2 Repeat Exercise 5.1 for a franchise deductible.

5.3 Repeat Example 5.6 for the model in Exercise 5.1 and a 5,000 deductible.

5.4 (*) Risk 1 has a Pareto distribution with parameters $\alpha > 2$ and θ. Risk 2 has a Pareto distribution with parameters 0.8α and θ. Each risk is covered by a separate policy, each with an ordinary deductible of k. Determine the expected cost per loss for risk 1. Determine the limit as k goes to infinity of

Table 5.1   Data for Exercise 5.5

x	$F(x)$	$E(X \wedge x)$
10,000	0.60	6,000
15,000	0.70	7,700
22,500	0.80	9,500
32,500	0.90	11,000
∞	1.00	20,000

the ratio of the expected cost per loss for risk 2 to the expected cost per loss for risk 1.

5.5 (*) Losses (prior to any deductibles being applied) have a distribution as reflected in Table 5.1. There is a per-loss ordinary deductible of 10,000. The deductible is then raised so that half the number of losses exceed the new deductible as exceeded the old deductible. Determine the percentage change in the expected cost per payment when the deductible is raised.

5.3   THE LOSS ELIMINATION RATIO AND THE EFFECT OF INFLATION FOR ORDINARY DEDUCTIBLES

A ratio that can be meaningful in evaluating the impact of a deductible is the loss elimination ratio.

Definition 5.7 *The **loss elimination ratio** is the ratio of the decrease in the expected payment with an ordinary deductible to the expected payment without the deductible.*

While many types of coverage modifications can decrease the expected payment, the term loss elimination ratio is reserved for the effect of changing the deductible. Without the deductible, the expected payment is $E(X)$. With the deductible, the expected payment (from Theorem 5.5) is $E(X)-E(X \wedge d)$. Therefore the loss elimination ratio is

$$\frac{E(X) - [E(X) - E(X \wedge d)]}{E(X)} = \frac{E(X \wedge d)}{E(X)}$$

provided $E(X)$ exists.

Example 5.8 *Determine the loss elimination ratio for the Pareto distribution with $\alpha = 3$ and $\theta = 2,000$ with an ordinary deductible of 500.*

From Example 5.6 we have a loss elimination ratio of $360/1,000 = 0.36$. Thus 36% of losses can be eliminated by introducing an ordinary deductible of 500.   □

Inflation increases costs, but it turns out that when there is a deductible the effect of inflation is magnified. First, some events that formerly produced losses below the deductible will now lead to payments. Second, the relative effect of inflation is magnified because the deductible is subtracted after inflation. For example, suppose an event formerly produced a loss of 600. With a 500 deductible the payment is 100. Inflation at 10% will increase the loss to 660 and the payment to 160, a 60% increase in the cost to the insurer.

Theorem 5.9 *For an ordinary deductible of d after uniform inflation of* $1+r$, *the expected cost per loss is*

$$(1 + r)\{E(X) - E[X \wedge d/(1 + r)]\}.$$

If $F[d/(1+r)] < 1$, *then the expected cost per payment is obtained by dividing by* $1 - F[d/(1 + r)]$.

Proof: After inflation, losses are given by the random variable $Y = (1+r)X$. From Theorem 4.19, $f_Y(y) = f_X[y/(1+r)]/(1+r)$ and $F_Y(y) = F_X[y/(1+r)]$. Using (3.8),

$$
\begin{aligned}
E(Y \wedge d) &= \int_0^d y f_Y(y) dy + d[1 - F_Y(d)] \\
&= \int_0^d \frac{y f_X[y/(1+r)]}{1+r} dy + d\left[1 - F_X\left(\frac{d}{1+r}\right)\right] \\
&= \int_0^{d/(1+r)} (1+r) x f_X(x) dx + d\left[1 - F_X\left(\frac{d}{1+r}\right)\right] \\
&= (1+r)\left\{\int_0^{d/(1+r)} x f_X(x) dx + \frac{d}{1+r}\left[1 - F_X\left(\frac{d}{1+r}\right)\right]\right\} \\
&= (1+r)E\left(X \wedge \frac{d}{1+r}\right)
\end{aligned}
$$

where the third line follows from the substitution $x = y/(1 + r)$. Noting that $E(Y) = (1 + r)E(X)$ completes the first statement of the theorem and the per-payment result follows from the relationship between the distribution functions of Y and X.   □

Example 5.10 *Determine the effect of inflation at 10% on an ordinary deductible of 500 applied to a Pareto distribution with* $\alpha = 3$ *and* $\theta = 2,000$.

From Example 5.6 the expected costs are 640 and 1,250 per loss and per payment respectively. With 10% inflation we need

$$
\begin{aligned}
E\left(X \wedge \frac{500}{1.1}\right) &= E(X \wedge 454.55) \\
&= \frac{2,000}{2}\left[1 - \left(\frac{2,000}{2,000 + 454.55}\right)^2\right] = 336.08.
\end{aligned}
$$

The expected cost per loss after inflation is $1.1(1,000 - 336.08) = 730.32$, an increase of 14.11%. On a per-payment basis we need

$$
\begin{aligned}
F_Y(500) &= F_X(454.55) \\
&= 1 - \left(\frac{2,000}{2,000 + 454.55}\right)^3 \\
&= 0.459.
\end{aligned}
$$

The expected cost per payment is $730.32/(1 - 0.459) = 1,350$, an increase of 8%. □

5.3.1   Exercises

5.6 Determine the loss elimination ratio for the distribution given below with an ordinary deductible of 5,000. This is the same model used in Exercise 5.1.

$$
F_4(x) = \begin{cases} 0, & x < 0, \\ 1 - 0.3e^{-0.00001x}, & x \geq 0. \end{cases}
$$

5.7 Determine the effect of inflation at 10% on an ordinary deductible of 5,000 applied to the distribution in Exercise 5.6.

5.8 (*) Losses have a lognormal distribution with $\mu = 7$ and $\sigma = 2$. There is a deductible of 2,000 and 10 losses are expected each year. Determine the loss elimination ratio. If there is uniform inflation of 20% but the deductible remains at 2,000, how many payments will be expected?

5.9 (*) Losses have a Pareto distribution with $\alpha = 2$ and $\theta = k$. There is an ordinary deductible of $2k$. Determine the loss elimination ratio before and after 100% inflation.

5.10 (*) Losses have an exponential distribution with a mean of 1,000. There is a deductible of 500. Determine the amount by which the deductible would have to be raised to double the loss elimination ratio.

5.11 (*) The values in Table 5.2 are available for a random variable X. There is a deductible of 15,000 per loss and no policy limit. Determine the expected cost per payment using X and then assuming 50% inflation (with the deductible remaining at 15,000).

5.12 (*) Losses have a lognormal distribution with $\mu = 6.9078$ and $\sigma = 1.5174$. Determine the ratio of the loss elimination ratio at 10,000 to the loss elimination ratio at 1,000. Then determine the percentage increase in the number of losses that exceed 1,000 if all losses are increased by 10%.

5.13 (*) Losses have a mean of 2,000. With a deductible of 1,000 the loss elimination ratio is 0.3. The probability of a loss being greater than 1,000 is 0.4. Determine the average size of a loss given it is less than or equal to 1,000.

Table 5.2   Data for Exercise 5.11

x	$F(x)$	$E(X \wedge x)$
10,000	0.60	6,000
15,000	0.70	7,700
22,500	0.80	9,500
∞	1.00	20,000

5.4   POLICY LIMITS

The opposite of a deductible is a policy limit. The typical policy limit arises in a contract where for losses below u the insurance pays the full loss but for losses above u the insurance pays only u. The effect of the limit is to produce a right censored random variable. It will have a mixed distribution with distribution and density function given by (where Y is the random variable after the limit has been imposed)

$$F_Y(y) = \begin{cases} F_X(y), & y < u, \\ 1, & y \geq u \end{cases}$$

and

$$f_Y(y) = \begin{cases} f_X(y), & y < u, \\ 1 - F_X(u), & y = u. \end{cases}$$

The effect of inflation can be calculated as follows.

Theorem 5.11 *For a policy limit of u, after uniform inflation of $1 + r$, the expected cost is $(1+r)E[X \wedge u/(1+r)]$.*

Proof: The expected cost is $E(Y \wedge u)$. The proof of Theorem 5.9 shows that this equals the expression given in this theorem.   □

For policy limits the concept of per payment and per loss is not relevant. All losses that produced payments prior to imposing the limit will produce payments after the limit is imposed.

Example 5.12 *Impose a limit of 3,000 on a Pareto distribution with $\alpha = 3$ and $\theta = 2,000$. Determine the expected cost per loss with the limit as well as the proportional reduction in expected cost. Repeat these calculations after 10% uniform inflation is applied.*

For this Pareto distribution, the expected cost is

$$E(X \wedge 3,000) = \frac{2,000}{2}\left[1 - \left(\frac{2,000}{2,000 + 3,000}\right)^2\right] = 840$$

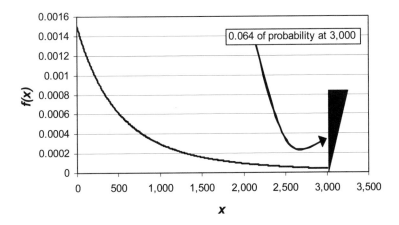

Fig. 5.2 Density function for Example 5.12.

and the proportional reduction is $(1{,}000 - 840)/1{,}000 = 0.16$. After inflation the expected cost is

$$1.1\mathrm{E}(X \wedge 3{,}000/1.1) = 1.1\frac{2{,}000}{2}\left[1 - \left(\frac{2{,}000}{2{,}000 + 3{,}000/1.1}\right)^{2}\right] = 903.11$$

for a proportional reduction of $(1{,}100 - 903.11)/1{,}100 = 0.179$. Also note that after inflation the expected cost has increased 7.51%, less than the general inflation rate. The effect is the opposite of the deductible—inflation is tempered, not exacerbated.

Figure 5.2 shows the density function for the right censored random variable. From 0 to 3,000 it matches the original Pareto distribution. The probability of exceeding 3,000, $\Pr(X > 3{,}000) = (2{,}000/5{,}000)^{3} = 0.064$ is concentrated at 3,000.   ☐

A policy limit and an ordinary deductible go together in the sense that, whichever applies to the insurance company's payments, the other applies to the policyholder's payments. For example, when the policy has a deductible of 500, the cost per loss to the policyholder is a random variable that is right censored at 500. When the policy has a limit of 3,000, the policyholder's payments are a variable that is left truncated and shifted (as in an ordinary deductible). The opposite of the franchise deductible is a coverage that right truncates any losses (see Exercise 3.12). This coverage is rarely, if ever, sold. (Would you buy a policy that pays you nothing if your loss exceeds u?)

5.4.1   Exercises

5.14 Determine the effect of 10% inflation on a policy limit of 150,000 on the following distribution. This is the same distribution used in Exercises 5.1 and 5.6.

$$F_4(x) = \begin{cases} 0, & x < 0 \\ 1 - 0.3e^{-0.00001x}, & x \geq 0. \end{cases}$$

5.15 (*) Let X has a Pareto distribution with $\alpha = 2$ and $\theta = 100$. Determine the range of the mean residual life function $e(d)$ as d ranges over all positive numbers. Then let $Y = 1.1X$. Determine the range of the ratio $e_Y(d)/e_X(d)$ as d ranges over all positive numbers. Finally, let Z be X right censored at 500 (that is, a limit of 500 is applied to X). Determine the range of $e_Z(d)$ as d ranges over the interval 0 to 500.

5.5   COINSURANCE, DEDUCTIBLES, AND LIMITS

The final common coverage modification is coinsurance. In this case the insurance company pays a proportion, α, of the loss and the policyholder pays the remaining fraction. If coinsurance is the only modification, this changes the loss variable X to the payment variable, $Y = \alpha X$. The effect of multiplication has already been covered. When all four items covered in this chapter are present (ordinary deductible, limit, coinsurance, and inflation), we create the following per-loss random variable:

$$Y^L = \begin{cases} 0, & X < \dfrac{d}{1+r}, \\ \alpha[(1+r)X - d], & \dfrac{d}{1+r} \leq X < \dfrac{u}{1+r},) \\ \alpha(u - d), & X \geq \dfrac{u}{1+r}. \end{cases}$$

For this definition, the quantities are applied in a particular order. In particular, the coinsurance is applied last. For the contract illustrated above, the policy limit is $\alpha(u - d)$, the maximum amount payable. In this definition, u is the loss above which no additional benefits are paid and will be called the **maximum covered loss**. For the per-payment variable, Y^P is undefined for $X < d/(1+r)$.

Previous results can be combined to produce the following theorem, given without proof.

Theorem 5.13 *For the per-loss variable,*

$$E(Y^L) = \alpha(1+r)\left[E\left(X \wedge \frac{u}{1+r}\right) - E\left(X \wedge \frac{d}{1+r}\right)\right].$$

The expected value of the per-payment variable is obtained as

$$E(Y^P) = \frac{E(Y^L)}{1 - F_X\left(\frac{d}{1+r}\right)}.$$

Higher moments are more difficult. The next theorem gives the formula for the second moment. The variance can then be obtained by subtracting the square of the mean.

Theorem 5.14 *For the per-loss variable*

$$
\begin{aligned}
E\left[(Y^L)^2\right] &= \alpha^2(1+r)^2\{E[(X \wedge u^*)^2] - E[(X \wedge d^*)^2] \\
&\quad - 2d^*E(X \wedge u^*) + 2d^*E(X \wedge d^*)\},
\end{aligned}
$$

where $u^* = u/(1+r)$ and $d^* = d/(1+r)$. For the second moment of the per-payment variable, divide this expression by $1 - F_X(d^*)$.

Proof: From the definition of Y^L,

$$
\begin{aligned}
E\left[(Y^L)^2\right] &= \int_{d^*}^{u^*} \alpha^2[(1+r)x - d]^2 f(x)dx + \int_{u^*}^{\infty} \alpha^2(u-d)^2 f(x)dx \\
\frac{E\left[(Y^L)^2\right]}{\alpha^2} &= (1+r)^2 \left[\int_0^{u^*} x^2 f(x)dx - \int_0^{d^*} x^2 f(x)dx\right] \\
&\quad - 2(1+r)d \left[\int_0^{u^*} xf(x)dx - \int_0^{d^*} xf(x)dx\right] \\
&\quad + d^2[F(u^*) - F(d^*)] + (u-d)^2[1 - F(u^*)] \\
&= (1+r)^2\{E[(X \wedge u^*)^2] - u^{*2}[1 - F(u^*)] \\
&\quad - E[(X \wedge d^*)^2] + d^{*2}[1 - F(d^*)]\} \\
&\quad - 2(1+r)^2 d^*\{E(X \wedge u^*) - u^*[1 - F(u^*)] \\
&\quad - E(X \wedge d^*) + d^*[1 - F(d^*)]\} \\
&\quad + (1+r)^2 d^{*2}[F(u^*) - F(d^*)] \\
&\quad + (1+r)^2(u^* - d^*)^2[1 - F(u^*)] \\
\frac{E\left[(Y^L)^2\right]}{[\alpha(1+r)]^2} &= E[(X \wedge u^*)^2] - E[(X \wedge d^*)^2] - 2d^*[E(X \wedge u^*) - E(X \wedge d^*)].
\end{aligned}
$$

$\square$

Example 5.15 *Determine the mean and standard deviation per loss for a Pareto distribution with $\alpha = 3$ and $\theta = 2,000$ with a deductible of 500 and a policy limit of 2,500. Note that the maximum covered loss is $u = 3,000$.*

From earlier examples, $E(X \wedge 500) = 360$ and $E(X \wedge 3,000) = 840$. The second limited moment is

$$
\begin{aligned}
E[(X \wedge u)^2] &= \int_0^u x^2 \frac{3(2,000)^3}{(x+2,000)^4} dx + u^2 \left(\frac{2,000}{u+2,000}\right)^3 \\
&= 3(2,000)^3 \int_{2,000}^{u+2,000} (y-2,000)^2 y^{-4} dy + u^2 \left(\frac{2,000}{u+2,000}\right)^3 \\
&= 3(2,000)^3 \left(-y^{-1} + 2,000y^{-2} - \frac{2,000^2}{3} y^{-3} \Big|_{2,000}^{u+2,000} \right) \\
&\quad + u^2 \left(\frac{2,000}{u+2,000}\right)^3 \\
&= 3(2,000)^3 \left[-\frac{1}{u+2,000} + \frac{2,000}{(u+2,000)^2} - \frac{2,000^2}{3(u+2,000)^3} \right] \\
&\quad + 3(2,000)^3 \left[\frac{1}{2,000} - \frac{2,000}{2,000^2} + \frac{2,000^2}{3(2,000)^3} \right] \\
&\quad + u^2 \left(\frac{2,000}{u+2,000}\right)^3 \\
&= (2,000)^2 - \left(\frac{2,000}{u+2,000}\right)^3 (2u+2,000)(u+2,000).
\end{aligned}
$$

Then, $E[(X \wedge 500)^2] = 160,000$ and $E[(X \wedge 3,000)^2] = 1,440,000$ and so

$$
\begin{aligned}
E(Y) &= 840 - 360 = 480 \\
E(Y^2) &= 1,440,000 - 160,000 - 2(500)(840) + 2(500)(360) = 800,000
\end{aligned}
$$

for a variance of $800,000 - 480^2 = 569,600$ and a standard deviation of 754.72.   □

5.5.1 Exercises

5.16 (*) You are given that $e(0) = 25$, $S(x) = 1 - x/w$, $0 \le x \le w$, and Y^P is the excess loss variable for $d = 10$. Determine the variance of Y^P.

5.17 (*) The loss ratio (R) is defined as total losses (L) divided by earned premiums (P). An agent will receive a bonus (B) if the loss ratio on his business is less than 0.7. The bonus is given as $B = P(0.7 - R)/3$ if this quantity is positive, otherwise it is zero. Let $P = 500,000$ and L have a Pareto distribution with parameters $\alpha = 3$ and $\theta = 600,000$. Determine the expected value of the bonus.

5.18 (*) Losses this year have a distribution such that $E(X \wedge d) = -0.025d^2 + 1.475d - 2.25$ for $d = 10, 11, 12, \ldots, 26$. Next year, losses will be uniformly higher by 10%. An insurance policy reimburses 100% of losses subject to a deductible of 11 up to a maximum reimbursement of 11. Determine the ratio of next year's reimbursements to this year's reimbursements.

5.19 (*) Losses have an exponential distribution with a mean of 1,000. An insurance company will pay the amount of each claim in excess of a deductible of 100. Determine the variance of the amount paid by the insurance company for one claim, including the possibility that the amount paid is zero.

5.20 (*) Total claims for a health plan have a Pareto distribution with $\alpha = 2$ and $\theta = 500$. The health plan implements an incentive to physicians that will pay a bonus of 50% of the amount by which total claims are less than 500; otherwise no bonus is paid. It is anticipated that with the incentive plan the claim distribution will change to become Pareto with $\alpha = 2$ and $\theta = K$. With the new distribution it turns out that expected claims plus the expected bonus is equal to expected claims prior to the bonus system. Determine the value of K.

5.21 (*) In year a, total expected losses are 10,000,000. Individual losses in year a have a Pareto distribution with $\alpha = 2$ and $\theta = 2,000$. A reinsurer pays the excess of each individual loss over 3,000. For this, the reinsurer is paid a premium equal to 110% of expected covered losses. In year b, losses will experience 5% inflation over year a, but the frequency of losses will not change. Determine the ratio of the premium in year b to the premium in year a.

5.22 (*) Losses have a uniform distribution from 0 to 50,000. There is a per-loss deductible of 5,000 and a policy limit of 20,000 (meaning that the maximum covered loss is 25,000). Determine the expected payment given that a payment has been made.

5.23 (*) Losses have a lognormal distribution with $\mu = 10$ and $\sigma = 1$. For losses below 50,000, no payment is made. For losses between 50,000 and 100,000, the full amount of the loss is paid. For losses in excess of 100,000 the limit of 100,000 is paid. Determine the expected cost per loss.

5.6   THE IMPACT OF DEDUCTIBLES ON CLAIM FREQUENCY

An important component in analyzing the effect of policy modifications pertains to the change in the frequency distribution of payments when the deductible (ordinary or franchise) is imposed or changed. When a deductible is imposed or increased, there will be fewer payments per period, while if a deductible is lowered, there will be more payments.

We can quantify this process, providing it can be assumed that the imposition of coverage modifications does not affect the process that produces losses or the type of individual who will purchase insurance. For example, those who buy a 250 deductible on an automobile property damage coverage may (correctly) view themselves as less likely to be involved in an accident than those who buy full coverage. Similarly, an employer may find that the rate of permanent disability declines when reduced benefits are provided to employees in the first few years of employment.

To begin, suppose X_j, the severity, represents the ground-up loss on the jth such loss and there are no coverage modifications. Let N^L denote the number of losses. Now consider a coverage modification such that v is the probability that a loss will result in a payment. For example, if there is a deductible of d, $v = \Pr(X > d)$. Next, define the indicator random variable I_j by $I_j = 1$ if the jth loss results in a payment and $I_j = 0$ otherwise. Then I_j has a Bernoulli distribution with parameter v and the pgf of I_j is $P_{I_j}(z) = 1 - v + vz$. Then $N^P = I_1 + \cdots + I_{N^L}$ represents the number of payments. If $I_1, I_2, \ldots$ are mutually independent and are also independent of N^L, then N^P has a compound distribution with N^L as the primary distribution and a Bernoulli secondary distribution. Thus

$$P_{N^P}(z) = P_{N^L}[P_{I_j}(z)] = P_{N^L}[1 + v(z - 1)].$$

In the important special case in which the distribution of N^L depends on a parameter θ such that

$$P_{N^L}(z) = P_{N^L}(z; \theta) = B[\theta(z - 1)],$$

where $B(z)$ is functionally independent of θ (as in Theorem 4.54), then

$$
\begin{aligned}
P_{N^P}(z) &= B[\theta(1 - v + vz - 1)] \\
&= B[v\theta(z - 1)] \\
&= P_{N^L}(z; v\theta).
\end{aligned}
$$

This implies that N^L and N^P are both from the same parametric family and only the parameter θ need be changed.

Example 5.16 *Demonstrate that the above result applies to the negative binomial distribution and illustrate the effect when a deductible of 250 is imposed on a negative binomial distribution with $r = 2$ and $\beta = 3$. Assume that losses have a Pareto distribution with $\alpha = 3$ and $\theta = 1{,}000$.*

The negative binomial pgf is $P_{N^L}(z) = [1 - \beta(z - 1)]^{-r}$. Here β takes on the role of θ in the result and $B(z) = (1 - z)^{-r}$. Then N^P must have a negative binomial distribution with $r^* = r$ and $\beta^* = v\beta$. For the particular situation described,

$$v = 1 - F(250) = \left(\frac{1{,}000}{1{,}000 + 250}\right)^3 = 0.512$$

and so $r^* = 2$ and $\beta^* = 3(0.512) = 1.536$.   □

This result may be generalized for zero-modified and zero-truncated distributions. Suppose N^L depends on parameters θ and α such that

$$P_{N^L}(z) = P_{N^L}(z; \theta, \alpha) = \alpha + (1 - \alpha)\frac{B[\theta(z - 1)] - B(-\theta)}{1 - B(-\theta)}. \quad (5.3)$$

Note that $\alpha = P_{N^L}(0) = \Pr(N^L = 0)$ and so is the modified probability at zero. It is also the case that, if $B[\theta(z-1)]$ is itself a pgf, then the pgf given in (5.3) is that for the corresponding zero-modified distribution. However, it is not necessary for $B[\theta(z-1)]$ to be a pgf in order for $P_{N^L}(z)$ as given in (5.3) to be a pgf. In particular, $B(z) = 1 + \ln(1 - z)$ yields the zero-modified (ZM) logarithmic distribution, even though there is no distribution with $B(z)$ as its pgf. Similarly, $B(z) = (1-z)^{-r}$ for $-1 < r < 0$ yields the ETNB distribution. A few algebraic steps reveal that for (5.3)

$$P_{N^P}(z) = P_{N^L}(z; v\theta, \alpha^*),$$

where $\alpha^* = \Pr(N^P = 0) = P_{N^P}(0) = P_{N^L}(1 - v; \theta, \alpha)$. It is expected that imposing a deductible will increase the value of α because periods with no payments will become more likely. In particular, if N^L is zero truncated, N^P will be zero modified.

Example 5.17 *Repeat the previous example, only now let the frequency distribution be zero-modified negative binomial with $r = 2$, $\beta = 3$, and $p_0^M = 0.4$.*

The pgf is

$$P_{N^L}(z) = p_0^M + (1 - p_0^M)\frac{[1 - \beta(z - 1)]^{-r} - (1 + \beta)^{-r}}{1 - (1 + \beta)^{-r}}.$$

Then $\alpha = p_0^M$ and $B(z) = (1 - z)^{-r}$. We then have $r^* = r$, $\beta^* = v\beta$, and

$$
\begin{aligned}
\alpha^* &= p_0^{M*} = p_0^M + (1 - p_0^M)\frac{[1 + v\beta)]^{-r} - (1 + \beta)^{-r}}{1 - (1 + \beta)^{-r}} \\
&= \frac{p_0^M - (1 + \beta)^{-r} + (1 + v\beta)^{-r} - p_0^M(1 + v\beta)^{-r}}{1 - (1 + \beta)^{-r}}.
\end{aligned}
$$

For the particular distribution given, the new parameters are $r^* = 2$, $\beta^* = 3(0.512) = 1.536$, and

$$p_0^{M*} = \frac{0.4 - 4^{-2} + 2.536^{-2} - 0.4(2.536)^{-2}}{1 - 4^{-2}} = 0.4595. \qquad \square$$

In applications, it may be the case that we want to determine the distribution of N^L from that of N^P. For example, data may have been collected on the number of payments in the presence of a deductible and from that data the parameters of N^P can be estimated. We may then want to know the distribution of payments if the deductible is removed. Arguing as before,

$$P_{N^L}(z) = P_{N^P}(1 - v^{-1} + zv^{-1}).$$

This implies that the formulas derived previously hold with v replaced by $1/v$. However, it is possible that the resulting pgf for N^L is not valid. In this case one of the modeling assumptions is invalid (for example, the assumption that changing the deductible does not change claim-related behavior).

Example 5.18 *Suppose payments on a policy with a deductible of 250 have the zero-modified negative binomial distribution with $r^* = 2$, $\beta^* = 1.536$, and $p_0^{M*} = 0.4595$. Losses have the Pareto distribution with $\alpha = 3$ and $\theta = 1,000$. Determine the distribution of the number of payments when the deductible is removed. Repeat this calculation assuming $p_0^{M*} = 0.002$.*

In this case the formulas use $v = 1/0.512 = 1.953125$ and so $r = 2$ and $\beta = 1.953125(1.536) = 3$. Also,

$$p_0^{M*} = \frac{0.4595 - 2.536^{-2} + 4^{-2} - 0.4595(4)^{-2}}{1 - 2.536^{-2}} = 0.4$$

as expected. For the second case,

$$p_0^{M*} = \frac{0.002 - 2.536^{-2} + 4^{-2} - 0.002(4)^{-2}}{1 - 2.536^{-2}} = -0.1079,$$

which is not a legitimate probability.   □

All members of the $(a, b, 0)$ and $(a, b, 1)$ classes meet the conditions of this section. Table 5.3 indicates how the parameters change when moving from N^L to N^P. If N^L has a compound distribution, then we can write $P_{N^L}(z) = P_1[P_2(z)]$ and therefore

$$P_{N^P}(z) = P_{N^L}[1 + v(z - 1)] = P_1\{P_2[1 + v(z - 1)]\}.$$

Thus N^P will also have a compound distribution with the secondary distribution modified as indicated. If the secondary distribution has an $(a, b, 0)$ distribution, then it can modified as in Table 5.3. The following example indicates the adjustment to be made if the secondary distribution has an $(a, b, 1)$ distribution.

Example 5.19 *Suppose N^L is Poisson–ETNB with $\lambda = 5$, $\beta = 0.3$, and $r = 4$. If $v = 0.5$, determine the distribution of N^P.*

From the discussion above, N^P is compound Poisson with $\lambda^* = 5$, but the secondary distribution is a zero-modified negative binomial with (from Table 5.3) $\beta^* = 0.5(0.3) = 0.15$,

$$p_0^{M*} = \frac{0 - 1.3^{-4} + 1.15^{-4} - 0(1.15)^{-4}}{1 - 1.3^{-4}} = 0.34103,$$

Table 5.3 Frequency adjustments

N^L	Parameters for N^P
Poisson	$\lambda^* = v\lambda$
ZM Poisson	$p_0^{M*} = \dfrac{p_0^M - e^{-\lambda} + e^{-v\lambda} - p_0^M e^{-v\lambda}}{1 - e^{-\lambda}}, \ \lambda^* = v\lambda$
Binomial	$q^* = vq$
ZM binomial	$p_0^{M*} = \dfrac{p_0^M - (1-q)^m + (1-vq)^m - p_0^M(1-vq)^m}{1-(1-q)^m}$
	$q^* = vq$
Negative binomial	$\beta^* = v\beta, \ r^* = r$
ZM negative	$p_0^{M*} = \dfrac{p_0^M - (1+\beta)^{-r} + (1+v\beta)^{-r} - p_0^M(1+v\beta)^{-r}}{1-(1+\beta)^{-r}}$
binomial	$\beta^* = v\beta, \ r^* = r$
ZM logarithmic	$p_0^{M*} = 1 - (1-p_0^M)\ln(1+v\beta)/\ln(1+\beta)$
	$\beta^* = v\beta$

and $r^* = 4$. This would be sufficient, except we have acquired the habit of using the ETNB as the secondary distribution. From Theorem 4.54 a compound Poisson distribution with a zero-modified secondary distribution is equivalent to a compound Poisson distribution with a zero-truncated secondary distribution. The Poisson parameter must be changed to $(1 - p_0^{M*})\lambda^*$. Therefore, N^P has a Poisson–ETNB distribution with $\lambda^* = (1 - 0.34103)5 = 3.29485$, $\beta^* = 0.15$, and $r^* = 4$. □

The results can be further generalized to an increase or decrease in the deductible. Let N^d be the frequency when the deductible is d and let N^{d^*} be the frequency when the deductible is d^*. Let $v = [1 - F_X(d^*)]/[1 - F_X(d)]$, and then Table 5.3 can be used to move from the parameters of N^d to the parameters of N^{d^*}. As long as $d^* > d$, we will have $v < 1$ and the formulas will lead to a legitimate distribution for N^{d^*}. This includes the special case of $d = 0$ that was used at the start of this section. If $d^* < d$, then $v > 1$ and there is no assurance that a legitimate distribution will result. This includes the special case $d^* = 0$ (removal of a deductible) covered earlier.

Finally, it should be noted that policy limits have no effect on the frequency distribution. Imposing, removing, or changing a limit will not change the number of payments made.

5.6.1 Exercises

5.24 A group life insurance policy has an accidental death rider. For ordinary deaths, the benefit is 10,000; however, for accidental deaths, the benefit is

20,000. The insureds are approximately the same age, so it is reasonable to assume they all have the same claim probabilities. Let them be 0.97 for no claim, 0.01 for an ordinary death claim, and 0.02 for an accidental death claim. A reinsurer has been asked to bid on providing an excess reinsurance that will pay 10,000 for each accidental death.

(a) The claim process can be modeled with a frequency component that has the Bernoulli distribution (the event is claim/no claim) and a two-point severity component (the probabilities are associated with the two claim levels, given that a claim occurred). Specify the probability distributions for the frequency and severity random variables.

(b) Suppose the reinsurer wants to retain the same frequency distribution. Determine the modified severity distribution that will reflect the reinsurer's payments.

(c) Determine the reinsurer's frequency and severity distributions when the severity distribution is to be conditional on a reinsurance payment being made.

5.25 Individual losses have a Pareto distribution with $\alpha = 2$ and $\theta = 1,000$. With a deductible of 500 the frequency distribution for the number of payments is Poisson–inverse Gaussian with $\lambda = 3$ and $\beta = 2$. If the deductible is raised to 1,000, determine the distribution for the number of payments. Also, determine the pdf of the severity distribution (per payment) when the new deductible is in place.

5.26 Losses have a Pareto distribution with $\alpha = 2$ and $\theta = 1,000$. The frequency distribution for a deductible of 500 is zero-truncated logarithmic with $\beta = 4$. Determine a model for the number of payments when the deductible is reduced to 0.

5.27 Suppose that the number of losses N^L has the Sibuya distribution (see Exercises 4.47 and 4.59) with pgf $P_{N^L}(z) = 1 - (1 - z)^{-r}$, where $-1 < r < 0$. Demonstrate that the number of payments has a zero-modified Sibuya distribution.

6

Aggregate loss models

6.1 INTRODUCTION

The purpose of this chapter is to develop models of aggregate losses, the total amount paid on all claims occurring in a fixed time period on a defined set of insurance contracts. There are two ways to go about adding the claims in order to obtain the total for the period.

One method is to record the payments as they are made and then add them up. In that case we can represent the aggregate losses as a sum, S, of a random number, N, of individual payment amounts $(X_1, X_2, \ldots, X_N)$. Hence,

$$S = X_1 + X_2 + \cdots + X_N, \quad N = 0, 1, 2, \ldots, \tag{6.1}$$

where $S = 0$ when $N = 0$.

Definition 6.1 _The **collective risk model** has the representation in_ (6.1) _with the X_js being independent and identically distributed (i.i.d.) random variables, unless otherwise specified. More formally, the independence assumptions are:_

1. _Conditional on $N = n$, the random variables $X_1, X_2, \ldots, X_n$ are i.i.d. random variables._

Loss Models: From Data to Decisions, Second Edition.
By Stuart A. Klugman, Harry H. Panjer, and Gordon E. Willmot
ISBN 0-471-21577-5   Copyright © 2004 John Wiley & Sons, Inc.

2. Conditional on $N = n$, the common distribution of the random variables $X_1, X_2, \ldots, X_n$ does not depend on n.

3. The distribution of N does not depend in any way on the values of $X_1, X_2, \ldots$.

An alternative model is given below

Definition 6.2 *The **individual risk model** represents the aggregate loss as a sum, $S = X_1 + \cdots + X_n$, of a fixed number, n, of insurance contracts. The loss amounts for the n contracts are $(X_1, X_2, \cdots, X_n)$, where the X_js are assumed to be independent but are not assumed to be identically distributed. The distribution of the X_js usually has a probability mass at zero, corresponding to the probability of no loss or payment.*

The individual risk model is used to add together the losses or payments from a fixed number of insurance contracts or sets of insurance contracts. It is used in modeling the losses of a group life or health insurance policy that covers a group of n employees. Each employee can have different coverage (life insurance benefit as a multiple of salary) and different levels of loss probabilities (different ages and health status).

In the special case where the X_js are identically distributed, the individual risk model becomes the special case of the collective risk model, with the distribution of N being the degenerate distribution with all of the probability at $N = n$; that is, $\Pr(N = n) = 1$.

The distribution of S in (6.1) is obtained from the distribution of N and the distribution of the X_js. Using this approach, the frequency and the severity of claims are modeled separately. The information about these distributions is used to obtain information about S. An alternative to this approach is to simply gather information about S (e.g., total losses each month for a period of months) and to use some model from Chapter 4 to model the distribution of S. Modeling the distribution of N and the distribution of the X_js separately has some distinct advantages:

1. The expected number of claims changes as the number of insured policies changes. Growth in the volume of business needs to be accounted for in forecasting the number of claims in future years based on past years' data.

2. The effects of general economic inflation and additional claims inflation are reflected in the losses incurred by insured parties and the claims paid by insurance companies. Such effects are often masked when insurance policies have deductibles and policy limits which do not depend on inflation and aggregate results are used.

3. The impact of changing individual deductibles and policy limits is more easily studied. This is done by changing the specification of the severity distribution.

4. The impact on claims frequencies of changing deductibles is better understood.

5. Data that are heterogeneous in terms of deductibles and limits can be combined to obtain the hypothetical loss size distribution. This is useful when data from several years in which policy provisions were changing are combined.

6. Models developed for noncovered losses to insureds, claim costs to insurers, and claim costs to reinsurers can be mutually consistent. This is useful for a direct insurer which is studying the consequence of shifting losses to a reinsurer.

7. The shape of the distribution of S depends on the shapes of both distributions of N and X. The understanding of the relative shapes is useful when modifying policy details. For example, if the severity distribution has a much heavier tail than the frequency distribution, the shape of the tail of the distribution of aggregate claims or losses will be determined by the severity distribution and will be insensitive to the choice of frequency distribution.

In summary, a more accurate and flexible model can be constructed by examining frequency and severity separately.

In constructing the model (6.1) for S, if N represents the actual number of losses to the insured, then the X_js can represent (i) the losses to the insured, (ii) the claim payments of the insurer, (iii) the claim payments of a reinsurer, or (iv) the deductibles (self-insurance) paid by the insured. In each case, the interpretation of S is different and the severity distribution can be constructed in a consistent manner.

Because the random variables N, $X_1, X_2, \ldots$, and S provide much of the focus for this chapter and the two that follow, we want to be especially careful when referring to them. We will refer to N as the **claim count random variable** and will refer to its distribution as the **claim count distribution**. The expression **number of claims** will also be used, and, occasionally, just **claims** will be used. Another term that will commonly be used is **frequency distribution**. The X_js are the **individual** or **single-loss random variables**. The modifier **individual** or **single** will be dropped when the reference is clear. In Chapter 5 a distinction was made between losses and payments. Strictly speaking, the X_js are payments because they represent a real cash transaction. However, the term **loss** is more customary, and we will continue with it. Another common term for the X_js is **severity**. Finally, S is the **aggregate loss random variable** or the **total loss random variable**.

Example 6.3 *An insurer estimates that individual losses to an insured follow a distribution with pdf $f_X(x)$. The insurer pays 80% of individual losses in excess of 1,000 with a maximum payment of 100,000. It reinsures that portion*

of any payments in excess of 50,000. *Develop models for each of the following:*
(a) the total loss preinsurance to the policyholder, (b) the aggregate loss to
the insurer prior to the reinsurance payment, (c) the aggregate loss to the
reinsurer, (d) the aggregate loss to the insurer, after the reinsurance payment,
and (e) the aggregate loss to the insured.

(a) The aggregate losses with no insurance are $S = X_1 + X_2 + \cdots + X_N$, where the X_js have the distribution with pdf $f_X(x)$.

(b) The aggregate payments by the insurer (before recovery of reinsurance) are $S = Y_1 + Y_2 + \cdots + Y_N$, where

$$Y_j = \begin{cases} 0, & X_j \leq 1{,}000, \\ 0.80(X_j - 1{,}000), & 1{,}000 < X_j \leq 126{,}000, \\ 100{,}000, & X_j > 126{,}000. \end{cases}$$

(c) The aggregate payments by the reinsurer are $S = Y_1 + Y_2 + \cdots + Y_N$, where

$$Y_j = \begin{cases} 0, & X_j \leq 63{,}500, \\ 0.80(X_j - 63{,}500), & 63{,}500 < X_j \leq 126{,}000, \\ 50{,}000, & X_j > 126{,}000. \end{cases}$$

(d) The aggregate costs to the insurer after recovery of reinsurance payments are $S = Y_1 + Y_2 + \cdots + Y_N$, where

$$Y_j = \begin{cases} 0, & X_j \leq 1{,}000, \\ 0.80(X_j - 1{,}000), & 1{,}000 < X_j \leq 63{,}500, \\ 50{,}000, & X_j > 63{,}500. \end{cases}$$

(e) The aggregate costs to the insured, that is, the uninsured costs, are $S = Y_1 + Y_2 + \cdots + Y_N$, where

$$Y_j = \begin{cases} X_j, & X_j \leq 1{,}000, \\ 800 + 0.20X_j, & 1{,}000 < X_j \leq 126{,}000, \\ X_j - 100{,}000, & X_j > 126{,}000. \end{cases} \qquad \square$$

6.1.1 Exercise

6.1 Show that the costs to the insured, the insurer, and the reinsurer in Example 6.3 sum to the aggregate loss.

6.2   MODEL CHOICES

In many cases of fitting frequency or severity distributions to data, several distributions may be good candidates for models. However, some distributions may be preferable for a variety of practical reasons.

In general, it is useful for the severity distribution to be a scale distribution (see Definition 4.2) because the choice of currency (e.g., U.S. dollars or British pounds) should not affect the result. Also, scale families are easy to adjust for inflationary effects over time (this is, in effect, a change in currency; e.g., 1994 U.S. dollars to 1995 U.S. dollars). When forecasting the costs for a future year, the anticipated rate of inflation can be factored in easily by adjusting the parameters.

A similar consideration applies to frequency distributions. As a block of an insurance company's business grows, the number of claims can be expected to grow, all other things being equal. If one chooses models that have probability generating functions of the form

$$P_N(z; \alpha) = Q(z)^\alpha \qquad (6.2)$$

for some parameter α, then the expected number of claims is proportional to α. Increasing the volume of business by $100r\%$ results in expected claims being proportional to $\alpha^* = (1 + r)\alpha$. This was discussed in Section 4.6.11. Because r is any value satisfying $r > -1$, the distributions satisfying (6.2) should allow α to take on any positive values. Such distributions can be shown to be infinitely divisible (see Definition 4.65).

A related consideration also suggests frequency distributions that are infinitely divisible. This relates to the concept of invariance over the time period of study. Ideally the model selected should not depend on the length of the time period used in the study of claims frequency. The expected frequency should be proportional to the length of the time period after any adjustment for growth in business. This means that a study conducted over a period of 10 years can be used to develop claims frequency distributions for periods of a month, a year, or any other period. Furthermore, the form of the distribution for a one-year period is the same as for a one-month period with a change of parameter. The parameter α corresponds to the length of a time period. For example, if $\alpha = 1.7$ in (6.2) for a one-month period, then the identical model with $\alpha = 20.4$ is an appropriate model for a one-year period.

Distributions that have a modification at zero are not of the form (6.2). However, it may still be desirable to use a zero-modified distribution if the physical situation suggests it. For example, if a certain proportion of policies never make a claim, due to duplication of coverage or other reason, it may be appropriate to use this same proportion in future periods for a policy selected at random.

6.2.1   Exercises

6.2 For pgfs satisfying (6.2), show that the mean is proportional to α.

6.3 Which of the distributions in Appendix B satisfy (6.2) for any positive value of α?

6.3   THE COMPOUND MODEL FOR AGGREGATE CLAIMS

Let S denote aggregate losses associated with a set of N observed claims $X_1, X_2, \cdots, X_N$ satisfying the independence assumptions following (6.1). The approach in this chapter is to:

1. Develop a model for the distribution of N based on data.

2. Develop a model for the common distribution of the X_js based on data.

3. Using these two models, carry out necessary calculations to obtain the distribution of S.

Completion of the first two steps follows the ideas developed elsewhere in this text. We now presume that these two models are developed and that we only need to carry out numerical work in obtaining solutions to problems associated with the distribution of S. These might involve pricing a stop-loss reinsurance contract, and they require analyzing the impact of changes in deductibles, coinsurance levels, and maximum payments on individual losses.
The random sum

$$S = X_1 + X_2 + \cdots + X_N$$

(where N has a counting distribution) has a distribution function

$$
\begin{aligned}
F_S(x) &= \Pr(S \le x) \\
&= \sum_{n=0}^{\infty} p_n \Pr(S \le x | N = n) \\
&= \sum_{n=0}^{\infty} p_n F_X^{*n}(x),
\end{aligned}
\tag{6.3}
$$

where $F_X(x) = \Pr(X \le x)$ is the common distribution function of the X_js and $p_n = \Pr(N = n)$. In (6.3), $F_X^{*n}(x)$ is the "n-fold convolution" of the cdf of X. It can be obtained as

$$
F_X^{*0}(x) = \begin{cases} 0, & x < 0, \\ 1, & x \ge 0, \end{cases}
$$

and

$$F_X^{*k}(x) = \int_{-\infty}^{\infty} F_X^{*(k-1)}(x-y)\, dF_X(y) \text{ for } k = 1, 2, \ldots . \qquad (6.4)$$

If X is a continuous random variable with probability zero on negative values, (6.4) reduces to

$$F_X^{*k}(x) = \int_0^x F_X^{*(k-1)}(x-y) f_X(y)\, dy \text{ for } k = 2, 3, \ldots .$$

For $k = 1$ this equation reduces to $F_X^{*1}(x) = F_X(x)$. By differentiating, the pdf is

$$f_X^{*k}(x) = \int_0^x f_X^{*(k-1)}(x-y) f_X(y)\, dy \text{ for } k = 2, 3, \ldots .$$

In the case of discrete random variables with positive probabilities at $0, 1, 2, \ldots$, Equation (6.4) reduces to

$$F_X^{*k}(x) = \sum_{y=0}^{x} F_X^{*(k-1)}(x-y) f_X(y) \text{ for } x = 0, 1, \ldots, \quad k = 2, 3, \ldots .$$

The corresponding pf is

$$f_X^{*k}(x) = \sum_{y=0}^{x} f_X^{*(k-1)}(x-y) f_X(y) \text{ for } x = 0, 1, \ldots, \quad k = 2, 3, \ldots .$$

The distribution (6.3) is called a **compound distribution** and the pf for the distribution of aggregate losses is

$$f_S(x) = \sum_{n=0}^{\infty} p_n f_X^{*n}(x).$$

Arguing as in Section 4.6.7, the pgf of S is

$$\begin{aligned}
P_S(z) &= \mathrm{E}[z^S] \\
&= \sum_{n=0}^{\infty} \mathrm{E}[z^{X_1 + X_2 + \cdots + X_n} | N = n] \Pr(N = n) \\
&= \sum_{n=0}^{\infty} \mathrm{E}\left[\prod_{j=1}^{n} z^{X_j} \right] \Pr(N = n) \\
&= \sum_{n=0}^{\infty} \Pr(N = n) [P_X(z)]^n \\
&= \mathrm{E}[P_X(z)^N] = P_N[P_X(z)] \qquad (6.5)
\end{aligned}$$

due to the independence of $X_1, \ldots, X_n$ for fixed n.

A similar relationship exists for the other generating functions. It is sometimes more convenient to use the characteristic function

$$\varphi_S(z) = E(e^{izS}) = P_N[\varphi_X(z)],$$

which always exists. Panjer and Willmot [106] use the Laplace transform

$$L_S(z) = E(e^{-zS}) = P_N[L_X(z)]$$

which always exists for random variables defined on nonnegative values. With regard to the moment generating function, we have

$$M_S(z) = P_N[M_X(z)].$$

The pgf of compound distributions was discussed in Section 4.6.7 where the "secondary" distribution plays the role of the claim size distribution in this chapter.

In the case where $P_N(z) = P_1[P_2(z)]$—that is, N is itself a compound distribution—$P_S(z) = P_1\{P_2[P_X(z)]\}$, which in itself produces no additional difficulties.

From (6.5), the moments of S can be obtained in terms of the moments of N and the X_js. The first three moments are

$$
\begin{aligned}
E(S) &= \mu'_{S1} = \mu'_{N1}\mu'_{X1} = E(N)E(X), \\
\mathrm{Var}(S) &= \mu_{S2} = \mu'_{N1}\mu_{X2} + \mu_{N2}(\mu'_{X1})^2, \\
E\{[S - E(S)]^3\} &= \mu_{S3} = \mu'_{N1}\mu_{X3} + 3\mu_{N2}\mu'_{X1}\mu_{X2} + \mu_{N3}(\mu'_{X1})^3.
\end{aligned}
\tag{6.6}
$$

Here, the first subscript indicates the appropriate random variable, the second subscript indicates the order of the moment, and the superscript is a prime ($'$) for raw moments (moments about the origin) and is unprimed for central moments (moments about the mean). The moments can be used on their own to provide approximations for probabilities of aggregate claims by matching the first few model and sample moments.

Example 6.4 *The observed mean (and standard deviation) of the number of claims and the individual losses over the past* 10 *months are* 6.7 (2.3) *and* 179,247 (52,141), *respectively. Determine the mean and variance of aggregate claims per month.*

$$
\begin{aligned}
E(S) &= 6.7(179,247) = 1,200,955, \\
\mathrm{Var}(S) &= 6.7(52,141)^2 + (2.3)^2(179,247)^2 \\
&= 1.88180 \times 10^{11}.
\end{aligned}
$$

Hence, the mean and standard deviation of aggregate claims are 1,200,955 and 433,797, respectively. □

Example 6.5 (Example 6.4 continued) *Using normal and lognormal distrib-utions as approximating distributions for aggregate claims, calculate the prob-ability that claims will exceed 140% of expected costs. That is,*

$$\Pr(S > 1.40 \times 1{,}200{,}955) = \Pr(S > 1{,}681{,}337).$$

For the normal distribution

$$
\begin{aligned}
\Pr(S > 1,681,337) &= \Pr\left(\frac{S - \mathrm{E}(S)}{\sqrt{\mathrm{Var}(S)}} > \frac{1,681,337 - 1,200,955}{433,797}\right)\\
&= \Pr(Z > 1.107) = 1 - \Phi(1.107) = 0.134.
\end{aligned}
$$

For the lognormal distribution, from Appendix A, the mean and second raw moment of the lognormal distribution are

$$\mathrm{E}(S) = \exp(\mu + \tfrac{1}{2}\sigma^2) \quad \text{and} \quad \mathrm{E}(S^2) = \exp(2\mu + 2\sigma^2).$$

Equating these to 1.200955×10^6 and $1.88180 \times 10^{11} + (1.200955 \times 10^6)^2 = 1.63047 \times 10^{12}$ and taking logarithms results in the following two equations in two unknowns:

$$\mu + \tfrac{1}{2}\sigma^2 = 13.99863, \quad 2\mu + 2\sigma^2 = 28.11989.$$

From this $\mu = 13.93731$ and $\sigma^2 = 0.1226361$. Then

$$
\begin{aligned}
\Pr(S > 1,681,337) &= 1 - \Phi\left[\frac{\ln 1,681,337 - 13.93731}{(0.1226361)^{0.5}}\right]\\
&= 1 - \Phi(1.135913) = 0.128.
\end{aligned}
$$

The normal distribution provides a good approximation when $\mathrm{E}(N)$ is large. In particular, if N has the Poisson, binomial, or negative binomial distribu-tion, a version of the central limit theorem indicates that, as λ, m, or r, respectively, goes to infinity, the distribution of S becomes normal. In this example, $\mathrm{E}(N)$ is small so the distribution of S is likely to be skewed. In this case the lognormal distribution may provide a good approximation, although there is no theory to support this choice. □

Example 6.6 (Group dental insurance) *Under a group dental insurance plan covering employees and their families, the premium for each married employee is the same regardless of the number of family members. The insurance com-pany has compiled statistics showing that the annual cost (adjusted to current dollars) of dental care per person for the benefits provided by the plan has the distribution in Table 6.1 (given in units of 25 dollars).*

Furthermore, the distribution of the number of persons per insurance cer-tificate (that is, per employee) receiving dental care in any year has the dis-tribution given in Table 6.2.

Table 6.1 Loss distribution for Example 6.6

x	$f_X(x)$
1	0.150
2	0.200
3	0.250
4	0.125
5	0.075
6	0.050
7	0.050
8	0.050
9	0.025
10	0.025

Table 6.2 Frequency distribution for Example 6.6

n	p_n
0	0.05
1	0.10
2	0.15
3	0.20
4	0.25
5	0.15
6	0.06
7	0.03
8	0.01

The insurer is now in a position to calculate the distribution of the cost per year per married employee in the group. The cost per married employee is

$$f_S(x) = \sum_{n=0}^{8} p_n f_X^{*n}(x).$$

Determine the pf of S up to 525. Determine the mean and standard deviation of total payments per employee.

The distribution up to amounts of 525 is given in Table 6.3. To obtain $f_S(x)$, each row of the matrix of convolutions of $f_X(x)$ is multiplied by the probabilities from the row below the table and the products are summed.

The reader may wish to verify using (6.6) that the first two moments of the distribution $f_S(x)$ are

$$E(S) = 12.58, \quad \text{Var}(S) = 58.7464.$$

Table 6.3   Aggregate probabilities for Example 6.6

x	f_X^{*0}	f_X^{*1}	f_X^{*2}	f_X^{*3}	f_X^{*4}	f_X^{*5}	f_X^{*6}	f_X^{*7}	f_X^{*8}	$f_S(x)$
0	1	0	0	0	0	0	0	0	0	.05000
1	0	.150	0	0	0	0	0	0	0	.01500
2	0	.200	.02250	0	0	0	0	0	0	.02338
3	0	.250	.06000	.00338	0	0	0	0	0	.03468
4	0	.125	.11500	.01350	.00051	0	0	0	0	.03258
5	0	.075	.13750	.03488	.00270	.00008	0	0	0	.03579
6	0	.050	.13500	.06144	.00878	.00051	.00001	0	0	.03981
7	0	.050	.10750	.08569	.01999	.00198	.00009	.00000	0	.04356
8	0	.050	.08813	.09750	.03580	.00549	.00042	.00002	.00000	.04752
9	0	.025	.07875	.09841	.05266	.01194	.00136	.00008	.00000	.04903
10	0	.025	.07063	.09338	.06682	.02138	.00345	.00031	.00002	.05190
11	0	0	.06250	.08813	.07597	.03282	.00726	.00091	.00007	.05138
12	0	0	.04500	.08370	.08068	.04450	.01305	.00218	.00022	.05119
13	0	0	.03125	.07673	.08266	.05486	.02062	.00448	.00060	.05030
14	0	0	.01750	.06689	.08278	.06314	.02930	.00808	.00138	.04818
15	0	0	.01125	.05377	.08081	.06934	.03826	.01304	.00279	.04576
16	0	0	.00750	.04125	.07584	.07361	.04677	.01919	.00505	.04281
17	0	0	.00500	.03052	.06811	.07578	.05438	.02616	.00829	.03938
18	0	0	.00313	.02267	.05854	.07552	.06080	.03352	.01254	.03575
19	0	0	.00125	.01673	.04878	.07263	.06573	.04083	.01768	.03197
20	0	0	.00063	.01186	.03977	.06747	.06882	.04775	.02351	.02832
21	0	0	0	.00800	.03187	.06079	.06982	.05389	.02977	.02479
p_n	.05	.10	.15	.20	.25	.15	.06	.03	.01	

Hence the annual cost of the dental plan has mean $12.58 \times 25 = 314.50$ dollars and standard deviation 191.6155 dollars. (Why can't the calculations be done from Table 6.3?)   □

It is common for insurance to be offered in which a deductible is applied to the aggregate losses for the period. When the losses occur to a policyholder it is called insurance coverage and when the losses occur to an insurance company it is called reinsurance coverage. The latter version is a common method for an insurance company to protect itself against an adverse year (as opposed to protecting against a single, very large claim). More formally, we present the following definition.

Definition 6.7 *Insurance on the aggregate losses, subject to a deductible, is called* **stop-loss insurance.** *The expected cost of this insurance is called the* **net stop-loss premium** *and can be computed as* $E[(S - d)_+]$, *where d is the deductible and the notation* $(\cdot)_+$ *means to use the value in parentheses if it is positive but to use zero otherwise.*

For any aggregate distribution,

$$E[(S - d)_+] = \int_d^\infty [1 - F_S(x)]\, dx.$$

If the distribution is continuous, the net stop-loss premium can be computed directly from the definition as

$$E[(S-d)_+] = \int_d^\infty (x-d)f_S(x)\,dx.$$

Similarly, for discrete random variables,

$$E[(S-d)_+] = \sum_{x>d}(x-d)f_S(x).$$

Any time there is an interval with no aggregate probability, the following result may simplify calculations.

Theorem 6.8 *Suppose* $\Pr(a < S < b) = 0$. *Then, for* $a \le d \le b$,

$$E[(S-d)_+] = \frac{b-d}{b-a}E[(S-a)_+] + \frac{d-a}{b-a}E[(S-b)_+].$$

That is, the net stop-loss premium can be calculated via linear interpolation.

Proof: From the assumption, $F_S(x) = F_S(a)$, $a \le x < b$. Then,

$$
\begin{aligned}
E[(S-d)_+] &= \int_d^\infty [1 - F_S(x)]\,dx \\
&= \int_a^\infty [1 - F_S(x)]\,dx - \int_a^d [1 - F_S(x)]\,dx \\
&= E[(S-a)_+] - \int_a^d [1 - F_S(a)]\,dx \\
&= E[(S-a)_+] - (d-a)[1 - F_S(a)]. \quad (6.7)
\end{aligned}
$$

Then, by setting $d = b$ in (6.7),

$$E[(S-b)_+] = E[(S-a)_+] - (b-a)[1 - F_S(a)]$$

and therefore

$$1 - F_S(a) = \frac{E[(S-a)_+] - E[(S-b)_+]}{b-a}.$$

Substituting this in (6.7) produces the desired result. □

Further simplification is available in the discrete case, provided S places probability at equally spaced values.

Theorem 6.9 *Assume* $\Pr(S = kh) = f_k \ge 0$ *for some fixed* $h > 0$ *and* $k = 0, 1, \dots$ *and* $\Pr(S = x) = 0$ *for all other* x. *Then, provided* $d = jh$, *with* j *a non-negative integer*

$$E[(S-d)_+] = h \sum_{m=0}^\infty \{1 - F_S[(m+j)h]\}.$$

Proof:

$$
\begin{aligned}
\mathrm{E}[(S-d)_+] &= \sum_{x>d}(x-d)f_S(x) \\
&= \sum_{k=j}^{\infty}(kh-jh)f_k \\
&= h\sum_{k=j}^{\infty}\sum_{m=0}^{k-j-1} f_k \\
&= h\sum_{m=0}^{\infty}\sum_{k=m+j+1}^{\infty} f_k \\
&= h\sum_{m=0}^{\infty}\{1-F_S[(m+j)h]\}.
\end{aligned}
$$
□

In the discrete case with probability at equally spaced values, a simple recursion holds.

Corollary 6.10 *Under the conditions of Theorem 6.9,*

$$
\mathrm{E}\{[S-(j+1)h]_+\} = \mathrm{E}[(S-jh)_+] - h[1-F_S(jh)].
$$

This result is easy to use because, when $d = 0$, $\mathrm{E}[(S-0)_+] = \mathrm{E}(S) = \mathrm{E}(N)\mathrm{E}(X)$, which can be obtained directly from the frequency and severity distributions.

Example 6.11 (Example 6.6 continued) *The insurer is examining the effect of imposing an aggregate deductible per employee. Determine the reduction in the net premium as a result of imposing deductibles of 25, 30, 50, and 100 dollars.*

From Table 6.3, the cdf at 0, 25, 50, and 75 dollars has values 0.05, 0.065, 0.08838, and 0.12306. With $\mathrm{E}(S) = 25(12.58) = 314.5$ we have

$$
\begin{aligned}
\mathrm{E}[(S-25)_+] &= 314.5 - 25(1-0.05) = 290.75, \\
\mathrm{E}[(S-50)_+] &= 290.75 - 25(1-0.065) = 267.375, \\
\mathrm{E}[(S-75)_+] &= 267.375 - 25(1-0.08838) = 244.5845, \\
\mathrm{E}[(S-100)_+] &= 244.5845 - 25(1-0.12306) = 222.661.
\end{aligned}
$$

From Theorem 6.8, $\mathrm{E}[(S-30)_+] = \frac{20}{25}290.75 + \frac{5}{25}267.375 = 286.07$. When compared to the original premium of 314.5, the reductions are 23.75, 28.43, 47.125, and 91.839 for the four deductibles.   □

6.3.1   Exercises

6.4 From (6.5), show that the relationships between the moments in (6.6) hold.

6.5 When an individual is admitted to the hospital, the hospital charges have the following characteristics:

1.

Charges	Mean	Standard deviation
Room	1,000	500
Other	500	300

2. The covariance between an individual's room charges and other charges is 100,000.

An insurer issues a policy that reimburses 100% for room charges and 80% for other charges. The number of hospital admissions has a Poisson distribution with parameter 4. Determine the mean and standard deviation of the insurer's payout for the policy.

6.6 Aggregate claims have been modeled by a compound negative binomial distribution with parameters $r = 15$ and $\beta = 5$. The claim amounts are uniformly distributed on the interval $(0, 10)$. Using the normal approximation, determine the premium such that the probability that claims will exceed premium is 0.05.

6.7 Automobile drivers can be divided into three homogeneous classes. The number of claims for each driver follows a Poisson distribution with parameter λ. Determine the variance of the number of claims for a randomly selected driver, using the following data.

Class	Proportion of population	λ
1	0.25	5
2	0.25	3
3	0.50	2

6.8 Assume X_1, X_2, and X_3 are mutually independent loss random variables with probability functions as given in Table 6.4. Determine the pf of $S = X_1 + X_2 + X_3$.

6.9 Assume X_1, X_2, and X_3 are mutually independent random variables with probability functions as given in Table 6.5. If $S = X_1 + X_2 + X_3$ and $f_S(5) = 0.06$, determine p.

Table 6.4 Distributions for Exercise 6.8

x	$f_1(x)$	$f_2(x)$	$f_3(x)$
0	0.90	0.50	0.25
1	0.10	0.30	0.25
2	0.00	0.20	0.25
3	0.00	0.00	0.25

Table 6.5 Distributions for Exercise 6.9

x	$f_1(x)$	$f_2(x)$	$f_3(x)$
0	p	0.6	0.25
1	$1-p$	0.2	0.25
2	0	0.1	0.25
3	0	0.1	0.25

6.10 Consider the following information about AIDS patients.

1. The conditional distribution of an individual's medical care costs, given that the individual does not have AIDS, has mean 1,000 and variance 250,000.

2. The conditional distribution of an individual's medical care costs, given that the individual does have AIDS, has mean 70,000 and variance 1,600,000.

3. The number of individuals with AIDS in a group of m randomly selected adults has a binomial distribution with parameters m and $q = 0.01$.

An insurance company determines premiums for a group as the mean plus10% of the standard deviation of the group's aggregate claims distribution. The premium for a group of 10 independent lives for which all individuals have been proven *not* to have AIDS is P. The premium for a group of 10 randomly selected adults is Q. Determine P/Q.

6.11 You have been asked by a city planner to analyze office cigarette smoking patterns. The planner has provided the information in Table 6.6 about the distribution of the number of cigarettes smoked during a workday.

The number of male employees in a randomly selected office of N employees has a binomial distribution with parameters N and 0.4. Determine the mean plus the standard deviation of the number of cigarettes smoked during a workday in a randomly selected office of eight employees.

6.12 For a certain group, aggregate claims are uniformly distributed over $(0, 10)$. Insurer A proposes stop-loss coverage with a deductible of 6 for a

Table 6.6   Data for Exercise 6.11

	Male	Female
Mean	6	3
Variance	64	31

premium equal to the expected stop-loss claims. Insurer B proposes group coverage with a premium of 7 and a dividend (a premium refund) equal to the excess, if any, of $7k$ over claims. Calculate k such that the expected cost to the group is equal under both proposals.

6.13 For a group health contract, aggregate claims are assumed to have an exponential distribution where the mean of the distribution is estimated by the group underwriter. Aggregate stop-loss insurance for total claims in excess of 125% of the expected claims is provided by a gross premium that is twice the expected stop-loss claims. You have discovered an error in the underwriter's method of calculating expected claims. The underwriter's estimate is 90% of the correct estimate. Determine the actual percentage loading in the premium.

6.14 A random loss, X, has the following probability function. You are given that $E(X) = 4$ and $E[(X - d)_+] = 2$. Determine d.

x	$f(x)$
0	0.05
1	0.06
2	0.25
3	0.22
4	0.10
5	0.05
6	0.05
7	0.05
8	0.05
9	0.12

6.15 A reinsurer pays aggregate claim amounts in excess of d, and in return it receives a stop-loss premium $E[(S - d)_+]$. You are given $E[(S - 100)_+] = 15$, $E[(S - 120)_+] = 10$, and the probability that the aggregate claim amounts are greater than 80 and less than or equal to 120 is 0. Determine the probability that the aggregate claim amounts are less than or equal to 80.

6.16 A loss random variable X has pdf $f(x) = \frac{1}{100}$, $0 < x < 100$. Two policies can be purchased to alleviate the financial impact of the loss.

$$A = \begin{cases} 0, & x < 50k, \\ \dfrac{x}{k} - 50, & x \geq 50k, \end{cases}$$

and

$$B = kx, \quad 0 < x < 100,$$

where A and B are the amounts paid when the loss is x. Both policies have the same net premium, that is, $E(A) = E(B)$. Determine k.

6.17 For a nursing home insurance policy, you are given that the average length of stay is 440 days and 30% of the stays are terminated in the first 30 days. These terminations are distributed uniformly during that period. The policy pays 20 per day for the first 30 days and 100 per day thereafter. Determine the expected benefits payable for a single stay.

6.18 An insurance portfolio produces N claims, where

n	$\Pr(N = n)$
0	0.5
1	0.4
3	0.1

Individual claim amounts have the following distribution:

x	$f_X(x)$
1	0.9
10	0.1

Individual claim amounts and N are mutually independent. Calculate the probability that the ratio of aggregate claims to expected claims will exceed 3.0.

6.19 A company sells group travel-accident life insurance with m payable in the event of a covered individual's death in a travel accident. The gross premium for a group is set equal to the expected value plus the standard deviation of the group's aggregate claims. The standard premium is based on the following assumptions:

1. All individual claims within the group are mutually independent and

2. $m^2 q(1-q) = 2,500$, where q is the probability of death by travel accident for an individual.

In a certain group of 100 lives, the independence assumption fails because three specific individuals always travel together. If one dies in an accident, all three are assumed to die. Determine the difference between this group's premium and the standard premium.

6.20 A life insurance company covers 16,000 lives for one-year term life insurance, as shown below.

Benefit amount	Number covered	Probability of claim
1	8,000	0.025
2	3,500	0.025
4	4,500	0.025

All claims are mutually independent. The insurance company's retention limit is 2 units per life. Reinsurance is purchased for 0.03 per unit. The probability that the insurance company's retained claims, S, plus cost of reinsurance will exceed 1,000 is $\Pr \left[\dfrac{S - \mathrm{E}(S)}{\sqrt{\mathrm{Var}(S)}} > K \right]$. Determine K using a normal approximation.

6.21 The probability density function of individual losses Y is

$$f(y) = \begin{cases} 0.02 \left(1 - \dfrac{y}{100}\right), & 0 < y < 100, \\ 0, & \text{elsewhere.} \end{cases}$$

The amount paid, Z, is 80% of that portion of the loss that exceeds a deductible of 10. Determine $\mathrm{E}(Z)$.

6.22 An individual loss distribution is normal with $\mu = 100$ and $\sigma^2 = 9$. The distribution for the number of claims, N, is given in Table 6.7. Determine the probability that aggregate claims exceed 100.

Table 6.7   Distribution for Exercise 6.22

n	$\Pr(N = n)$
0	0.5
1	0.2
2	0.2
3	0.1

Table 6.8   Distribution for Exercise 6.23

n	$f(n)$
0	1/16
1	1/4
2	3/8
3	1/4
4	1/16

6.23 An employer self-insures a life insurance program with the following characteristics:

1. Given that a claim has occurred, the claim amount is 2,000 with probability 0.4 and 3,000 with probability 0.6,

2. The number of claims has the distribution given in Table 6.8.

The employer purchases aggregate stop-loss coverage that limits the employer's annual claims cost to 5,000. The aggregate stop-loss coverage costs 1,472. Determine the employer's expected annual cost of the program, including the cost of stop-loss coverage.

6.24 The probability that an individual admitted to the hospital will stay k days or less is $1-0.8^k$ for $k = 0, 1, 2, \ldots$. A hospital indemnity policy provides a fixed amount per day for the 4th day through the 10th day (that is, for a maximum of 7 days). Determine the percentage increase in the expected cost per admission if the maximum number of days paid is increased from 7 to 14.

6.25 The probability density function of aggregate claims, S, is given by $f_S(x) = 3x^{-4}$, $x \geq 1$. The relative loading θ and the value λ are selected so that
$$\Pr[S \leq (1+\theta)\mathrm{E}(S)] = \Pr\left[S \leq \mathrm{E}(S) + \lambda\sqrt{\mathrm{Var}(S)}\right] = 0.90.$$

Calculate λ and θ.

6.4   ANALYTIC RESULTS

For most choices of distributions of N and the X_js, the compound distributional values can only be obtained numerically. Subsequent sections in this chapter are devoted to such numerical procedures.

However, for certain combinations of choices, simple analytic results are available, thus reducing the computational problems considerably.

Example 6.12 (Compound geometric–exponential) *Suppose $X_1, X_2, \ldots$ are i.i.d. with common exponential distribution with mean θ and mgf $M_X(z) = (1-\theta z)^{-1}$. Suppose that N has a geometric distribution with parameter β and pgf $P_N(z) = [1 - \beta(z-1)]^{-1}$ (see Appendix B). Determine the distribution of S.*

The mgf of S is

$$
\begin{aligned}
M_S(z) &= P_N[M_X(z)] \\
&= \{1 - \beta[(1-\theta z)^{-1} - 1]\}^{-1} \\
&= \frac{1}{1+\beta}1 + \frac{\beta}{1+\beta}[1 - \theta(1+\beta)z]^{-1}
\end{aligned}
$$

with a bit of algebra.

This is a two-point mixture of a degenerate distribution with probability 1 at zero and an exponential distribution with mean $\theta(1 + \beta)$. Hence, $\Pr(S = 0) = (1 + \beta)^{-1}$, and for $x > 0$, S has pdf

$$
f_S(x) = \frac{\beta}{\theta(1 + \beta)^2} \exp\left[-\frac{x}{\theta(1 + \beta)}\right].
$$

It has a point mass of $(1+\beta)^{-1}$ at zero and an exponentially decaying density over the positive axis. Its cdf can be written as

$$
F_S(x) = 1 - \frac{\beta}{1 + \beta} \exp\left[-\frac{x}{\theta(1 + \beta)}\right], \quad x \geq 0.
$$

It has a jump at zero and is continuous otherwise. This example will arise again in Chapter 8 in connection with ruin theory.   □

Example 6.13 (Exponential severities) *Determine the cdf of S for any compound distribution with exponential severities.*

The mgf of the sum of n independent exponential random variables each with mean θ is

$$
M_{X_1+X_2+\cdots+X_n}(z) = (1 - \theta z)^{-n},
$$

which is the mgf of the gamma distribution with cdf

$$
F_X^{*n}(x) = \Gamma\left(n; \frac{x}{\theta}\right)
$$

(see Appendix A). For integer values of α, the values of $\Gamma(\alpha; x)$ can be calculated exactly (see Appendix A for the derivation) as

$$
\Gamma(n; x) = 1 - \sum_{j=0}^{n-1} \frac{x^j e^{-x}}{j!}, \quad n = 1, 2, 3, \ldots . \tag{6.8}
$$

From (6.3)

$$F_S(x) = p_0 + \sum_{n=1}^{\infty} p_n \Gamma\left(n; \frac{x}{\theta}\right).$$

Substituting in (6.8) yields

$$F_S(x) = 1 - \sum_{n=1}^{\infty} p_n \sum_{j=0}^{n-1} \frac{(x/\theta)^j e^{-x/\theta}}{j!}, \qquad x \geq 0. \tag{6.9}$$

Interchanging the order of summation yields

$$\begin{aligned}
F_S(x) &= 1 - e^{-x/\theta} \sum_{j=0}^{\infty} \frac{(x/\theta)^j}{j!} \sum_{n=j+1}^{\infty} p_n \\
&= 1 - e^{-x/\theta} \sum_{j=0}^{\infty} \bar{P}_j \frac{(x/\theta)^j}{j!}, \qquad x \geq 0,
\end{aligned}$$

where $\bar{P}_j = \sum_{n=j+1}^{\infty} p_n$ for $j = 0, 1, \ldots$. $\qquad\square$

The approach of Example 6.13 may be extended to the larger class of mixed Erlang severity distributions, as shown in Exercise 6.35.

For frequency distributions which assign positive probability to all nonnegative integers, (6.9) can be evaluated by taking sufficient terms in the first summation. For distributions for which $\Pr(N > n^*) = 0$, the first summation becomes finite. For example, for the binomial frequency distribution, (6.9) becomes

$$F_S(x) = 1 - \sum_{n=1}^{m} \binom{m}{n} q^n (1-q)^{m-n} \sum_{j=0}^{n-1} \frac{(x/\theta)^j e^{-x/\theta}}{j!}. \tag{6.10}$$

Example 6.14 (Compound negative binomial–exponential) *Determine the distribution of S when the frequency distribution is negative binomial with an integer value for the parameter r and the severity distribution is exponential.*

The mgf of S is

$$\begin{aligned}
M_S(z) &= P_N[M_X(z)] \\
&= P_N[(1-\theta z)^{-1}] \\
&= \{1 - \beta[(1-\theta z)^{-1} - 1]\}^{-r}.
\end{aligned}$$

With a bit of algebra, this can be rewritten as

$$M_S(z) = \left(1 + \frac{\beta}{1+\beta}\{[1 - \theta(1+\beta)z]^{-1} - 1\}\right)^r$$

which is of the form

$$M_S(z) = P_N^*[M_X^*(z)]$$

where

$$P_N^*(z) = \left[1 + \frac{\beta}{1+\beta}(z-1)\right]^r,$$

the pgf of the binomial distribution with parameters r and $\beta/(1+\beta)$, and $M_X^*(z)$ is the mgf of the exponential distribution with mean $\theta(1+\beta)$.

This transformation reduces the computation of the distribution function to the finite sum of the form of (6.10), that is,

$$
\begin{aligned}
F_S(x) \;=\; & 1 - \sum_{n=1}^{r} \binom{r}{n}\left(\frac{\beta}{1+\beta}\right)^n\left(\frac{1}{1+\beta}\right)^{r-n} \\
& \times \sum_{j=0}^{n-1} \frac{[x\theta^{-1}(1+\beta)^{-1}]^j e^{-x\theta^{-1}(1+\beta)^{-1}}}{j!}.
\end{aligned}
$$

□

Example 6.15 (Severity distributions closed under convolution) *A distribution is said to be **closed under convolution** if adding i.i.d. members of a family produces another member of that family. Further assume that adding n members of a family produces a member with all but one parameter unchanged and the remaining parameter is multiplied by n. Determine the distribution of S when the severity distribution has this property.*

The condition means that, if $f_X(x; a)$ is the pf of each X_j, then the pf of $X_1 + X_2 + \cdots + X_n$ is $f_X(x; na)$. This means that

$$
\begin{aligned}
f_S(x) \;&=\; \sum_{n=1}^{\infty} p_n f_X^{*n}(x; a) \\
&=\; \sum_{n=1}^{\infty} p_n f_X(x; na),
\end{aligned}
$$

eliminating the need to carry out evaluation of the convolution. Severity distributions that are closed under convolution include the gamma and inverse Gaussian distributions. See Exercise 6.26.

□

6.4.1 Exercises

6.26 The following questions concern closure under convolution.

(a) Show that the gamma and inverse Gaussian distributions are closed under convolution. Show that the gamma distribution has the additional property mentioned in Example 6.15.

(b) Discrete distributions can also be used as severity distributions. Which of the distributions in Appendix B are closed under convolution? How can this information be used in simplifying calculation of compound probabilities of the form (4.20)?

6.27 A compound negative binomial distribution has parameters $\beta = 1$, $r = 2$, and severity distribution $\{f_X(x); \ x = 0, 1, 2, \ldots\}$. How do the parameters of the distribution change if the severity distribution is $\{g_X(x) = f_X(x)/[1 - f_X(0)]; \ x = 1, 2, \ldots\}$ but the aggregate claims distribution remains unchanged?

6.28 Consider the compound logarithmic distribution with exponential severity distribution.

(a) Show that the density of aggregate losses may be expressed as

$$f_S(x) = \frac{1}{\ln(1 + \beta)} \sum_{n=1}^{\infty} \frac{1}{n!} \left[\frac{\beta}{\theta(1 + \beta)} \right]^n x^{n-1} e^{-x/\theta}.$$

(b) Reduce this to

$$f_S(x) = \frac{\exp\{-x/[\theta(1 + \beta)]\} - \exp(-x/\theta)}{x \ln(1 + \beta)}.$$

6.29 An insurance policy reimburses aggregate incurred expenses at the rate of 80% of the first 1,000 in excess of 100, 90% of the next 1,000, and 100% thereafter. Express the expected cost of this coverage in terms of $R_d = \mathrm{E}[(S - d)_+]$ for different values of d.

6.30 The number of accidents incurred by an insured driver in a single year has a Poisson distribution with parameter $\lambda = 2$. If an accident occurs, the probability that the damage amount exceeds the deductible is 0.25. The number of claims and the damage amounts are independent. What is the probability that there will be no damages exceeding the deductible in a single year?

6.31 The aggregate loss distribution is modeled by an insurance company using an exponential distribution. However, the mean is uncertain. The company uses a uniform distribution (2,000,000, 4,000,000) to express its view of what the mean should be. Determine the expected aggregate losses.

6.32 A group hospital indemnity policy provides benefits at a continuous rate of 100 per day of hospital confinement for a maximum of 30 days. Benefits for partial days of confinement are prorated. The length of hospital confinement in days, T, has the following continuance (survival) function for $0 \le t \le 30$:

$$
\Pr(T \ge t) = \begin{cases}
1 - 0.04t, & 0 \le t \le 10, \\
0.95 - 0.035t, & 10 < t \le 20, \\
0.65 - 0.02t, & 20 < t \le 30.
\end{cases}
$$

For a policy period, each member's probability of a single hospital admission is 0.1 and of more than one admission is 0. Determine the pure premium per member, ignoring the time value of money.

6.33 Medical and dental claims are assumed to be independent with compound Poisson distributions as follows:

Claim type	Claim amount distribution	λ
Medical claims	Uniform $(0, 1{,}000)$	2
Dental claims	Uniform $(0, 200)$	3

Let X be the amount of a given claim under a policy which covers both medical and dental claims. Determine $E[(X - 100)_+]$, the expected cost (in excess of 100) of any given claim.

6.34 For a certain insured, the distribution of aggregate claims is binomial with parameters $m = 12$ and $q = 0.25$. The insurer will pay a dividend, D, equal to the excess of 80% of the premium over claims, if positive. The premium is 5. Determine $E[D]$.

6.35 Consider a severity distribution which is a finite mixture of gamma distributions with integer shape parameters (such gamma distributions are called Erlang distributions), that is, which may be expressed as

$$
f_X(x) = \sum_{k=1}^{r} q_k \frac{\theta^{-k} x^{k-1} e^{-x/\theta}}{(k-1)!}, \quad x > 0.
$$

(a) Show that the moment generating function may be written as

$$
M_X(z) = Q\{(1 - \theta z)^{-1}\},
$$

where

$$
Q(z) = \sum_{k=1}^{r} q_k z^k
$$

is the pgf of the distribution $\{q_1, q_2, \ldots, q_r\}$. Thus interpret $f_X(x)$ as the pf of a compound distribution.

(b) Show that the mgf of S is

$$M_S(z) = C\{(1 - \theta z)^{-1}\},$$

where

$$C(z) = \sum_{k=0}^{\infty} c_k z^k = P_N\{Q(z)\}.$$

(c) Describe how the distribution $\{c_k;\ k = 0, 1, 2, \ldots\}$ may be calculated recursively if the number of claims distribution is a member of the $(a, b, 1)$ class (Section 4.6.6).

(d) Show that the distribution function of S is given by

$$
\begin{aligned}
F_S(x) &= 1 - \sum_{n=1}^{\infty} c_n \sum_{j=0}^{n-1} \frac{(x/\theta)^j e^{-x/\theta}}{j!} \\
&= 1 - e^{-x/\theta} \sum_{j=0}^{\infty} \bar{C}_j \frac{(x/\theta)^j}{j!}, \quad x \geq 0,
\end{aligned}
$$

where $\bar{C}_j = \sum_{n=j+1}^{\infty} c_n$.

6.5 COMPUTING THE AGGREGATE CLAIMS DISTRIBUTION

The computation of the compound distribution function

$$F_S(x) = \sum_{n=0}^{\infty} p_n F_X^{*n}(x) \tag{6.11}$$

or the corresponding probability (density) function is generally not an easy task, even in the simplest of cases. In this section we discuss a number of approaches to numerical evaluation of (6.11) for specific choices of the frequency and severity distributions as well as for arbitrary choices of one or both distributions.

One approach is to use an **approximating distribution** to avoid direct calculation of (6.11). This approach was used in Example 6.5 where the method of moments was used to estimate the parameters of the approximating distribution. The advantage of this method is that it is simple and easy to apply. However, the disadvantages are significant. First, there is no way of knowing how good the approximation is. Choosing different approximating distributions can result in very different results, particularly in the right-hand tail of the distribution. Of course, the approximation should improve as more moments are used; but after four moments, one quickly runs out of distributions!

The approximating distribution may also fail to accommodate special features of the true distribution. For example, when the loss distribution is of the continuous type and there is a maximum possible claim (for example, when there is a policy limit), the severity distribution may have a point mass ("atom" or "spike") at the maximum. The true aggregate claims distribution is of the mixed type with spikes at integral multiples of the maximum corresponding to $1, 2, 3, \ldots$ claims at the maximum. These spikes, if large, can have a significant effect on the probabilities near such multiples. These jumps in the aggregate claims distribution function cannot be replicated by a smooth approximating distribution.

The second method to evaluate (6.11) or the corresponding pdf is **direct calculation**. The most difficult (or computer intensive) part is the evaluation of the n-fold convolutions of the severity distribution for $n = 2, 3, 4, \ldots$. In some situations, there is an analytic form—for example, when the severity distribution is closed under convolution, as defined in Example 6.15 and illustrated in Examples 6.12–6.14. Otherwise the convolutions need to be evaluated numerically using

$$F_X^{*k}(x) = \int_{-\infty}^{\infty} F_X^{*(k-1)}(x - y) \, dF_X(y). \tag{6.12}$$

When the losses are limited to nonnegative values (as is usually the case), the range of integration becomes finite, reducing (6.12) to

$$F_X^{*k}(x) = \int_{0-}^{x} F_X^{*(k-1)}(x - y) \, dF_X(y). \tag{6.13}$$

These integrals are written in Lebesgue–Stieltjes form because of possible jumps in the cdf $F_X(x)$ at zero and at other points.[1] Numerical evaluation of (6.13) requires numerical integration methods. Because of the first term inside the integral, (6.13) needs to be evaluated for all possible values of x. This quickly becomes technically overpowering!

A simple way to avoid these technical problems is to replace the severity distribution by a discrete distribution defined at multiples $0, 1, 2 \ldots$ of some convenient monetary unit such as 1,000. This reduces (6.13) to (in terms of the new monetary unit)

$$F_X^{*k}(x) = \sum_{y=0}^{x} F_X^{*(k-1)}(x - y) f_X(y).$$

The corresponding pf is

$$f_X^{*k}(x) = \sum_{y=0}^{x} f_X^{*(k-1)}(x - y) f_X(y).$$

---

[1] Without going into the formal definition of the Lebesgue–Stieltjes integral, it suffices to interpret $\int g(y) \, dF_X(y)$ as to be evaluated by integrating $g(y) f_X(y)$ over those y values for which X has a continuous distribution and then adding $g(y_i) \Pr(X = y_i)$ over those points where $\Pr(X = y_i) > 0$. This allows for a single notation to be used for continuous, discrete, and mixed random variables.

In practice, the monetary unit can be made sufficiently small to accommodate spikes at maximum insurance amounts. One needs only the spike to be a multiple of the monetary unit to have it located at exactly the right point. As the monetary unit of measurement becomes small, the discrete distribution function needs to approach the true distribution function. The simplest approach is to round all amounts to the nearest multiple of the monetary unit; for example, round all losses or claims to the nearest 1,000. More sophisticated methods will be discussed later in this chapter.

When the severity distribution is defined on nonnegative integers $0, 1, 2, \ldots$, calculating $f_X^{*k}(x)$ for integral x requires $x + 1$ multiplications. Then carrying out these calculations for all possible values of k and x up to n requires a number of multiplications that are of order n^3, written as $O(n^3)$, to obtain the distribution of (6.11) for $x = 0$ to $x = n$. When the maximum value, n, for which the aggregate claims distribution is calculated is large, the number of computations quickly becomes prohibitive, even for fast computers. For example, in real applications n can easily be as large as 1,000. This requires about 10^9 multiplications. Further, if $\Pr(X = 0) > 0$, an infinite number of calculations are required to obtain any single probability. This is because $F_X^{*n}(x) > 0$ for all n and all x and so the sum in (6.11) contains an infinite number of terms. When $\Pr(X = 0) = 0$, we have $F_X^{*n}(x) = 0$ for $n > x$ and so (6.11) will have no more than $x + 1$ positive terms. Table 6.3 provides an example of this latter case.

Alternative methods to more quickly evaluate the aggregate claims distribution are discussed in the next two sections. The first such method, **the recursive method**, reduces the number of computations discussed above to $O(n^2)$, which is a considerable savings in computer time, a reduction of about 99.9% when $n = 1,000$ compared to direct calculation. However, the method is limited to certain frequency distributions. Fortunately, it includes all frequency distributions discussed in Section 4.6 and Appendix B.

The second such method, **the inversion method**, numerically inverts a transform, such as the characteristic function, using a general or specialized inversion software package. Two versions of this method are discussed in this chapter.

6.6 THE RECURSIVE METHOD

Suppose that the severity distribution $f_X(x)$ is defined on $0, 1, 2, \ldots, m$ representing multiples of some convenient monetary unit. The number m represents the largest possible payment and could be infinite. Further, suppose that the frequency distribution, p_k, is a member of the $(a, b, 1)$ class and therefore satisfies

$$p_k = \left(a + \frac{b}{k} \right) p_{k-1}, \quad k = 2, 3, 4, \ldots .$$

Then the following result holds.

Theorem 6.16 *For the* $(a, b, 1)$ *class,*

$$f_S(x) = \frac{[p_1 - (a + b)p_0]f_X(x) + \sum_{y=1}^{x \wedge m} (a + by/x)f_X(y)f_S(x - y)}{1 - af_X(0)}, \quad (6.14)$$

noting that $x \wedge m$ *is notation for* $\min(x, m)$.

Proof: This result is identical to Theorem 4.49 with appropriate substitution of notation and recognition that the argument of $f_X(x)$ cannot exceed m. $\square$

Corollary 6.17 *For the* $(a, b, 0)$ *class, the result* (6.14) *reduces to*

$$f_S(x) = \frac{\sum_{y=1}^{x \wedge m} (a + by/x) f_X(y)f_S(x - y)}{1 - af_X(0)}. \quad (6.15)$$

Note that when the severity distribution has no probability at zero, the denominator of (6.14) and (6.15) equals 1. Further, in the case of the Poisson distribution, (6.15) reduces to

$$f_S(x) = \frac{\lambda}{x} \sum_{y=1}^{x \wedge m} yf_X(y)f_S(x - y), \quad x = 1, 2, \ldots. \quad (6.16)$$

The starting value of the recursive schemes (6.14) and (6.15) is $f_S(0) = P_N[f_X(0)]$ following Theorem 4.51 with an appropriate change of notation. In the case of the Poisson distribution we have

$$f_S(0) = e^{-\lambda[1 - f_X(0)]}.$$

Starting values for other frequency distributions are found in Appendix D.

6.6.1   Applications to compound frequency models

When the frequency distribution can be represented as a compound distribution (e.g., Neyman Type A, Poisson–inverse Gaussian) involving only distributions from the $(a, b, 0)$ or $(a, b, 1)$ classes, the recursive formula (6.14) can be used two or more times to obtain the aggregate claims distribution. If the frequency distribution can be written as

$$P_N(z) = P_1[P_2(z)],$$

then the aggregate claims distribution has pgf

$$\begin{aligned} P_S(z) &= P_N[P_X(z)] \\ &= P_1\{P_2[P_X(z)]\}, \end{aligned}$$

which can be rewritten as

$$P_S(z) = P_1[P_{S_1}(z)] \quad (6.17)$$

where

$$P_{S_1}(z) = P_2[P_X(z)]. \tag{6.18}$$

Now (6.18) is the same form as an aggregate claims distribution. Thus, if $P_2(z)$ is in the $(a, b, 0)$ or $(a, b, 1)$ class, the distribution of S_1 can be calculated using (6.14). The resulting distribution is the "severity" distribution in (6.18). Thus, a second application of (6.14) to (6.17) results in the distribution of S.

The following example illustrates the use of this algorithm.

Example 6.18 *The number of claims has a Poisson–ETNB distribution with Poisson parameter* $\lambda = 2$ *and ETNB parameters* $\beta = 3$ *and* $r = 0.2$. *The claim size distribution has probabilities* 0.3, 0.5, *and* 0.2 *at* 0, 10, *and* 20, *respectively. Determine the total claims distribution recursively.*

In the above terminology, N has pgf $P_N(z) = P_1[P_2(z)]$, where $P_1(z)$ and $P_2(z)$ are the Poisson and ETNB pgfs, respectively. Then the total dollars of claims has pgf $P_S(z) = P_1[P_{S_1}(z)]$, where $P_{S_1}(z) = P_2[P_X(z)]$ is a compound ETNB pgf. We will first compute the distribution of S_1. We have (in monetary units of 10) $f_X(0) = 0.3$, $f_X(1) = 0.5$, and $f_X(2) = 0.2$. In order to use the compound ETNB recursion, we start with

$$
\begin{aligned}
f_{S_1}(0) &= P_2[f_X(0)] \\
&= \frac{\{1 + \beta[1 - f_X(0)]\}^{-r} - (1 + \beta)^{-r}}{1 - (1 + \beta)^{-r}} \\
&= \frac{\{1 + 3(1 - 0.3)\}^{-0.2} - (1 + 3)^{-0.2}}{1 - (1 + 3)^{-0.2}} \\
&= 0.16369.
\end{aligned}
$$

The remaining values of $f_{S_1}(x)$ may be obtained from (6.14) with S replaced by S_1. In this case we have $a = 3/(1+3) = 0.75$, $b = (0.2-1)a = -0.6$, $p_0 = 0$ and $p_1 = (0.2)(3)/[(1+3)^{0.2+1} - (1+3)] = 0.46947$. Then (6.14) becomes

$$
\begin{aligned}
f_{S_1}(x) &= \frac{[0.46947 - (0.75 - 0.6)(0)]\, f_X(x) + \sum_{y=1}^{x}(0.75 - 0.6y/x)\, f_X(y) f_{S_1}(x - y)}{1 - (0.75)(0.3)} \\
&= 0.60577 f_X(x) + 1.29032 \sum_{y=1}^{x}\left(0.75 - 0.6\frac{y}{x}\right) f_X(y) f_{S_1}(x - y).
\end{aligned}
$$

The first few probabilities are

$$
\begin{aligned}
f_{S_1}(1) &= 0.60577(0.5) + 1.29032\left[0.75 - 0.6\left(\tfrac{1}{1}\right)\right](0.5)(0.16369) \\
&= 0.31873, \\
f_{S_1}(2) &= 0.60577(0.2) + 1.29032\left\{\left[0.75 - 0.6\left(\tfrac{1}{2}\right)\right](0.5)(0.31873)\right. \\
&\quad \left. + \left[0.75 - 0.6\left(\tfrac{2}{2}\right)\right](0.2)(0.16369)\right\} = 0.22002, \\
f_{S_1}(3) &= 1.29032\left\{\left[0.75 - 0.6\left(\tfrac{1}{3}\right)\right](0.5)(0.22002)\right. \\
&\quad \left. + \left[0.75 - 0.6\left(\tfrac{2}{3}\right)\right](0.2)(0.31873)\right\} = 0.10686, \\
f_{S_1}(4) &= 1.29032\left\{\left[0.75 - 0.6\left(\tfrac{1}{4}\right)\right](0.5)(0.10686)\right. \\
&\quad \left. + \left[0.75 - 0.6\left(\tfrac{2}{4}\right)\right](0.2)(0.22002)\right\} = 0.06692.
\end{aligned}
$$

We now turn to evaluation of the distribution of S with compound Poisson pgf

$$
P_S(z) = P_1\left[P_{S_1}(z)\right] = e^{\lambda\left[P_{S_1}(z)-1\right]}.
$$

Thus the distribution

$$
\{f_{S_1}(x); x = 0, 1, 2, \ldots\}
$$

becomes the "secondary" or "claim size" distribution in an application of the compound Poisson recursive formula. Therefore,

$$
f_S(0) = P_S(0) = e^{\lambda\left[P_{S_1}(0)-1\right]} = e^{\lambda\left[f_{S_1}(0)-1\right]} = e^{2(0.16369-1)} = 0.18775.
$$

The remaining probabilities may be found from the recursive formula

$$
f_S(x) = \frac{2}{x}\sum_{y=1}^{x} y f_{S_1}(y) f_S(x-y), \quad x = 1, 2, \ldots .
$$

The first few probabilities are

$$
\begin{aligned}
f_S(1) &= 2\left(\tfrac{1}{1}\right)(0.31873)(0.18775) = 0.11968, \\
f_S(2) &= 2\left(\tfrac{1}{2}\right)(0.31873)(0.11968) + 2\left(\tfrac{2}{2}\right)(0.22002)(0.18775) = 0.12076, \\
f_S(3) &= 2\left(\tfrac{1}{3}\right)(0.31873)(0.12076) + 2\left(\tfrac{2}{3}\right)(0.22002)(0.11968) \\
&\quad + 2\left(\tfrac{3}{3}\right)(0.10686)(0.18775) = 0.10090, \\
f_S(4) &= 2\left(\tfrac{1}{4}\right)(0.31873)(0.10090) + 2\left(\tfrac{2}{4}\right)(0.22002)(0.12076) \\
&\quad + 2\left(\tfrac{3}{4}\right)(0.10686)(0.11968) + 2\left(\tfrac{4}{4}\right)(0.06692)(0.18775) \\
&= 0.08696.
\end{aligned}
$$

$\square$

This simple idea can be extended to higher levels of compounding by repeatedly applying the same concepts. The computer time required to carry out two applications will be about twice that of one application of (6.14).

However, the total number of computations is still of order $O(x^2)$ rather than $O(x^3)$ as in the direct method.

When the severity distribution has a maximum possible value at m, the computations are speeded up even more because the sum in (6.14) will be restricted to at most m nonzero terms. In this case, then, the computations can be considered to be of order $O(x)$.

6.6.2   Underflow/overflow problems

The recursion (6.14) starts with the calculated value of $P(S = 0) = P_N[f_X(0)]$. For large insurance portfolios, this probability is very small, sometimes smaller than the smallest number that can be represented on the computer. When this occurs, this initial value is represented on the computer as zero and the recursion (6.14) fails. This problem can be overcome in several different ways (see Panjer and Willmot [105]). One of the easiest ways is to start with an arbitrary set of values for $f_S(0), f_S(1), \ldots, f_S(k)$ such as $(0, 0, 0, \ldots, 0, 1)$, where k is sufficiently far to the left in the distribution so that $F_S(k)$ is still negligible. Setting k to a point that lies six standard deviations to the left of the mean is usually sufficient. Recursion (6.14) is used to generate values of the distribution with this set of starting values until the values are consistently less than $f_S(k)$. The "probabilities" are then summed and divided by the sum so that the "true" probabilities add to 1. Trial and error will dictate how small k should be for a particular problem.

Another method to obtain probabilities when the starting value is too small is to carry out the calculations for a subset of the portfolio. For example, for the Poisson distribution with mean λ, find a value of $\lambda^* = \lambda/2^n$ so that the probability at zero is representable on the computer when λ^* is used as the Poisson mean. Equation (6.14) is now used to obtain the aggregate claims distribution when λ^* is used as the Poisson mean. If $P_*(z)$ is the pgf of the aggregate claims using Poisson mean λ^*, then $P_S(z) = [P_*(z)]^{2^n}$. Hence one can obtain successively the distributions with pgfs $[P_*(z)]^2$, $[P_*(z)]^4$, $[P_*(z)]^8, \ldots, [P_*(z)]^{2^n}$ by convoluting the result at each stage with itself. This requires an additional n convolutions in carrying out the calculations but involves no approximations. This procedure can be carried out for any frequency distributions that are closed under convolution. For the negative binomial distribution, the analogous procedure starts with $r^* = r/2^n$. For the binomial distribution, the parameter m must be integer valued. A slight modification can be used. Let $m^* = \lfloor m/2^n \rfloor$ when $\lfloor \cdot \rfloor$ indicates the *integer part of* function. When the n convolutions are carried out, one still needs to carry out the calculations using (6.14) for parameter $m - m^*2^n$. This result is then convoluted with the result of the n convolutions. For compound frequency distributions, only the primary distribution needs to be closed under convolution.

6.6.3   Numerical stability

Any recursive formula requires accurate computation of values because each such value will be used in computing subsequent values. Recursive schemes suffer the risk of errors propagating through all subsequent values and potentially blowing up. In the recursive formula (6.14), errors are introduced through rounding or truncation at each stage because computers represent numbers with a finite number of significant digits. The question about stability is, *"How fast do the errors in the calculations grow as the computed values are used in successive computations?"*

The question of error propagation in recursive formulas has been a subject of study of numerical analysts. This work has been extended by Panjer and Wang [104] to study the recursive formula (6.14). The analysis is quite complicated and well beyond the scope of this book. However, some general conclusions can be made here.

Errors are introduced in subsequent values through the summation

$$\sum_{y=1}^{x}\left(a+\frac{by}{x}\right)f_X(y)f_S(x-y)$$

in recursion (6.14). In the extreme right-hand tail of the distribution of S, this sum is positive (or at least nonnegative), and subsequent values of the sum will be decreasing. The sum will stay positive, even with rounding errors, when each of the three factors in each term in the sum is positive. In this case, the recursive formula is stable, producing relative errors that do not grow fast. For the Poisson and negative binomial based distributions, the factors in each term are always positive.

On the other hand, for the binomial distribution, the sum can have negative terms because a is negative, b is positive, and y/x is a positive function not exceeding 1. In this case, the negative terms can cause the successive values to blow up with alternating signs. When this occurs, the nonsensical results are immediately obvious. Although this does not happen frequently in practice, the reader should be aware of this possibility in models based on the binomial distribution.

6.6.4   Continuous severity

The recursive method has been developed for discrete severity distributions, while it is customary to use continuous distributions for severity. In the case of continuous severities, the analog of the recursion (6.14) is an integral equation, the solution of which is the aggregate claims distribution.

Theorem 6.19 *For the $(a, b, 1)$ class of frequency distributions and any continuous severity distribution with probability on the positive real line, the fol-*

lowing integral equation holds:

$$f_S(x) = p_1 f_X(x) + \int_0^x \left(a + \frac{by}{x} \right) f_X(y) f_S(x-y)\, dy. \qquad (6.19)$$

The proof of this result is beyond the scope of this book. For a detailed proof, see Theorems 6.14.1 and 6.16.1 of Panjer and Willmot [106], along with the associated corollaries. They consider the more general (a, b, m) class of distributions, which allow for arbitrary modification of m initial values of the distribution. Note that the initial term is $p_1 f_X(x)$, not $[p_1 - (a+b)p_0] f_X(x)$ as in (6.14). Also, (6.19) holds for members of the $(a, b, 0)$ class as well.

Integral equations of the form (6.19) are Volterra integral equations of the second kind. Numerical solution of this type of integral equation has been studied in the text by Baker [10]. We will develop a method using a discrete approximation of the severity distribution in order to use the recursive method (6.14) and avoid the more complicated methods of Baker [10].

6.6.5 Constructing arithmetic distributions

In order to implement recursive methods, the easiest approach is to construct a discrete severity distribution on multiples of a convenient unit of measurement h, the **span**. Such a distribution is called arithmetic because it is defined on the nonnegative integers. In order to arithmetize a distribution, it is important to preserve the properties of the original distribution both locally through the range of the distribution and globally—that is, for the entire distribution. This should preserve the general shape of the distribution and at the same time preserve global quantities such as moments.

The methods suggested here apply to the discretization (arithmetization) of continuous, mixed, and nonarithmetic discrete distributions.

6.6.5.1 Method of rounding (mass dispersal) Let f_j denote the probability placed at jh, $j = 0, 1, 2, \ldots$. Then set[2]

$$
\begin{aligned}
f_0 &= \Pr\left(X < \frac{h}{2} \right) = F_X\left(\frac{h}{2} - 0 \right), \\
f_j &= \Pr\left(jh - \frac{h}{2} \le X < jh + \frac{h}{2} \right) \\
&= F_X\left(jh + \frac{h}{2} - 0 \right) - F_X\left(jh - \frac{h}{2} - 0 \right), \quad j = 1, 2, \ldots .
\end{aligned}
$$

This method splits the probability between $(j+1)h$ and jh and assigns it to $j+1$ and j. This, in effect, rounds all amounts to the nearest convenient monetary unit, h, the span of the distribution.

---

[2] The notation $F_X(x-0)$ indicates that discrete probability at x should not be included. For continuous distributions this will make no difference.

6.6.5.2 Method of local moment matching   In this method we construct an arithmetic distribution that matches p moments of the arithmetic and the true severity distributions. Consider an arbitrary interval of length ph, denoted by $[x_k, x_k + ph)$. We will locate point masses $m_0^k, m_1^k, \cdots, m_p^k$ at points x_k, $x_k + h, \cdots, x_k + ph$ so that the first p moments are preserved. The system of $p + 1$ equations reflecting these conditions is

$$\sum_{j=0}^{p} (x_k + jh)^r m_j^k = \int_{x_k-0}^{x_k+ph-0} x^r dF_X(x), \quad r = 0, 1, 2, \ldots, p, \tag{6.20}$$

where the notation "-0" at the limits of the integral indicates that discrete probability at x_k is to be included but discrete probability at $x_k + ph$ is to be excluded.

Arrange the intervals so that $x_{k+1} = x_k + ph$ and so the endpoints coincide. Then the point masses at the endpoints are added together. With $x_0 = 0$, the resulting discrete distribution has successive probabilities:

$$\begin{array}{llll} f_0 = m_0^0, & f_1 = m_1^0, & f_2 = m_2^0, \ldots, \\ f_p = m_p^0 + m_0^1, & f_{p+1} = m_1^1, & f_{p+2} = m_2^1, \ldots. \end{array} \tag{6.21}$$

By summing (6.20) for all possible values of k, with $x_0 = 0$, it is clear that the first p moments are preserved for the entire distribution and that the probabilities add to 1 exactly. It only remains to solve the system of equations (6.20).

Theorem 6.20 *The solution of* (6.20) *is*

$$m_j^k = \int_{x_k-0}^{x_k+ph-0} \prod_{i \neq j} \frac{x - x_k - ih}{(j-i)h} dF_X(x), \quad j = 0, 1, \ldots, p. \tag{6.22}$$

Proof: The Lagrange formula for collocation of a polynomial $f(y)$ at points $y_0, y_1, \ldots, y_n$ is

$$f(y) = \sum_{j=0}^{n} f(y_j) \prod_{i \neq j} \frac{y - y_i}{y_j - y_i}.$$

Applying this formula to the polynomial $f(y) = y^r$ over the points $x_k, x_k + h, \ldots, x_k + ph$ yields

$$x^r = \sum_{j=0}^{p} (x_k + jh)^r \prod_{i \neq j} \frac{x - x_k - ih}{(j-i)h}, \quad r = 0, 1, \ldots, p.$$

Integrating over the interval $[x_k, x_k + ph)$ with respect to the severity distribution results in

$$\int_{x_k-0}^{x_k+ph-0} x^r dF_X(x) = \sum_{j=0}^{p} (x_k + jh)^r m_j^k,$$

where m_j^k is given by (6.22). Hence, the solution (6.22) preserves the first p moments, as required.   □

Example 6.21 *Suppose X has the exponential distribution with pdf $f(x) = 0.1e^{-0.1x}$. Use a span of $h = 2$ to discretize this distribution by the method of rounding and by matching the first moment.*

For the method of rounding, the general formulas are

$$\begin{aligned} f_0 &= F(1) = 1 - e^{-0.1(1)} = 0.09516, \\ f_j &= F(2j+1) - F(2j-1) = e^{-0.1(2j-1)} - e^{-0.1(2j+1)}. \end{aligned}$$

The first few values are given in Table 6.9.

For matching the first moment we have $p = 1$ and $x_k = 2k$. The key equations become

$$\begin{aligned} m_0^k &= \int_{2k}^{2k+2} \frac{x - 2k - 2}{-2}(0.1)e^{-0.1x}dx = 5e^{-0.1(2k+2)} - 4e^{-0.1(2k)}, \\ m_1^k &= \int_{2k}^{2k+2} \frac{x - 2k}{2}(0.1)e^{-0.1x}dx = -6e^{-0.1(2k+2)} + 5e^{-0.1(2k)}, \end{aligned}$$

and then

$$\begin{aligned} f_0 &= m_0^0 = 5e^{-0.2} - 4 = 0.09365, \\ f_j &= m_1^{j-1} + m_0^j = 5e^{-0.1(2j-2)} - 10e^{-0.1(2j)} + 5e^{-0.1(2j+2)}. \end{aligned}$$

The first few values also are given in Table 6.9. A more direct solution for matching the first moment is provided in Exercise 6.36.   □

This method of local moment matching was introduced by Gerber and Jones [44] and Gerber[43] and further studied by Panjer and Lutek [103] for a variety of empirical and analytical severity distributions. In assessing the impact of errors on aggregate stop-loss net premiums (aggregate excess-of-loss pure premiums), Panjer and Lutek [103] found that two moments were usually sufficient and that adding a third moment requirement adds only marginally to the accuracy. Furthermore, the rounding method and the first-moment method ($p = 1$) had similar errors while the second-moment method ($p = 2$) provided significant improvement. The specific formulas for the method of rounding and the method of matching the first moment are given in Appendix E. A reason to favor matching zero or one moment is that the resulting probabilities will always be nonnegative. When matching two or more moments, this cannot be guaranteed.

The methods described here are qualitatively similar to numerical methods used to solve Volterra integral equations such as (6.19) developed in numerical analysis (see, for example, Baker [10]).

Table 6.9   Discretization of the exponential distribution by two methods

j	f_j rounding	f_j matching
0	0.09516	0.09365
1	0.16402	0.16429
2	0.13429	0.13451
3	0.10995	0.11013
4	0.09002	0.09017
5	0.07370	0.07382
6	0.06034	0.06044
7	0.04940	0.04948
8	0.04045	0.04051
9	0.03311	0.03317
10	0.02711	0.02716

6.6.6   Exercises

6.36 Show that the method of local moment matching with $k = 1$ (matching total probability and the mean) using (6.21) and (6.22) results in

$$f_0 = 1 - \frac{E[X \wedge h]}{h}$$

$$f_i = \frac{2E[X \wedge ih] - E[X \wedge (i-1)h] - E[X \wedge (i+1)h]}{h}, \quad i = 1, 2, \ldots,$$

and that $\{f_i; \ i = 0, 1, 2, \ldots\}$ forms a valid distribution with the same mean as the original severity distribution. Using the formula given here, verify the formula given in Example 6.21.

6.37 You are the agent for a baseball player who desires an incentive contract that will pay the amounts given in Table 6.10. The number of times at bat has a Poisson distribution with $k = 200$. The parameter x is determined so that the probability of the player earning at least 4,000,000 is 0.95. Determine the player's expected compensation.

Table 6.10   Data for Exercise 6.37

Type of hit	Probability of hit per time at bat	Compensation per hit
Single	0.14	x
Double	0.05	$2x$
Triple	0.02	$3x$
Home run	0.03	$4x$

6.38 A weighted average of two Poisson distributions

$$p_k = w \frac{e^{-\lambda_1} \lambda_1^k}{k!} + (1-w) \frac{e^{-\lambda_2} \lambda_2^k}{k!}$$

has been used by some authors e.g., Tröbliger [130] to treat drivers as either "good" or "bad" (see Example 4.64).

(a) Find the pgf $P_N(z)$ of the number of losses in terms of the two pgfs $P_1(z)$ and $P_2(z)$ of the number of losses of the two types of drivers.

(b) Let $f_X(x)$ denote a severity distribution defined on the nonnegative integers. How can (6.16) be used to compute the distribution of aggregate claims for the entire group?

(c) Can this be extended to other frequency distributions?

6.39 A compound Poisson aggregate loss model has five expected claims per year. The severity distribution is defined on positive multiples of 1,000. Given that $f_S(1) = e^{-5}$ and $f_S(2) = \frac{5}{2} e^{-5}$, determine $f_X(2)$.

6.40 For a compound Poisson distribution, $\lambda = 6$ and individual losses have pf $f_X(1) = f_X(2) = f_X(4) = \frac{1}{3}$. Some of the pf values for the aggregate distribution S are given in Table 6.11. Determine $f_S(6)$.

6.41 Consider the $(a, b, 0)$ class of frequency distributions and any severity distribution defined on the positive integers $\{1, 2, \ldots, M < \infty\}$, where M is the maximum possible single loss.

(a) Show that for the compound distribution the following backward recursion holds:

$$f_X(x) = \frac{f_S(x+M) - \sum_{y=1}^{M-1} \left(a + b \frac{M-y}{x+M} \right) f_X(M-y) f_S(x+y)}{\left(a + b \frac{M}{x+M} \right) f_X(M)}.$$

Table 6.11   Data for Exercise 6.40

x	$f_S(x)$
3	0.0132
4	0.0215
5	0.0271
6	$f_S(6)$
7	0.0410

(b) For the binomial (m, q) frequency distribution, how can the above formula be used to obtain the distribution of aggregate losses? See Panjer and Wang [104].

6.42 Aggregate claims are compound Poisson with $\lambda = 2$, $f_X(1) = \frac{1}{4}$, and $f_X(2) = \frac{3}{4}$. For a premium of 6 an insurer covers aggregate claims and agrees to pay a dividend (a refund of premium) equal to the excess, if any, of 75% of the premium over 100% of the claims. Determine the excess of premium over expected claims and dividends.

6.43 On a given day, a physician provides medical care to N_A adults and N_C children. Assume N_A and N_C have Poisson distributions with parameters 3 and 2, respectively. The distributions of length of care per patient are as follows:

	Adult	Child
1 hour	0.4	0.9
2 hour	0.6	0.1

Let N_A, N_C, and the lengths of care for all individuals be independent. The physician charges 200 per hour of patient care. Determine the probability that the office income on a given day is less than or equal to 800.

6.44 A group policyholder's aggregate claims, S, has a compound Poisson distribution with $\lambda = 1$ and all claim amounts equal to 2. The insurer pays the group the following dividend:

$$D = \begin{cases} 6 - S, & S < 6, \\ 0, & S \geq 6. \end{cases}$$

Determine $E[D]$.

6.45 You are given two independent compound Poisson random variables S_1 and S_2, where $f_j(x)$, $j = 1, 2$, are the two single-claim size distributions. You are given $\lambda_1 = \lambda_2 = 1$, $f_1(1) = 1$, and $f_2(1) = f_2(2) = 0.5$. Let $F_X(x)$ be the single-claim size distribution function associated with the compound distribution $S = S_1 + S_2$. Calculate $F_X^{*4}(6)$.

6.46 The variable S has a compound Poisson claims distribution with the following:

1. Individual claim amounts equal to 1, 2, or 3.

2. $E(S) = 56$.

3. $Var(S) = 126$.

Table 6.12   Data for Exercise 6.48

Deductible	Net premium
4	0.20
5	0.10
6	0.04
7	0.02

4. $\lambda = 29$.

Determine the expected number of claims of size 2.

6.47 For a compound Poisson distribution with positive integer claim amounts, the probability function follows:

$$f_S(x) = \frac{1}{x}[0.16 f_S(x-1) + k f_S(x-2) + 0.72 f_S(x-3)], \quad x = 1, 2, 3, \ldots .$$

The expected value of aggregate claims is 1.68. Determine the expected number of claims.

6.48 For a portfolio of policies you are given the following:

1. The number of claims has a Poisson distribution.

2. Claim amounts can be 1, 2, or 3.

3. A stop-loss reinsurance contract has net premiums for various deductibles as given in Table 6.12.

Determine the probability that aggregate claims will be either 5 or 6.

6.49 For group disability income insurance, the expected number of disabilities per year is 1 per 100 lives covered. The continuance (survival) function for the length of a disability in days, Y, is

$$\Pr(Y > y) = 1 - \frac{y}{10}, \quad y = 0, 1, \ldots, 10.$$

The benefit is 20 per day following a five-day waiting period. Using a compound Poisson distribution, determine the variance of aggregate claims for a group of 1,500 independent lives.

6.50 A population has two classes of drivers. The number of accidents per individual driver has a geometric distribution. For a driver selected at random from Class I, the geometric distribution parameter has a uniform distribution over the interval $(0, 1)$. Twenty-five percent of the drivers are in Class I. All drivers in Class II have expected number of claims 0.25. For a driver selected at random from this population, determine the probability of exactly two accidents.

Note: The following two Exercises require the use of a computer.

6.51 A policy covers physical damage incurred by the trucks in a company's fleet. The number of losses in a year has a Poisson distribution with $\lambda = 5$. The amount of a single loss has a gamma distribution with $\alpha = 0.5$ and $\theta = 2,500$. The insurance contract pays a maximum annual benefit of 20,000. Determine the probability that the maximum benefit will be paid. Use a span of 100 and the method of rounding.

6.52 An individual has purchased health insurance for which he pays 10 for each physician visit and 5 for each prescription. The probability that a payment will be 10 is 0.25, and the probability that it will be 5 is 0.75. The total number of payments per year has the Poisson–Poisson (Neyman Type A) distribution with $\lambda_1 = 10$ and $\lambda_2 = 4$. Determine the probability that total payments in one year will exceed 400. Compare your answer to a normal approximation.

6.53 Demonstrate that if the exponential distribution is discretized by the method of rounding, the resulting discrete distribution is a ZM geometric distribution.

6.7   THE IMPACT OF INDIVIDUAL POLICY MODIFICATIONS ON AGGREGATE PAYMENTS

In Section 5.6 the manner in which individual deductibles (both ordinary and franchise) affect both the individual loss amounts and the claim frequency distribution was discussed. In this section we will consider the impact on aggregate losses. It is worth noting that both individual coinsurance and individual policy limits have an impact on the individual losses but not on the frequency of such losses, so we will focus primarily on the deductible issues in what follows. We also remark that we continue to assume that the presence of policy modifications does not have an underwriting impact on the individual loss distribution through an effect on the risk characteristics of the insured population, an issue which was discussed in Section 5.6. That is, the *ground-up* distribution of the individual loss amount X is assumed to be unaffected by the policy modifications, and only the payments themselves are affected.

From the standpoint of the aggregate losses, the relevant facts are now described. Regardless of whether the deductible is of the ordinary or franchise type, we shall assume that an individual loss results in a payment with probability v. The individual ground-up loss random variable X has policy modifications (including deductibles) applied, so that a payment is then made. Individual payments may then be viewed on a *per-loss* basis, where the amount of such payment, denoted by Y^L, will be 0 if the loss results in no payment. Thus, on a per-loss basis, the payment amount is determined on each and every loss. Alternatively, individual payments may also be viewed on a *per-payment* basis. In this case, the amount of payment is denoted by Y^P, and on this basis payment amounts are only determined on losses which actually result in a nonzero payment being made. Therefore, by definition, $\Pr(Y^P = 0) = 0$, and the distribution of Y^P is the conditional distribution of Y^L given that $Y^L > 0$. Notationally, we write $Y^P = Y^L | Y^L > 0$. Therefore, the cumulative distribution functions are related by

$$F_{Y^L}(y) = (1 - v) + v F_{Y^P}(y), \quad y \geq 0,$$

because $1 - v = \Pr(Y^L = 0) = F_{Y^L}(0)$ (recall that Y^L has a discrete probability mass point $1 - v$ at 0, even if X and hence Y^P and Y^L have continuous probability density functions for $y > 0$). The moment generating functions of Y^L and Y^P are thus related by

$$M_{Y^L}(t) = (1 - v) + v M_{Y^P}(t), \tag{6.23}$$

which may be restated in terms of expectations as

$$\mathrm{E}(e^{tY^L}) = \mathrm{E}(e^{tY^L} | Y^L = 0)\Pr\left(Y^L = 0\right) + \mathrm{E}(e^{tY^L} | Y^L > 0)\Pr\left(Y^L > 0\right).$$

It follows from Section 5.6 that the number of losses N^L and the number of payments N^P are related through their probability generating functions by

$$P_{N^P}(z) = P_{N^L}(1 - v + vz), \tag{6.24}$$

where $P_{N^P}(z) = \mathrm{E}\left(z^{N^P}\right)$ and $P_{N^L}(z) = \mathrm{E}\left(z^{N^L}\right)$.

We now turn to the analysis of the aggregate payments. On a per loss basis, the total payments may be expressed as $S = Y_1^L + Y_2^L + \cdots + Y_{N^L}^L$ with $S = 0$ if $N^L = 0$ and where Y_j^L is the payment amount on the jth loss. Alternatively, ignoring losses on which no payment is made, we may express the total payments on a per-payment basis as $S = Y_1^P + Y_2^P + \cdots + Y_{N^P}^P$ with $S = 0$ if $N^P = 0$, and Y_j^P is the payment amount on the jth loss, which results in a nonzero payment. Clearly, S may be represented in two distinct ways on an aggregate basis. Of course, the moment generating function of S on a per-loss basis is

$$M_S(t) = \mathrm{E}\left(e^{tS}\right) = P_{N^L}\left[M_{Y^L}(t)\right], \tag{6.25}$$

whereas on a per-payment basis we have

$$M_S(t) = \mathrm{E}\left(e^{tS}\right) = P_{N^P}\left[M_{Y^P}(t)\right]. \tag{6.26}$$

Obviously, (6.25) and (6.26) are equal, as may be seen from (6.23) and (6.24). That is,

$$P_{N^L}\left[M_{Y^L}(t)\right] = P_{N^L}\left[1 - v + v M_{Y^P}(t)\right] = P_{N^P}\left[M_{Y^P}(t)\right].$$

Consequently, any analysis of the aggregate payments S may be done on either a per-loss basis [with compound representation (6.25) for the moment generating function] or on a per payment basis [with (6.26) as the compound moment generating function]. The basis selected should obviously be determined by whatever is more suitable for the particular situation at hand. While by no means a hard-and-fast rule, the authors have found it more convenient to use the per-loss basis to evaluate moments of S. In particular, the formulas given in Section 5.5 for the individual mean and variance are on a per-loss basis, and the mean and variance of the aggregate payments S may be computed using these and (6.6) but with N replaced by N^L and X by Y^L.

On the other hand, if the (approximated) distribution of S is of interest, then a payment basis is normally to be preferred. The reason for this choice is that on a per-loss basis underflow problems may result if $E(N^L)$ is large, and computer storage problems may occur due to the presence of a large number of zero probabilities in the distribution of Y^L, particularly if a franchise deductible is employed. Also, for convenience, we normally elect to apply policy modifications to the individual loss distribution first and then discretize (if necessary), rather than discretizing and then applying policy modifications to the discretized distributions. This issue is only relevant if the deductible and policy limit are not integer multiples of the discretization span, however. The following example illustrates these ideas.

Example 6.22 *The number of ground-up losses is Poisson distributed with mean $\lambda = 3$. The individual loss distribution is Pareto with parameters $\alpha = 4$ and $\theta = 10$. An individual ordinary deductible of 6, coinsurance of 75%, and an individual loss limit of 24 (before application of the deductible and coinsurance) are all applied. Determine the mean, variance, and distribution of aggregate payments.*

We will first compute the mean and variance on a per-loss basis. The mean number of losses is $E(N^L) = 3$, and the mean individual payment on a per loss basis is (using Theorem 5.13 with $r = 0$ and the Pareto distribution)

$$E(Y^L) = 0.75\left[E(X \wedge 24) - E(X \wedge 6)\right] = 0.75(3.2485 - 2.5195) = 0.54675.$$

The mean of the aggregate payments is thus

$$E(S) = E(N^L)E(Y^L) = (3)(0.54675) = 1.64.$$

The second moment of the individual payments on a per-loss basis is, using Theorem 5.14 with $r = 0$ and the Pareto distribution,

$$
\begin{aligned}
E\left[(Y^L)^2\right] &= (0.75)^2\{E\left[(X \wedge 24)^2\right] - E\left[(X \wedge 6)^2\right] \\
&\quad -2(6)E(X \wedge 24) + 2(6)E(X \wedge 6)\} \\
&= (0.75)^2\left[26.3790 - 10.5469 - 12(3.2485) + 12(2.5195)\right] \\
&= 3.98481.
\end{aligned}
$$

In order to compute the variance of aggregate payments, we do not need to explicitly determine $\text{Var}(Y^L)$ because S is compound Poisson distributed, which implies [using (4.27), for example] that

$$\text{Var}(S) = \lambda E\left[(Y^L)^2\right] = 3(3.98481) = 11.9544 = (3.46)^2.$$

In order to compute the (approximate) distribution of S, we will use the per payment basis. First note that $v = Pr(X > 6) = [10/(10+6)]^4 = 0.15259$, and the number of payments N^P is Poisson distributed with mean $E(N^P) = \lambda v = 3(0.15259) = 0.45776$. Let $Z = X - 6|X > 6$, so that Z is the individual payment random variable with only a deductible of 6. Then

$$Pr(Z > z) = \frac{Pr(X > z + 6)}{Pr(X > 6)}.$$

With coinsurance of 75%, $Y^P = 0.75Z$ has cumulative distribution function

$$F_{Y^P}(y) = 1 - Pr(0.75Z > y) = 1 - \frac{Pr(X > 6 + y/0.75)}{Pr(X > 6)}.$$

That is, for y less than the maximum payment of $(0.75)(24 - 6) = 13.5$,

$$F_{Y^P}(y) = \frac{Pr(X > 6) - Pr(X > 6 + y/0.75)}{Pr(X > 6)}, \quad y < 13.5,$$

and $F_{Y^P}(y) = 1$ for $y \geq 13.5$. We then discretize the distribution of Y^P (we thus apply the policy modifications first and then discretize) using a span of 2.25 and the method of rounding. This yields $f_0 = F_{Y^P}(1.125) = 0.30124$, $f_1 = F_{Y^P}(3.375) - F_{Y^P}(1.125) = 0.32768$, and so on. In this situation care must be exercised in evaluation of f_6, and we have $f_6 = F_{Y^P}(14.625) - F_{Y^P}(12.375) = 1 - 0.94126 = 0.05874$. Then $f_n = 1 - 1 = 0$ for $n = 7, 8, \ldots$. The approximate distribution of S may then be computed using the compound Poisson recursive formula, namely, $g_0 = e^{-0.45776(1-0.30124)} = 0.72625$, and

$$g_k = \frac{0.45776}{k} \sum_{j=1}^{k} j f_j g_{k-j}, \quad k = 1, 2, 3, \ldots.$$

Thus, $g_1 = (0.45776)(1)(0.32768)(0.72625) = 0.10894$, for example.   □

6.7.1   Exercises

6.54 Suppose that the number of ground-up losses N^L has probability generating function $P_{N^L}(z) = B[\theta(z-1)]$, where θ is a parameter and B is functionally independent of θ. The individual ground-up loss distribution is exponential with cumulative distribution function $F_X(x) = 1 - e^{-\mu x}$, $x \geq 0$. Individual losses are subject to an ordinary deductible of d and coinsurance of

α. Demonstrate that the aggregate payments, on a per-payment basis, have compound moment generating function given by (6.26), where N^P has the same distribution as N^L but with θ replaced by $\theta e^{-\mu d}$ and Y^P has the same distribution as X but with μ replaced by μ/α.

6.55 A ground-up model of individual losses has the gamma distribution with parameters $\alpha = 2$ and $\theta = 100$. The number of losses has the negative binomial distribution with $r = 2$ and $\beta = 1.5$. An ordinary deductible of 50 and a loss limit of 175 (before imposition of the deductible) are applied to each individual loss.

(a) Determine the mean and variance of the aggregate payments on a per-loss basis.

(b) Determine the distribution of the number of payments.

(c) Determine the cumulative distribution function of the amount Y^P of a payment given that a payment is made.

(d) Discretize the severity distribution from (c) using the method of rounding and a span of 40.

(e) Use the recursive formula to calculate the discretized distribution of aggregate payments up to a discretized amount paid of 120.

6.8 CALCULATIONS WITH APPROXIMATE DISTRIBUTIONS

Whenever the severity distribution is calculated using an approximate method, the result is, of course, an approximation to the true aggregate distribution. In particular, the true aggregate distribution is often continuous (except, perhaps, with discrete probability at zero or at an aggregate censoring limit) while the approximate distribution either is discrete with probability at equally spaced values as with recursion and Fast Fourier Transform (FFT), is discrete with probability $1/n$ at arbitrary values as with simulation, or has a piecewise linear distribution function as with Heckman–Meyers. In this section we introduce reasonable ways to obtain values of $F_S(x)$ and $E[(S \wedge x)^k]$ from those approximating distributions. In all cases we assume that the true distribution of aggregate payments is continuous, except perhaps with discrete probability at $S = 0$.

6.8.1 Arithmetic distributions

For recursion and the FFT, the approximating distribution can be written as $p_0, p_1, \ldots$, where $p_j = \Pr(S^* = jh)$ and S^* refers to the approximating distribution. While several methods of undiscretizing this distribution are possible, we will introduce only one. It assumes we can obtain $g_0 = \Pr(S = 0)$, the true probability that aggregate payments are zero. The method is based

Table 6.13 Discrete approximation to the aggregate payments distribution

j	x	$f_X(x)$	$p_j = f_{S^*}(x)$
0	0	0.009934	0.335556
1	2	0.019605	0.004415
2	4	0.019216	0.004386
3	6	0.018836	0.004356
4	8	0.018463	0.004327
5	10	0.018097	0.004299
6	12	0.017739	0.004270
7	14	0.017388	0.004242
8	16	0.017043	0.004214
9	18	0.016706	0.004186
10	20	0.016375	0.004158

on constructing a continuous approximation to S^* by assuming the probability p_j is uniformly spread over the interval $(j - \frac{1}{2})h$ to $(j + \frac{1}{2})h$ for $j = 1, 2, \ldots$. For the interval from 0 to $h/2$, a discrete probability of g_0 is placed at zero and the remaining probability, $p_0 - g_0$, is spread uniformly over the interval. Let S^{**} be the random variable with this mixed distribution. All quantities of interest are then computed using S^{**}.

Example 6.23 *Let N have the geometric distribution with $\beta = 2$ and let X have the exponential distribution with $\theta = 100$. Use recursion with a span of 2 to approximate the aggregate distribution and then obtain a continuous approximation.*

The exponential distribution was discretized using the method which preserves the first moment. The probabilities appear in Table 6.13. Also presented are the aggregate probabilities computed using the recursive formula. We also note that $g_0 = \Pr(N = 0) = (1 + \beta)^{-1} = \frac{1}{3}$. For $j = 1, 2, \ldots$ the continuous approximation has pdf $f_{S^{**}}(x) = f_{S^*}(2j)/2$, $2j - 1 < x \le 2j + 1$. We also have $\Pr(S^{**} = 0) = \frac{1}{3}$ and $f_{S^{**}}(x) = (0.335556 - \frac{1}{3})/1 = 0.002223$, $0 < x \le 1$. $\square$

Returning to the original problem, it is possible to work out the general formulas for the basic quantities. For the cdf,

$$
\begin{aligned}
F_{S^{**}}(x) &= g_0 + \int_0^x \frac{p_0 - g_0}{h/2} ds \\
&= g_0 + \frac{2x}{h}(p_0 - g_0), \quad 0 \le x \le \frac{h}{2},
\end{aligned}
$$

and

$$
\begin{aligned}
F_{S^{**}}(x) &= \sum_{i=0}^{j-1} p_i + \int_{(j-1/2)h}^{x} \frac{p_j}{h}\, ds \\
&= \sum_{i=0}^{j-1} p_i + \frac{x - (j-1/2)h}{h} p_j, \quad \left(j - \frac{1}{2}\right) h < x \le \left(j + \frac{1}{2}\right) h.
\end{aligned}
$$

For the limited expected value (LEV),

$$
\begin{aligned}
\mathrm{E}[(S^{**} \wedge x)^k] &= 0^k g_0 + \int_0^x s^k \frac{p_0 - g_0}{h/2}\, ds + x^k [1 - F_{S^{**}}(x)] \\
&= \frac{2x^{k+1}(p_0 - g_0)}{h(k+1)} + x^k [1 - F_{S^{**}}(x)], \quad 0 < x \le \frac{h}{2},
\end{aligned}
$$

and

$$
\begin{aligned}
\mathrm{E}[(S^{**} \wedge x)^k] &= 0^k g_0 + \int_0^{h/2} s^k \frac{p_0 - g_0}{h/2}\, ds + \sum_{i=1}^{j-1} \int_{(i-1/2)h}^{(i+1/2)h} s^k \frac{p_i}{h}\, ds \\
&\quad + \int_{(j-1/2)h}^{x} s^k \frac{p_j}{h}\, ds + x^k [1 - F_{S^{**}}(x)] \\
&= \frac{(h/2)^k (p_0 - g_0)}{k+1} + \sum_{i=1}^{j-1} \frac{h^k[(i+1/2)^{k+1} - (i-1/2)^{k+1}]}{k+1} p_i \\
&\quad + \frac{x^{k+1} - [(j-1/2)h]^{k+1}}{h(k+1)} p_j \\
&\quad + x^k [1 - F_{S^{**}}(x)], \quad \left(j - \frac{1}{2}\right) h < x \le \left(j + \frac{1}{2}\right) h.
\end{aligned}
$$

For $k = 1$ this reduces to

$$
\mathrm{E}(S^{**} \wedge x) = \begin{cases}
x(1 - g_0) - \dfrac{x^2}{h}(p_0 - g_0), & 0 < x \le \dfrac{h}{2}, \\[2mm]
\dfrac{h}{4}(p_0 - g_0) + \displaystyle\sum_{i=1}^{j-1} ihp_i + \dfrac{x^2 - [(j-1/2)h]^2}{2h} p_j \\[2mm]
\quad + x[1 - F_{S^{**}}(x)], & \left(j - \dfrac{1}{2}\right) h < x \le \left(j + \dfrac{1}{2}\right) h.
\end{cases}
$$

$$
\text{(6.27)}
$$

These formulas are summarized in Appendix E.

Example 6.24 (Example 6.23 continued) *Compute the cdf and LEV at integral values from 1 to 10 using S^*, S^{**}, and the exact distribution of aggregate losses.*

The exact distribution is available for this example. It was developed in Example 6.12 where it was determined that $\Pr(S = 0) = (1 + \beta)^{-1} = \frac{1}{3}$ and

Table 6.14 Comparison of true aggregate payment values and two approximations

	cdf			LEV		
x	S	S^*	S^{**}	S	S^*	S^{**}
1	0.335552	0.335556	0.335556	0.66556	0.66444	0.66556
2	0.337763	0.339971	0.337763	1.32890	1.32889	1.32890
3	0.339967	0.339971	0.339970	1.99003	1.98892	1.99003
4	0.342163	0.344357	0.342163	2.64897	2.64895	2.64896
5	0.344352	0.344357	0.344356	3.30571	3.30459	3.30570
6	0.346534	0.348713	0.346534	3.96027	3.96023	3.96025
7	0.348709	0.348713	0.348712	4.61264	4.61152	4.61263
8	0.350876	0.353040	0.350876	5.26285	5.26281	5.26284
9	0.353036	0.353040	0.353039	5.91089	5.90977	5.91088
10	0.355189	0.357339	0.355189	6.55678	6.55673	6.55676

the pdf for the continuous part is

$$f_S(x) = \frac{\beta}{\theta(1+\beta)^2} \exp\left[-\frac{x}{\theta(1+\beta)}\right] = \frac{2}{900}e^{-x/300}, \quad x > 0.$$

From this we have

$$F_S(x) = \tfrac{1}{3} + \int_0^x \frac{2}{900}e^{-s/300}\,ds = 1 - \tfrac{2}{3}e^{-x/300}$$

and

$$E(S \wedge x) = \int_0^x \frac{2s}{900}e^{-s/300}\,ds + x\tfrac{2}{3}e^{-x/300} = 200(1 - e^{-x/300}).$$

The requested values are given in Table 6.14.   □

6.8.2   Empirical distributions

When the approximate distribution is obtained by simulation (the simulation process is discussed in Chapter 17), the result is an empirical distribution. Unlike approximations produced by recursion or the FFT, simulation does not place the probabilities at equally spaced values. This makes it less clear how the approximate distribution should be smoothed. On the other hand, simulation usually involves tens or hundreds of thousands of points, and therefore the individual points are likely to be close to each other. For these reasons it seems sufficient to simply use the empirical distribution as the answer. That is, all calculations should be done using the approximate empirical random variable, S^*. The formulas for the commonly required quantities are very simple. Let $x_1, x_2, \ldots, x_n$ be the simulated values. Then

$$F_{S^*}(x) = \frac{\text{number of } x_j \leq x}{n}$$

Table 6.15   Simulated values of aggregate losses

j	x_j	j	x_j
1–331	0	346	6.15
332	0.04	347	6.26
333	0.12	348	6.58
334	0.89	349	6.68
335	1.76	350	6.71
336	2.16	351	6.82
337	3.13	352	7.76
338	3.40	353	8.23
339	4.38	354	8.67
340	4.78	355	8.77
341	4.95	356	8.85
342	5.04	357	9.18
343	5.07	358	9.88
344	5.81	359	10.12
345	5.94		

and

$$\mathrm{E}[(S^* \wedge x)^k] = \frac{1}{n} \sum_{x_j < x} x_j^k + x^k[1 - F_{S^*}(x)].$$

Example 6.25 (Example 6.23 continued) *Simulate 1,000 observations from the compound model with geometric frequency and exponential severity. Use the results to obtain values of the cdf and LEV for the integers from 1 to 10. The small sample size was selected so that only about 30 values between zero and 10 (not including zero) are expected.*

The simulations produced an aggregate payment of zero 331 times. The set of nonzero values that were less than 10 plus the first value past 10 are presented in Table 6.15. Other than zero, none of the values appeared more than once in the simulation. The requested values from the empirical distribution along with the true values are given in Table 6.16.   □

6.8.3   Piecewise linear cdf

When using the Heckman–Meyers inversion method (to be introduced in Section 6.9.2), the output is approximate values of the cdf $F_S(x)$ at any set of desired values. The values are approximate because the severity distribution function is required to be piecewise linear and because approximate integration is used. Let $S^{\#}$ denote an arbitrary random variable with cdf values as given by the Heckman–Meyers method at arbitrarily selected points $0 = x_1 < x_2 < \cdots < x_n$ and let $F_j = F_{S^{\#}}(x_j)$. Also, set $F_n = 1$ so that

Table 6.16 Empirical and smoothed values from a simulation

x	$F_{S^*}(x)$	$F_S(x)$	$E(S^* \wedge x)$	$E(S \wedge x)$
0	0.331	0.333	0.0000	0.0000
1	0.334	0.336	0.6671	0.6656
2	0.335	0.338	1.3328	1.3289
3	0.336	0.340	1.9970	1.9900
4	0.338	0.342	2.6595	2.6490
5	0.341	0.344	3.3206	3.3057
6	0.345	0.347	3.9775	3.9603
7	0.351	0.349	4.6297	4.6126
8	0.352	0.351	5.2784	5.2629
9	0.356	0.353	5.9250	5.9109
10	0.358	0.355	6.5680	6.5568

no probability is lost. The easiest way to complete the description of the smoothed distribution is to connect these points with straight lines. Let $S^{\#\#}$ be the random variable with this particular cdf. Intermediate values of the cdf of $S^{\#\#}$ are found by interpolation.

$$F_{S^{\#\#}}(x) = \frac{(x - x_{j-1})F_j + (x_j - x)F_{j-1}}{x_j - x_{j-1}}.$$

The formula for the limited expected value is (for $x_{j-1} < x \le x_j$)

$$\begin{aligned}
E[(S^{\#\#} \wedge x)^k] &= \sum_{i=2}^{j-1} \int_{x_{i-1}}^{x_i} s^k \frac{F_i - F_{i-1}}{x_i - x_{i-1}}\, ds \\
&+ \int_{x_{j-1}}^{x} s^k \frac{F_j - F_{j-1}}{x_j - x_{j-1}}\, ds + x^k[1 - F_{S^{\#\#}}(x)] \\
&= \sum_{i=2}^{j-1} \frac{(x_i^{k+1} - x_{i-1}^{k+1})(F_i - F_{i-1})}{(k+1)(x_i - x_{i-1})} \\
&+ \frac{(x^{k+1} - x_{j-1}^{k+1})(F_j - F_{j-1})}{(k+1)(x_j - x_{j-1})} \\
&+ x^k \left[1 - \frac{(x - x_{j-1})F_j + (x_j - x)F_{j-1}}{x_j - x_{j-1}}\right],
\end{aligned}$$

and when $k = 1$,

$$\begin{aligned}
E(S^{\#\#} \wedge x) &= \sum_{i=2}^{j-1} \frac{(x_i + x_{i-1})(F_i - F_{i-1})}{2} + \frac{(x^2 - x_{j-1}^2)(F_j - F_{j-1})}{2(x_j - x_{j-1})} \\
&+ x \left[1 - \frac{(x - x_{j-1})F_j + (x_j - x)F_{j-1}}{x_j - x_{j-1}}\right].
\end{aligned}$$

6.8.4   Exercises

6.56 Let the frequency (of losses) distribution be negative binomial with $r = 2$ and $\beta = 2$. Let the severity distribution (of losses) have the gamma distribution with $\alpha = 4$ and $\theta = 25$. Determine $F_S(200)$ and $E(S \wedge 200)$ for an ordinary per-loss deductible of 25. Use the recursive formula to obtain the aggregate distribution and use a discretization interval of 5 with the method of rounding to discretize the severity distribution.

6.57 *(Exercise 6.51 continued)* Recall that the number of claims has a Poisson distribution with $\lambda = 5$ and the amount of a single claim has a gamma distribution with $\alpha = 0.5$ and $\theta = 2,500$. Determine the mean, standard deviation, and 90th percentile of payments by the insurance company under each of the following coverages. Any computational method may be used.

(a) A maximum aggregate payment of 20,000.

(b) A per-claim ordinary deductible of 100 and a per claim maximum payment of 10,000. There is no aggregate maximum payment.

(c) A per-claim ordinary deductible of 100 with no maximum payment. There is an aggregate ordinary deductible of 15,000, an aggregate coinsurance factor of 0.8, and a maximum insurance payment of 20,000. This corresponds to an aggregate reinsurance provision.

6.58 *(Exercise 6.52 continued)* Recall that the number of payments has the Poisson–Poisson distribution with $\lambda_1 = 10$ and $\lambda_2 = 4$ while the payment per claim by the insured is 5 with probability 0.75 and 10 with probability 0.25. Determine the expected payment by the insured under each of the following situations. Any computational method may be used.

(a) A maximum payment of 400.

(b) A coinsurance arrangement where the insured pays 100% up to an aggregate total of 300 and then pays 20% of aggregate payments above 300.

6.9   INVERSION METHODS

Inversion methods discussed in this section are used to obtain numerically the probability function, or some related function such as a net stop-loss premium (aggregate excess-of-loss pure premium), from a known expression for a transform, such as the pgf, mgf, or cf of the desired function.

Compound distributions lend themselves naturally to this approach because their transforms are compound functions and are easily evaluated when both frequency and severity components are known. The pgf and cf of the aggregate loss distribution are

$$P_S(z) = P_N[P_X(z)]$$

and

$$\varphi_S(z) = \mathrm{E}[e^{iSz}] = P_N[\varphi_X(z)], \tag{6.28}$$

respectively. The characteristic function always exists and is unique. Conversely, for a given characteristic function, there always exists a unique distribution. The objective of inversion methods is to obtain the distribution numerically from the characteristic function (6.28).

It is worth mentioning that there has recently been much research in other areas of applied probability on obtaining the distribution numerically from the associated Laplace–Stieltjes transform. These techniques are applicable to the evaluation of compound distributions in the present context but will not be discussed further here. A good survey is [2], pp. 257–323.

6.9.1 Fast Fourier transform

The FFT is an algorithm that can be used for inverting characteristic functions to obtain densities of discrete random variables. The FFT comes from the field of signal processing. It was first used for the inversion of characteristic functions of compound distributions by Bertram [14] and is explained in detail with applications to aggregate loss calculation by Robertson [111].

Definition 6.26 *For any continuous function* $f(x)$, *the **Fourier transform** is the mapping*

$$\tilde{f}(z) = \int_{-\infty}^{\infty} f(x)e^{izx}\, dx. \tag{6.29}$$

The original function can be recovered from its Fourier transform as

$$f(x) = \frac{1}{2\pi} \int_{-\infty}^{\infty} \tilde{f}(z)e^{-izx}\, dz.$$

When $f(x)$ is a probability density function, $\tilde{f}(z)$ is its characteristic function. For our applications, $f(x)$ will be real valued. From (6.29), $\tilde{f}(z)$ is complex valued. When $f(x)$ is a probability function of a discrete (or mixed) distribution, the definitions can easily be generalized (see, for example, Fisz [38]).

Definition 6.27 *Let* f_x *denote a function defined for all integer values of* x *that is periodic with period length* n *(that is,* $f_{x+n} = f_x$ *for all* x*). For the vector* $(f_0, f_1, \ldots, f_{n-1})$, *the **discrete Fourier transform** is the mapping* $\tilde{f}_x$, $x = \ldots, -1, 0, 1, \ldots$, *defined by*

$$\tilde{f}_k = \sum_{j=0}^{n-1} f_j \exp\left(\frac{2\pi i}{n} jk\right), \quad k = \ldots, -1, 0, 1, \ldots. \tag{6.30}$$

This mapping is bijective. In addition, $\tilde{f}_k$ is also periodic with period length n. The inverse mapping is

$$f_j = \frac{1}{n} \sum_{k=0}^{n-1} \tilde{f}_k \exp\left(-\frac{2\pi i}{n}kj\right), \quad j = \ldots, -1, 0, 1, \ldots . \qquad (6.31)$$

This inverse mapping recovers the values of the original function.

Because of the periodic nature of f and $\tilde{f}$, we can think of the discrete Fourier transform as a bijective mapping of n points into n points. From (6.30), it is clear that, in order to obtain n values of $\tilde{f}_k$, the number of terms that need to be evaluated is of order n^2, that is, $O(n^2)$.

The **Fast Fourier Transform (FFT)** is an algorithm that reduces the number of computations required to be of order $O(n \ln_2 n)$. This can be a dramatic reduction in computations when n is large. The algorithm exploits the property that a discrete Fourier transform of length n can be rewritten as the sum of two discrete transforms, each of length $n/2$, the first consisting of the even-numbered points and the second consisting of the odd-numbered points.

$$
\begin{aligned}
\tilde{f}_k &= \sum_{j=0}^{n-1} f_j \exp\left(\frac{2\pi i}{n}jk\right) \\
&= \sum_{j=0}^{n/2-1} f_{2j} \exp\left(\frac{2\pi i}{n}2jk\right) + \sum_{j=0}^{n/2-1} f_{2j+1} \exp\left[\frac{2\pi i}{n}(2j+1)k\right] \\
&= \sum_{j=0}^{m-1} f_{2j} \exp\left(\frac{2\pi i}{m}jk\right) + \exp\left(\frac{2\pi i}{n}k\right) \sum_{j=0}^{m-1} f_{2j+1} \exp\left(\frac{2\pi i}{m}jk\right),
\end{aligned}
$$

when $m = n/2$. Hence

$$\tilde{f}_k = \tilde{f}_k^a + \exp\left(\frac{2\pi i}{n}k\right)\tilde{f}_k^b. \qquad (6.32)$$

These can, in turn, be written as the sum of two transforms of length $m/2$. This can be continued successively. For the lengths $n/2$, $m/2$, $\ldots$ to be integers, the FFT algorithm begins with a vector of length $n = 2^r$. The successive writing of the transforms into transforms of half the length will result, after r times, in transforms of length 1. Knowing the transform of length 1 will allow one to successively compose the transforms of length 2, 2^2, 2^3, $\ldots, 2^r$ by simple addition using (6.32). Details of the methodology are found in Press et al. [107].

In our applications, we use the FFT to invert the characteristic function when discretization of the severity distribution is done. This is carried out as follows:

1. Discretize the severity distribution using some methods such as those described in the previous section, obtaining the discretized severity distribution

$$f_X(0), f_X(1), \ldots, f_X(n-1),$$

where $n = 2^r$ for some integer r and n is the number of points desired in the distribution $f_S(x)$ of aggregate claims.

2. Apply the FFT to this vector of values, obtaining $\varphi_X(z)$, the characteristic function of the **discretized** distribution. The result is also a vector of $n = 2^r$ values.

3. Transform this vector using the pgf transformation of the claim frequency distribution, obtaining $\varphi_S(z) = P_N[\varphi_X(z)]$, which is the characteristic function, that is, the discrete Fourier transform of the aggregate claims distribution, a vector of $n = 2^r$ values.

4. Apply the Inverse Fast Fourier Transform (IFFT), which is identical to the FFT except for a sign change and a division by n [see (6.31)]. This gives a vector of length $n = 2^r$ values representing the exact distribution of aggregate claims for the discretized severity model.

The FFT procedure requires a discretization of the severity distribution. When the number of points in the severity distribution is less than $n = 2^r$, the severity distribution vector must be padded with zeros until it is of length n.

When the severity distribution places probability on values beyond $x = n$, as is the case with most distributions discussed in Chapter 4, the probability that is missed in the right-hand tail beyond n can introduce some minor error in the final solution because the function and its transform are both assumed to be periodic with period n, when in reality they are not. The authors suggest putting all the remaining probability at the final point at $x = n$ so that the probabilities add up to 1 exactly. This allows for periodicity to be used for the severity distribution in the FFT algorithm and ensures that the final set of aggregate probabilities will sum to 1. However, it is imperative that n be selected to be large enough so that most all the aggregate probability occurs by the nth point. The following example provides an extreme illustration.

Example 6.28 *Suppose the random variable X takes on the values 1, 2, and 3 with probabilities 0.5, 0.4, and 0.1, respectively. Further suppose the number of claims has the Poisson distribution with parameter $\lambda = 3$. Use the FFT to obtain the distribution of S using $n = 8$ and $n = 4{,}096$.*

In either case, the probability distribution of X is completed by adding one zero at the beginning (because S places probability at zero, the initial representation of X must also have the probability at zero given) and either 4 or 4,092 zeros at the end. The results from employing the FFT and IFFT

Table 6.17   Aggregate probabilities computed by the FFT and IFFT

s	$n = 8$ $f_S(s)$	$n = 4,096$ $f_S(s)$
0	0.11227	0.04979
1	0.11821	0.07468
2	0.14470	0.11575
3	0.15100	0.13256
4	0.14727	0.13597
5	0.13194	0.12525
6	0.10941	0.10558
7	0.08518	0.08305

appear in Table 6.17. For the case $n = 8$, the eight probabilities sum to 1. For the case $n = 4,096$, the probabilities also sum to 1, but there is not room here to show them all. It is easy to apply the recursive formula to this problem, which verifies that all of the entries for $n = 4,096$ are accurate to the five decimal places presented. On the other hand, with $n = 8$, the FFT gives values that are clearly distorted. If any generalization can be made, it is that more of the extra probability has been added to the smaller values of S.   □

Because the FFT and IFFT algorithms are available in many computer software packages and because the computer code is short, easy to write, and available (e.g., [107], pp. 411–412), no further technical details about the algorithm are given here. The reader can read any one of numerous books dealing with FFTs for a more detailed understanding of the algorithm. The technical details which allow the speeding up of the calculations from $O(n^2)$ to $O(n \ln_2 n)$ relate to the detailed properties of the discrete Fourier transform. Robertson [111] gives a good explanation of the FFT as applied to calculating the distribution of aggregate claims.

6.9.2   Direct numerical inversion

The inversion of the characteristic function (6.28) has been done using approximate integration methods by Heckman and Meyers [51] in the case of Poisson, binomial, and negative binomial claim frequencies and continuous severity distributions. The method is easily extended to other frequency distributions.

In this method, the severity distribution function is replaced by a piecewise linear distribution. It further uses a maximum single-loss amount so the cdf jumps to 1 at the maximum possible individual loss. The range of the severity random variable is divided into intervals of possibly unequal length. The remaining steps parallel those of the FFT method. Consider the cdf of the severity distribution $F_X(x)$, $0 \le x < \infty$. Let $0 = x_0 < x_1 < \cdots < x_n$ be arbitrarily selected loss values. Then the probability that losses lie in the interval $(x_{k-1}, x_k]$ is given by $f_k = F_X(x_k) - F_X(x_{k-1})$. Using a uniform density d_k over this interval results in the approximating density function $f^*(x) = d_k = f_k/(x_k - x_{k-1})$ for $x_{k-1} < x \le x_k$. Any remaining probability $f_{n+1} = 1 - F_X(x_n)$ is placed as a spike at x_n. This approximating pdf is selected to make evaluation of the cf easy. It is not required for direct inversion. The cf of the approximating severity distribution is

$$\varphi_X(z) = \int_0^\infty e^{izx}\, dF_X(x)$$

$$= \sum_{k=1}^n \int_{x_{k-1}}^{x_k} d_k e^{izx}\, dx + f_{n+1} e^{izx_n}$$

$$= \sum_{k=1}^n d_k \frac{e^{izx_k} - e^{izx_{k-1}}}{iz} + f_{n+1} e^{izx_n}.$$

The cf can be separated into real and imaginary parts by using Euler's formula

$$e^{i\theta} = \cos(\theta) + i\sin(\theta).$$

Then the real part of the cf is

$$a(z) = \text{Re}[\varphi_X(z)] = \frac{1}{z}\sum_{k=1}^n d_k[\sin(zx_k) - \sin(zx_{k-1})]$$
$$+ f_{n+1}\cos(zx_n)$$

and the imaginary part is

$$b(z) = \text{Im}[\varphi_X(z)] = \frac{1}{z}\sum_{k=1}^n d_k[\cos(zx_{k-1}) - \cos(zx_k)]$$
$$+ f_{n+1}\sin(zx_n).$$

The cf of aggregate losses (6.28) is obtained as

$$\varphi_S(z) = P_N[\varphi_X(z)] = P_N[a(z) + ib(z)],$$

which can be rewritten as

$$\varphi_S(z) = r(z)e^{i\theta(z)}$$

because it is complex valued.

The distribution of aggregate claims is obtained as

$$F_S(x) = \frac{1}{2} + \frac{1}{\pi}\int_0^\infty \frac{r(z/\sigma)}{z}\sin\left(\frac{zx}{\sigma} - \frac{\theta z}{\sigma}\right) dz, \qquad (6.33)$$

where σ is the standard deviation of the distribution of aggregate losses. Approximate integration techniques are used to evaluate (6.33) for any value of x. The reader is referred to Heckman and Meyers [51] for details. They also obtain the net stop-loss (excess pure) premium for the aggregate loss distribution as

$$
\begin{aligned}
P(d) &= \mathrm{E}[(S-d)_+] = \int_d^\infty (s-d)\, dF_S(s) \\
&= \frac{\sigma}{\pi} \int_0^\infty \frac{r(z/\sigma)}{z^2} \left[\cos\left(\frac{\theta z}{\sigma}\right) - \cos\left(\frac{zd}{\sigma} - \frac{\theta z}{\sigma}\right) \right] dz \\
&\quad + \mu - \frac{d}{2}
\end{aligned}
\tag{6.34}
$$

from (6.33), where μ is the mean of the aggregate loss distribution and d is the deductible.

Equation (6.33) provides only a single value of the distribution, while (6.34) provides only one value of the premium, but it does so quickly. The error of approximation depends on the spacing of the numerical integration method but is controllable.

6.9.3   Exercise

6.59 Repeat Exercises 6.51 and 6.52 using the inversion method.

6.10   COMPARISON OF METHODS

The recursive method has some significant advantages. The time required to compute an entire distribution of n points is reduced to $O(n^2)$ from $O(n^3)$ for the direct convolution method. Furthermore, it provides exact values when the severity distribution is itself discrete (arithmetic). The only source of error is in the discretization of the severity distribution. Except for binomial models, the calculations are guaranteed to be numerically stable. This method is very easy to program in a few lines of computer code. However, it has a few disadvantages. The recursive method only works for the classes of frequency distributions described in Section 4.6. Using distributions not based on the $(a, b, 0)$ and $(a, b, 1)$ classes requires modification of the formula or developing a new recursion. Numerous other recursions have recently been developed in the actuarial and statistical literature.

The FFT method is easy to use in that it uses standard routines available with many software packages. It is faster than the recursive method when n is large because it requires calculations of order $n \ln_2 n$ rather than n^2. However, if the severity distribution has a fixed (and not too large) number of points, the recursive method will require fewer computations because the sum in (6.14) will have at most m terms, reducing the order of required computations to be of order n, rather than n^2 in the case of no upper limit of the severity. The FFT method can be extended to the case where the severity distribution can take on negative values. Like the recursive method, it produces the entire distribution.

The direct inversion method has been demonstrated to be very fast in calculating a single value of the aggregate distribution or the net stop-loss (excess pure) premium for a single deductible d. However, it requires a major computer programming effort. It has been developed by Heckman and Meyers [51] specifically for $(a, b, 0)$ frequency models. It is possible to generalize the computer code to handle any distribution with a pgf that is a relatively simple function. This method is much faster than the recursive method when the expected number of claims is large. The speed does not depend on the size of λ in the case of the Poisson frequency model. In addition to being complicated to program, the method involves approximate integration whose errors depend on the method and interval size.

Through the use of transforms, both the FFT and inversion methods are able to handle convolutions efficiently. For example, suppose a reinsurance agreement was to cover the aggregate losses of three groups, each with unique frequency and severity distributions. If S_i, $i = 1, 2, 3$, are the aggregate losses for each group, the characteristic function for the total aggregate losses $S = S_1 + S_2 + S_3$ is $\varphi_S(z) = \varphi_{S_1}(z)\varphi_{S_2}(z)\varphi_{S_3}(z)$ and so the only extra work is some multiplications prior to the inversion step. The recursive method does not accommodate convolutions as easily.

The Heckman–Meyers method has some technical difficulties when being applied to severity distributions that are of the discrete type or have some anomalies, such as heaping of losses at some round number (e.g., 1,000,000). At any jump in the severity distribution function, a very short interval containing the jump needs to be defined in setting up the points $(x_1, x_2, \ldots, x_n)$.

We save a discussion of simulation for last because it differs greatly from the other methods. For those not familiar with this method, an introduction is provided in Chapter 17. The major advantage is a big one. If you can carefully articulate the model, you should be able to obtain the aggregate distribution by simulation. The programming effort may take a little time but can be done in a straightforward manner. Today's computers will conduct the simulation in a reasonable amount of time. Most of the analytic methods were developed as a response to the excessive computing time that simulations used to require. That is less of a problem now. On the other hand, it is difficult to write a general-purpose simulation program. Instead, it is possibly necessary to write a new routine as each problem occurs. Thus it is probably best to save the simulation approach for those problems that cannot be solved by the other methods. Then, of course, it is worth the effort because there is no alternative.

One other drawback of simulation occurs in extremely low frequency situations (which is where recursion excels). For example, consider an individual excess-of-loss reinsurance in which reinsurance benefits are paid on individual losses above 1,000,000, an event which occurs about 1 time in 100, but when it does, the tail is extremely long (for example, a Pareto distribution with small α). The simulation will have to discard 99% of the generated losses and then will need a large number of those that exceed the deductible (due to the large variation in losses). It may take a long time to obtain a reliable answer. One possible solution for simulation is to work with the conditional distribution of the loss variable, given that a payment has been made.

No method is clearly superior for all problems. Each method has both advantages and disadvantages when compared with the others. What we really have is an embarrassment of riches. Twenty-five years ago, actuaries wondered if there would ever be effective methods for determining aggregate distributions. Today we can choose from several.

6.11   THE INDIVIDUAL RISK MODEL

6.11.1   Parametric approximation

The **individual risk model** represents the aggregate loss as a fixed sum of independent (but not necessarily identically distributed) random variables:

$$S = X_1 + X_2 + \cdots + X_n.$$

This is usually thought of as the sum of the losses from n insurance contracts, for example, n persons covered under a group insurance policy.

The individual risk model was originally developed for life insurance in which the probability of death within a year is q_j and the fixed benefit paid for the death of the jth person is b_j. In this case, the distribution of the loss to the insurer for the jth policy is

$$f_{X_j}(x) = \begin{cases} 1 - q_j, & x = 0, \\ q_j, & x = b_j. \end{cases}$$

In this case the mean and variance of aggregate losses are

$$\mathrm{E}(S) = \sum_{j=1}^{n} b_j q_j$$

and

$$\mathrm{Var}(S) = \sum_{j=1}^{n} b_j^2 q_j (1 - q_j)$$

because the X_js are assumed to be independent. Then, the pgf of aggregate losses is

$$P_S(z) = \prod_{j=1}^{n} (1 - q_j + q_j z^{b_j}). \tag{6.35}$$

In the special case where all the risks are identical with $q_j = q$ and $b_j = 1$, the pgf reduces to

$$P_S(z) = [1 + q(z - 1)]^n,$$

and in this case S has a binomial distribution.

The individual risk model can be generalized as follows. Let $X_j = I_j B_j$, where $I_1, \ldots, I_n$, $B_1, \ldots, B_n$ are independent. The random variable I_j is an indicator variable that takes on the value 1 with probability q_j and the value 0 with probability $1 - q_j$. This variable indicates whether or not the jth policy produced a payment. The random variable B_j can have any distribution and represents the amount of the payment in respect of the jth policy given that a payment was made. In the life insurance case, B_j is degenerate, with all probability on the value b_j. If we let $\mu_j = E(B_j)$ and $\sigma_j^2 = \text{Var}(B_j)$ then

$$E(S) = \sum_{j=1}^{n} q_j \mu_j \tag{6.36}$$

and

$$\text{Var}(S) = \sum_{j=1}^{n} [q_j \sigma_j^2 + q_j(1 - q_j)\mu_j^2]. \tag{6.37}$$

You are asked to verify these formulas in Exercise 6.60. The following example is a simple version of this situation.

Example 6.29 *Consider a group life insurance contract with an accidental death benefit. Assume that for all members the probability of death in the next year is 0.01 and that 30% of deaths are accidental. For 50 employees the benefit for an ordinary death is 50,000 and for an accidental death it is 100,000. For the remaining 25 employees the benefits are 75,000 and 150,000, respectively. Develop an individual risk model and determine its mean and variance.*

For all 75 employees $q_j = 0.01$. For 50 employees, B_j takes on the value 50,000 with probability 0.7 and 100,000 with probability 0.3. For them, $\mu_j = 65,000$ and $\sigma_j^2 = 525,000,000$. For the remaining 25 employees B_j takes on the value 75,000 with probability 0.7 and 150,000 with probability 0.3. For them, $\mu_j = 97,500$ and $\sigma_j^2 = 1,181,250,000$. Then

$$\begin{aligned} E(S) &= 50(0.01)(65,000) + 25(0.01)(97,500) \\ &= 56,875 \end{aligned}$$

and

$$\begin{aligned} \text{Var}(S) &= 50(0.01)(525,000,000) + 50(0.01)(0.99)(65,000)^2 \\ &\quad + 25(0.01)(1,181,250,000) + 25(0.01)(0.99)(97,500)^2 \\ &= 5,001,984,375. \end{aligned}$$

Table 6.18   Employee data for Example 6.30

Employee, j	Age (years)	Sex	Benefit, b_j	Mortality rate, q_j
1	20	M	15,000	0.00149
2	23	M	16,000	0.00142
3	27	M	20,000	0.00128
4	30	M	28,000	0.00122
5	31	M	31,000	0.00123
6	46	M	18,000	0.00353
7	47	M	26,000	0.00394
8	49	M	24,000	0.00484
9	64	M	60,000	0.02182
10	17	F	14,000	0.00050
11	22	F	17,000	0.00050
12	26	F	19,000	0.00054
13	37	F	30,000	0.00103
14	55	F	55,000	0.00479
Total			373,000	

□

When the risks are different, the probabilities defined by pgf (6.35) can be computed exactly or approximately. A normal, gamma, lognormal, or any other distribution can be used to approximate the distribution. This is usually done by matching the first few moments. Because the normal, gamma, and lognormal distributions each have two parameters, the mean and variance are sufficient.

Example 6.30 (Group life insurance) *A small manufacturing business has a group life insurance contract on its 14 permanent employees. The actuary for the insurer has selected a mortality table to represent the mortality of the group. Each employee is insured for the amount of his or her salary rounded up to the next 1,000 dollars. The group's data are given in Table 6.18.*

If the insurer adds a 45% relative loading to the net (pure) premium, what are the chances that it will lose money in a given year? Use the normal and lognormal approximations.

The mean and variance of the aggregate losses for the group are

$$E(S) = \sum_{j=1}^{14} b_j q_j = 2,054.41$$

and

$$\text{Var}(S) = \sum_{j=1}^{14} b_j^2 q_j (1 - q_j) = 1.02534 \times 10^8.$$

The premium being charged is $1.45 \times 2,054.41 = 2{,}978.89$. For the normal approximation (in units of 1,000), the mean is 2.05441 and the variance is 102.534. Then the probability of a loss is

$$
\begin{aligned}
\Pr(S > 2.97889) \ &= \ \Pr\left[Z > \frac{2.97889 - 2.05441}{(102.534)^{1/2}}\right] \\
&\doteq \ \Pr(Z > 0.0913) \\
&= \ 0.46 \text{ or } 46\%.
\end{aligned}
$$

For the lognormal approximation (as in Example 6.5)

$$\mu + \tfrac{1}{2}\sigma^2 = \ln 2.05441 = 0.719989$$

and

$$2\mu + 2\sigma^2 = \ln(102.534 + 2.05441^2) = 4.670533.$$

From this $\mu = -0.895289$ and $\sigma^2 = 3.230555$. Then

$$
\begin{aligned}
\Pr(S > 2.97889) \ &= \ 1 - \Phi\left[\frac{\ln 2.97889 + 0.895289}{(3.230555)^{1/2}}\right] \\
&= \ 1 - \Phi(1.105) \\
&= \ 0.13 \text{ or } 13\%. \qquad \square
\end{aligned}
$$

In the next subsection we present several ways of obtaining the exact distribution of S for the case where the benefit amounts are fixed.

6.11.2   Exact calculation of the aggregate distribution

6.11.2.1   Direct calculation   The pf of aggregate losses is given by

$$f_S(x) = f_{X_1} * f_{X_2} * \cdots * f_{X_n}(x), \tag{6.38}$$

where

$$f_{X_j}(x) = \begin{cases} p_j = 1 - q_j, & x = 0, \\ q_j, & x = b_j. \end{cases}$$

The density (6.38) can be calculated recursively over the partial sums $S_j = S_{j-1} + X_j$ for $j = 2, 3, \ldots, n$ beginning with $S_1 = X_1$. Then

$$
\begin{aligned}
f_{S_j}(x) \ &= \ \begin{cases} f_{S_{j-1}}(x) f_{X_j}(0), & x < b_j, \\ f_{S_{j-1}}(x) f_{X_j}(0) + f_{S_{j-1}}(x - b_j) f_{X_j}(b_j), & x \geq b_j, \end{cases} \\
&= \ \begin{cases} p_j f_{S_{j-1}}(x), & x < b_j, \\ p_j f_{S_{j-1}}(x) + q_j f_{S_{j-1}}(x - b_j), & x \geq b_j. \end{cases}
\end{aligned}
$$

Table 6.19   Cumulative probabilities for Example 6.31

x	$F_S(x)$	x	$F_S(x)$	x	$F_S(x)$	x	$F_S(x)$
0	0.95273905	20	0.96157969	40	0.97335098	60	0.99933062
1	0.95273905	21	0.96157969	41	0.97335892	61	0.99933187
2	0.95273905	22	0.96157969	42	0.97338128	62	0.99933191
3	0.95273905	23	0.96157969	43	0.97338740	63	0.99933193
4	0.95273905	24	0.96621337	44	0.97340884	64	0.99933198
5	0.95273905	25	0.96621337	45	0.97341351	65	0.99933202
6	0.95273905	26	0.96998201	46	0.97342561	66	0.99933206
7	0.95273905	27	0.96998201	47	0.97342840	67	0.99933209
8	0.95273905	28	0.97114577	48	0.97343397	68	0.99933217
9	0.95273905	29	0.97114648	49	0.97343866	69	0.99933450
10	0.95273905	30	0.97212950	50	0.97345889	70	0.99934141
11	0.95273905	31	0.97330507	51	0.97346040	71	0.99934796
12	0.95273905	32	0.97330747	52	0.97346606	72	0.99935031
13	0.95273905	33	0.97331344	53	0.97346608	73	0.99936659
14	0.95321566	34	0.97331962	54	0.97347547	74	0.99937973
15	0.95463736	35	0.97332386	55	0.97806678	75	0.99941735
16	0.95599217	36	0.97332585	56	0.97807068	76	0.99944759
17	0.95646878	37	0.97332829	57	0.97807536	77	0.99945823
18	0.95984386	38	0.97333493	58	0.97807660	78	0.99953355
19	0.96035862	39	0.97334251	59	0.97807808	79	0.99956734

If we wish to calculate the distribution of total claims up to some value r, the computer time involved, as measured by the number of multiplications, can be seen to be of order nr. If both r and n are large (e.g., $r = 10,000$ and $n = 10,000$), the number of computations can be prohibitive.

Example 6.31 (Example 6.30 continued) *Use the direct method to determine the pf of S as well as the probability required in Example* 6.30.

$$
\begin{aligned}
f_{S_1}(0) &= 0.99851, \\
f_{S_1}(15) &= 0.00149, \\
f_{S_2}(0) &= p_2 f_{S_1}(0) = 0.99709212, \\
f_{S_2}(15) &= p_2 f_{S_1}(15) = 0.00148788, \\
f_{S_2}(16) &= p_2 f_{S_1}(16) + q_2 f_{S_1}(0) = 0.00141788, \\
f_{S_2}(31) &= p_2 f_{S_1}(31) + q_2 f_{S_1}(15) = 0.0000021158.
\end{aligned}
$$

The final values of the cdf $F_S(x)$ for $x = 0, \ldots, 79$ are given in Table 6.19. From Table 6.19, the probability of exceeding 2,978.89 is seen to be 0.047, which shows that both approximations in Example 6.30 are poor.   □

This approach is reasonable when n is not too large, but for larger groups an alternative method is needed.

6.11.2.2 Recursive calculation   The following approach allows for the distribution to be calculated recursively based on De Pril [26]. We first divide the portfolio into subportfolios according to policy size and claim probability. Let n_{ij} be the number of policies with benefit i (where $i = 1, 2, \ldots, r$)[3] and claim probability q_j (where $j = 1, 2, \ldots, m$). Then the pgf of total claims may be written as

$$P_S(z) = \prod_{i=1}^{r} \prod_{j=1}^{m} (1 - q_j + q_j z^i)^{n_{ij}}.$$

The logarithm of the pgf is

$$\ln P_S(z) = \sum_{i=1}^{r} \sum_{j=1}^{m} n_{ij} \ln(1 - q_j + q_j z^i). \tag{6.39}$$

We now differentiate (6.39) to obtain

$$P_S'(z) = P_S(z) \left[\sum_{i=1}^{r} \sum_{j=1}^{m} i q_j n_{ij} z^{i-1} (1 - q_j + q_j z^i)^{-1} \right]. \tag{6.40}$$

Setting $z = 1$ in (6.40) yields the mean of the total claims distribution, namely

$$E(S) = P_S'(1) = \sum_{i=1}^{r} \sum_{j=1}^{m} i q_j n_{ij}.$$

Now, (6.40) may be rewritten as

$$
\begin{aligned}
z P_S'(z) &= P_S(z) \left[\sum_{i=1}^{r} \sum_{j=1}^{m} i n_{ij} \left(\frac{q_j}{1 - q_j} z^i \right) \left(1 + \frac{q_j}{1 - q_j} z^i \right)^{-1} \right] \\
&= P_S(z) \left[\sum_{i=1}^{r} \sum_{j=1}^{m} i n_{ij} \sum_{k=1}^{\infty} (-1)^{k-1} \left(\frac{q_j}{1 - q_j} \right)^k z^{ik} \right] \tag{6.41}
\end{aligned}
$$

for $|z| < \min_{i,j} [q_j^{-1}(1 - q_j)]^{1/i}$. The second term on the right-hand side of (6.41) may be rewritten as

$$\sum_{i=1}^{r} \sum_{k=1}^{\infty} h(i, k) z^{ik},$$

where

$$h(i, k) = i(-1)^{k-1} \sum_{j=1}^{m} n_{ij} \left(\frac{q_j}{1 - q_j} \right)^k. \tag{6.42}$$

---

[3] As in the discretization of severity distributions, it is necessary that the benefit amounts be in arithmetic progression. However, the monetary unit need not be 1. For example, $i = 1, 2, \ldots$ could represent benefit amounts of 5,000, 10,000, \ldots .

Thus, (6.41) may be written as

$$zP'_S(z) = P_S(z) \left[\sum_{i=1}^{r} \sum_{k=1}^{\infty} h(i,k)z^{ik} \right]. \tag{6.43}$$

The coefficient of z^x on the left-hand side of (6.43) is $xf_S(x)$, where $f_S(x)$ is the coefficient of z^x in $P_S(z)$. The right-hand side of (6.43) is a convolution, and the coefficient of z^x is thus given by

$$\sum_{ik \le x} h(i,k)f_S(x-ik). \tag{6.44}$$

A simpler way of writing (6.44) is

$$\sum_{i=1}^{x} \sum_{k=1}^{\lfloor x/i \rfloor} h(i,k)f_S(x-ik)$$

where $\lfloor \cdot \rfloor$ denotes the greatest integer function, that is, the largest integer that is less than or equal to the argument. Finally, because $h(i,k) = 0$ if $i > x$, one may equate coefficients of z^x on both sides of (6.43) and divide by x to obtain

$$f_S(x) = \frac{1}{x} \sum_{i=1}^{x \wedge r} \sum_{k=1}^{\lfloor x/i \rfloor} h(i,k)f_S(x-ik), \quad x \ge 1. \tag{6.45}$$

Now,

$$f_S(0) = P_S(0) = \prod_{i=1}^{r} \prod_{j=1}^{m} (1-q_j)^{n_{ij}}, \tag{6.46}$$

and from (6.45),

$$
\begin{aligned}
f_S(1) &= h(1,1)f_S(0), \\
f_S(2) &= \tfrac{1}{2}\{h(1,1)f_S(1) + [h(1,2) + h(2,1)]f_S(0)\}, \\
& \vdots
\end{aligned}
$$

The probabilities $\{f_S(x); \ x = 1, 2, \ldots\}$ may be calculated recursively using (6.45), beginning with (6.46).

It can be seen from (6.42) that $h(i,k)$ is a weighted sum of the kth power of $q_j/(1-q_j)$, $j = 1, 2, \ldots, m$. When q_j is close to zero, $[q_j/(1-q_j)]^k$ is small. Consequently, the magnitude of $h(i,k)$ decreases rapidly as k increases. This suggests that the inner summation in (6.45) can be limited to a small number of terms without significant loss of accuracy in computations while speeding up the computations considerably.

If we limit k to a maximum of K terms, let

$$f_S^{(K)}(x) = \frac{1}{x} \sum_{i=1}^{x \wedge r} \sum_{k=1}^{K \wedge \lfloor x/i \rfloor} h(i,k)f_S^{(K)}(x-ik) \tag{6.47}$$

Table 6.20   Values of n_{ij} for Example 6.32

j	$1000q_j$	14	15	16	17	18	19	20	24	26	28	30	31	55	60
1	0.50	1	0	0	1	0	0	0	0	0	0	0	0	0	0
2	0.54	0	0	0	0	0	1	0	0	0	0	0	0	0	0
3	1.03	0	0	0	0	0	0	0	0	0	0	1	0	0	0
4	1.22	0	0	0	0	0	0	0	0	0	1	0	0	0	0
5	1.23	0	0	0	0	0	0	0	0	0	0	0	1	0	0
6	1.28	0	0	0	0	0	0	1	0	0	0	0	0	0	0
7	1.42	0	0	1	0	0	0	0	0	0	0	0	0	0	0
8	1.49	0	1	0	0	0	0	0	0	0	0	0	0	0	0
9	3.53	0	0	0	0	1	0	0	0	0	0	0	0	0	0
10	3.94	0	0	0	0	0	0	0	0	1	0	0	0	0	0
11	4.79	0	0	0	0	0	0	0	0	0	0	0	0	1	0
12	4.84	0	0	0	0	0	0	0	1	0	0	0	0	0	0
13	21.82	0	0	0	0	0	0	0	0	0	0	0	0	0	1

denote the approximation using at most K terms in (6.45). In a later paper, De Pril [27] shows that, if $q_j < \frac{1}{2}$, $j = 1, 2, \ldots, m$, then

$$\sum_{x=0}^{M} |f_S(x) - f_S^{(K)}(x)| < e^{\delta(K)} - 1, \tag{6.48}$$

where

$$\delta(K) = \frac{1}{K+1} \sum_{i=1}^{r} \sum_{j=1}^{m} n_{ij} \frac{1 - q_j}{1 - 2q_j} \left(\frac{q_j}{1 - q_j} \right)^{K+1} \tag{6.49}$$

and $M = \sum_{i=1}^{r} \sum_{j=1}^{m} i n_{ij}$ is the maximum possible aggregate claim amount. The value of $\delta(K)$ is easily calculated for any value of K. Equation (6.48) provides an upper bound on the sum of the absolute errors over the entire distribution of aggregate claims and can be used to guarantee accuracy of results when a limited number of terms is used in (6.47).

Example 6.32 (Example 6.30 continued) *Determine the exact distribution of aggregate losses using the recursive method.*

The values of q_j and the nonzero rows of the matrix of n_{ij} values are given in Table 6.20.

Using (6.49), we find that $\delta(1) = 5.947 \times 10^{-4}$, $\delta(2) = 3.900 \times 10^{-6}$, $\delta(3) = 6.369 \times 10^{-8}$, and $\delta(4) = 1.131 \times 10^{-9}$. Hence, (6.47) with $K = 4$ will give us about 8 decimal place accuracy. The (nonzero) values of $h(i, k)$ computed using (6.42) are given in Table 6.21.

The values of $f_S(x)$ and the associated cdf $F_S(x)$ calculated using (6.47) with $K = 4$ and (6.46) are given in Table 6.22.

Table 6.21   Values of $h(i, k)$ for Example 6.32

		$h(i, k)$		
i	$k = 1$	$k = 2$	$k = 3$	$k = 4$
14	7.0035018×10^{-3}	$-3.5035025 \times 10^{-6}$	1.7526276×10^{-9}	$-8.7675218 \times 10^{-13}$
15	2.2383351×10^{-2}	$-3.3400962 \times 10^{-5}$	4.9841694×10^{-8}	$-7.4374944 \times 10^{-11}$
16	2.2752309×10^{-2}	$-3.2354221 \times 10^{-5}$	4.6008325×10^{-8}	$-6.5424723 \times 10^{-11}$
17	8.5042522×10^{-3}	$-4.2542531 \times 10^{-6}$	2.1281907×10^{-9}	$-1.0646277 \times 10^{-12}$
18	6.3765090×10^{-2}	$-2.2588816 \times 10^{-4}$	8.0020991×10^{-7}	$-2.8347477 \times 10^{-9}$
19	1.0265543×10^{-2}	$-5.5463884 \times 10^{-6}$	2.9966680×10^{-9}	$-1.6190750 \times 10^{-12}$
20	2.5632810×10^{-2}	$-3.2852048 \times 10^{-5}$	4.2104515×10^{-8}	$-5.3962851 \times 10^{-11}$
24	1.1672495×10^{-1}	$-5.6769638 \times 10^{-4}$	2.7610139×10^{-6}	$-1.3428300 \times 10^{-8}$
26	1.0284521×10^{-1}	$-4.0681297 \times 10^{-4}$	1.6091833×10^{-6}	$-6.3652612 \times 10^{-9}$
28	3.4201726×10^{-2}	$-4.1777074 \times 10^{-5}$	5.1030287×10^{-8}	$-6.2332996 \times 10^{-11}$
30	3.0931860×10^{-2}	$-3.1892665 \times 10^{-5}$	3.2883315×10^{-8}	$-3.3904736 \times 10^{-11}$
31	3.8176959×10^{-2}	$-4.7015487 \times 10^{-5}$	5.7900266×10^{-8}	$-7.1305033 \times 10^{-11}$
55	2.6471800×10^{-1}	$-1.2741022 \times 10^{-3}$	6.1323232×10^{-6}	$-2.9515207 \times 10^{-8}$
60	1.3384040	$-2.9855420 \times 10^{-2}$	6.6597689×10^{-4}	$-1.4855768 \times 10^{-5}$

It can be seen that the values in the last column of this table are identical to the corresponding values from Example 6.31 based on the direct method. This method is especially useful when there are a large number of lives in a group insurance contract.   □

Example 6.33 (An expanded group) *For the purpose of illustrating the effect of the size of the portfolio, consider a portfolio consisting of 1,400 independent lives, with exactly 100 lives like each life in the group life portfolio of Example 6.30. Determine the exact distribution of total losses.*

The values of n_{ij} are now either 100 or 0. From (6.42), it can be seen that each $h(i, k)$ is now 100 times larger than that of the previous example. The distribution of total claims can be computed as in the previous example. In Table 6.23 we give some values of the distribution function of total claims (as before, x is measured in units of 1,000).

From Example 6.30, the mean and variance of total claims for this portfolio of 1,400 lives are $\mu_1 = 205,441$ and $\mu_2 = 1.0253356 \times 10^{10}$. Also, the coefficient of skewness is calculated as $\mu_3(\mu_2)^{-3/2} = 0.5267345$, which is exactly one-tenth of the value of 5.267345 for the corresponding group of 14 lives. This indicates that the distribution is much more symmetric.   □

There are numerous papers on the subject of the individual risk model. De Pril [28] develops a generalization of this method to the case where the loss can take on more than one value.

Table 6.22 Aggregate probabilities for Example 6.32

x	$f_S(x)$	$F_S(x)$	x	$f_S(x)$	$F_S(x)$
0	9.5273905×10^{-1}	0.95273905	38	6.6436439×10^{-6}	0.97333493
14	4.7660783×10^{-4}	0.95321566	39	7.5742253×10^{-6}	0.97334251
15	1.4216995×10^{-3}	0.95463736	40	8.4744508×10^{-6}	0.97335098
16	1.3548133×10^{-3}	0.95599217	41	7.9416543×10^{-6}	0.97335892
17	4.7660783×10^{-4}	0.95646878	42	2.2356100×10^{-5}	0.97338128
18	3.3750829×10^{-3}	0.95984386	43	6.1253961×10^{-6}	0.97338740
19	5.1475706×10^{-4}	0.96035862	44	2.1435448×10^{-5}	0.97340884
20	1.2210690×10^{-3}	0.96157969	45	4.6721584×10^{-6}	0.97341351
24	4.6336840×10^{-3}	0.96621337	46	1.2100769×10^{-5}	0.97342561
26	3.7686403×10^{-3}	0.96998201	47	2.7915140×10^{-6}	0.97342840
28	1.1637614×10^{-3}	0.97114577	48	5.5621896×10^{-5}	0.97343397
29	7.1120536×10^{-7}	0.97114649	49	4.6964950×10^{-6}	0.97343866
30	9.8301077×10^{-4}	0.97212950	50	2.0226469×10^{-5}	0.97345889
31	1.1755723×10^{-3}	0.97330507	51	1.5103585×10^{-6}	0.97346040
32	2.3995910×10^{-6}	0.97330747	52	5.6661624×10^{-6}	0.97346607
33	5.9716305×10^{-6}	0.97331344	53	1.3705553×10^{-8}	0.97346608
34	6.1784053×10^{-6}	0.97331962	54	9.3923168×10^{-6}	0.97347547
35	4.2424878×10^{-6}	0.97332386	55	4.5913084×10^{-3}	0.97806678
36	1.9938909×10^{-6}	0.97332585	56	3.9003832×10^{-6}	0.97807068
37	2.4343694×10^{-6}	0.97332829	57	4.6823253×10^{-6}	0.97807536

6.11.3 Compound Poisson approximation

Because of the computational complexity of calculating the distribution of to-tal claims for a portfolio of n risks using the individual risk model, it has been popular to attempt to approximate the distribution by using the compound Poisson distribution. As was seen in Section 6.5, use of the compound Pois-son allows calculation of the total claims distribution by using a very simple recursive procedure or by using the Fast Fourier Transform. The pgf (6.35) of aggregate losses is

$$P_S(z) = \prod_{j=1}^{n} [1 + q_j(z^{b_j} - 1)].$$

By taking logarithms and using a Taylor series expansion of $\ln[1 + q_j(z^{b_j} - 1)]$, we obtain

$$\ln P_S(z) = \sum_{j=1}^{n} \sum_{k=1}^{\infty} \frac{(-1)^{k+1}}{k} [q_j(z^{b_j} - 1)]^k.$$

Table 6.23 Aggregate distribution for Example 6.33

x	$F_S(x)$	x	$F_S(x)$	x	$F_S(x)$	x	$F_S(x)$
0	0.00789581	200	0.51793382	400	0.96031865	600	0.99927281
8	0.00789581	208	0.55208736	408	0.96528977	608	0.99939248
16	0.01059183	216	0.57594360	416	0.96999808	616	0.99950270
24	0.01906263	224	0.60583632	424	0.97360199	624	0.99958630
32	0.02561396	232	0.63412023	432	0.97694855	632	0.99965590
40	0.02979597	240	0.66687534	440	0.98031827	640	0.99971784
48	0.03774849	248	0.68632432	448	0.98297484	648	0.99976679
56	0.04770335	256	0.71292641	456	0.98515668	656	0.99980876
64	0.06976756	264	0.73984823	464	0.98728185	664	0.99984205
72	0.07610528	272	0.76061061	472	0.98914069	672	0.99987063
80	0.10013432	280	0.78007667	480	0.99068429	680	0.99989481
88	0.12399672	288	0.80016248	488	0.99194854	688	0.99991371
96	0.13839960	296	0.82073766	496	0.99321771	696	0.99992950
104	0.15945674	304	0.83672920	504	0.99421982	704	0.99994275
112	0.18004988	312	0.85121374	512	0.99504627	712	0.99995364
120	0.22162539	320	0.86849112	520	0.99580992	720	0.99996222
128	0.23569706	328	0.88253629	528	0.99644624	728	0.99996932
136	0.26335063	336	0.89343529	536	0.99701494	736	0.99997545
144	0.30172723	344	0.90530546	544	0.99745896	744	0.99998004
152	0.33041683	352	0.91610001	552	0.99785787	752	0.99998383
160	0.35497038	360	0.92599796	560	0.99821941	760	0.99998707
168	0.38635038	368	0.93340851	568	0.99850204	768	0.99998955
176	0.42177800	376	0.94180939	576	0.99873887	776	0.99999162
184	0.45476409	384	0.94903173	584	0.99895067	784	0.99999326
192	0.47881084	392	0.95482932	592	0.99912971	792	0.99999461

Retaining only the first term in the inner sum yields the approximation

$$\ln P_S(z) \doteq \sum_{j=1}^{n} q_j \left(z^{b_j} - 1\right)$$

$$= \lambda \sum_{j=1}^{n} \frac{\lambda_j}{\lambda} \left(z^{b_j} - 1\right), \tag{6.50}$$

where $\lambda_j = q_j$ and $\lambda = \sum_{j=1}^{n} \lambda_j$. This results in

$$P_S(z) \doteq \exp\{\lambda[P_X(z) - 1]\},$$

which is the pgf of a compound Poisson distribution with individual loss distribution pgf

$$P_X(z) = \frac{1}{\lambda} \sum_{j=1}^{n} \lambda_j z^{b_j}. \tag{6.51}$$

Table 6.24   Aggregate distribution for Example 6.34

x	$F_S(x)$	x	$F_S(x)$	x	$F_S(x)$	x	$F_S(x)$
0	0.9530099	20	0.9618348	40	0.9735771	60	0.9990974
1	0.9530099	21	0.9618348	41	0.9735850	61	0.9990986
2	0.9530099	22	0.9618348	42	0.9736072	62	0.9990994
3	0.9530099	23	0.9618348	43	0.9736133	63	0.9990995
4	0.9530099	24	0.9664473	44	0.9736346	64	0.9990995
5	0.9530099	25	0.9664473	45	0.9736393	65	0.9990996
6	0.9530099	26	0.9702022	46	0.9736513	66	0.9990997
7	0.9530099	27	0.9702022	47	0.9736541	67	0.9990997
8	0.9530099	28	0.9713650	48	0.9736708	68	0.9990998
9	0.9530099	29	0.9713657	49	0.9736755	69	0.9991022
10	0.9530099	30	0.9723490	50	0.9736956	70	0.9991091
11	0.9530099	31	0.9735235	51	0.9736971	71	0.9991156
12	0.9530099	32	0.9735268	52	0.9737101	72	0.9991179
13	0.9530099	33	0.9735328	53	0.9737102	73	0.9991341
14	0.9534864	34	0.9735391	54	0.9737195	74	0.9991470
15	0.9549064	35	0.9735433	55	0.9782901	75	0.9991839
16	0.9562597	36	0.9735512	56	0.9782947	76	0.9992135
17	0.9567362	37	0.9735536	57	0.9782994	77	0.9992239
18	0.9601003	38	0.9735604	58	0.9783006	78	0.9992973
19	0.9606149	39	0.9735679	59	0.9783021	79	0.9993307

This distribution has pf

$$\Pr(X = x) = \frac{1}{\lambda} \sum_{\{j:b_j=x\}} \lambda_j. \tag{6.52}$$

The numerator sums all probabilities associated with amount b_j.

Note that the means of the frequency distribution and the aggregate loss distribution match those of the exact distribution.

Example 6.34 (Example 6.30 continued) *Consider the group life case of Example 6.30. Derive a compound Poisson approximation.*

Using the compound Poisson approximation of this section with Poisson parameter $\lambda = \sum q_j = 0.04813$, the distribution function given in Table 6.24 is obtained.

When these values are compared to those of Example 6.31, it can be seen that the maximum error of 0.0002708 occurs at $x = 0$.   □

Some closely related approximations have been used. One popular one is to let λ_j in (6.50) be set to

$$\lambda_j = -\ln(1 - q_j), \quad j = 1, 2, \ldots, n. \tag{6.53}$$

This matches the *no-loss* probability $1 - q_j$ with the no-loss probability of the Poisson distribution, $e^{-\lambda_j}$. This effectively replaces each life in the group by a Poisson distribution. This approximation is appropriate in the context of a group life insurance contract where a life is "replaced" upon death, leaving the Poisson intensity unchanged by the death. Naturally the expected number of losses is greater than $\sum_{j=1}^{n} q_j$. An alternative choice was proposed by Kornya [79]. It used $\lambda_j = q_j/(1 - q_j)$ in (6.50). It results in an expected number of losses that exceeds that using (6.53) (see Exercise 6.61).

6.11.3.1 *More than one possible loss amount*

It was noted in the beginning of this section that there may be more than one possible loss amount. Again let B_j be the random variable that measures the amount of the loss given that there was a loss and let $X_j = I_j B_j$. Then

$$P_{X_j}(z) = [1 - q_j + q_j P_{B_j}(z)].$$

The pgf corresponding to (6.35) is

$$P_S(z) = \prod_{j=1}^{n} [1 - q_j + q_j P_{B_j}(z)].$$

Although it is possible to extend the exact computational methods to this case, it is quite cumbersome. However, the compound Poisson approximation based on matching of moments (6.50) simply requires replacing z^{b_j} by $P_{B_j}(z)$. Then, the pgf of the severity distribution (6.51) becomes

$$P_X(z) = \frac{1}{\lambda} \sum_{j=1}^{n} \lambda_j P_{B_j}(z),$$

and so

$$f_X(x) = \frac{1}{\lambda} \sum_{j=1}^{n} \lambda_j f_{B_j}(x), \qquad (6.54)$$

which is a weighted average of the n individual severity densities. Extensions to continuous severity distributions also satisfy (6.54) for all values of x.

Example 6.35 (Example 6.29 continued) *Develop compound Poisson approximations using all three methods suggested here. Compute the mean and variance for each approximation and compare it to the exact value.*

Using the method that matches the mean, we have $\lambda = 50(0.01) + 25(0.01) = 0.75$. The severity distribution is

$$f_X(50,000) = \frac{50(0.01)(0.7)}{0.75} = 0.4667,$$

$$f_X(75,000) = \frac{25(0.01)(0.7)}{0.75} = 0.2333,$$

$$f_X(100,000) = \frac{50(0.01)(0.3)}{0.75} = 0.2000,$$

$$f_X(150,000) = \frac{25(0.01)(0.3)}{0.75} = 0.1000.$$

The mean is $\lambda E(X) = 0.75(75{,}833.33) = 56{,}875$, which matches the exact value, and the variance is $\lambda E(X^2) = 0.75(6{,}729{,}166{,}667) = 5{,}046{,}875{,}000$, which exceeds the exact value.

For the method that preserves the probability of no losses, $\lambda = -75 \ln(0.99) = 0.753775$. For this method, the severity distribution turns out to be exactly the same as before (this is due to the fact that all individuals have the same value of q_j). Thus the mean is 57,161 and the variance is 5,072,278,876, both of which exceed the previous approximate values.

Using Kornya's method, $\lambda = 75(0.01)/0.99 = 0.757576$ and again the severity distribution is unchanged. The mean is 57,449 and the variance is 5,097,853,535, which are the largest values of all.   □

6.11.4   Exercises

6.60 Derive (6.36) and (6.37).

6.61 Demonstrate that the compound Poisson model given by $\lambda_j = q_j$ and (6.52) produces a model with the same mean as the exact distribution but with a larger variance. Then show that the one using $\lambda_j = -\ln(1 - q_j)$ must produce a larger mean and even larger variance, and finally show that the one using $\lambda_j = q_j/(1 - q_j)$ must produce the largest mean and variance of all.

6.62 Individual members of an insured group have independent claims. The claim distribution has the statistics given in Table 6.25.

The premium for a group with future claims S is the mean of S plus 2 times the standard deviation of S. If the genders of the members of a group of m members are not known, the number of males is assumed to have a binomial distribution with parameters m and $q = 0.4$. Let A be the premium for a group of 100 for which the genders of the members are not known and let B is the premium for a group of 40 males and 60 females. Determine A/B.

6.63 An insurance company assumes claim probabilities for persons covered by its group life insurance contracts as given in Table 6.26.

A group of mutually independent lives has coverage of 1,000 per life. The company assumes that 20% of the lives are smokers. Based on this assumption, the premium is set equal to 110% of expected claims. If 30% of the lives are smokers, the probability that claims will exceed the premium is less than

Table 6.25   Data for Exercise 6.62

	Mean	Variance
Males	2	4
Females	4	10

Table 6.26   Data for Exercise 6.63

Class	Probability of claim
Smoker	0.02
Nonsmoker	0.01

0.20. Using the normal approximation, determine the minimum number of lives which must be in the group.

6.64 Based on the individual risk model with independent claims, the cumulative distribution function of aggregate claims for a portfolio of life insurance policies is as in Table 6.27.

One policy with face amount 100 and probability of claim 0.20 is increased in face amount to 200. Determine the probability that aggregate claims for the revised portfolio will not exceed 500.

6.65 A group life insurance contract covering independent lives is rated in the three age groupings as given in Table 6.28. The insurer prices the contract

Table 6.27   Distribution for Exercise 6.64

x	$F_S(x)$
0	0.40
100	0.58
200	0.64
300	0.69
400	0.70
500	0.78
600	0.96
700	1.00

Table 6.28   Data for Exercise 6.65

Age group	Number in age group	Probability of claim per life	Mean of the exponential distribution of claim amounts
18–35	400	0.03	5
36–50	300	0.07	3
51–65	200	0.10	2

Table 6.29   Data for Exercise 6.66

Service	Probability of claim	Distribution of annual charges given that a claim occcurs	
		Mean	Variance
Office visits	0.7	160	4,900
Surgery	0.2	600	20,000
Other services	0.5	240	8,100

so that the probability that claims will exceed the premium is 0.05. Using the normal approximation, determine the premium that the insurer will charge.

6.66 The probability model for the distribution of annual claims per member in a health plan is shown in Table 6.29. Independence of costs and occurrences among services and members is assumed. Using the normal approximation, determine the minimum number of members that a plan must have such that the probability that actual charges will exceed 115% of the expected charges is less than 0.10.

6.67 An insurer has a portfolio of independent risks as given in Table 6.30. The insurer sets α and k such that aggregate claims have expected value 100,000 and minimum variance. Determine α.

6.68 An insurance company has a portfolio of independent one-year term life policies as given in Table 6.31. The actuary approximates the distribution of claims in the individual model using the compound Poisson model in which the expected number of claims is the same as in the individual model. Determine

Table 6.30   Data for Exercise 6.67

Class	Probability of claim	Benefit	Number of risks
Standard	0.2	k	3,500
Substandard	0.6	αk	2,000

Table 6.31   Data for Exercise 6.68

Class	Number in class	Benefit amount	Probability of a claim
1	500	x	0.01
2	500	$2x$	0.02

Table 6.32 Data for Exercise 6.69

Class	Benefit amount	Probability of death	Number of policies
1	100,000	0.10	500
2	200,000	0.02	500
3	300,000	0.02	500
4	200,000	0.10	300
5	200,000	0.10	500

the maximum value of x such that the variance of the compound Poisson approximation is less than 4,500.

6.69 An insurance company sold one-year term life insurance on a group of 2,300 independent lives as given in Table 6.32.

The insurance company reinsures amounts in excess of 100,000 on each life. The reinsurer wishes to charge a premium that is sufficient to guarantee that it will lose money 5% of the time on such groups. Obtain the appropriate premium by each of the following ways.

(a) Using a normal approximation to the aggregate claims distribution.

(b) Using a lognormal approximation.

(c) Using a gamma approximation.

(d) Using the compound Poisson approximation which matches the means.

(e) Carrying out the calculations exactly (using the method developed by De Pril or some other method). This requires a computer.

7

Discrete-time ruin models

7.1 INTRODUCTION

The risk assumed with a portfolio of insurance contracts is difficult to assess, but it is nevertheless important to attempt to do so in order to ensure the viability of an insurance operation. The distribution of total claims over a fixed period of time is an obvious input parameter to such a process, and this quantity has been the subject of the previous chapters.

In this chapter we take a multiperiod approach in which the fortunes of the policy, portfolio, or company are followed over time. The most common use of this approach is **ruin theory**, in which the quantity of interest is the amount of surplus, with ruin occurring when the surplus becomes negative. In order to track surplus we must model more than the claim payments. We must include premiums, investment income, and expenses, along with any other item that impacts the cash flow.

The models described in this and the next chapter are quite simple and idealized in order to maintain mathematical simplicity. Consequently the output from the analysis should not be viewed as a representation of absolute reality, but rather as important additional information on the risk associated with the portfolio of business. Such information is useful for long-run financial planning and maintenance of the insurer's solvency.

Loss Models: From Data to Decisions, Second Edition.
By Stuart A. Klugman, Harry H. Panjer, and Gordon E. Willmot
ISBN 0-471-21577-5   Copyright © 2004 John Wiley & Sons, Inc.

This chapter is organized into two parts. The first part (Section 7.2) introduces process models. The appropriate definitions are made and the terms of ruin theory defined. The second part (Section 7.3) analyzes discrete-time models. This can be done with the tools presented in the previous chapters. An analysis of continuous-time models is covered in the next chapter. This requires an introduction to stochastic processes. Two processes are analyzed: the compound Poisson process and Brownian motion. The compound Poisson process has been the standard model for ruin analysis in actuarial science, while Brownian motion has found considerable use in modern financial theory and also can be used as an approximation to the compound Poisson process.

7.2 PROCESS MODELS FOR INSURANCE

7.2.1 Processes

The major difference between this chapter and the earlier ones is that we now want to view the evolution of the portfolio over time. With that in mind, we define two kinds of processes. We note that, while processes that involve random events are usually called **stochastic processes**, we will not employ the modifier "stochastic" and instead trust that the context will make it clear which processes are random and which are not.

Definition 7.1 *A **continuous-time process** is denoted $\{X_t; t \geq 0\}$. If there are random elements, it is sufficient to specify the joint distribution of $(X_{t_1}, \ldots, X_{t_n})$ for all $t_1, \ldots, t_n$ and any n.*

In general, it is insufficient to describe the process by specifying the distribution of X_t for arbitrary t. Many processes have correlations between the values observed at different times.

Example 7.2 *Let $\{S_t; t \geq 0\}$ be the total losses paid from time 0 to time t. Indicate how the collective risk model of Chapter 6 may be used to describe this process.*

For the joint distribution of $(S_{t_1}, \ldots, S_{t_n})$, suppose $t_1 < \cdots < t_n$. Let $W_j = S_{t_j} - S_{t_{j-1}}$ with $S_{t_0} = S_0 = 0$. Let the W_j have independent distributions given by the collective risk model. The individual loss distributions could be identical while the frequency distribution would have a mean that is proportional to the length of the time period, $t_j - t_{j-1}$. An example of a realization of this process (called a **sample path**) is given in Figure 7.1. □

It is usually easier to describe a process if it does not change much over time. Two specific ways in which this can happen are defined below.

Definition 7.3 *A process has **independent increments** if the random variables $X_t - X_s$ and $X_u - X_v$ are independent whenever $s < t \leq v < u$.*

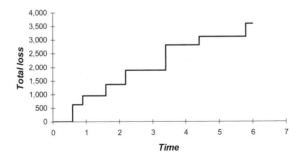

Fig. 7.1 Continuous total loss process, S_t.

This property indicates that the movement in the process in any one period is independent of the movement in a different, nonoverlapping period.

Definition 7.4 *A process has* **stationary increments** *if the distribution of $X_t - X_s$ depends on t and s only through the difference $t - s$.*

This property implies that the movement does not depend on the date. In other words, you cannot tell what time it is by looking at increments in the process.

Most business organizations do not continuously monitor their status. Instead, it is checked at regular intervals. This leads to the other kind of process.

Definition 7.5 *A* **discrete-time process** *is denoted by $\{X_t; t = 0, 1, 2, \ldots\}$. If there are random elements, it is sufficient to specify the joint distribution of $(X_{t_1}, \ldots, X_{t_n})$ for integer t_i and any n.*

A discrete-time process can be derived from a continuous-time process by just writing down the values of X_t at integral times. In this chapter, all discrete-time processes will take measurements at the end of each observation period, such as a month, quarter, or year.

Example 7.6 (Example 7.2 continued) *Convert the process to a discrete time process with stationary, independent increments.*

Let $X_1, X_2, \ldots$ be the amount of the total losses in each period where the X_js are i.i.d. and each X_j has a compound distribution. Then let the total loss process be $S_t = X_1 + \cdots + X_t$. The process has stationary increments because $S_t - S_s = X_{s+1} + \cdots + X_t$ and its distribution depends only on the number of X_js, which is $t - s$. The property of independent increments follows directly from the independence of the X_js. Figure 7.2 is the discrete-time version of Figure 7.1. □

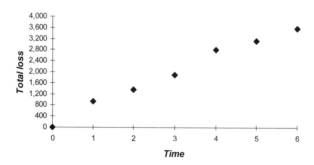

Fig. 7.2   Discrete total loss process, $\tilde{S}_t$.

7.2.2   An insurance model

The earlier examples have already illustrated most of the model we will use for the insurance process. We are interested in the **surplus process** $\{U_t; t \geq 0\}$ (or perhaps its discrete-time version, $\{U_t; t = 0, 1, \ldots\}$), which measures the surplus of the portfolio at time t. We begin at time zero with $u = U_0$, the **initial surplus**. We think of the surplus in the accounting sense in that it represents excess funds that would not be needed if the portfolio terminated today. For an ongoing concern, a positive value provides protection against adversity. The surplus at time t is

$$U_t = U_0 + P_t - S_t,$$

where $\{P_t; t \geq 0\}$ is the premium process which measures all premiums (net of expenses) collected up to time t, and $\{S_t; t \geq 0\}$ is the loss process, which measures all losses paid up to time t. We make the following observations:

1. P_t may be written or earned premiums, as appropriate;

2. S_t may be paid or incurred losses, again, as appropriate; and

3. P_t may depend on S_u for $u < t$. For example, dividends based on favorable past loss experience may reduce the current premium.

It is possible, though not necessary, to separate the frequency and severity components of S_t. Let $\{N_t; t \geq 0\}$ be the claims process which records the number of claims as of time t. Then let $S_t = X_1 + \cdots + X_{N_t}$. The sequence $\{X_1, X_2, \ldots\}$ need not consist of i.i.d. variables. However, if it does and the sequence is independent of N_t for all t, then S_t will have a compound distribution.

We now look at two special cases of the surplus process. These are the only ones that will be studied.

7.2.2.1 A discrete-time model Let the increment in the surplus process in year t be defined as

$$W_t = P_t - P_{t-1} - S_t + S_{t-1}, \ t = 1, 2, \ldots .$$

Then the progression of surplus is

$$U_t = U_{t-1} + W_t, \ t = 1, 2, \ldots .$$

It will be relatively easy to learn about the distribution of $\{U_t; t = 1, 2, \ldots\}$ provided that the random variable W_t either is independent of the other W_ts or only depends on the value of U_{t-1}. The dependency of W_t on U_{t-1} allows us to pay a dividend based on the surplus at the end of the previous year (because W_t depends on P_t).

In Section 7.3, two methods of determining the distribution of the U_ts will be presented. These will be computationally intensive, but given enough time and resources, the answers are easy to obtain.

7.2.2.2 A continuous-time model In most cases it is extremely difficult to analyze continuous-time models. This is because the joint distribution must be developed at every time point, not just at a countable set of time points. One model that has been extensively analyzed is the compound Poisson claim process where premiums are collected at a constant continuous nonrandom rate,

$$P_t = (1 + \theta)\mathrm{E}(S_1)t,$$

and the total loss process is $S_t = X_1 + \cdots + X_{N_t}$, where $\{N_t; t \geq 0\}$ is the Poisson process. This process is discussed in detail in Section 8.1.1. It suffices for now to note that for any period the number of losses has the Poisson distribution with a mean that is proportional to the length of the time period.

Because this model is more difficult to work with, the entire next chapter will be devoted to its development and analysis. We are now ready to define the quantity of interest, the one that measures the portfolio's chance for success.

7.2.3 Ruin

The main purpose for building a process model is to determine if the portfolio will survive over time. The probability of survival can be defined in four different ways.

Definition 7.7 *The **continuous-time, infinite-horizon survival probability** is given by*

$$\phi(u) = \Pr(U_t \geq 0 \ for \ all \ t \geq 0 | U_0 = u).$$

Here we continuously check the surplus and demand that the portfolio be solvent forever. Both continuous checking and a requirement that the portfolio survive forever are unrealistic. In practice, it is more likely that surplus is checked at regular intervals. While we would like our portfolio to last forever, it is too much to ask that our model be capable of forecasting infinitely far into the future. A more useful quantity follows.

Definition 7.8 *The **discrete-time, finite-horizon survival probability** is given by*

$$\tilde{\phi}(u,\tau) = \Pr(U_t \geq 0 \text{ for all } t = 0, 1, \ldots, \tau | U_0 = u).$$

Here the portfolio is required to survive τ periods (usually years), and we only check at the end of each period. There are two intermediate cases.

Definition 7.9 *The **continuous-time, finite-horizon survival probability** is given by*

$$\phi(u,\tau) = \Pr(U_t \geq 0 \text{ for all } 0 \leq t \leq \tau | U_0 = u)$$

*and the **discrete-time, infinite-horizon survival probability** is given by*

$$\tilde{\phi}(u) = \Pr(U_t \geq 0 \text{ for all } t = 0, 1, \ldots | U_0 = u).$$

It should be clear that the following inequalities hold:

$$\tilde{\phi}(u,\tau) \geq \tilde{\phi}(u) \geq \phi(u)$$

and

$$\tilde{\phi}(u,\tau) \geq \phi(u,\tau) \geq \phi(u).$$

There are also some limits that should be equally obvious. They are

$$\lim_{\tau \to \infty} \phi(u,\tau) = \phi(u)$$

and

$$\lim_{\tau \to \infty} \tilde{\phi}(u,\tau) = \tilde{\phi}(u).$$

In many cases, convergence is rapid. This means that the choice of a finite or infinite horizon should depend as much on the ease of calculation as on the appropriateness of the model. We will find that, if the Poisson process holds, infinite-horizon probabilities are easier to obtain. For other cases, the finite-horizon calculation may be easier.

Although we have not defined notation to express them, there is another pair of limits. As the frequency with which surplus is checked increases (that is, the number of times per year), the discrete-time survival probabilities converge to their continuous-time counterparts.

As this subsection refers to ruin, we close by defining the probability of ruin.

Definition 7.10 *The **continuous-time, infinite-horizon ruin probability** is given by*

$$\psi(u) = 1 - \phi(u)$$

and the other three ruin probabilities are defined and denoted in a similar manner.

7.3 DISCRETE, FINITE-TIME RUIN PROBABILITIES

7.3.1 The discrete-time process

Let P_t be the premium collected in the tth period and let S_t be the losses paid in the tth period. We also add one generalization. Let C_t be any cash flow other than the collection of premiums and the payment of losses. The most significant cash flow is the earning of investment income on the surplus available at the beginning of the period. The surplus at the end of the tth period is then

$$U_t = u + \sum_{j=1}^{t}(P_j + C_j - S_j) = U_{t-1} + P_t + C_t - S_t.$$

The final assumption is that, given U_{t-1}, the random variable $W_t = P_t + C_t - S_t$ depends only upon U_{t-1} and not upon any other previous experience. This makes $\{U_t; t = 1, 2, \ldots\}$ a **Markov process**.

In order to evaluate ruin probabilities, we consider a second process defined as follows. First, define

$$
\begin{aligned}
W_t^* &= \begin{cases} 0, & U_{t-1}^* < 0, \\ W_t, & U_{t-1}^* \geq 0, \end{cases} \\
U_t^* &= U_{t-1}^* + W_t^*,
\end{aligned}
\tag{7.1}
$$

where the new process starts with $U_0^* = u$. In this case, the finite-horizon survival probability is

$$\tilde{\phi}(u, \tau) = \Pr(U_\tau^* \geq 0).$$

The reason we need only check U_t^* at time τ is that, once ruined, this process is not allowed to become nonnegative. The following example illustrates this distinction and is a preview of the method presented in detail in the next subsection.

Example 7.11 *Consider a process with an initial surplus of 2, a fixed annual premium of 3, and losses of either 0 or 6 with probabilities 0.6 and 0.4, respectively. There are no other cash flows. Determine $\tilde{\phi}(2, 2)$.*

There are only two possible values for U_1, 5 and -1, with probabilities 0.6 and 0.4. In each year, W_t takes the values 3 and -3 with probabilities 0.6 and 0.4. For year 2, there are four possible ways for the process to end. They are listed in Table 7.1. Then, $\tilde{\phi}(2, 2) = 0.36 + 0.24 = 0.60$. Note that for U_2 the process would continue for cases 3 and 4, producing values of 2 and -4. But our process is not allowed to recover from ruin and so case 3 must be forced to remain negative. □

Table 7.1 Calculations for Example 7.11

Case	U_1	W_2	W_2^*	U_2^*	Probability
1	5	3	3	8	0.36
2	5	-3	-3	2	0.24
3	-1	3	0	-1	0.24
4	-1	-3	0	-1	0.16

7.3.2 Evaluating the probability of ruin

There are three ways to evaluate the ruin probability. One way that is always available is simulation. Just as the aggregate loss distribution can be simulated, the progress of surplus can also be simulated. For extremely complicated models (for example, one encompassing medical benefits, including hospitalization, prescription drugs, and outpatient visits as well as random inflation, interest rates, and utilization rates), this may be the only way to proceed. For more modest settings the other two methods will work well. The first is a brute force method that has few restrictions, and the second is an inversion method that has some restrictions.

7.3.2.1 Evaluation by convolutions For any practical use of this method, the distributions of all the random variables involved should be discrete and have finite support. If they are not, some discrete approximation should be constructed. The calculation is done recursively, using (7.1). For notational purposes, suppose we have obtained the discrete pf of U_{t-1}^*. Then the ruin probability is $\tilde{\psi}(u, t-1) = \Pr(U_{t-1}^* < 0)$ and the distribution of nonnegative surplus is $f_j = \Pr(U_{t-1}^* = u_j)$, $j = 1, 2, \ldots, n$, where $u_j \geq 0$ for all j and u_n is the largest possible value of U_{t-1}^*. We have assumed that for each positive value of U_{t-1}^* the distribution of W_t is known. Let $g_{j,k} = \Pr(W_t = w_{j,k} | U_{t-1}^* = u_j)$. We have left open the possibility that even the values W_t may depend on u_j. We then obtain the probabilities of U_t^* by convolution. First,

$$
\begin{aligned}
\tilde{\psi}(u, t) &= \tilde{\psi}(u, t-1) + \Pr(U_{t-1}^* \geq 0 \text{ and } U_{t-1}^* + W_t < 0) \\
&= \tilde{\psi}(u, t-1) + \sum_{j=1}^{n} \Pr(U_{t-1}^* + W_t < 0 | U_{t-1}^* = u_j) \Pr(U_{t-1}^* = u_j) \\
&= \tilde{\psi}(u, t-1) + \sum_{j=1}^{n} \Pr(u_j + W_t < 0 | U_{t-1}^* = u_j) f_j \\
&= \tilde{\psi}(u, t-1) + \sum_{j=1}^{n} \sum_{w_{j,k} < -u_j} g_{j,k} f_j.
\end{aligned}
$$

Then,

$$
\begin{aligned}
\Pr(U_t^* = x) &= \Pr(U_{t-1}^* \geq 0 \text{ and } U_{t-1}^* + W_t = x) \\
&= \sum_{j=1}^{n} \Pr(U_{t-1}^* \geq 0 \text{ and } U_{t-1}^* + W_t = x | U_{t-1}^* = u_j) \\
&\quad \times \Pr(U_{t-1}^* = u_j) \\
&= \sum_{j=1}^{n} \Pr(u_j + W_t = x | U_{t-1}^* = u_j) f_j \\
&= \sum_{j=1}^{n} \sum_{w_{j,k}+u_j=x} g_{j,k} f_j.
\end{aligned}
$$

Although these formulas look a bit intimidating, they are fairly easy to implement. Consider the following example.

Example 7.12 *Suppose that annual losses can assume the values 0, 2, 4, and 6, with probabilities 0.4, 0.3, 0.2, and 0.1, respectively. Further suppose that the initial surplus is 2, and a premium of 2.5 is collected at the beginning of each year. Interest is earned at 10% on any surplus available at the beginning of the year because losses are paid at the end of the year. In addition, a rebate of 0.5 is given in any year in which there are no losses. Determine the survival probability at the end of each of the first two years.*

First note that the rebate cannot be such that it is applied to the next year's premium. Doing so would require that we begin the year not only knowing the surplus but also if a rebate was to be provided.

At time zero, $\tilde{\psi}(2,0) = 0$ and $f_1 = \Pr(U_0^* = 2) = 1$. The possible values of $w_{1,k}$ are given in Table 7.2 along with the probabilities, $g_{1,k}$.

For example, $w_{1,1}$ is based on a premium of 2.5, interest of 0.45 (on the surplus after collection of the premium), a loss payment of 0, and a rebate of 0.5. To evaluate $\tilde{\psi}(2,1)$, observe that the only value of $w_{1,k}$ which is below $-u_1 = -2$ is $w_{1,4}$ and so $\tilde{\psi}(2,1) = 0.1$. It is also easy to see that the only values of x that will have positive probability are those that have $2+w_{1,k} > 0$. This gives the values for the distribution of U_1^* as in Table 7.3.

Table 7.2 w and g for Example 7.12

k	$w_{1,k}$	$g_{1,k}$
1	2.45	0.4
2	0.95	0.3
3	−1.05	0.2
4	−3.05	0.1

Table 7.3 U_1^* for Example 7.12

j	u_j	f_j
1	0.95	0.2
2	2.95	0.3
3	4.45	0.4

Table 7.4 $u + w$ and g for Example 7.12

j	u_j	f_j	k 1	2	3	4
1	0.95	0.2	3.295, 0.4	1.795, 0.3	−0.205, 0.2	−2.205, 0.1
2	2.95	0.3	5.495, 0.4	3.995, 0.3	1.995, 0.2	−0.005, 0.1
3	4.45	0.4	7.145, 0.4	5.645, 0.3	3.645, 0.2	1.645, 0.1

The remaining probability is at $\Pr(U_1^* = -1.05) = 0.1$.

One way to visualize year 2 is with a two-way table providing all of the combinations of u_j and $w_{j,k}$. The entries in Table 7.4 are $u_j + w_{j,k}$, $g_{j,k}$. Only the sums need be presented because they are the only interesting quantities.

The joint probability for any cell is the product of f_j from that row and the probability in that cell. The addition to $\tilde{\psi}(2,1)$ is the probability for all the cells with negative entries, that is,

$$\tilde{\psi}(2,2) = 0.1 + 0.2(0.2) + 0.2(0.1) + 0.3(0.1) = 0.19.$$

There are no duplicate values for $w_{i,k}$, so the best we can do is to put the values in order and note that they are the new u_j values for the beginning of year 3. They are listed in Table 7.5.

Table 7.5 u for Example 7.12

j	u_j	f_j
1	1.645	0.04
2	1.795	0.06
3	1.995	0.06
4	3.295	0.08
5	3.645	0.08
6	3.995	0.09
7	5.495	0.12
8	5.645	0.12
9	7.145	0.16

Table 7.6 Probabilities for Example 7.13

j	u_j	f_j
1	0	0.0134
2	2	0.189225
3	4	0.258975
4	6	0.2568
5	8	0.0916

The probabilities total 0.81, the complement of $\tilde{\psi}(2,2)$. By the earlier definition, the remaining 0.19 probability is associated with $U_2^* < 0$.   □

It should be easy to see that the number of possible u values as well as the number of decimal places can increase rapidly. At some point, rounding would seem to be a good idea. A simple way to do this is to demand that at each period the only allowable u values are some multiple of h, a span that may need to increase from period to period. When probability is assigned to some value that is not a multiple of h, it is distributed to the two nearest values in a way that will preserve the mean (spreading to more values could preserve higher moments).

Example 7.13 (Example 7.12 continued) *Distribute the probabilities for the surplus at the end of year 2 using a span of $h = 2$.*

The probability of 0.04 at 1.645 must be distributed to the points 0 and 2. To preserve the mean, $0.355(0.04)/2 = 0.0071$ is placed at zero and the remaining 0.0329 is placed at 2. The expected value is $0.0071(0) + 0.0329(2) = 0.0658$, which matches the original value of $0.04(1.645)$. The value 0.355 is the distance from the point in question (1.645) to the next span point (2), and the denominator is the span. The probability is then placed at the previous span point. The resulting approximate distribution is given in Table 7.6.   □

7.3.2.2 Evaluation by inversion   One of the strengths of the inversion method is that the act of computing a convolution is reduced to a few multiplications. This is true, provided that the random variables are independent. In this case that means that W_t is independent of U_{t-1}. We use a different approach with regard to keeping track of ruin (earlier that was accomplished by freezing U_t^* upon ruin). This idea could also be applied to the direct convolution approach. This time, let U_t^{**} be U_t conditioned on $U_t \geq 0$. At the end of each period, all probability associated with ruin is redistributed over the outcomes producing nonnegative surplus. The year-by-year analysis proceeds as follows:

1. Determine $\varphi_{1,t}(z) = \mathrm{E}(e^{izU_{t-1}^{**}})$, the characteristic function of U_{t-1}^{**}.

2. Determine $\varphi_{2,t}(z) = \mathrm{E}(e^{izW_t})$, the characteristic function of W_t.

3. Then $\varphi_{3,t}(z) = \varphi_{1,t}(z) \cdot \varphi_{2,t}(z)$ is the characteristic function of $U_{t-1}^{**} + W_t$.

4. Use inversion to determine $f_t(u)$, the pf of $U_{t-1}^{**} + W_t$.

5. Let $r_t = \Pr(U_{t-1}^{**} + W_t < 0)$. This is the probability that, given survival to time $t - 1$, the portfolio is ruined at time t.

6. Then $f_t^{**}(u) = f_t(u)/(1 - r_t)$ for $u \geq 0$ is the pf of U_t^{**}.

7. The probability of ruin by time t is then $\tilde{\psi}(u, t) = \tilde{\psi}(u, t - 1) + r_t[1 - \tilde{\psi}(u, t - 1)]$.

The process is initiated by noting that the pf of U_1 can be obtained directly by observing that $U_1 = u + W_1$, so all that needs to be done is to shift the arguments of the pf of W_1 by u.

Example 7.14 *Aggregate losses for one year are 0, 2, 4, and 6 with proba-bilities 0.4, 0.3, 0.2, and 0.1, respectively. Premiums of 2.5 are collected at the beginning of the year and initial surplus is 2. Determine the probability of ruin within the first two years using the Fast Fourier Transform (FFT).*

The pf of W_t is the same in all years and is given in Table 7.7. With an initial surplus of 2 it is easy to obtain the distribution of U_1. It is given in Table 7.8. This immediately gives $\tilde{\psi}(2, 1) = 0.1$ and the distribution of U_1^{**} is given in Table 7.9.

Table 7.7   pf of W_t for Example 7.14

w	$\Pr(W = w)$
-3.5	0.1
-1.5	0.2
0.5	0.3
2.5	0.4

Table 7.8   pf of U_1 for Example 7.14

u	$\Pr(U_1 = u)$
-1.5	0.1
0.5	0.2
2.5	0.3
4.5	0.4

Table 7.9 pf of U_1^{**} for Example 7.14

u	$\Pr(U_1^{**} = u)$
0.5	2/9
2.5	3/9
4.5	4/9

In order for the FFT to work in a simple manner, it is best to have all amounts be positive. This can be accomplished by adding 3.5 to each variable. The shifted distributions are given in the second and third columns of Table 7.10. Anticipating that the shifted $U_1^{**} + W_2$ will take on values from 0 to 14 with a span of 2, we observe that eight values are required. This is already a power of 2, so no extra zeros need be added. In Table 7.10 the fourth and fifth columns provide the FFT of the two input variables. They are followed by the product of the two characteristic functions and then ultimately by the inverse of this characteristic function. The last column is the pf we seek. Of course, in this case it would have been trivial to perform the convolutions, but this way we can also verify that the FFT and its inverse do what they are supposed to.

Table 7.10   Year 2 ruin calculation for Example 7.14

u	$f_1^{**}(u)$	$f_W(u)$	$\varphi_{1,2}/8$	$\varphi_{2,2}/8$
0	0	1/10	0.125	0.125
2	0	2/10	$-0.08502 - 0.05724i$	$-0.00518 - 0.09053i$
4	2/9	3/10	$0.02778 + 0.04167i$	$-0.025 + 0.025i$
6	3/9	4/10	$-0.02609 - 0.00169i$	$0.03018 - 0.01553i$
8	4/9	0	0.04167	-0.025
10	0	0	$-0.02609 + 0.00169i$	$0.03018 + 0.01553i$
12	0	0	$0.02778 - 0.04167i$	$-0.025 - 0.25i$
14	0	0	$-0.08502 + 0.05724i$	$-0.00518 + 0.09053i$

u	$\varphi_{3,2}/64$	$f_2(u)$
0	0.01563	0
2	$-0.00474 + 0.00799i$	0
4	$-0.00174 - 0.00035i$	2/90
6	$-0.00081 + 0.00035i$	7/90
8	-0.00104	16/90
10	$-0.00081 - 0.00035i$	25/90
12	$-0.00174 + 0.00035i$	24/90
14	$-0.00474 - 0.00799i$	16/90

Table 7.11 Distribution of surplus after year 2 for Example 7.14

u	$\Pr(U_1^{**} + W_2 = u)$	$\Pr(U_2^{**} = u)$
-3	2/90	0
-1	7/90	0
1	16/90	16/81
3	25/90	25/81
5	24/90	24/81
7	16/90	16/81

We must note that the probabilities in the last column are shifted by 7. The actual distribution of the sum is given in Table 7.11. We see that $\frac{9}{90} = \frac{1}{10}$ of the probability is associated with negative values and so $\tilde{\psi}(2,2) = 0.1 + 0.9(0.1) = 0.19$. The conditional distribution U_2^{**} is also given in Table 7.11.□

7.3.3 Exercises

7.1 The total claims paid in a year can be 0, 5, 10, 15, or 20 with probabilities 0.4, 0.3, 0.15, 0.1, and 0.05, respectively. Annual premiums of 6 are collected at the beginning of each year. Interest of 10% is earned on any funds available at the beginning of the year, and claims are paid at the end of the year.

(a) Determine $\tilde{\psi}(2,3)$ exactly.

(b) Determine $\tilde{\psi}(2,3)$, but after the premium is added and the interest credited, discretize the resulting distribution with a span of 5.

7.2 Repeat Exercise 7.1 using the FFT and rediscretizing to maintain a span of 5.

8

Continuous-time ruin models

8.1 INTRODUCTION

In this chapter we turn to models that examine surplus continuously over time. Because these models tend to be difficult to analyze, we begin by restricting attention to models in which the number of claims has a Poisson distribution. In the discrete-time case we found that answers could be obtained by brute force. For the continuous case we find that exact, analytic solutions can be obtained for some situations, and that approximations and an upper bound can be obtained for many situations. In this section we introduce the Poisson process and the continuous-time approach to ruin.

8.1.1 The Poisson process

We consider the basic properties of the Poisson process $\{N_t; \ t \geq 0\}$ representing the number of claims on a portfolio of business. Thus, N_t is the number of claims in $(0, t]$. A formal definition of a Poisson process is now given.

Definition 8.1 *The number-of-claims process* $\{N_t; \ t \geq 0\}$ *is a* ***Poisson process*** *with rate* $\lambda > 0$ *if the following three conditions hold:*

1. $N_0 = 0$.

Loss Models: From Data to Decisions, Second Edition.
By Stuart A. Klugman, Harry H. Panjer, and Gordon E. Willmot
ISBN 0-471-21577-5   Copyright © 2004 John Wiley & Sons, Inc.

2. *The process has stationary and independent increments.*

3. *The number of claims in an interval of length t is Poisson distributed with mean λt. That is, for all $s, t > 0$ we have*

$$\Pr(N_{t+s} - N_s = n) = \frac{(\lambda t)^n e^{-\lambda t}}{n!}, \quad n = 0, 1, \ldots . \quad (8.1)$$

Stationary increments means that the distribution of the number of claims in a fixed interval depends only on the length of the interval and not on when the interval occurs so, for example, there is no trend effect. **Independent increments** means that the number of claims in an interval is statistically independent of the number of claims in any previous interval (not overlapping the present interval). Together, **stationary and independent increments** imply that the process can be thought of intuitively as starting over at any point in time. Actually, the assumption of stationarity in Condition 2 in the definition is not necessary because it is implied by Condition 3, but it is stated for clarity.

An important property of the Poisson process is that the times between claims are independent and identically exponentially distributed, each with mean $1/\lambda$. To see this, let W_j be the time between the $(j-1)$th and jth claims for $j = 1, 2, \ldots$, where W_1 is the time of the first claim. Then,

$$\Pr(W_1 > t) = \Pr(N_t = 0) = e^{-\lambda t},$$

and so W_1 is exponential with mean $1/\lambda$. Also,

$$
\begin{aligned}
\Pr(W_2 > t | W_1 = s) &= \Pr(W_1 + W_2 > s + t | W_1 = s) \\
&= \Pr(N_{t+s} = 1 | N_s = 1) \\
&= \Pr(N_{t+s} - N_s = 0 | N_s = 1) \\
&= \Pr(N_{t+s} - N_s = 0)
\end{aligned}
$$

because the increments are independent. From Condition 3, we then have

$$\Pr(W_2 > t | W_1 = s) = e^{-\lambda t}.$$

Because this is true for all s, $\Pr(W_2 > t) = e^{-\lambda t}$ and W_2 is independent of W_1. Similarly, $W_3, W_4, W_5, \ldots$ are independent and exponentially distributed, each with mean $1/\lambda$.

Finally, we remark that, from a fixed point in time $t_0 \geq 0$ the time until the next claim occurs is also exponentially distributed with mean $1/\lambda$, due to the memoryless property of the exponential distribution. That is, if the nth claim occurred s time units before t_0, the probability that the next claim occurs at least t time units after t_0 is $\Pr(W_{n+1} > t + s | W_{n+1} > s) = e^{-\lambda t}$, which is the same exponential survival function no matter what s and n happen to be.

8.1.2   The continuous-time problem

The model for claims payments will be the compound Poisson process. A formal definition follows.

Definition 8.2 *Let the number of claims process $\{N_t;\ t \geq 0\}$ be a Poisson process with rate λ. Let the individual losses $\{X_1, X_2, \ldots\}$ be independent and identically distributed positive random variables, independent of N_t, each with cumulative distribution function $F(x)$ and mean $\mu < \infty$. Thus X_j is the amount of the jth loss. Let S_t be the total loss in $(0, t]$. It is given by $S_t = 0$ if $N_t = 0$ and $S_t = \sum_{j=1}^{N_t} X_j$ if $N_t > 0$. Then, for fixed t, S_t has a compound Poisson distribution. The process $\{S_t;\ t \geq 0\}$ is said to be a **compound Poisson process**. Because $\{N_t;\ t \geq 0\}$ has stationary and independent increments, so does $\{S_t; t \geq 0\}$. Also,*

$$\mathrm{E}(S_t) = \mathrm{E}(N_t)\mathrm{E}(X_j) = (\lambda t)(\mu) = \lambda \mu t.$$

We assume that premiums are payable continuously at constant rate c per unit time. That is, the total net premium in $(0, t]$ is ct and we ignore interest for mathematical simplicity. We further assume that net premiums have a positive loading, that is, $ct > \mathrm{E}(S_t)$, which implies that $c > \lambda \mu$. Thus let

$$c = (1 + \theta)\lambda \mu, \tag{8.2}$$

where $\theta > 0$ is called the **relative security loading** or **premium loading factor**.

For our model, we have now specified the loss and premium processes. The surplus process is thus

$$U_t = u + ct - S_t, \quad t \geq 0,$$

where $u = U_0$ is the initial surplus. We say that ruin occurs if U_t ever becomes negative, and survival occurs otherwise. Thus, the infinite-time survival probability is defined as

$$\phi(u) = \Pr(U_t \geq 0 \text{ for all } t \geq 0 | U_0 = u),$$

and the infinite-time ruin probability is

$$\psi(u) = 1 - \phi(u).$$

Our goal is to analyze $\phi(u)$ and/or $\psi(u)$.

8.2   THE ADJUSTMENT COEFFICIENT AND LUNDBERG'S INEQUALITY

In this section we determine a special quantity and then show that it can be used to obtain a bound on the value of $\psi(u)$. While it is only a bound, it is easy to obtain, and as an upper bound it provides a conservative estimate.

8.2.1   The adjustment coefficient

It is difficult to motivate the definition of the adjustment coefficient from a physical standpoint, so we just state it. We adopt the notational convention that X is an arbitrary claim size random variable in what follows.

Definition 8.3 *Let $t = \kappa$ be the smallest positive solution to the equation*

$$1 + (1 + \theta)\mu t = M_X(t), \tag{8.3}$$

*where $M_X(t) = \mathrm{E}(e^{tX})$ is the moment generating function of the claim severity random variable X. If such a value exists, it is called the **adjustment coefficient**.*

To see that there may be a solution, consider the two lines in the (t, y) plane given by $y_1(t) = 1 + (1 + \theta)\mu t$ and $y_2(t) = M_X(t) = \mathrm{E}(e^{tX})$. Now, $y_1(t)$ is a straight line with positive slope $(1 + \theta)\mu$. The mgf may not exist at all or may exist only for some values of t. Assume for this discussion that the mgf exists for all nonnegative t. Then $y_2'(t) = \mathrm{E}(Xe^{tX}) > 0$ and $y_2''(t) = \mathrm{E}(X^2 e^{tX}) > 0$. Because $y_1(0) = y_2(0) = 1$, the two curves intersect when $t = 0$. But $y_2'(0) = \mathrm{E}(X) = \mu < (1 + \theta)\mu = y_1'(0)$. Thus, as t increases from 0 the curve $y_2(t)$ initially falls below $y_1(t)$, but because $y_2'(t) > 0$ and $y_2''(t) > 0$, eventually $y_2(t)$ will cross $y_1(t)$ at a point $\kappa > 0$. The point κ is the adjustment coefficient.

We remark that there may not be a positive solution to (8.3), for example, if the single claim amount distribution has no moment generating function (e.g., Pareto, lognormal).

Example 8.4 (Exponential claim amounts) *If X has an exponential distribution with mean μ, determine the adjustment coefficient.*

We have $F(x) = 1 - e^{-x/\mu}$, $x \geq 0$. Then, $M_X(t) = (1 - \mu t)^{-1}$, $t < \mu^{-1}$. Thus, from (8.3), κ satisfies

$$1 + (1 + \theta)\mu\kappa = (1 - \mu\kappa)^{-1}. \tag{8.4}$$

As noted earlier, $\kappa = 0$ is one solution and the positive solution is $\kappa = \theta/[\mu(1+\theta)]$. The graph in Figure 8.1 displays plots of the left- and right-hand sides of (8.4) for the case $\theta = 0.2$ and $\mu = 1$. They intersect at 0 and at the adjustment coefficient, $\kappa = 0.2/1.2 = 0.1667$. □

Example 8.5 (A gamma distribution) *Suppose that the relative security loading is $\theta = 2$ and the gamma distribution has $\alpha = 2$. To avoid confusion, let β be the scale parameter for the gamma distribution. Determine the adjustment coefficient.*

The single claim size density is

$$f(x) = \beta^{-2}xe^{-x/\beta}, \quad x > 0.$$

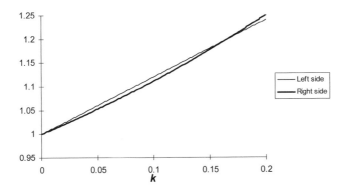

Fig. 8.1 Left and right sides of the adjustment coefficient equation.

For the gamma distribution $\mu = 2\beta$ and

$$M_X(t) = \int_0^\infty e^{tx} f(x)\, dx = (1 - \beta t)^{-2}, \quad t < \frac{1}{\beta}.$$

Then from (8.3) we obtain

$$1 + 6\kappa\beta = (1 - \beta\kappa)^{-2},$$

which may be rearranged as

$$6\beta^3\kappa^3 - 11\beta^2\kappa^2 + 4\beta\kappa = 0.$$

This is easily factored as

$$\kappa\beta(2\kappa\beta - 1)(3\kappa\beta - 4) = 0.$$

The adjustment coefficient is the only root that solves the original equation,[1] namely $\kappa = 1/(2\beta)$. □

For general claim amount distributions, it is not possible to explicitly solve for κ as was done in the above two examples. Normally, one must resort to numerical methods, many of which require an initial guess as to the value of

---

[1] Of the two roots, the larger one, $4/(3\beta)$, is not a legitimate argument for the mgf. The mgf exists only for values less than $1/\beta$. When solving such equations, the adjustment coefficient will always be the smallest positive solution.

κ. To find such a value, note that for (8.3) we may write

$$
\begin{aligned}
1 + (1+\theta)\mu\kappa &= \mathrm{E}(e^{\kappa X}) \\
&= \mathrm{E}(1 + \kappa X + \tfrac{1}{2}\kappa^2 X^2 + \cdots) \\
&> \mathrm{E}(1 + \kappa X + \tfrac{1}{2}\kappa^2 X^2) \\
&= 1 + \kappa\mu + \tfrac{1}{2}\kappa^2 \mathrm{E}(X^2).
\end{aligned}
$$

Then subtraction of $1 + \kappa\mu$ from both sides of the inequality and division by κ results in

$$
\kappa < \frac{2\theta\mu}{\mathrm{E}(X^2)}. \tag{8.5}
$$

The right-hand side of (8.5) is usually a satisfactory initial value of κ. Other inequalities for κ are given in the exercises.

Example 8.6 *The aggregate loss random variable has variance equal to three times the mean. Determine a bound on the adjustment coefficient.*

For the compound Poisson distribution, $\mathrm{E}(S_t) = \lambda\mu t$, $\mathrm{Var}(S_t) = \lambda t\mathrm{E}(X^2)$, and so $\mathrm{E}(X^2) = 3\mu$. Hence, from (8.5), $\kappa < 2\theta/3$. $\quad\square$

Define

$$
H(t) = 1 + (1+\theta)\mu t - M_X(t). \tag{8.6}
$$

Then the adjustment coefficient $\kappa > 0$ satisfies $H(\kappa) = 0$. To solve this equation, use the Newton–Raphson formula,

$$
\kappa_{j+1} = \kappa_j - \frac{H(\kappa_j)}{H'(\kappa_j)},
$$

where

$$
H'(t) = (1+\theta)\mu - M_X'(t)
$$

beginning with an initial value κ_0. Because $H(0) = 0$, care must be taken so as not to converge to the value 0.

Example 8.7 *Suppose the Poisson parameter is $\lambda = 4$ and the premium rate is $c = 7$. Further suppose the individual loss amount distribution is given by*

$$
\mathrm{Pr}(X = 1) = 0.6, \ \mathrm{Pr}(X = 2) = 0.4.
$$

Determine the adjustment coefficient.

We have

$$
\mu = E(X) = (1)(0.6) + (2)(0.4) = 1.4
$$

and

$$
\mathrm{E}(X^2) = (1)^2(0.6) + (2)^2(0.4) = 2.2.
$$

Then $\theta = c(\lambda\mu)^{-1} - 1 = 7(5.6)^{-1} - 1 = 0.25$. From (8.5), we know that κ must be less than $\kappa_0 = 2(0.25)(1.4)/2.2 = 0.3182$. Now,

$$M_X(t) = 0.6e^t + 0.4e^{2t}$$

and so from (8.6)

$$H(t) = 1 + 1.75t - 0.6e^t - 0.4e^{2t}.$$

We also have

$$M_X'(t) = (1e^t)(0.6) + (2e^{2t})(0.4)$$

and so

$$H'(t) = 1.75 - 0.6e^t - 0.8e^{2t}.$$

Our initial guess is $\kappa_0 = 0.3182$. Then $H(\kappa_0) = -0.02381$ and $H'(\kappa_0) = -0.5865$. Thus, an updated estimate of κ is

$$\kappa_1 = 0.3182 - \frac{-0.02381}{-0.5865} = 0.2776.$$

Then $H(0.2776) = -0.003091$, $H'(0.2776) = -0.4358$, and

$$\kappa_2 = 0.2776 - \frac{-0.003091}{-0.4358} = 0.2705.$$

Continuing in this fashion, we get $\kappa_3 = 0.2703$, $\kappa_4 = 0.2703$, and so the adjustment coefficient $\kappa = 0.2703$ to four decimal places of accuracy. $\qquad\square$

There is another form for the adjustment coefficient equation (8.3) which is often useful. In particular, the following is an alternative definition of κ:

$$1 + \theta = \int_0^\infty e^{\kappa x} f_e(x)\, dx, \tag{8.7}$$

where

$$f_e(x) = \frac{1 - F(x)}{\mu}, \quad x > 0, \tag{8.8}$$

is the equilibrium probability density function discussed in Section 4.3.3.
To see that (8.7) is equivalent to (8.3), note that

$$\int_0^\infty e^{\kappa x} f_e(x)\, dx = \frac{M_X(\kappa) - 1}{\mu\kappa}$$

from Exercise 4.15. Thus replacement of $M_X(\kappa)$ by $1 + (1 + \theta)\mu\kappa$ in this expression yields (8.7).

8.2.2   Lundberg's inequality

The first main use of the adjustment coefficient lies in the following result.

Theorem 8.8 *Suppose $\kappa > 0$ satisfies (8.3). Then the probability of ruin $\psi(u)$ satisfies*

$$\psi(u) \leq e^{-\kappa u}, \quad u \geq 0. \tag{8.9}$$

Proof: Let $\psi_n(u)$ be the probability that ruin occurs on or before the nth claim for $n = 0, 1, 2, \ldots$. We will prove by induction on n that $\psi_n(u) \leq e^{-\kappa u}$. Obviously, $\psi_0(u) = 0 \leq e^{-\kappa u}$. Now assume that $\psi_n(u) \leq e^{-\kappa u}$ and we wish to show that $\psi_{n+1}(u) \leq e^{-\kappa u}$. Let us consider what happens on the first claim. The time until the first claim occurs is exponential with probability density function $\lambda e^{-\lambda t}$. If the claim occurs at time $t > 0$, the surplus available to pay the claim at time t is $u + ct$. Thus, ruin occurs on the first claim if the amount of the claim exceeds $u + ct$. The probability that this happens is $1 - F(u + ct)$. If the amount of the claim is x, where $0 \leq x \leq u + ct$, ruin does not occur on the first claim. After payment of the claim, there is still a surplus of $u + ct - x$ remaining. Ruin can still occur on the next n claims. Because the surplus process has stationary and independent increments, this is the same probability as if we had started at the time of the first claim with initial reserve $u + ct - x$ and been ruined in the first n claims. Thus, by the law of total probability, we have the recursive equation[2]

$$\psi_{n+1}(u) = \int_0^\infty \left[1 - F(u + ct) + \int_0^{u+ct} \psi_n(u + ct - x)\, dF(x) \right] \lambda e^{-\lambda t}\, dt.$$

Thus, using the inductive hypothesis,

$$
\begin{aligned}
\psi_{n+1}(u) &= \int_0^\infty \left[\int_{u+ct}^\infty dF(x) + \int_0^{u+ct} \psi_n(u + ct - x) dF(x) \right] \lambda e^{-\lambda t}\, dt \\
&\leq \int_0^\infty \left[\int_{u+ct}^\infty e^{-\kappa(u+ct-x)}\, dF(x) \right. \\
&\qquad \left. + \int_0^{u+ct} e^{-\kappa(u+ct-x)}\, dF(x) \right] \lambda e^{-\lambda t}\, dt,
\end{aligned}
$$

---

[2] The Stieltjes integral notation "$dF(x)$" may be viewed as a notational convention to cover the situation where X is discrete, continuous, or mixed. In the continuous case, replace $dF(x)$ by $f(x)dx$ and proceed in the usual Riemann integral fashion. In the discrete case, the integral is simply notation for the usual sum involving the probability mass function.

where we have also used the fact that $-\kappa(u + ct - x) > 0$ when $x > u + ct$. Combining the two inner integrals gives

$$
\begin{aligned}
\psi_{n+1}(u) &\leq \int_0^\infty \left[\int_0^\infty e^{-\kappa(u+ct-x)}\, dF(x)\right] \lambda e^{-\lambda t}\, dt \\
&= \lambda e^{-\kappa u} \int_0^\infty e^{-\kappa ct} \left[\int_0^\infty e^{\kappa x}\, dF(x)\right] e^{-\lambda t}\, dt \\
&= \lambda e^{-\kappa u} \int_0^\infty e^{-(\lambda+\kappa c)t} \left[M_X(\kappa)\right] dt \\
&= \lambda M_X(\kappa) e^{-\kappa u} \int_0^\infty e^{-(\lambda+\kappa c)t}\, dt \\
&= \frac{\lambda M_X(\kappa)}{\lambda + \kappa c} e^{-\kappa u}.
\end{aligned}
$$

But from (8.3) and (8.2)

$$
\lambda M_X(\kappa) = \lambda[1 + (1+\theta)\kappa\mu] = \lambda + \kappa(1+\theta)\lambda\mu = \lambda + \kappa c
$$

and so $\psi_{n+1}(u) \leq e^{-\kappa u}$. Therefore, $\psi_n(u) \leq e^{-\kappa u}$ for all n and so $\psi(u) = \lim_{n\to\infty} \psi_n(u) \leq e^{-\kappa u}$. $\square$

This result is important because it may be used to examine the interplay between the level of surplus u and the premium loading θ, both parameters which are under the control of the insurer. Suppose one is willing to tolerate a probability of ruin of α (e.g., $\alpha = 0.01$) and a surplus of u is available. Then a loading of

$$
\theta = \frac{u\left\{E\left[\exp\left(-\dfrac{\ln\alpha}{u}X\right)\right] - 1\right\}}{-\mu\ln\alpha} - 1
$$

ensures that (8.3) is satisfied by $\kappa = (-\ln\alpha)/u$. Then, by Theorem 8.8, $\psi(u) \leq e^{-\kappa u} = e^{\ln\alpha} = \alpha$. On the other hand, if a specified loading of θ is desired, the surplus u required to ensure a ruin probability of no more than α is given by

$$
u = \frac{-\ln\alpha}{\kappa}
$$

because $\psi(u) \leq e^{-\kappa u} = e^{\ln\alpha} = \alpha$ as before.
   Also, (8.9) allows us to show that

$$
\psi(\infty) = \lim_{u\to\infty} \psi(u) = 0. \tag{8.10}
$$

Because the ruin probability is also nonnegative, we have

$$
0 \leq \psi(u) \leq e^{-\kappa u} \tag{8.11}
$$

and thus

$$0 \leq \lim_{u \to \infty} \psi(u) \leq \lim_{u \to \infty} e^{-\kappa u} = 0,$$

which establishes (8.10). We then have that for the survival probability

$$\phi(\infty) = 1. \tag{8.12}$$

8.2.3 Exercises

8.1 Calculate the adjustment coefficient if $\theta = 0.32$ and the claim size distribution is the same as that of Example 8.5.

8.2 Calculate the adjustment coefficient if the individual loss size density is $f(x) = \sqrt{\beta/(\pi x)}e^{-\beta x}$, $x > 0$.

8.3 Calculate the adjustment coefficient if $c = 3$, $\lambda = 4$, and the individual loss size density is $f(x) = e^{-2x} + \frac{3}{2}e^{-3x}$, $x > 0$. Do not use an iterative numerical procedure.

8.4 If $c = 2.99$, $\lambda = 1$, and the individual loss size distribution is given by $\Pr(X = 1) = 0.2$, $\Pr(X = 2) = 0.3$, and $\Pr(X = 3) = 0.5$, use the Newton–Raphson procedure to numerically obtain the adjustment coefficient.

8.5 Repeat Exercise 8.3 using the Newton–Raphson procedure beginning with an initial estimate based on (8.5).

8.6 Suppose that $E(X^3)$ is known where X is a generic individual loss amount random variable. Prove that the adjustment coefficient κ satisfies

$$\kappa < \frac{-3E(X^2) + \sqrt{9[E(X^2)]^2 + 240\mu E(X^3)}}{2E(X^3)}.$$

Also prove that the right-hand side of this inequality is strictly less than the bound given in (8.5), namely $2\theta\mu/E(X^2)$.

8.7 Recall that, if $g''(x) \geq 0$, Jensen's inequality implies $E[g(Y)] \geq g[E(Y)]$. Also, from Section 4.3.3,

$$\int_0^\infty x f_e(x)\, dx = \frac{E(X^2)}{2\mu},$$

where $f_e(x)$ is defined by (8.8).

(a) Use (8.7) and the above results to show that

$$\kappa \leq \frac{2\mu \ln(1+\theta)}{E(X^2)}.$$

(b) Show that $\ln(1 + \theta) < \theta$ for $\theta > 0$ and thus the inequality in (a) is tighter than that from (8.5). *Hint*: Consider $h(\theta) = \theta - \ln(1 + \theta)$, $\theta > 0$.

(c) If there is a maximum claim size of m, show that (8.7) becomes

$$1 + \theta = \int_0^m e^{\kappa x} f_e(x) \, dx.$$

Show that the right-hand side of this equality satisfies

$$\int_0^m e^{\kappa x} f_e(x) \, dx \leq e^{\kappa m}$$

and hence that

$$\kappa \geq \frac{1}{m} \ln(1 + \theta).$$

8.8 In Section 4.3.3 it was shown that, if $F(x)$ has an increasing mean residual life [which is implied if $F(x)$ has a decreasing hazard rate], then

$$\int_x^\infty f_e(y) \, dy \geq 1 - F(x), \quad x \geq 0.$$

(a) Let Y have probability density function $f_e(y)$, $y \geq 0$, and let X have cumulative distribution function $F(x)$. Show that

$$\Pr(Y > y) \geq \Pr(X > y), \quad y \geq 0$$

and hence that

$$\Pr(e^{\kappa Y} > t) \geq \Pr(e^{\kappa X} > t), \quad t \geq 1.$$

(b) Use (a) to show that $E(e^{\kappa Y}) \geq E(e^{\kappa X})$.

(c) Use (b) to show that $\kappa \leq \theta / [\mu(1 + \theta)]$.

(d) Prove that, if the above inequality is reversed,

$$\kappa \geq \frac{\theta}{\mu(1 + \theta)}.$$

8.9 Suppose that $\kappa > 0$ satisfies (8.3) and also that

$$S(x) \leq \rho e^{-\kappa x} \int_x^\infty e^{\kappa y} \, dF(y) \tag{8.13}$$

for $0 < \rho \leq 1$, where $S(x) = 1 - F(x)$. Prove that $\psi(u) \leq \rho e^{-\kappa u}$, $u \geq 0$. *Hint*: Use the method of Theorem 8.8.

8.10 Continue the previous exercise. Use integration by parts to show that

$$\int_x^\infty e^{\kappa y}\, dF(y) = e^{\kappa x} S(x) + \kappa \int_x^\infty e^{\kappa y} S(y)\, dy, \quad x \geq 0.$$

8.11 Suppose $F(x)$ has a decreasing hazard rate (Section 4.3.3). Prove that $S(y) \geq S(x)S(y-x)$, $x \geq 0$, $y \geq x$. Then use Exercise 8.10 to show that (8.13) is satisfied with $\rho^{-1} = \mathrm{E}(e^{\kappa X})$. Use (8.3) to conclude that

$$\psi(x) \leq [1 + (1+\theta)\kappa\mu]^{-1} e^{-\kappa x}, \quad x \geq 0.$$

8.12 Suppose $F(x)$ has a hazard rate $\mu(x) = -(d/dx)\ln S(x)$ which satisfies $\mu(x) \leq m < \infty$, $x \geq 0$. Use the result in Exercise 8.10 to show that (8.13) is satisfied with $\rho = 1 - \kappa/m$ and thus

$$\psi(x) \leq (1 - \kappa/m)e^{-\kappa x}, \quad x \geq 0.$$

Hint: Show that, for $y > x$, $S(y) \geq S(x)e^{-(y-x)m}$.

8.3 AN INTEGRODIFFERENTIAL EQUATION

We now consider the problem of finding an explicit formula for the ruin probability $\psi(u)$ or (equivalently) the survival probability $\phi(u)$. It will be useful in what follows to consider a slightly more general function.

Definition 8.9 $G(u, y) = \Pr(ruin\ occurs\ with\ initial\ reserve\ u\ and\ deficit\ immediately\ after\ ruin\ occurs\ is\ at\ most\ y)$, $u \geq 0, y \geq 0$.

For the event described, the surplus immediately after ruin is between 0 and $-y$. We then have

$$\psi(u) = \lim_{y \to \infty} G(u, y), \quad u \geq 0. \tag{8.14}$$

We have the following result.

Theorem 8.10 *The function $G(u, y)$ satisfies the equation*

$$\frac{\partial}{\partial u}G(u, y) = \frac{\lambda}{c}G(u, y) - \frac{\lambda}{c}\int_0^u G(u-x, y)\, dF(x) - \frac{\lambda}{c}[F(u+y) - F(u)],$$
$$u \geq 0. \tag{8.15}$$

Proof: Let us again consider what happens with the first claim. The time of the first claim has the exponential probability density function $\lambda e^{-\lambda t}$, and the surplus available to pay the first claim at time t is $u + ct$. If the amount of the claim is x, where $0 \leq x \leq u + ct$, then the first claim does not cause ruin but reduces the surplus to $u + ct - x$. By the stationary and independent increments property, ruin with a deficit of at most y would then occur thereafter with probability $G(u + ct - x, y)$. The only other possibility for ruin to occur with a deficit of at most y is that the first claim does cause ruin, that is, it occurs for an amount x where $x > u + ct$ but $x \leq u + ct + y$ because, if $x > u + ct + y$, the deficit would then exceed y. The probability that the claim amount x satisfies $u + ct < x \leq u + ct + y$ is $F(u + ct + y) - F(u + ct)$. Consequently, by the law of total probability, we have

$$G(u, y) = \int_0^\infty \left[\int_0^{u+ct} G(u + ct - x, y)dF(x) \right.$$

$$\left. + F(u + ct + y) - F(u + ct) \right] \lambda e^{-\lambda t} dt.$$

We wish to differentiate this expression with respect to u, and in order to do so, it is convenient to change the variable of integration from t to $z = u + ct$. Thus, $t = (z - u)/c$ and $dt = dz/c$. Then with this change of variable we have

$$G(u, y) = \frac{\lambda}{c} e^{(\lambda/c)u} \int_u^\infty e^{-(\lambda/c)z} \left[\int_0^z G(z - x, y)dF(x) + F(z + y) - F(z) \right] dz.$$

Recall from the fundamental theorem of calculus that, if k is a function, then $\frac{d}{du} \int_u^\infty k(z)dz = -k(u)$, and we may differentiate with the help of the product rule to obtain

$$\frac{\partial}{\partial u} G(u, y) = \frac{\lambda}{c} G(u, y) + \frac{\lambda}{c} e^{(\lambda/c)u} \left\{ -e^{-(\lambda/c)u} \left[\int_0^u G(u - x, y)dF(x) \right. \right.$$

$$\left. \left. + F(u + y) - F(u) \right] \right\},$$

from which the result follows.   □

We now determine an explicit formula for $G(0, y)$.

Theorem 8.11 *The function* $G(0, y)$ *is given by*

$$G(0, y) = \frac{\lambda}{c} \int_0^y [1 - F(x)]dx, \quad y \geq 0. \tag{8.16}$$

Proof: First note that

$$0 \leq G(u, y) \leq \psi(u) \leq e^{-\kappa u}$$

and thus

$$0 \leq G(\infty, y) = \lim_{u \to \infty} G(u, y) \leq \lim_{u \to \infty} e^{-\kappa u} = 0,$$

and therefore $G(\infty, y) = 0$. Also,

$$\int_0^\infty G(u, y) \, du \leq \int_0^\infty e^{-\kappa u} \, du = \kappa^{-1} < \infty.$$

Thus let $\tau(y) = \int_0^\infty G(u, y) du$ and we know that $0 < \tau(y) < \infty$. Then, integrate (8.15) with respect to u from 0 to ∞ to get, using the above,

$$-G(0, y) = \frac{\lambda}{c} \tau(y) - \frac{\lambda}{c} \int_0^\infty \int_0^u G(u-x, y) \, dF(x) \, du - \frac{\lambda}{c} \int_0^\infty [F(u+y) - F(u)] \, du.$$

Interchanging the order of integration in the double integral yields

$$G(0, y) = -\frac{\lambda}{c} \tau(y) + \frac{\lambda}{c} \int_0^\infty \int_x^\infty G(u - x, y) \, du \, dF(x)$$
$$+ \frac{\lambda}{c} \int_0^\infty [F(u + y) - F(u)] \, du$$

and changing the variable of integration from u to $v = u - x$ in the inner integral of the double integral results in

$$G(0, y) = -\frac{\lambda}{c} \tau(y) + \frac{\lambda}{c} \int_0^\infty \int_0^\infty G(v, y) \, dv \, dF(x)$$
$$+ \frac{\lambda}{c} \int_0^\infty [F(u + y) - F(u)] \, du$$
$$= -\frac{\lambda}{c} \tau(y) + \frac{\lambda}{c} \int_0^\infty \tau(y) \, dF(x) + \frac{\lambda}{c} \int_0^\infty [F(u + y) - F(u)] \, du.$$

Because $\int_0^\infty dF(x) = 1$, the first two terms on the right-hand side cancel, and so

$$G(0, y) = \frac{\lambda}{c} \int_0^\infty [F(u + y) - F(u)] \, du$$
$$= \frac{\lambda}{c} \int_0^\infty [1 - F(u)] \, du - \frac{\lambda}{c} \int_0^\infty [1 - F(u + y)] \, du.$$

Then change the variable from u to $x = u$ in the first integral and from u to $x = u + y$ in the second integral. The result is

$$G(0, y) = \frac{\lambda}{c} \int_0^\infty [1 - F(x)] \, dx - \frac{\lambda}{c} \int_y^\infty [1 - F(x)] \, dx = \frac{\lambda}{c} \int_0^y [1 - F(x)] \, dx. \qquad \square$$

We remark that (8.16) holds even if there is no adjustment coefficient. The function $G(0, y)$ is itself of considerable interest in its own right, but for now we shall return to the analysis of $\phi(u)$.

Theorem 8.12 *The survival probability with no initial reserve satisfies*

$$\phi(0) = \frac{\theta}{1 + \theta}. \qquad (8.17)$$

Proof: Recall that $\mu = \int_0^\infty [1 - F(x)]\, dx$ and note that from (8.16)

$$\psi(0) = \lim_{y \to \infty} G(0, y) = \frac{\lambda}{c} \int_0^\infty [1 - F(x)]\, dx = \frac{\lambda\mu}{c} = \frac{1}{1+\theta}.$$

Thus, $\phi(0) = 1 - \psi(0) = \theta/(1+\theta)$. □

The general solution to $\phi(u)$ may be obtained from the following integro-differential equation subject to the initial condition (8.17).

Theorem 8.13 *The probability of ultimate survival $\phi(u)$ satisfies*

$$\phi'(u) = \frac{\lambda}{c}\phi(u) - \frac{\lambda}{c}\int_0^u \phi(u - x)\, dF(x), \quad u \geq 0. \tag{8.18}$$

Proof: From (8.15) with $y \to \infty$ and (8.14),

$$\psi'(u) = \frac{\lambda}{c}\psi(u) - \frac{\lambda}{c}\int_0^u \psi(u - x)\, dF(x) - \frac{\lambda}{c}[1 - F(u)], \quad u \geq 0. \tag{8.19}$$

In terms of the survival probability $\phi(u) = 1 - \psi(u)$, (8.19) may be expressed as

$$
\begin{aligned}
-\phi'(u) &= \frac{\lambda}{c}[1 - \phi(u)] - \frac{\lambda}{c}\int_0^u [1 - \phi(u - x)]\, dF(x) - \frac{\lambda}{c}[1 - F(u)] \\
&= -\frac{\lambda}{c}\phi(u) - \frac{\lambda}{c}\int_0^u dF(x) + \frac{\lambda}{c}\int_0^u \phi(u - x)\, dF(x) + \frac{\lambda}{c}F(u) \\
&= -\frac{\lambda}{c}\phi(u) + \frac{\lambda}{c}\int_0^u \phi(u - x)\, dF(x)
\end{aligned}
$$

because $F(u) = \int_0^u dF(x)$. The result then follows. □

It is largely a matter of taste whether one uses (8.18) or (8.19). We shall often use (8.18) because it is slightly simpler algebraically. Unfortunately, the solution for general $F(x)$ is rather complicated and we shall defer this general solution to Section 8.4. At this point we shall obtain the solution for one special choice of $F(x)$.

Example 8.14 (The exponential distribution) *Suppose, as in Example 8.4, that $F(x) = 1 - e^{-x/\mu}$, $x \geq 0$. Determine $\phi(u)$.*

In this case (8.18) becomes

$$\phi'(u) = \frac{\lambda}{c}\phi(u) - \frac{\lambda}{\mu c}\int_0^u \phi(u - x)e^{-x/\mu}\, dx.$$

Change variables in the integral from x to $y = u - x$ to obtain

$$\phi'(u) = \frac{\lambda}{c}\phi(u) - \frac{\lambda}{\mu c}e^{-u/\mu}\int_0^u \phi(y)e^{y/\mu}\,dy. \tag{8.20}$$

We wish to eliminate the integral term in (8.20) so we differentiate with respect to u. This gives

$$\phi''(u) = \frac{\lambda}{c}\phi'(u) + \frac{\lambda}{\mu^2 c}e^{-u/\mu}\int_0^u \phi(y)e^{y/\mu}\,dy - \frac{\lambda}{\mu c}\phi(u).$$

The integral term can be eliminated using (8.20) to produce

$$\phi''(u) = \frac{\lambda}{c}\phi'(u) - \frac{\lambda}{\mu c}\phi(u) + \frac{1}{\mu}\left[\frac{\lambda}{c}\phi(u) - \phi'(u)\right],$$

which simplifies to

$$\phi''(u) = \left(\frac{\lambda}{c} - \frac{1}{\mu}\right)\phi'(u) = -\frac{\theta}{\mu(1+\theta)}\phi'(u).$$

After multiplication by the integrating factor $e^{\theta u/[\mu(1+\theta)]}$, this may be rewritten as

$$\frac{d}{du}\left[e^{\theta u/[\mu(1+\theta)]}\phi'(u)\right] = 0.$$

Integrating with respect to u gives

$$e^{\theta u/[\mu(1+\theta)]}\phi'(u) = K_1.$$

From (8.20) with $u = 0$ and using (8.17), we thus have

$$K_1 = \phi'(0) = \frac{\lambda}{c}\frac{\theta}{1+\theta} = \frac{\lambda}{\lambda\mu(1+\theta)}\frac{\theta}{1+\theta} = \frac{\theta}{\mu(1+\theta)^2}.$$

Thus,

$$\phi'(u) = \frac{\theta}{\mu(1+\theta)^2}\exp\left[-\frac{\theta u}{\mu(1+\theta)}\right],$$

which may be integrated again to give

$$\phi(u) = -\frac{1}{1+\theta}\exp\left[-\frac{\theta u}{\mu(1+\theta)}\right] + K_2.$$

Now (8.17) gives $\phi(0) = \theta/(1+\theta)$, and so with $u = 0$ we have $K_2 = 1$. Thus

$$\phi(u) = 1 - \frac{1}{1+\theta}\exp\left[-\frac{\theta u}{\mu(1+\theta)}\right]$$

is the required probability.   □

8.3.1   Exercises

8.13 Suppose that the claim size distribution is exponential with $F(x) = 1 - e^{-x/\mu}$ as in Example 8.14.

(a) Prove, using (8.15), that $G(u, y) = \psi(u)F(y)$ in this case.

(b) Prove that the distribution of the deficit immediately after ruin occurs, given that ruin does occur, has the same exponential distribution given above.

8.14 This exercise involves the derivation of integral equations called defective renewal equations for $G(u, y)$ and $\psi(u)$. These may be used to derive various properties of these functions.

(a) Integrate (8.15) over u from 0 to t and use (8.16) to show that

$$
\begin{aligned}
G(t, y) \;=\; & \frac{\lambda}{c}\Lambda(t, y) - \frac{\lambda}{c}\int_0^t \Lambda(t - x, y)dF(x) \\
& + \frac{\lambda}{c}\int_0^y [1 - F(x)]dx - \frac{\lambda}{c}\int_0^t [1 - F(u)]du \\
& + \frac{\lambda}{c}\int_0^t [1 - F(u + y)]du,
\end{aligned}
$$

where $\Lambda(x, y) = \int_0^x G(v, y)dv$.

(b) Use integration by parts on the integral $\int_0^t \Lambda(t-x, y)dF(x)$ to show from (a) that

$$
\begin{aligned}
G(t, y) \;=\; & \frac{\lambda}{c}\Lambda(t, y) - \frac{\lambda}{c}\int_0^t G(t - x, y)F(x)dx \\
& + \frac{\lambda}{c}\int_0^{y+t} [1 - F(x)]dx - \frac{\lambda}{c}\int_0^t [1 - F(u)]du.
\end{aligned}
$$

(c) Prove using (b) that

$$
G(u, y) = \frac{\lambda}{c}\int_0^u G(u - x, y)[1 - F(x)]dx + \frac{\lambda}{c}\int_u^{y+u} [1 - F(x)]dx.
$$

(d) Prove that

$$
\psi(u) = \frac{\lambda}{c}\int_0^u \psi(u - x)[1 - F(x)]dx + \frac{\lambda}{c}\int_u^{\infty} [1 - F(x)]dx.
$$

8.4   THE MAXIMUM AGGREGATE LOSS

We now derive the general solution to the integrodifferential equation (8.18) subject to the boundary conditions (8.12) and (8.17).

Beginning with an initial reserve u, the probability that the surplus will ever fall below the initial level u is $\psi(0)$ because the surplus process has stationary and independent increments. Thus the probability of dropping below the initial level u is the same for all u, but we know that when $u = 0$ it is $\psi(0)$.

The key result is that, given that there is a drop below the initial level u, the random variable Y which represents the amount of this initial drop has the equilibrium probability density function $f_e(y)$, where $f_e(y)$ is given by (8.8).

Theorem 8.15 *Given that there is a drop below the initial level u, the random variable Y which represents the amount of this initial drop has probability density function $f_e(y) = [1 - F(y)]/\mu$.*

Proof: Recall the function $G(u, y)$ from Definition 8.9. Because the surplus process has stationary and independent increments, $G(0, y)$ also represents the probability that the surplus drops below its initial level, and the amount of this drop is at most y. Thus, using Theorem 8.11, the amount of the drop, given that there is a drop, has cumulative distribution function

$$
\begin{aligned}
\Pr(Y \leq y) &= \frac{G(0, y)}{\psi(0)} \\
&= \frac{\lambda}{c\psi(0)} \int_0^y [1 - F(u)]\, du \\
&= \frac{1}{\mu} \int_0^y [1 - F(u)]\, du
\end{aligned}
$$

and the result follows by differentiation.   □

If there is a drop of y, the surplus immediately after the drop is $u - y$, and because the surplus process has stationary and independent increments, ruin occurs thereafter with probability $\psi(u - y)$, provided $u - y$ is nonnegative; otherwise ruin would have already occurred. The probability of a second drop is $\psi(0)$, and the amount of the second drop also has density $f_e(y)$ and is independent of the first drop. Due to the memoryless property of the Poisson process, the process "starts over" after each drop. Therefore, the total number of drops K is geometrically distributed, that is, $\Pr(K = 0) = 1 - \psi(0)$, $\Pr(K = 1) = [1 - \psi(0)]\psi(0)$, and more generally,

$$
\Pr(K = k) = [1 - \psi(0)][\psi(0)]^k = \frac{\theta}{1 + \theta}\left(\frac{1}{1 + \theta}\right)^k, \quad k = 0, 1, 2, \ldots,
$$

because $\psi(0) = 1/(1 + \theta)$. The usual geometric parameter β (in Appendix B) is thus $1/\theta$ in this case.

After a drop, the surplus immediately begins to increase again. Thus, the lowest level of the surplus is $u - L$, where L, called the **maximum aggregate**

loss, is the total of all the drop amounts. Let Y_j be the amount of the jth drop, and because the surplus process has stationary and independent increments, $\{Y_1, Y_2, \ldots\}$ is a sequence of independent and identically distributed random variables [each with density $f_e(y)$]. Because the number of drops is K, it follows that

$$L = Y_1 + Y_2 + \cdots + Y_K$$

with $L = 0$ if $K = 0$. Thus, L is a compound geometric random variable with "claim size density" $f_e(y)$.

Clearly, ultimate survival beginning with initial reserve u occurs if the maximum aggregate loss L does not exceed u, that is,

$$\phi(u) = \Pr(L \le u), \quad u \ge 0.$$

Let $F_e^{*0}(y) = 0$ if $y < 0$ and 1 if $y \ge 0$. Also $F_e^{*k}(y) = \Pr\{Y_1 + Y_2 + \cdots + Y_k \le y\}$ is the cumulative distribution function of the k-fold convolution of the distribution of Y with itself. We then have the general solution, namely,

$$\phi(u) = \sum_{k=0}^{\infty} \frac{\theta}{1+\theta} \left(\frac{1}{1+\theta}\right)^k F_e^{*k}(u), \quad u \ge 0.$$

In terms of the ruin probability, this general solution may be expressed as

$$\psi(u) = \sum_{k=1}^{\infty} \frac{\theta}{1+\theta} \left(\frac{1}{1+\theta}\right)^k S_e^{*k}(u), \quad u \ge 0,$$

where $S_e^{*k}(y) = 1 - F_e^{*k}(y)$. Evidently, $\psi(u)$ is the survival function associated with the compound geometric random variable L, and analytic solutions may be obtained in a similar manner as to those obtained in Section 6.4. An analytic solution for the important Erlang mixture claim severity pdf[3]

$$f(x) = \sum_{k=1}^{r} q_k \frac{\beta^{-k} x^{k-1} e^{-x/\beta}}{(k-1)!},$$

where the q_k are positive weights that sum to 1, may be found in Exercise 8.17, and for some other claim severity distributions in the next section.

We may also compute ruin probabilities numerically by computing the cumulative distribution function of a compound geometric distribution using any of the techniques described in Chapter 6.

Example 8.16 *Suppose the individual loss distribution is Pareto with $\alpha = 3$ and a mean of 500. Let the security loading be $\theta = 0.2$. Determine $\phi(u)$ for $u = 100, 200, 300, \ldots$.*

---

[3] Any continuous positive probability density function may be approximated arbitrarily accurately by an Erlang mixture pdf, as shown by Tijms [129], p. 163. An Erlang distribution is a gamma distribution for which the shape parameter α must be an integer.

Table 8.1   Survival probabilites, Pareto losses

u	$\phi(u)$	u	$\phi(u)$
100	0.193	5,000	0.687
200	0.216	7,500	0.787
300	0.238	10,000	0.852
500	0.276	15,000	0.923
1,000	0.355	20,000	0.958
2,000	0.473	25,000	0.975
3,000	0.561		

We first require the cdf, $F_e(u)$. It can be found from its pdf

$$
f_e(u) = \frac{1 - F(u)}{\mu} = \frac{1 - \left[1 - \left(\dfrac{1,000}{1,000 + u}\right)^3\right]}{500}
$$

$$
= \frac{1}{500}\left(\frac{1,000}{1,000 + u}\right)^3,
$$

which happens to be the density function of a Pareto distribution with $\alpha = 2$ and a mean of 1,000. This new Pareto distribution is the severity distribution for a compound geometric distribution where the parameter is $\beta = 1/\theta = 5$. The compound geometric distribution can be evaluated using any of the techniques in Chapter 6. We used the recursive formula with a discretization which preserves the mean and a span of $h = 5$. The cumulative probabilities are then obtained by summing the discrete probabilities generated by the recursive formula. The values appear in Table 8.1.   □

8.4.1   Exercises

8.15 Suppose the number of claims follows the Poisson process and the amount of an individual claim is exponentially distributed with mean 100. The relative security loading is $\theta = 0.1$. Determine $\psi(1,000)$ by using the method of this section. Use the method of rounding with a span of 50 to discretize the exponential distribution. Compare your answer to the exact ruin probability (see Example 8.14).

8.16 Consider the problem of Example 8.5 with $\beta = 50$. Use the method of this section (with discretization by rounding and a span of 1) to approximate $\psi(200)$. Compare your answer to the exact ruin probability which may be found in Example 8.19.

8.17 Suppose that the claim severity pdf is given by

$$f(x) = \sum_{k=1}^{r} q_k \frac{\beta^{-k} x^{k-1} e^{-x/\beta}}{(k-1)!}, \quad x > 0,$$

where $\sum_{k=1}^{r} q_k = 1$. Note that this is a mixture of gamma densities.

(a) Show that

$$f_e(x) = \sum_{k=1}^{r} q_k^* \frac{\beta^{-k} x^{k-1} e^{-x/\beta}}{(k-1)!}, \quad x > 0,$$

where

$$q_k^* = \frac{\sum_{j=k}^{r} q_j}{\sum_{j=1}^{r} j q_j}, \quad k = 1, 2, \ldots, r,$$

and also show that $\sum_{k=1}^{r} q_k^* = 1$.

(b) Define

$$Q^*(z) = \sum_{k=1}^{r} q_k^* z^k$$

and use the results of Exercise 6.35 to show that

$$\psi(u) = \sum_{n=1}^{\infty} c_n \sum_{j=0}^{n-1} \frac{(u/\beta)^j e^{-u/\beta}}{j!}, \quad u \geq 0,$$

where

$$C(z) = \left\{ 1 - \frac{1}{\theta}[Q^*(z) - 1] \right\}^{-1}$$

is a compound geometric pgf, with probabilities which may be computed recursively by $c_0 = \theta(1+\theta)^{-1}$ and

$$c_k = \frac{1}{1+\theta} \sum_{j=1}^{k} q_j^* c_{k-j}, \quad k = 1, 2, \ldots,$$

where $q_j^* = 0$ if $j \neq 1, 2, \ldots, r$.

(c) Use (b) to show that

$$\psi(u) = e^{-u/\beta} \sum_{j=0}^{\infty} \bar{C}_j \frac{(u/\beta)^j}{j!}, \quad u \geq 0,$$

where $\bar{C}_j = \sum_{k=j+1}^{\infty} c_k$, $j = 0, 1, \ldots$. Then use (b) to show that the $\bar{C}_n$s may be computed recursively from

$$\bar{C}_n = \frac{1}{1+\theta} \sum_{k=1}^{n} q_k^* \bar{C}_{n-k} + \frac{1}{1+\theta} \sum_{k=n+1}^{\infty} q_k^*, \quad n = 1, 2, \ldots,$$

beginning with $\bar{C}_0 = (1+\theta)^{-1}$.

8.18   (a) Using Exercise 8.14(c) prove that

$$G(u, y) = \frac{1}{1+\theta} \int_0^u G(u-x, y) f_e(x) dx + \frac{1}{1+\theta} \int_u^{y+u} f_e(x) dx,$$

where $G(u, y)$ is defined in Section 8.3, and using Exercise 8.14(d) that

$$\psi(u) = \frac{1}{1+\theta} \int_0^u \psi(u-x) f_e(x) dx + \frac{1}{1+\theta} \int_u^{\infty} f_e(x) dx,$$

where $f_e(x)$ is given by (8.8).

(b) Prove the results in (a) directly by using probabilistic arguments. *Hint:* Condition on the amount of the first drop in surplus and use the law of total probability.

8.5   CRAMER'S ASYMPTOTIC RUIN FORMULA AND TIJMS' APPROXIMATION

There is another very useful piece of information regarding the ruin probability which involves the adjustment coefficient κ. The following theorem gives a result known as Cramér's asymptotic ruin formula. The notation $a(x) \sim b(x)$, $x \to \infty$, means $\lim_{x \to \infty} a(x)/b(x) = 1$.

Theorem 8.17 *Suppose $\kappa > 0$ satisfies (8.3). Then the ruin probability satisfies*

$$\psi(u) \sim C e^{-\kappa u}, \quad u \to \infty, \tag{8.21}$$

where

$$C = \frac{\mu\theta}{M_X'(\kappa) - \mu(1+\theta)}, \tag{8.22}$$

and $M_X(t) = E(e^{tX}) = \int_0^{\infty} e^{tx} dF(x)$ is the moment generating function of the claim severity random variable X.

Proof: The proof of this result is complicated and utilizes the key renewal theorem together with a defective renewal equation for $\psi(u)$ which may be found in Exercise 8.14(d), or equivalently in Exercise 8.18(a). The interested reader should see Rolski et. al. [113], Sec. 5.4.2 for details.   □

Thus, in addition to Lundberg's inequality given by Theorem 8.8, the ruin probability behaves like an exponential function for large u. Note that, for

Lundberg's inequality (8.9) to hold, it must be the case that C given by (8.22) must satisfy $C \le 1$. Also, although (8.21) is an asymptotic approximation, it is known to be quite accurate even for u which is not too large (particularly if the relative security loading θ is itself not too large). Before continuing, let us consider an important special case.

Example 8.18 (The exponential distribution) *If $F(x) = 1 - e^{-x/\mu}$, $x \ge 0$, determine the asymptotic ruin formula.*

We found in Example 8.4 that the adjustment coefficient was given by $\kappa = \theta/[\mu(1+\theta)]$ and $M_X(t) = (1 - \mu t)^{-1}$. Thus,

$$M_X'(t) = \frac{d}{dt}(1 - \mu t)^{-1} = \mu(1 - \mu t)^{-2}.$$

Also,

$$M_X'(\kappa) = \mu(1 - \mu\kappa)^{-2} = \mu[1 - \theta(1+\theta)^{-1}]^{-2} = \mu(1+\theta)^2.$$

Thus, from (8.22),

$$C = \frac{\mu\theta}{\mu(1+\theta)^2 - \mu(1+\theta)} = \frac{\theta}{(1+\theta)(1+\theta-1)} = \frac{1}{1+\theta}.$$

The asymptotic formula (8.21) becomes

$$\psi(u) \sim \frac{1}{1+\theta} \exp\left[-\frac{\theta u}{\mu(1+\theta)}\right], \quad u \to \infty.$$

This is the exact ruin probability as was demonstrated in Example 8.14.   □

In cases other than when $F(x)$ is the exponential distribution, the exact solution for $\psi(u)$ is more complicated (including in particular the general compound geometric solution given in Section 8.4). A simple analytic approximation was suggested by Tijms [129], pp. 271–272 to take advantage of the accuracy for large u of Cramér's asymptotic ruin formula given in Theorem 8.17. The idea is to add an exponential term to (8.21) to improve the accuracy for small u as well. Thus, the Tijms approximation is defined as

$$\psi_T(u) = \left(\frac{1}{1+\theta} - C\right) e^{-u/\alpha} + Ce^{-\kappa u}, \quad u \ge 0, \tag{8.23}$$

where α is chosen so that the approximation also matches the compound geometric mean of the maximum aggregate loss. As shown in Section 4.3.3, the mean of the amount of the drop in surplus (in the terminology of Section 8.4) is $E(Y) = \int_0^\infty y f_e(y) dy = E(X^2)/(2\mu)$, where $\mu = E(X)$ and X is a generic claim severity random variable. Similarly, the number of drops in surplus K is geometrically distributed with parameter $1/\theta$, so from Appendix

B we have $E(K) = 1/\theta$. Because the maximum aggregate loss is the compound geometric random variable L, it follows from (6.6) that its mean is

$$E(L) = E(K)E(Y) = \frac{E(X^2)}{2\mu\theta}.$$

But $\psi(u) = \Pr(L > u)$, and from (3.9) on page 32 with $k = 1$ and $u = \infty$ we have $E(L) = \int_0^\infty \psi(u)du$. Therefore, in order that the Tijms approximation match the mean, we need to replace $\psi(u)$ by $\psi_T(u)$ in the integral. Thus from (8.23)

$$\begin{aligned}
\int_0^\infty \psi_T(u)du &= \left(\frac{1}{1+\theta} - C\right)\int_0^\infty e^{-u/\alpha}du + C\int_0^\infty e^{-\kappa u}du \\
&= \alpha\left(\frac{1}{1+\theta} - C\right) + \frac{C}{\kappa},
\end{aligned}$$

and equating this to $E(L)$ yields

$$\alpha\left(\frac{1}{1+\theta} - C\right) + \frac{C}{\kappa} = \frac{E(X^2)}{2\mu\theta},$$

which may be solved for α to give

$$\alpha = \frac{E(X^2)/(2\mu\theta) - C/\kappa}{1/(1+\theta) - C}. \tag{8.24}$$

To summarize, Tijms' approximation to the ruin probability is given by (8.23), with α given by (8.24).

In addition to providing a simple analytic approximation which is of good quality, Tijms' approximation $\psi_T(u)$ has the added benefit of exactly reproducing the true value of $\psi(u)$ in some cases. (Some insight into this phenomenon is provided by Exercise 8.21.) In particular, it can be shown that $\psi_T(u) = \psi(u)$ if the claim size pdf is of the form $f(x) = p(\beta^{-1}e^{-x/\beta}) + (1 - p)(\beta^{-2}xe^{-x/\beta})$, $x \geq 0$, with $0 \leq p < 1$ (of course, if $p = 1$, this is the exponential density for which Tijms' approximation is not used). We have the following example.

Example 8.19 (A gamma distribution with a shape parameter[4] of 2) *As in Example 8.5, suppose that $\theta = 2$, and the single claim size density is $f(x) = \beta^{-2}xe^{-x/\beta}$, $x \geq 0$. Determine the Tijms approximation to the ruin probability.*

The moment generating function is $M_X(t) = (1 - \beta t)^{-2}$, $t < 1/\beta$, from which one finds that $M_X'(t) = 2\beta(1 - \beta t)^{-3}$, and $\mu = M_X'(0) = 2\beta$. As shown

---

[4] For a gamma distribution, the shape parameter is the one denoted by α in Appendix A and is not to be confused with the value of α in the Tijms approximation.

in Example 8.5, the adjustment coefficient $\kappa > 0$ satisfies $1 + (1 + \theta)\kappa\mu = M_X(\kappa)$, which in this example becomes $1 + 6\beta\kappa = (1 - \beta\kappa)^{-2}$ and is given by $\kappa = 1/(2\beta)$. We will first compute Cramér's asymptotic ruin formula. We have $M_X'(\kappa) = M_X'[1/(2\beta)] = 2\beta(1 - \frac{1}{2})^{-3} = 16\beta$. Thus, (8.22) yields

$$C = \frac{(2\beta)(2)}{16\beta - (2\beta)(1 + 2)} = \frac{2}{5},$$

and from (8.21), $\psi(u) \sim \frac{2}{5}e^{-u/(2\beta)}, u \to \infty$. We next turn to Tijms' approximation given by (8.23), which becomes in this case

$$\psi_T(u) = \left(\frac{1}{1+2} - \frac{2}{5}\right) e^{-u/\alpha} + \frac{2}{5}e^{-u/(2\beta)} = \frac{2}{5}e^{-u/(2\beta)} - \frac{1}{15}e^{-u/\alpha}.$$

It remains to compute α. We have $M_X''(t) = 6\beta^2(1 - \beta t)^{-4}$, from which it follows that $E(X^2) = M_X''(0) = 6\beta^2$. The amount of the drop in surplus has mean $E(Y) = E(X^2)/(2\mu) = 6\beta^2/(4\beta) = 3\beta/2$. Because the number of drops has mean $E(K) = 1/\theta = \frac{1}{2}$, the maximum aggregate loss has mean $E(L) = E(K)E(Y) = 3\beta/4$, and α must satisfy $E(L) = \int_0^\infty \psi_T(u)du$, or equivalently (8.24). That is, α is given by[5]

$$\alpha = \frac{\frac{3\beta}{4} - \frac{2}{5}(2\beta)}{\frac{1}{1+2} - \frac{2}{5}} = \frac{3\beta}{4}.$$

Tijms' approximation thus becomes

$$\psi_T(u) = \frac{2}{5}e^{-u/(2\beta)} - \frac{1}{15}e^{-4u/(3\beta)}, \quad u \geq 0.$$

As mentioned above, $\psi(u) = \psi_T(u)$ in this case. $\qquad\qquad\square$

Another class of claim severity distributions for which the Tijms approximation is exactly equal to the true ruin probability is that, with probability density function of the form $f(x) = p(\beta_1 e^{-\beta_1 x}) + (1 - p)(\beta_2 e^{-\beta_2 x})$, $x \geq 0$. If $0 < p < 1$, then this distribution is a mixture of two exponentials, whereas if, $p = \beta_2/(\beta_2 - \beta_1)$ then the distribution, referred to as a combination of two exponentials, is that of the sum of two independent exponential random variables with means β_1 and β_2, where $\beta_1 \neq \beta_2$. The next example illustrates these ideas.

---

[5] It is actually not a coincidence that $1/\alpha$ is the other root of the adjustment coefficient equation, as may be seen from Example 8.5. It is instructive to compute α in this manner, however, because this approach is applicable in general for arbitrary claim size distributions, including those in which Tijms' approximation does not exactly reproduce the true ruin probability.

Example 8.20 (A mixture of exponential distributions) *Suppose that $\theta = \frac{4}{11}$ and the single claim size density is $f(x) = e^{-3x} + 10e^{-5x}/3, \ x \geq 0$. Determine the Tijms approximation to the ruin probability.*

First we note that the moment generating function is

$$M_X(t) = \int_0^\infty e^{tx} f(x) dx = (3 - t)^{-1} + \tfrac{10}{3}(5 - t)^{-1}.$$

Thus, $M_X'(t) = (3-t)^{-2} + \frac{10}{3}(5-t)^{-2}$, from which it follows that $\mu = M_X'(0) = \frac{1}{9} + \frac{10}{75} = \frac{11}{45}$. Equation (8.3) then implies that the adjustment coefficient $\kappa > 0$ satisfies $1 + \frac{1}{3}\kappa = (3 - \kappa)^{-1} + \frac{10}{3}(5 - \kappa)^{-1}$. Multiplication by $3(3 - \kappa)(5 - \kappa)$ yields

$$3(\kappa - 3)(\kappa - 5) + \kappa(\kappa - 3)(\kappa - 5) = 3(5 - \kappa) + 10(3 - \kappa).$$

That is,

$$3(\kappa^2 - 8\kappa + 15) + \kappa^3 - 8\kappa^2 + 15\kappa = 45 - 13\kappa.$$

Rearrangement yields

$$0 = \kappa^3 - 5\kappa^2 + 4\kappa = \kappa(\kappa - 1)(\kappa - 4),$$

and $\kappa = 1$ because it is the smallest positive root.

Next, we determine Cramér's asymptotic formula. Equation (8.22) becomes, with $M_X'(\kappa) = M_X'(1) = \frac{1}{4} + \frac{10}{3}\frac{1}{16} = \frac{11}{24}$,

$$C = \frac{\left(\frac{11}{45}\right)\left(\frac{4}{11}\right)}{\frac{11}{24} - \left(\frac{11}{45}\right)\left(\frac{15}{11}\right)} = \frac{32}{45},$$

and thus Cramér's asymptotic formula is $\psi(u) \sim \frac{32}{45}e^{-u}, u \to \infty$.

Equation (8.23) then becomes

$$\psi_T(u) = \left(\frac{1}{1 + \frac{4}{11}} - \frac{32}{45}\right)e^{-u/\alpha} + \frac{32}{45}e^{-u} = \frac{1}{45}e^{-u/\alpha} + \frac{32}{45}e^{-u}.$$

In order to compute α, we note that $M_X''(t) = 2(3 - t)^{-3} + \frac{20}{3}(5 - t)^{-3}$, and thus $E(X^2) = M_X''(0) = \frac{2}{27} + \frac{20}{3}\left(\frac{1}{125}\right) = \frac{86}{675}$. The mean of the maximum aggregate loss is therefore

$$E(L) = \frac{E(X^2)}{2\mu\theta} = \frac{\frac{86}{675}}{2\left(\frac{11}{45}\right)\left(\frac{4}{11}\right)} = \frac{43}{60}.$$

Equation (8.24) then yields

$$\alpha = \frac{\frac{43}{60} - \frac{32}{45}}{\frac{1}{1+\frac{4}{11}} - \frac{32}{45}} = \frac{1}{4},$$

and so Tijms' approximation becomes $\psi_T(u) = \frac{1}{45}e^{-4u} + \frac{32}{45}e^{-u}$. As mentioned above, $\psi(u) = \psi_T(u)$ in this case also. □

It is not hard to see from (8.23) that $\psi_T(u) \sim Ce^{-\kappa u}$, $u \to \infty$, if $\kappa < 1/\alpha$. In this situation, $\psi_T(u)$ will equal $\psi(u)$ when $u = 0$ and when $u \to \infty$ as well as matching the compound geometric mean. It can be shown that a sufficient condition for the asymptotic agreement between $\psi_T(u)$ and $\psi(u)$ to hold as $u \to \infty$ is that the nonexponential claim size cumulative distribution function $F(x)$ has either a nondecreasing or nonincreasing mean residual life function [which is implied if $F(x)$ has a nonincreasing or nondecreasing hazard rate, as discussed in Section 4.3.3]. It is also interesting to note that $\psi_T(x) > Ce^{-\kappa x}$ in the former case and $\psi_T(x) < Ce^{-\kappa x}$ in the latter case. See Willmot [137] for proofs of these facts.

The following example illustrates the accuracy of Cramér's asymptotic formula and Tijms' approximation.

Example 8.21 (A gamma distribution with a shape parameter of 3) *Suppose the claim severity distribution is a gamma distribution with a mean of 1 and density given by* $f(x) = 27x^2e^{-3x}/2$, $x \geq 0$. *Determine the exact ruin probability, Cramér's asymptotic ruin formula, and Tijms' approximation when the relative security loading θ in each is* $0.25, 1$, *and* 4, *and the initial surplus u is* $0.10, 0.25, 0.50, 0.75$, *and* 1.

The moment generating function is $M_X(t) = (1 - t/3)^{-3}$.

The exact values of $\psi(u)$ may be obtained using the algorithm presented in Exercise 8.17. That is, $\psi(u) = e^{-3u}\sum_{j=0}^{\infty}\bar{C}_j(3u)^j/j!$, $u \geq 0$, where the $\bar{C}_j$s may be computed recursively using

$$\bar{C}_j = \frac{1}{1+\theta}\sum_{k=1}^{j}q_k^*\bar{C}_{j-k} + \frac{1}{1+\theta}\sum_{k=j+1}^{\infty}q_k^*, \quad j = 1,2,3,\ldots,$$

with $\bar{C}_0 = 1/(1+\theta), q_1^* = q_2^* = q_3^* = \frac{1}{3}$, and $q_k^* = 0$ otherwise. The required values are listed in Table 8.2 under the heading titled Exact.

Cramér's asymptotic ruin probabilities are given by the approximation (8.21), with κ obtained from (8.3) numerically for each value of θ using the Newton–Raphson approach described in Section 8.2.1. The coefficient C is then obtained from (8.22). The required values are listed in Table 8.2 under the heading titled Cramér.

Tijms' approximation is obtained using (8.23) with α satisfying (8.24), and the values are listed in Table 8.2 under the heading titled 'Tijms.'

The values in the table, which may also be found in Tijms [129], p. 272 and Willmot [137], demonstrate that Tijms' approximation is an accurate approximation to the true value in this situation, particularly for small θ. Cramér's asymptotic formula is also remarkably accurate for small θ and u. Because this gamma distribution has an increasing hazard rate (as discussed

Table 8.2   Ruin probabilities with gamma losses

θ	u	Exact	Cramér	Tijms
0.25	0.10	0.7834	0.8076	0.7844
	0.25	0.7562	0.7708	0.7571
	0.50	0.7074	0.7131	0.7074
	0.75	0.6577	0.6597	0.6573
	1.00	0.6097	0.6103	0.6093
1.00	0.10	0.4744	0.5332	0.4764
	0.25	0.4342	0.4700	0.4361
	0.50	0.3664	0.3809	0.3665
	0.75	0.3033	0.3088	0.3026
	1.00	0.2484	0.2502	0.2476
4.00	0.10	0.1839	0.2654	0.1859
	0.25	0.1594	0.2106	0.1615
	0.50	0.1209	0.1432	0.1212
	0.75	0.0882	0.0974	0.0875
	1.00	0.0626	0.0663	0.0618

in Example 4.17), Tijms' approximate ruin probabilities are guaranteed to be smaller than Cramér's asymptotic ruin probabilities, and this may be seen to be true from the table. It also follows that the exact values, Cramér's asymptotic values, and Tijms' approximate values all must converge as $u \to \infty$, but the agreement can be seen to be fairly close even for $u = 1$. $\qquad \square$

8.5.1   Exercises

8.19 Show that (8.22) may be reexpressed as

$$C = \frac{\theta}{\kappa E(Ye^{\kappa Y})},$$

where Y has pdf $f_e(y)$. Hence prove for the problem of Exercise 8.17 that

$$\psi(u) \sim \frac{\theta}{\kappa \beta \sum_{j=1}^{r} jq_j^*(1 - \beta\kappa)^{-j-1}} e^{-\kappa u}, \quad u \to \infty,$$

where $\kappa > 0$ satisfies

$$1 + \theta = Q^*[(1 - \beta\kappa)^{-1}] = \sum_{j=1}^{r} q_j^*(1 - \beta\kappa)^{-j}.$$

8.20 Recall the function $G(u, y)$ defined in Section 8.3. It can be shown using the result of Exercise 8.14(c) that Cramér's asymptotic ruin formula may be generalized to

$$G(u, y) \sim C(y)e^{-\kappa u}, \quad u \to \infty,$$

where

$$C(y) = \frac{\mu\kappa \int_0^\infty e^{\kappa t} \int_y^{t+y} f_e(x)dx \, dt}{M_X'(\kappa) - \mu(1 + \theta)}.$$

(a) Demonstrate that Cramér's asymptotic ruin formula is recovered as $y \to \infty$.

(b) Demonstrate using Exercise 8.13 that the above asymptotic formula for $G(u, y)$ is an equality for all u in the exponential claims case with $F(x) = 1 - e^{-x/\mu}$.

8.21 Suppose that the following formula for the ruin probability is known to hold:

$$\psi(u) = C_1 e^{-r_1 u} + C_2 e^{-r_2 u}, \quad u \geq 0,$$

where $C_1 \neq 0, C_2 \neq 0$, and (without loss of generality) $0 < r_1 < r_2$.

(a) Determine the relative security loading θ.

(b) Determine the adjustment coefficient κ.

(c) Prove that $0 < C_1 \leq 1$.

(d) Determine Cramér's asymptotic ruin formula.

(e) Prove that $\psi_T(u) = \psi(u)$, where $\psi_T(u)$ is Tijms' approximation to the ruin probability.

8.22 Suppose that $\theta = \frac{4}{5}$ and the claim size density is given by $f(x) = (1 + 6x)e^{-3x}$, $x \geq 0$.

(a) Determine Cramér's asymptotic ruin formula.

(b) Determine the ruin probability $\psi(u)$.

8.23 Suppose that $\theta = \frac{3}{11}$ and the claim size density is given by $f(x) = 2e^{-4x} + \frac{7}{2}e^{-7x}$, $x \geq 0$.

(a) Determine Cramér's asymptotic ruin formula.

(b) Determine the ruin probability $\psi(u)$.

8.24 Suppose that $\theta = \frac{3}{5}$ and the claim size density is given by $f(x) = 3e^{-4x} + \frac{1}{2}e^{-2x}$, $x \geq 0$.

(a) Determine Cramér's asymptotic ruin formula.

(b) Determine the ruin probability $\psi(u)$.

8.25 Suppose that $\theta = \frac{7}{5}$ and the claim size density is the convolution of two exponential distributions given by $f(x) = \int_0^x 3e^{-3(x-y)}2e^{-2y}dy$, $x \geq 0$.

(a) Determine Cramér's asymptotic ruin formula.

(b) Determine the ruin probability $\psi(u)$.

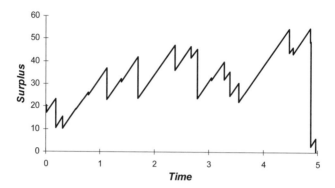

Fig. 8.2   Sample path for a Poisson surplus process.

8.6   THE BROWNIAN MOTION RISK PROCESS

In this section, we study the relationship between Brownian motion (the Wiener process) and the surplus process $\{U_t;\ t \geq 0\}$, where

$$U_t = u + ct - S_t, \quad t \geq 0 \tag{8.25}$$

and $\{S_t;\ t \geq 0\}$ is the total loss process defined by

$$S_t = X_1 + X_2 + \cdots + X_{N_t}, \quad t \geq 0,$$

where $\{N_t;\ t \geq 0\}$ is a Poisson process with rate λ and $S_t = 0$ when $N_t = 0$. As earlier in this chapter we assume that the individual losses $\{X_1, X_2, \ldots\}$ are independently and identically distributed positive random variables whose moment generating function exists. The surplus process $\{U_t;\ t \geq 0\}$ increases continuously with slope c, the premium rate per unit time, and has successive downward jumps of $\{X_1, X_2, \ldots\}$ at random jump times $\{T_1, T_2, \ldots\}$, as illustrated by Figure 8.2. In that figure, $u = 20$, $c = 35$, $\lambda = 3$, and X has an exponential distribution with mean 10.
   Let

$$Z_t = U_t - u = ct - S_t, \quad t \geq 0. \tag{8.26}$$

Then $Z_0 = 0$. Because S_t has a compound distribution, the process $\{Z_t;\ t \geq 0\}$ has mean

$$
\begin{aligned}
\mathrm{E}(Z_t) &= ct - \mathrm{E}(S_t) \\
&= ct - \lambda t \mathrm{E}(X)
\end{aligned}
$$

and variance

$$\mathrm{Var}(Z_t) = \lambda t \mathrm{E}(X^2).$$

We now introduce the corresponding stochastic process based on Brownian motion.

Definition 8.22 *A continuous-time stochastic process* $\{W_t;\ t \geq 0\}$ *is a **Brownian motion** process if*

1. *$W_0 = 0$;*

2. *$\{W_t,\ t \geq 0\}$ has stationary and independent increments; and*

3. *for every $t > 0$, W_t is normally distributed with mean 0 and variance $\sigma^2 t$.*

The Brownian motion process, also called the **Wiener process** or **white noise**, has been used extensively in describing various physical phenomena. When $\sigma^2 = 1$, it is called **standard Brownian motion**. The English botanist Robert Brown discovered the process in 1827 and used it to describe the continuous irregular motion of a particle immersed in a liquid or gas. In 1905 Albert Einstein explained this motion by postulating perpetual collision of the particle with the surrounding medium. Norbert Wiener provided the analytical description of the process in a series of papers beginning in 1918. Since then it has been used in many areas of application from quantum mechanics to describing price levels on the stock market. It has become the key model underpinning modern financial theory.

Definition 8.23 *A continuous-time stochastic process* $\{W_t;\ t \geq 0\}$ *is called a **Brownian motion with drift** process if it satisfies the properties of a Brownian motion process except that W_t has mean μt rather than 0, for some $\mu > 0$.*

A Brownian motion with drift is illustrated in Figure 8.3. This process has $u = 20$, $\mu = 5$, and $\sigma^2 = 600$. The illustrated process has an initial surplus of 20, so the mean of W_t is $20 + 5t$. Technically, $W_t - 20$ is a Brownian motion with drift process.

We now show how the surplus process (8.26) based on the compound Poisson risk process is related to the Brownian motion with drift process. We will take a limit of the process (8.26) as the expected number of downward jumps becomes large and simultaneously the size of the jumps becomes small. Because the Brownian motion with drift process is characterized by the infinitesimal mean μ and infinitesimal variance σ^2, we force the mean and variance functions to be the same for the two processes. In this way, the Brownian motion with drift can be thought of as an approximation to the compound Poisson–based surplus process. Similarly, the compound Poisson process can be used as an approximation for Brownian motion.

Let

$$\mu = c - \lambda E[X]$$

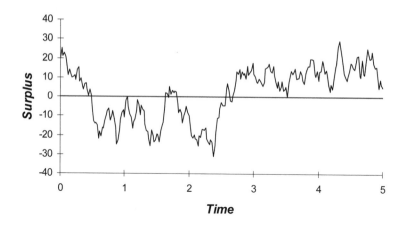

Fig. 8.3 Sample path for a Brownian motion with drift.

and

$$\sigma^2 = \lambda E[X^2]$$

denote the infinitesimal mean and variance of the Brownian motion with drift process. Then

$$\lambda = \frac{\sigma^2}{E[X^2]} \tag{8.27}$$

and

$$c = \mu + \sigma^2 \frac{E[X]}{E[X^2]}. \tag{8.28}$$

Now, in order to take limits, we can treat the jump size X as a scaled version of some other random variable Y, so that $X = \alpha Y$, where Y has fixed mean and variance. Then

$$\lambda = \frac{\sigma^2}{E[Y^2]} \cdot \frac{1}{\alpha^2}$$

and

$$c = \mu + \sigma^2 \frac{E[Y]}{E[Y^2]} \cdot \frac{1}{\alpha}.$$

Then, in order for $\lambda \to \infty$, we let $\alpha \to 0$.

Because the process $\{S_t;\ t \geq 0\}$ is a continuous-time process with stationary and independent increments, so are the processes $\{U_t;\ t \geq 0\}$ and $\{Z_t;\ t \geq 0\}$. This will then also be the case for the limiting process. Because $Z_0 = 0$, we only need to establish that for every t, in the limit, Z_t is normally distributed with mean μt and variance $\sigma^2 t$ according to Definitions 8.22 and

8.23. We do this by looking at the moment generating function of Z_t.

$$
\begin{aligned}
M_{Z_t}(r) &= M_{ct-S_t}(r) \\
&= \mathrm{E}\{\exp[r(ct - S_t)]\} \\
&= \exp(t\{rc + \lambda[M_X(-r) - 1]\}).
\end{aligned}
$$

Then

$$
\begin{aligned}
\frac{\ln M_{Z_t}(r)}{t} &= rc + \lambda[M_X(-r) - 1] \\
&= r[\mu + \lambda \mathrm{E}(X)] \\
&\quad + \lambda\left[1 - r\mathrm{E}(X) + \frac{r^2}{2!}\mathrm{E}(X^2) - \frac{r^3}{3!}\mathrm{E}(X^3) + \cdots - 1\right] \\
&= r\mu + \frac{r^2}{2}\lambda\mathrm{E}(X^2) - \lambda\left[\frac{r^3}{3!}\mathrm{E}(X^3) - \frac{r^4}{4!}\mathrm{E}(X^4) + \cdots\right] \\
&= r\mu + \frac{r^2}{2}\sigma^2 - \lambda\alpha^2\left[\alpha\frac{r^3}{3!}\mathrm{E}(Y^3) - \alpha^2\frac{r^4}{4!}\mathrm{E}(Y^4) + \cdots\right] \\
&= r\mu + \frac{r^2}{2}\sigma^2 - \sigma^2\left[\alpha\frac{r^3}{3!}\frac{\mathrm{E}(Y^3)}{\mathrm{E}(Y^2)} - \alpha^2\frac{r^4}{4!}\frac{\mathrm{E}(Y^4)}{\mathrm{E}(Y^2)} + \cdots\right].
\end{aligned}
$$

Because all terms except α are fixed, as $\alpha \to 0$, we have

$$
\lim_{\alpha \to 0} M_{Z_t}(r) = \exp\left(r\mu t + \frac{r^2}{2}\sigma^2 t\right),
$$

which is the mgf of the normal distribution with mean μt and $\sigma^2 t$. This establishes that the limiting process is Brownian motion with drift.

From Figure 8.2, it is clear that the process U_t is differentiable everywhere except at jump points. As the number of jump points increases indefinitely, the process becomes **nowhere differentiable**. Another property of a Brownian motion process is that **its paths are continuous functions of t with probability 1**. Intuitively, this occurs because the jump sizes become small as $\alpha \to 0$.

Finally, the total distance traveled in $(0, t]$ by the process U_t is

$$
\begin{aligned}
D &= ct + S_t \\
&= ct + X_1 + \cdots + X_{N_t},
\end{aligned}
$$

which has expected value

$$
\begin{aligned}
\mathrm{E}[D] &= ct + \lambda t \mathrm{E}[X] \\
&= t\left[\mu + \sigma^2\frac{\mathrm{E}(Y)}{\mathrm{E}(Y^2)}\frac{1}{\alpha} + \sigma^2\frac{\mathrm{E}(Y)}{\mathrm{E}(Y^2)}\frac{1}{\alpha}\right] \\
&= t\left[\mu + 2\sigma^2\frac{\mathrm{E}(Y)}{\mathrm{E}(Y^2)}\frac{1}{\alpha}\right].
\end{aligned}
$$

This quantity becomes indefinitely large as $\alpha \to 0$. Hence, we have

$$\lim_{\alpha \to 0} \mathrm{E}[D] = \infty.$$

This means that the expected distance traveled in a finite time interval is infinitely large! For a more rigorous discussion of the properties of the Brownian motion process, the text by Karlin and Taylor [71], Ch. 7 is recommended.

Because $Z_t = U_t - u$, we can just add u to the Brownian motion with drift process and then use (8.27) and (8.28) to develop an approximation for the process (8.26). Of course, the larger the value of λ and the smaller the jumps, the better will be the approximation. For a very large block of insurance policies (for example, for an entire company), this may be appropriate. In this case, the probability of ultimate ruin and the distribution of time until ruin are easily obtained from the approximating Brownian motion with drift process. This is done in the next section. Similarly, if a process is known to be Brownian motion with drift, a compound Poisson surplus process can be used as an approximation.

8.7 BROWNIAN MOTION AND THE PROBABILITY OF RUIN

Let $\{W_t;\ t \geq 0\}$ denote the Brownian motion with drift process with mean function μt and variance function $\sigma^2 t$. Let $U_t = u + W_t$ denote the Brownian motion with drift process with initial surplus $U_0 = u$.

We consider the probability of ruin in a finite time interval $(0, \tau)$ as well as the distribution of time until ruin if ruin occurs. Let $T = \min_{t>0}\{t : U_t < 0\}$ be the time at which ruin occurs (with $T = \infty$ if ruin does not occur). Letting $\tau \to \infty$ will give ultimate ruin probabilities.

The probability of ruin before time τ can be expressed as

$$
\begin{aligned}
\psi(u, \tau) &= 1 - \phi(u, \tau) \\
&= \Pr\{T < \tau\} \\
&= \Pr\left\{\min_{0<t<\tau} U_t < 0\right\} \\
&= \Pr\left\{\min_{0<t<\tau} W_t < -U_0\right\} \\
&= \Pr\left\{\min_{0<t<\tau} W_t < -u\right\}.
\end{aligned}
$$

Theorem 8.24 *For the process U_t described above, the ruin probability is given by*

$$\psi(u, \tau) = \Phi\left(-\frac{u + \mu\tau}{\sqrt{\sigma^2\tau}}\right) + \exp\left(-\frac{2\mu}{\sigma^2}u\right)\Phi\left(-\frac{u - \mu\tau}{\sqrt{\sigma^2\tau}}\right), \tag{8.29}$$

where $\Phi(\cdot)$ is the cdf of the standard normal distribution.

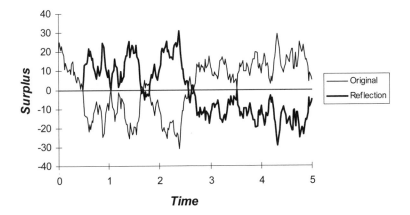

Fig. 8.4 Type B sample path and its reflection.

Proof: Any sample path of U_t with a final level $U_\tau < 0$ must have first crossed the barrier $U_t = 0$ at some time $T < \tau$. For any such path U_t, we define a new path U_t^* which is the same as the original sample path for all $t < T$ but is the reflection about the barrier $U_t = 0$ of the original sample path for all $t > T$. Then

$$U_t^* = \begin{cases} U_t, & t \le T, \\ \\ -U_t, & t > T. \end{cases} \tag{8.30}$$

The reflected path U_t^* has final value $U_\tau^* = -U_\tau$. These are illustrated in Figure 8.4, which is based on the sample path in Figure 8.3.

Now consider any path that crosses the barrier $U_t = 0$ in the time interval $(0, \tau)$. Any such path is one of two possible types:

Type A: One that has a final value of $U_\tau < 0$.

Type B: One that has a final value of $U_\tau > 0$.

Any path of Type B is a reflection of some other path of Type A. Hence, sample paths can be considered in reflecting pairs. The probability of ruin at some time in $(0, \tau)$ is the total probability of all such pairs:

$$\psi(u, \tau) = \Pr\{T < \tau\} = \Pr\left\{ \min_{0 < t < \tau} U_t < 0 \right\},$$

where it is understood that all probabilities are conditional on $U_0 = u$. This probability is obtained by considering all original paths of Type A with final values $U_\tau = x < 0$. By adding all the corresponding reflecting paths U_t^* as well, all possible paths that cross the ruin barrier are considered. Note that the case $U_\tau = 0$ has been left out. The probability of this happening is zero and so this event can be ignored. In Figure 8.4 the original sample path ended at a positive surplus value and so is of Type B. The reflection is of Type A.

Let A_x and B_x denote the sets of all possible paths of Types A and B respectively, which end at $U_\tau = x$ for Type A and $U_\tau = -x$ for Type B. Further let $\Pr\{A_x\}$ and $\Pr\{B_x\}$ denote the total probability associated with the paths in the sets.[6] Hence the probability of ruin is

$$\Pr\{T < \tau\} = \int_{-\infty}^{0} \Pr\{U_\tau = x\} \frac{\Pr\{A_x\} + \Pr\{B_x\}}{\Pr\{U_\tau = x\}} \, dx. \qquad (8.31)$$

Because A_x is the set of all possible paths ending at x,

$$\Pr\{A_x\} = \Pr\{U_\tau = x\},$$

where the right-hand side is the pdf of U_τ. Then

$$\Pr\{T < \tau\} = \int_{-\infty}^{0} \Pr\{U_\tau = x\} \left[1 + \frac{\Pr\{B_x\}}{\Pr\{A_x\}} \right] dx. \qquad (8.32)$$

Because $U_t - u$ is a Brownian motion with drift process, U_τ is normally distributed with mean $u + \mu\tau$ and variance $\sigma^2\tau$, and so

$$\Pr\{U_\tau = x\} = (2\pi\sigma^2\tau)^{-1/2} \exp\left[-\frac{(x - u - \mu\tau)^2}{2\sigma^2\tau} \right].$$

To obtain $\Pr\{B_x\}/\Pr\{A_x\}$, we condition on all possible ruin times T. Then

$$\frac{\Pr\{B_x\}}{\Pr\{A_x\}} = \frac{\int_0^\tau \Pr\{B_x | T = t\} \Pr\{T = t\} \, dt}{\int_0^\tau \Pr\{A_x | T = t\} \Pr\{T = t\} \, dt}$$

$$= \frac{\int_0^\tau \Pr\{U_\tau = -x | T = t\} \Pr\{T = t\} \, dt}{\int_0^\tau \Pr\{U_\tau = x | T = t\} \Pr\{T = t\} \, dt}.$$

The conditional pdf of $U_\tau | T = t$ is the same as the pdf of $U_\tau - U_t$ because $T = t$ implies $U_t = 0$. The process U_t has independent increments and so

---

[6] We are abusing probability notation here. The actual probability of these events is zero. What is being called a probability is really a probability density which can be integrated to produce probabilities for sets which have positive probability.

$U_\tau - U_t$ has a normal distribution. Then,

$$
\begin{aligned}
\Pr\{U_\tau = x | T = t\} &= \Pr\{U_\tau - U_t = x\} \\
&= \frac{\exp\left\{-\dfrac{[x - \mu(\tau - t)]^2}{2\sigma^2(\tau - t)}\right\}}{\sqrt{2\pi\sigma^2(\tau - t)}} \\
&= \frac{\exp\left\{-\dfrac{x^2 - 2x\mu(\tau - t) + \mu^2(\tau - t)^2}{2\sigma^2(\tau - t)}\right\}}{\sqrt{2\pi\sigma^2(\tau - t)}} \\
&= \exp\left(\frac{x\mu}{\sigma^2}\right) \frac{\exp\left\{-\dfrac{x^2 + \mu^2(\tau - t)^2}{2\sigma^2(\tau - t)}\right\}}{\sqrt{2\pi\sigma^2(\tau - t)}}.
\end{aligned}
$$

Similarly, by replacing x with $-x$,

$$
\Pr\{U_\tau = -x | T = t\} = \frac{\exp\left(-\dfrac{x\mu}{\sigma^2}\right) \exp\left\{-\dfrac{x^2 + \mu^2(\tau - t)^2}{2\sigma^2(\tau - t)}\right\}}{\sqrt{2\pi\sigma^2(\tau - t)}}.
$$

We then have

$$
\begin{aligned}
\frac{\Pr\{B_x\}}{\Pr\{A_x\}} &= \frac{\displaystyle\int_0^\tau \frac{\exp\left(-\dfrac{x\mu}{\sigma^2}\right) \exp\left\{-\dfrac{x^2 + \mu^2(\tau - t)^2}{2\sigma^2(\tau - t)}\right\}}{\sqrt{2\pi\sigma^2(\tau - t)}} \Pr\{T = t\}\, dt}{\displaystyle\int_0^\tau \frac{\exp\left(\dfrac{x\mu}{\sigma^2}\right) \exp\left\{-\dfrac{x^2 + \mu^2(\tau - t)^2}{2\sigma^2(\tau - t)}\right\}}{\sqrt{2\pi\sigma^2(\tau - t)}} \Pr\{T = t\}\, dt} \\
&= \exp\left(-\frac{2\mu x}{\sigma^2}\right).
\end{aligned}
$$

Then from (8.31)

$$
\begin{aligned}
\psi(u,\tau) &= \Pr\{T < \tau\} \\
&= \int_{-\infty}^{0} \Pr\{U_\tau = x\} \left[1 + \frac{\Pr\{B_x\}}{\Pr\{A_x\}}\right] dx \\
&= \Phi\left(\frac{-u - \mu\tau}{\sqrt{\sigma^2\tau}}\right) \\
&\quad + \int_{-\infty}^{0} (2\pi\sigma^2\tau)^{-1/2} \exp\left[-\frac{(x - u - \mu\tau)^2}{2\sigma^2\tau} - \frac{2\mu x}{\sigma^2}\right] dx \\
&= \Phi\left(-\frac{u + \mu\tau}{\sqrt{\sigma^2\tau}}\right) \\
&\quad + \int_{-\infty}^{0} (2\pi\sigma^2\tau)^{-1/2} \exp\left[-\frac{(x - u + \mu\tau)^2 + 4\mu u\tau}{2\sigma^2\tau}\right] dx \\
&= \Phi\left(-\frac{u + \mu\tau}{\sqrt{\sigma^2\tau}}\right) + \exp\left(-\frac{2\mu}{\sigma^2}u\right)\Phi\left(-\frac{u - \mu\tau}{\sqrt{\sigma^2\tau}}\right). \qquad \square
\end{aligned}
$$

Corollary 8.25 *The probability of ultimate ruin is given by*

$$
\psi(u) = 1 - \phi(u) = \Pr\{T < \infty\} = \exp\left(-\frac{2\mu}{\sigma^2}u\right). \tag{8.33}
$$

By letting $\tau \to \infty$, this result follows from Theorem 8.24. It should be noted that the distribution (8.29) is a **defective distribution** because the cdf does not approach 1 as $\tau \to \infty$. The corresponding proper distribution is obtained by conditioning on ultimate ruin.

Corollary 8.26 *The distribution of the time until ruin given that it occurs is given by*

$$
\begin{aligned}
\frac{\psi(u,\tau)}{\psi(u)} &= \Pr\{T < \tau | T < \infty\} \\
&= \exp\left(\frac{2\mu}{\sigma^2}u\right)\Phi\left(-\frac{u + \mu\tau}{\sqrt{\sigma^2\tau}}\right) + \Phi\left(-\frac{u - \mu\tau}{\sqrt{\sigma^2\tau}}\right), \tau > 0. (8.34)
\end{aligned}
$$

Corollary 8.27 *The probability density function of the time until ruin is given by*

$$
f_T(\tau) = \frac{u}{\sqrt{2\pi\sigma^2}}\tau^{-3/2}\exp\left[-\frac{(u - \mu\tau)^2}{2\sigma^2\tau}\right], \quad \tau > 0. \tag{8.35}
$$

This is obtained by differentiation of (8.34) with respect to τ. It is not hard to see, using Appendix A, that if $\mu > 0$ then (8.35) is the pdf of an inverse Gaussian distribution with mean u/μ and variance $u\sigma^2/\mu^3$. With $\mu = 0$, ruin is certain and the time until ruin (8.35) has pdf

$$
f_T(\tau) = \frac{u}{\sqrt{2\pi\sigma^2}}\tau^{-3/2}\exp\left(-\frac{u^2}{2\sigma^2\tau}\right), \quad \tau > 0,
$$

and cdf [from (8.34)]

$$F_T(\tau) = 2\Phi\left(-\frac{u}{\sigma\tau^{1/2}}\right), \quad \tau > 0.$$

This distribution is the **one-sided stable law with index 1/2**.

These results can be used as approximations for the original surplus process (8.26) based on the compound Poisson model. In this situation $c = (1 + \theta)\lambda E(X)$ where θ is the relative premium loading. We do this by substituting back using (8.27) and (8.28).

Then, for the process (8.26) from (8.29), (8.33), and (8.35), we have

$$\psi(u,\tau) \doteq \Phi\left[-\frac{u + \theta\lambda\tau E(X)}{\sqrt{\lambda\tau E(X^2)}}\right]$$

$$+ \exp\left[-\frac{2E(X)}{E(X^2)}\theta u\right]\Phi\left[-\frac{u - \theta\lambda\tau E(X)}{\sqrt{\lambda\tau E(X^2)}}\right], \quad u > 0, \ \tau > 0,$$

$$\psi(u) \doteq \exp\left[-\frac{2E(X)}{E(X^2)}\theta u\right], \qquad\qquad u > 0,$$

and

$$f_T(\tau) \doteq \frac{u}{\sqrt{2\pi\lambda E(X^2)}}\tau^{-3/2}\exp\left\{-\frac{[u - \theta\lambda\tau E(X)]^2}{2\lambda\tau E(X^2)}\right\}, \quad \tau > 0.$$

Then, for any compound Poisson-based process, it is easy to get simple numerical approximations. For example, the expected time until ruin, given that it occurs, is

$$E(T) = \frac{u}{\mu} = \frac{u}{\theta\lambda E(X)}. \qquad (8.36)$$

Naturally, the accuracy of this approximation depends on the relative sizes of the quantities involved.

It should be noted from (8.36) that the expected time of ruin, given that it occurs, depends (as we might expect) on the four key quantities which describe the surplus process. A higher initial surplus (u) increases the time to ruin, while increasing any of the other components decreases the expected time. This may appear surprising at first, but, for example, increasing the loading increases the rate of expected growth in surplus, making ruin difficult. Therefore, if ruin should occur, it will have to happen soon, before the high loading leads to large gains. If λ is large, the company is essentially much larger and events happen more quickly. Therefore, ruin, if it happens, will occur sooner. Finally, a large value of $E(X)$ makes it easier for an early claim to wipe out the initial surplus.

All these are completely intuitive. However, formula (8.36) shows how each factor can have an influence on the expected ruin time.

On a final note, it is also possible to use the compound Poisson-based risk process Z_t as an approximation for a Brownian motion process. For known drift and variance parameters μ and σ^2, one can use (8.27) and (8.28) to obtain

$$\mu = \theta \lambda \mathrm{E}(X), \tag{8.37}$$

$$\sigma^2 = \lambda \mathrm{E}(X^2). \tag{8.38}$$

It is convenient to fix the jump sizes so that $\mathrm{E}(X) = k$, say, and $\mathrm{E}(X^2) = k^2$. Then we have

$$\lambda = \frac{\sigma^2}{k^2}, \tag{8.39}$$

$$\theta = \frac{\mu}{\lambda k} = \frac{\mu}{\sigma^2} k. \tag{8.40}$$

When μ and σ^2 are fixed, choosing a value of k fixes λ and θ. Hence, the Poisson-based process can be used to approximate the Brownian motion with accuracy determined only by the parameter k. The smaller the value of k, the smaller the jump sizes and the larger the number of jumps per unit time.

Hence, simulation of the Brownian motion process can be done using the Poisson-based process. To simulate the Poisson-based process, the waiting times between successive events are generated first because these are exponentially distributed with mean $1/\lambda$. As k becomes small, λ becomes large and the mean waiting time becomes small.

Part III

Construction of empirical models

9

Review of mathematical statistics

9.1 INTRODUCTION

Before studying empirical models and then parametric models, we review some concepts from mathematical statistics. Mathematical statistics is a broad subject that includes many topics not covered in this chapter. For those that are covered, it is assumed that the reader has had some prior exposure. The topics of greatest importance for constructing actuarial models are estimation and hypothesis testing. Because the Bayesian approach to statistical inference is often either ignored or treated lightly in introductory mathematical statistics texts and courses, it receives more in-depth coverage in this text in Section 12.4. Bayesian methodology also provides the basis for the credibility methods covered in Chapter 16.

To see the need for methods of statistical inference, consider the case where your boss needs a model for basic dental payments. One option is to simply announce the model. You announce that it is the lognormal distribution with $\mu = 5.1239$ and $\sigma = 1.0345$ (the many decimal places are designed to give your announcement an aura of precision). When your boss, or a regulator, or an attorney who has put you on the witness stand asks you how you know that to be so, it will likely not be sufficient to answer that "I just know these

Loss Models: From Data to Decisions, Second Edition.
By Stuart A. Klugman, Harry H. Panjer, and Gordon E. Willmot
ISBN 0-471-21577-5   Copyright © 2004 John Wiley & Sons, Inc.

things." It may not even be sufficient to announce that your friend at Gamma Dental uses that model.

An alternative is to collect some data and use it to formulate a model. Most distributional models have two components. The first is a name, such as "Pareto." The second is the set of values of parameters that complete the specification. Matters would be simpler if modeling could be done in that order. Most of the time we need to fix the parameters that go with a named model before we can decide if we want to use that type of model.

Because the parameter estimates are based on a sample from the population and not the entire population, the results will not be the true values. It is important to have an idea of the potential error. One way to express this is with an interval estimate. That is, rather than announcing a particular value, a range of plausible values is presented.

When named parametric distributions are used, the parameterizations used are those from Appendices A and B.

9.2   POINT ESTIMATION

9.2.1   Introduction

Regardless of how a model is estimated, it is extremely unlikely that the estimated model will exactly match the true distribution. Ideally, we would like to be able to measure the error we will be making when using the estimated model. But this is clearly impossible! If we knew the amount of error we had made, we could adjust our estimate by that amount and then have no error at all. The best we can do is discover how much error is inherent in repeated use of the *procedure*, as opposed to how much error we made with our current estimate. Therefore, this section is about the quality of the ensemble of answers produced from the procedure, not about the quality of a particular answer.

This is an important point with regard to actuarial practice. What is important is that an appropriate procedure be used, with everyone understanding that even the best procedure can lead to a poor result once the random future outcome has been revealed. This point is stated nicely in a Society of Actuaries principles draft ([124], pp. 779–780) regarding the level of adequacy of a provision for a block of life risk obligations (that is, the probability that the company will have enough money to meet its contractual obligations):

> The indicated level of adequacy is prospective, but the actuarial model is generally validated against past experience. It is incorrect to conclude on the basis of subsequent experience that the actuarial assumptions were inappropriate or that the indicated level of adequacy was overstated or understated.

When constructing models, there are a number of types of error. Several will not be covered here. Among them are model error (choosing the wrong model) and sampling frame error (trying to draw inferences about a population that differs from the one sampled). An example of model error is selecting a Pareto distribution when the true distribution is Weibull. An example of sampling frame error is sampling claims from policies sold by independent agents in order to price policies sold over the Internet.

The type of error we can measure is that due to using a sample from the population to make inferences about the entire population. Errors occur when the items sampled do not represent the population. As noted earlier, we cannot know if the particular items sampled today do or do not represent the population. We can, however, estimate the extent to which estimators are affected by the possibility of a nonrepresentative sample.

The approach taken in this section is to consider all the samples that might be taken from the population. Each such sample leads to an estimated quantity (for example, a probability, a parameter value, or a moment). We do not expect the estimated quantities to always match the true value. For a sensible estimation procedure we do expect that for some samples the quantity will match the true value, for many it will be close, and for only a few it will be quite different. If we can construct a measure of how well the set of potential estimates matches the true value, we have a handle on the quality of our estimation procedure. The approach outlined here is often called the *classical* or *frequentist* approach to estimation.

Finally, we need a word about the difference between *estimate* and *estimator*. The former refers to the specific value obtained when applying an estimation procedure to a set of numbers. The latter refers to a rule or formula that produces the estimate. An estimate is a number or function while an estimator is a random variable or a random function. Usually, both the words and the context will make clear which is being referred to.

9.2.2   Measures of quality

9.2.2.1 Introduction There are a number of ways to measure the quality of an estimator. Three of them are discussed here. Two examples will be used throughout to illustrate them.

Example 9.1 *A population contains the values 1, 3, 5, and 9. We want to estimate the population mean by taking a sample of size 2 with replacement.*

Example 9.2 *A population has the exponential distribution with a mean of θ. We want to estimate the population mean by taking a sample of size 3 with replacement.*

Both examples are clearly artificial in that we know the answers prior to sampling (4.5 and θ). However, that knowledge will make apparent the error in the procedure we select. For practical applications, we will need to be able to estimate the error when we do not know the true value of the quantity being estimated.

9.2.2.2 Unbiasedness When constructing an estimator, it would be good if, on average, the errors we make cancel each other out. More formally, let θ be the quantity we want to estimate. Let $\hat{\theta}$ be the random variable that represents the estimator and let $E(\hat{\theta}|\theta)$ be the expected value of the estimator $\hat{\theta}$ when θ is the true parameter value.

Definition 9.3 *An estimator,* $\hat{\theta}$*, is **unbiased** if* $E(\hat{\theta}|\theta) = \theta$ *for all* θ*. The **bias** is* $\text{bias}_{\hat{\theta}}(\theta) = E(\hat{\theta}|\theta) - \theta$*.*

The bias depends on the estimator being used and may also depend on the particular value of θ.

Example 9.4 *For Example 9.1 determine the bias of the sample mean as an estimator of the population mean.*

The population mean is $\theta = 4.5$. The sample mean is the average of the two observations. It is also the estimator we would use employing the empirical approach. In all cases, we assume that sampling is random. In other words, every sample of size n has the same chance of being drawn. Such sampling also implies that any member of the population has the same chance of being observed as any other member. For this example, there are 16 equally likely ways the sample could have turned out. They are listed below.

1,1	1,3	1,5	1,9	3,1	3,3	3,5	3,9
5,1	5,3	5,5	5,9	9,1	9,3	9,5	9,9

This leads to the following 16 equally likely values for the sample mean:

1	2	3	5	2	3	4	6
3	4	5	7	5	6	7	9

Combining the common values, the sample mean, usually denoted $\bar{X}$, has the following probability distribution:

x	1	2	3	4	5	6	7	9
$p_{\bar{X}}(x)$	1/16	2/16	3/16	2/16	3/16	2/16	2/16	1/16

The expected value of the estimator is

$$E(\bar{X}) = [1(1) + 2(2) + 3(3) + 4(2) + 5(3) + 6(2) + 7(2) + 9(1)]/16 = 4.5$$

and so the sample mean is an unbiased estimator of the population mean for this example. $\square$

Example 9.5 *For Example 9.2 determine the bias of the sample mean and the sample median as estimators of the population mean.*

The sample mean is $\bar{X} = (X_1 + X_2 + X_3)/3$, where each X_j represents one of the observations from the exponential population. Its expected value is

$$
\begin{aligned}
\mathrm{E}(\bar{X}) &= \mathrm{E}\left(\frac{X_1 + X_2 + X_3}{3}\right) = \tfrac{1}{3}\left[\mathrm{E}(X_1) + \mathrm{E}(X_2) + \mathrm{E}(X_3)\right] \\
&= \tfrac{1}{3}(\theta + \theta + \theta) = \theta
\end{aligned}
$$

and therefore the sample mean is an unbiased estimator of the population mean.

Investigating the sample median is a bit more difficult. The distribution function of the middle of three observations can be found as follows, using Y as the random variable of interest and X as the random variable for an observation from the population:

$$
\begin{aligned}
F_Y(y) &= \Pr(Y \le y) = \Pr(X_1, X_2, X_3 \le y) + \Pr(X_1, X_2 \le y, X_3 > y) \\
&\quad + \Pr(X_1, X_3 \le y, X_2 > y) + \Pr(X_2, X_3 \le y, X_1 > y) \\
&= F_X(y)^3 + 3F_X(y)^2[1 - F_X(y)] \\
&= [1 - e^{-y/\theta}]^3 + 3[1 - e^{-y/\theta}]^2 e^{-y/\theta}.
\end{aligned}
$$

The density function is

$$
f_Y(y) = F_Y'(y) = \frac{6}{\theta}\left(e^{-2y/\theta} - e^{-3y/\theta}\right).
$$

The expected value of this estimator is

$$
\begin{aligned}
\mathrm{E}(Y|\theta) &= \int_0^\infty y\frac{6}{\theta}\left(e^{-2y/\theta} - e^{-3y/\theta}\right)dy \\
&= \frac{5\theta}{6}.
\end{aligned}
$$

This estimator is clearly biased,[1] with $\mathrm{bias}_Y(\theta) = 5\theta/6 - \theta = -\theta/6$. On average, this estimator underestimates the true value. It is also easy to see that the sample median can be turned into an unbiased estimator by multiplying it by 1.2. □

For Example 9.2 we have two estimators (the sample mean and 1.2 times the sample median) that are both unbiased. We will need additional criteria to decide which one we prefer.

---

[1] The sample median is not likely to be a good estimator of the population mean. This example studies it for comparison purposes. Because the population median is $\theta \ln 2$, the sample median is biased for the population median.

Some estimators exhibit a small amount of bias, which vanishes as the sample size goes to infinity.

Definition 9.6 *Let $\hat{\theta}_n$ be an estimator of θ based on a sample size of n. The estimator is **asymptotically unbiased** if*

$$\lim_{n \to \infty} E(\hat{\theta}_n | \theta) = \theta$$

for all θ.

Example 9.7 *Suppose a random variable has the uniform distribution on the interval $(0, \theta)$. Consider the estimator $\hat{\theta}_n = \max(X_1, \ldots, X_n)$. Show that this estimator is asymptotically unbiased.*

Let Y_n be the maximum from a sample of size n. Then

$$
\begin{aligned}
F_{Y_n}(y) &= \Pr(Y_n \le y) = \Pr(X_1 \le y, \ldots, X_n \le y) \\
&= [F_X(y)]^n \\
&= (y/\theta)^n \\
f_{Y_n}(y) &= \frac{ny^{n-1}}{\theta^n}, \quad 0 < y < \theta.
\end{aligned}
$$

The expected value is

$$E(Y_n | \theta) = \int_0^\theta ny^n \theta^{-n} dy = \frac{n}{n+1} y^{n+1} \theta^{-n} \Big|_0^\theta = \frac{n\theta}{n+1}.$$

As $n \to \infty$, the limit is θ, making this estimator asymptotically unbiased. $\square$

9.2.2.3 Consistency

A second desirable property of an estimator is that it works well for extremely large samples. Slightly more formally, as the sample size goes to infinity, the probability that the estimator is in error by more than a small amount goes to zero. A formal definition follows.

Definition 9.8 *An estimator is **consistent** (often called, in this context, **weakly consistent**) if, for all $\delta > 0$ and any θ,*

$$\lim_{n \to \infty} \Pr(|\hat{\theta}_n - \theta| > \delta) = 0.$$

A sufficient (although not necessary) condition for weak consistency is that the estimator be asymptotically unbiased and $\mathrm{Var}(\hat{\theta}_n) \to 0$.

Example 9.9 *Prove that, if the variance of a random variable is finite, the sample mean is a consistent estimator of the population mean.*

From Exercise 9.2, the sample mean is unbiased. In addition,

$$\mathrm{Var}(\bar{X}) = \mathrm{Var}\left(\frac{1}{n}\sum_{j=1}^{n}X_j\right)$$

$$= \frac{1}{n^2}\sum_{j=1}^{n}\mathrm{Var}(X_j)$$

$$= \frac{\mathrm{Var}(X)}{n} \to 0.$$

The second step follows from assuming that the observations are independent.   □

Example 9.10 *Show that the maximum observation from a uniform distribution on the interval $(0, \theta)$ is a consistent estimator of θ.*

From Example 9.7, the maximum is asymptotically unbiased. The second moment is

$$E(Y_n^2) = \int_0^\theta ny^{n+1}\theta^{-n}\,dy = \frac{n}{n+2}y^{n+2}\theta^{-n}\Big|_0^\theta = \frac{n\theta^2}{n+2}$$

and then

$$\mathrm{Var}(Y_n) = \frac{n\theta^2}{n+2} - \left(\frac{n\theta}{n+1}\right)^2 = \frac{n\theta^2}{(n+2)(n+1)^2} \to 0.$$ □

9.2.2.4 Mean-squared error   While consistency is nice, most estimators have this property. What would be truly impressive is an estimator that is not only correct on average but comes very close most of the time and, in particular, comes closer than rival estimators. One measure for a finite sample is motivated by the definition of consistency. The quality of an estimator could be measured by the probability that it gets within δ of the true value—that is, by measuring $\Pr(|\hat{\theta}_n - \theta| < \delta)$. But the choice of δ is arbitrary and we prefer measures that cannot be altered to suit the investigator's whim. Then we might consider $E(|\hat{\theta}_n - \theta|)$, the average absolute error. But we know that working with absolute values often presents unpleasant mathematical challenges, and so the following has become widely accepted as a measure of accuracy.

Definition 9.11 *The **mean-squared error** (**MSE**) of an estimator is*

$$\mathrm{MSE}_{\hat{\theta}}(\theta) = E[(\hat{\theta} - \theta)^2|\theta].$$

Note that the MSE is a function of the true value of the parameter. An estimator may perform extremely well for some values of the parameter but poorly for others.

Example 9.12 *Consider the estimator* $\hat{\theta} = 5$ *of an unknown parameter* θ. *The MSE is* $(5 - \theta)^2$, *which is very small when* θ *is near 5 but becomes poor for other values. Of course this estimate is both biased and inconsistent unless* θ *is exactly equal to 5.*

A result that follows directly from the various definitions is

$$\text{MSE}_{\hat{\theta}}(\theta) = \text{E}\{[\hat{\theta} - \text{E}(\hat{\theta}|\theta) + \text{E}(\hat{\theta}|\theta) - \theta]^2|\theta\} = \text{Var}(\hat{\theta}|\theta) + [\text{bias}_{\hat{\theta}}(\theta)]^2. \quad (9.1)$$

If we restrict attention to only unbiased estimators, the best such could be defined as follows.

Definition 9.13 *An estimator,* $\hat{\theta}$, *is called a* **uniformly minimum variance unbiased estimator (UMVUE)** *if it is unbiased and for any true value of* θ *there is no other unbiased estimator that has a smaller variance.*

Because we are looking only at unbiased estimators, it would have been equally effective to make the definition in terms of MSE. We could also generalize the definition by looking for estimators that are uniformly best with regard to MSE, but the previous example indicates why that is not feasible. There are a few theorems that can assist with the determination of UMVUEs. However, such estimators are difficult to determine. On the other hand, MSE is still a useful criterion for comparing two alternative estimators.

Example 9.14 *For Example 9.2 compare the MSEs of the sample mean and* 1.2 *times the sample median.*

The sample mean has variance

$$\frac{\text{Var}(X)}{3} = \frac{\theta^2}{3}.$$

When multiplied by 1.2, the sample median has second moment

$$
\begin{aligned}
\text{E}[(1.2Y)^2] &= 1.44 \int_0^\infty y^2 \frac{6}{\theta} \left(e^{-2y/\theta} - e^{-3y/\theta} \right) dy \\
&= 1.44 \frac{6}{\theta} \left[y^2 \left(\frac{-\theta}{2} e^{-2y/\theta} + \frac{\theta}{3} e^{-3y/\theta} \right) \right. \\
&\qquad\qquad -2y \left(\frac{\theta^2}{4} e^{-2y/\theta} - \frac{\theta^2}{9} e^{-3y/\theta} \right) \\
&\qquad\qquad \left. +2 \left(\frac{-\theta^3}{8} e^{-2y/\theta} + \frac{\theta^3}{27} e^{-3y/\theta} \right) \right]\Big|_0^\infty \\
&= \frac{8.64}{\theta} \left(\frac{2\theta^3}{8} - \frac{2\theta^3}{27} \right) = \frac{38\theta^2}{25}
\end{aligned}
$$

for a variance of

$$\frac{38\theta^2}{25} - \theta^2 = \frac{13\theta^2}{25} > \frac{\theta^2}{3}.$$

The sample mean has the smaller MSE regardless of the true value of θ. Therefore, for this problem, it is a superior estimator of θ.   □

Example 9.15 *For the uniform distribution on the interval $(0, \theta)$ compare the MSE of the estimators $2\bar{X}$ and $[(n+1)/n] \max(X_1, \ldots, X_n)$. Also evaluate the MSE of $\max(X_1, \ldots, X_n)$.*

The first two estimators are unbiased, so it is sufficient to compare their variances. For twice the sample mean,

$$\mathrm{Var}(2\bar{X}) = \frac{4}{n}\,\mathrm{Var}(X) = \frac{4\theta^2}{12n} = \frac{\theta^2}{3n}.$$

For the adjusted maximum, the second moment is

$$\mathrm{E}\left[\left(\frac{n+1}{n}Y_n\right)^2\right] = \frac{(n+1)^2}{n^2}\,\frac{n\theta^2}{n+2} = \frac{(n+1)^2\theta^2}{(n+2)n}$$

for a variance of

$$\frac{(n+1)^2\theta^2}{(n+2)n} - \theta^2 = \frac{\theta^2}{n(n+2)}.$$

Except for the case $n = 1$ (and then the two estimators are identical), the one based on the maximum has the smaller MSE. The third estimator is biased. For it, the MSE is

$$\frac{n\theta^2}{(n+2)(n+1)^2} + \left(\frac{n\theta}{n+1} - \theta\right)^2 = \frac{2\theta^2}{(n+1)(n+2)},$$

which is also larger than that for the adjusted maximum.   □

9.2.3   Exercises

9.1 For Example 9.1, show that the mean of three observations drawn without replacement is an unbiased estimator of the population mean while the median of three observations drawn without replacement is a biased estimator of the population mean.

9.2 Prove that for random samples the sample mean is always an unbiased estimator of the population mean.

9.3 Let X have the uniform distribution over the range $(\theta - 2, \theta + 2)$. That is, $f_X(x) = 0.25$, $\theta - 2 < x < \theta + 2$. Show that the median from a sample of size 3 is an unbiased estimator of θ.

9.4 Explain why the sample mean may not be a consistent estimator of the population mean for a Pareto distribution.

9.5 For the sample of size 3 in Exercise 9.3, compare the MSE of the sample mean and median as estimates of θ.

9.6 (*) You are given two independent estimators of an unknown quantity θ. For estimator A, $\mathrm{E}(\hat{\theta}_A) = 1{,}000$ and $\mathrm{Var}(\hat{\theta}_A) = 160{,}000$, while for estimator B, $\mathrm{E}(\hat{\theta}_B) = 1{,}200$ and $\mathrm{Var}(\hat{\theta}_B) = 40{,}000$. Estimator C is a weighted average, $\hat{\theta}_C = w\hat{\theta}_A + (1-w)\hat{\theta}_B$. Determine the value of w that minimizes $\mathrm{Var}(\hat{\theta}_C)$.

9.7 (*) A population of losses has the Pareto distribution (see Appendix A) with $\theta = 6{,}000$ and α unknown. Simulation of the results from maximum likelihood estimation based on samples of size 10 has indicated that $\mathrm{E}(\hat{\alpha}) = 2.2$ and $\mathrm{MSE}(\hat{\alpha}) = 1$. Determine $\mathrm{Var}(\hat{\alpha})$ if it is known that $\alpha = 2$.

9.8 (*) Two instruments are available for measuring a particular nonzero distance. The random variable X represents a measurement with the first instrument, and the random variable Y with the second instrument. Assume X and Y are independent with $\mathrm{E}(X) = 0.8m$, $\mathrm{E}(Y) = m$, $\mathrm{Var}(X) = m^2$, and $\mathrm{Var}(Y) = 1.5m^2$, where m is the true distance. Consider estimators of m that are of the form $Z = \alpha X + \beta Y$. Determine the values of α and β that make Z a UMVUE within the class of estimators of this form.

9.9 A population contains six members, with values 1, 1, 2, 3, 5, and 10. A random sample of size 3 is drawn without replacement. In each case the objective is to estimate the population mean. *Note:* A spreadsheet with an optimization routine may be the best way to solve this problem.

   (a) Determine the bias, variance, and MSE of the sample mean.

   (b) Determine the bias, variance, and MSE of the sample median.

   (c) Determine the bias, variance, and MSE of the sample midrange (the average of the largest and smallest observations).

   (d) Consider an arbitrary estimator of the form $aX_{(1)} + bX_{(2)} + cX_{(3)}$, where $X_{(1)} \leq X_{(2)} \leq X_{(3)}$, are the sample order statistics.

      i. Determine a restriction on the values of a, b, and c that will assure that the estimator is unbiased.

      ii. Determine the values of a, b, and c that will produce the unbiased estimator with the smallest variance.

      iii. Determine the values of a, b, and c that will produce the (possibly biased) estimator with the smallest MSE.

9.10 (*) Two different estimators, $\hat{\theta}_1$ and $\hat{\theta}_2$, are being considered. To test their performance, 75 trials have been simulated, each with the true value set at $\theta = 2$. The following totals were obtained:

$$\sum_{j=1}^{75} \hat{\theta}_{1j} = 165, \ \sum_{j=1}^{75} \hat{\theta}_{1j}^2 = 375, \ \sum_{j=1}^{75} \hat{\theta}_{2j} = 147, \ \sum_{j=1}^{75} \hat{\theta}_{2j}^2 = 312,$$

where $\hat{\theta}_{ij}$ is the estimate based on the jth simulation using estimator $\hat{\theta}_i$. Estimate the MSE for each estimator and determine the **relative efficiency** (the ratio of the MSEs).

9.3 INTERVAL ESTIMATION

All of the estimators discussed to this point have been **point estimators**. That is, the estimation process produces a single value that represents our best attempt to determine the value of the unknown population quantity. While that value may be a good one, we do not expect it to exactly match the true value. A more useful statement is often provided by an **interval estimator**. Instead of a single value, the result of the estimation process is a range of possible numbers, any of which is likely to be the true value. A specific type of interval estimator is the confidence interval.

Definition 9.16 *A* $100(1-\alpha)\%$ ***confidence interval*** *for a parameter θ is a pair of random values, L and U, computed from a random sample such that* $\Pr(L \leq \theta \leq U) \geq 1 - \alpha$ *for all θ.*

Note that this definition does not uniquely specify the interval. Because the definition is a probability statement and must hold for all θ, it says nothing about whether or not a particular interval encloses the true value of θ from a particular population. Instead, the **level of confidence**, $1-\alpha$, is a property of the method used to obtain L and U and not of the particular values obtained. The proper interpretation is that, if we use a particular interval estimator over and over on a variety of samples, at least $100(1-\alpha)\%$ of the time our interval will enclose the true value.

Constructing confidence intervals is usually very difficult. For example, we know that, if a population has a normal distribution with unknown mean and variance, a $100(1-\alpha)\%$ confidence interval for the mean uses

$$L = \bar{X} - t_{\alpha/2,n-1}s/\sqrt{n}, \quad U = \bar{X} + t_{\alpha/2,n-1}s/\sqrt{n}, \tag{9.2}$$

where $s = \sqrt{\sum_{j=1}^{n}(X_j - \bar{X})^2/(n-1)}$ and $t_{\alpha/2,b}$ is the $100(1 - \alpha/2)$th percentile of the t distribution with b degrees of freedom. But it takes a great deal of effort to verify that this is correct (see, for example, [58], p. 214).

However, there is a method for constructing approximate confidence intervals that is often accessible. Suppose we have a point estimator $\hat{\theta}$ of parameter θ such that $\mathrm{E}(\hat{\theta}) \doteq \theta$, $\mathrm{Var}(\hat{\theta}) \doteq v(\theta)$, and $\hat{\theta}$ has approximately a normal distribution. Theorem 12.13 shows that this is often the case. With all these approximations, we have that approximately

$$1 - \alpha \doteq \Pr\left(-z_{\alpha/2} \leq \frac{\hat{\theta} - \theta}{\sqrt{v(\theta)}} \leq z_{\alpha/2}\right), \tag{9.3}$$

where $z_{\alpha/2}$ is the $100(1-\alpha/2)$th percentile of the standard normal distribution. Solving for θ produces the desired interval. Sometimes this is difficult to do (due to the appearance of θ in the denominator) and so, if necessary, replace $v(\theta)$ in (9.3) with $v(\hat{\theta})$ to obtain a further approximation,

$$1 - \alpha \doteq \Pr\left(\hat{\theta} - z_{\alpha/2}\sqrt{v(\hat{\theta})} \leq \theta \leq \hat{\theta} + z_{\alpha/2}\sqrt{v(\hat{\theta})}\right). \tag{9.4}$$

Example 9.17 *Use (9.4) to construct an approximate 95% confidence interval for the mean of a normal population with unknown variance.*

Use $\hat{\theta} = \bar{X}$ and then note that $\mathrm{E}(\hat{\theta}) = \theta$, $\mathrm{Var}(\hat{\theta}) = \sigma^2/n$, and $\hat{\theta}$ does have a normal distribution. The confidence interval is then $\bar{X} \pm 1.96 s/\sqrt{n}$. Because $t_{.025,n-1} > 1.96$, this approximate interval must be narrower than the exact interval given by (9.2). That means that our level of confidence is something less than 95%. □

Example 9.18 *Use (9.3) and (9.4) to construct approximate 95% confidence intervals for the mean of a Poisson distribution. Obtain intervals for the particular case where $n = 25$ and $\bar{x} = 0.12$.*

Let $\hat{\theta} = \bar{X}$, the sample mean. For the Poisson distribution, $\mathrm{E}(\hat{\theta}) = \mathrm{E}(X) = \theta$ and $v(\theta) = \mathrm{Var}(\bar{X}) = \mathrm{Var}(X)/n = \theta/n$. For the first interval

$$0.95 \doteq \Pr\left(-1.96 \leq \frac{\bar{X} - \theta}{\sqrt{\theta/n}} \leq 1.96\right)$$

is true if and only if

$$|\bar{X} - \theta| \leq 1.96\sqrt{\frac{\theta}{n}},$$

which is equivalent to

$$(\bar{X} - \theta)^2 \leq \frac{3.8416\theta}{n}$$

or

$$\theta^2 - \theta\left(2\bar{X} + \frac{3.8416}{n}\right) + \bar{X}^2 \leq 0.$$

Solving the quadratic produces the interval

$$\bar{X} + \frac{1.9208}{n} \pm \frac{1}{2}\sqrt{\frac{15.3664\bar{X} + 3.8416^2/n}{n}}$$

and for this problem the interval is 0.197 ± 0.156.

For the second approximation the interval is $\bar{X} \pm 1.96\sqrt{\bar{X}/n}$ and for the example it is 0.12 ± 0.136. This interval extends below zero (which is not possible for the true value of θ). This is because (9.4) is too crude an approximation in this case. □

9.3.1   Exercise

9.11 Let $x_1, \ldots, x_n$ be a random sample from a population with pdf $f(x) = \theta^{-1} e^{-x/\theta}$, $x > 0$. This exponential distribution has a mean of θ and a variance of θ^2. Consider the sample mean, $\bar{X}$, as an estimator of θ. It turns out that $\bar{X}/\theta$ has a gamma distribution with $\alpha = n$ and $\theta = 1/n$, where in the second expression the "θ" on the left is the parameter of the gamma distribution. For a sample of size 50 and a sample mean of 275, develop 95% confidence intervals by each of the following methods. In each case, if the formula requires the true value of θ, substitute the estimated value.

(a) Use the gamma distribution to determine an exact interval.

(b) Use a normal approximation, estimating the variance prior to solving the inequalities as in (9.4).

(c) Use a normal approximation, estimating θ after solving the inequalities as in Example 9.18.

9.4   TESTS OF HYPOTHESES

Hypothesis testing is covered in detail in most mathematical statistics texts. This review will be fairly straightforward and will not address philosophical issues or consider alternative approaches. A hypothesis test begins with two hypotheses, one called the null and one called the alternative. The traditional notation is H_0 for the null hypothesis and H_1 for the alternative hypothesis. The two hypotheses are not treated symmetrically. Reversing them may alter the results. To illustrate this process, a simple example will be used.

Example 9.19 *Your company has been basing its premiums on an assumption that the average claim is 1,200. You want to raise the premium and a regulator has insisted that you provide evidence that the average now exceeds 1,200. To provide such evidence, the following numbers have been obtained. What are the hypotheses for this problem?*

27	82	115	126	155	161	243	294	340	384
457	680	855	877	974	1,193	1,340	1,884	2,558	15,743

Let μ be the population mean. One hypothesis (the one you claim is true) is that $\mu > 1,200$. Because hypothesis tests must present an either/or situation, the other hypothesis must be $\mu \leq 1,200$. The only remaining task is to decide which of them is the null hypothesis. Whenever the universe of continuous possibilities is divided in two there is likely to be a boundary that needs to be assigned to one hypothesis or the other. The hypothesis that includes the boundary must be the null hypothesis. Therefore, the problem can be succinctly stated as:

$$H_0 \;:\; \mu \leq 1{,}200$$
$$H_1 \;:\; \mu > 1{,}200.$$

□

The decision is made by calculating a quantity called a **test statistic**. It is a function of the observations and is treated as a random variable. That is, in designing the test procedure we are concerned with the samples that might have been obtained and not with the particular sample that was obtained. The test specification is completed by constructing a **rejection region**. It is a subset of the possible values of the test statistic. If the value of the test statistic for the observed sample is in the rejection region, the null hypothesis is rejected and the alternative hypothesis is announced as the result that is supported by the data. Otherwise, the null hypothesis is not rejected (more on this later). The boundaries of the rejection region (other than plus or minus infinity) are called the **critical values**.

Example 9.20 (Example 9.19 continued) *Complete the test using the test statistic and rejection region that is promoted in most statistics books. Assume that the population has a normal distribution with standard deviation 3,435.*

The traditional test statistic for this problem is

$$z = \frac{\bar{x} - 1{,}200}{3{,}435/\sqrt{20}} = 0.292$$

and the null hypothesis is rejected if $z > 1.645$. Because 0.292 is less than 1.645, the null hypothesis is not rejected. The data do not support the assertion that the average claim exceeds 1,200.   □

The test in the previous example was constructed to meet certain objectives. The first objective is to control what is called the Type I error. It is the error made when the test rejects the null hypothesis in a situation where it happens to be true. In the example, the null hypothesis can be true in more than one way. This leads to the most common measure of the propensity of a test to make a Type I error.

Definition 9.21 *The **significance level** of a hypothesis test is the probability of making a Type I error given that the null hypothesis is true. If it can be true in more than one way, the level of significance is the maximum of such probabilities. The significance level is usually denoted by the letter α.*

This is a conservative definition in that it looks at the worst case. It is typically a case that is on the boundary between the two hypotheses.

Example 9.22 *Determine the level of significance for the test in Example 9.20.*

Begin by computing the probability of making a Type I error when the null hypothesis is true with $\mu = 1{,}200$. Then,

$$\Pr(Z > 1.645|\mu = 1{,}200) = 0.05.$$

That is because the assumptions imply that Z has a standard normal distribution.

Now suppose μ has a value that is below 1,200. Then

$$\Pr\left(\frac{\bar{X} - 1{,}200}{3{,}435/\sqrt{20}} > 1.645\right)$$

$$= \Pr\left(\frac{\bar{X} - \mu + \mu - 1{,}200}{3{,}435/\sqrt{20}} > 1.645\right)$$

$$= \Pr\left(\frac{\bar{X} - \mu}{3{,}435/\sqrt{20}} > 1.645 - \frac{\mu - 1{,}200}{3{,}435/\sqrt{20}}\right).$$

Because μ is known to be less than 1,200, the right-hand side is always greater than 1.645. The left-hand side has a standard normal distribution and therefore the probability is less than 0.05. Therefore the significance level is 0.05.□

The significance level is usually set in advance and is often between 1 and 10%. The second objective is to keep the Type II error (not rejecting the null hypothesis when the alternative is true) probability small. Generally, attempts to reduce the probability of one type of error increase the probability of the other. The best we can do once the significance level has been set is to make the Type II error as small as possible, though there is no assurance that the probability will be a small number. The best test is one that meets the following requirement.

Definition 9.23 *A hypothesis test is **uniformly most powerful** if no other test exists that has the same or lower significance level and for a particular value within the alternative hypothesis has a smaller probability of making a Type II error.*

Example 9.24 (Example 9.22 continued) *Determine the probability of making a Type II error when the alternative hypothesis is true with $\mu = 2{,}000$.*

$$\Pr\left(\frac{\bar{X} - 1{,}200}{3{,}435/\sqrt{20}} < 1.645|\mu = 2{,}000\right)$$

$$= \Pr(\bar{X} - 1{,}200 < 1{,}263.51|\mu = 2{,}000)$$

$$= \Pr(\bar{X} < 2{,}463.51|\mu = 2{,}000)$$

$$= \Pr\left(\frac{\bar{X} - 2{,}000}{3{,}435/\sqrt{20}} < \frac{2{,}463.51 - 2{,}000}{3{,}435/\sqrt{20}} = 0.6035\right) = 0.7269.$$

For this value of μ, the test is not very powerful, having over a 70% chance of making a Type II error. Nevertheless (though this is not easy to prove), the test used is the most powerful test for this problem.   □

Because the Type II error probability can be high, it is customary to not make a strong statement when the null hypothesis is not rejected. Rather than say we choose or accept the null hypothesis, we say that we fail to reject it. That is, there was not enough evidence in the sample to make a strong argument in favor of the alternative hypothesis, so we take no stand at all.

A common criticism of this approach to hypothesis testing is that the choice of the significance level is arbitrary. In fact, by changing the significance level, any result can be obtained.

Example 9.25 (Example 9.24 continued) *Complete the test using a significance level of $\alpha = 0.45$. Then determine the range of significance levels for which the null hypothesis is rejected and for which it is not rejected.*

Because $\Pr(Z > 0.1257) = 0.45$, the null hypothesis is rejected when

$$\frac{\bar{X} - 1{,}200}{3{,}435/\sqrt{20}} > 0.1257.$$

In this example, the test statistic is 0.292, which is in the rejection region, and thus the null hypothesis is rejected. Of course, few people would place confidence in the results of a test that was designed to make errors 45% of the time. Because $\Pr(Z > 0.292) = 0.3851$, the null hypothesis is rejected for those who select a significance level that is greater than 38.51% and is not rejected by those who use a significance level that is less than 38.51%.   □

Few people are willing to make errors 38.51% of the time. Announcing this figure is more persuasive than the earlier conclusion based on a 5% significance level. When a significance level is used, readers are left to wonder what the outcome would have been with other significance levels. The value of 38.51% is called a p-value. A working definition is:

Definition 9.26 *For a hypothesis test, the **p-value** is the probability that the test statistic takes on a value that is less in agreement with the null hypothesis than the value obtained from the sample. Tests conducted at a significance level that is greater than the p-value will lead to a rejection of the null hypothesis, while tests conducted at a significance level that is smaller than the p-value will lead to a failure to reject the null hypothesis.*

Also, because the p-value must be between 0 and 1, it is on a scale that carries some meaning. The closer to zero the value is, the more support the data give to the alternative hypothesis. Common practice is that values above

10% indicate that the data provide no evidence in support of the alternative hypothesis, while values below 1% indicate strong support for the alternative hypothesis. Values in between indicate uncertainty as to the appropriate conclusion and may call for more data or a more careful look at the data or the experiment that produced it.

9.4.1 Exercise

9.12 (*Exercise 9.11 continued*) Test $H_0 : \theta \geq 325$ vs $H_1 : \theta < 325$ using a significance level of 5% and the sample mean as the test statistic. Also, compute the p-value. Do this using the exact distribution of the test statistic and a normal approximation.

10

Estimation for complete data

10.1 INTRODUCTION

The material in this and the next chapter has been traditionally presented under the heading of "survival models" with the accompanying notion that the techniques are useful only when studying lifetime distributions. Standard texts on the subject such as Klein and Moeschberger [74] and Lawless [81] contain examples that are exclusively oriented in that direction. However, as will be seen in these two chapters, the same problems that occur when modeling lifetime occur when modeling payment amount. The examples we present will be of both types. To emphasize that point, some of the starred exercises were taken from the former Society of Actuaries Course 160 exam, but the setting was changed to a payment environment. Only a handful of references are presented, most of the results being well developed in the survival models literature. Readers wanting more detail and proofs should consult a text dedicated to the subject, such as the ones mentioned above.

In this chapter it is assumed that the type of model is known but not the full description of the model. In Chapter 4, models were divided into two types—data-dependent and parametric. The definitions are repeated below.

Definition 10.1 *A **data-dependent distribution** is at least as complex as the data or knowledge that produced it and the number of "parameters" increases as the number of data points or amount of knowledge increases.*

Definition 10.2 *A **parametric distribution** is a set of distribution functions, each member of which is determined by specifying one or more values called **parameters**. The number of parameters is fixed and finite.*

Here, only two data-dependent distributions will be considered. They depend on the data in similar ways. The simplest definitions for the two types considered appear below.

Definition 10.3 *The **empirical distribution** is obtained by assigning probability $1/n$ to each data point.*

Definition 10.4 *A **kernel smoothed distribution** is obtained by replacing each data point with a continuous random variable and then assigning probability $1/n$ to each such random variable. The random variables used must be identical except for a location or scale change that is related to its associated data point.*

Note that the empirical distribution is a special type of kernel smoothed distribution in which the random variable assigns probability 1 to the data point. An alternative to the empirical distribution that is similar in spirit but produces different numbers will also be presented. In Chapter 11 it will be shown how the definition can be modified to account for data that have been altered through censoring and truncation. With regard to kernel smoothing, there are several distributions that could be used, a few of which are introduced in Section 11.3.

Throughout this part, four examples will used repeatedly. Because they are simply data sets, they will be referred to as Data Sets A, B, C and D.

Data Set A *This data set is well-known in the casualty actuarial literature. It was first analyzed in the paper [30] by Dropkin in 1959. He collected data from 1956–1958 on the number of accidents by one driver in one year. The results for 94,935 drivers are in Table 10.1.*

Data Set B *These numbers are artificial. They represent the amounts paid on workers compensation medical benefits but are not related to any particular policy or set of policyholders. These payments are the full amount of the loss. A random sample of 20 payments is given in Table 10.2.*

Data Set C *These observations represent payments on 227 claims from a general liability insurance policy. The data are in Table 10.3.*

Data Set D *These numbers are artificial. They represent the time at which a five-year term insurance policy terminates. For some policyholders, termination is by death, for some it is by surrender (the cancellation of the insurance*

Table 10.1 Data Set A

Number of accidents	Number of drivers
0	81,714
1	11,306
2	1,618
3	250
4	40
5 or more	7

Table 10.2 Data Set B

27	82	115	126	155	161	243	294	340	384
457	680	855	877	974	1,193	1,340	1,884	2,558	15,743

Table 10.3 Data Set C

Payment range	Number of payments
0–7,500	99
7,500–17,500	42
17,500–32,500	29
32,500–67,500	28
67,500–125,000	17
125,000–300,000	9
Over 300,000	3

contract), and for the remainder it is expiration of the five-year period. Two separate versions are presented. For Data Set $D1$ (*Table* 10.4) there were 30 policies observed from issue. For each, both the time of death and time of surrender are presented, provided they were before the expiration of the five-year period. Of course, normally we do not know the time of death of policyholders who surrender and we do not know when policyholders who died would have surrendered had they not died. Note that the final 12 policyholders survived both death and surrender to the end of the five-year period.

For Data Set $D2$ (*Table* 10.5), only the time of the first event is observed. In addition, there are 10 more policyholders who were first observed at some time after the policy was issued. The table presents the results for all 40 policies. The column headed "First observed" gives the duration at which the policy was first observed; the column headed "Last observed" gives the duration at which the policy was last observed; and the column headed "Event" is coded "s" for surrender, "d" for death, and "e" for expiration of the five-year period.

Table 10.4   Data Set D1

Policyholder	Time of death	Time of surrender
1	–	0.1
2	4.8	0.5
3	–	0.8
4	0.8	3.9
5	3.1	1.8
6	–	1.8
7	–	2.1
8	–	2.5
9	–	2.8
10	2.9	4.6
11	2.9	4.6
12	–	3.9
13	4.0	–
14	–	4.0
15	–	4.1
16	4.8	–
17	–	4.8
18	–	4.8
19–30	–	–

When observations are collected from a probability distribution, the ideal situation is to have the (essentially) exact[1] value of each observation. This case is referred to as "complete, individual data." This is the case in Data Sets B and D1. There are two reasons why exact data may not be available. One is grouping, in which all that is recorded is the range of values in which the observation belongs. This is the case for Data Set C and for Data Set A for those with five or more accidents.

A second reason that exact values may not be available is the presence of censoring or truncation. When data are censored from below, observations below a given value are known to be below that value but the exact value is unknown. When data are censored from above, observations above a given value are known to be above that value but the exact value is unknown. Note that censoring effectively creates grouped data. When the data are grouped in the first place, censoring has no effect. For example, the data in Data Set C may have been censored from above at 300,000, but we cannot know for sure

---

[1]Some measurements are never exact. Ages may be rounded to the nearest whole number, monetary amounts to the nearest dollar, car mileage to the nearest tenth of a mile, and so on. This text is not concerned with such rounding errors. Rounded values will be treated as if they are exact.

Table 10.5 Data Set D2

Policy	First observed	Last observed	Event	Policy	First observed	Last observed	Event
1	0	0.1	s	16	0	4.8	d
2	0	0.5	s	17	0	4.8	s
3	0	0.8	s	18	0	4.8	s
4	0	0.8	d	19-30	0	5.0	e
5	0	1.8	s	31	0.3	5.0	e
6	0	1.8	s	32	0.7	5.0	e
7	0	2.1	s	33	1.0	4.1	d
8	0	2.5	s	34	1.8	3.1	d
9	0	2.8	s	35	2.1	3.9	s
10	0	2.9	d	36	2.9	5.0	e
11	0	2.9	d	37	2.9	4.8	s
12	0	3.9	s	38	3.2	4.0	d
13	0	4.0	d	39	3.4	5.0	e
14	0	4.0	s	40	3.9	5.0	e
15	0	4.1	s				

from the data set and that knowledge has no effect on how we treat the data. On the other hand, were Data Set B to be censored at 1,000, we would have 15 individual observations and then 5 grouped observations in the interval from 1,000 to infinity.

In insurance settings, censoring from above is fairly common. For example, if a policy pays no more than 100,000 for an accident any time the loss is above 100,000 the actual amount will be unknown but we will know that it happened. In Data Set D2 we have random censoring. Consider the fifth policy in the table. When the "other information" is not available, all that is known about the time of death is that it will be after 1.8 years. All of the policies are censored at 5 years by the nature of the policy itself. Also, note that Data Set A has been censored from above at 5. This is more common language than to say that Data Set A has some individual data and some grouped data.

When data are truncated from below, observations below a given value are not recorded. Truncation from above implies that observations above a given value are not recorded. In insurance settings, truncation from below is fairly common. If an automobile physical damage policy has a per claim deductible of 250, any losses below 250 will not come to the attention of the insurance company and so will not appear in any data sets. Data Set D2 has observations 31–40 truncated from below at varying values. Data sets may have truncation forced on them. For example, if Data Set B were to be truncated from below at 250, the first 7 observations would disappear and the remaining 13 would be unchanged.

10.2   THE EMPIRICAL DISTRIBUTION FOR COMPLETE, INDIVIDUAL DATA

As noted in Definition 10.3, the empirical distribution assigns probability $1/n$ to each data point. That works well when the value of each data point is recorded. An alternative definition follows:

Definition 10.5 *The **empirical distribution function** is*

$$F_n(x) = \frac{number\ of\ observations \le x}{n},$$

where n is the total number of observations.

Example 10.6 *Provide the empirical probability functions for the data in Data Sets A and B. For Data Set A also provide the empirical distribution function. For Data Set A assume all seven drivers who had five or more accidents had exactly five accidents.*

For notation, a subscript of the sample size (or of n if the sample size is not known) will be used to indicate an empirical function. Without the subscript, the function represents the true function for the underlying random variable. For Data Set A, the estimated probability function is

$$p_{94,935}(x) = \begin{cases} 81,714/94,935 = 0.860736, & x = 0, \\ 11,306/94,935 = 0.119092, & x = 1, \\ 1,618/94,935 = 0.017043, & x = 2, \\ 250/94,935 = 0.002633, & x = 3, \\ 40/94,935 = 0.000421, & x = 4, \\ 7/94,935 = 0.000074, & x = 5, \end{cases}$$

where the values add to 0.999999 due to rounding. The distribution function is a step function with jumps at each data point.

$$F_{94,935}(x) = \begin{cases} 0/94,935 = 0.000000, & x < 0, \\ 81,714/94,935 = 0.860736, & 0 \le x < 1, \\ 93,020/94,935 = 0.979828, & 1 \le x < 2, \\ 94,638/94,935 = 0.996872, & 2 \le x < 3, \\ 94,888/94,935 = 0.999505, & 3 \le x < 4, \\ 94,928/94,935 = 0.999926, & 4 \le x < 5, \\ 94,935/94,935 = 1.000000, & x \ge 5. \end{cases}$$

For Data Set B,

$$p_{20}(x) = \begin{cases} 0.05, & x = 27, \\ 0.05, & x = 82, \\ 0.05, & x = 115, \\ \vdots & \vdots \\ 0.05, & x = 15,743. \end{cases}$$

□

As noted in the example, the empirical model is a discrete distribution. Therefore, the derivative required to create the density and hazard rate functions cannot be taken. The closest we can come, in an empirical sense, to estimating the hazard rate function is to estimate the cumulative hazard rate function, defined as follows.

Definition 10.7 *The **cumulative hazard rate function** is defined as*

$$H(x) = -\ln S(x).$$

The name comes from the fact that, if $S(x)$ is differentiable,

$$H'(x) = -\frac{S'(x)}{S(x)} = \frac{f(x)}{S(x)} = h(x)$$

and then

$$H(x) = \int_{-\infty}^{x} h(y)dy.$$

The distribution function can be obtained from $F(x) = 1 - S(x) = 1 - e^{-H(x)}$. Therefore, estimating the cumulative hazard function provides an alternative way to estimate the distribution function.

In order to define empirical estimates, some additional notation is needed. For a sample of size n, let $y_1 < y_2 < \cdots < y_k$ be the k unique values that appear in the sample, where k must be less than or equal to n. Let s_j be the number of times the observation y_j appears in the sample. Thus, $\sum_{j=1}^{k} s_j = n$. Also of interest is the number of observations in the data set that are greater than or equal to a given value. Both the observations and the number of observations are referred to as the **risk set**. Let $r_j = \sum_{i=j}^{k} s_i$ be the number of observations greater than or equal to y_j. Using this notation, the empirical distribution function is

$$F_n(x) = \begin{cases} 0, & x < y_1, \\ 1 - \frac{r_j}{n}, & y_{j-1} \le x < y_j, \ j = 2, \ldots, k, \\ 1, & x \ge y_k. \end{cases}$$

Example 10.8 *Consider a data set containing the numbers 1.0, 1.3, 1.5, 1.5, 2.1, 2.1, 2.1, and 2.8. Determine the quantities described in the previous paragraph and then obtain the empirical distribution function.*

There are five unique values and thus $k = 5$. Values of y_j, s_j, and r_j are given in Table 10.6.

Table 10.6   Values for Example 10.8

j	y_j	s_j	r_j
1	1.0	1	8
2	1.3	1	7
3	1.5	2	6
4	2.1	3	4
5	2.8	1	1

$$F_8(x) = \begin{cases} 0, & x < 1.0, \\ 1 - \frac{7}{8} = 0.125, & 1.0 \le x < 1.3, \\ 1 - \frac{6}{8} = 0.250, & 1.3 \le x < 1.5, \\ 1 - \frac{4}{8} = 0.500, & 1.5 \le x < 2.1, \\ 1 - \frac{1}{8} = 0.875, & 2.1 \le x < 2.8, \\ 1, & x \ge 2.8. \end{cases} \qquad \square$$

Definition 10.9 *The **Nelson–Åalen estimate** ([1],[99]) of the cumulative hazard rate function is*

$$\hat{H}(x) = \begin{cases} 0, & x < y_1, \\ \sum_{i=1}^{j-1} \frac{s_i}{r_i}, & y_{j-1} \le x < y_j, \ j = 2, \dots, k, \\ \sum_{i=1}^{k} \frac{s_i}{r_i}, & x \ge y_k. \end{cases}$$

Because this is a step function, its derivatives (which would provide an estimate of the hazard rate function) are not interesting. An intuitive derivation of this estimator can be found on page 302.

Example 10.10 *Determine the Nelson–Åalen estimate for the previous example.*

We have

$$\hat{H}(x) = \begin{cases} 0, & x < 1.0, \\ \frac{1}{8} = 0.125, & 1.0 \le x < 1.3, \\ 0.125 + \frac{1}{7} = 0.268, & 1.3 \le x < 1.5, \\ 0.268 + \frac{2}{6} = 0.601, & 1.5 \le x < 2.1, \\ 0.601 + \frac{3}{4} = 1.351, & 2.1 \le x < 2.8, \\ 1.351 + \frac{1}{1} = 2.351, & x \ge 2.8. \end{cases}$$

Table 10.7 Data for Example 10.11

j	y_j	s_j	r_j	$S_{30}(x)$	$\hat{H}(x)$	$\hat{S}(x) = e^{-\hat{H}(x)}$
1	0.8	1	30	$\frac{29}{30} = 0.9667$	$\frac{1}{30} = 0.0333$	0.9672
2	2.9	2	29	$\frac{27}{30} = 0.9000$	$0.0333 + \frac{2}{29} = 0.1023$	0.9028
3	3.1	1	27	$\frac{26}{30} = 0.8667$	$0.1023 + \frac{1}{27} = 0.1393$	0.8700
4	4.0	1	26	$\frac{25}{30} = 0.8333$	$0.1393 + \frac{1}{26} = 0.1778$	0.8371
5	4.8	2	25	$\frac{23}{30} = 0.7667$	$0.1778 + \frac{2}{25} = 0.2578$	0.7727

These values can be used to produce an alternative estimate of the distribution function via exponentiation. For example, for $1.5 \leq x < 2.1$, the estimate is $\hat{F}(x) = 1 - e^{-0.601} = 0.452$, which is not equal to the empirical estimate of 0.5. When a function is estimated by other methods, the function has a caret (hat) placed on it. □

Example 10.11 *Determine the empirical survival function and Nelson–Åalen estimate of the cumulative hazard rate function for the time to death for Data Set D1. Estimate the survival function from the Nelson–Åalen estimate. Assume that the death time is known for those who surrender.*

The calculations are in Table 10.7. For the empirical functions, the values given are for the interval from (and including) the current y value to (but not including) the next y value. □

For this particular problem, where it is known that all policyholders terminate at time 5, results past 5 are not interesting. The methods of obtaining an empirical distribution that have been introduced work only when the individual observations are available and there is no truncation or censoring. The following chapter will introduce modifications for those situations.

10.2.1 Exercises

10.1 Obtain the empirical distribution function and the Nelson–Åalen estimate of the distribution function for the time to surrender using Data Set D1. Assume that the surrender time is known for those who die.

10.2 The data in Table 10.8 are from *Loss Distributions* [59], p. 128. It represents the total damage done by 35 hurricanes between the years 1949 and 1980. The losses have been adjusted for inflation (using the Residential Construction Index) to be in 1981 dollars. The entries represent all hurricanes for which the trended loss was in excess of 5,000,000.

Table 10.8   Trended hurricane losses

Year	Loss (10^3)	Year	Loss (10^3)	Year	Loss (10^3)
1964	6,766	1964	40,596	1975	192,013
1968	7,123	1949	41,409	1972	198,446
1971	10,562	1959	47,905	1964	227,338
1956	14,474	1950	49,397	1960	329,511
1961	15,351	1954	52,600	1961	361,200
1966	16,983	1973	59,917	1969	421,680
1955	18,383	1980	63,123	1954	513,586
1958	19,030	1964	77,809	1954	545,778
1974	25,304	1955	102,942	1970	750,389
1959	29,112	1967	103,217	1979	863,881
1971	30,146	1957	123,680	1965	1,638,000
1976	33,727	1979	140,136		

The federal government is considering funding a program that would provide 100% payment for all damages for any hurricane causing damage in excess of 5,000,000. You have been asked to make some preliminary estimates.

(a) Estimate the mean, standard deviation, coefficient of variation, and skewness for the population of hurricane losses.

(b) Estimate the first and second limited moments at 500,000,000.

10.3 (*) There have been 30 claims recorded in a random sampling of claims. There were 2 claims for 2,000, 6 for 4,000, 12 for 6,000, and 10 for 8,000. Determine the empirical skewness coefficient.

10.3   EMPIRICAL DISTRIBUTIONS FOR GROUPED DATA

For grouped data, construction of the empirical distribution as defined previously is not possible. However, it is possible to approximate the empirical distribution. The strategy is to obtain values of the empirical distribution function wherever possible and then connect those values in some reasonable way. For grouped data, the distribution function is usually approximated by connecting the points with straight lines. Other interpolation methods are discussed in Chapter 15. For notation, let the group boundaries be $c_0 < c_1 < \cdots < c_k$, where often $c_0 = 0$ and $c_k = \infty$. The number of observations falling between c_{j-1} and c_j is denoted n_j with $\sum_{j=1}^{k} n_j = n$. For such data, we are able to determine the empirical distribution at each group boundary. That is, $F_n(c_j) = (1/n) \sum_{i=1}^{j} n_i$. Note that no rule is proposed for observations that fall on a group boundary. There is no correct approach, but whatever approach is used, consistency in assignment of observations to groups should be used. You will note that in Data Set C it is not possible to tell how the assignments were made. If we had that knowledge, it would not affect any subsequent calculations.[2]

Definition 10.12 *For grouped data, the distribution function obtained by connecting the values of the empirical distribution function at the group boundaries with straight lines is called the* **ogive.** *The formula is*

$$F_n(x) = \frac{c_j - x}{c_j - c_{j-1}} F_n(c_{j-1}) + \frac{x - c_{j-1}}{c_j - c_{j-1}} F_n(c_j), \ c_{j-1} \le x \le c_j.$$

This function is differentiable at all values except group boundaries. Therefore the density function can be obtained. To completely specify the density function, it will arbitrarily be made right-continuous.

Definition 10.13 *For grouped data, the empirical density function can be obtained by differentiating the ogive. The resulting function is called a* **histogram.** *The formula is*

$$f_n(x) = \frac{F_n(c_j) - F_n(c_{j-1})}{c_j - c_{j-1}} = \frac{n_j}{n(c_j - c_{j-1})}, \ c_{j-1} \le x < c_j.$$

Many computer programs that produce histograms actually create a bar chart with bar heights proportional to n_j/n. This is acceptable if the groups have equal width, but if not, then the above formula is needed. The advantage of this approach is that the histogram is indeed a density function, and among other things, areas under the histogram can be used to obtain empirical probabilities.

Example 10.14 *Construct the ogive and histogram for Data Set C.*

The distribution function is

$$F_{227}(x) = \begin{cases} 0.000058150x, & 0 \le x \le 7{,}500, \\ 0.29736 + 0.000018502x, & 7{,}500 \le x \le 17{,}500, \\ 0.47210 + 0.000008517x, & 17{,}500 \le x \le 32{,}500, \\ 0.63436 + 0.000003524x, & 32{,}500 \le x \le 67{,}500, \\ 0.78433 + 0.000001302x, & 67{,}500 \le x \le 125{,}000, \\ 0.91882 + 0.000000227x, & 125{,}000 \le x \le 300{,}000, \\ \text{undefined}, & x > 300{,}000, \end{cases}$$

where, for example, for the range $32{,}500 \le x \le 67{,}500$ the calculation is

$$F_{227}(x) = \frac{67{,}500 - x}{67{,}500 - 32{,}500} \frac{170}{227} + \frac{x - 32{,}500}{67{,}500 - 32{,}500} \frac{198}{227}.$$

The value is undefined above 300,000 because the last interval has a width of infinity. A graph of the ogive for values up to 125,000 appears in Figure 10.1.

---

[2] Technically, for the interval from c_{j-1} to c_j, $x = c_j$ should be included and $x = c_{j-1}$ excluded in order for $F_n(c_j)$ to be the empirical distribution function.

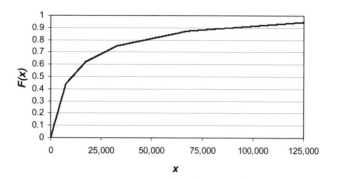

Fig. 10.1 Ogive for general liability losses.

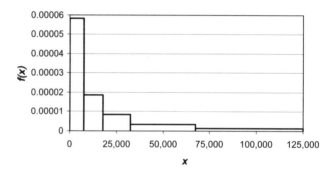

Fig. 10.2 Histogram of general liability losses.

The derivative is simply a step function with the following values.

$$
f_{227}(x) = \begin{cases}
0.000058150, & 0 \leq x < 7{,}500, \\
0.000018502, & 7{,}500 \leq x < 17{,}500, \\
0.000008517, & 17{,}500 \leq x < 32{,}500, \\
0.000003524, & 32{,}500 \leq x < 67{,}500, \\
0.000001302, & 67{,}500 \leq x < 125{,}000, \\
0.000000227, & 125{,}000 \leq x < 300{,}000, \\
\text{undefined}, & x \geq 300{,}000.
\end{cases}
$$

A graph of the function up to 125,000 appears in Figure 10.2.   □

Table 10.9 Data for Exercise 10.4

Payment range	Number of payments
0–25	6
25–50	24
50–75	30
75–100	31
100–150	57
150–250	80
250–500	85
500–1000	54
1000–2000	15
2000–4000	10
Over 4000	0

10.3.1 Exercises

10.4 Construct the ogive and histogram for the data in Table 10.9.

10.5 (*) The following 20 wind losses (in millions of dollars) were recorded in one year:

$$1 \quad 1 \quad 1 \quad 1 \quad 1 \quad 2 \quad 2 \quad 3 \quad 3 \quad 4$$
$$6 \quad 6 \quad 8 \quad 10 \quad 13 \quad 14 \quad 15 \quad 18 \quad 22 \quad 25$$

   (a) Construct an ogive based on using class boundaries at 0.5, 2.5, 8.5, 15.5, and 29.5.

   (b) Construct a histogram using the same boundaries as in part (a).

10.6 The data in Table 10.10 are from Herzog and Laverty [54]. A certain class of 15-year mortgages was followed from issue until December 31, 1993. The issues were split into those that were refinances of existing mortgages and those that were original issues. Each entry in the table provides the number of issues and the percentage of them that were still in effect after the indicated number of years. Draw as much of the two ogives (on the same graph) as is possible from the data. Does it appear from the ogives that the lifetime variable (time to mortgage termination) has a different distribution for refinanced versus original issues?

10.7 (*) The data in Table 10.11 were collected (units are millions of dollars). Construct the histogram.

10.8 (*) Forty losses have been observed. Sixteen are between 1 and $\frac{4}{3}$ and those 16 losses total 20. Ten losses are between $\frac{4}{3}$ and 2 with a total of 15. Ten more are between 2 and 4 with a total of 35. The remaining 4 losses

Table 10.10   Data for Exercise 10.6

	Refinances		Original	
Years	No. issued	Survived	No. issued	Survived
1.5	42,300	99.97	12,813	99.88
2.5	9,756	99.82	18,787	99.43
3.5	1,550	99.03	22,513	98.81
4.5	1,256	98.41	21,420	98.26
5.5	1,619	97.78	26,790	97.45

Table 10.11   Data for Exercise 10.7

Loss	No. of observations
0–2	25
2–10	10
10–100	10
100–1,000	5

are greater than 4. Using the empirical model based on these observations, determine $E(X \wedge 2)$.

10.9 (*) A sample of size 2,000 contains 1,700 observations that are no greater than 6,000, 30 that are greater than 6,000 but no greater than 7,000, and 270 that are greater than 7,000. The total amount of the 30 observations that are between 6,000 and 7,000 is 200,000. The value of $E(X \wedge 6,000)$ for the empirical distribution associated with these observations is 1,810. Determine $E(X \wedge 7,000)$ for the empirical distribution.

11

Estimation for modified data

11.1 POINT ESTIMATION

It is not unusual for data to be incomplete due to censoring or truncation. The formal definitions are as follows.

Definition 11.1 *An observation is **truncated from below** (also called **left truncated**) at d if when it is below d it is not recorded but when it is above d it is recorded at its observed value.*
*An observation is **truncated from above** (also called **right truncated**) at u if when it is above u it is not recorded but when it is below u it is recorded at its observed value.*
*An observation is **censored from below** (also called **left censored**) at d if, when it is below d it is recorded as being equal to d but when it is above d it is recorded at its observed value.*
*An observation is **censored from above** (also called **right censored**) at u if, when it is above u it is recorded as being equal to u but when it is below u it is recorded at its observed value.*

The most common occurrences are left truncation and right censoring. Left truncation occurs when an ordinary deductible of d is applied. When a policyholder has a loss below d, he or she knows no benefits will be paid and so

Loss Models: From Data to Decisions, Second Edition.
By Stuart A. Klugman, Harry H. Panjer, and Gordon E. Willmot
ISBN 0-471-21577-5   Copyright © 2004 John Wiley & Sons, Inc.

does not inform the insurer. When the loss is above d, the amount of the loss will be reported. A policy limit is an example of right censoring. When the amount of the loss exceeds u, benefits beyond that value are not paid and so the exact value is not recorded. However, it is known that a loss of at least u has occurred.

When constructing a mortality table, it is impractical to follow people from birth to death. It is more common to follow a group of people of varying ages for a few years. When a person joins a study, he or she is alive at that time. This person's age at death must be at least as great as the age at entry to the study and thus has been left truncated. If the person is alive when the study ends, right censoring has occurred. The person's age at death is not known, but it is known that it is at least as large as the age when the study ended. Right censoring also affects those who leave the study prior to its end due to surrender.

Because left truncation and right censoring are the most common occurrences in actuarial work, they are the only cases that will be covered in this chapter. To save words, *truncated* will always mean truncated from below and *censored* will always mean censored from above.

When trying to construct an empirical distribution from truncated or censored data, the first task is to create notation to summarize the data. For individual data, there are three facts that are needed. First is the truncation point for that observation. Let that value be d_j for the jth observation. If there was no truncation, $d_j = 0$. The second is the observation itself. The notation used will depend on whether or not that observation was censored. If it was not censored, let its value be x_j. If it was censored, let its value be u_j. When this subject is presented more formally, a distinction is made between the case where the censoring point is known in advance and where it is not. For example, a liability insurance policy with a policy limit usually has the censoring point known prior to the receipt of any claims. On the other hand, in a mortality study of insured lives, those that surrender their policy do so at an age that was not known when the policy was sold. In this chapter no distinction will be made between the two cases.

To perform the estimation, the raw data must be summarized in a useful manner. The most interesting values are the uncensored observations. Let $y_1 < y_2 < \cdots < y_k$ be the k unique values of the x_js that appear in the sample, where k must be less than or equal to the number of uncensored observations. Let s_j be the number of times the uncensored observation y_j appears in the sample. The final important quantity is the **risk set** at the jth ordered observation y_j and is denoted r_j. When thinking in terms of a mortality study, the risk set comprises the individuals who are under observation at that age. Included are all who die (have x values) at that age or later and all who are censored (have u values) at that age or later. However, those who are first observed (have d values) at that age or later were not under observation at that time. The formula is

$$r_j = (\text{number of } x_i\text{s } \geq y_j) + (\text{number of } u_i\text{s } \geq y_j) - (\text{number of } d_i\text{s} \geq y_j).$$

Alternatively, because the total number of d_is is equal to the total number of x_is and u_is, we also have

$$r_j = (\text{number of } d_i\text{s} < y_j) - (\text{number of } x_i\text{s } < y_j) - (\text{number of } u_i\text{s } < y_j).$$
(11.1)

This latter version is a bit easier to conceptualize because it includes all who have entered the study prior to the given age less those who have already left. The key point is that the risk set is the number of people observed alive at age y_j. If the data are loss amounts, the risk set is the number of policies with observed loss amounts (either the actual amount or the maximum amount due to a policy limit) greater than or equal to y_j less those with deductibles greater than or equal to y_j. This also leads to a recursive version of the formula,

$$
\begin{aligned}
r_j = {} & r_{j-1} + (\text{number of } d_i\text{s between } y_{j-1} \text{ and } y_j) \\
& -(\text{number of } x_i\text{s between } y_{j-1} \text{ and } y_j) \\
& -(\text{number of } u_i\text{s between } y_{j-1} \text{ and } y_j),
\end{aligned}
$$
(11.2)

where *between* is interpreted to mean greater than or equal to y_{j-1} and less than y_j and r_0 is set equal to 0.

Example 11.2 *Using Data Set D2, calculate the above quantities using both* (11.1) *and* (11.2).

The calculations appear in Tables 11.1 and 11.2.   □

Despite all the work we have done to this point, we have yet to produce an estimator of the survival function. The one most commonly used is called the **Kaplan–Meier product–limit Estimator** [70]. Begin with $S(0) = 1$. Because no one died prior to y_1, the survival function remains at 1 until this value. Thinking conditionally, just before y_1, there were r_1 people available to die, of which s_1 did so. Thus, the probability of surviving past y_1 is $(r_1 - s_1)/r_1$. This becomes the value of $S(y_1)$ and the survival function remains at that value until y_2. Again, thinking conditionally, the new survival value at y_2 is $S(y_1)(r_2 - s_2)/r_2$. The general formula is

$$
S_n(t) = \begin{cases}
1, & 0 \leq t < y_1, \\[2mm]
\prod_{i=1}^{j-1} \left(\dfrac{r_i - s_i}{r_i} \right), & y_{j-1} \leq t < y_j,\ j = 2, \ldots, k, \\[4mm]
\prod_{i=1}^{k} \left(\dfrac{r_i - s_i}{r_i} \right) \text{ or } 0, & t \geq y_k.
\end{cases}
$$

Table 11.1   Values for Example 11.2

i	d_i	x_i	u_i	i	d_i	x_i	u_i
1	0	–	0.1	16	0	4.8	–
2	0	–	0.5	17	0	–	4.8
3	0	–	0.8	18	0	–	4.8
4	0	0.8	–	19–30	0	–	5.0
5	0	–	1.8	31	0.3	–	5.0
6	0	–	1.8	32	0.7	–	5.0
7	0	–	2.1	33	1.0	4.1	–
8	0	–	2.5	34	1.8	3.1	–
9	0	–	2.8	35	2.1	–	3.9
10	0	2.9	–	36	2.9	–	5.0
11	0	2.9	–	37	2.9	–	4.8
12	0	–	3.9	38	3.2	4.0	–
13	0	4.0	–	39	3.4	–	5.0
14	0	–	4.0	40	3.9	–	5.0
15	0	–	4.1				

Table 11.2   Risk set calculations for Example 11.2

j	y_j	s_j	r_j
1	0.8	1	$32 - 0 - 2 = 30$ or $0 + 32 - 0 - 2 = 30$
2	2.9	2	$35 - 1 - 8 = 26$ or $30 + 3 - 1 - 6 = 26$
3	3.1	1	$37 - 3 - 8 = 26$ or $26 + 2 - 2 - 0 = 26$
4	4.0	2	$40 - 4 - 10 = 26$ or $26 + 3 - 1 - 2 = 26$
5	4.1	1	$40 - 6 - 11 = 23$ or $26 + 0 - 2 - 1 = 23$
6	4.8	1	$40 - 7 - 12 = 21$ or $23 + 0 - 1 - 1 = 21$

If $s_k = r_k$, then $S(t) = 0$ for $t \geq y_k$ makes sense. Everyone in the sample has died by that value and so, empirically, survival past that age is not possible. However, due to censoring, it is possible that at the age of the last death there were still people alive but all were censored prior to death. We know that survival past the last observed death age is possible, but there is no empirical data available to complete the survival function. One option (the first one used in the above formula) is to keep the function at its last value. This is clearly the largest reasonable choice. Another option is to declare the function to be zero past the last observed age, whether it is an observed death or a censored age. This is the smallest reasonable choice and makes it possible to calculate moments. An intermediate option is to use an exponential curve to reduce the value from its current level to zero. Let $w = \max\{x_1, \ldots, x_n, u_1, \ldots, u_n\}$.

Then, for $t \geq w$,

$$S_n(t) = e^{(t/w) \ln s^*} = (s^*)^{t/w}, \text{ where } s^* = \prod_{i=1}^{k} \left(\frac{r_i - s_i}{r_i} \right).$$

There is an alternative method of obtaining the values of s_j and r_j that is more suitable for Excel® spreadsheet work.[1] The steps are as follows:

1. There should be one row for each data point. The points need not be in any particular order.

2. Each row should have three entries. The first entry should be d_j, the second entry should be u_j or x_j (there can be only one of these). The third entry should be the letter "x" (without the quotes) if the second entry is an x-value (an observed value) and should be the letter "u" if the second entry is a u-value (a censored value). Assume, for example, that the d_js occupy cells B6:B45, the u_js and x_js occupy C6:C45, and the x/u letters occupy D6:D45.

3. Create the columns for x, r, and s as follows.

4. For the ordered observed values (say they should begin in cell F2, start with the lowest d-value. The formula in F2 is =MIN(B6:B45).

5. Then in cell F3 enter the formula

    =MIN(IF(C$6:C$45>F2,IF(D$6:D$45="x",C$6:C$45,1E36),1E36)).

    Because this is an array formula, it must be entered with Ctrl-Shift-Enter. Copy this formula into cells F4, F5, and so on until the value 1E36 appears. Column F should now contain the unique, ordered, y-values.

6. In cell G3 enter the formula

    =COUNTIF(B$6:B$45,"<"&F3)-COUNTIF(C$6:C$45,"<"&F3).

    Copy this formula into cells G4, G5, and so on until values appear across from all but the last value in column F. This column contains the risk set values.

7. In cell H3 enter the formula

    =SUM(IF(C$6:C$45=F3,IF(D$6:D$45="x",1,0),0)).

---

[1] This scheme was devised by Charles Thayer and improved by Margie Rosenberg. It is a great improvement over the author's scheme presented in earlier drafts. These instructions work with Office XP and should work in a similar manner for other versions.

Enter this array formula with Ctrl-Shift-Enter and then copy it into H4, H5, and so on to match the rows of column G. This column contains the s-values.

8. Begin the calculation of $S(y)$ by entering a 1 in cell I2

9. Calculate the next $S(y)$ value by entering the following formula in cell I3.

$$=\text{I2*(G3} - \text{H3)/G3}.$$

Then copy this formula into cells I4, I5, and so on to complete the process.

Example 11.3 *Determine the Kaplan–Meier estimate for Data Set D2.*

Based on the previous example, we have

$$S_{40}(t) = \begin{cases} 1, & 0 \le t < 0.8, \\ \frac{30-1}{30} = 0.9667, & 0.8 \le t < 2.9, \\ 0.9667\frac{26-2}{26} = 0.8923, & 2.9 \le t < 3.1, \\ 0.8923\frac{26-1}{26} = 0.8580, & 3.1 \le t < 4.0, \\ 0.8580\frac{26-2}{26} = 0.7920, & 4.0 \le t < 4.1, \\ 0.7920\frac{23-1}{23} = 0.7576, & 4.1 \le t < 4.8, \\ 0.7576\frac{21-1}{21} = 0.7215, & 4.8 \le t < 5.0, \\ 0.7215 \text{ or } 0 \text{ or } 0.7215^{t/5.0}, & t \ge 5.0. \end{cases}$$

□

An alternative to the Kaplan–Meier estimate is a modification of the Nelson–Åalen estimate introduced earlier. As before, this method directly estimates the cumulative hazard rate function. The following is an intuitive derivation of this estimator. Let $r(t)$ be the risk set at any time t and let $h(t)$ be the hazard rate function. Also, let $s(t)$ be the expected total number of observed deaths prior to time t. It is reasonable to conclude that

$$s(t) = \int_0^t r(u)h(u)du.$$

Taking derivatives,

$$ds(t) = r(t)h(t)dt.$$

Then,

$$\frac{ds(t)}{r(t)} = h(t)dt.$$

Integrating both sides yields

$$\int_0^t \frac{ds(u)}{r(u)} = \int_0^t h(t)dt = H(t).$$

Now replace the true expected count $s(t)$ by $\hat{s}(t)$, the observed number of deaths by time t. It is a step function, increasing by s_i at each death time. Therefore, the left-hand side becomes

$$\sum_{t_i \leq t} \frac{s_i}{r_i},$$

which defines the estimator, $\hat{H}(t)$. The Nelson–Åalen estimator is

$$\hat{H}(t) = \begin{cases} 0, & 0 \leq t < y_1, \\ \sum_{i=1}^{j-1} \frac{s_i}{r_i}, & y_{j-1} \leq t < y_j, \ j = 2, \ldots, k, \\ \sum_{i=1}^{k} \frac{s_i}{r_i}, & t \geq y_k, \end{cases}$$

and then

$$\hat{S}(t) = e^{-\hat{H}(t)}.$$

For $t \geq w$, alternative estimates are $\hat{S}(t) = 0$ and $\hat{S}(t) = \hat{S}(y_k)^{t/w}$.

Example 11.4 *Determine the Nelson–Åalen estimate of the survival function for Data Set D2.*

$$\hat{H}(t) = \begin{cases} 0, & 0 \leq t < 0.8, \\ \frac{1}{30} = 0.0333, & 0.8 \leq t < 2.9, \\ 0.0333 + \frac{2}{26} = 0.1103, & 2.9 \leq t < 3.1, \\ 0.1103 + \frac{1}{26} = 0.1487, & 3.1 \leq t < 4.0, \\ 0.1487 + \frac{2}{26} = 0.2256, & 4.0 \leq t < 4.1, \\ 0.2256 + \frac{1}{23} = 0.2691, & 4.1 \leq t < 4.8, \\ 0.2691 + \frac{1}{21} = 0.3167, & t \geq 4.8. \end{cases}$$

$$\hat{S}(t) = \begin{cases} 1, & 0 \leq t < 0.8, \quad \rightarrow S(0) \\ e^{-0.0333} = 0.9672, & 0.8 \leq t < 2.9, \\ e^{-0.1103} = 0.8956, & 2.9 \leq t < 3.1, \\ e^{-0.1487} = 0.8618, & 3.1 \leq t < 4.0, \\ e^{-0.2256} = 0.7980, & 4.0 \leq t < 4.1, \\ e^{-0.2691} = 0.7641, & 4.1 \leq t < 4.8, \\ e^{-0.3167} = 0.7285, & 4.8 \leq t < 5.0, \quad \rightarrow S(4.8) \\ 0.7285 \text{ or } 0 \text{ or } 0.7285^{t/5.0}, & t \geq 5.0. \end{cases} \qquad \square$$

It is important to note that when the data are truncated the resulting distribution function is the distribution function for payments given that they are above the smallest truncation point (that is, the smallest d value). Empirically, there is no information about observations below that value, and thus there can be no information for that range. It should be noted that all the notation and formulas in this section are consistent with those in Section 10.2. If it turns out that there was no censoring or truncation, using the formulas in this section will lead to the same results as when using the empirical formulas in Section 10.2.

11.1.1   Exercises

11.1 Repeat Example 11.2, treating "surrender" as "death." The easiest way to do this is to reverse the x and u labels and then use the above formula. In this case death produces censoring because those who die are lost to observation and thus their surrender time is never observed. Treat those who lasted the entire five years as surrenders at that time.

11.2 Determine the Kaplan–Meier estimate for the time to surrender for Data Set D2. Treat those who lasted the entire five years as surrenders at that time.

11.3 Determine the Nelson–Åalen estimate of $H(t)$ and $S(t)$ for Data Set D2 where the variable is time to surrender.

11.4 Determine the Kaplan–Meier and Nelson–Åalen estimates of the distribution function of the amount of a workers compensation loss. First do this using the raw data from Data Set B. Then repeat the exercise, modifying the data by left truncation at 100 and right censoring at 1,000.

11.5 (*) You are given the following times of first claim for five randomly selected auto insurance policies: 1, 2, 3, 4, 5. You are later told that one of the five times given is actually the time of policy lapse but you are not told which one. The smallest product-limit estimate of $S(4)$, the probability that the first claim occurs after time 4, would result if which of the given times arose from the lapsed policy?

11.6 (*) For a mortality study with right censored data, you are given the information in Table 11.3. Calculate the estimate of the survival function at time 12 using the Nelson–Åalen estimate.

11.7 (*) Three hundred mice were observed at birth. An additional 20 mice were first observed at age 2 (days) and 30 more were first observed at age 4. There were 6 deaths at age 1, 10 at age 3, 10 at age 4, a at age 5, b at age 9, and 6 at age 12. In addition, 45 mice were lost to observation at age 7, 35 at age 10, and 15 at age 13. The following product-limit estimates were obtained: $S_{350}(7) = 0.892$ and $S_{350}(13) = 0.856$. Determine the values of a and b.

Table 11.3 Data for Exercise 11.6

Time t_j	Number of deaths, s_j	Number at risk, r_j
5	2	15
7	1	12
10	1	10
12	2	6

11.8 (*) Let n be the number of lives observed from birth. None were cen-sored and no two lives died at the same age. At the time of the ninth death, the Nelson–Åalen estimate of the cumulative hazard rate is 0.511 and at the time of the tenth death it is 0.588. Estimate the value of the survival function at the time of the third death.

11.9 (*) All members of a study joined at birth; however, some may leave the study by means other than death. At the time of the third death, there was one death (that is, $s_3 = 1$); at the time of the fourth death there were two deaths; and at the time of the fifth death there was one death. The following product-limit estimates were obtained: $S_n(y_3) = 0.72$, $S_n(y_4) = 0.60$, and $S_n(y_5) = 0.50$. Determine the number of censored observations between times y_4 and y_5. Assume no observations were censored at the death times.

11.2 MEANS, VARIANCES, AND INTERVAL ESTIMATION

When all of the information is available, working with the empirical estimate of the survival function is straightforward.

Example 11.5 *Demonstrate that for complete data the empirical estimator of the survival function is unbiased and consistent.*

Recall that the empirical estimate of $S(x)$ is $S_n(x) = Y/n$, where Y is the number of observations in the sample that are greater than x. Then Y must have a binomial distribution with parameters n and $S(x)$. Then,

$$E[S_n(x)] = E\left(\frac{Y}{n}\right) = \frac{nS(x)}{n} = S(x),$$

demonstrating that the estimator is unbiased. The variance is

$$Var[S_n(x)] = Var\left(\frac{Y}{n}\right) = \frac{S(x)[1 - S(x)]}{n},$$

which has a limit of zero, thus verifying consistency.   □

In order to make use of the result, the best we can do for the variance is estimate it. It is unlikely we know the value of $S(x)$ because that is the quantity we are trying to estimate. The estimated variance is given by

$$\widehat{\text{Var}}[S_n(x)] = \frac{S_n(x)[1 - S_n(x)]}{n}.$$

The same results hold for empirically estimated probabilities. Let $p = \Pr(a < X \leq b)$. The empirical estimate of p is $\hat{p} = S_n(a) - S_n(b)$. Arguments similar to those used in the example above verify that $\hat{p}$ is unbiased and consistent, with $\text{Var}(\hat{p}) = p(1-p)/n$.

When doing mortality studies or evaluating the effect of deductibles, we sometimes are more interested in estimating conditional quantities.

Example 11.6 *Using the full information from the observations in Data Set D1, empirically estimate q_2 and estimate the variance of this estimator.*

For this data set, $n = 30$. By duration 2, one had died, and by duration 3, three had died. Thus, $S_{30}(2) = \frac{29}{30}$ and $S_{30}(3) = \frac{27}{30}$. The empirical estimate is

$$\hat{q}_2 = \frac{S_{30}(2) - S_{30}(3)}{S_{30}(2)} = \frac{2}{29}.$$

The challenge is in trying to evaluate the mean and variance of this estimator. Let X be the number of deaths between durations 0 and 2 and let Y be the number of deaths between durations 2 and 3. Then $\hat{q}_2 = Y/(30 - X)$. It should be clear that it is not possible to evaluate $\text{E}(\hat{q}_2)$ because with positive probability X will equal 30 and the estimator will not be defined.[2] The usual solution is to obtain a conditional estimate of the variance. That is, given there were 29 people alive at duration 2, determine the variance. Then the only random quantity is Y and we have

$$\widehat{\text{Var}}\left[\hat{q}_2 | S_{30}(2) = \tfrac{29}{30}\right] = \frac{(2/29)(27/29)}{29}.$$

□

In general, let n be the initial sample, n_x the number alive at age x, and n_y the number alive at age y. Then,

$$\widehat{\text{Var}}(_{y-x}\hat{q}_x | n_x) = \widehat{\text{Var}}(_{y-x}\hat{p}_x | n_x) = \frac{(n_x - n_y)(n_y)}{n_x^3}.$$

---

[2] This is a situation where the Bayesian approach (introduced in Section 12.4) works better. Bayesian analyses proceed from the data as observed and are not concerned with other values that might have been observed. If $X = 30$, there is no estimate to worry about, while if $X < 30$, analysis can proceed.

Example 11.7 *Using Data Set B, empirically estimate the probability that a payment will be at least* 1,000 *when there is a deductible of* 250.

Empirically, there were 13 losses above the deductible, of which 4 exceeded 1,250 (the loss that produces a payment of 1,000). The empirical estimate is $\frac{4}{13}$. Using survival function notation, the estimator is $S_{20}(1250)/S_{20}(250)$. Once again, only a conditional variance can be obtained. The estimated variance is $4(9)/13^3$. □

For grouped data, there is no problem if the survival function is to be estimated at a boundary. For interpolated values using the ogive, it is a bit more complex.

Example 11.8 *Determine the expected value and variance of the estimators of the survival function and density function using the ogive and histogram, respectively.*

Suppose the value of x is between the boundaries c_{j-1} and c_j. Let Y be the number of observations at or below c_{j-1} and let Z be the number of observations above c_{j-1} and at or below c_j. Then

$$S_n(x) = 1 - \frac{Y(c_j - c_{j-1}) + Z(x - c_{j-1})}{n(c_j - c_{j-1})}$$

and

$$
\begin{aligned}
E[S_n(x)] &= 1 - \frac{n[1 - S(c_{j-1})](c_j - c_{j-1}) + n[S(c_{j-1}) - S(c_j)](x - c_{j-1})}{n(c_j - c_{j-1})} \\
&= S(c_{j-1})\frac{c_j - x}{c_j - c_{j-1}} + S(c_j)\frac{x - c_{j-1}}{c_j - c_{j-1}}.
\end{aligned}
$$

This estimator is biased (although it is an unbiased estimator of the true interpolated value). The variance is

$$Var[S_n(x)] = \frac{\begin{array}{c}(c_j - c_{j-1})^2\,Var(Y) + (x - c_{j-1})^2\,Var(Z) \\ +2(c_j - c_{j-1})(x - c_{j-1})\,Cov(Y,Z)\end{array}}{[n(c_j - c_{j-1})]^2},$$

where $Var(Y) = nS(c_{j-1})[1 - S(c_{j-1})]$, $Var(Z) = n[S(c_{j-1}) - S(c_j)][1 - S(c_{j-1}) + S(c_j)]$, and $Cov(Y,Z) = -n[1 - S(c_{j-1})][S(c_{j-1}) - S(c_j)]$. For the density estimate,

$$f_n(x) = \frac{Z}{n(c_j - c_{j-1})}$$

and

$$E[f_n(x)] = \frac{S(c_{j-1}) - S(c_j)}{c_j - c_{j-1}},$$

which is biased for the true density function. The variance is

$$\text{Var}[f_n(x)] = \frac{[S(c_{j-1}) - S(c_j)][1 - S(c_{j-1}) + S(c_j)]}{n(c_j - c_{j-1})^2}.$$

□

Example 11.9 *For Data Set C estimate* $S(10{,}000)$, $f(10{,}000)$, *and the variance of your estimators.*

The point estimates are

$$S_{227}(10{,}000) = 1 - \frac{99(17{,}500 - 7{,}500) + 42(10{,}000 - 7{,}500)}{227(17{,}500 - 7{,}500)} = 0.51762,$$

$$f_{227}(10{,}000) = \frac{42}{227(17{,}500 - 7{,}500)} = 0.000018502.$$

The estimated variances are

$$\widehat{\text{Var}}[S_{227}(10{,}000)] = \frac{1}{227(10{,}000)^2} \left[10{,}000^2 \frac{99}{227} \frac{128}{227} + 2{,}500^2 \frac{42}{227} \frac{185}{227} \right.$$

$$\left. - 2(10{,}000)(2{,}500) \frac{99}{227} \frac{42}{227} \right]$$

$$= 0.00094713$$

and

$$\widehat{\text{Var}}[f_{227}(10{,}000)] = \frac{\frac{42}{227} \frac{185}{227}}{227(10{,}000)^2} = 6.6427 \times 10^{-12}.$$

□

Discrete data such as in Data Set A can be considered a special form of grouped data. Each discrete possibility is similar to an interval.

Example 11.10 *Demonstrate that for a discrete random variable the empirical estimator of a particular outcome is unbiased and consistent and derive its variance.*

Let N_j be the number of times the value x_j was observed in the sample. Then N_j has a binomial distribution with parameters n and $p(x_j)$. The empirical estimator is $p_n(x_j) = N_j/n$ and

$$\text{E}[p_n(x_j)] = \text{E}\left(\frac{N_j}{n}\right) = \frac{np(x_j)}{n} = p(x_j),$$

demonstrating that it is unbiased. Also,

$$\text{Var}[p_n(x_j)] = \text{Var}\left(\frac{N_j}{n}\right) = \frac{np(x_j)[1 - p(x_j)]}{n^2} = \frac{p(x_j)[1 - p(x_j)]}{n},$$

which goes to zero as $n \to \infty$, demonstrating consistency.   □

Example 11.11 *For Data Set A determine the empirical estimate of $p(2)$ and estimate its variance.*

The empirical estimate is

$$p_{94,935}(2) = \frac{1,618}{94,935} = 0.017043$$

and its estimated variance is

$$\frac{0.017043(0.982957)}{94,935} = 1.76466 \times 10^{-7}.$$ □

It is possible to use the variances to construct confidence intervals for the unknown probability.

Example 11.12 *Use (9.3) and (9.4) to construct approximate 95% confidence intervals for $p(2)$ using Data Set A.*

From (9.3),

$$0.95 = \Pr\left(-1.96 \leq \frac{p_n(2) - p(2)}{\sqrt{p(2)[1 - p(2)]/n}} \leq 1.96\right).$$

Solve this by making the inequality an equality and then squaring both sides to obtain [dropping the argument of (2) for simplicity],

$$\frac{(p_n - p)^2 n}{p(1 - p)} = 1.96^2,$$
$$np_n^2 - 2npp_n + np^2 = 1.96^2 p - 1.96^2 p^2,$$
$$0 = (n + 1.96^2)p^2 - (2np_n + 1.96^2)p + np_n^2.$$

The solution is

$$p = \frac{2np_n + 1.96^2 \pm \sqrt{(2np_n + 1.96^2)^2 - 4(n + 1.96^2)np_n^2}}{2(n + 1.96^2)},$$

which provides the two endpoints of the confidence interval. Inserting the numbers from Data Set A ($p_n = 0.017043$, $n = 94,935$) produces a confidence interval of $(0.016239, 0.017886)$.

Equation (9.4) provides the confidence interval directly as

$$p_n \pm 1.96\sqrt{\frac{p_n(1 - p_n)}{n}}.$$

Inserting the numbers from Data Set A gives 0.017043 ± 0.000823 for an interval of $(0.016220, 0.017866)$. The answers for the two methods are very similar, which is to be expected when the sample size is large. The results are reasonable because it is well known that the normal distribution is a good approximation to the binomial. $\qquad\square$

When data are censored or truncated, the matter becomes more complex. Counts no longer have the binomial distribution and therefore the distribution of the estimator is harder to obtain. While there are proofs available to back up the results presented here, they will not be provided. Instead, an attempt will be made to indicate why the results are reasonable.

Consider the Kaplan–Meier product-limit estimator of $S(t)$. It is the product of a number of terms of the form $(r_j - s_j)/r_j$, where r_j was viewed as the number available to die at age y_j and s_j is the number who actually did so. Assume that the death ages and the number available to die are fixed, so that the value of s_j is the only random quantity. As a random variable, S_j has a binomial distribution based on a sample of r_j lives and success probability $[S(y_{j-1}) - S(y_j)]/S(y_{j-1})$. The probability arises from the fact that those available to die were known to be alive at the previous death age. For one of these terms,

$$
\mathrm{E}\left(\frac{r_j - S_j}{r_j}\right) = \frac{r_j - r_j[S(y_{j-1}) - S(y_j)]/S(y_{j-1})}{r_j} = \frac{S(y_j)}{S(y_{j-1})}.
$$

That is, this ratio is an unbiased estimator of the probability of surviving from one death age to the next one. Furthermore,

$$
\begin{aligned}
\mathrm{Var}\left(\frac{r_j - S_j}{r_j}\right) &= \frac{r_j \dfrac{S(y_{j-1}) - S(y_j)}{S(y_{j-1})}\left[1 - \dfrac{S(y_{j-1}) - S(y_j)}{S(y_{j-1})}\right]}{r_j^2} \\
&= \frac{[S(y_{j-1}) - S(y_j)]S(y_j)}{r_j S(y_{j-1})^2}.
\end{aligned}
$$

Now consider the estimated survival probability at one of the death ages. Its expected value is

$$
\begin{aligned}
\mathrm{E}[\hat{S}(y_j)] &= \mathrm{E}\left[\prod_{i=1}^{j}\left(\frac{r_i - S_i}{r_i}\right)\right] = \prod_{i=1}^{j}\mathrm{E}\left(\frac{r_i - S_i}{r_i}\right) \\
&= \prod_{i=1}^{j}\frac{S(y_i)}{S(y_{i-1})} = \frac{S(y_j)}{S(y_0)},
\end{aligned}
$$

where y_0 is the smallest observed age in the sample. In order to bring the expectation inside the product, it was assumed that the S values are independent. The result demonstrates that at the death ages the estimator is unbiased.

With regard to the variance, we first need a general result concerning the variance of a product of independent random variables. Let $X_1, \ldots, X_n$ be independent random variables where $E(X_j) = \mu_j$ and $Var(X_j) = \sigma_j^2$. Then,

$$
\begin{aligned}
Var(X_1 \cdots X_n) &= E(X_1^2 \cdots X_n^2) - E(X_1 \cdots X_n)^2 \\
&= E(X_1^2) \cdots E(X_n^2) - E(X_1)^2 \cdots E(X_n)^2 \\
&= (\mu_1^2 + \sigma_1^2) \cdots (\mu_n^2 + \sigma_n^2) - \mu_1^2 \cdots \mu_n^2.
\end{aligned}
$$

For the product-limit estimator,

$$
\begin{aligned}
Var[S_n(y_j)] &= Var\left[\prod_{i=1}^{j}\left(\frac{r_i - S_i}{r_i}\right)\right] \\
&= \prod_{i=1}^{j}\left[\frac{S(y_i)^2}{S(y_{i-1})^2} + \frac{[S(y_{i-1}) - S(y_i)]S(y_i)}{r_i S(y_{i-1})^2}\right] - \frac{S(y_j)^2}{S(y_0)^2} \\
&= \prod_{i=1}^{j}\left[\frac{r_i S(y_i)^2 + [S(y_{i-1}) - S(y_i)]S(y_i)}{r_i S(y_{i-1})^2}\right] - \frac{S(y_j)^2}{S(y_0)^2} \\
&= \prod_{i=1}^{j}\left[\frac{S(y_i)^2}{S(y_{i-1})^2}\frac{r_i S(y_i) + [S(y_{i-1}) - S(y_i)]}{r_i S(y_i)}\right] - \frac{S(y_j)^2}{S(y_0)^2} \\
&= \frac{S(y_j)^2}{S(y_0)^2}\left\{\prod_{i=1}^{j}\left[1 + \frac{S(y_{i-1}) - S(y_i)}{r_i S(y_i)}\right] - 1\right\}.
\end{aligned}
$$

This formula is unpleasant to work with, so the following approximation is often used. It is based on the fact that for any set of small numbers $a_1, \ldots, a_n$ the product $(1+a_1)\cdots(1+a_n)$ is approximately $1+a_1+\cdots+a_n$. This follows because the missing terms are all products of two or more of the a_is. If they are all small to begin with, the products will be even smaller and so can be ignored. Applying this produces the approximation

$$
Var[S_n(y_j)] \doteq \left[\frac{S(y_j)}{S(y_0)}\right]^2 \sum_{i=1}^{j}\frac{S(y_{i-1}) - S(y_i)}{r_i S(y_i)}.
$$

Because it is unlikely that the survival function is known, an estimated value needs to be inserted. Recall that the estimated value of $S(y_j)$ is actually conditional on being alive at age y_0. Also, $(r_i - s_i)/r_i$ is an estimate of $S(y_i)/S(y_{i-1})$. Then,

$$
\widehat{Var}[S_n(y_j)] \doteq S_n(y_j)^2 \sum_{i=1}^{j}\frac{s_i}{r_i(r_i - s_i)}. \tag{11.3}
$$

Equation (11.3) is known as Greenwood's approximation. It is the only version that will be used in this text.

Example 11.13 *Using Data Set D1, estimate the variance of $S_{30}(3)$ both directly and using Greenwood's formula. Do the same for $_2\hat{q}_3$.*

Because there is no censoring or truncation, the empirical formula can be used to directly estimate this variance. There were three deaths out of 30 individuals, and therefore

$$\widehat{\text{Var}}[S_{30}(3)] = \frac{(3/30)(27/30)}{30} = \frac{81}{30^3}.$$

For Greenwood's approximation, $r_1 = 30$, $s_1 = 1$, $r_2 = 29$, and $s_2 = 2$. The approximation is

$$\left(\frac{27}{30}\right)^2 \left(\frac{1}{30(29)} + \frac{2}{29(27)}\right) = \frac{81}{30^3}.$$

It can be demonstrated that when there is no censoring or truncation the two formulas will always produce the same answer. Recall that the development of Greenwood's formula produced the variance only at death ages. The convention for non-death ages is to take the sum up to the last death age that is less than or equal to the age under consideration.

With regard to $_2\hat{q}_3$, arguing as in Example 11.6 produces an estimated (conditional) variance of

$$\widehat{\text{Var}}(_2\hat{q}_3) = \frac{(4/27)(23/27)}{27} = \frac{92}{27^3}.$$

For Greenwood's formula, we first must note that we are estimating

$$_2q_3 = \frac{S(3) - S(5)}{S(3)} = 1 - \frac{S(5)}{S(3)}.$$

As with the empirical estimate, all calculations must be done given the 27 people alive at duration 3. Furthermore, the variance of $_2\hat{q}_3$ is the same as the variance of $\hat{S}(5)$ using only information from duration 3 and beyond. Starting from duration 3 there are three death times, 3.1, 4.0, and 4.8, with $r_1 = 27$, $r_2 = 26$, $r_3 = 25$, $s_1 = 1$, $s_2 = 1$, and $s_3 = 2$. Greenwood's approximation is

$$\left(\frac{23}{27}\right)^2 \left(\frac{1}{27(26)} + \frac{1}{26(25)} + \frac{2}{25(23)}\right) = \frac{92}{27^3}.$$

□

Example 11.14 *Repeat the previous example, this time using all 40 observations in Data Set D2 and the incomplete information due to censoring and truncation.*

For this example, the direct empirical approach is not available. That is because it is unclear what the sample size is (it varies over time as subjects enter and leave due to truncation and censoring). From Example 11.2, the relevant values within the first three years are $r_1 = 30$, $r_2 = 26$, $s_1 = 1$, and $s_2 = 2$. From Example 11.3, $S_{40}(3) = 0.8923$. Then, Greenwood's estimate is

$$(0.8923)^2 \left(\frac{1}{30(29)} + \frac{2}{26(24)} \right) = 0.0034671.$$

An approximate 95% confidence interval can be constructed using the normal approximation. It is

$$0.8923 \pm 1.96\sqrt{0.0034671} = 0.8923 \pm 0.1154,$$

which corresponds to the interval $(0.7769, 1.0077)$. For small sample sizes, it is possible that the confidence intervals admit values less than 0 or greater than 1.

With regard to $_2\hat{q}_3$, the relevant quantities are (starting at duration 3, but using the subscripts from the earlier examples for these data) $r_3 = 26$, $r_4 = 26$, $r_5 = 23$, $r_6 = 21$, $s_3 = 1$, $s_4 = 2$, $s_5 = 1$, and $s_6 = 1$. This gives an estimated variance of

$$\left(\frac{0.7215}{0.8923} \right)^2 \left(\frac{1}{26(25)} + \frac{2}{26(24)} + \frac{1}{23(22)} + \frac{1}{21(20)} \right) = 0.0059502.$$

□

The previous example indicated that the usual method of constructing a confidence interval can lead to an unacceptable result. An alternative approach can be constructed as follows. Let $Y = \ln[-\ln S_n(t)]$. Using the delta method (see Theorem 12.17), the variance of Y can be approximated as follows. The function of interest is $g(x) = \ln(-\ln x)$. Its derivative is

$$g'(x) = \frac{1}{-\ln x} \frac{-1}{x} = \frac{1}{x \ln x}.$$

According to the delta method, the variance of Y can be approximated by

$$\{g'[\mathrm{E}(S_n(t))]\}^2 \, \mathrm{Var}[S_n(t)] = \frac{\mathrm{Var}[S_n(t)]}{[S_n(t) \ln S_n(t)]^2}$$

where we have used the fact that $S_n(t)$ is an unbiased estimator of $S(t)$. Then, an estimated 95% confidence interval for $\theta = \ln[-\ln S(t)]$ is

$$\ln[-\ln S_n(t)] \pm 1.96 \frac{\sqrt{\widehat{\mathrm{Var}[S_n(t)]}}}{S_n(t) \ln S_n(t)}.$$

Because $S(t) = \exp(-e^\theta)$, putting each endpoint through this formula will provide a confidence interval for $S(t)$. For the upper limit we have (where

$\hat{v} = \widehat{\text{Var}}[S_n(t)])$

$$\exp\left\{-e^{\ln[-\ln S_n(t)]+1.96\sqrt{\hat{v}}/[S_n(t)\ln S_n(t)]}\right\}$$

$$= \exp\left\{[\ln S_n(t)]e^{1.96\sqrt{\hat{v}}/[S_n(t)\ln S_n(t)]}\right\}$$

$$= S_n(t)^U, \quad U = \exp\left[\frac{1.96\sqrt{\hat{v}}}{S_n(t)\ln S_n(t)}\right].$$

Similarly, the lower limit is $S_n(t)^{1/U}$. This interval will always be inside the range zero to 1 and is referred to as the log-transformed confidence interval.

Example 11.15 *Obtain the log-transformed confidence interval for $S(3)$ as in Example 11.14.*

We have

$$U = \exp\left[\frac{1.96\sqrt{0.0034671}}{0.8923\ln(0.8923)}\right] = 0.32142.$$

The lower limit of the interval is $0.8923^{1/0.32142} = 0.70150$ and the upper limit is $0.8923^{0.32142} = 0.96404.$ □

Similar results are available for the Nelson–Åalen estimator. An intuitive derivation of a variance estimate proceeds as follows. As in the derivation for the Kaplan–Meier estimator, all results are obtained assuming the risk set numbers are known, not random. The number of deaths at death time t_i has approximately a Poisson distribution[3] with parameter $r_i h(t_i)$ and so its variance is $r_i h(t_i)$, which can be approximated by $r_i(s_i/r_i) = s_i$. Then (also assuming independence),

$$\widehat{\text{Var}}[\hat{H}(y_j)] = \widehat{\text{Var}}\left(\sum_{i=1}^{j}\frac{s_i}{r_i}\right) = \sum_{i=1}^{j}\frac{\widehat{\text{Var}}(s_i)}{r_i^2} \doteq \sum_{i=1}^{j}\frac{s_i}{r_i^2}.$$

The linear confidence interval is simply

$$\hat{H}(t) \pm z_{\alpha/2}\sqrt{\widehat{\text{Var}}[\hat{H}(y_j)]}.$$

A log-transformed interval similar to the one developed for the survival function[4] is

$$\hat{H}(t)U, \text{ where } U = \exp\left[\pm\frac{z_{\alpha/2}\sqrt{\widehat{Var}[\hat{H}(y_j)]}}{\hat{H}(t)}\right].$$

---

[3] A binomial assumption (as was used for the Kaplan-Meier derivation) could also have been made. Similarly, a Poisson assumption could have been used for the Kaplan-Meier derivation. The formulas given here are the ones most commonly used.

[4] The derivation of this interval uses the transformation $Y = \ln\hat{H}(t)$.

Example 11.16 *Construct an approximate 95% confidence interval for $H(3)$ by each formula using all 40 observations in Data Set D2.*

The point estimate is $\hat{H}(3) = \frac{1}{30} + \frac{2}{26} = 0.11026$. The estimated variance is $\frac{1}{30^2} + \frac{2}{26^2} = 0.0040697$. The linear confidence interval is

$$0.11026 \pm 1.96\sqrt{0.0040697} = 0.11026 \pm 0.12504$$

for an interval of $(-0.01478, 0.23530)$. For the log-transformed interval,

$$U = \exp\left[\pm\frac{1.96(0.0040697)^{1/2}}{0.11026}\right] = \exp(\pm 1.13402) = 0.32174 \text{ to } 3.10813.$$

The interval is $0.11026(0.32174) = 0.03548$ to $0.11026(3.10813) = 0.34270$. □

11.2.1   Exercises

11.10 Using the full information from Data Set D1, empirically estimate q_j for $j = 0, \ldots, 4$ and $_5p_0$ where the variable of interest is time of surrender. Estimate the variance of each of your estimators. Identify which estimated variances are conditional. Interpret $_5q_0$ as the probability of surrendering before the five years expire.

11.11 For Data Set A determine the empirical estimate of the probability of having two or more accidents and estimate its variance.

11.12 Repeat Example 11.13 using time to surrender as the variable.

11.13 Repeat Example 11.14 using time to surrender as the variable. Interpret $_2q_3$ as the probability of surrendering before the five years expire.

11.14 Obtain the log-transformed confidence interval for $S(3)$ in Exercise 11.13.

11.15 Construct 95% confidence intervals for $H(3)$ by each formula using all 40 observations in Data Set D2 with surrender being the variable of interest.

11.16 (*) Ten individuals were observed from birth. All were observed until death. Table 11.4 gives the death ages. Let V_1 denote the estimated conditional variance of $_3\hat{q}_7$ if calculated without any distribution assumption. Let V_2 denote the conditional variance of $_3\hat{q}_7$ if calculated knowing that the survival function is $S(t) = 1 - t/15$. Determine $V_1 - V_2$.

11.17 (*) For the interval from zero to one year, the exposure (r) is 15 and the number of deaths (s) is 3. For the interval from one to two years the exposure is 80 and the number of deaths is 24. For two to three years the values are 25 and 5; for three to four years they are 60 and 6; and for four to

Table 11.4   Data for Exercise 11.16

Age	Number of deaths
2	1
3	1
5	1
7	2
10	1
12	2
13	1
14	1

five years they are 10 and 3. Determine Greenwood's approximation to the variance of $\hat{S}(4)$.

11.18 (*) Observations can be censored, but there is no truncation. Let y_j and y_{j+1} be consecutive death ages. A 95% linear confidence interval for $H(y_j)$ using the Nelson–Åalen estimator is $(0.07125, 0.22875)$ while a similar interval for $H(y_{j+1})$ is $(0.15607, 0.38635)$. Determine s_{j+1}.

11.19 (*) A mortality study is conducted on 50 lives, all observed from age 0. At age 15 there were two deaths; at age 17 there were three censored observations; at age 25 there were four deaths; at age 30 there were c censored observations; at age 32 there were eight deaths; and at age 40 there were two deaths. Let S be the product-limit estimate of $S(35)$ and let V be the Greenwood estimate of this estimator's variance. You are given $V/S^2 = 0.011467$. Determine the value of c.

11.20 (*) Fifteen cancer patients were observed from the time of diagnosis until the earlier of death or 36 months from diagnosis. Deaths occurred as follows: At 15 months there were /two2 deaths; at 20 months there were three deaths; at 24 months there were two deaths; at 30 months there were d deaths; at 34 months there were two deaths; and at 36 months there was one death. The Nelson–Åalen estimate of $H(35)$ is 1.5641. Determine the variance of this estimator.

11.21 (*) You are given the values in Table 11.5. Determine the standard deviation of the Nelson–Åalen estimator of the cumulative hazard function at time 20.

11.3   KERNEL DENSITY MODELS

One problem with empirical distributions is that they are always discrete. If it is known that the true distribution is continuous, the empirical distribution

Table 11.5   Data for Exercise 11.21

y_j	r_j	s_j
1	100	15
8	65	20
17	40	13
25	31	31

may be viewed as a poor approximation. In this section, a method of obtaining a smooth, empirical-like distribution is introduced. Recall from Definition 10.4 that the idea is to replace each discrete piece of probability by a continuous random variable. While not necessary, it is customary that the continuous variable have a mean equal to the value of the point it replaces. This ensures that the kernel estimate has the same mean as the empirical estimate. One way to think about such a model is that it produces the final observed value in two steps. The first step is to draw a value at random from the empirical distribution. The second step is to draw a value at random from a continuous distribution whose mean is equal to the value drawn at the first step. The selected continuous distribution is called the kernel.

For notation, let $p(y_j)$ be the probability assigned to the value y_j ($j = 1, \ldots, k$) by the empirical distribution. Let $K_y(x)$ be a distribution function for a continuous distribution such that its mean is y. Let $k_y(x)$ be the corresponding density function.

Definition 11.17 *A **kernel density estimator** of a distribution function is*

$$\hat{F}(x) = \sum_{j=1}^{k} p(y_j) K_{y_j}(x)$$

and the estimator of the density function is

$$\hat{f}(x) = \sum_{j=1}^{k} p(y_j) k_{y_j}(x).$$

The function $k_y(x)$ is called the kernel. Three kernels will now be introduced.

Definition 11.18 *The **uniform kernel** is given by*

$$
k_y(x) = \begin{cases} 0, & x < y - b, \\ \dfrac{1}{2b}, & y - b \le x \le y + b, \\ 0, & x > y + b, \end{cases}
$$

$$
K_y(x) = \begin{cases} 0, & x < y - b, \\ \dfrac{x - y + b}{2b}, & y - b \le x \le y + b, \\ 1, & x > y + b. \end{cases}
$$

*The **triangular kernel** is given by*

$$
k_y(x) = \begin{cases} 0, & x < y - b, \\ \dfrac{x - y + b}{b^2}, & y - b \le x \le y, \\ \dfrac{y + b - x}{b^2}, & y \le x \le y + b, \\ 0, & x > y + b, \end{cases}
$$

$$
K_y(x) = \begin{cases} 0, & x < y - b, \\ \dfrac{(x - y + b)^2}{2b^2}, & y - b \le x \le y, \\ 1 - \dfrac{(y + b - x)^2}{2b^2}, & y \le x \le y + b, \\ 1, & x > y + b. \end{cases}
$$

*The **gamma** kernel is given by letting the kernel have a gamma distribution with shape parameter α and scale parameter y/α. That is,*

$$
k_y(x) = \frac{x^{\alpha - 1} e^{-x\alpha/y}}{(y/\alpha)^\alpha \Gamma(\alpha)}.
$$

Note that the gamma distribution has a mean of $\alpha(y/\alpha) = y$ and a variance of $\alpha(y/\alpha)^2 = y^2/\alpha$.

In each case there is a parameter that relates to the spread of the kernel. In the first two cases it is the value of $b > 0$, which is called the bandwidth. In the gamma case, the value of α controls the spread, with a larger value indicating a smaller spread. There are other kernels that cover the range from zero to infinity.

Example 11.19 *Determine the kernel density estimate for Example 10.8 using each of the three kernels.*

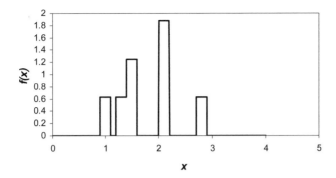

Fig. 11.1   Uniform kernel density with bandwidth 0.1.

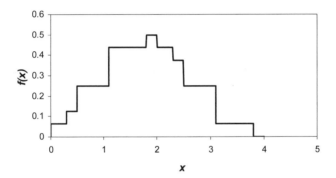

Fig. 11.2   Uniform kernel density with bandwidth 1.0.

The empirical distribution places probability $\frac{1}{8}$ at 1.0, $\frac{1}{8}$ at 1.3, $\frac{2}{8}$ at 1.5, $\frac{3}{8}$ at 2.1, and $\frac{1}{8}$ at 2.8. For a uniform kernel with a bandwidth of 0.1 we do not get much separation. The data point at 1.0 is replaced by a horizontal density function running from 0.9 to 1.1 with a height of $\frac{1}{8}\frac{1}{2(0.1)} = 0.625$. On the other hand, with a bandwidth of 1.0 that same data point is replaced by a horizontal density function running from 0.0 to 2.0 with a height of $\frac{1}{8}\frac{1}{2(1)} = 0.0625$. Figures 11.1 and 11.2 provide plots of the density functions.

It should be clear that the larger bandwidth provides more smoothing. In the limit, as the bandwidth approaches zero, the kernel density estimate matches the empirical estimate. Note that, if the bandwidth is too large, probability will be assigned to negative values, which may be an undesirable result. Methods exist for dealing with that issue, but they will not be presented here.

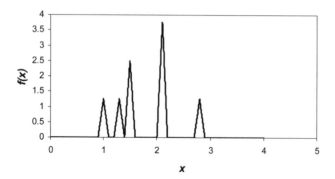

Fig. 11.3   Triangular kernel density with bandwidth 0.1.

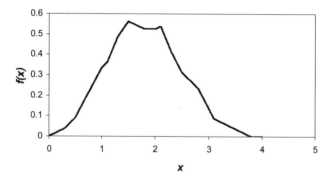

Fig. 11.4   Triangular kernel density with bandwidth 1.0.

For the triangular kernel, each point is replaced by a triangle. Pictures for the same two bandwidths used previously appear in Figures 11.3 and 11.4.

Once again, the larger bandwidth provides more smoothing. The gamma kernel simply provides a mixture of gamma distributions where each data point provides the mean and the empirical probabilities provide the weights. The density function is

$$f_\alpha(x) = \sum_{j=1}^{5} p(y_j) \frac{x^{\alpha-1} e^{-x\alpha/y_j}}{(y_j/\alpha)^\alpha \Gamma(\alpha)}$$

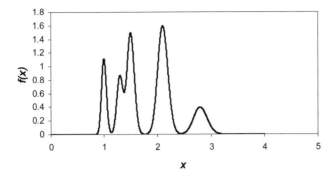

Fig. 11.5 Gamma kernel density with $\alpha = 500$.

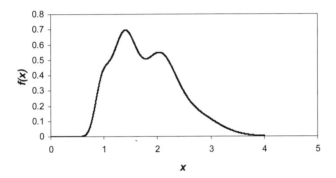

Fig. 11.6 Gamma kernel density with $\alpha = 50$.

and is graphed in Figures 11.5 and 11.6 for two α values.[5] For this kernel, decreasing the value of α increases the amount of smoothing. Further discussion of the gamma kernel can be found in [23], where the author recommends $\alpha = \sqrt{n}/(\hat{\mu}'_4/\hat{\mu}'_2 - 1)^{1/2}$. $\qquad\Box$

11.3.1 Exercises

11.22 Provide the formula for the Pareto kernel.

---

[5] When computing values of the density function, overflow and underflow problems can be reduced by computing the logarithm of the elements of the ratio, that is, $(\alpha - 1)\ln x - x\alpha/y_j - \alpha \ln(y_j/\alpha) - \ln \Gamma(\alpha)$, and then exponentiating the result.

Table 11.6   Data for Exercise 11.24

t_j	s_j	r_j
10	1	20
34	1	19
47	1	18
75	1	17
156	1	16
171	1	15

11.23 Construct a kernel density estimate for the time to surrender for Data Set D2. Be aware of the fact that this is a mixed distribution (probability is continuous from 0 to 5 but is discrete at 5).

11.24 (*) You are given the data in Table 11.6 on time to death. Using the uniform kernel with a bandwidth of 60, determine $\hat{f}(100)$.

11.4 APPROXIMATIONS FOR LARGE DATA SETS

11.4.1 Introduction

When there are large amounts of data, constructing the Kaplan–Meier estimate may require more sorting and counting than can be justified by the results. This is especially true if values of the distribution function are not needed at each value. For example, if the goal is to construct a mortality table, values are needed only at integral ages. The finer details of mortality table construction and alternative methods can be found in the texts by Batten [11] and London [85]. While the context for the examples presented here will be the construction of mortality tables, the methods can apply anytime the data have been rounded.

Suppose there are intervals given as $c_0 < c_1 < \cdots < c_k$. Let d_j be the number of observations that are left truncated at a value in the interval $[c_j, c_{j+1})$. In a mortality study, this would be a count of the lives that were first observed at an age in the given range. Similarly, let u_j be the number of observations that are right censored at a value in the interval $(c_j, c_{j+1}]$. Note the difference in the endpoints of the two intervals. This is necessary because truncation is possible at the left end of the first interval but not at the right end of the last interval. The reverse is true for censoring. Note that all observations are to contribute to some d_j, but only observations that are actually censored can contribute to some u_j. Let x_j be the number of uncensored observations in the interval $(c_j, c_{j+1}]$. Then $n = \sum_{j=0}^{k-1} d_j = \sum_{j=0}^{k-1}(u_j + x_j)$ where n is the sample size. The computational advantage is that one pass through the data set allows these values to be accumulated and from there only this reduced set of values needs to be processed.

11.4.2   Kaplan–Meier type approximations

In order to apply the Kaplan–Meier formula, assumptions must be made about the location of the values within each interval. The simplest is to assume that all of the uncensored observations in an interval occur at the same value within that interval, say c_j^*, that all left truncated values are less than c_j^*, and that all right censored values are greater than or equal to c_j^*. The risk set at c_j^* is $r_j = \sum_{i=0}^{j} d_i - \sum_{i=0}^{j-1}(u_i + x_i)$. Rather than place all probability at the c_j^* values (as is done by the Kaplan–Meier method), it is customary to evaluate the distribution function at the given endpoints and then smooth the function by interpolation (usually linear) between successive values. Then,

$$\hat{F}(c_0) = 0,$$

$$\hat{F}(c_j) = 1 - \prod_{i=0}^{j-1}\left(1 - \frac{x_i}{r_i}\right), \quad j = 1, 2, \dots, k. \tag{11.4}$$

Let

$$q_j = c_{j+1} - c_j q_{c_j} = \frac{S(c_j) - S(c_{j+1})}{S(c_j)}.$$

From (11.4),

$$\hat{q}_j = \frac{\prod_{i=0}^{j-1}\left(1 - \frac{x_i}{r_i}\right) - \prod_{i=0}^{j}\left(1 - \frac{x_i}{r_i}\right)}{\prod_{i=0}^{j-1}\left(1 - \frac{x_i}{r_i}\right)} = 1 - \left(1 - \frac{x_j}{r_j}\right) = \frac{x_j}{r_j}. \tag{11.5}$$

This is the traditional form of a life table estimator where the numerator has the number of observed deaths and the denominator is a measure of exposure (the number of lives available to die). For this formula, all who enter the study prior to or during the current interval are given a chance to die and all who have left prior to the interval are removed from consideration. If dollar amounts are being studied and the boundaries include all the possible values for deductibles and limits, this formula produces the exact product-limit estimate at the given values. For mortality studies, this is equivalent to having all lives enter on their birthdays (which may be true if insuring ages are used, see Exercise 11.26) and surrender on birthdays.

Equation (11.5) can be generalized as follows. Let $P_j = \sum_{i=0}^{j-1}(d_i - u_i - x_i)$, the number of people under observation at age c_j. Continue to assume that all the uncensored observations occur at a fixed point in the interval. Further assume that at this time $100\alpha\%$ of those who will enter (be counted in d_j) have done so and that $100\beta\%$ of those who will be censored (be counted in u_j) have done so. Then the risk set is $r_j = P_j + \alpha d_j - \beta u_j$. Equation (11.5) is obtained by setting $\alpha = 1$ and $\beta = 0$. An alternative is to set $\alpha = \beta = 0.5$. This is equivalent to having the entrants and exits spread uniformly throughout the interval. The result is $r_j = P_j + 0.5(d_j - u_j)$. Because $P_{j+1} = P_j + d_j - u_j - x_j$, this can be rewritten as

$$r_j = 0.5(P_j + P_{j+1} + x_j), \tag{11.6}$$

a formula commonly used in constructing mortality tables. At times it may be necessary to make different assumptions for different intervals, as illustrated in Example 11.20.

11.4.3   Multiple-decrement tables

The goal of all the estimation procedures in this text is to deduce the probability distribution for the variable of interest in the absence of truncation and censoring. For loss data, that would be the probabilities if there were no deductible or limit. For lifetime data it would be the probabilities if we could follow people from birth to death. In the language of *Actuarial Mathematics* [16], these are called *single-decrement rates* and are denoted q'_j. It is often desired to create a table of *multiple-decrement probabilities*, denoted q_j. A superscript identifies the decrement of interest. For example, suppose the decrements were death (d), withdrawal (w), and retirement (r). Then $q_j^{\prime(w)}$ is the probability that a person age c_j withdraws prior to age c_{j+1} in an environment where death and retirement are not possible while $q_j^{(r)}$ is the probability that a person age c_j retires prior to age c_{j+1} in an environment where prior death or withdrawal eliminates the chance of retirement. Multiple-decrement tables are often constructed by obtaining the single-decrement rates from different sources and then combining with a formula such as

$$q_j^{(g)} = \frac{\ln(1 - q_j^{\prime(g)})}{\ln(1 - q_j^{(T)})} q_j^{(T)}, \quad q_j^{(T)} = 1 - \prod_{g=1}^{m}(1 - q_j^{\prime(g)}), \tag{11.7}$$

where g represents an arbitrary decrement and m is the total number of decrements.

Example 11.20 *Estimate both single- and multiple-decrement quantities using Data Set D2 and the methods of this section. Make reasonable assumptions.*

First consider the decrement death. In the notation of this section, the relevant quantities are in Table 11.7. For this setting, more than one assumption is needed. For $d_0 = 32$ it is clear that the 30 values that are exactly zero should be treated as such (policies followed from the beginning) while

Table 11.7 Single-decrement calculations for Example 11.20

j	d_j	u_j	x_j	P_j	r_j	$q_j'^{(d)}$	$\hat{F}(j)$
0	32	3	1	0	29.5	0.0339	0.0000
1	2	2	0	28	28.0	0.0000	0.0339
2	3	3	2	28	28.0	0.0714	0.0339
3	3	3	3	26	26.0	0.1154	0.1029
4	0	21	2	23	21.0	0.0952	0.2064
5							0.2820

Table 11.8 Multiple-decrement calculations for Example 11.20

j	$q_j'^{(d)}$	$q_j'^{(w)}$	$q_j^{(T)}$	$q_j^{(d)}$	$q_j^{(w)}$
0	0.0339	0.0984	0.1289	0.0322	0.0967
1	0.0000	0.0690	0.0690	0.0000	0.0690
2	0.0714	0.1053	0.1692	0.0676	0.1015
3	0.1154	0.1154	0.2175	0.1087	0.1087
4	0.0952	0.1818	0.2597	0.0864	0.1733

the 2 policies that entered after issue require an assumption. It makes sense to assume a uniform spread. Then $r_0 = 30 + 0.5(2) - 0.5(3) = 29.5$. The other r values are calculated using (11.6), noting that policy 33 is assumed to enter at mid-duration, 1.5. Also note that the 17 policies that were still active after five years are all assumed to be censored at time 5, rather than be spread uniformly through the fifth year.

For withdrawals the values of $q_j'^{(w)}$ are given in Table 11.8 along with the calculated multiple decrement values using (11.7).   □

Example 11.21 *Loss data for policies with deductibles of* 0, 250, *and* 500 *and policy limits of* 5,000, 7,500, *and* 10,000 *were collected. The data are in Table* 11.9. *Use the methods of this section to estimate the distribution function for losses.*

The calculations appear in Table 11.10. Because the deductibles and limits are at the endpoints of intervals, the only reasonable assumption is $\alpha = 1$ and $\beta = 0$.   □

11.4.4   Exercises

11.25 Verify the calculations in Table 11.8.

11.26 When life insurance policies are issued, it is customary to assign a whole-number age to the insured and then the premium associated with that

Table 11.9   Data for Example 11.21

Range	Deductible 0	Deductible 250	Deductible 500	Total
0–100	15			15
100–250	16			16
250–500	34	96		130
500–1,000	73	175	251	499
1,000–2,500	131	339	478	948
2,500–5,000	83	213	311	607
5,000–7,500	12	48	88	148
7,500–10,000	1	4	11	16
At 5,000	7	17	18	42
At 7,500	5	10	15	30
At 10,000	2	1	4	7
Total	379	903	1,176	2,458

Table 11.10   Calculations for Example 11.21

c_j	d_j	u_j	x_j	P_j	r_j	$q_j'^{(d)}$	$\hat{F}(c_j)$
0	379	0	15	0	379	0.0396	0.0000
100	0	0	16	364	364	0.0440	0.0396
250	903	0	130	348	1,251	0.1039	0.0818
500	1,176	0	499	1,121	2,297	0.2172	0.1772
1,000	0	0	948	1,798	1,798	0.5273	0.3560
2,500	0	42	607	850	850	0.7141	0.6955
5,000	0	30	148	201	201	0.7363	0.9130
7,500	0	7	16	23	23	0.6957	0.9770
10,000							0.9930

age is charged. The interpretation of q_x changes from "What is the probability someone having their xth birthday dies in the next year?" to "What is the probability that a person who was assigned age $x - k$ at issue k years ago dies in the next year?" Such age assignments are called "insuring ages" and effectively move the birthday to the policy issue date. As a result, insured lives tend to enter observation on their birthday (artificially assigned as the policy issue date). This makes the d value exact (with $\alpha = 1$) rather than approximate. However, withdrawal can take place at any time, making $\beta =$

Table 11.11   Data for Exercise 11.26

d	u	x	d	u	x
45	46.0		45	45.8	
45	46.0		46	47.0	
45		45.3	46	47.0	
45		46.7	46	46.3	
45		45.4	46		46.2
45	47.0		46		46.4
45	45.4		46	46.9	

Table 11.12   Data for Exercise 11.27

Deductible	Payment	Deductible	Payment
250	2,221	500	3,660
250	2,500*	500	215
250	207	500	1,302
250	3,735	500	10,000*
250	5,000*	1,000	1,643
250	517	1,000	3,395
250	5,743	1,000	3,981
500	2,500*	1,000	3,836
500	525	1,000	5,000*
500	4,393	1,000	1,850
500	5,000*	1,000	6,722

*Amount paid was at the policy limit

0.5 a reasonable assumption.[6] For the data in Table 11.11 estimate q_{45} and q_{46} using both the exact Kaplan–Meier estimate and the method of this section.

11.27 Twenty-two insurance payments are recorded in Table 11.12. Use the fewest reasonable number of intervals and the method of this section to estimate the probability that a policy with a deductible of 500 will have a payment in excess of 5,000.

---

[6] However, just as in Example 11.20 where different d values received different treatment, here there can be u values that deserve different treatment. Observation of an individual can end because the individual leaves or because the observation period ends. For studies of insured lives it is common for observation to end at a policy anniversary and thus at a whole-number insuring age. For them, $\beta = 0$ is an appropriate assumption.

Part IV

Parametric statistical methods

12

Parameter estimation

If a phenomenon is to be modeled using a parametric model, it is necessary to assign values to the parameters. This could be done arbitrarily, but it would seem to be more reasonable to base the assignment on observations from that phenomenon. In particular, we will assume that n independent observations have been collected. For some of the techniques it will be further assumed that all the observations are from the same random variable. For others, that restriction will be relaxed.

The methods introduced in Section 12.1 are relatively easy to implement but tend to give poor results. Section 12.2 covers maximum likelihood estimation. This method is more difficult to use but has superior statistical properties and is considerably more flexible.

12.1 METHOD OF MOMENTS AND PERCENTILE MATCHING

For these methods we assume that all n observations are from the same parametric distribution. In particular, let the distribution function be given by

$$F(x|\boldsymbol{\theta}), \quad \boldsymbol{\theta}^T = (\theta_1, \theta_2, \ldots, \theta_p)$$

Loss Models: From Data to Decisions, Second Edition.
By Stuart A. Klugman, Harry H. Panjer, and Gordon E. Willmot
ISBN 0-471-21577-5   Copyright © 2004 John Wiley & Sons, Inc.

where $\boldsymbol{\theta}^T$ is the transpose of $\boldsymbol{\theta}$. That is, $\boldsymbol{\theta}$ is a column vector containing the p parameters to be estimated. Furthermore, let $\mu'_k(\boldsymbol{\theta}) = E(X^k|\boldsymbol{\theta})$ be the kth raw moment and let $\pi_g(\boldsymbol{\theta})$ be the $100g$th percentile of the random variable. That is, $F[\pi_g(\boldsymbol{\theta})|\boldsymbol{\theta}] = g$. If the distribution function is continuous, there will be at least one solution to that equation.

For a sample of n independent observations from this random variable, let $\hat{\mu}'_k = \frac{1}{n}\sum_{j=1}^n x_j^k$ be the empirical estimate of the kth moment and let $\hat{\pi}_g$ be the empirical estimate of the $100g$th percentile

Definition 12.1 *A* ***method-of-moments estimate*** *of $\boldsymbol{\theta}$ is any solution of the p equations*

$$\mu'_k(\boldsymbol{\theta}) = \hat{\mu}'_k, \quad k = 1, 2, \ldots, p.$$

The motivation for this estimator is that it produces a model that has the same first p raw moments as the data (as represented by the empirical distribution). The traditional definition of the method of moments uses positive integers for the moments. Arbitrary negative or fractional moments could also be used. In particular, when estimating parameters for inverse distributions, matching negative moments may be a superior approach.[1]

Example 12.2 *Use the method of moments to estimate parameters for the exponential, gamma, and Pareto distributions for Data Set B from Chapter 10.*

The first two sample moments are

$$
\begin{aligned}
\hat{\mu}'_1 &= \tfrac{1}{20}(27 + \cdots + 15{,}743) = 1{,}424.4, \\
\hat{\mu}'_2 &= \tfrac{1}{20}(27^2 + \cdots + 15{,}743^2) = 13{,}238{,}441.9.
\end{aligned}
$$

For the exponential distribution the equation is

$$\theta = 1{,}424.4$$

with the obvious solution, $\hat{\theta} = 1{,}424.4$.

For the gamma distribution, the two equations are

$$
\begin{aligned}
E(X) &= \alpha\theta = 1{,}424.4, \\
E(X^2) &= \alpha(\alpha+1)\theta^2 = 13{,}238{,}441.9.
\end{aligned}
$$

Dividing the second equation by the square of the first equation yields

$$\frac{\alpha+1}{\alpha} = 6.52489, \quad 1 = 5.52489\alpha$$

---

[1]One advantage is that with appropriate moments selected the equations must have a solution within the range of allowable parameter values.

and so $\hat{\alpha} = 1/5.52489 = 0.18100$ and $\hat{\theta} = 1{,}424.4/0.18100 = 7{,}869.61$.

For the Pareto distribution, the two equations are

$$E(X) \;=\; \frac{\theta}{\alpha - 1} = 1{,}424.4,$$

$$E(X^2) \;=\; \frac{2\theta^2}{(\alpha - 1)(\alpha - 2)} = 13{,}238{,}441.9.$$

Dividing the second equation by the square of the first equation yields

$$\frac{2(\alpha - 1)}{(\alpha - 2)} = 6.52489$$

with a solution of $\hat{\alpha} = 2.442$ and then $\hat{\theta} = 1{,}424.4(1.442) = 2{,}053.985$.   □

There is no guarantee that the equations will have a solution or, if there is a solution, that it will be unique.

Definition 12.3 *A **percentile matching estimate** of θ is any solution of the p equations*

$$\pi_{g_k}(\boldsymbol{\theta}) = \hat{\pi}_{g_k}, \;\; k = 1, 2, \dots, p,$$

where $g_1, g_2, \dots, g_p$ are p arbitrarily chosen percentiles. From the definition of percentile, the equations can also be written

$$F(\hat{\pi}_{g_k}|\boldsymbol{\theta}) = g_k, \;\; k = 1, 2, \dots, p.$$

The motivation for this estimator is that it produces a model with p percentiles that match the data (as represented by the empirical distribution). As with the method of moments, there is no guarantee that the equations will have a solution or, if there is a solution, that it will be unique. One problem with this definition is that percentiles for discrete random variables (such as the empirical distribution) are not always well defined. For example, Data Set B has 20 observations. Any number between 384 and 457 has 10 observations below and 10 above and so could serve as the median. The convention is to use the midpoint. However, for other percentiles, there is no "official" interpolation scheme.[2] The following definition will be used here.

Definition 12.4 *The **smoothed empirical estimate** of a percentile is found by*

$$\hat{\pi}_g \;=\; (1 - h)x_{(j)} + hx_{(j+1)}, \text{ where}$$

$$j \;=\; \lfloor (n + 1)g \rfloor \text{ and } h = (n + 1)g - j.$$

---

[2] Hyndman and Fan [65] present nine different methods. They recommend a slight modification of the one presented here using $j = \lfloor g(n + \tfrac{1}{3}) + \tfrac{1}{3} \rfloor$ and $h = g(n + \tfrac{1}{3}) + \tfrac{1}{3} - j$.

Here $\lfloor \cdot \rfloor$ indicates the greatest integer function and $x_{(1)} \le x_{(2)} \le \cdots \le x_{(n)}$ are the order statistics from the sample.

Unless there are two or more data points with the same value, no two percentiles will have the same value. One feature of this definition is that $\hat{\pi}_g$ cannot be obtained for $g < 1/(n+1)$ or $g > n/(n+1)$. This seems reasonable as we should not expect to be able to infer the value of large or small percentiles from small samples. We will use the smoothed version whenever an empirical percentile estimate is called for.

Example 12.5 *Use percentile matching to estimate parameters for the exponential and Pareto distributions for Data Set B.*

For the exponential distribution, select the 50th percentile. The empirical estimate is the traditional median of $\hat{\pi}_{0.5} = (384 + 457)/2 = 420.5$ and the equation to solve is

$$
\begin{aligned}
0.5 &= F(420.5|\theta) = 1 - e^{-420.5/\theta}, \\
\ln 0.5 &= \frac{-420.5}{\theta}, \\
\hat{\theta} &= \frac{-420.5}{\ln 0.5} = 606.65.
\end{aligned}
$$

For the Pareto distribution, select the 30th and 80th percentiles. The smoothed empirical estimates are found as follows:

$$
\begin{aligned}
\text{30th:} \quad j &= \lfloor 21(0.3) \rfloor = \lfloor 6.3 \rfloor = 6, \ h = 6.3 - 6 = 0.3, \\
\hat{\pi}_{0.3} &= 0.7(161) + 0.3(243) = 185.6, \\
\text{80th:} \quad j &= \lfloor 21(0.8) \rfloor = \lfloor 16.8 \rfloor = 16, \ h = 16.8 - 16 = 0.8, \\
\hat{\pi}_{0.8} &= 0.2(1{,}193) + 0.8(1{,}340) = 1{,}310.6.
\end{aligned}
$$

The equations to solve are

$$
\begin{aligned}
0.3 &= F(185.6) = 1 - \left(\frac{\theta}{185.6 + \theta} \right)^{\alpha}, \\
0.8 &= F(1{,}310.6) = 1 - \left(\frac{\theta}{1310.6 + \theta} \right)^{\alpha}, \\
\ln 0.7 &= -0.356675 = \alpha \ln \left(\frac{\theta}{185.6 + \theta} \right), \\
\ln 0.2 &= -1.609438 = \alpha \ln \left(\frac{\theta}{1{,}310.6 + \theta} \right), \\
\frac{-1.609438}{-0.356675} &= 4.512338 = \frac{\ln \left(\frac{\theta}{1{,}310.6 + \theta} \right)}{\ln \left(\frac{\theta}{185.6 + \theta} \right)}.
\end{aligned}
$$

Any of the methods from Appendix F can be used to solve this equation for $\hat{\theta} = 715.03$. Then, from the first equation,

$$0.3 = 1 - \left(\frac{715.03}{185.6 + 715.03}\right)^\alpha,$$

which yields $\hat{\alpha} = 1.54559$. $\square$

The estimates are much different from those obtained in Example 12.2. This is one indication that these methods may not be particularly reliable.

12.1.1 Exercises

12.1 Determine the method-of-moments estimate for an exponential model for Data Set B with observations censored at 250.

12.2 Determine the method-of-moments estimate for a lognormal model for Data Set B.

12.3 (*) The 20th and 80th percentiles from a sample are 5 and 12 respectively. Using the percentile matching method, estimate $S(8)$ assuming the population has a Weibull distribution.

12.4 (*) From a sample you are given that the mean is 35,000, the standard deviation is 75,000, the median is 10,000, and the 90th percentile is 100,000. Using the percentile matching method, estimate the parameters of a Weibull distribution.

12.5 (*) A sample of size 5 produced the values 4, 5, 21, 99, and 421. You fit a Pareto distribution using the method of moments. Determine the 95th percentile of the fitted distribution.

12.6 (*) In year 1 there are 100 claims with an average size of 10,000 and in year 2 there are 200 claims with an average size of 12,500. Inflation increases the size of all claims by 10% per year. A Pareto distribution with $\alpha = 3$ and θ unknown is used to model the claim size distribution. Estimate θ for year 3 using the method of moments.

12.7 (*) From a random sample the 20th percentile is 18.25 and the 80th percentile is 35.8. Estimate the parameters of a lognormal distribution using percentile matching and then use these estimates to estimate the probability of observing a value in excess of 30.

12.8 (*) A claim process is a mixture of two random variables A and B, where A has an exponential distribution with a mean of 1 and B has an exponential distribution with a mean of 10. A weight of p is assigned to distribution A and

$1 - p$ to distribution B. The standard deviation of the mixture is 2. Estimate p by the method of moments.

12.9 (*) A random sample of 20 observations has been ordered as follows:

$$12 \quad 16 \quad 20 \quad 23 \quad 26 \quad 28 \quad 30 \quad 32 \quad 33 \quad 35$$
$$36 \quad 38 \quad 39 \quad 40 \quad 41 \quad 43 \quad 45 \quad 47 \quad 50 \quad 57$$

Determine the 60th sample percentile using the smoothed empirical estimate.

12.10 (*) The following 20 wind losses (in millions of dollars) were recorded in one year:

$$1 \quad 1 \quad 1 \quad 1 \quad 1 \quad 2 \quad 2 \quad 3 \quad 3 \quad 4$$
$$6 \quad 6 \quad 8 \quad 10 \quad 13 \quad 14 \quad 15 \quad 18 \quad 22 \quad 25$$

Determine the sample 75th percentile using the smoothed empirical estimate.

12.11 (*) The observations 1,000, 850, 750, 1,100, 1,250, and 900 were obtained as a random sample from a gamma distribution with unknown parameters α and θ. Estimate these parameters by the method-of-moments.

12.12 (*) A random sample of claims has been drawn from a loglogistic distribution. In the sample, 80% of the claims exceed 100 and 20% exceed 400. Estimate the loglogistic parameters by percentile matching.

12.13 (*) Let $x_1, \ldots, x_n$ be a random sample from a population with cdf $F(x) = x^p$, $0 < x < 1$. Determine the method of moments estimate of p.

12.14 (*) A random sample of 10 claims obtained from a gamma distribution is given below:

$$1,500 \quad 6,000 \quad 3,500 \quad 3,800 \quad 1,800 \quad 5,500 \quad 4,800 \quad 4,200 \quad 3,900 \quad 3,000$$

Estimate α and θ by the method of moments.

12.15 (*) A random sample of five claims from a lognormal distribution is given below:

$$500 \quad 1,000 \quad 1,500 \quad 2,500 \quad 4,500.$$

Estimate μ and σ by the method of moments. Estimate the probability that a loss will exceed 4,500.

12.16 (*) The random variable X has pdf $f(x) = \beta^{-2} x \exp(-0.5x^2/\beta^2)$, x, $\beta > 0$. For this random variable, $E(X) = (\beta/2)\sqrt{2\pi}$ and $\mathrm{Var}(X) = 2\beta^2 - \pi\beta^2/2$. You are given the following five observations:

$$4.9 \quad 1.8 \quad 3.4 \quad 6.9 \quad 4.0$$

Table 12.1   Data for Exercise 12.18

No. of claims	No. of policies
0	9,048
1	905
2	45
3	2
4+	0

Table 12.2   Data for Exercise 12.19

No. of claims	No. of policies
0	861
1	121
2	13
3	3
4	1
5	0
6	1
7+	0

Determine the method-of-moments estimate of β.

12.17 The random variable X has pdf $f(x) = \alpha \lambda^{\alpha} (\lambda + x)^{-\alpha-1}$, $x, \alpha, \lambda > 0$. It is known that $\lambda = 1,000$. You are given the following five observations:

$$43 \quad 145 \quad 233 \quad 396 \quad 775$$

Determine the method of moments estimate of α.

12.18 Use the data in Table 12.1 to determine the method-of-moments estimate of the parameters of the negative binomial model.

12.19 Use the data in Table 12.2 to determine the method-of-moments estimate of the parameters of the negative binomial model.

12.2   MAXIMUM LIKELIHOOD ESTIMATION

12.2.1   Introduction

Estimation by the method of moments and percentile matching is often easy to do, but these estimators tend to perform poorly. The main reason for this is that they use a few features of the data, rather than the entire set of observations. It is particularly important to use as much information as possible when the population has a heavy right tail. For example, when estimating parameters for the normal distribution, the sample mean and variance are sufficient.[3] However, when estimating parameters for a Pareto distribution, it is important to know all the extreme observations in order to successfully estimate α. Another drawback of these methods is that they require that all the observations are from the same random variable. Otherwise, it is not clear what to use for the population moments or percentiles. For example, if half the observations have a deductible of 50 and half have a deductible of 100, it is not clear to what the sample mean should be equated.[4] Finally, these methods allow the analyst to make arbitrary decisions regarding the moments or percentiles to use.

There are a variety of estimators that use the individual data points. All of them are implemented by setting an objective function and then determining the parameter values that optimize that function. For example, we could estimate parameters by minimizing the maximum difference between the distribution function for the parametric model and the distribution function for the Nelson–Åalen estimate. Of the many possibilities, the only one used here is the maximum likelihood estimator. The general form of this estimator is presented in this introduction. This is followed with useful special cases.

To define the maximum likelihood estimator, let the data set consist of n events $A_1, \ldots, A_n$, where A_j is whatever was observed for the jth observation. For example, A_j may consist of a single point or an interval. The latter arises with grouped data or when there is censoring. For example, when there is censoring at u and a censored observation is observed, the observed event is the interval from u to infinity. Further assume that the event A_j results from observing the random variable X_j. The random variables $X_1, \ldots, X_n$ need not have the same probability distribution, but their distributions must depend on the same parameter vector, $\boldsymbol{\theta}$. In addition, the random variables are assumed to be independent.

Definition 12.6 *The **likelihood function** is*

$$L(\boldsymbol{\theta}) = \prod_{j=1}^{n} \Pr(X_j \in A_j | \boldsymbol{\theta})$$

*and the **maximum likelihood estimate** of $\boldsymbol{\theta}$ is the vector that maximizes the likelihood function.[5]*

---

[3] This applies both in the formal statistical definition of sufficiency (not covered here) and in the conventional sense. If the population has a normal distribution, the sample mean and variance convey as much information as the original observations.

[4] One way to rectify that drawback is to first determine a data-dependent model such as the Kaplan-Meier estimate. Then use percentiles or moments from that model.

[5] Some authors write the likelihood function as $L(\boldsymbol{\theta}|\mathbf{x})$, where the vector $\mathbf{x}$ represents the observed data. Because observed data can take many forms, the dependence of the likelihood function on the data is suppressed in the notation.

There is no guarantee that the function has a maximum at eligible parameter values. It is possible that as various parameters become zero or infinite the likelihood function will continue to increase. Care must be taken when maximizing this function because there may be local maxima in addition to the global maximum. Often, it is not possible to analytically maximize the likelihood function (by setting partial derivatives equal to zero). Numerical approaches, such as those outlined in Appendix F, will usually be needed.

Because the observations are assumed to be independent, the product in the definition represents the joint probability $\Pr(X_1 \in A_1, \ldots, X_n \in A_n | \boldsymbol{\theta})$, that is, the likelihood function is the probability of obtaining the sample results that were obtained, given a particular parameter value. The estimate is then the parameter value that produces the model under which the actual observations are most likely to be observed. One of the major attractions of this estimator is that it is almost always available. That is, if you can write an expression for the desired probabilities, you can execute this method. If you cannot write and evaluate an expression for probabilities using your model, there is no point in postulating that model in the first place because you will not be able to use it to solve your problem.

Example 12.7 *Suppose the data in Data Set B were censored at 250. Determine the maximum likelihood estimate of θ for an exponential distribution.*

The first seven data points are uncensored. For them, the set A_j contains the single point equal to the observation x_j. When calculating the likelihood function for a single point for a continuous model, it is necessary to interpret $\Pr(X_j = x_j) = f(x_j)$. That is, the density function should be used. Thus the first seven terms of the product are

$$f(27)f(82) \cdots f(243) = \theta^{-1}e^{-27/\theta}\theta^{-1}e^{-82/\theta} \cdots \theta^{-1}e^{-243/\theta} = \theta^{-7}e^{-909/\theta}.$$

For the final 13 terms, the set A_j is the interval from 250 to infinity and therefore $\Pr(X_j \in A_j) = \Pr(X_j > 250) = e^{-250/\theta}$. There are 13 such factors making the likelihood function

$$L(\theta) = \theta^{-7}e^{-909/\theta}(e^{-250/\theta})^{13} = \theta^{-7}e^{-4,159/\theta}.$$

It is easier to maximize the logarithm of the likelihood function. Because it occurs so often, we denote the **loglikelihood function** as $l(\boldsymbol{\theta}) = \ln L(\boldsymbol{\theta})$. Then

$$\begin{aligned} l(\theta) &= -7\ln\theta - 4{,}159\theta^{-1}, \\ l'(\theta) &= -7\theta^{-1} + 4{,}159\theta^{-2} = 0, \\ \hat{\theta} &= \frac{4{,}159}{7} = 594.14. \end{aligned}$$

In this case, the calculus technique of setting the first derivative equal to zero is easy to do. Also, evaluating the second derivative at this solution produces a negative number, verifying that this solution is a maximum.   □

12.2.2   Complete, individual data

When there is no truncation, and no censoring and the value of each observation is recorded, it is easy to write the loglikelihood function.

$$L(\boldsymbol{\theta}) = \prod_{j=1}^{n} f_{X_j}(x_j|\boldsymbol{\theta}), \quad l(\boldsymbol{\theta}) = \sum_{j=1}^{n} \ln f_{X_j}(x_j|\boldsymbol{\theta}).$$

The notation indicates that it is not necessary for each observation to come from the same distribution.

Example 12.8 *Using Data Set B determine the maximum likelihood estimates for an exponential distribution, for a gamma distribution where α is known to equal 2, and for a gamma distribution where both parameters are unknown.*

For the exponential distribution, the general solution is

$$
\begin{aligned}
l(\theta) &= \sum_{j=1}^{n} \left(-\ln\theta - x_j\theta^{-1} \right) = -n\ln\theta - n\bar{x}\theta^{-1}, \\
l'(\theta) &= -n\theta^{-1} + n\bar{x}\theta^{-2} = 0, \\
n\theta &= n\bar{x}, \\
\hat{\theta} &= \bar{x}.
\end{aligned}
$$

For Data Set B, $\hat{\theta} = \bar{x} = 1{,}424.4$. The value of the loglikelihood function is -165.23. For this situation the method-of-moments and maximum likelihood estimates are identical.

For the gamma distribution with $\alpha = 2$,

$$
\begin{aligned}
f(x|\theta) &= \frac{x^{2-1}e^{-x/\theta}}{\Gamma(2)\theta^2} = x\theta^{-2}e^{-x/\theta}, \\
\ln f(x|\theta) &= \ln x - 2\ln\theta - x\theta^{-1}, \\
l(\theta) &= \sum_{j=1}^{n} \ln x_j - 2n\ln\theta - n\bar{x}\theta^{-1}, \\
l'(\theta) &= -2n\theta^{-1} + n\bar{x}\theta^{-2} = 0, \\
\hat{\theta} &= \tfrac{1}{2}\bar{x}.
\end{aligned}
$$

For Data Set B, $\hat{\theta} = 1{,}424.4/2 = 712.2$ and the value of the loglikelihood function is -179.98. Again, this estimate is the same as the method of moments estimate.

For the gamma distribution with unknown parameters the equation is not as simple.

$$
\begin{aligned}
f(x|\alpha, \theta) &= \frac{x^{\alpha-1}e^{-x/\theta}}{\Gamma(\alpha)\theta^{\alpha}}, \\
\ln f(x|\alpha, \theta) &= (\alpha - 1)\ln x - x\theta^{-1} - \ln\Gamma(\alpha) - \alpha\ln\theta.
\end{aligned}
$$

The partial derivative with respect to α requires the derivative of the gamma function. The resulting equation cannot be solved analytically. Using numerical methods, the estimates are $\hat{\alpha} = 0.55616$ and $\hat{\theta} = 2{,}561.1$ and the value of the loglikelihood function is -162.29. These do not match the method-of-moments estimates. ☐

12.2.3 Complete, grouped data

When data are complete and grouped, the observations may be summarized as follows. Begin with a set of numbers $c_0 < c_1 < \cdots < c_k$, where c_0 is the smallest possible observation (often zero) and c_k is the largest possible observation (often infinity). From the sample, let n_j be the number of observations in the interval $(c_{j-1}, c_j]$. For such data, the likelihood function is

$$L(\boldsymbol{\theta}) = \prod_{j=1}^{k} [F(c_j|\boldsymbol{\theta}) - F(c_{j-1}|\boldsymbol{\theta})]^{n_j}$$

and its logarithm is

$$l(\boldsymbol{\theta}) = \sum_{j=1}^{k} n_j \ln[F(c_j|\boldsymbol{\theta}) - F(c_{j-1}|\boldsymbol{\theta})].$$

Example 12.9 *From Data Set C, determine the maximum likelihood estimate for an exponential distribution.*

The loglikelihood function is

$$
\begin{aligned}
l(\theta) &= 99 \ln[F(7{,}500) - F(0)] + 42 \ln[F(17{,}500) - F(7{,}500)] + \cdots \\
&\quad + 3 \ln[1 - F(300{,}000)] \\
&= 99 \ln(1 - e^{-7{,}500/\theta}) + 42 \ln(e^{-7{,}500/\theta} - e^{-17{,}500/\theta}) + \cdots \\
&\quad + 3 \ln e^{-300{,}000/\theta}.
\end{aligned}
$$

A numerical routine is needed to produce $\hat{\theta} = 29{,}721$ and the value of the loglikelihood function is -406.03. ☐

12.2.4 Truncated or censored data

When data are censored, there is no additional complication. As noted in Example 12.7, right censoring simply creates an interval running from the censoring point to infinity. In that example, data below the censoring point were individual data, and so the likelihood function contains both density and distribution function terms.

Truncated data present more of a challenge. There are two ways to proceed. One is to shift the data by subtracting the truncation point from each observation. The other is to accept the fact that there is no information about values below the truncation point but then attempt to fit a model for the original population.

Example 12.10 *Assume the values in Data Set B had been truncated from below at 200. Using both methods, estimate the value of α for a Pareto distribution with $\theta = 800$ known. Then use the model to estimate the cost per payment with deductibles of 0, 200, and 400.*

Using the shifting approach, the values become 43, 94, 140, 184, 257, 480, 655, 677, 774, 993, 1,140, 1,684, 2,358, and 15,543. The likelihood function is

$$
L(\alpha) = \prod_{j=1}^{14} \frac{\alpha(800^\alpha)}{(800 + x_j)^{\alpha+1}},
$$

$$
\begin{aligned}
l(\alpha) &= \sum_{j=1}^{14} [\ln \alpha + \alpha \ln 800 - (\alpha + 1) \ln(x_j + 800)] \\
&= 14 \ln \alpha + 93.5846\alpha - 103.969(\alpha + 1) \\
&= 14 \ln \alpha - 103.969 - 10.384\alpha, \\
l'(\alpha) &= 14\alpha^{-1} - 10.384, \\
\hat{\alpha} &= \frac{14}{10.384} = 1.3482.
\end{aligned}
$$

Because the data have been shifted, it is not possible to estimate the cost with no deductible. With a deductible of 200, the expected cost is the expected value of the estimated Pareto distribution, $800/0.3482 = 2{,}298$. Raising the deductible to 400 is equivalent to imposing a deductible of 200 on the modeled distribution. From Theorem 5.13, the expected cost per payment is

$$
\frac{E(X) - E(X \wedge 200)}{1 - F(200)} = \frac{\dfrac{800}{0.3482}\left(\dfrac{800}{200+800}\right)^{0.3482}}{\left(\dfrac{800}{200+800}\right)^{1.3482}} = \frac{1{,}000}{0.3482} = 2{,}872.
$$

For the unshifted approach we need to ask the key question required when constructing the likelihood function. That is, what is the probability of observing each value knowing that values under 200 are omitted from the data set? This becomes a conditional probability and therefore the likelihood function is (where the x_j values are now the original values)

$$L(\alpha) = \prod_{j=1}^{14} \frac{f(x_j|\alpha)}{1 - F(200|\alpha)} = \prod_{j=1}^{14} \left[\frac{\alpha(800^\alpha)}{(800 + x_j)^{\alpha+1}} \middle/ \left(\frac{800}{800 + 200} \right)^\alpha \right]$$

$$= \prod_{j=1}^{14} \frac{\alpha(1{,}000^\alpha)}{(800 + x_j)^{\alpha+1}},$$

$$l(\alpha) = 14 \ln \alpha + 14\alpha \ln 1{,}000 - (\alpha + 1) \sum_{j=1}^{14} \ln(800 + x_j),$$

$$= 14 \ln \alpha + 96.709\alpha - (\alpha + 1)105.810,$$

$$l'(\alpha) = 14\alpha^{-1} - 9.101,$$

$$\hat{\alpha} = 1.5383.$$

This model is for losses with no deductible, and therefore the expected cost without a deductible is $800/0.5383 = 1{,}486$. Imposing deductibles of 200 and 400 produces the following results:

$$\frac{E(X) - E(X \wedge 200)}{1 - F(200)} = \frac{1{,}000}{0.5383} = 1{,}858,$$

$$\frac{E(X) - E(X \wedge 400)}{1 - F(400)} = \frac{1{,}200}{0.5383} = 2{,}229. \qquad \square$$

It should now be clear that the contribution to the likelihood function can be written for most any observation. The following two steps summarize the process:

1. For the numerator, use $f(x)$ if the exact value, x, of the observation is known. If it is only known that the observation is between y and z, use $F(z) - F(y)$.

2. For the denominator, let d be the truncation point (use zero if there is no truncation). The denominator is then $1 - F(d)$.

Example 12.11 *Determine Pareto and gamma models for the time to death for Data Set D2.*

Table 12.3 shows how the likelihood function is constructed for these values. For deaths, the time is known and so the exact value of x is available. For surrenders or those reaching time 5, the observation is censored and therefore death is known to be some time in the interval from the surrender time, y, to infinity. In the table, $z = \infty$ is not noted because all interval observations end at infinity. The likelihood function must be maximized numerically. For the Pareto distribution there is no solution. The likelihood function keeps getting

Table 12.3   Likelihood function for Example 12.11

Obs.	x, y	d	L	Obs.	x, y	d	L
1	$y = 0.1$	0	$1 - F(0.1)$	16	$x = 4.8$	0	$f(4.8)$
2	$y = 0.5$	0	$1 - F(0.5)$	17	$y = 4.8$	0	$1 - F(4.8)$
3	$y = 0.8$	0	$1 - F(0.8)$	18	$y = 4.8$	0	$1 - F(4.8)$
4	$x = 0.8$	0	$f(0.8)$	19-30	$y = 5.0$	0	$1 - F(5.0)$
5	$y = 1.8$	0	$1 - F(1.8)$	31	$y = 5.0$	0.3	$\frac{1-F(5.0)}{1-F(0.3)}$
6	$y = 1.8$	0	$1 - F(1.8)$	32	$y = 5.0$	0.7	$\frac{1-F(5.0)}{1-F(0.7)}$
7	$y = 2.1$	0	$1 - F(2.1)$	33	$x = 4.1$	1.0	$\frac{f(4.1)}{1-F(1.0)}$
8	$y = 2.5$	0	$1 - F(2.5)$	34	$x = 3.1$	1.8	$\frac{f(3.1)}{1-F(1.8)}$
9	$y = 2.8$	0	$1 - F(2.8)$	35	$y = 3.9$	2.1	$\frac{1-F(3.9)}{1-F(2.1)}$
10	$x = 2.9$	0	$f(2.9)$	36	$y = 5.0$	2.9	$\frac{1-F(5.0)}{1-F(2.9)}$
11	$x = 2.9$	0	$f(2.9)$	37	$y = 4.8$	2.9	$\frac{1-F(4.8)}{1-F(2.9)}$
12	$y = 3.9$	0	$1 - F(3.9)$	38	$x = 4.0$	3.2	$\frac{f(4.0)}{1-F(3.2)}$
13	$x = 4.0$	0	$f(4.0)$	39	$y = 5.0$	3.4	$\frac{1-F(5.0)}{1-F(3.4)}$
14	$y = 4.0$	0	$1 - F(4.0)$	40	$y = 5.0$	3.9	$\frac{1-F(5.0)}{1-F(3.9)}$
15	$y = 4.1$	0	$1 - F(4.1)$				

larger as α and θ get larger.[6] For the gamma distribution the maximum is at $\hat{\alpha} = 2.617$ and $\hat{\theta} = 3.311$. □

Discrete data present no additional problems.

Example 12.12 *For Data Set A, assume that the seven drivers with five or more accidents all had exactly five accidents. Determine the maximum likelihood estimate for a Poisson distribution and for a binomial distribution with $m = 8$.*

In general, for a discrete distribution with complete data, the likelihood function is

$$L(\boldsymbol{\theta}) = \prod_{j=1}^{\infty} [p(x_j|\boldsymbol{\theta})]^{n_j},$$

where x_j is one of the observed values, $p(x_j|\boldsymbol{\theta})$ is the probability of observing x_j, and n_x is the number of times x was observed in the sample. For the

---

[6] For a Pareto distribution, the limit as the parameters α and θ become infinite with the ratio being held constant is an exponential distribution. Thus, for this example, the exponential distribution is a better model (as measured by the likelihood function) than any Pareto model.

Poisson distribution

$$L(\lambda) = \prod_{x=0}^{\infty} \left(\frac{e^{-\lambda} \lambda^x}{x!} \right)^{n_x} = \prod_{x=0}^{\infty} \frac{e^{-n_x \lambda} \lambda^{x n_x}}{(x!)^{n_x}},$$

$$l(\lambda) = \sum_{x=0}^{\infty} (-n_x \lambda + x n_x \ln \lambda - n_x \ln x!) = -n\lambda + n\bar{x} \ln \lambda - \sum_{x=0}^{\infty} n_x \ln x!,$$

$$l'(\lambda) = -n + \frac{n\bar{x}}{\lambda} = 0,$$

$$\hat{\lambda} = \bar{x}.$$

For the binomial distribution

$$L(q) = \prod_{x=0}^{m} \left[\binom{m}{x} q^x (1-q)^{m-x} \right]^{n_x} = \prod_{x=0}^{m} \frac{m!^{n_x} q^{x n_x} (1-q)^{(m-x)n_x}}{(x!)^{n_x} [(m-x)!]^{n_x}},$$

$$l(q) = \sum_{x=0}^{m} [n_x \ln m! + x n_x \ln q + (m-x)n_x \ln(1-q)]$$

$$- \sum_{x=0}^{m} [n_x \ln x! + n_x \ln(m-x)!],$$

$$l'(q) = \sum_{x=0}^{m} \frac{x n_x}{q} - \frac{(m-x)n_x}{1-q} = \frac{n\bar{x}}{q} - \frac{mn - n\bar{x}}{1-q} = 0,$$

$$\hat{q} = \frac{\bar{x}}{m}.$$

For this problem, $\bar{x} = [81{,}714(0) + 11{,}306(1) + 1{,}618(2) + 250(3) + 40(4) + 7(5)]/94{,}935 = 0.16313$. Therefore, for the Poisson distribution $\hat{\lambda} = 0.16313$, and for the binomial distribution $\hat{q} = 0.16313/8 = 0.02039$.   □

In Exercise 12.25 you are asked to estimate the Poisson parameter when the actual values for those with five or more accidents are not known.

12.2.5   Exercises

12.20 Repeat Example 12.8 using the inverse exponential, inverse gamma with $\alpha = 2$, and inverse gamma distributions. Compare your estimates with the method-of-moments estimates.

12.21 From Data Set C, determine the maximum likelihood estimates for gamma, inverse exponential, and inverse gamma distributions.

12.22 Determine maximum likelihood estimates for Data Set B using the inverse exponential, gamma, and inverse gamma distributions. Assume the

q et exponentiel

Table 12.4   Data for Exercise 12.27

Age last observed	Cause
1.7	Death
1.5	Censoring
2.6	Censoring
3.3	Death
3.5	Censoring

data have been censored at 250 and then compare your answers to those obtained in Example 12.8 and Exercise 12.20.

12.23 Repeat Example 12.10 using a Pareto distribution with both parameters unknown.

12.24 Repeat Example 12.11, this time finding the distribution of the time to surrender.

12.25 Repeat Example 12.12, but this time assume that the actual values for the seven drivers who have five or more accidents are unknown. Note that this is a case of censoring.

12.26 (*) Lives are observed in order to estimate q_{35}. Ten lives are first observed at age 35.4 and 6 die prior to age 36 while the other 4 survive to age 36. An additional 20 lives are first observed at age 35 and 8 die prior to age 36 with the other 12 surviving to age 36. Determine the maximum likelihood estimate of q_{35} given that the time to death from age 35 has density function $f(t) = w$, $0 \le t \le 1$, with $f(t)$ unspecified for $t > 1$.

12.27 (*) The model has hazard rate function $h(t) = \lambda_1$, $0 \le t < 2$, and $h(t) = \lambda_2$, $t \ge 2$. Five items are observed from age zero, with the results in Table 12.4. Determine the maximum likelihood estimates of λ_1 and λ_2.

12.28 (*) Your goal is to estimate q_x. The time to death for a person age x has a constant density function. In a mortality study, 10 lives were first observed at age x. Of them, 1 died and 1 was removed from observation alive at age $x + 0.5$. Determine the maximum likelihood estimate of q_x.

12.29 (*) Ten lives are subject to the survival function

$$S(t) = \left(1 - \frac{t}{k}\right)^{1/2}, \quad 0 \le t \le k,$$

where t is time since birth. There are 10 lives observed from birth. At time 10, 2 of the lives die and the other 8 are withdrawn from observation. Determine the maximum likelihood estimate of k.

12.30 (*) Five hundred losses are observed. Five of the losses are 1,100, 3,200, 3,300, 3,500, and 3,900. All that is known about the other 495 losses is that they exceed 4,000. Determine the maximum likelihood estimate of the mean of an exponential model.

12.31 (*) One hundred people are observed at age 35. Of them, 15 leave the study at age 35.6, 10 die sometime between ages 35 and 35.6, and 3 die sometime after age 35.6 but before age 36. The remaining 72 people survive to age 36. Determine the product-limit estimate of q_{35} and the maximum likelihood estimate of q_{35}. For the latter, assume the time to death is uniform between ages 35 and 36.

12.32 (*) The survival function is $S(t) = 1 - t/w$, $0 \le t \le w$. Five claims were studied in order to estimate the distribution of the time from reporting to settlement. After five years, four of the claims were settled, the times being 1, 3, 4, and 4. Actuary X then estimates w using maximum likelihood. Actuary Y prefers to wait until all claims are settled. The fifth claim is settled after six years, at which time actuary Y estimates w by maximum likelihood. Determine the two estimates.

12.33 (*) Four automobile engines were first observed when they were three years old. They were then observed for r additional years. By that time three of the engines had failed, with the failure ages being 4, 5, and 7. The fourth engine was still working at age $3 + r$. The survival function has the uniform distribution on the interval 0 to w. The maximum likelihood estimate of w is 13.67. Determine r.

12.34 (*) Ten claims were observed. The values of seven of them (in thousands) were 3, 7, 8, 12, 12, 13, and 14. The remaining three claims were all censored at 15. The proposed model has a hazard rate function given by

$$h(t) = \begin{cases} \lambda_1, & 0 < t < 5, \\ \lambda_2, & 5 \le t < 10, \\ \lambda_3, & t \ge 10. \end{cases}$$

Determine the maximum likelihood estimates of the three parameters.

12.35 (*) You are given the five observations 521, 658, 702, 819, and 1,217. Your model is the single-parameter Pareto distribution with distribution function

$$F(x) = 1 - \left(\frac{500}{x}\right)^\alpha, \quad x > 500, \ \alpha > 0.$$

Determine the maximum likelihood estimate of α.

12.36 (*) You have observed the following five claim severities: 11.0, 15.2, 18.0, 21.0, and 25.8. Determine the maximum likelihood estimate of μ for the following model:

$$f(x) = \frac{1}{\sqrt{2\pi x}} \exp\left[-\frac{1}{2x}(x - \mu)^2\right], \quad x, \mu > 0.$$

12.37 (*) A random sample of size 5 is taken from a Weibull distribution with $\tau = 2$. Two of the sample observations are known to exceed 50 and the three remaining observations are 20, 30, and 45. Determine the maximum likelihood estimate of θ.

12.38 (*) Phil and Sylvia are competitors in the light bulb business. Sylvia advertises that her light bulbs burn twice as long as Phil's. You were able to test 20 of Phil's bulbs and 10 of Sylvia's. You assumed that both of their bulbs have an exponential distribution with time measured in hours. You have separately estimated the parameters as $\hat{\theta}_P = 1,000$ and $\hat{\theta}_S = 1,500$ for Phil and Sylvia respectively, using maximum likelihood. Using all 30 observations, determine $\hat{\theta}^*$, the maximum likelihood estimate of θ_P restricted by Sylvia's claim that $\theta_S = 2\theta_P$.

12.39 (*) A sample of 100 losses revealed that 62 were below 1,000 and 38 were above 1,000. An exponential distribution with mean θ is considered. Using only the given information, determine the maximum likelihood estimate of θ. Now suppose you are also given that the 62 losses that were below 1,000 totalled 28,140 while the total for the 38 above 1,000 remains unknown. Using this additional information, determine the maximum likelihood estimate of θ.

12.40 (*) The following values were calculated from a random sample of 10 losses:

$$\sum_{j=1}^{10} x_j^{-2} = 0.00033674, \quad \sum_{j=1}^{10} x_j^{-1} = 0.023999,$$

$$\sum_{j=1}^{10} x_j^{-0.5} = 0.34445, \quad \sum_{j=1}^{10} x_j^{0.5} = 488.97$$

$$\sum_{j=1}^{10} x_j = 31,939, \quad \sum_{j=1}^{10} x_j^2 = 211,498,983.$$

Losses come from a Weibull distribution with $\tau = 0.5$ [so $F(x) = 1 - e^{-(x/\theta)^{0.5}}$]. Determine the maximum likelihood estimate of θ.

12.41 (*) For claims reported in 1997, the number settled in 1997 (year 0) was unknown, the number settled in 1998 (year 1) was 3, and the number settled in 1999 (year 2) was 1. The number settled after 1999 is unknown. For claims reported in 1998 there were 5 settled in year 0, 2 settled in year 1, and the number settled after year 1 is unknown. For claims reported in 1999 there were 4 settled in year 0 and the number settled after year 0 is unknown. Let N be the year in which a randomly selected claim is settled and assume that it has probability function $\Pr(N = n) = p_n = (1 - p)p^n$, $n = 0, 1, 2, \ldots$. Determine the maximum likelihood estimate of p.

12.42 (*) A sample of n independent observations $x_1, \ldots, x_n$ came from a distribution with a pdf of $f(x) = 2\theta x \exp(-\theta x^2)$, $x > 0$. Determine the maximum likelihood estimator (mle) of θ.

12.43 (*) Let $x_1, \ldots, x_n$ be a random sample from a population with cdf $F(x) = x^p$, $0 < x < 1$. Determine the mle of p.

12.44 A random sample of 10 claims obtained from a gamma distribution is given below:

$$1,500 \quad 6,000 \quad 3,500 \quad 3,800 \quad 1,800 \quad 5,500 \quad 4,800 \quad 4,200 \quad 3,900 \quad 3,000$$

(a) (*) Suppose it is known that $\alpha = 12$. Determine the maximum likelihood estimate of θ.

(b) Determine the maximum likelihood estimates of α and θ.

12.45 A random sample of five claims from a lognormal distribution is given below:

$$500 \quad 1,000 \quad 1,500 \quad 2,500 \quad 4,500$$

Estimate μ and σ by maximum likelihood. Estimate the probability that a loss will exceed 4,500.

12.46 (*) Let $x_1, \ldots, x_n$ be a random sample from a random variable with pdf $f(x) = \theta^{-1} e^{-x/\theta}$, $x > 0$. Determine the maximum likelihood estimator of θ.

12.47 (*) The random variable X has pdf $f(x) = \beta^{-2} x \exp(-0.5 x^2 / \beta^2)$, x, $\beta > 0$. For this random variable, $E(X) = (\beta/2)\sqrt{2\pi}$ and $Var(X) = 2\beta^2 - \pi\beta^2/2$. You are given the following five observations:

$$4.9 \quad 1.8 \quad 3.4 \quad 6.9 \quad 4.0$$

Determine the maximum likelihood estimate of β.

12.48 (*) Let $x_1, \ldots, x_n$ be a random sample from a random variable with cdf $F(x) = 1 - x^{-\alpha}$, $x > 1$, $\alpha > 0$. Determine the maximum likelihood estimator of α.

12.49 (*) The random variable X has pdf $f(x) = \alpha \lambda^\alpha (\lambda + x)^{-\alpha-1}$, $x, \alpha, \lambda > 0$. It is known that $\lambda = 1,000$. You are given the following five observations:

$$43 \quad 145 \quad 233 \quad 396 \quad 775$$

Determine the maximum likelihood estimate of α.

Table 12.5   Data for Exercise 12.51

Loss	No. of observations	Loss	No. of observations
0–25	5	350–500	17
25–50	37	500–750	13
50–75	28	750–1000	12
75–100	31	1,000–1,500	3
100–125	23	1,500–2,500	5
125–150	9	2,500–5,000	5
150–200	22	5,000–10,000	3
200–250	17	10,000–25,000	3
250–350	15	25,000–	2

$\rightarrow$ **12.50** The following 20 observations were collected. It is desired to estimate $\Pr(X > 200)$. When a parametric model is called for, use the single-parameter Pareto distribution for which $F(x) = 1 - (100/x)^\alpha$, $x > 100$, $\alpha > 0$.

$$
\begin{array}{cccccccccc}
132 & 149 & 476 & 147 & 135 & 110 & 176 & 107 & 147 & 165 \\
135 & 117 & 110 & 111 & 226 & 108 & 102 & 108 & 227 & 102
\end{array}
$$

(a) Determine the empirical estimate of $\Pr(X > 200)$.

(b) Determine the method-of-moments estimate of the single-parameter Pareto parameter α and use it to estimate $\Pr(X > 200)$.

(c) Determine the maximum likelihood estimate of the single-parameter Pareto parameter α and use it to estimate $\Pr(X > 200)$.

12.51 The data in Table 12.5 presents the results of a sample of 250 losses. Consider the inverse exponential distribution with cdf $F(x) = e^{-\theta/x}$, $x > 0$, $\theta > 0$. Determine the maximum likelihood estimate of θ.

12.52 Consider the inverse Gaussian distribution with density given by

$$
f_X(x) = \left(\frac{\theta}{2\pi x^3} \right)^{1/2} \exp\left[-\frac{\theta}{2x} \left(\frac{x - \mu}{\mu} \right)^2 \right], \quad x > 0.
$$

(a) Show that

$$
\sum_{j=1}^{n} \frac{(x_j - \mu)^2}{x_j} = \mu^2 \sum_{j=1}^{n} \left(\frac{1}{x_j} - \frac{1}{\bar{x}} \right) + \frac{n}{\bar{x}} (\bar{x} - \mu)^2,
$$

where $\bar{x} = (1/n) \sum_{j=1}^{n} x_j$.

(b) For a sample $(x_1, \cdots, x_n)$, show that the maximum likelihood estimates of μ and θ are

$$
\hat{\mu} = \bar{x}
$$

and

$$\hat{\theta} = \frac{n}{\displaystyle\sum_{j=1}^{n}\left(\frac{1}{x_j} - \frac{1}{\bar{x}}\right)}.$$

12.53 Suppose that $X_1, \ldots, X_n$ are independent and normally distributed with mean $\mathrm{E}(X_j) = \mu$ and $\mathrm{Var}(X_j) = (\theta m_j)^{-1}$, where $m_j > 0$ is a known constant. Prove that the maximum likelihood estimates of μ and θ are

$$\hat{\mu} = \bar{X}$$

and

$$\hat{\theta} = n\left[\sum_{j=1}^{n} m_j(X_j - \bar{X})^2\right]^{-1}$$

where $\bar{X} = (1/m)\sum_{j=1}^{n} m_j X_j$ and $m = \sum_{j=1}^{n} m_j$.

12.3 VARIANCE AND INTERVAL ESTIMATION

In general, it is not easy to determine the variance of complicated estimators such as the maximum likelihood estimator. However, it is possible to approximate the variance. The key is a theorem that can be found in most mathematical statistics books. The particular version stated here and its multi-parameter generalization is taken from [112] and stated without proof. Recall that $L(\theta)$ is the likelihood function and $l(\theta)$ its logarithm. All of the results assume that the population has a distribution that is a member of the chosen parametric family.

Theorem 12.13 *Assume that the pdf (pf in the discrete case) $f(x; \theta)$ satisfies the following for θ in an interval containing the true value (replace integrals by sums for discrete variables):*

(i) $\ln f(x; \theta)$ is three times differentiable with respect to θ.

(ii) $\int \frac{\partial}{\partial \theta} f(x; \theta)\, dx = 0$. This implies that the derivative may be taken outside the integral and so we are just differentiating the constant 1.[7]

(iii) $\int \frac{\partial^2}{\partial \theta^2} f(x; \theta)\, dx = 0$. This is the same concept for the second derivative.

---

[7] The integrals in *(ii)* and *(iii)* are to be evaluated over the range of x values for which $f(x; \theta) > 0$.

(iv) $-\infty < \int f(x;\theta)\dfrac{\partial^2}{\partial\theta^2}\ln f(x;\theta)\,dx < 0$. *This establishes that the indicated integral exists and that the location where the derivative is zero is a maximum.*

(v) There exists a function $H(x)$ *such that* $\int H(x)f(x;\theta)\,dx < \infty$ *with* $\left|\dfrac{\partial^3}{\partial\theta^3}\ln f(x;\theta)\right| < H(x)$. *This makes sure that the population is not overpopulated with regard to extreme values.*

Then the following results hold:

(a) As $n \to \infty$, *the probability that the likelihood equation* $[L'(\theta) = 0]$ *has a solution goes to 1.*

(b) As $n \to \infty$, *the distribution of the maximum likelihood estimator* $\hat{\theta}_n$ *converges to a normal distribution with mean* θ *and variance such that* $I(\theta)\,\mathrm{Var}(\hat{\theta}_n) \to 1$, *where*

$$
\begin{aligned}
I(\theta) &= -n\mathrm{E}\left[\frac{\partial^2}{\partial\theta^2}\ln f(X;\theta)\right] = -n\int f(x;\theta)\frac{\partial^2}{\partial\theta^2}\ln f(x;\theta)\,dx\\
&= n\mathrm{E}\left[\left(\frac{\partial}{\partial\theta}\ln f(X;\theta)\right)^2\right] = n\int f(x;\theta)\left(\frac{\partial}{\partial\theta}\ln f(x;\theta)\right)^2 dx.
\end{aligned}
$$

For any z, the last statement is to be interpreted as

$$
\lim_{n\to\infty}\mathrm{Pr}\left(\frac{\hat{\theta}_n - \theta}{[I(\theta)]^{-1/2}} < z\right) = \Phi(z)
$$

and therefore $[I(\theta)]^{-1}$ is a useful approximation for $\mathrm{Var}(\hat{\theta}_n)$. The quantity $I(\theta)$ is called the **information** (sometimes more specifically, **Fisher's information**). It follows from this result that the maximum likelihood estimator is asymptotically unbiased and consistent. The conditions in statements *(i)*–*(v)* are often referred to as "mild regularity conditions." A skeptic would translate this statement as "conditions that are almost always true but are often difficult to establish, so we'll just assume they hold in our case." Their purpose is to ensure that the density function is fairly smooth with regard to changes in the parameter and that there is nothing unusual about the density itself.[8]

The results stated above assume that the sample consists of independent and identically distributed random observations. A more general version of

---

[8] For an example of a situation where these conditions do not hold, see Exercise 12.55.

the result uses the logarithm of the likelihood function:

$$I(\theta) = -\mathrm{E}\left[\frac{\partial^2}{\partial \theta^2}l(\theta)\right] = \mathrm{E}\left[\left(\frac{\partial}{\partial \theta}l(\theta)\right)^2\right].$$

The only requirement here is that the same parameter value apply to each observation.

If there is more than one parameter, the only change is that the vector of maximum likelihood estimates now has an asymptotic multivariate normal distribution. The covariance matrix[9] of this distribution is obtained from the inverse of the matrix with (r, s)th element,

$$
\begin{aligned}
\mathbf{I}(\boldsymbol{\theta})_{rs} &= -\mathrm{E}\left[\frac{\partial^2}{\partial \theta_s\, \partial \theta_r}l(\boldsymbol{\theta})\right] = -n\mathrm{E}\left[\frac{\partial^2}{\partial \theta_s\, \partial \theta_r}\ln f(X;\boldsymbol{\theta})\right] \\
&= \mathrm{E}\left[\frac{\partial}{\partial \theta_r}l(\boldsymbol{\theta})\frac{\partial}{\partial \theta_s}l(\boldsymbol{\theta})\right] = n\mathrm{E}\left[\frac{\partial}{\partial \theta_r}\ln f(X;\boldsymbol{\theta})\frac{\partial}{\partial \theta_s}\ln f(X;\boldsymbol{\theta})\right].
\end{aligned}
$$

The first expression on each line is always correct. The second expression assumes that the likelihood is the product of n identical densities. This matrix is often called the **information matrix**. The information matrix also forms the Cramér–Rao lower bound. That is, under the usual conditions, no unbiased estimator has a smaller variance than that given by the inverse of the information. Therefore, at least asymptotically, no unbiased estimator is more accurate than the maximum likelihood estimator.

Example 12.14 *Estimate the covariance matrix of the maximum likelihood estimator for the lognormal distribution. Then apply this result to Data Set B.*

The likelihood function and its logarithm are

$$
L(\mu, \sigma) = \prod_{j=1}^{n}\frac{1}{x_j\sigma\sqrt{2\pi}}\exp\left[-\frac{(\ln x_j - \mu)^2}{2\sigma^2}\right],
$$

$$
l(\mu, \sigma) = \sum_{j=1}^{n}\left[-\ln x_j - \ln\sigma - \frac{1}{2}\ln(2\pi) - \frac{1}{2}\left(\frac{\ln x_j - \mu}{\sigma}\right)^2\right].
$$

The first partial derivatives are

$$
\frac{\partial l}{\partial \mu} = \sum_{j=1}^{n}\frac{\ln x_j - \mu}{\sigma^2} \quad \text{and} \quad \frac{\partial l}{\partial \sigma} = -\frac{n}{\sigma} + \sum_{j=1}^{n}\frac{(\ln x_j - \mu)^2}{\sigma^3}.
$$

---

[9] For any multivariate random variable the covariance matrix has the variances of the individual random variables on the main diagonal and covariances in the off-diagonal positions.

The second partial derivatives are

$$\frac{\partial^2 l}{\partial \mu^2} = -\frac{n}{\sigma^2},$$

$$\frac{\partial^2 l}{\partial \sigma \, \partial \mu} = -2 \sum_{j=1}^{n} \frac{\ln x_j - \mu}{\sigma^3},$$

$$\frac{\partial^2 l}{\partial \sigma^2} = \frac{n}{\sigma^2} - 3 \sum_{j=1}^{n} \frac{(\ln x_j - \mu)^2}{\sigma^4}.$$

The expected values are ($\ln X_j$ has a normal distribution with mean μ and standard deviation σ)

$$\mathrm{E}\left(\frac{\partial^2 l}{\partial \mu^2}\right) = -\frac{n}{\sigma^2},$$

$$\mathrm{E}\left(\frac{\partial^2 l}{\partial \mu \, \partial \sigma}\right) = 0,$$

$$\mathrm{E}\left(\frac{\partial^2 l}{\partial \sigma^2}\right) = -\frac{2n}{\sigma^2}.$$

Changing the signs and inverting produce an estimate of the covariance matrix (it is an estimate because Theorem 12.13 only provides the covariance matrix in the limit). It is

$$\begin{bmatrix} \dfrac{\sigma^2}{n} & 0 \\ 0 & \dfrac{\sigma^2}{2n} \end{bmatrix}.$$

For the lognormal distribution, the maximum likelihood estimates are the solutions to the two equations

$$\sum_{j=1}^{n} \frac{\ln x_j - \mu}{\sigma^2} = 0 \ \text{ and } \ -\frac{n}{\sigma} + \sum_{j=1}^{n} \frac{(\ln x_j - \mu)^2}{\sigma^3} = 0.$$

From the first equation $\hat{\mu} = (1/n)\sum_{j=1}^{n} \ln x_j$, and from the second equation $\hat{\sigma}^2 = (1/n)\sum_{j=1}^{n}(\ln x_j - \hat{\mu})^2$. For Data Set B the values are $\hat{\mu} = 6.1379$ and $\hat{\sigma}^2 = 1.9305$ or $\hat{\sigma} = 1.3894$. With regard to the covariance matrix the true values are needed. The best we can do is substitute the estimated values to obtain

$$\widehat{\mathrm{Var}}(\hat{\mu}, \hat{\sigma}) = \begin{bmatrix} 0.0965 & 0 \\ 0 & 0.0483 \end{bmatrix}. \tag{12.1}$$

The multiple "hats" in the expression indicate that this is an estimate of the variance of the estimators.   □

The zeros off the diagonal indicate that the two parameter estimates are asymptotically uncorrelated. For the particular case of the lognormal distribution, that is also true for any sample size. One thing we could do with this information is construct approximate 95% confidence intervals for the true parameter values. These would be 1.96 standard deviations on either side of the estimate:

$$\mu \quad : \quad 6.1379 \pm 1.96(0.0965)^{1/2} = 6.1379 \pm 0.6089,$$
$$\sigma \quad : \quad 1.3894 \pm 1.96(0.0483)^{1/2} = 1.3894 \pm 0.4308.$$

To obtain the information matrix, it is necessary to take both derivatives and expected values. This is not always easy to do. A way to avoid this problem is to simply not take the expected value. Rather than working with the number that results from the expectation, use the observed data points. The result is called the **observed information**.

Example 12.15 *Estimate the covariance in the previous example using the observed information.*

Substituting the observations into the second derivatives produces

$$\frac{\partial^2 l}{\partial \mu^2} = -\frac{n}{\sigma^2} = -\frac{20}{\sigma^2},$$

$$\frac{\partial^2 l}{\partial \sigma \, \partial \mu} = -2 \sum_{j=1}^{n} \frac{\ln x_j - \mu}{\sigma^3} = -2 \frac{122.7576 - 20\mu}{\sigma^3},$$

$$\frac{\partial^2 l}{\partial \sigma^2} = \frac{n}{\sigma^2} - 3 \sum_{j=1}^{n} \frac{(\ln x_j - \mu)^2}{\sigma^4} = \frac{20}{\sigma^2} - 3 \frac{792.0801 - 245.5152\mu + 20\mu^2}{\sigma^4}.$$

Inserting the parameter estimates produces the negatives of the entries of the observed information,

$$\frac{\partial^2 l}{\partial \mu^2} = -10.3600, \quad \frac{\partial^2 l}{\partial \sigma \, \partial \mu} = 0, \quad \frac{\partial^2 l}{\partial \sigma^2} = -20.7190.$$

Changing the signs and inverting produce the same values as in (12.1). This is a feature of the lognormal distribution that need not hold for other models. $\square$

Sometimes it is not even possible to take the derivative. In that case an approximate second derivative can be used. A reasonable approximation is

$$\frac{\partial^2 f(\boldsymbol{\theta})}{\partial \theta_i \, \partial \theta_j} \doteq \frac{1}{h_i h_j} [f(\boldsymbol{\theta} + \tfrac{1}{2} h_i \mathbf{e}_i + \tfrac{1}{2} h_j \mathbf{e}_j) - f(\boldsymbol{\theta} + \tfrac{1}{2} h_i \mathbf{e}_i - \tfrac{1}{2} h_j \mathbf{e}_j)$$
$$- f(\boldsymbol{\theta} - \tfrac{1}{2} h_i \mathbf{e}_i + \tfrac{1}{2} h_j \mathbf{e}_j) + f(\boldsymbol{\theta} - \tfrac{1}{2} h_i \mathbf{e}_i - \tfrac{1}{2} h_j \mathbf{e}_j)],$$

where $\mathbf{e}_i$ is a vector with all zeros except for a 1 in the ith position and $h_i = \theta_i/10^v$, where v is one-third the number of significant digits used in calculations.

Example 12.16 *Repeat the previous example using approximate derivatives.*

Assume that there are 15 significant digits being used. Then $h_1 = 6.1379/10^5$ and $h_2 = 1.3894/10^5$. Reasonably close values are 0.00006 and 0.00001. The first approximation is

$$
\begin{aligned}
\frac{\partial^2 l}{\partial \mu^2} &\doteq \frac{l(6.13796, 1.3894) - 2l(6.1379, 1.3894) + l(6.13784, 1.3894)}{(0.00006)^2} \\
&= \frac{-157.71389308198 - 2(-157.71389304968) + (-157.71389305468)}{(0.00006)^2} \\
&= -10.3604.
\end{aligned}
$$

The other two approximations are

$$
\frac{\partial^2 l}{\partial \sigma \, \partial \mu} \doteq 0.0003, \quad \frac{\partial^2 l}{\partial \sigma^2} \doteq -20.7208.
$$

We see that here the approximation works very well.   □

The information matrix provides a method for assessing the quality of the maximum likelihood estimators of a distribution's parameters. However, we are often more interested in a quantity that is a function of the parameters. For example, we might be interested in the lognormal mean as an estimate of the population mean. That is, we want to use $\exp(\hat{\mu} + \hat{\sigma}^2/2)$ as an estimate of the population mean, where the maximum likelihood estimates of the parameters are used. It is very difficult to evaluate the mean and variance of this random variable because it is a complex function of two variables that already have complex distributions. The following theorem (from [108]) can help. The method is often called the **delta method**.

Theorem 12.17 *Let $\mathbf{X}_n = (X_{1n}, \ldots, X_{kn})^T$ be a multivariate random variable of dimension k based on a sample of size n. Assume that $\mathbf{X}$ is asymptotically normal with mean $\boldsymbol{\theta}$ and covariance matrix $\boldsymbol{\Sigma}/n$, where neither $\boldsymbol{\theta}$ nor $\boldsymbol{\Sigma}$ depend on n. Let g be a function of k variables that is totally differentiable. Let $G_n = g(X_{1n}, \ldots, X_{kn})$. Then G_n is asymptotically normal with mean $g(\boldsymbol{\theta})$ and variance $(\partial \mathbf{g})^T \boldsymbol{\Sigma} (\partial \mathbf{g})/n$, where $\partial \mathbf{g}$ is the vector of first derivatives, that is, $\partial \mathbf{g} = (\partial g/\partial \theta_1, \ldots, \partial g/\partial \theta_k)^T$ and it is to be evaluated at $\boldsymbol{\theta}$, the true parameters of the original random variable.*

The statement of the theorem is hard to decipher. The Xs are the estimators and g is the function of the parameters that are being estimated. For a model with one parameter, the theorem reduces to the following statement:

Let $\hat{\theta}$ be an estimator of θ that has an asymptotic normal distribution with mean θ and variance σ^2/n. Then $g(\hat{\theta})$ has an asymptotic normal distribution with mean $g(\theta)$ and asymptotic variance $[g'(\theta)](\sigma^2/n)[g'(\theta)] = g'(\theta)^2\sigma^2/n$.

Example 12.18 *Use the delta method to approximate the variance of the maximum likelihood estimator of the probability that an observation from an exponential distribution exceeds 200. Apply this result to Data Set B.*

From Example 12.8 we know that the maximum likelihood estimate of the exponential parameter is the sample mean. We are asked to estimate $p = \Pr(X > 200) = \exp(-200/\theta)$. The maximum likelihood estimate is $\hat{p} = \exp(-200/\hat{\theta}) = \exp(-200/\bar{x})$. Determining the mean and variance of this quantity is not easy. But we do know that $\mathrm{Var}(\bar{X}) = \mathrm{Var}(X)/n = \theta^2/n$. Furthermore,

$$g(\theta) = e^{-200/\theta}, \quad g'(\theta) = 200\theta^{-2}e^{-200/\theta},$$

and therefore the delta method gives

$$\mathrm{Var}(\hat{p}) \doteq \frac{(200\theta^{-2}e^{-200/\theta})^2\theta^2}{n} = \frac{40{,}000\theta^{-2}e^{-400/\theta}}{n}.$$

For Data Set B,

$$\bar{x} = 1{,}424.4,$$
$$\hat{p} = \exp\left(-\frac{200}{1{,}424.4}\right) = 0.86900$$
$$\widehat{\mathrm{Var}}(\hat{p}) = \frac{40{,}000(1{,}424.4)^{-2}\exp(-400/1{,}424.4)}{20} = 0.0007444.$$

A 95% confidence interval for p is $0.869 \pm 1.96\sqrt{0.0007444}$ or 0.869 ± 0.053. $\square$

Example 12.19 *Construct a 95% confidence interval for the mean of a lognormal population using Data Set B. Compare this to the more traditional confidence interval based on the sample mean.*

From Example 12.14 we have $\hat{\mu} = 6.1379$ and $\hat{\sigma} = 1.3894$ and an estimated covariance matrix of

$$\frac{\hat{\Sigma}}{n} = \begin{bmatrix} 0.0965 & 0 \\ 0 & 0.0483 \end{bmatrix}.$$

The function is $g(\mu, \sigma) = \exp(\mu + \sigma^2/2)$. The partial derivatives are

$$\frac{\partial g}{\partial \mu} = \exp\left(\mu + \tfrac{1}{2}\sigma^2\right)$$
$$\frac{\partial g}{\partial \sigma} = \sigma\exp\left(\mu + \tfrac{1}{2}\sigma^2\right)$$

and the estimates of these quantities are 1,215.75 and 1,689.16, respectively. The delta method produces the following approximation:

$$\widehat{\text{Var}}[g(\hat{\mu}, \hat{\sigma})] = [\; 1{,}215.75 \quad 1{,}689.16 \;] \begin{bmatrix} 0.0965 & 0 \\ 0 & 0.0483 \end{bmatrix} \begin{bmatrix} 1{,}215.75 \\ 1{,}689.16 \end{bmatrix}$$

$$= 280{,}444.$$

The confidence interval is $1{,}215.75 \pm 1.96\sqrt{280{,}444}$ or $1{,}215.75 \pm 1{,}037.96$.

The customary confidence interval for a population mean is $\bar{x} \pm 1.96s/\sqrt{n}$ where is s^2 is the sample variance. For Data Set B the interval is $1{,}424.4 \pm 1.96(3{,}435.04)/\sqrt{20}$ or $1{,}424.4 \pm 1{,}505.47$. It is not surprising that this is a wider interval because we know that (for a lognormal population) the maximum likelihood estimator is asymptotically UMVUE.   □

12.3.1 Exercises

12.54 Determine 95% confidence intervals for the parameters of exponential and gamma models for Data Set B. The likelihood function and maximum likelihood estimates were determined in Example 12.8.

12.55 Let X have a uniform distribution on the interval from 0 to θ. Show that the maximum likelihood estimator is $\hat{\theta} = \max(X_1, \ldots, X_n)$. Use Examples 9.7 and 9.10 to show that this estimator is asymptotically unbiased and to obtain its variance. Show that Theorem 12.13 yields a negative estimate of the variance and that item (ii) in the conditions does not hold.

12.56 Use the delta method to construct a 95% confidence interval for the mean of a gamma distribution using Data Set B. Preliminary calculations are in Exercise 12.54.

12.57 (*) For a lognormal distribution with parameters μ and σ you are given that the maximum likelihood estimates are $\hat{\mu} = 4.215$ and $\hat{\sigma} = 1.093$. The estimated covariance matrix of $(\hat{\mu}, \hat{\sigma})$ is

$$\begin{bmatrix} 0.1195 & 0 \\ 0 & 0.0597 \end{bmatrix}.$$

The mean of a lognormal distribution is given by $\exp(\mu + \sigma^2/2)$. Estimate the variance of the maximum likelihood estimator of the mean of this lognormal distribution using the delta method.

12.58 (*) A distribution has two parameters, α and β. A sample of size 10 produced the following loglikelihood function:

$$l(\alpha, \beta) = -2.5\alpha^2 - 3\alpha\beta - \beta^2 + 50\alpha + 2\beta + k,$$

where k is a constant. Estimate the covariance matrix of the maximum likelihood estimator $(\hat{\alpha}, \hat{\beta})$.

12.59 In Exercise 12.39 two maximum likelihood estimates were obtained for the same model. The second estimate was based on more information than the first one. It would be reasonable to expect that the second estimate is more accurate. Confirm this by estimating the variance of each of the two estimators. Do your calculations using the observed likelihood.

12.60 This is a continuation of Exercise 12.43. Let $x_1, \ldots, x_n$ be a random sample from a population with cdf $F(x) = x^p$, $0 < x < 1$.

    (a) Determine the asymptotic variance of the maximum likelihood estimator of p.

    (b) Use your answer to obtain a general formula for a 95% confidence interval for p.

    (c) Determine the maximum likelihood estimator of $E(X)$ and obtain its asymptotic variance and a formula for a 95% confidence interval.

12.61 This is a continuation of Exercise 12.46. Let $x_1, \ldots, x_n$ be a random sample from a population with pdf $f(x) = \theta^{-1}e^{-x/\theta}$, $x > 0$.

    (a) Determine the asymptotic variance of the maximum likelihood estimator of θ.

    (b) (*) Use your answer to obtain a general formula for a 95% confidence interval for θ.

    (c) Determine the maximum likelihood estimator of $\text{Var}(X)$ and obtain its asymptotic variance and a formula for a 95% confidence interval.

12.62 (*) A sample of size 40 has been taken from a population with pdf $f(x) = (2\pi\theta)^{-1/2}e^{-x^2/(2\theta)}$, $-\infty < x < \infty$, $\theta > 0$. The maximum likelihood estimate of θ is $\hat{\theta} = 2$. Approximate the MSE of $\hat{\theta}$.

12.63 Four observations were made from a random variable having the density function $f(x) = 2\lambda x e^{-\lambda x^2}$, $x, \lambda > 0$. Exactly one of the four observations was less than 2.

    (a) (*) Determine the maximum likelihood estimator of λ.

    (b) Approximate the variance of the maximum likelihood estimator of λ.

12.64 Estimate the covariance matrix of the maximum likelihood estimators for the data in Exercise 12.44 with both α and θ unknown. Do this by computing approximate derivatives of the loglikelihood. Then construct a 95% confidence interval for the mean.

12.65 Estimate the variance of the maximum likelihood estimator for Exercise 12.49 and use it to construct a 95% confidence interval for $E(X \wedge 500)$.

12.66 Consider a random sample of size n from a Weibull distribution. For this exercise, write the Weibull survival function as

$$S(x) = \exp\left\{-\left[\frac{\Gamma(1+\tau^{-1})x}{\mu}\right]^{\tau}\right\}.$$

For this exercise, assume that τ is known and that only μ is to be estimated.

(a) Show that $E(X) = \mu$.

(b) Show that the maximum likelihood estimate of μ is

$$\hat{\mu} = \Gamma(1+\tau^{-1})\left(\frac{1}{n}\sum_{j=1}^{n}x_j^{\tau}\right)^{1/\tau}.$$

(c) Show that using the observed information produces the variance estimate

$$V\hat{ar}(\hat{\mu}) = \frac{\hat{\mu}}{n\tau^2}.$$

where μ is replaced by $\hat{\mu}$.

(d) Show that using the information (again replacing μ with $\hat{\mu}$) produces the same variance estimate as in part (c).

(e) Show that $\hat{\mu}$ has a transformed gamma distribution with $\alpha = n, \theta = \mu n^{-1/\tau}$, and $\tau = \tau$. Use this to obtain the exact variance of $\hat{\mu}$ (as a function of μ). Hint - The variable X^{τ} has an exponential distribution and so the variable $\sum_{j=1}^{n}X_j^{\tau}$ has a gamma distribution with first parameter equal to n and second parameter equal to the mean of the exponential distribution.

12.4 BAYESIAN ESTIMATION

All of the previous discussion on estimation has assumed a frequentist approach. That is, the population distribution is fixed but unknown, and our decisions are concerned not only with the sample we obtained from the population but also with the possibilities attached to other samples that might have been obtained. The Bayesian approach assumes that only the data actually observed are relevant and it is the population that is variable. For parameter estimation the following definitions describe the process and then Bayes' theorem provides the solution.

12.4.1 Definitions and Bayes' theorem

Definition 12.20 *The **prior distribution** is a probability distribution over the space of possible parameter values. It is denoted $\pi(\theta)$ and represents our*

opinion concerning the relative chances that various values of θ are the true value of the parameter.

As before, the parameter θ may be scalar or vector valued. Determination of the prior distribution has always been one of the barriers to the widespread acceptance of Bayesian methods. It is almost certainly the case that your experience has provided some insights about possible parameter values before the first data point has been observed. (If you have no such opinions, perhaps the wisdom of the person who assigned this task to you should be questioned.) The difficulty is translating this knowledge into a probability distribution. An excellent discussion about prior distributions and the foundations of Bayesian analysis can be found in Lindley [83], and for a discussion about issues surrounding the choice of Bayesian versus frequentist methods, see Efron [32]. The book by Klugman [77] contains more detail on the Bayesian approach along with several actuarial applications. More recent articles applying Bayesian methods to actuarial problems include [25], [101], [119], and [133]. A good source for a thorough mathematical treatment of Bayesian methods is the text by Berger [13]. In recent years many advancements in Bayesian calculations have occurred. A good resource is [22]. Scollnik [118] has demonstrated how the computer program WINBUGS can be used to provide Bayesian solutions to actuarial problems.

Due to the difficulty of finding a prior distribution that is convincing (you will have to convince others that your prior opinions are valid) and the possibility that you may really have no prior opinion, the definition of prior distribution can be loosened.

Definition 12.21 *An **improper prior distribution** is one for which the probabilities (or pdf) are nonnegative but their sum (or integral) is infinite.*

A great deal of research has gone into the determination of a so-called **noninformative** or **vague** prior. Its purpose is to reflect minimal knowledge. Universal agreement on the best way to construct a vague prior does not exist. However, there is agreement that the appropriate noninformative prior for a scale parameter is $\pi(\theta) = 1/\theta, \theta > 0$. Note that this is an improper prior.

For a Bayesian analysis, the model is no different than before.

Definition 12.22 *The **model distribution** is the probability distribution for the data as collected given a particular value for the parameter. Its pdf is denoted $f_{\mathbf{X}|\Theta}(\mathbf{x}|\theta)$, where vector notation for $\mathbf{x}$ is used to remind us that all the data appear here. Also note that this is identical to the likelihood function and so that name may also be used at times.*

If the vector of observations $\mathbf{x} = (x_1, \ldots, x_n)^T$ consists of independent and identically distributed random variables, then

$$f_{\mathbf{X}|\Theta}(\mathbf{x}|\theta) = f_{X|\Theta}(x_1|\theta) \cdots f_{X|\Theta}(x_n|\theta).$$

We use concepts from multivariate statistics to obtain two more definitions. In both cases, as well as in the following, integrals should be replaced by sums if the distributions are discrete.

Definition 12.23 *The **joint distribution** has pdf*

$$f_{\mathbf{X},\Theta}(\mathbf{x}, \theta) = f_{\mathbf{X}|\Theta}(\mathbf{x}|\theta)\pi(\theta).$$

Definition 12.24 *The **marginal distribution** of* $\mathbf{x}$ *has pdf*

$$f_{\mathbf{X}}(\mathbf{x}) = \int f_{\mathbf{X}|\Theta}(\mathbf{x}|\theta)\pi(\theta)\, d\theta.$$

Compare this definition to that of a mixture distribution given by (4.4) on page 59. The final two quantities of interest are the following.

Definition 12.25 *The **posterior distribution** is the conditional probability distribution of the parameters given the observed data. It is denoted* $\pi_{\Theta|\mathbf{X}}(\theta|\mathbf{x})$.

Definition 12.26 *The **predictive distribution** is the conditional probability distribution of a new observation* y *given the data* $\mathbf{x}$. *It is denoted* $f_{Y|\mathbf{X}}(y|\mathbf{x})$.[10]

These last two items are the key output of a Bayesian analysis. The posterior distribution tells us how our opinion about the parameter has changed once we have observed the data. The predictive distribution tells us what the next observation might look like given the information contained in the data (as well as, implicitly, our prior opinion). Bayes' theorem tells us how to compute the posterior distribution.

Theorem 12.27 *The posterior distribution can be computed as*

$$\pi_{\Theta|\mathbf{X}}(\theta|\mathbf{x}) = \frac{f_{\mathbf{X}|\Theta}(\mathbf{x}|\theta)\pi(\theta)}{\displaystyle\int f_{\mathbf{X}|\Theta}(\mathbf{x}|\theta)\pi(\theta)\, d\theta} \tag{12.2}$$

while the predictive distribution can be computed as

$$f_{Y|\mathbf{X}}(y|\mathbf{x}) = \int f_{Y|\Theta}(y|\theta)\pi_{\Theta|\mathbf{X}}(\theta|\mathbf{x})\, d\theta, \tag{12.3}$$

where $f_{Y|\Theta}(y|\theta)$ *is the pdf of the new observation, given the parameter value.*

---

[10]In this section and in any subsequent Bayesian discussions, we reserve $f(\cdot)$ for distributions concerning observations (such as the model and predictive distributions) and $\pi(\cdot)$ for distributions concerning parameters (such as the prior and posterior distributions). The arguments will usually make it clear which particular distribution is being used. To make matters explicit, we also employ subscripts to enable us to keep track of the random variables.

The predictive distribution can be interpreted as a mixture distribution where the mixing is with respect to the posterior distribution. The following example illustrates the above definitions and results. The setting, though not the data, is taken from Meyers [92].

Example 12.28 *The following amounts were paid on a hospital liability policy:*

$$125 \quad 132 \quad 141 \quad 107 \quad 133 \quad 319 \quad 126 \quad 104 \quad 145 \quad 223$$

The amount of a single payment has the single-parameter Pareto distribution with $\theta = 100$ and α unknown. The prior distribution has the gamma distribution with $\alpha = 2$ and $\theta = 1$. Determine all of the relevant Bayesian quantities.

The prior density has a gamma distribution and is

$$\pi(\alpha) = \alpha e^{-\alpha}, \quad \alpha > 0,$$

while the model is (evaluated at the data points)

$$f_{\mathbf{X}|A}(\mathbf{x}|\alpha) = \frac{\alpha^{10}(100)^{10\alpha}}{\left(\prod_{j=1}^{10} x_j^{\alpha+1}\right)} = \alpha^{10} e^{-3.801121\alpha - 49.852823}.$$

The joint density of $\mathbf{x}$ and A is (again evaluated at the data points)

$$f_{\mathbf{X},A}(\mathbf{x}, \alpha) = \alpha^{11} e^{-4.801121\alpha - 49.852823}.$$

The posterior distribution of α is

$$\pi_{A|\mathbf{X}}(\alpha|\mathbf{x}) = \frac{\alpha^{11} e^{-4.801121\alpha - 49.852823}}{\int_0^\infty \alpha^{11} e^{-4.801121\alpha - 49.852823} \, d\alpha} = \frac{\alpha^{11} e^{-4.801121\alpha}}{(11!)(1/4.801121)^{12}}. \quad (12.4)$$

There is no need to evaluate the integral in the denominator. Because we know that the result must be a probability distribution, the denominator is just the appropriate normalizing constant. A look at the numerator reveals that we have a gamma distribution with $\alpha = 12$ and $\theta = 1/4.801121$.

The predictive distribution is

$$\begin{aligned}
f_{Y|\mathbf{X}}(y|\mathbf{x}) &= \int_0^\infty \frac{\alpha 100^\alpha}{y^{\alpha+1}} \frac{\alpha^{11} e^{-4.801121\alpha}}{(11!)(1/4.801121)^{12}} \, d\alpha \\
&= \frac{1}{y(11!)(1/4.801121)^{12}} \int_0^\infty \alpha^{12} e^{-(0.195951 + \ln y)\alpha} \, d\alpha \\
&= \frac{1}{y(11!)(1/4.801121)^{12}} \frac{(12!)}{(0.195951 + \ln y)^{13}} \\
&= \frac{12(4.801121)^{12}}{y(0.195951 + \ln y)^{13}}, \quad y > 100. \quad (12.5)
\end{aligned}$$

While this density function may not look familiar, you are asked to show in Exercise 12.67 that $\ln Y - \ln 100$ has the Pareto distribution.   □

12.4.2   Inference and prediction

In one sense the analysis is complete. We begin with a distribution that quantifies our knowledge about the parameter and/or the next observation and we end with a revised distribution. But we have a suspicion that your boss may not be satisfied if you produce a distribution in response to his or her request. No doubt a specific number, perhaps with a margin for error, is what is desired. The usual Bayesian solution is to pose a loss function.

Definition 12.29 *A **loss function** $l_j(\hat{\theta}_j, \theta_j)$ describes the penalty paid by the investigator when $\hat{\theta}_j$ is the estimate and θ_j is the true value of the jth parameter.*

It would also be possible to have a multidimensional loss function $l(\widehat{\boldsymbol{\theta}}, \boldsymbol{\theta})$ which allowed the loss to depend simultaneously on the errors in the various parameter estimates.

Definition 12.30 *The **Bayes estimate** for a given loss function is the one that minimizes the expected loss given the posterior distribution of the parameter in question.*

The three most commonly used loss functions are defined as follows.

Definition 12.31 *For **squared-error loss** the loss function is (all subscripts are dropped for convenience) $l(\hat{\theta}, \theta) = (\hat{\theta} - \theta)^2$. For **absolute loss** it is $l(\hat{\theta}, \theta) = |\hat{\theta} - \theta|$. For **zero–one loss** it is $l(\hat{\theta}, \theta) = 0$ if $\hat{\theta} = \theta$ and is 1 otherwise.*

The following theorem indicates the Bayes estimates for these three common loss functions.

Theorem 12.32 *For squared-error loss the Bayes estimate is the mean of the posterior distribution, for absolute loss it is a median, and for zero–one loss it is a mode.*

Note that there is no guarantee that the posterior mean exists or that the posterior median or mode will be unique. When not otherwise specified, the term *Bayes estimate* will refer to the posterior mean.

Example 12.33 (Example 12.28 continued) *Determine the three Bayes estimates of α.*

The mean of the posterior gamma distribution is $\alpha\theta = 12/4.801121 = 2.499416$. The median of 2.430342 must be determined numerically while the mode is $(\alpha - 1)\theta = 11/4.801121 = 2.291132$. Note that the α used here is the parameter of the posterior gamma distribution, not the α for the single-parameter Pareto distribution that we are trying to estimate.   □

For forecasting purposes, the expected value of the predictive distribution is often of interest. It can be thought of as providing a point estimate of the $(n+1)$th observation given the first n observations and the prior distribution. It is

$$
\begin{aligned}
E(Y|\mathbf{x}) &= \int y f_{Y|\mathbf{X}}(y|\mathbf{x})dy \\
&= \int y \int f_{Y|\Theta}(y|\theta)\pi_{\Theta|\mathbf{X}}(\theta|\mathbf{x})d\theta dy \\
&= \int \pi_{\Theta|\mathbf{X}}(\theta|\mathbf{x}) \int y f_{Y|\Theta}(y|\theta)dy d\theta \\
&= \int E(Y|\theta)\pi_{\Theta|\mathbf{X}}(\theta|\mathbf{x})d\theta.
\end{aligned} \tag{12.6}
$$

Equation (12.6) can be interpreted as a weighted average using the posterior distribution as weights.

Example 12.34 (Example 12.28 continued) *Determine the expected value of the* 11*th observation, given the first* 10.

For the single-parameter Pareto distribution, $E(Y|\alpha) = 100\alpha/(\alpha - 1)$ for $\alpha > 1$. Because the posterior distribution assigns positive probability to values of $\alpha \leq 1$, the expected value of the predictive distribution is not defined. □

The Bayesian equivalent of a confidence interval is easy to construct. The following definition will suffice.

Definition 12.35 *The points* $a < b$ *define a* $100(1 - \alpha)\%$ **credibility interval** *for* θ_j *provided that* $\Pr(a \leq \Theta_j \leq b|\mathbf{x}) \geq 1 - \alpha$.

The use of the term credibility has no relationship to its use in actuarial analyses as developed in Chapter 16. The inequality is present for the case where the posterior distribution of θ_j is discrete. Then it may not be possible for the probability to be exactly $1 - \alpha$. This definition does not produce a unique solution. The following theorem indicates one way to produce a unique interval.

Theorem 12.36 *If the posterior random variable* $\theta_j|\mathbf{x}$ *is continuous and unimodal, then the* $100(1 - \alpha)\%$ *credibility interval with smallest width* $b - a$ *is the unique solution to*

$$
\begin{aligned}
\int_a^b \pi_{\Theta_j|\mathbf{X}}(\theta_j|\mathbf{x})\,d\theta_j &= 1 - \alpha, \\
\pi_{\Theta|\mathbf{X}}(a|\mathbf{x}) &= \pi_{\Theta|\mathbf{X}}(b|\mathbf{x}).
\end{aligned}
$$

This interval is a special case of a highest posterior density (*HPD*) *credibility set.*

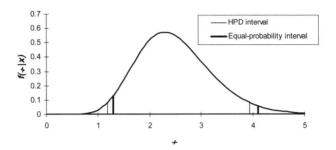

Fig. 12.1 Two Bayesian credibility intervals.

The following example may clarify the theorem.

Example 12.37 (Example 12.28 continued) *Determine the shortest 95% credibility interval for the parameter* α. *Also determine the interval that places 2.5% probability at each end.*

The two equations from Theorem 12.36 are

$$\Pr(a \leq A \leq b|\mathbf{x}) = \Gamma(12; 4.801121b) - \Gamma(12; 4.801121a) = 0.95,$$
$$a^{11}e^{-4.801121a} = b^{11}e^{-4.801121b}.$$

and numerical methods can be used to find the solution $a = 1.1832$ and $b = 3.9384$. The width of this interval is 2.7552.

Placing 2.5% probability at each end yields the two equations

$$\Gamma(12; 4.801121b) = 0.975, \quad \Gamma(12; 4.801121a) = 0.025.$$

This solution requires either access to the inverse of the incomplete gamma function or the use of root-finding techniques with the incomplete gamma function itself. The solution is $a = 1.2915$ and $b = 4.0995$. The width is 2.8080, wider than the first interval. Figure 12.1 shows the difference in the two intervals. The solid vertical bars represent the HPD interval. The total area to the left and right of these bars is 0.05. Any other 95% interval must also have this probability. To create the interval with 0.025 probability on each side, both bars must be moved to the right. To subtract the same probability on the right end that is added on the left end, the right limit must be moved a greater distance because the posterior density is lower over that interval than it is on the left end. This must lead to a wider interval. □

The following definition provides the equivalent result for any posterior distribution.

Definition 12.38 *For any posterior distribution the* $100(1-\alpha)\%$ **HPD credibility set** *is the set of parameter values* C *such that*

$$\Pr(\theta_j \in C) \geq 1 - \alpha \tag{12.7}$$

and

$$C = \{\theta_j : \pi_{\Theta_j|\mathbf{X}}(\theta_j|\mathbf{x}) \geq c\} \text{ for some } c,$$

where c *is the largest value for which the inequality* (12.7) *holds.*

This set may be the union of several intervals (which can happen with a multimodal posterior distribution). This definition produces the set of minimum total width that has the required posterior probability. Construction of the set is done by starting with a high value of c and then lowering it. As it decreases, the set C gets larger, as does the probability. The process continues until the probability reaches $1 - \alpha$. It should be obvious to see how the definition can be extended to the construction of a simultaneous credibility set for a vector of parameters, $\boldsymbol{\theta}$.

Sometimes it is the case that, while computing posterior probabilities is difficult, computing posterior moments may be easy. We can then use the Bayesian central limit theorem. The following is a paraphrase from Berger [13], p. 224.

Theorem 12.39 *If* $\pi(\theta)$ *and* $f_{\mathbf{X}|\Theta}(\mathbf{x}|\theta)$ *are both twice differentiable in the elements of* θ *and other commonly satisfied assumptions hold, then the posterior distribution of* Θ *given* $\mathbf{X} = \mathbf{x}$ *is asymptotically normal.*

The "commonly satisfied assumptions" are like those in Theorem 12.13. As in that theorem, it is possible to do further approximations. In particular, the asymptotic normal distribution also results if the posterior mode is substituted for the posterior mean and/or if the posterior covariance matrix is estimated by inverting the matrix of second partial derivatives of the negative logarithm of the posterior density.

Example 12.40 (Example 12.28 continued) *Construct a 95% credibility interval for* α *using the Bayesian central limit theorem.*

The posterior distribution has a mean of 2.499416 and a variance of $\alpha\theta^2 = 0.520590$. Using the normal approximation, the credibility interval is $2.499416 \pm 1.96(0.520590)^{1/2}$, which produces $a = 1.0852$ and $b = 3.9136$. This interval (with regard to the normal approximation) is HPD due to the symmetry of the normal distribution.

The approximation is centered at the posterior mode of 2.291132 (see Example 12.33). The second derivative of the negative logarithm of the posterior density [from (12.4)] is

$$-\frac{d^2}{d\alpha^2} \ln\left[\frac{\alpha^{11}e^{-4.801121\alpha}}{(11!)(1/4.801121)^{12}}\right] = \frac{11}{\alpha^2}.$$

The variance estimate is the reciprocal. Evaluated at the modal estimate of α we get $(2.291132)^2/11 = 0.477208$ for a credibility interval of $2.29113 \pm 1.96(0.477208)^{1/2}$, which produces $a = 0.9372$ and $b = 3.6451$. ☐

The same concepts can apply to the predictive distribution. However, the Bayesian central limit theorem does not help here because the predictive sample has only one member. The only potential use for it is that for a large original sample size we can replace the true posterior distribution in (12.3) with a multivariate normal distribution.

Example 12.41 (Example 12.28 continued) *Construct a 95% highest density prediction interval for the next observation.*

It is easy to see that the predictive density function (12.5) is strictly decreasing. Therefore the region with highest density runs from $a = 100$ to b. The value of b is determined from

$$
\begin{aligned}
0.95 &= \int_{100}^{b} \frac{12(4.801121)^{12}}{y(0.195951 + \ln y)^{13}} \, dy \\
&= \int_{0}^{\ln(b/100)} \frac{12(4.801121)^{12}}{(4.801121 + x)^{13}} \, dx \\
&= 1 - \left[\frac{4.801121}{4.801121 + \ln(b/100)} \right]^{12}
\end{aligned}
$$

and the solution is $b = 390.1840$. It is interesting to note that the mode of the predictive distribution is 100 (because the pdf is strictly decreasing) while the mean is infinite (with $b = \infty$ and an additional y in the integrand, after the transformation, the integrand is like $e^x x^{-13}$, which goes to infinity as x goes to infinity). ☐

The following example revisits a calculation done in Section 4.6.3. There the negative binomial distribution was derived as a gamma mixture of Poisson variables. The following example shows how the same calculations arise in a Bayesian context.

Example 12.42 *The number of claims in one year on a given policy is known to have a Poisson distribution. The parameter is not known, but the prior distribution has a gamma distribution with parameters α and θ. Suppose in the past year the policy had x claims. Use Bayesian methods to estimate the number of claims in the next year. Then repeat these calculations assuming claim counts for the past n years, $x_1, \ldots, x_n$.*

The key distributions are (where $x = 0, 1, \ldots, \lambda, \alpha, \theta > 0$):

Prior:
$$\pi(\lambda) = \frac{\lambda^{\alpha-1} e^{-\lambda/\theta}}{\Gamma(\alpha)\theta^\alpha}$$

Model:
$$p(x|\lambda) = \frac{\lambda^x e^{-\lambda}}{x!}$$

Joint:
$$p(x, \lambda) = \frac{\lambda^{x+\alpha-1} e^{-(1+1/\theta)\lambda}}{x!\Gamma(\alpha)\theta^\alpha}$$

Marginal:
$$p(x) = \int_0^\infty \frac{\lambda^{x+\alpha-1} e^{-(1+1/\theta)\lambda}}{x!\Gamma(\alpha)\theta^\alpha} d\lambda$$
$$= \frac{\Gamma(x+\alpha)}{x!\Gamma(\alpha)\theta^\alpha(1+1/\theta)^{x+\alpha}}$$
$$= \binom{x+\alpha-1}{x}\left(\frac{1}{1+\theta}\right)^\alpha\left(\frac{\theta}{1+\theta}\right)^x$$

Posterior:
$$\pi(\lambda|x) = \frac{\lambda^{x+\alpha-1} e^{-(1+1/\theta)\lambda}}{x!\Gamma(\alpha)\theta^\alpha} \Big/ \frac{\Gamma(x+\alpha)}{x!\Gamma(\alpha)\theta^\alpha(1+1/\theta)^{x+\alpha}}$$
$$= \frac{\lambda^{x+\alpha-1} e^{-(1+1/\theta)\lambda}(1+1/\theta)^{x+\alpha}}{\Gamma(x+\alpha)}$$

The marginal distribution is negative binomial with $r = \alpha$ and $\beta = \theta$. The posterior distribution is gamma with shape parameter "α" equal to $x + \alpha$ and scale parameter "θ" equal to $(1 + 1/\theta)^{-1} = \theta/(1 + \theta)$. The Bayes estimate of the Poisson parameter is the posterior mean, $(x + \alpha)\theta/(1 + \theta)$. For the predictive distribution, (12.3) gives

$$
\begin{aligned}
p(y|x) &= \int_0^\infty \frac{\lambda^y e^{-\lambda}}{y!} \frac{\lambda^{x+\alpha-1} e^{-(1+1/\theta)\lambda}(1+1/\theta)^{x+\alpha}}{\Gamma(x+\alpha)} d\lambda \\
&= \frac{(1+1/\theta)^{x+\alpha}}{y!\Gamma(x+\alpha)} \int_0^\infty \lambda^{y+x+\alpha-1} e^{-(2+1/\theta)\lambda} d\lambda \\
&= \frac{(1+1/\theta)^{x+\alpha}\Gamma(y+x+\alpha)}{y!\Gamma(x+\alpha)(2+1/\theta)^{y+x+\alpha}}, \quad y = 0, 1, \ldots,
\end{aligned}
$$

and some rearranging shows this to be a negative binomial distribution with $r = x + \alpha$ and $\beta = \theta/(1 + \theta)$. The expected number of claims for the next year is $(x + \alpha)\theta/(1 + \theta)$. Alternatively, from (12.6),

$$E(Y|x) = \int_0^\infty \lambda \frac{\lambda^{x+\alpha-1} e^{-(1+1/\theta)\lambda}(1+1/\theta)^{x+\alpha}}{\Gamma(x+\alpha)} d\lambda = \frac{(x+\alpha)\theta}{1+\theta}.$$

For a sample of size n, the key change is that the model distribution is now

$$p(\mathbf{x}|\lambda) = \frac{\lambda^{x_1+\cdots+x_n} e^{-n\lambda}}{x_1!\cdots x_n!}.$$

Following this through, the posterior distribution is still gamma, now with shape parameter $x_1 + \cdots + x_n + \alpha = n\bar{x} + \alpha$ and scale parameter $\theta/(1 + n\theta)$. The predictive distribution is still negative binomial, now with $r = n\bar{x} + \alpha$ and $\beta = \theta/(1 + n\theta)$. $\qquad\qquad\qquad\qquad\qquad\qquad\qquad\qquad\qquad\qquad\qquad\square$

When only moments are needed, the double-expectation formulas can be very useful. Provided the moments exist, for any random variables X and Y,

$$
\begin{aligned}
\mathrm{E}(Y) &= \mathrm{E}[\mathrm{E}(Y|X)], & (12.8) \\
\mathrm{Var}(Y) &= \mathrm{E}[\mathrm{Var}(Y|X)] + \mathrm{Var}[\mathrm{E}(Y|X)]. & (12.9)
\end{aligned}
$$

For the predictive distribution,

$$
\begin{aligned}
\mathrm{E}(Y|\mathbf{x}) &= \mathrm{E}_{\Theta|\mathbf{x}}[\mathrm{E}(Y|\Theta, \mathbf{x})] \\
&= \mathrm{E}_{\Theta|\mathbf{x}}[\mathrm{E}(Y|\Theta)]
\end{aligned}
$$

and

$$
\begin{aligned}
\mathrm{Var}(Y|\mathbf{x}) &= \mathrm{E}_{\Theta|\mathbf{x}}[\mathrm{Var}(Y|\Theta, \mathbf{x})] + \mathrm{Var}_{\Theta|\mathbf{x}}[\mathrm{E}(Y|\Theta, \mathbf{x})] \\
&= \mathrm{E}_{\Theta|\mathbf{x}}[\mathrm{Var}(Y|\Theta)] + \mathrm{Var}_{\Theta|\mathbf{x}}[\mathrm{E}(Y|\Theta)].
\end{aligned}
$$

The simplification on the inner expected value and variance results from the fact that, if Θ is known, the value of $\mathbf{x}$ provides no additional information about the distribution of Y. This is simply a restatement of (12.6).

Example 12.43 *Apply these formulas to obtain the predictive mean and variance for the previous example. Then anticipate the credibility formulas of Chapter 16.*

The predictive mean uses $\mathrm{E}(Y|\lambda) = \lambda$. Then,

$$
\mathrm{E}(Y|\mathbf{x}) = \mathrm{E}(\lambda|\mathbf{x}) = \frac{(n\bar{x} + \alpha)\theta}{1 + n\theta}.
$$

The predictive variance uses $\mathrm{Var}(Y|\lambda) = \lambda$, and then

$$
\begin{aligned}
\mathrm{Var}(Y|\mathbf{x}) &= \mathrm{E}(\lambda|\mathbf{x}) + \mathrm{Var}(\lambda|\mathbf{x}) \\
&= \frac{(n\bar{x} + \alpha)\theta}{1 + n\theta} + \frac{(n\bar{x} + \alpha)\theta^2}{(1 + n\theta)^2} \\
&= (n\bar{x} + \alpha)\frac{\theta}{1 + n\theta}\left(1 + \frac{\theta}{1 + n\theta}\right).
\end{aligned}
$$

These agree with the mean and variance of the known negative binomial distribution for y. However, these quantities were obtained from moments of the model (Poisson) and posterior (gamma) distributions. The predictive mean can be written as

$$
\frac{n\theta}{1 + n\theta}\bar{x} + \frac{1}{1 + n\theta}\alpha\theta,
$$

which is a weighted average of the mean of the data and the mean of the prior distribution. Note that as the sample size increases more weight is placed on the data and less on the prior opinion. The variance of the prior distribution can be increased by letting θ become large. As it should, this also increases the weight placed on the data. The credibility formulas in Chapter 16 generally consist of weighted averages of an estimate from the data and a prior opinion. □

12.4.3 Conjugate prior distributions and the linear exponential family

A large parametric family that includes many of the distributions we have encountered so far has a special use in Bayesian analysis. The definition is as follows:

Definition 12.44 *A random variable X (discrete or continuous) has a distribution which is from the **linear exponential family** if its pf may be parameterized in terms of a parameter θ and expressed as*

$$f(x;\theta) = \frac{p(x)e^{-\theta x}}{q(\theta)}. \tag{12.10}$$

*The function $p(x)$ depends only on x (not on θ), and the function $q(\theta)$ is a normalizing constant. Also, the support of the random variable must not depend on θ. The parameter θ is called the **natural parameter** of the distribution.*

Example 12.45 *Show that the exponential distribution is of the form (12.10).*

The pdf is

$$f(x;\beta) = \beta^{-1}e^{-\beta^{-1}x}.$$

If we let $\theta = 1/\beta$, then the pdf is

$$f(x;\theta) = \frac{1e^{-\theta x}}{\theta^{-1}},$$

which is of the form (12.10) with $p(x) = 1$ and $q(\theta) = 1/\theta$. □

Example 12.46 *Show that the Poisson distribution is a member of the linear exponential family.*

The pf is

$$f(x;\lambda) = \frac{\lambda^x e^{-\lambda}}{x!} = \frac{(1/x!)e^{-(-\ln\lambda)x}}{e^\lambda}.$$

If we let $\theta = -\ln\lambda$, then the pf is

$$f(x;\theta) = \frac{(1/x!)e^{-\theta x}}{e^{e^{-\theta}}},$$

which is of the form (12.10) with $p(x) = 1/x!$ and $q(\theta) = e^{e^{-\theta}}$. Note that in this parameterization the Poisson mean is $e^{-\theta}$. $\quad\square$

Example 12.47 *Show that the normal distribution with mean μ and known variance v is a member of the linear exponential family.*

The pdf is

$$
\begin{aligned}
f(x; \mu, v) &= (2\pi v)^{-1/2} \exp\left[-\frac{1}{2v}(x - \mu)^2\right] \\
&= (2\pi v)^{-1/2} \exp\left(-\frac{x^2}{2v} + \frac{\mu}{v}x - \frac{\mu^2}{2v}\right) \\
&= \frac{(2\pi v)^{-1/2} \exp\left(-\dfrac{x^2}{2v}\right) \exp\left(\dfrac{\mu}{v}x\right)}{\exp\left(\dfrac{\mu^2}{2v}\right)}.
\end{aligned}
$$

If we let $\theta = -\mu/v$, the pdf is

$$
f(x; \theta, v) = \frac{(2\pi v)^{-1/2} \exp\left(-\dfrac{x^2}{2v}\right) \exp\left(-\theta x\right)}{\exp\left(\dfrac{\theta^2 v}{2}\right)},
$$

which is of the form (12.10) with $p(x) = (2\pi v)^{-1/2} \exp[-x^2/(2v)]$, and $q(\theta) = \exp(\theta^2 v/2)$. $\quad\square$

We now find the mean and variance of the distribution defined by (12.10). First, note that
$$
\ln f(x; \theta) = \ln p(x) - \theta x - \ln q(\theta).
$$

Differentiate with respect to θ to obtain

$$
\frac{\partial}{\partial \theta} f(x; \theta) = \left[-x - \frac{q'(\theta)}{q(\theta)}\right] f(x; \theta). \tag{12.11}
$$

Integrate (or sum) over the range of x (known not to depend on θ) to obtain

$$
\int \frac{\partial}{\partial \theta} f(x; \theta)\, dx = -\int x f(x; \theta)\, dx - \frac{q'(\theta)}{q(\theta)} \int f(x; \theta)\, dx.
$$

On the left-hand side, interchange the order of differentiation and integration (or summation) to obtain

$$
\frac{\partial}{\partial \theta}\left[\int f(x; \theta)\, dx\right] = -\int x f(x; \theta)\, dx - \frac{q'(\theta)}{q(\theta)} \int f(x; \theta)\, dx.
$$

We know that $\int f(x;\theta)\,dx = 1$ and $\int x f(x;\theta)\,dx = \mathrm{E}(X)$ and thus

$$\frac{\partial}{\partial\theta}(1) = -\mathrm{E}(X) - \frac{q'(\theta)}{q(\theta)}.$$

In other words, the mean is

$$\mathrm{E}(X) = \mu(\theta) = -\frac{q'(\theta)}{q(\theta)} = -\frac{d}{d\theta}\ln q(\theta). \qquad (12.12)$$

To obtain the variance, (12.11) may first be rewritten as

$$\frac{\partial}{\partial\theta}f(x;\theta) = -[x - \mu(\theta)]f(x;\theta).$$

Differentiate again with respect to θ to obtain

$$\begin{aligned}
\frac{\partial^2}{\partial\theta^2}f(x;\theta) &= \mu'(\theta)f(x;\theta) - [x - \mu(\theta)]\frac{\partial}{\partial\theta}f(x;\theta) \\
&= \mu'(\theta)f(x;\theta) + [x - \mu(\theta)]^2 f(x;\theta).
\end{aligned}$$

Again, integrate over the range of x to obtain

$$\int \frac{\partial^2}{\partial\theta^2}f(x,\theta)\,dx = \mu'(\theta)\int f(x;\theta)\,dx + \int [x - \mu(\theta)]^2 f(x;\theta)\,dx.$$

In other words

$$\int [x - \mu(\theta)]^2 f(x;\theta)\,dx = -\mu'(\theta) + \frac{\partial^2}{\partial\theta^2}\int f(x;\theta)\,dx.$$

Because $\mu(\theta)$ is the mean, the left-hand side is the variance (by definition), and then because the second term on the right-hand side is zero, we obtain

$$\mathrm{Var}(X) = v(\theta) = -\mu'(\theta) = -\frac{d^2}{d\theta^2}\ln q(\theta). \qquad (12.13)$$

In Example 12.42 it turned out the posterior distribution was of the same type as the prior distribution (gamma). This makes calculations relatively easy. A definition of this concept follows.

Definition 12.48 *A prior distribution is said to be a **conjugate prior distribution** for a given model if the resulting posterior distribution is of the same type as the prior (but perhaps with different parameters).*

The following theorem shows that, if the model is a member of the linear exponential family, a conjugate prior distribution is easy to find.

Theorem 12.49 *Suppose that given* $\Theta = \theta$ *the random variables* $X_1, \ldots, X_n$ *are independent and identically distributed with pf*

$$f_{X_j|\Theta}(X_j|\theta) = \frac{p(x_j)e^{-\theta x_j}}{q(\theta)},$$

where Θ *has pdf*

$$\pi(\theta) = \frac{[q(\theta)]^{-k}e^{-\theta\mu k}}{c(\mu, k)},$$

where k *and* μ *are parameters of the distribution and* $c(\mu, k)$ *is the normalizing constant. Then the posterior pf* $\pi_{\Theta|\mathbf{X}}(\theta|\mathbf{x})$ *is of the same form as* $\pi(\theta)$.

Proof: The posterior distribution is

$$\pi\left(\theta|\mathbf{x}\right) \propto \frac{\left[\prod_{j=1}^{n} p(x_j)\right] e^{-\theta\Sigma x_j}}{q(\theta)^n} \frac{[q(\theta)]^{-k}e^{-\theta\mu k}}{c(\mu, k)}$$

$$\propto [q(\theta)]^{-(k+n)} \exp\left[\left(-\theta\frac{\mu k + \sum x_j}{k+n}\right)(k+n)\right]$$

$$\propto [q(\theta)]^{-k^*} \exp(-\theta\mu^* k^*),$$

which is of the same form as $\pi(\theta)$ with parameters

$$k^* = k + n,$$
$$\mu^* = \frac{\mu k + \sum x_j}{k+n} = \frac{k}{k+n}\mu + \frac{n}{k+n}\overline{x}.$$

$\square$

Example 12.50 *Show that for the Poisson model the conjugate prior as given in Theorem 12.49 is the gamma distribution.*

From Example 12.46 we have that $q(\theta) = \exp(e^{-\theta})$ and $\lambda = \exp(-\theta)$. The prior as given by the theorem is

$$\pi(\theta) \propto \left[\exp(e^{-\theta})\right]^{-k} \exp(-\theta\mu k).$$

Then the prior density for λ is

$$\pi(\lambda) \propto [\exp(\lambda)]^{-k}\lambda^{\mu k}\lambda^{-1} = \lambda^{\mu k-1}e^{-\lambda k},$$

which is a gamma distribution with $\alpha = \mu k$ and $\theta = 1/k$. The term λ^{-1} appears because it is $|d\theta/d\lambda|$, which is needed for the change of variable. $\square$

12.4.4   Computational issues

It should be obvious by now that all Bayesian analyses proceed by taking integrals or sums. So at least conceptually it is always possible to do a Bayesian analysis. However, only in rare cases are the integrals or sums easy to do, and that means most Bayesian analyses will require numerical integration. While one-dimensional integrations are easy to do to a high degree of accuracy, multidimensional integrals are much more difficult to approximate. A great deal of effort has been expended with regard to solving this problem. A number of ingenious methods have been developed. Some of them are summarized in Klugman [77]. However, the one that is widely used today is called Markov chain Monte Carlo simulation. A good discussion of this method can be found in [118] and actuarial applications can be found in [21] and [119].

There is another way which completely avoids computational problems. This is illustrated using the example (in an abbreviated form) from Meyers [92], which also employed this technique. The example also shows how a Bayesian analysis is used to estimate a function of parameters.

Example 12.51 *Data were collected on 100 losses in excess of 100,000. The single-parameter Pareto distribution is to be used with $\theta = 100,000$ and α unknown. The objective is to estimate the layer average severity for the layer from 1,000,000 to 5,000,000. For the observations, $\sum_{j=1}^{100} \ln x_j = 1{,}208.4354$.*

The model density is

$$
\begin{aligned}
f_{\mathbf{X}|A}(\mathbf{x}|\alpha) &= \prod_{j=1}^{100} \frac{\alpha(100{,}000)^{\alpha}}{x_j^{\alpha+1}} \\
&= \exp\left[100\ln\alpha + 100\alpha\ln 100{,}000 - (\alpha+1)\sum_{j=1}^{100}\ln x_j\right] \\
&= \exp\left(100\ln\alpha - \frac{100\alpha}{1.75} - 1{,}208.4354\right).
\end{aligned}
$$

The density appears in column 3 of Table 12.6. To prevent computer overflow, the value 1,208.4354 was not subtracted prior to exponentiation. This makes the entries proportional to the true density function. The prior density is given in the second column. It was chosen based on a belief that the true value is in the range 1–2.5 and is more likely to be near 1.5 than at the ends. The posterior density is then obtained using (12.2). The elements of the numerator are found in column 4. The denominator is no longer an integral but a sum. The sum is at the bottom of column 4 and then the scaled values are in column 5.

We can see from column 5 that the posterior mode is at $\alpha = 1.7$, as compared to the maximum likelihood estimate of 1.75 (see Exercise 12.69). The posterior mean of α could be found by adding the product of columns 1 and 5. Here we are interested in a layer average severity. For this problem it

Table 12.6 Bayesian estimation of a layer average severity

α	$\pi(\alpha)$	$f(\mathbf{x}\vert\alpha)$	$\pi(\alpha)f(\mathbf{x}\vert\alpha)$	$\pi(\alpha\vert\mathbf{x})$	LAS(α)	$\pi\times L^*$	$\pi(\alpha\vert\mathbf{x})l(\alpha)^2$
1.0	0.0400	1.52×10^{-25}	6.10×10^{-27}	0.0000	160,944	0	6,433
1.1	0.0496	6.93×10^{-24}	3.44×10^{-25}	0.0000	118,085	2	195,201
1.2	0.0592	1.37×10^{-22}	8.13×10^{-24}	0.0003	86,826	29	2,496,935
1.3	0.0688	1.36×10^{-21}	9.33×10^{-23}	0.0038	63,979	243	15,558,906
1.4	0.0784	7.40×10^{-21}	5.80×10^{-22}	0.0236	47,245	1,116	52,737,840
1.5	0.0880	2.42×10^{-20}	2.13×10^{-21}	0.0867	34,961	3,033	106,021,739
1.6	0.0832	5.07×10^{-20}	4.22×10^{-21}	0.1718	25,926	4,454	115,480,050
1.7	0.0784	7.18×10^{-20}	5.63×10^{-21}	0.2293	19,265	4,418	85,110,453
1.8	0.0736	7.19×10^{-20}	5.29×10^{-21}	0.2156	14,344	3,093	44,366,353
1.9	0.0688	5.29×10^{-20}	3.64×10^{-21}	0.1482	10,702	1,586	16,972,802
2.0	0.0640	2.95×10^{-20}	1.89×10^{-21}	0.0768	8,000	614	4,915,383
2.1	0.0592	1.28×10^{-20}	7.57×10^{-22}	0.0308	5,992	185	1,106,259
2.2	0.0544	4.42×10^{-21}	2.40×10^{-22}	0.0098	4,496	44	197,840
2.3	0.0496	1.24×10^{-21}	6.16×10^{-23}	0.0025	3,380	8	28,650
2.4	0.0448	2.89×10^{-22}	1.29×10^{-23}	0.0005	2,545	1	3,413
2.5	0.0400	5.65×10^{-23}	2.26×10^{-24}	0.0001	1,920	0	339
	1.0000		2.46×10^{-20}	1.0000		18,827	445,198,597

$^*\pi(\alpha\vert\mathbf{x})$LAS($\alpha$)

is

$$
\begin{aligned}
\text{LAS}(\alpha) &= \text{E}(X \wedge 5{,}000{,}000) - \text{E}(X \wedge 1{,}000{,}000) \\
&= \frac{100{,}000^{\alpha}}{\alpha - 1}\left(\frac{1}{1{,}000{,}000^{\alpha-1}} - \frac{1}{5{,}000{,}000^{\alpha-1}}\right), \quad \alpha \neq 1, \\
&= 100{,}000\left(\ln 5{,}000{,}000 - \ln 1{,}000{,}000\right), \quad \alpha = 1.
\end{aligned}
$$

Values of LAS(α) for the 16 possible values of α appear in column 6. The last two columns are then used to obtain the posterior expected values of the layer average severity. The point estimate is the posterior mean, 18,827. The posterior standard deviation is

$$
\sqrt{445{,}198{,}597 - 18{,}827^2} = 9{,}526.
$$

We can also use columns 5 and 6 to construct a credibility interval. Discarding the first five rows and the last four rows eliminates 0.0406 of posterior probability. That leaves (5,992, 34,961) as a 96% credibility interval for the layer average severity. Part of Meyers' paper was the observation that even with a fairly large sample the accuracy of the estimate is poor.

The discrete approximation to the prior distribution could be refined by using many more than 16 values. This adds little to the spreadsheet effort. The number was kept small here only for display purposes.   □

12.4.5 Exercises

12.67 Show that, if Y is the predictive distribution in Example 12.28, then $\ln Y - \ln 100$ has the Pareto distribution.

12.68 Determine the posterior distribution of α in Example 12.28 if the prior distribution is an arbitrary gamma distribution. To avoid confusion, denote the first parameter of this gamma distribution by γ. Next determine a particular combination of gamma parameters so that the posterior mean is the maximum likelihood estimate of α regardless of the specific values of $x_1, \ldots, x_n$. Is this prior improper?

12.69 For Example 12.51 demonstrate that the maximum likelihood estimate of α is 1.75.

12.70 Let $x_1, \ldots, x_n$ be a random sample from a lognormal distribution with unknown parameters μ and σ. Let the prior density be $\pi(\mu, \sigma) = \sigma^{-1}$.

   (a) Write the posterior pdf of μ and σ up to a constant of proportionality.

   (b) Determine Bayesian estimators of μ and σ by using the posterior mode.

   (c) Fix σ at the posterior mode as determined in part (b) and then determine the exact (conditional) pdf of μ. Then use it to determine a 95% HPD credibility interval for μ.

12.71 A random sample of size 100 has been taken from a gamma distribution with α known to be 2, but θ unknown. For this sample, $\sum_{j=1}^{100} x_j = 30{,}000$. The prior distribution for θ is inverse gamma with β taking the role of α and λ taking the role of θ.

   (a) Determine the exact posterior distribution of θ. At this point the values of β and λ have yet to be specified.

   (b) The population mean is 2θ. Determine the posterior mean of 2θ using the prior distribution first with $\beta = \lambda = 0$ [this is equivalent to $\pi(\theta) = \theta^{-1}$] and then with $\beta = 2$ and $\lambda = 250$ (which is a prior mean of 250). Then, in each case, determine a 95% credibility interval with 2.5% probability on each side.

   (c) Determine the posterior variance of 2θ and use the Bayesian central limit theorem to construct a 95% credibility interval for 2θ using each of the two prior distributions given in part (b).

   (d) Determine the maximum likelihood estimate of θ and then use the estimated variance to construct a 95% confidence interval for 2θ.

12.72 Suppose that given $\Theta = \theta$ the random variables $X_1, \ldots, X_n$ are independent and binomially distributed with pf

$$f_{X_j|\Theta}(x_j|\theta) = \binom{K_j}{x_j} \theta^{x_j}(1-\theta)^{K_j - x_j}, \quad x_j = 0, 1, \ldots, K_j,$$

and Θ itself is beta distributed with parameters a and b and pdf

$$\pi(\theta) = \frac{\Gamma(a+b)}{\Gamma(a)\Gamma(b)} \theta^{a-1}(1-\theta)^{b-1}, \quad 0 < \theta < 1.$$

(a) Verify that the marginal pf of X_j is

$$f_{X_j}(x_j) = \frac{\binom{-a}{x_j}\binom{-b}{K_j - x_j}}{\binom{-a-b}{K_j}}, \quad x_j = 0, 1, \ldots, K_j,$$

and $E(X_j) = aK_j/(a+b)$. This distribution is termed the binomial–beta or negative hypergeometric distribution.

(b) Determine the posterior pdf $\pi_{\Theta|\mathbf{X}}(\theta|\mathbf{x})$ and the posterior mean $E(\Theta|\mathbf{x})$.

12.73 Suppose that given $\Theta = \theta$ the random variables $X_1, \ldots, X_n$ are independent and identically exponentially distributed with pdf

$$f_{X_j|\Theta}(x_j|\theta) = \theta e^{-\theta x_j}, \quad x_j > 0,$$

and Θ is itself gamma distributed with parameters $\alpha > 1$ and $\beta > 0$,

$$\pi(\theta) = \frac{\theta^{\alpha-1}e^{-\theta/\beta}}{\Gamma(\alpha)\beta^{\alpha}}, \quad \theta > 0.$$

(a) Verify that the marginal pdf of X_j is

$$f_{X_j}(x_j) = \alpha \beta^{-\alpha}(\beta^{-1} + x_j)^{-\alpha-1}, \quad x_j > 0,$$

and

$$E(X_j) = \frac{1}{\beta(\alpha-1)}.$$

This distribution is one form of the Pareto distribution.

(b) Determine the posterior pdf $\pi_{\Theta|\mathbf{X}}(\theta|\mathbf{x})$ and the posterior mean $E(\Theta|\mathbf{x})$.

12.74 Suppose that given $\Theta = \theta$ the random variables $X_1, \ldots, X_n$ are independent and identically negative binomially distributed with parameters r and θ with pf

$$f_{X_j|\Theta}(x_j|\theta) = \binom{r + x_j - 1}{x_j} \theta^r (1-\theta)^{x_j}, \quad x_j = 0, 1, 2, \ldots,$$

and Θ itself is beta distributed with parameters a and b and pdf

$$\pi(\theta) = \frac{\Gamma(a+b)}{\Gamma(a)\Gamma(b)}\theta^{a-1}(1-\theta)^{b-1}, \quad 0 < \theta < 1.$$

(a) Verify that the marginal pf of X_j is

$$f_{X_j}(x_j) = \frac{\Gamma(r+x_j)}{\Gamma(r)x_j!}\frac{\Gamma(a+b)}{\Gamma(a)\Gamma(b)}\frac{\Gamma(a+r)\Gamma(b+x_j)}{\Gamma(a+r+b+x_j)}, \quad x_j = 0,1,2,\ldots,$$

and

$$E(X_j) = \frac{rb}{a-1}.$$

This distribution is termed the **generalized Waring distribution**. The special case where $b = 1$ is the **Waring distribution** and the **Yule distribution** if $r = 1$ and $b = 1$.

(b) Determine the posterior pdf $f_{\Theta|\mathbf{X}}(\theta|\mathbf{x})$ and the posterior mean $E(\Theta|\mathbf{x})$.

12.75 Suppose that given $\Theta = \theta$ the random variables $X_1,\ldots,X_n$ are independent and identically normally distributed with mean μ and variance θ^{-1} and Θ is gamma distributed with parameters α and (θ replaced by) $1/\beta$.

(a) Verify that the marginal pdf of X_j is

$$f_{X_j}(x_j) = \frac{\Gamma(\alpha+\frac{1}{2})}{\sqrt{2\pi\beta}\,\Gamma(\alpha)}\left[1 + \frac{1}{2\beta}(x_j-\mu)^2\right]^{-\alpha-1/2}, \quad -\infty < x_j < \infty,$$

which is a form of the t-distribution.

(b) Determine the posterior pdf $f_{\Theta|\mathbf{X}}(\theta|\mathbf{x})$ and the posterior mean $E(\theta|\mathbf{x})$.

12.76 Prove that the binomial distribution with pf

$$f(x;p) = \binom{n}{x}p^x(1-p)^{n-x}$$

is of the form (12.10) and identify θ, $p(x)$, and $q(\theta)$.

12.77 Consider the negative binomial distribution with pf

$$f(x;\alpha,\beta) = \frac{\Gamma(\alpha+x)}{\Gamma(\alpha)x!}\left(\frac{\beta}{1+\beta}\right)^\alpha\left(\frac{1}{1+\beta}\right)^x.$$

If α is fixed, show that $f(x;\alpha,\beta)$ is of the form (12.10) and identify θ, $p(x)$, and $q(\theta)$.

12.78 Suppose $X_1, \ldots, X_n$ are independent and identically distributed with distribution (12.10). Prove that the maximum likelihood estimate of the mean is the sample mean. In other words, if $\hat{\theta}$ is the maximum likelihood estimator of θ, prove that

$$\widehat{\mu(\theta)} = \mu(\hat{\theta}) = \bar{X}.$$

12.79 Consider the generalization of (12.10) given by

$$f(x; \theta) = \frac{p(m, x) e^{-m\theta x}}{[q(\theta)]^m},$$

where m is a known parameter. Prove that the mean is still given by (12.12) but the variance is given by $v(\theta)/m$, where $v(\theta)$ is given by (12.13).

12.80 Let $X_1, \ldots, X_n$ be independent and identically distributed conditional on Θ with pf

$$f_{X_j|\Theta}(x_j|\theta) = \frac{p(x_j) e^{-\theta x_j}}{q(\theta)}.$$

Let $S = X_1 + \cdots + X_n$.

(a) Show that, conditional on Θ, S has pf of the form

$$f_{S|\Theta}(s|\theta) = \frac{p_n(s) e^{-\theta s}}{[q(\theta)]^n},$$

where $p_n(s)$ does not depend on θ.

(b) Prove that the posterior distribution $\pi_{\Theta|\mathbf{X}}(\theta|\mathbf{x})$ is the same as the (conditional) distribution of $\Theta|S$,

$$\pi_{\Theta|\mathbf{X}}(\theta|\mathbf{x}) = \frac{f_{S|\Theta}(s|\theta) \pi(\theta)}{f_S(s)},$$

where $\pi(\theta)$ is the pf of Θ and $f_S(s)$ is the marginal pf of S.

12.81 Suppose that given N the random variable X is binomially distributed with parameters N and p.

(a) Show that, if N is Poisson distributed, so is X (unconditionally) and identify the parameters.

(b) Show that, if N is binomially distributed, so is X (unconditionally) and identify the parameters.

(c) Show that, if N is negative binomially distributed, so is X (unconditionally) and identify the parameters.

12.82 (*) A die is selected at random from an urn that contains two six-sided dice. Die number 1 has three faces with the number 2 while one face each has the numbers 1, 3, and 4. Die number 2 has three faces with the number 4 while one face each has the numbers 1, 2, and 3. The first five rolls of the die yielded the numbers 2, 3, 4, 1, and 4 in that order. Determine the probability that the selected die was die number 2.

12.83 (*) The number of claims in a year, Y, has a distribution which depends on a parameter θ. As a random variable, Θ has the uniform distribution on the interval $(0, 1)$. The unconditional probability that Y is 0 is greater than 0.35. For each conditional pf given below, determine if it is possible that it is the true conditional pf of Y.

(a) $\Pr(Y = y|\theta) = e^{-\theta}\theta^y/y!$.

(b) $\Pr(Y = y|\theta) = (y + 1)\theta^2(1 - \theta)^y$.

(c) $\Pr(Y = y|\theta) = \binom{2}{y}\theta^y(1 - \theta)^{2-y}$.

12.84 (*) Your prior distribution concerning the unknown value of H is $\Pr(H = \frac{1}{4}) = \frac{4}{5}$ and $\Pr(H = \frac{1}{2}) = \frac{1}{5}$. The observation from a single experiment has distribution $\Pr(D = d|H = h) = h^d(1 - h)^{1-d}$ for $d = 0, 1$. The result of a single experiment is $d = 1$. Determine the posterior distribution of H.

12.85 (*) The number of claims in one year, Y, has the Poisson distribution with parameter θ. The parameter θ has the exponential distribution with pdf $\pi(\theta) = e^{-\theta}$. A particular insured had no claims in one year. Determine the posterior distribution of θ for this insured.

12.86 (*) The number of claims in one year, Y, has the Poisson distribution with parameter θ. The prior distribution has the gamma distribution with pdf $\pi(\theta) = \theta e^{-\theta}$. There was one claim in one year. Determine the posterior pdf of θ.

12.87 (*) Each individual car's claim count has a Poisson distribution with parameter λ. All individual cars have the same parameter. The prior distribution is gamma with parameters $\alpha = 50$ and $\theta = 1/500$. In a two-year period, the insurer covers 750 and 1,100 cars in years 1 and 2, respectively. There were 65 and 112 claims in years one and two, respectively. Determine the coefficient of variation of the posterior gamma distribution.

12.88 (*) The number of claims, r, made by an individual in one year has the binomial distribution with pf $f(r) = \binom{3}{r}\theta^r(1 - \theta)^{3-r}$. The prior distribution for θ has pdf $\pi(\theta) = 6(\theta - \theta^2)$. There was one claim in a one-year period. Determine the posterior pdf of θ.

12.89 (*) The number of claims for an individual in one year has a Poisson distribution with parameter λ. The prior distribution for λ has the gamma distribution with mean 0.14 and variance 0.0004. During the past two years a total of 110 claims has been observed. In each year there were 310 policies in force. Determine the expected value and variance of the posterior distribution of λ.

12.90 (*) The number of claims for an individual in one year has a Poisson distribution with parameter λ. The prior distribution for λ is exponential with an expected value of 2. There were three claims in the first year. Determine the posterior distribution of λ.

12.91 (*) The number of claims in one year has the binomial distribution with $n = 3$ and θ unknown. The prior distribution for θ is beta with pdf $\pi(\theta) = 2800\theta^3(1-\theta)^4$, $0 < \theta < 1$. Two claims were observed. Determine each of the following.

(a) The posterior distribution of θ.

(b) The expected value of θ from the posterior distribution.

12.92 (*) An individual risk has exactly one claim each year. The amount of the single claim has an exponential distribution with pdf $f(x) = te^{-tx}$, $x > 0$. The parameter t has a prior distribution with pdf $\pi(t) = te^{-t}$. A claim of 5 has been observed. Determine the posterior pdf of t.

12.93 Suppose that given $\Theta_1 = \theta_1$ and $\Theta_2 = \theta_2$ the random variables $X_1, \ldots,$ X_n are independent and identically normally distributed with mean θ_1 and variance θ_2^{-1}. Suppose also that the conditional distribution of Θ_1 given $\Theta_2 = \theta_2$ is a normal distribution with mean μ and variance σ^2/θ_2 and Θ_2 is gamma distributed with parameters α and $\theta = 1/\beta$.

(a) Show that the posterior conditional distribution of Θ_1 given $\Theta_2 = \theta_2$ is normally distributed with mean

$$\mu_* = \frac{1}{1+n\sigma^2}\mu + \frac{n\sigma^2}{1+n\sigma^2}\overline{x}$$

and variance

$$\sigma_*^2 = \frac{\sigma^2}{\theta_2(1+n\sigma^2)}$$

and the posterior marginal distribution of Θ_2 is gamma distributed with parameters

$$\alpha_* = \alpha + \frac{n}{2}$$

and

$$\beta_* = \beta + \frac{1}{2}\sum_{i=1}^{n}(x_i - \overline{x})^2 + \frac{n(\overline{x}-\mu)^2}{2(1+n\sigma^2)}.$$

(b) Find the posterior marginal means $E(\Theta_1|\mathbf{x})$ and $E(\Theta_2|\mathbf{x})$.

Table 12.7 Number of hospital liability claims by year

Year	Number of claims
1985	6
1986	2
1987	3
1988	0
1989	2
1990	1
1991	2
1992	5
1993	1
1994	3

Table 12.8 Hospital liability claims by frequency

Frequency (k)	Number of observations (n_k)
0	1
1	2
2	3
3	2
4	0
5	1
6	1
7+	0

12.5 ESTIMATION FOR DISCRETE DISTRIBUTIONS

12.5.1 Poisson

The principles of estimation discussed earlier in this chapter for continuous models can be applied equally to frequency distributions. We will now illustrate the methods of estimation by fitting a Poisson model.

Example 12.52 *A hospital liability policy has experienced the number of claims over a 10-year period given in Table* 12.7. *Estimate the Poisson parameter using the method of moments and the method of maximum likelihood.*

These data can be summarized in a different way. We can count the number of years in which exactly zero claims occurred, one claim occurred, and so on, as in Table 12.8.

The total number of claims for the period 1985–1994 is 25. Hence, the average number of claims per year is 2.5. The average can also be computed from Table 12.8. Let n_k denote the number of years in which a frequency of exactly k claims occurred. The expected frequency (sample mean) is

$$\bar{x} = \frac{\sum_{k=0}^{\infty} kn_k}{\sum_{k=0}^{\infty} n_k},$$

where n_k represents the number of observed values at frequency k. Hence the method-of-moments estimate of the Poisson parameter is $\hat{\lambda} = 2.5$.

Maximum likelihood estimation can easily be carried out on these data. The likelihood contribution of an observation of k is p_k. Then the likelihood for the entire set of observations is

$$L = \prod_{k=0}^{\infty} p_k^{n_k}$$

and the loglikelihood is

$$l = \sum_{k=0}^{\infty} n_k \ln p_k.$$

The likelihood and loglikelihood functions are considered to be functions of the unknown parameters. In the case of the Poisson distribution, there is only one parameter, making the maximization easy.

For the Poisson distribution,

$$p_k = \frac{e^{-\lambda}\lambda^k}{k!}$$

and

$$\ln p_k = -\lambda + k \ln \lambda - \ln k!.$$

The loglikelihood is

$$\begin{aligned} l &= \sum_{k=0}^{\infty} n_k(-\lambda + k \ln \lambda - \ln k!) \\ &= -\lambda n + \sum_{k=0}^{\infty} k\, n_k \ln \lambda - \sum_{k=0}^{\infty} n_k \ln k!, \end{aligned}$$

where $n = \sum_{k=0}^{\infty} n_k$ is the sample size. Differentiating the loglikelihood with respect to λ, we obtain

$$\frac{dl}{d\lambda} = -n + \sum_{k=0}^{\infty} k\, n_k \frac{1}{\lambda}.$$

By setting the derivative of the loglikelihood to zero, the maximum likelihood estimate is obtained as the solution of the resulting equation. The estimator is then

$$\hat{\lambda} = \frac{\sum_{k=0}^{\infty} kn_k}{n} = \bar{x}.$$

From this it can be seen that for the Poisson distribution the maximum likelihood and the method-of-moments estimators are identical.

If N has a Poisson distribution with mean λ, then

$$E(\hat{\lambda}) = E(N) = \lambda$$

and

$$\mathrm{Var}(\hat{\lambda}) = \frac{\mathrm{Var}(N)}{n} = \frac{\lambda}{n}.$$

Hence, $\hat{\lambda}$ is unbiased and consistent. From Theorem 12.13, the maximum likelihood estimator is asymptotically normally distributed with mean λ and variance

$$
\begin{aligned}
\mathrm{Var}(\hat{\lambda}) &= \left\{ -n\mathrm{E}\left[\frac{d^2}{d\lambda^2} \ln p_N \right] \right\}^{-1} \\
&= \left\{ -n\mathrm{E}\left[\frac{d^2}{d\lambda^2} (-\lambda + N \ln \lambda - \ln N!) \right] \right\}^{-1} \\
&= \left[n\mathrm{E}(N/\lambda^2) \right]^{-1} \\
&= \left(n\lambda^{-1} \right)^{-1} = \frac{\lambda}{n}.
\end{aligned}
$$

In this case the asymptotic approximation to the variance is equal to its true value. From this information, we can construct an approximate 95% confidence interval for the true value of the parameter. The interval is $\hat{\lambda} \pm 1.96(\hat{\lambda}/n)^{1/2}$. For this example, the interval becomes $(1.52, 3.48)$. This confidence interval is only an approximation because it relies on large sample theory. The sample size is very small and such a confidence interval should be used with caution. □

The formulas presented so far have assumed that the counts at each observed frequency are known. Occasionally, data are collected so that this is not given. The most common example is to have a final entry given as $k+$, where the count is the number of times k or more claims were observed. If n_{k+} is the number of times this was observed, the contribution to the likelihood function is

$$(p_k + p_{k+1} + \cdots)^{n_{k+}} = (1 - p_0 - \cdots - p_{k-1})^{n_{k+}}.$$

The same adjustments apply to grouped frequency data of any kind. Suppose there were five observations at frequencies 3–5. The contribution to the likelihood function is

$$(p_3 + p_4 + p_5)^5.$$

Table 12.9   Data for Example 12.53

No. of claims/day	Observed no. of days
0	47
1	97
2	109
3	62
4	25
5	16
6+	9

Example 12.53 *For the data in Table 12.9[11] determine the maximum likelihood estimate for the Poisson distribution.*

The likelihood function is

$$L = p_0^{47} p_1^{97} p_2^{109} p_3^{62} p_4^{25} p_5^{16} (1 - p_0 - p_1 - p_2 - p_3 - p_4 - p_5)^9,$$

and when written as a function of λ, it becomes somewhat complicated. While the derivative can be taken, solving the equation when it is set equal to zero will require numerical methods. It may be just as easy to use a numerical method to directly maximize the function. A reasonable starting value can be obtained by assuming that all nine observations were exactly at 6 and then using the sample mean. Of course, this will understate the true maximum likelihood estimate, but should be a good place to start. For this particular example, the maximum likelihood estimate is $\hat{\lambda} = 2.0226$, which is very close to the value obtained when all the counts were recorded.   □

12.5.2   Negative binomial

The moment equations are

$$r\beta = \frac{\sum_{k=0}^{\infty} k n_k}{n} = \bar{x} \tag{12.14}$$

and

$$r\beta(1 + \beta) = \frac{\sum_{k=0}^{\infty} k^2 n_k}{n} - \left(\frac{\sum_{k=0}^{\infty} k n_k}{n} \right)^2 = s^2 \tag{12.15}$$

with solutions $\hat{\beta} = (s^2/\bar{x}) - 1$ and $\hat{r} = \bar{x}/\hat{\beta}$. Note that this variance estimate is obtained by dividing by n, not $n - 1$. This is a common, though not required,

---

[11] This is the same data as will be analyzed in Example 13.15 except the observations at 6 or more have been combined.

approach when using the method of moments. Also note that, if $s^2 < \bar{x}$, the estimate of β will be negative, an inadmissible value.

Example 12.54 (Example 12.52 continued) *Estimate the negative binomial parameters by the method of moments.*

The sample mean and the sample variance are 2.5 and 3.05 (verify this), respectively, and the estimates of the parameters are $\hat{r} = 11.364$ and $\hat{\beta} = 0.22$.   □

When compared to the Poisson distribution with the same mean, it can be seen that β is a measure of "extra-Poisson" variation. A value of $\beta = 0$ means no extra-Poisson variation, while a value of $\beta = 0.22$ implies a 22% increase in the variance when compared to the Poisson distribution with the same mean.
We now examine maximum likelihood estimation. The loglikelihood for the negative binomial distribution is

$$
\begin{aligned}
l &= \sum_{k=0}^{\infty} n_k \ln p_k \\
&= \sum_{k=0}^{\infty} n_k \left[\ln \binom{r+k-1}{k} - r\ln(1+\beta) + k\ln\beta - k\ln(1+\beta) \right].
\end{aligned}
$$

The loglikelihood is a function of the two parameters β and r. In order to find the maximum of the loglikelihood, we differentiate with respect to each of the parameters, set the derivatives equal to zero, and solve for the parameters. The derivatives of the loglikelihood are

$$
\frac{\partial l}{\partial \beta} = \sum_{k=0}^{\infty} n_k \left(\frac{k}{\beta} - \frac{r+k}{1+\beta} \right) \tag{12.16}
$$

and

$$
\begin{aligned}
\frac{\partial l}{\partial r} &= -\sum_{k=0}^{\infty} n_k \ln(1+\beta) + \sum_{k=0}^{\infty} n_k \frac{\partial}{\partial r} \ln \frac{(r+k-1)\cdots r}{k!} \\
&= -n\ln(1+\beta) + \sum_{k=0}^{\infty} n_k \frac{\partial}{\partial r} \ln \prod_{m=0}^{k-1} (r+m) \\
&= -n\ln(1+\beta) + \sum_{k=0}^{\infty} n_k \frac{\partial}{\partial r} \sum_{m=0}^{k-1} \ln(r+m) \\
&= -n\ln(1+\beta) + \sum_{k=1}^{\infty} n_k \sum_{m=0}^{k-1} \frac{1}{r+m}. \tag{12.17}
\end{aligned}
$$

Setting these equations to zero yields

$$\hat{\mu} = \hat{r}\hat{\beta} = \frac{\sum_{k=0}^{\infty} k n_k}{n} = \bar{x} \tag{12.18}$$

and

$$n \ln(1 + \hat{\beta}) = \sum_{k=1}^{\infty} n_k \left(\sum_{m=0}^{k-1} \frac{1}{\hat{r} + m} \right). \tag{12.19}$$

Note that the maximum likelihood estimator of the mean is the sample mean (as, by definition, in the method of moments). Equations (12.18) and (12.19) can be solved numerically. Replacing $\hat{\beta}$ in (12.19) by $\hat{\mu}/\hat{r}$ yields the equation

$$H(\hat{r}) = n \ln \left(1 + \frac{\bar{x}}{\hat{r}} \right) - \sum_{k=1}^{\infty} n_k \left(\sum_{m=0}^{k-1} \frac{1}{\hat{r} + m} \right) = 0. \tag{12.20}$$

If the right-hand side of (12.15) is greater than the right-hand side of (12.14), it can be shown that there is a unique solution of (12.20). If not, then the negative binomial model is probably not a good model to use because the sample variance does not exceed the sample mean.[12]

Equation (12.20) can be solved numerically for $\hat{r}$ using the Newton–Raphson method. The required equation for the kth iteration is

$$r_k = r_{k-1} - \frac{H(r_{k-1})}{H'(r_{k-1})}.$$

A useful starting value for r_0 is the moment-based estimator of r. Of course, any numerical root-finding method (e.g., bisection, secant) may be used.

The loglikelihood is a function of two variables. It can be maximized directly using methods like those described in Appendix F. For the case of the negative binomial distribution with complete data, because we know the estimator of the mean must be the sample mean, setting $\beta = \bar{x}/r$ reduces this to a one-dimensional problem.

Example 12.55 *Determine the maximum likelihood estimates of the negative binomial parameters for the data in Example 12.52.*

The maximum occurs at $\hat{r} = 10.9650$ and $\hat{\beta} = 0.227998$. □

Example 12.56 *Tröbliger [130] studied the driving habits of 23,589 automobile drivers in a class of automobile insurance by counting the number of*

---

[12] In other words, when the sample variance is less than or equal to the mean, the loglikelihood function will not have a maximum. The function will keep increasing as r goes to infinity and β goes to zero with the product remaining constant. This effectively says that the negative binomial distribution that best matches the data is the Poisson distribution that is a limiting case.

Table 12.10   Two models for automobile claims frequency

No. of claims/year	No. of drivers	Poisson expected	Negative binomial expected
0	20,592	20,420.9	20,596.8
1	2,651	2,945.1	2,631.0
2	297	212.4	318.4
3	41	10.2	37.8
4	7	0.4	4.4
5	0	0.0	0.5
6	1	0.0	0.1
7+	0	0.0	0.0
Parameters		$\lambda = 0.144220$	$r = 1.11790$ $\beta = 0.129010$
Loglikelihood		$-10{,}297.84$	$-10{,}223.42$

accidents per driver in a one-year time period. The data as well as fitted Poisson and negative binomial distributions are given in Table 12.10. Based on the information presented, which distribution appears to provide a better model?

The expected counts are found by multiplying the sample size (23,589) by the probability assigned by the model. It is clear that the negative binomial probabilities produce expected counts that are much closer to those that were observed. In addition, the loglikelihood function is maximized at a significantly higher value. Formal procedures for model selection (including what it means to be *significantly higher*) are discussed in Chapter 13. However, in this case, the superiority of the negative binomial model is apparent.   □

12.5.3 Binomial

The binomial distribution has two parameters, m and q. Frequently, the value of m is known and fixed. In this case, only one parameter, q, needs to be estimated. In many insurance situations, q is interpreted as the probability of some event such as death or disability. In such cases the value of q is usually estimated as

$$\hat{q} = \frac{\text{number of observed events}}{\text{maximum number of possible events}},$$

which is the method-of-moments estimator when m is known.

In situations where frequency data are in the form of the previous examples in this chapter, the value of the parameter m, the largest possible observation, may be known and fixed or unknown. In any case, m must be no smaller than the largest observation. The loglikelihood is

$$
\begin{aligned}
l &= \sum_{k=0}^{m} n_k \ln p_k \\
&= \sum_{k=0}^{m} n_k \left[\ln \binom{m}{k} + k \ln q + (m - k) \ln(1 - q) \right].
\end{aligned}
$$

When m is known and fixed, one needs only maximize l with respect to q.

$$
\frac{\partial l}{\partial q} = \frac{1}{q} \sum_{k=0}^{m} k n_k - \frac{1}{1 - q} \sum_{k=0}^{m} (m - k) n_k.
$$

Setting this equal to zero yields

$$
\hat{q} = \frac{1}{m} \frac{\sum_{k=0}^{m} k n_k}{\sum_{k=0}^{m} n_k},
$$

which is the sample proportion of observed events. For the method of moments, with m fixed, the estimator of q is the same as the maximum likelihood estimator because the moment equation is

$$
mq = \frac{\sum_{k=0}^{m} k n_k}{\sum_{k=0}^{m} n_k}.
$$

When m is unknown, the maximum likelihood estimator of q is

$$
\hat{q} = \frac{1}{\hat{m}} \frac{\sum_{k=0}^{\infty} k n_k}{\sum_{k=0}^{\infty} n_k}, \tag{12.21}
$$

where $\hat{m}$ is the maximum likelihood estimate of m. An easy way to approach the maximum likelihood estimation of m and q is to create a *likelihood profile* for various possible values of m as follows:

Step 1:   Start with $\hat{m}$ equal to the largest observation.
Step 2:   Obtain $\hat{q}$ using (12.21).
Step 3:   Calculate the loglikelihood at these values.
Step 4:   Increase $\hat{m}$ by 1.
Step 5:   Repeat steps 2–4 until a maximum is found.

As with the negative binomial, there need not be a pair of parameters that maximizes the likelihood function. In particular, if the sample mean is less than or equal to the sample variance, the procedure above will lead to ever increasing loglikelihood values as the value of $\hat{m}$ is increased. Once again, the trend is toward a Poisson model. This can be checked out using the data from Example 12.52.

Table 12.11   Number of claims per policy

No. of claims/policy	No. of policies
0	5,367
1	5,893
2	2,870
3	842
4	163
5	23
6	1
7	1
8+	0

Example 12.57 *The number of claims per policy during a one-year period for a block of 15,160 insurance policies are given in Table 12.11. Obtain moment-based and maximum likelihood estimators.*

The sample mean and variance are 0.985422 and 0.890355, respectively. The variance is smaller than the mean, suggesting the binomial as a reasonable distribution to try. The method of moments leads to

$$mq = 0.985422$$

and

$$mq(1 - q) = 0.890355.$$

Hence, $\hat{q} = 0.096474$ and $\hat{m} = 10.21440$. However, m can only take on integer values. We choose $\hat{m} = 10$ by rounding. Then we adjust the estimate of $\hat{q}$ to 0.0985422 from the first moment equation. Doing this will result in a model variance which differs from the sample variance because $10(0.0985422)(1 - 0.0985422) = 0.888316$. This shows one of the pitfalls of using the method of moments with integer-valued parameters.

We now turn to maximum likelihood estimation. From the data $m \geq 7$. If m is known, then only q needs to be estimated. If m is unknown, then we can produce a likelihood profile by maximizing the likelihood for fixed values of m starting at 7 and increasing until a maximum is found. The results are in Table 12.12.

The largest loglikelihood value occurs at $m = 10$. If, a priori, the value of m is unknown, then the maximum likelihood estimates of the parameters are $\hat{m} = 10$ and $\hat{q} = 0.0985422$. This is the same as the adjusted moment estimates. This is not necessarily the case for all data sets.   □

Table 12.12 Binomial likelihood profile

$\hat{m}$	$\hat{q}$	$-$Loglikelihood
7	0.140775	19,273.56
8	0.123178	19,265.37
9	0.109491	19,262.02
10	0.098542	19,260.98
11	0.089584	19,261.11
12	0.082119	19,261.84

12.5.4 The $(a, b, 1)$ class

Estimation of the parameters for the $(a, b, 1)$ class follows the same general principles that were used in connection with the $(a, b, 0)$ class.

Assuming that the data are in the same form as the previous examples, the likelihood is, using (4.13),

$$L = \left(p_0^M\right)^{n_0} \prod_{k=1}^{\infty} (p_k^M)^{n_k} = \left(p_0^M\right)^{n_0} \prod_{k=1}^{\infty} \left[(1 - p_0^M)p_k^T\right]^{n_k}.$$

The loglikelihood is,

$$
\begin{aligned}
l &= n_0 \ln p_0^M + \sum_{k=1}^{\infty} n_k \left[\ln(1 - p_0^M) + \ln p_k^T\right] \\
&= n_0 \ln p_0^M + \sum_{k=1}^{\infty} n_k \ln(1 - p_0^M) + \sum_{k=1}^{\infty} n_k \left[\ln p_k - \ln(1 - p_0)\right],
\end{aligned}
$$

where the last statement follows from $p_k^T = p_k/(1-p_0)$. The three parameters of the $(a, b, 1)$ class are p_0^M, a, and b, where a and b determine $p_1, p_2, \ldots$.

Then it can be seen that

$$l = l_0 + l_1$$

with

$$l_0 = n_0 \ln p_0^M + \sum_{k=1}^{\infty} n_k \ln(1 - p_0^M),$$

$$l_1 = \sum_{k=1}^{\infty} n_k \left[\ln p_k - \ln(1 - p_0)\right],$$

where l_0 depends only on the parameter p_0^M and l_1 is independent of p_0^M, depending only on a and b. This simplifies the maximization because

$$\frac{\partial l}{\partial p_0^M} = \frac{\partial l_0}{\partial p_0^M} = \frac{n_0}{p_0^M} - \sum_{k=1}^{\infty} \frac{n_k}{1 - p_0^M} = \frac{n_0}{p_0^M} - \frac{n - n_0}{1 - p_0^M},$$

resulting in

$$\hat{p}_0^M = \frac{n_0}{n},$$

the proportion of observations at zero. This is the natural estimator because p_0^M represents the probability of an observation of zero.

Similarly, because the likelihood factors conveniently, the estimation of a and b is independent of p_0^M. Note that although a and b are parameters maximization should not be done with respect to them. That is because not all values of a and b produce admissible probability distributions.[13] For the zero-modified Poisson distribution, the relevant part of the loglikelihood is

$$
\begin{aligned}
l_1 &= \sum_{k=1}^{\infty} n_k \left[\ln \frac{e^{-\lambda}\lambda^k}{k!} - \ln(1 - e^{-\lambda}) \right] \\
&= -(n - n_0)\lambda + \left(\sum_{k=1}^{\infty} k\, n_k \right) \ln \lambda - (n - n_0)\ln(1 - e^{-\lambda}) + c \\
&= -(n - n_0)[\lambda + \ln(1 - e^{-\lambda})] + n\bar{x}\ln\lambda + c,
\end{aligned}
$$

where $\bar{x} = \frac{1}{n}\sum_{k=0}^{\infty} k n_k$ is the sample mean, $n = \sum_{k=0}^{\infty} n_k$, and c is independent of λ. Hence,

$$
\begin{aligned}
\frac{\partial l_1}{\partial \lambda} &= -(n - n_0) - (n - n_0)\frac{e^{-\lambda}}{1 - e^{-\lambda}} + n\frac{\bar{x}}{\lambda} \\
&= -\frac{n - n_0}{1 - e^{-\lambda}} + \frac{n\bar{x}}{\lambda}.
\end{aligned}
$$

Setting this to zero yields

$$\bar{x}(1 - e^{-\lambda}) = \frac{n - n_0}{n}\lambda. \tag{12.22}$$

By graphing each side as a function of λ, it is clear that, if $n_0 > 0$, there exist exactly two roots: one is $\lambda = 0$, the other is $\lambda > 0$. Equation (12.22) can be solved numerically to obtain $\hat{\lambda}$. Note that, because $\hat{p}_0^M = n_0/n$ and $p_0 = e^{-\lambda}$, (12.22) can be rewritten as

$$\bar{x} = \frac{1 - \hat{p}_0^M}{1 - p_0}\lambda. \tag{12.23}$$

Because the right-hand side of (12.23) is the theoretical mean of the zero-modified Poisson distribution (when $\hat{p}_0^M$ is replaced with p_0^M), (12.23) is a

---

[13] Maximization can be done with respect to any parameterization because maximum likelihood estimation is invariant under parameter transformations. However, it is more difficult to maximize over bounded regions because numerical methods are difficult to constrain and analytic methods will fail due to a lack of differentiability. Therefore, estimation is usually done with respect to particular class members, such as the Poisson.

moment equation. Hence, an alternative estimation method yielding the same results as the maximum likelihood method is to equate p_0^M to the sample proportion at zero and the theoretical mean to the sample mean. This suggests that, by fixing the zero probability to the observed proportion at zero and equating the low order moments, a modified moment method can be used to get starting values for numerical maximization of the likelihood function. Because the maximum likelihood method has better asymptotic properties, it is preferable to use the modified moment method only to obtain starting values.

For the purpose of obtaining estimates of the asymptotic variance of the maximum likelihood estimator of λ, it is easy to obtain

$$\frac{\partial^2 l_1}{\partial \lambda^2} = (n - n_0)\frac{e^{-\lambda}}{(1 - e^{-\lambda})^2} - \frac{n\bar{x}}{\lambda^2},$$

and the expected value is obtained by observing that $E(\bar{x}) = (1 - p_0^M)\lambda/(1 - e^{-\lambda})$. Finally, p_0^M may be replaced by its estimator, n_0/n. The variance of $\hat{p}_0^M$ is obtained by observing that the numerator, n_0, has a binomial distribution and therefore the variance is $p_0^M(1 - p_0^M)/n$.

For the zero-modified binomial distribution,

$$
\begin{aligned}
l_1 &= \sum_{k=1}^{m} n_k \left\{ \ln\left[\binom{m}{k} q^k (1 - q)^{m-k}\right] - \ln[1 - (1 - q)^m] \right\} \\
&= \left(\sum_{k=1}^{m} k n_k\right) \ln q + \sum_{k=1}^{m} (m - k) n_k \ln(1 - q) \\
&\quad - \sum_{k=1}^{m} n_k \ln[1 - (1 - q)^m] + c \\
&= n\bar{x} \ln q + m(n - n_0) \ln(1 - q) - n\bar{x} \ln(1 - q) \\
&\quad - (n - n_0) \ln[1 - (1 - q)^m] + c
\end{aligned}
$$

where c does not depend on q and

$$\frac{\partial l_1}{\partial q} = \frac{n\bar{x}}{q} - \frac{m(n - n_0)}{1 - q} + \frac{n\bar{x}}{1 - q} - \frac{(n - n_0)m(1 - q)^{m-1}}{1 - (1 - q)^m}.$$

Setting this to zero yields

$$\bar{x} = \frac{1 - \hat{p}_0^M}{1 - p_0} mq, \tag{12.24}$$

where we recall that $p_0 = (1 - q)^m$. This equation matches the theoretical mean with the sample mean.

If m is known and fixed, the maximum likelihood estimator of p_0^M is still

$$\hat{p}_0^M = \frac{n_0}{n}.$$

However, even with m known, (12.24) must be solved numerically for q. When m is unknown and also needs to be estimated, the above procedure can be followed for different values of m until the maximum of the likelihood function is obtained.

The zero-modified negative binomial (or extended truncated negative binomial) distribution is a bit more complicated because three parameters need to be estimated. Of course, the maximum likelihood estimator of p_0^M is $\hat{p}_0^M = n_0/n$ as before, reducing the problem to the estimation of r and β. The part of the loglikelihood relevant to r and β is

$$l_1 = \sum_{k=1}^{\infty} n_k \ln p_k - (n - n_0) \ln(1 - p_0). \tag{12.25}$$

Hence

$$l_1 = \sum_{k=1}^{\infty} n_k \ln \left[\binom{k+r-1}{k} \left(\frac{1}{1+\beta} \right)^r \left(\frac{\beta}{1+\beta} \right)^k \right]$$
$$- (n - n_0) \ln \left[1 - \left(\frac{1}{1+\beta} \right)^r \right]. \tag{12.26}$$

This function needs to be maximized over the (r, β) plane to obtain the maximum likelihood estimates. This can be done numerically using maximization procedures such as those described in Appendix F. Starting values can be obtained by the modified moment method by setting $\hat{p}_0^M = n_0/n$ and equating the first two moments of the distribution to the first two sample moments. It is generally easier to use raw moments (moments about the origin) than central moments for this purpose. In practice, it may be more convenient to maximize (12.25) rather than (12.26) because one can take advantage of the recursive scheme

$$p_k = p_{k-1} \left(a + \frac{b}{k} \right)$$

in evaluating (12.25). This makes computer programming a bit easier.

For zero-truncated distributions there is no need to estimate the probability at zero because it is known to be zero. The remaining parameters are estimated using the same formulas developed for the zero-modified distributions.

Example 12.58 *The data set in Table* 12.13 *comes from Beard et al.* [12]. *Determine a model that adequately describes the data.*

When a Poisson distribution is fitted to it, the resulting fit is very poor. There is too much probability for one accident and two little at subsequent values. The geometric distribution is tried as a one-parameter alternative. It has loglikelihood

Table 12.13   Fitted distributions to Beard data

Accidents	Observed	Poisson	Geometric	ZM Poisson	ZM geom.
0	370,412	369,246.9	372,206.5	370,412.0	370,412.0
1	46,545	48,643.6	43,325.8	46,432.1	46,555.2
2	3,935	3,204.1	5,043.2	4,138.6	3,913.6
3	317	140.7	587.0	245.9	329.0
4	28	4.6	68.3	11.0	27.7
5	3	0.1	8.0	0.4	2.3
6+	0	0.0	1.0	0.0	0.2
Parameters		λ: 0.13174	β: 0.13174	p_0^M: 0.87934	p_0^M: 0.87934
				λ: 0.17827	β: 0.091780
Loglikelihood		$-171{,}373$	$-171{,}479$	$-171{,}160$	$-171{,}133$

$$
\begin{aligned}
l &= -n\ln(1+\beta) + \sum_{k=1}^{\infty} n_k \ln\left(\frac{\beta}{1+\beta}\right)^k \\
&= -n\ln(1+\beta) + \sum_{k=1}^{\infty} kn_k[\ln\beta - \ln(1+\beta)] \\
&= -n\ln(1+\beta) + n\bar{x}[\ln\beta - \ln(1+\beta)] \\
&= -(n+n\bar{x})\ln(1+\beta) + n\bar{x}\ln\beta,
\end{aligned}
$$

where $\bar{x} = \sum_{k=1}^{\infty} k\, n_k/n$ and $n = \sum_{k=0}^{\infty} n_k$.
Differentiation reveals that the loglikelihood has a maximum at

$$
\hat{\beta} = \bar{x}.
$$

A qualitative look at the numbers indicates that the zero-modified geometric distribution matches the data better than the other three models considered. A formal analysis is done in Example 13.16.   □

12.5.5   Compound models

For the method of moments, the first few moments can be matched with the sample moments. The system of equations can be solved to obtain the moment based estimators. Note that the number of parameters in the compound model is the sum of the number of parameters in the primary and secondary distributions. The first two theoretical moments for compound distributions are

$$
\begin{aligned}
\mathrm{E}(S) &= \mathrm{E}(N)\mathrm{E}(M) \\
\mathrm{Var}(S) &= \mathrm{E}(N)\,\mathrm{Var}(M) + \mathrm{E}(M)^2\,\mathrm{Var}(N).
\end{aligned}
$$

These results were developed in Chapter 6. The first three moments for the compound Poisson distribution are given in (4.27).

Maximum likelihood estimation is also carried out as before. The loglikelihood to be maximized is

$$l = \sum_{k=0}^{\infty} n_k \ln g_k.$$

When g_k is the probability of a compound distribution, the loglikelihood can be maximized numerically. The first and second derivatives of the loglikelihood can be obtained by using approximate differentiation methods as applied directly to the loglikelihood function at the maximum value.

Example 12.59 *Determine various properties of the Poisson–zero-truncated geometric distribution. This distribution is also called the Polya–Aeppli distribution.*

For the zero-truncated geometric distribution the pgf is

$$P_2(z) = \frac{[1 - \beta(z - 1)]^{-1} - (1 + \beta)^{-1}}{1 - (1 + \beta)^{-1}}$$

and therefore the pgf of the Polya–Aeppli distribution is

$$
\begin{aligned}
P(z) &= P_1[P_2(z)] = \exp\left(\lambda\left\{\frac{[1 - \beta(z - 1)]^{-1} - (1 + \beta)^{-1}}{1 - (1 + \beta)^{-1}} - 1\right\}\right) \\
&= \exp\left\{\lambda\frac{[1 - \beta(z - 1)]^{-1} - 1}{1 - (1 + \beta)^{-1}}\right\}.
\end{aligned}
$$

The mean is

$$P'(1) = \lambda(1 + \beta)$$

and the variance is

$$P''(1) + P'(1) - [P'(1)]^2 = \lambda(1 + \beta)(1 + 2\beta).$$

Alternatively, $E(N) = \mathrm{Var}(N) = \lambda$, $E(M) = 1 + \beta$, and $\mathrm{Var}(M) = \beta(1 + \beta)$. Then,

$$
\begin{aligned}
E(S) &= \lambda(1 + \beta), \\
\mathrm{Var}(S) &= \lambda\beta(1 + \beta) + \lambda(1 + \beta)^2 = \lambda(1 + \beta)(1 + 2\beta).
\end{aligned}
$$

From Theorem 4.51, the probability at zero is

$$g_0 = P_1(0) = e^{-\lambda}.$$

The successive values of g_k are computed easily using the compound Poisson recursion

$$g_k = \frac{\lambda}{k}\sum_{j=1}^{k} j f_j g_{k-j}, \qquad k = 1, 2, 3, \dots, \tag{12.27}$$

Table 12.14 Automobile claims by year

Year	Exposure	Claims
1986	2,145	207
1987	2,452	227
1988	3,112	341
1989	3,458	335
1990	3,698	362
1991	3,872	359

where $f_j = \beta^{j-1}/(1+\beta)^j$, $j = 1, 2, \ldots$. For any values of λ and β, the loglikelihood function can be easily evaluated. ☐

Example 13.17 provides a data set for which the Polya–Aeppli distribution is a good choice.

Another useful compound Poisson distribution is the Poisson–extended truncated negative binomial (Poisson–ETNB) distribution. Although it does not matter if the secondary distribution is modified or truncated, we prefer the truncated version here so that the parameter r may be extended.[14] Special cases are: $r = 1$, which is the Poisson–geometric (also called Polya–Aeppli); $r \to 0$, which is the Poisson–logarithmic (negative binomial); and $r = -0.5$, which is called the Poisson–inverse Gaussian. This name is not consistent with the others. Here the inverse Gaussian distribution is a mixing distribution (see Section 4.6.9). Example 13.18 provides a data set for which the Poisson–inverse Gaussian distribution is a good choice.

12.5.6   Effect of exposure on maximum likelihood estimation

In Section 4.6.11 the effect of exposure on discrete distributions was discussed. When aggregate data from a large group of insureds is obtained, maximum likelihood estimation is still possible. The following example illustrates this for the Poisson distribution.

Example 12.60 *Determine the maximum likelihood estimate of the Poisson parameter for the data in Table* 12.14.

Let λ be the Poisson parameter for a single exposure. If year k has e_k exposures, then the number of claims has a Poisson distribution with parameter

---

[14] This does not contradict Theorem 4.54. When $-1 < r < 0$, it is still the case that changing the probability at zero will not produce new distributions. What is true is that there is no probability at zero which will lead to an ordinary $(a, b, 0)$ negative binomial secondary distribution.

λe_k. If n_k is the number of claims in year k, the likelihood function is

$$L = \prod_{k=1}^{6} \frac{e^{-\lambda e_k} (\lambda e_k)^{n_k}}{n_k!}.$$

The maximum likelihood estimate is found by

$$l = \ln L = \sum_{k=1}^{6} [-\lambda e_k + n_k \ln(\lambda e_k) - \ln(n_k!)],$$

$$\frac{\partial l}{\partial \lambda} = \sum_{k=1}^{6} \left(-e_k + n_k \lambda^{-1}\right) = 0,$$

$$\hat{\lambda} = \frac{\sum_{k=1}^{6} n_k}{\sum_{k=1}^{6} e_k} = \frac{1,831}{18,737} = 0.09772.$$

$\square$

In this example the answer is what we expected it to be, the average number of claims per exposure. This technique will work for any distribution in the $(a, b, 0)^{15}$ and compound classes. But care must be taken in the interpretation of the model. For example, if we use a negative binomial distribution, we are assuming that each exposure unit produces claims according to a negative binomial distribution. This is different from assuming that total claims have a negative binomial distribution because they arise from individuals who each have a Poisson distribution but with different parameters.

12.5.7 Exercises

12.94 Assume that the binomial parameter m is known. Consider the maximum likelihood estimator of q.

(a) Show that the maximum likelihood estimator is unbiased.

(b) Determine the variance of the maximum likelihood estimator.

(c) Show that the asymptotic variance as given in Theorem 12.13 is the same as that developed in part (b).

(d) Determine a simple formula for a confidence interval using (9.4) on page 276 that is based on replacing q with $\hat{q}$ in the variance term.

(e) Determine a more complicated formula for a confidence interval using (9.3) that is not based on such a replacement. This should be done in a manner similar to that used in Example 11.12 on page 309.

---

[15] For the binomial distribution, the usual problem that m must be an integer remains.

Table 12.15   Data for Exercise 12.96

No. of claims	No. of policies
0	9,048
1	905
2	45
3	2
4+	0

12.95 Use (12.18) to determine the maximum likelihood estimator of β for the geometric distribution. In addition, determine the variance of the maximum likelihood estimator and verify that it matches the asymptotic variance as given in Theorem 12.13.

12.96 A portfolio of 10,000 risks produced the claim counts in Table 12.15.

(a) Determine the maximum likelihood estimate of λ for a Poisson model and then determine a 95% confidence interval for λ.

(b) Determine the maximum likelihood estimate of β for a geometric model and then determine a 95% confidence interval for β.

(c) Determine the maximum likelihood estimate of r and β for a negative binomial model.

(d) Assume that $m = 4$. Determine the maximum likelihood estimate of q of the binomial model.

(e) Construct 95% confidence intervals for q using the methods developed in parts (d) and (e) of Exercise 12.94.

(f) Determine the maximum likelihood estimate of m and q by constructing a likelihood profile.

12.97 An automobile insurance policy provides benefits for accidents caused by both underinsured and uninsured motorists. Data on 1,000 policies revealed the information in Table 12.16.

(a) Determine the maximum likelihood estimate of λ for a Poisson model for each of the variables N_1 = number of underinsured claims and N_2 = number of uninsured claims.

(b) Assume that N_1 and N_2 are independent. Use Theorem 4.37 on page 74 to determine a model for $N = N_1 + N_2$.

12.98 An alternative method of obtaining a model for N in Exercise 12.97 would be to record the total number of underinsured and uninsured claims for each of the 1,000 policies. Suppose this was done and the results were as in Table 12.17.

Table 12.16 Data for Exercise 12.97

No. of claims	Underinsured	Uninsured
0	901	947
1	92	50
2	5	2
3	1	1
4	1	0
5+	0	0

Table 12.17 Data for Exercise 12.98

No. of claims	No. of policies
0	861
1	121
2	13
3	3
4	1
5	0
6	1
7+	0

(a) Determine the maximum likelihood estimate of λ for a Poisson model.

(b) The answer to part (a) matched the answer to part (c) of the previous exercise. Demonstrate that this must always be so.

(c) Determine the maximum likelihood estimate of β for a geometric model.

(d) Determine the maximum likelihood estimate of r and β for a negative binomial model.

(e) Assume that $m = 7$. Determine the maximum likelihood estimate of q of the binomial model.

(f) Determine the maximum likelihood estimates of m and q by constructing a likelihood profile.

12.99 The data in Table 12.18 represent the number of prescriptions filled in one year for a group of elderly members of a group insurance plan.

(a) Determine the maximum likelihood estimate of λ for a Poisson model.

(b) Determine the maximum likelihood estimate of β for a geometric model and then determine a 95% confidence interval for β.

Table 12.18   Data for Exercise 12.99

No. of prescriptions	Frequency	No. of prescriptions	Frequency
0	82	16–20	40
1–3	49	21–25	38
4–6	47	26–35	52
7–10	47	36–	91
11–15	57		

(c) Determine the maximum likelihood estimates of r and β for a negative binomial model.

12.6   BIVARIATE MODELS

12.6.1   Introduction

At times a bivariate distribution with dependent variables is the appropriate model. One such situation is a joint life annuity or insurance. Here the timing of the payments depends on the first or second death of two individuals. Because these individuals are often related (typically spouses), the times of death will be dependent. As another example, in casualty insurances it is common to record the expenses that are directly related to the payment of the loss, referred to as the allocated loss adjustment expenses (ALAE). The loss and the ALAE are usually strongly positively correlated.

There are a variety of sources for bivariate and multivariate models. Among them are the books by Hutchinson and Lai ([64]), Kotz, Balakrishnan, and Johnson ([80]), and Mardia ([89]). However, most of the distributions have marginal distributions that are not of interest for actuarial applications or have the parameters related in an unsuitable manner (for example, a bivariate gamma distribution in which both X and Y must have the same value for α). One exception is the bivariate lognormal distribution for which the logarithms of the two variables have a bivariate normal distribution.

Of more interest and practical value are methods which construct bivariate models from known marginal distributions. For example, suppose it were known that losses have the Pareto distribution and that ALAE have the gamma distribution. Then those parameters could be estimated (and the models themselves determined) from the marginal data. Then they could be combined into a bivariate distribution that introduces a degree of association between the two variables. Among the methods available, the copula has received a lot of attention in the actuarial literature and is the only one that will be covered here.

Table 12.19   Twenty-four losses with ALAE

Loss	ALAE	Loss	ALAE
1,500	301	11,750	2,530
2,000	3,043	12,500	165
2,500	415	14,000	175
2,500	4,940	14,750	28,217
4,500	395	15,000	2,072
5,000	25	17,500	6,328
5,750	34,474	19,833	212
7,000	50	30,000	2,172
7,000	10,593	33,033	7,845
7,500	50	44,887	2,178
9,000	406	62,500	12,251
10,000	1,174	210,000	7,357

12.6.2   Copulas

Copula distributions are created using a function, also called a copula. This function must itself be a legitimate bivariate distribution function over the unit square with uniform marginals. Denote the two marginal distribution functions $F_X(x)$ and $F_Y(y)$ and the copula function $C(u, v)$. The bivariate distribution function created by the three is then

$$F_{X,Y}(x, y) = C[F_X(x), F_Y(y)].$$

A simple but fairly useless example is the copula $C(u, v) = uv$. This creates the bivariate distribution function $F_{X,Y}(x, y) = F_X(x)F_Y(y)$, which is true for independent variables.

A good general introduction is [42] and an introduction for actuaries can be found in [40]. The paper by Frees, Carriere, and Valdez, [39] works with Frank's copula for a study of joint lifetimes. An expanded version of the example presented here can be found in [78]. The last two cited papers show how to write the likelihood function under various truncations and censoring.

Example 12.61 *The loss and ALAE were recorded for each of* 24 *claims* (*Table* 12.19). *Determine a model for the joint distribution using Frank's copula with Pareto distributions for both marginals.*

Frank's copula is (where $\log_\alpha$ means the logarithm base α)

$$C(u, v) = \log_\alpha \left[1 + \frac{(\alpha^u - 1)(\alpha^v - 1)}{\alpha - 1} \right], \qquad (12.28)$$

where the parameter α controls the degree of association between the two variables. Values of α less than 1 indicate a positive association, values greater than 1 indicate an inverse association, and 1 indicates independence. If we let β and θ be the parameters of the marginal Pareto distribution for X (where θ is the scale parameter) and let γ and τ be the parameters for Y (with τ the scale parameter), the bivariate distribution function is

$$F(x,y) = \log_\alpha \left\{ 1 + \frac{[\alpha^{1-(1+x/\theta)^{-\beta}} - 1][\alpha^{1-(1+y/\tau)^{-\gamma}} - 1]}{\alpha - 1} \right\}.$$

Taking partial derivatives with respect to x and y provides the joint density function

$$f(x,y) = \frac{(\alpha - 1)\dfrac{\beta\gamma}{\theta\tau}\alpha^{2-(1+x/\theta)^{-\beta}-(1+y/\tau)^{-\gamma}} \times (1+x/\theta)^{-\beta-1}(1+y/\tau)^{-\gamma-1}\ln\alpha}{\{\alpha - 1 + [\alpha^{1-(1+x/\theta)^{-\beta}} - 1][\alpha^{1-(1+y/\tau)^{-\gamma}} - 1]\}^2}.$$

Starting values for the four Pareto parameters were obtained by finding the maximum likelihood estimates for the two marginal distributions. Simplex maximization yields the estimates $\hat{\alpha} = 0.133024$, $\hat{\beta} = 2.59889$, $\hat{\theta} = 36{,}141.4$, $\hat{\gamma} = 0.759943$, and $\hat{\tau} = 803.839$. The positive association is apparent and could be tested. One way is to use the likelihood ratio test discussed in Chapter 13. It turns out that with the small sample size there is not sufficient evidence to be sure there is a positive association. □

A number of results concerning Frank's copula can be found in the paper by Genest [41]. Two are presented here. To simulate an (X, Y) pair, begin by simulating the X value from the marginal distribution. This can be done using the standard inversion technique. Follow this by simulating a value of Y from the conditional distribution of Y given $X = x$. To do this, first note that the distribution function is

$$F_{Y|X}(y|x) = \frac{(\partial/\partial x)F(x,y)}{f_X(x)}.$$

For Frank's copula we have

$$\frac{\partial}{\partial x}F(x,y) = f_X(x)\frac{\partial}{\partial u}C(u,v)\big|_{u=F_X(x),v=F_Y(y)}$$

$$= \frac{f_X(x)\alpha^{F_X(x)}[\alpha^{F_Y(y)} - 1]}{\alpha - 1 + [\alpha^{F_X(x)} - 1][\alpha^{F_Y(y)} - 1]}.$$

To simulate a conditional value of Y using the inversion method discussed in Chapter 17, obtain a uniform(0,1) random number r and solve the equation

$$\frac{\alpha^{F_X(x)}[\alpha^{F_Y(y)} - 1]}{\alpha - 1 + [\alpha^{F_X(x)} - 1][\alpha^{F_Y(y)} - 1]} = r$$

for $F_Y(y)$ to obtain

$$\alpha^{F_Y(y)} = 1 + \frac{r(\alpha - 1)}{\alpha^{F_X(x)}(1 - r) + r}$$

or

$$F_Y(y) = \frac{1}{\ln \alpha} \ln \left[1 + \frac{r(\alpha - 1)}{\alpha^{F_X(x)}(1 - r) + r} \right].$$

The right-hand side is a number and then the distribution function of Y can be inverted to solve for the simulated value.

The regression function can be found from

$$
\begin{aligned}
E(Y|X = x) &= \int \left[1 - F_{Y|x}(y|x) \right] dy \\
&= \int \left\{ 1 - \frac{\alpha^{F_X(x)} [\alpha^{F_Y(y)} - 1]}{\alpha - 1 + [\alpha^{F_X(x)} - 1][\alpha^{F_Y(y)} - 1]} \right\} dy,
\end{aligned}
$$

but it is likely that the integral will have to be done numerically.

12.6.3 Exercise

12.100 Consider the data set in Table 12.19. Fit a bivariate distribution using Frank's copula where each marginal distribution has the inverse exponential distribution.

12.7 MODELS WITH COVARIATES

12.7.1 Introduction

It may be that the distribution of the random variable of interest depends on certain characteristics of the underlying situation. For example, the distribution of time to death may be related to the individual's age, gender, smoking status, blood pressure, height, and weight. Or, consider the number of automobile accidents a vehicle has in a year. The distribution of this variable might be related to the number of miles it is driven, where it is driven, and various characteristics of the primary driver such as age, gender, marital status, and driving history.

Example 12.62 *Suppose we believe that the distribution of the number of accidents a driver has in a year is related to the driver's age and gender. Provide three approaches to modeling this situation.*

Of course there is no limit to the number of models that could be considered. Three that might be used are given below.

1. Construct a model for each combination of gender and age. Collect data separately for each combination and construct each model separately. Either parametric or data-dependent models could be selected.

2. Construct a single, fully parametric model for this situation. As an example, the number of accidents for a given driver could be assumed to have the Poisson distribution with parameter λ. The value of λ is then assumed to depend on the age x and the gender ($g = 1$ for males, $g = 0$ for females) in some way such as

$$\lambda = (\alpha_0 + \alpha_1 x + \alpha_2 x^2)\beta^g.$$

3. Begin with a model for the density, distribution, or hazard rate function that is similar to a data-dependent model. Then use the age and gender to modify this function. For example, select a survival function $S_0(n)$ and then the survival function for a particular driver might be

$$S(n|x, g) = [S_0(n)]^{(\alpha_0 + \alpha_1 x + \alpha_2 x^2)\beta^g} . \qquad \Box$$

While there is nothing wrong with the first approach, it is not very interesting. It just asks us to repeat the modeling process over and over as we move from one combination to another. The second approach is a single parametric model that can also be analyzed with techniques already discussed, but it is clearly more parsimonious. The third model's hybrid nature implies that additional effort will be needed to implement it.

The third model would be a good choice when there is no obvious distributional model for a given individual. In the case of automobile drivers, the Poisson distribution is a reasonable choice and so the second model may be the best approach. If the variable is time to death, a data-dependent model such as a life table may be appropriate.

The advantage of the second and third approaches over the first one is that for some of the combinations there may be very few observations. In this case, the parsimony afforded by the second and third models may allow the limited information to still be useful. For example, suppose our task was to estimate the 80 entries in a life table running from age 20 through age 99 for four gender/smoker combinations. Using the ideas in model 1 above there are 320 items to estimate. Using the ideas in model 3 there would be 83 items to estimate.[16]

---

[16] There would be 80 items needed to estimate the survival function for one of the four combinations. The other three combinations each add one more item, the power to which the survival function is to be raised.

12.7.2   Proportional hazards models

A particular model that is relatively easy to work with is the Cox proportional hazards model.

Definition 12.63 *Given a baseline hazard rate function $h_0(t)$ and values $z_1, \ldots, z_p$ associated with a particular individual, the **Cox proportional hazards model** for that person is given by the hazard rate function*

$$h(x|\mathbf{z}) = h_0(x)c(\beta_1 z_1 + \cdots + \beta_p z_p) = h_0(x)c(\boldsymbol{\beta}^T \mathbf{z}),$$

*where $c(y)$ is any function that takes on only positive values, $\mathbf{z} = (z_1, \ldots, z_p)^T$ is a column vector of the z values (called **covariates**), and $\boldsymbol{\beta} = (\beta_1, \ldots, \beta_p)^T$ is a column vector of coefficients.*

The only function that will be used here is $c(y) = e^y$. One advantage of this function is that it must be positive. The name for this model is fitting because if the ratio of the hazard rate functions for two individuals is taken, the ratio will be constant. That is, one person's hazard rate function is proportional to any other person's hazard rate function. Our goal is to estimate the baseline hazard rate function $h_0(t)$ and the vector of coefficients $\boldsymbol{\beta}$.

Example 12.64 *Suppose the size of a homeowner's fire insurance claim as a percentage of the house's value depends upon the age of the house and the type of construction (wood or brick). Develop a Cox proportional hazards model for this situation. Also, indicate the difference between wood and brick houses of the same age.*

Let $z_1 = age$ (a nonnegative whole number) and $z_2 = 1$ if the construction is wood and $z_2 = 0$ if the construction is brick. Then the hazard rate function for a given house is

$$h(x|z_1, z_2) = h_0(x)e^{\beta_1 z_1 + \beta_2 z_2}.$$

One consequence of this model is that, regardless of the age, the effect of switching from brick to wood is the same. For two houses of age z_1 we have

$$h_{wood}(x) = h_0(x)e^{\beta_1 z_1 + \beta_2} = h_{brick}(x)e^{\beta_2}.$$

The effect on the survival function is

$$
\begin{aligned}
S_{wood}(x) &= \exp\left[-\int_0^x h_{wood}(y)dy\right] = \exp\left[-\int_0^x h_{brick}(y)e^{\beta_2}dy\right] \\
&= [S_{brick}(x)]^{\exp(\beta_2)}.
\end{aligned}
$$

$\square$

The baseline hazard rate function can be estimated using either a parametric model or a data-dependent model. The remainder of the model is

Table 12.20   Fire insurance payments

z_1	z_2	Payment
10	0	70
20	0	22
30	0	90*
40	0	81
50	0	8
10	1	51
20	1	95*
30	1	55
40	1	85*
50	1	93

*The payment was made at the policy limit.

parametric. In the spirit of this text, we will use maximum likelihood for estimation of β_1 and β_2. We will begin with a fully parametric example.

Example 12.65 *For the fire insurance example,* 10 *payments are in Table 12.20. All values are expressed as a percentage of the house's value. Estimate the parameters of the Cox proportional hazards model using maximum likelihood and both an exponential and a beta distribution for the baseline hazard rate function. There is no deductible on these policies, but there is a policy limit (which differs by policy).*

In order to construct the likelihood function, we need the density and survival functions. Let $c_j = \exp(\boldsymbol{\beta}^T \mathbf{z})$ be the Cox multiplier for the jth observation. Then, as noted in the previous example, $S_j(x) = S_0(x)^{c_j}$, where $S_0(x)$ is the baseline distribution. The density function is

$$
\begin{aligned}
f_j(x) &= -S_j'(x) = -c_j S_0(x)^{c_j - 1} S_0'(x) \\
&= c_j S_0(x)^{c_j - 1} f_0(x).
\end{aligned}
$$

For the exponential distribution,

$$
S_j(x) = [e^{-x/\theta}]^{c_j} = e^{-c_j x/\theta} \text{ and } f_j(x) = \left(\frac{c_j}{\theta}\right) e^{-c_j x/\theta}
$$

and for the beta distribution,

$$
\begin{aligned}
S_j(x) &= [1 - \beta(a, b; x)]^{c_j}, \text{ and} \\
f_j(x) &= c_j [1 - \beta(a, b; x)]^{c_j - 1} \frac{\Gamma(a+b)}{\Gamma(a)\Gamma(b)} x^{a-1} (1-x)^{b-1},
\end{aligned}
$$

where $\beta(a, b; x)$ is the distribution function for a beta distribution with parameters a and b [available in Excel® as BETADIST(x,a,b)]. The gamma function is available in Excel® as EXP(GAMMALN(a)). For policies with payments not at the limit, the contribution to the likelihood function is the density function while for those paid at the limit it is the survival function. In both cases, the likelihood function is sufficiently complex that it is not worth writing out. The parameter estimates for the exponential model are $\hat{\beta}_1 = 0.00319$, $\hat{\beta}_2 = -0.63722$, and $\hat{\theta} = 0.74041$. The value of the logarithm of the likelihood function is -6.1379. For the beta model, the estimates are $\hat{\beta}_1 = -0.00315$, $\hat{\beta}_2 = -0.77847$, $\hat{a} = 1.03706$, and $\hat{b} = 0.81442$. The value of the logarithm of the likelihood function is -4.2155. Using the Schwarz Bayesian criterion (see Section 13.5.3), an improvement of $\ln(10)/2 = 1.1513$ is needed to justify a fourth parameter. The beta model is preferred. If an estimate of the information matrix is desired, the only reasonable strategy is to take numerical derivatives of the loglikelihood.   □

An alternative is to construct a data-dependent model for the baseline hazard rate. Let $R(y_j)$ be the set of observations that are in the risk set for uncensored observation y_j.[17] Rather than obtain the true likelihood value, it is easier to obtain what is called the *partial likelihood* value. It is a conditional value. Rather than asking, "What is the probability of observing a value of y_j?" we ask, "Given that it is known there is an uncensored observation of y_j, what is the probability that it was the policy that had that value? Do this conditioned on equalling or exceeding that value." This method allows us to estimate the β coefficients separately from the baseline hazard rate. Notation can become a bit awkward here. Let j^* identify the observation that produced the uncensored observation of y_j. Then the contribution to the likelihood function for that policy is

$$\frac{f_{j^*}(y_j)/S_{j^*}(y_j)}{\sum_{i \in R(y_j)} f_i(y_j)/S_i(y_j)} = \frac{c_{j^*} f_0(y_j)/S_0(y_j)}{\sum_{i \in R(y_j)} c_i f_0(y_j)/S_0(y_j)} = \frac{c_{j^*}}{\sum_{i \in R(y_j)} c_i}.$$

Example 12.66 *Use the partial likelihood to estimate β_1 and β_2.*

The ordered, uncensored values are 8, 22, 51, 55, 70, 81, and 93. The calculation of the contribution to the likelihood function is in Table 12.21.

The product is maximized when $\hat{\beta}_1 = -0.00373$ and $\hat{\beta}_2 = -0.91994$ and the logarithm of the partial likelihood is -11.9889. When β_1 is forced to be zero, the maximum is at $\hat{\beta}_2 = -0.93708$ and the logarithm of the partial likelihood is -11.9968. There is no evidence in this sample that age of the house has an impact when using this model.   □

Three issues remain. One is to estimate the baseline hazard rate function, one is to deal with the case where there are multiple observations at the same

---

[17]Recall from Section 11.1 that $y_1, y_2, \ldots$ represent the ordered, unique values from the set of uncensored observations. The risk set was also defined in that section.

Table 12.21   Fire insurance likelihood

Value	y	c	Contribution to L
8	8	$c_1 = \exp(50\beta_1)$	$\dfrac{c_1}{c_1+\cdots+c_{10}}$
22	22	$c_2 = \exp(20\beta_1)$	$\dfrac{c_2}{c_2+\cdots+c_{10}}$
51	51	$c_3 = \exp(10\beta_1 + \beta_2)$	$\dfrac{c_3}{c_3+\cdots+c_{10}}$
55	55	$c_4 = \exp(30\beta_1 + \beta_2)$	$\dfrac{c_4}{c_4+\cdots+c_{10}}$
70	70	$c_5 = \exp(10\beta_1)$	$\dfrac{c_5}{c_5+\cdots+c_{10}}$
81	81	$c_6 = \exp(40\beta_1)$	$\dfrac{c_6}{c_6+\cdots+c_{10}}$
85		$c_7 = \exp(40\beta_1 + \beta_2)$	
90		$c_8 = \exp(30\beta_1)$	
93	93	$c_9 = \exp(50\beta_1 + \beta_2)$	$\dfrac{c_9}{c_9+c_{10}}$
95		$c_{10} = \exp(20\beta_1 + \beta_2)$	

value, and the final one is to estimate the variances of estimators. For the second problem, there are a number of approaches in the literature. The question raised earlier could be rephrased as "Given that it is known there are s_j uncensored observations of y_j, what is the probability that it was the s_j policies that actually had that value? Do this conditioned on equalling or exceeding that value." A direct interpretation of this statement would have the numerator reflect the probability of the s_j observations that were observed. The denominator would be based on all subsets of $R(y_j)$ with s_j members. This is a lot of work. A simplified version due to Breslow treats each of the s_j observations separately but, for the denominator, uses the same risk set for all of them. The effect is to require no change from the algorithm introduced above.

Example 12.67 *In the previous example, suppose that the observation of 81 had actually been 70. Give the contribution to the partial likelihood function for these two observations.*

Using the notation from that example, the contribution for the first observation of 70 would still be $c_5/(c_5+\cdots+c_{10})$. However, the second observation of 70 would now contribute $c_6/(c_5+\cdots+c_{10})$. Note that the numerator has not changed (it is still c_6); however, the denominator reflects the fact that there are six observations in $R(70)$. $\square$

With regard to estimating the hazard rate function, we first note that the cumulative hazard rate function is

$$H(t|\mathbf{z}) = \int_0^t h(u|\mathbf{z})du = \int_0^t h_0(u)c\,du = H_0(t)c.$$

Table 12.22   Fire insurance baseline survival function

Value	y	c	Jump	$\hat{H}_0(y)$	$\hat{S}_0(y)$
8	8	0.8300	$\frac{1}{0.8300+\cdots+0.3699} = 0.1597$	0.1597	0.8524
22	22	0.9282	$\frac{1}{0.9282+\cdots+0.3699} = 0.1841$	0.3438	0.7091
51	51	0.3840	$\frac{1}{0.3840+\cdots+0.3699} = 0.2220$	0.5658	0.5679
55	55	0.3564	$\frac{1}{0.3564+\cdots+0.3699} = 0.2427$	0.8086	0.4455
70	70	0.9634	$\frac{1}{0.9634+\cdots+0.3699} = 0.2657$	1.0743	0.3415
81	81	0.8615	$\frac{1}{0.8615+\cdots+0.3699} = 0.3572$	1.4315	0.2390
85		0.3434			
90		0.8942			
93	93	0.3308	$\frac{1}{0.3308+0.3699} = 1.4271$	2.8586	0.0574
95		0.3699			

To employ an analog of the Nelson–Åalen estimate, we use

$$\hat{H}_0(t) = \sum_{y_j \leq t} \frac{s_j}{\sum_{i \in R(y_j)} c_i}.$$

That is, the outer sum is taken over all uncensored observations less than or equal to t. The numerator is the number of observations having an uncensored value equal to y_j and the denominator, rather than having the number in the risk set, adds their c values. As usual, the baseline survival function is estimated as $\hat{S}_0(t) = \exp[-\hat{H}_0(t)]$.

Example 12.68 *For the continuing example (using the original values), estimate the baseline survival function and then estimate the probability that a claim for a 35-year-old wood house will exceed 80% of the house's value. Compare this to the value obtained from the beta distribution model obtained earlier.*

Using the estimates obtained earlier, the 10 c values are as given in Table 12.22. Also included is the jump in the cumulative hazard estimate, followed by the estimate of the cumulative hazard function itself. Values for that function apply from the given y value up to, but not including, the next y value.

For the house as described, $c = \exp[-0.00373(35) - 0.91994(1)] = 0.34977$. The estimated probability is $0.3415^{0.34977} = 0.68674$. From the beta distribution, $\hat{S}_0(0.8) = 0.27732$ and $c = \exp[-0.00315(35) - 0.77847(1)] = 0.41118$, which gives an estimated probability of $0.27732^{0.41118} = 0.59015$. □

With regard to variance estimates, the logarithm of the partial likelihood function is

$$l(\boldsymbol{\beta}) = \sum_{j^*} \ln \frac{c_{j^*}}{\sum_{i \in R(y_j)} c_i},$$

where the sum is taken over all observations that produced an uncensored value. Taking the first partial derivative with respect to β_g produces

$$\frac{\partial}{\partial \beta_g} l(\boldsymbol{\beta}) = \sum_{j^*} \left[\frac{1}{c_{j^*}} \frac{\partial c_{j^*}}{\partial \beta_g} - \frac{1}{\sum_{i \in R(y_j)} c_i} \frac{\partial}{\partial \beta_g} \sum_{i \in R(y_j)} c_i \right].$$

To simplify this expression, note that

$$\frac{\partial c_{j^*}}{\partial \beta_g} = \frac{\partial e^{\beta_1 z_{j^*1} + \beta_2 z_{j^*2} + \cdots + \beta_p z_{j^*p}}}{\partial \beta_g} = z_{j^*g} c_{j^*},$$

where z_{j^*g} is the value of z_g for subject j^*. The derivative is

$$\frac{\partial}{\partial \beta_g} l(\boldsymbol{\beta}) = \sum_{j^*} \left[z_{j^*g} - \frac{\sum_{i \in R(y_j)} z_{ig} c_i}{\sum_{i \in R(y_j)} c_i} \right].$$

The negative second partial derivative is

$$-\frac{\partial^2}{\partial \beta_h \beta_g} l(\boldsymbol{\beta})$$

$$= \sum_{j^*} \left[\frac{\sum_{i \in R(y_j)} z_{ig} z_{ih} c_i}{\sum_{i \in R(y_j)} c_i} - \frac{\left(\sum_{i \in R(y_j)} z_{ig} c_i \right) \left(\sum_{i \in R(y_j)} z_{ih} c_i \right)}{\left(\sum_{i \in R(y_j)} c_i \right)^2} \right].$$

Using the estimated values, these partial derivatives provide an estimate of the information matrix.

Example 12.69 *Obtain the information matrix and estimated covariance matrix for the continuing example. Then use this to produce a 95% confidence interval for the relative risk of a wood house versus a brick house of the same age.*

Consider the entry in the outer sum for the observation with $z_1 = 50$ and $z_2 = 1$. The risk set contains this observation (with a value of 93 and $c = 0.330802$) and the censored observation with $z_1 = 20$ and $z_2 = 1$ (with a value of 95 and $c = 0.369924$). For the derivative with respect to β_1 and β_2 the entry is

$$\frac{50(1)(0.330802) + 20(1)(0.369924)}{0.330802 + 0.369924}$$
$$- \frac{[50(0.330802) + 20(0.369924)][1(0.330802) + 1(0.369924)]}{(0.330802 + 0.369924)^2} = 0.$$

Summing such items and doing the same for the other partial derivatives yield the information matrix and its inverse, the covariance matrix.

$$I = \begin{bmatrix} 1171.054 & 5.976519 \\ 5.976519 & 1.322283 \end{bmatrix}, \widehat{\mathrm{Var}} = \begin{bmatrix} 0.000874 & -0.00395 \\ -0.00395 & 0.774125 \end{bmatrix}.$$

The relative risk is the ratio of the c values for the two cases. For a house of age x, the relative risk of wood versus brick is $e^{z_1\beta_1+\beta_2}/e^{z_1\beta_1} = e^{\beta_2}$. A 95% confidence interval for β_2 is $-0.91994 \pm 1.96\sqrt{0.774125}$ or $(-2.6444, 0.80455)$. Exponentiating the endpoints gives the confidence interval for the relative risk, $(0.07105, 2.2357)$. $\square$

12.7.3 The generalized linear and accelerated failure time models

The proportional hazards model requires a particular relationship between survival functions. For actuarial purposes it may not be the most appropriate because it is difficult to interpret the meaning of multiplying a hazard rate function by a constant (or, equivalently, raising a survival function to a power).[18] It may be more useful to relate the covariates to a quantity of direct interest, such as the expected value. Linear models, such as the standard multiple regression model are inadequate because they tend to rely on the normal distribution, a model not suitable for most phenomena of interest to actuaries. The generalized linear model drops that restriction and so may be more useful. A comprehensive reference is [90] and actuarial papers using the model include [47], [61], [93], and [97]. The definition of this model given below is slightly more general than the usual one.

Definition 12.70 *Suppose a parametric distribution has parameters μ and $\boldsymbol{\theta}$, where μ is the mean and $\boldsymbol{\theta}$ is a vector of additional parameters. Let its cdf be $F(x|\mu, \boldsymbol{\theta})$. The mean must not depend on the additional parameters and the additional parameters must not depend on the mean. Let $\mathbf{z}$ be a vector of covariates for an individual, let $\boldsymbol{\beta}$ be a vector of coefficients, and let $\eta(\mu)$ and $c(y)$ be functions. The generalized linear model then states that the random variable, X, has as its distribution function*

$$F(x|\mathbf{z}, \boldsymbol{\theta}) = F(x|\mu, \boldsymbol{\theta}),$$

where μ is such that $\eta(\mu) = c(\boldsymbol{\beta}^T\mathbf{z})$.

The model indicates that the mean of an individual observation is related to the covariates through a particular set of functions. Normally, these functions do not involve parameters, but instead are used to provide a good fit or to ensure that only legitimate values of μ are encountered.

---

[18]However, it is not uncommon in life insurance to incorporate a given health risk (such as obesity) by multiplying the values of q_x by a constant. This is not much different from multiplying the hazard rate function by a constant.

Example 12.71 *Demonstrate that the ordinary linear regression model is a special case of the generalized linear model.*

For ordinary linear regression, X has a normal distribution with $\mu = \mu$ and $\theta = \sigma^2$. Both η and c are the identity function, resulting in $\mu = \boldsymbol{\beta}^T \mathbf{z}$.   □

The model presented here is more general than the one usually used where only a few distributions are allowed for X. The reason is that, for these distributions, it has been possible to develop the full set of regression tools, such as residual analysis. Computer packages that implement the generalized linear model use only these distributions.

For many of the distributions we have been using, the mean is not a parameter. However, it could be. For example, we could parameterize the Pareto distribution by setting $\mu = \theta/(\alpha-1)$ or, equivalently, replacing θ with $\mu(\alpha-1)$. The distribution function is now

$$F(x|\mu, \alpha) = 1 - \left[\frac{\mu(\alpha - 1)}{\mu(\alpha - 1) + x} \right]^\alpha, \quad \mu > 0, \ \alpha > 1.$$

Note the restriction on α in the parameter space.

Example 12.72 *Construct a generalized linear model for the data set in Example 12.65 using a beta distribution for the loss model.*

The beta distribution as parameterized in Appendix A has a mean of $\mu = a/(a+b)$. Let the other parameter be $\theta = b$. One way of linking the covariates to the mean is to use $\eta(\mu) = \mu/(1 - \mu)$ and $c(\boldsymbol{\beta}^T \mathbf{z}) = \exp(\boldsymbol{\beta}^T \mathbf{z})$. Setting these equal and solving yields

$$\mu = \frac{\exp(\boldsymbol{\beta}^T \mathbf{z})}{1 + \exp(\boldsymbol{\beta}^T \mathbf{z})}.$$

Solving the first two equations yields $a = b\mu/(1-\mu) = b\exp(\boldsymbol{\beta}^T \mathbf{z})$. Maximum likelihood estimation proceeds by using a factor of $f(x)$ for each uncensored observation and $1 - F(x)$ for each censored observation. For each observation, the beta distribution uses the parameter b directly, and the parameter a from the value of b and the covariates for that observation. Because there is no baseline distribution, the expression $\boldsymbol{\beta}^T \mathbf{z}$ must include a constant term. Maximizing the likelihood function yields the estimates $\hat{b} = 0.5775$, $\hat{\beta}_0 = 0.2130$, $\hat{\beta}_1 = 0.0018$, and $\hat{\beta}_2 = 1.0940$. As in Example 12.65, the impact of age is negligible. One advantage of this model is that the mean is directly linked to the covariates.   □

A model that is similar in spirit to the generalized linear model is the accelerated failure time model as described below.

Definition 12.73 *The **accelerated failure time model** is defined from*

$$S(x|\mathbf{z}, \boldsymbol{\beta}) = S_0(xe^{-\boldsymbol{\beta}^T \mathbf{z}}). \tag{12.29}$$

Table 12.23 Data for Example 12.74

Age	Male (0) 100	125	150	Female (1) 100	125	150
50	13	12	85	3	12	49
51	11	21	95	7	13	53
52	8	8	105	8	13	69
53	10	20	113	12	16	61
54	8	11	109	12	15	60
55	13	22	126	8	12	68
56	19	16	142	11	11	96
57	9	19	145	5	19	97
58	17	23	155	5	17	93
59	14	28	182	9	14	96

To see that, provided the mean exists, it is a generalized linear model, first note that, (assuming $S(0) = 1$),

$$E(X|\mathbf{z}, \boldsymbol{\beta}) = \int_0^\infty S_0(xe^{-\boldsymbol{\beta}^T\mathbf{z}})dx = \int_0^\infty e^{\boldsymbol{\beta}^T\mathbf{z}} S_0(y)dy = \exp(\boldsymbol{\beta}^T\mathbf{z})E_0(X),$$

thus relating the mean of the distribution to the covariates. The name comes from the fact that the covariates effectively change the age. A person age x whose covariates are $\mathbf{z}$ has a future lifetime with the same distribution as a person for whom $\mathbf{z} = 0$ and is age $xe^{-\boldsymbol{\beta}^T\mathbf{z}}$. If the baseline distribution has a scale parameter, then the effect of the covariates is to multiply that scale parameter by a constant. So, if θ is the scale parameter for the baseline distribution then a person with covariate $\mathbf{z}$ will have the same distribution, but with scale parameter $\exp(\boldsymbol{\beta}^T\mathbf{z})\theta$. Unlike the generalized linear model, it is not necessary for the mean to exist before this model can be used.

Example 12.74 *A mortality study at ages 50–59 included people of both genders and with systolic blood pressure of 100, 125, or 150. For each of the 6 combinations and at each of the 10 ages, 1,000 people were observed and the number of deaths recorded. The data appear in Table 12.23. Develop and estimate the parameters for an accelerated failure time model based on the Gompertz distribution.*

The Gompertz distribution has hazard rate function $h(x) = Bc^x$ which implies a survival function of $S_0(x) = \exp[-B(c^x - 1)/\ln c]$ as the baseline distribution. Let the covariates be $z_1 = 0$ for males and $z_1 = 1$ for females and let z_2 be the blood pressure. For an individual insured, let $\gamma = \exp(\beta_1 z_1 + \beta_2 z_2)$. The accelerated failure time model implies that

$$S(x|\gamma) = S_0\left(\frac{x}{\gamma}\right) = \exp\left[-\frac{B(c^{x/\gamma} - 1)}{\ln c}\right].$$

Let $c^* = c^{1/\gamma}$ and let $B^* = B/\gamma$. Then,

$$S(x|\gamma) = \exp\left[-\frac{B^*\gamma(c^{*x}-1)}{\gamma \ln c^*}\right] = \exp\left[-\frac{B^*(c^{*x}-1)}{\ln c^*}\right],$$

and so the distribution remains Gompertz with new parameters as indicated. For each age,

$$q_x|\gamma = 1 - \frac{S(x+1|\gamma)}{S(x|\gamma)} = 1 - \exp\left[-\frac{B^*c^{*x}(c^*-1)}{\ln c^*}\right].$$

If there are d_x deaths at age x, the contribution to the loglikelihood function (where a binomial distribution has been assumed for the number of deaths) is

$$d_x \ln q_x + (1000 - d_x) \ln(1 - q_x).$$

The likelihood function is maximized at $B = 0.000243$, $c = 1.00866$, $\beta_1 = 0.110$, and $\beta_2 = -0.0144$. Being female multiplies the expected lifetime (from birth) by a factor of $\exp(0.110) = 1.116$. An increase of 25 in blood pressure lowers the expected lifetime by $1 - \exp[-25(0.0144)] = 0.302$, or a 30.2% decrease. $\quad\square$

12.7.4   Exercises

12.101 Suppose the 40 observations in Data Set D2 in Chapter 10 were from four types of policyholders. Observations 1, 5, ... are from male smokers, observations 2, 6, ... are from male nonsmokers, observations 3, 7, ... are from female smokers, and observations 4, 8, ... are from female nonsmokers. You are to construct a model for the time to surrender and then use the model to estimate the probability of surrendering in the first year for each of the four cases. Construct each of the following three models:

   (a) Use four different Nelson–Åalen estimates, keeping the four groups separate.

   (b) Use a proportional hazards model where the baseline distribution has the exponential distribution.

   (c) Use a proportional hazards model with an empirical estimate of the baseline distribution.

12.102 (*) The duration of a strike follows a Cox proportional hazards model in which the baseline distribution has an exponential distribution. The only variable used is the index of industrial production. When the index has a value of 10, the <u>mean</u> duration of a strike is 0.2060 years. When the index has a value of 25, the <u>median</u> duration is 0.0411 years. Determine the probability that a strike will have a duration of more than one year if the index has a value of 5.

12.103 (*) A Cox proportional hazards model has $z_1 = 1$ for males and $z_1 = 0$ for females and $z_2 = 1$ for adults and $z_2 = 0$ for children. The maximum likelihood estimates of the coefficients are $\hat{\beta}_1 = 0.25$ and $\hat{\beta}_2 = -0.45$. The covariance matrix of the estimators is

$$\begin{bmatrix} 0.36 & 0.10 \\ 0.10 & 0.20 \end{bmatrix}.$$

Determine a 95% linear confidence interval for $\beta_1 - \beta_2$ and then use the result to obtain a confidence interval for the relative risk of a male child compared to a female adult.

12.104 (*) Four insureds were observed from birth to death. The two from Class A died at times 1 and 9 while the two from Class B died at times 2 and 4. A proportional hazards model uses $z_1 = 1$ for Class B and 0 for Class A. Let $b = \hat{\beta}_1$. Estimate the cumulative hazard rate at time 3 for a member of Class A.

12.105 (*) A Cox proportional hazards model has three covariates. The life that died first has values $1, 0, 0$ for z_1, z_2, z_3. The second to die has values $0, 1, 0$ and the third to die has values $0, 0, 1$. Determine the partial likelihood function (as a function of β_1, β_2, and β_3).

12.106 Repeat Example 12.72 using only construction type and not age.

12.107 Repeat Example 12.74 using a proportional hazards model with a Gompertz baseline distribution.

12.108 Repeat Example 12.74 using an accelerated failure time model with a gamma baseline distribution.

13

Model selection

13.1 INTRODUCTION

When using data to build a model, the process must end with the announcement of a "winner." While qualifications, limitations, caveats, and other attempts to escape full responsibility are appropriate, and often necessary, a commitment to a solution is often required. In this chapter we look at a variety of ways to evaluate a model and compare competing models. But we must also remember that whatever model we select it is only an approximation of reality. This is reflected in the following modeler's motto[1]:

> All models are wrong, but some models are useful.

Thus, our goal is to determine a model that is good enough to use to answer the question. The challenge here is that the definition of *good enough* will depend on the particular application. Another important modeling point is that a solid understanding of the question will guide you to the answer. The following quote from John Tukey [131], pp. 13–14 sums this up:

> Far better an approximate answer to the right question, which is often vague, than an exact answer to the wrong question, which can always be made precise.

---

[1]It is usually attributed to George Box.

Loss Models: From Data to Decisions, Second Edition.
By Stuart A. Klugman, Harry H. Panjer, and Gordon E. Willmot
ISBN 0-471-21577-5   Copyright © 2004 John Wiley & Sons, Inc.

In this chapter, a specific modeling strategy will be considered. Our preference is to have a single approach that can be used for any probabilistic modeling situation. A consequence is that for any particular modeling situation there may be a better (more reliable or more accurate) approach. For example, while maximum likelihood is a good estimation method for most settings, it may not be the best[2] for certain distributions. A literature search will turn up methods that have been optimized for specific distributions, but they will not be mentioned here. Similarly, many of the hypothesis tests used here give approximate results. For specific cases, better approximations, or maybe even exact results, are available. They will also be bypassed. The goal here is to outline a method that will give reasonable answers most of the time and be adaptable to a variety of situations.

This chapter assumes the reader has a basic understanding of statistical hypothesis testing as reviewed in Chapter 9. The remaining sections cover a variety of evaluation and selection tools. Each tool has its own strengths and weaknesses, and it is possible for different tools to lead to different models. This makes modeling as much art as science. At times, in real-world applications, the model's purpose may lead the analyst to favor one tool over another.

13.2 REPRESENTATIONS OF THE DATA AND MODEL

All the approaches to be presented attempt to compare the proposed model to the data or to another model. The proposed model is represented by either its density or distribution function or perhaps some functional of these quantities such as the limited expected value function or the mean residual life function. The data can be represented by the empirical distribution function or a histogram. The graphs are easy to construct when there is individual, complete data. When there is grouping or observations have been truncated or censored, difficulties arise. Here, the only cases to be covered are those where all the data have been truncated at the same value (which could be zero) and are all censored at the same value (which could be infinity). Extensions to the case of multiple truncation or censoring points are detailed in [109].[3] It should be noted that the need for such representations applies only to continuous models. For discrete data, issues of censoring, truncation, and grouping rarely apply. The data can easily be represented by the relative or cumulative frequencies at each possible observation.

---

[2]There are many definitions of "best." Combining the Cramér-Rao lower bound with Theorem 12.13 indicates that maximum likelihood estimators are asymptotically optimal using unbiasedness and minimum variance as the definition of best.

[3]Because the Kaplan-Meier estimate can be used to represent data with multiple truncation or censoring points, constructing graphical comparisons of the model and data is not difficult. The major challenge is generalizing the hypothesis tests to this situation.

Table 13.1   Data Set B with highest value changed

27	82	115	126	155	161	243	294	340	384
457	680	855	877	974	1,193	1,340	1,884	2,558	3,476

With regard to representing the data, the empirical distribution function will be used for individual data and the histogram will be used for grouped data.

In order to compare the model to truncated data, we begin by noting that the empirical distribution begins at the truncation point and represents conditional values (that is, they are the distribution and density function given that the observation exceeds the truncation point). In order to make a comparison to the empirical values, the model must also be truncated. Let the truncation point in the data set be t. The modified functions are

$$F^*(x) = \begin{cases} 0, & x < t, \\ \dfrac{F(x) - F(t)}{1 - F(t)}, & x \geq t, \end{cases}$$

$$f^*(x) = \begin{cases} 0, & x < t, \\ \dfrac{f(x)}{1 - F(t)}, & x \geq t. \end{cases}$$

In this chapter, when a distribution function or density function is indicated, a subscript equal to the sample size indicates that it is the empirical model (from Kaplan–Meier, Nelson–Åalen, the ogive, etc.) while no adornment or the use of an asterisk (*), indicates the estimated parametric model. There is no notation for the true, underlying distribution because it is unknown and unknowable.

13.3 GRAPHICAL COMPARISON OF THE DENSITY AND DISTRIBUTION FUNCTIONS

The most direct way to see how well the model and data match up is to plot the respective density and distribution functions.

Example 13.1 *Consider Data Sets B and C. However, for this example and all that follow, in Data Set B replace the value at 15,743 with 3,476 (this is to allow the graphs to fit comfortably on a page). These data sets are reproduced here in Tables 13.1 and 13.2. Truncate Data Set B at 50 and Data Set C at 7,500. Estimate the parameter of an exponential model for each data set. Plot the appropriate functions and comment on the quality of the fit of the model. Repeat this for Data Set B censored at 1,000 (without any truncation).*

Table 13.2 Data Set C

Payment range	Number of payments
0–7,500	99
7,500–17,500	42
17,500–32,500	29
32,500–67,500	28
67,500–125,000	17
125,000–300,000	9
Over 300,000	3

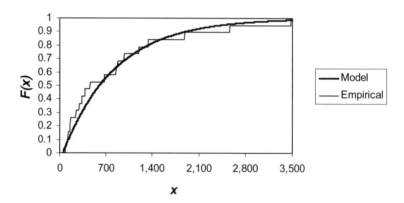

Fig. 13.1 Model vs. data cdf plot for Data Set B truncated at 50.

For Data Set B, there are 19 observations (the first observation is removed due to truncation). A typical contribution to the likelihood function is $f(82)/[1 - F(50)]$. The maximum likelihood estimate of the exponential parameter is $\hat{\theta} = 802.32$. The empirical distribution function starts at 50 and jumps $1/19$ at each data point. The distribution function, using a truncation point of 50, is

$$F^*(x) = \frac{1 - e^{-x/802.32} - \left(1 - e^{-50/802.32}\right)}{1 - \left(1 - e^{-50/802.32}\right)} = 1 - e^{-(x-50)/802.32}.$$

Figure 13.1 presents a plot of these two functions.

The fit is not as good as we might like because the model understates the distribution function at smaller values of x and overstates the distribution

Exponential fit

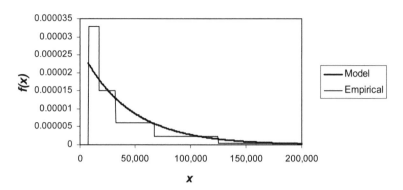

Fig. 13.2 Model vs. data density plot for Data Set C truncated at 7,500.

function at larger values of x. This is not good because it means that tail probabilities are understated.

For Data Set C, the likelihood function uses the truncated values. For example, the contribution to the likelihood function for the first interval is

$$\left[\frac{F(17,500) - F(7,500)}{1 - F(7,500)}\right]^{42}.$$

The maximum likelihood estimate is $\hat{\theta} = 44{,}253$. The height of the first histogram bar is

$$\frac{42}{128(17,500 - 7,500)} = 0.0000328$$

and the last bar is for the interval from 125,000 to 300,000 (a bar cannot be constructed for the interval from 300,000 to infinity). The density function must be truncated at 7,500 and becomes

$$
\begin{aligned}
f^*(x) &= \frac{f(x)}{1 - F(7,500)} = \frac{44,253^{-1}e^{-x/44,253}}{1 - (1 - e^{-7,500/44,253})} \\
&= \frac{e^{-(x-7,500)/44,253}}{44,253}, \quad x > 7,500.
\end{aligned}
$$

The plot of the density function versus the histogram is given Figure 13.2.

The exponential model understates the early probabilities. It is hard to tell from the picture how the curves compare above 125,000.

For Data Set B modified with a limit, the maximum likelihood estimate is $\hat{\theta} = 718.00$. When constructing the plot, the empirical distribution function must stop at 1,000. The plot appears in Figure 13.3.

Exponential fit

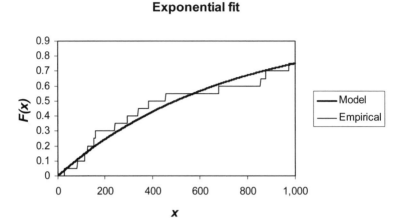

Fig. 13.3 Model vs. data cdf plot for Data Set B censored at 1,000.

Once again, the exponential model does not fit well.   □

When the model's distribution function is close to the empirical distribution function, it is difficult to make small distinctions. Among the many ways to amplify those distinctions, two will be presented here. The first is to simply plot the difference of the two functions. That is, if $F_n(x)$ is the empirical distribution function and $F^*(x)$ is the model distribution function, plot $D(x) = F_n(x) - F^*(x)$.

Example 13.2 *Plot $D(x)$ for the previous example.*

For Data Set B truncated at 50, the plot appears in Figure 13.4. The lack of fit for this model is magnified in this plot.

There is no corresponding plot for grouped data. For Data Set B censored at 1,000, the plot must again end at that value. It appears in Figure 13.5. The lack of fit continues to be apparent.   □

Another way to highlight any differences is the *p–p* plot, which is also called a probability plot. The plot is created by ordering the observations as $x_1 \leq \cdots \leq x_n$. A point is then plotted corresponding to each value. The coordinates to plot are $(F_n(x_j), F^*(x_j))$.[4] If the model fits well, the plotted

---

[4]In the first edition of this text this plot was incorrectly called a *q-q* plot. There is a plot that goes by that name, but it will not be introduced here.

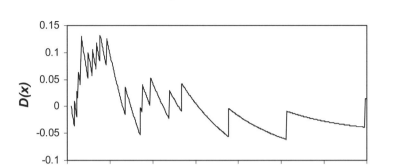

Fig. 13.4 Model vs. data $D(x)$ plot for Data Set B truncated at 50.

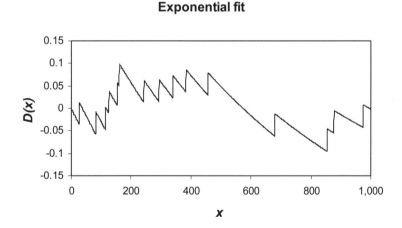

Fig. 13.5 Model vs. data $D(x)$ plot for Data Set B censored at 1,000.

points will be near the 45° line running from $(0,0)$ to $(1,1)$. However, for this to be the case, a different definition of the empirical distribution function is needed. It can be shown that the expected value of $F_n(x_j)$ is $j/(n+1)$ and therefore the empirical distribution should be that value and not the usual j/n. If two observations have the same value, either plot both points (they

Exponential fit

Fig. 13.6   p–p for Data Set B truncated at 50.

would have the same "y" value but different "x" values) or plot a single value by averaging the two "x" values.

Example 13.3 *Create a p–p plot for the continuing example.*

For Data Set B truncated at 50, $n = 19$ and one of the observed values is $x = 82$. The empirical value is $F_n(82) = \frac{1}{20} = 0.05$. The other coordinate is

$$F^*(82) = 1 - e^{-(82-50)/802.32} = 0.0391.$$

One of the plotted points will be $(0.05, 0.0391)$. The complete picture appears in Figure 13.6.

From the lower left part of the plot it is clear that the exponential model places less probability on small values than the data call for. A similar plot can be constructed for Data Set B censored at 1,000 and it appears in Figure 13.7.

This plot ends at about 0.75 because that is the highest probability observed prior to the censoring point at 1,000. There are no empirical values at higher probabilities. Again, the exponential model tends to underestimate the empirical values.   □

13.3.1   Exercises

13.1 Repeat Example 13.1 using a Weibull model in place of the exponential model.

Exponential fit

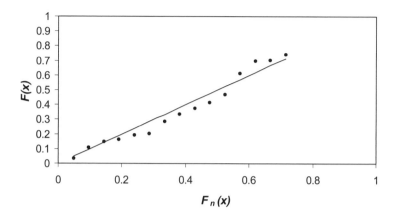

Fig. 13.7 *p–p* plot for Data Set B censored at 1,000.

13.2 Repeat Example 13.2 for a Weibull model.

13.3 Repeat Example 13.3 for a Weibull model.

13.4 HYPOTHESIS TESTS

A picture may be worth many words, but sometimes it is best to replace the impressions conveyed by pictures with mathematical demonstrations. One such demonstration is a test of the hypotheses

H_0 : The data came from a population with the stated model.

H_1 : The data did not come from such a population.

The test statistic is usually a measure of how close the model distribution function is to the empirical distribution function. When the null hypothesis completely specifies the model (for example, an exponential distribution with mean 100), critical values are well known. However, it is more often the case that the null hypothesis states the name of the model but not its parameters. When the parameters are estimated from the data, the test statistic tends to be smaller than it would have been had the parameter values been prespecified. That is because the estimation method itself tries to choose parameters that produce a distribution that is close to the data. In that case, the tests become approximate. Because rejection of the null hypothesis occurs for large values of the test statistic, the approximation tends to increase the probability of a

Type II error while lowering the probability of a Type I error.[5] For actuarial modeling this is likely to be an acceptable trade-off.

One method of avoiding the approximation is to randomly divide the sample in half. Use one half to estimate the parameters and then use the other half to conduct the hypothesis test. Once the model is selected, the full data set could be used to reestimate the parameters.

13.4.1   Kolmogorov–Smirnov test

Let t be the left truncation point ($t = 0$ if there is no truncation) and let u be the right censoring point ($u = \infty$ if there is no censoring). Then, the test statistic is

$$D = \max_{t \leq x \leq u} |F_n(x) - F^*(x)|.$$

This test should only be used on individual data. This is to ensure that the step function $F_n(x)$ is well defined. Also, the model distribution function $F^*(x)$ is assumed to be continuous over the relevant range.

Example 13.4 *Calculate D for Example* 13.1.

Table 13.3 provides the needed values. Because the empirical distribution function jumps at each data point, the model distribution function must be compared both before and after the jump. The values just before the jump are denoted $F_n(x-)$ in the table. The maximum is $D = 0.1340$.

For Data Set B censored at 1,000, 15 of the 20 observations are uncensored. Table 13.4 illustrates the needed calculations. The maximum is $D = 0.0991$. □

All that remains is to determine the critical value. Commonly used critical values for this test are $1.22/\sqrt{n}$ for $\alpha = 0.10$, $1.36/\sqrt{n}$ for $\alpha = 0.05$, and $1.63/\sqrt{n}$ for $\alpha = 0.01$. When $u < \infty$, the critical value should be smaller because there is less opportunity for the difference to become large. Modifications for this phenomenon exist in the literature (see [125], for example, which also includes tables of critical values for specific null distribution models), and one such modification is given in [109] but will not be introduced here.

Example 13.5 *Complete the Kolmogorov–Smirnov test for the previous example.*

For Data Set B truncated at 50 the sample size is 19. The critical value at a 5% significance level is $1.36/\sqrt{19} = 0.3120$. Because $0.1340 < 0.3120$, the null hypothesis is not rejected and the exponential distribution is a plausible

---

[5]Among the tests presented here, only the chi-square test has a built-in correction for this situation. Modifications for the other tests have been developed, but they will not be presented here.

Table 13.3 Calculation of D for Example 13.4

x	$F^*(x)$	$F_n(x-)$	$F_n(x)$	Maximum difference
82	0.0391	0.0000	0.0526	0.0391
115	0.0778	0.0526	0.1053	0.0275
126	0.0904	0.1053	0.1579	0.0675
155	0.1227	0.1579	0.2105	0.0878
161	0.1292	0.2105	0.2632	0.1340
243	0.2138	0.2632	0.3158	0.1020
294	0.2622	0.3158	0.3684	0.1062
340	0.3033	0.3684	0.4211	0.1178
384	0.3405	0.4211	0.4737	0.1332
457	0.3979	0.4737	0.5263	0.1284
680	0.5440	0.5263	0.5789	0.0349
855	0.6333	0.5789	0.6316	0.0544
877	0.6433	0.6316	0.6842	0.0409
974	0.6839	0.6842	0.7368	0.0529
1,193	0.7594	0.7368	0.7895	0.0301
1,340	0.7997	0.7895	0.8421	0.0424
1,884	0.8983	0.8421	0.8947	0.0562
2,558	0.9561	0.8947	0.9474	0.0614
3,476	0.9860	0.9474	1.0000	0.0386

model. While it is unlikely that the exponential model is appropriate for this population, the sample size is too small to lead to that conclusion. For Data Set B censored at 1,000 the sample size is 20 and so the critical value is $1.36/\sqrt{20} = 0.3041$ and the exponential model is again viewed as being plausible. $\qquad\square$

For both this test and the Anderson–Darling test that follows, the critical values are correct only when the null hypothesis completely specifies the model. When the data set is used to estimate parameters for the null hypothesized distribution (as in the example), the correct critical value is smaller. For both tests, the change depends on the particular distribution that is hypothesized and maybe even on the particular true values of the parameters. An indication of how simulation can be used for this situation is presented in Section 17.2.4.

Table 13.4 Calculation of D for Example 13.4 with censoring

x	$F^*(x)$	$F_n(x-)$	$F_n(x)$	Maximum difference
27	0.0369	0.00	0.05	0.0369
82	0.1079	0.05	0.10	0.0579
115	0.1480	0.10	0.15	0.0480
126	0.1610	0.15	0.20	0.0390
155	0.1942	0.20	0.25	0.0558
161	0.2009	0.25	0.30	0.0991
243	0.2871	0.30	0.35	0.0629
294	0.3360	0.35	0.40	0.0640
340	0.3772	0.40	0.45	0.0728
384	0.4142	0.45	0.50	0.0858
457	0.4709	0.50	0.55	0.0791
680	0.6121	0.55	0.60	0.0621
855	0.6960	0.60	0.65	0.0960
877	0.7052	0.65	0.70	0.0552
974	0.7425	0.70	0.75	0.0425
1000	0.7516	0.75	0.75	0.0016

13.4.2 Anderson–Darling test

This test is similar to the Kolmogorov–Smirnov test, but uses a different measure of the difference between the two distribution functions. The test statistic is

$$A^2 = n \int_t^u \frac{[F_n(x) - F^*(x)]^2}{F^*(x)[1 - F^*(x)]} f^*(x)dx.$$

That is, it is a weighted average of the squared differences between the empirical and model distribution functions. Note that when x is close to t or to u the weights might be very large due to the small value of one of the factors in the denominator. This test statistic tends to place more emphasis on good fit in the tails than in the middle of the distribution. Calculating with this formula appears to be challenging. However, for individual data (so this is another test that does not work for grouped data), the integral simplifies to

$$A^2 = -nF^*(u) + n\sum_{j=0}^{k}[1 - F_n(y_j)]^2\{\ln[1 - F^*(y_j)] - \ln[1 - F^*(y_{j+1})]\}$$

$$+ n\sum_{j=1}^{k} F_n(y_j)^2[\ln F^*(y_{j+1}) - \ln F^*(y_j)],$$

where the unique noncensored data points are $t = y_0 < y_1 < \cdots < y_k < y_{k+1} = u$. Note that when $u = \infty$ the last term of the first sum is zero

Table 13.5   Anderson–Darling test for Example 13.6

j	y_j	$F^*(x)$	$F_n(x)$	Summand
0	50	0.0000	0.0000	0.0399
1	82	0.0391	0.0526	0.0388
2	115	0.0778	0.1053	0.0126
3	126	0.0904	0.1579	0.0332
4	155	0.1227	0.2105	0.0070
5	161	0.1292	0.2632	0.0904
6	243	0.2138	0.3158	0.0501
7	294	0.2622	0.3684	0.0426
8	340	0.3033	0.4211	0.0389
9	384	0.3405	0.4737	0.0601
10	457	0.3979	0.5263	0.1490
11	680	0.5440	0.5789	0.0897
12	855	0.6333	0.6316	0.0099
13	877	0.6433	0.6842	0.0407
14	974	0.6839	0.7368	0.0758
15	1,193	0.7594	0.7895	0.0403
16	1,340	0.7997	0.8421	0.0994
17	1,884	0.8983	0.8947	0.0592
18	2,558	0.9561	0.9474	0.0308
19	3,476	0.9860	1.0000	0.0141
20	∞	1.0000	1.0000	

[evaluating the formula as written will ask for $\ln(0)$]. The critical values are 1.933, 2.492, and 3.857 for 10, 5, and 1% significance levels, respectively. As with the Kolmogorov–Smirnov test, the critical value should be smaller when $u < \infty$.

Example 13.6 *Perform the Anderson–Darling test for the continuing example.*

For Data Set B truncated at 50, there are 19 data points. The calculation is in Table 13.5, where "summand" refers to the sum of the corresponding terms from the two sums. The total is 1.0226 and the test statistic is $-19(1) + 19(1.0226) = 0.4292$. Because the test statistic is less than the critical value of 2.492, the exponential model is viewed as plausible.

For Data Set B censored at 1,000, the results are in Table 13.6. The total is 0.7602 and the test statistic is $-20(0.7516) + 20(0.7602) = 0.1713$. Because the test statistic does not exceed the critical value of 2.492, the exponential model is viewed as plausible. □

Table 13.6   Anderson–Darling calculation for Example 13.6 with censored data

j	y_j	$F^*(x)$	$F_n^*(x)$	Summand
0	0	0.0000	0.00	0.0376
1	27	0.0369	0.05	0.0718
2	82	0.1079	0.10	0.0404
3	115	0.1480	0.15	0.0130
4	126	0.1610	0.20	0.0334
5	155	0.1942	0.25	0.0068
6	161	0.2009	0.30	0.0881
7	243	0.2871	0.35	0.0493
8	294	0.3360	0.40	0.0416
9	340	0.3772	0.45	0.0375
10	384	0.4142	0.50	0.0575
11	457	0.4709	0.55	0.1423
12	680	0.6121	0.60	0.0852
13	855	0.6960	0.65	0.0093
14	877	0.7052	0.70	0.0374
15	974	0.7425	0.75	0.0092
16	1000	0.7516	0.75	

13.4.3   Chi-square goodness-of-fit test

Unlike the previous two tests, this test allows for some discretion. It begins with the selection of $k - 1$ arbitrary values, $t = c_0 < c_1 < \cdots < c_k = \infty$. Let $\hat{p}_j = F^*(c_j) - F^*(c_{j-1})$ be the probability a truncated observation falls in the interval from c_{j-1} to c_j. Similarly, let $p_{nj} = F_n(c_j) - F_n(c_{j-1})$ be the same probability according to the empirical distribution. The test statistic is then

$$\chi^2 = \sum_{j=1}^{k} \frac{n(\hat{p}_j - p_{nj})^2}{\hat{p}_j},$$

where n is the sample size. Another way to write the formula is to let $E_j = n\hat{p}_j$ be the number of expected observations in the interval (assuming that the hypothesized model is true) and $O_j = np_{nj}$ be the number of observations in the interval. Then,

$$\chi^2 = \sum_{j=1}^{k} \frac{(E_j - O_j)^2}{E_j}.$$

The critical value for this test comes from the chi-square distribution with degrees of freedom equal to the number of terms in the sum (k) minus 1 minus the number of estimated parameters. There are a number of rules that have been proposed for deciding when the test is reasonably accurate. They center around the values of $E_j = n\hat{p}_j$. The most conservative states that each must

Table 13.7 Data Set B truncated at 50

Range	$\hat{p}$	Expected	Observed	χ^2
50–150	0.1172	2.227	3	0.2687
150–250	0.1035	1.966	3	0.5444
250–500	0.2087	3.964	4	0.0003
500–1,000	0.2647	5.029	4	0.2105
1,000–2,000	0.2180	4.143	3	0.3152
2,000–∞	0.0880	1.672	2	0.0644
Total	1	19	19	1.4034

be at least 5. Some authors claim that values as low as 1 are acceptable. All agree the test works best when the values are about equal from term to term. If the data are grouped, there is little choice but to use the groups as given, although adjacent groups could be combined to increase E_j. For individual data, the data can be grouped for the purpose of performing this test.[6]

Example 13.7 *Perform the chi-square goodness-of-fit test for the exponential distribution for the continuing example.*

All three data sets can be evaluated with this test. For Data Set B truncated at 50, establish boundaries at 50, 150, 250, 500, 1000, 2000, and infinity. The calculations appear in Table 13.7. The total is $\chi^2 = 1.4034$. With four degrees of freedom (6 rows minus 1 minus 1 estimated parameter) the critical value for a test at a 5% significance level is 9.4877 (this can be obtained with the Excel$^{\circledR}$ function CHIINV(.05,4)) and the p-value is 0.8436 [from CHIDIST(1.4034,4)]. The exponential model is a good fit.

For Data Set B censored at 1,000, the first interval is from 0–150 and the last interval is from 1,000–∞. Unlike the previous two tests, the censored observations can be used. The calculations are in Table 13.8. The total is $\chi^2 = 0.5951$. With three degrees of freedom (5 rows minus 1 minus 1 estimated parameter) the critical value for a test at a 5% significance level is 7.8147 and the p-value is 0.8976. The exponential model is a good fit.

For Data Set C the groups are already in place. The results are given Table 13.9. The test statistic is $\chi^2 = 61.913$. There are four degrees of freedom for a critical value of 9.488. The p-value is about 10^{-12}. There is clear evidence that the exponential model is not appropriate. A more accurate test would

---

[6] Moore [95] cites a number of rules. Among them are (1) An expected frequency of at least 1 for all cells and and an expected frequency of at least 5 for 80% of the cells; (2) an average count per cell of at least 4 when testing at the 1% significance level and an average count of at least 2 when testing at the 5% significance level; and (3) A sample size of at least 10, at least 3 cells, and the ratio of the square of the sample size to the number of cells at least 10.

Table 13.8 Data Set B censored at 1,000

Range	$\hat{p}$	Expected	Observed	χ^2
0–150	0.1885	3.771	4	0.0139
150–250	0.1055	2.110	3	0.3754
250–500	0.2076	4.152	4	0.0055
500–1,000	0.2500	5.000	4	0.2000
1,000–∞	0.2484	4.968	5	0.0002
Total	1	20	20	0.5951

Table 13.9 Data Set C

Range	$\hat{p}$	Expected	Observed	χ^2
7,500–17,500	0.2023	25.889	42	10.026
17,500–32,500	0.2293	29.356	29	0.004
32,500–67,500	0.3107	39.765	28	3.481
67,500–125,000	0.1874	23.993	17	2.038
125,000–300,000	0.0689	8.824	9	0.003
300,000–∞	0.0013	0.172	3	46.360
Total	1	128	128	61.913

combine the last two groups (because the expected count in the last group is less than 1). The group from 125,000 to infinity has an expected count of 8.997 and an observed count of 12 for a contribution of 1.002. The test statistic is now 16.552 and with three degrees of freedom the p-value is 0.00087. The test continues to reject the exponential model.   □

Sometimes, the test can be modified to fit different situations. The following example illustrates this for aggregate frequency data.

Example 13.8 *Conduct an approximate goodness-of-fit test for the Poisson model determined in Example* 12.60. *The data are repeated in Table* 13.10.

For each year we are assuming that the number of claims is the result of the sum of a number (given by the exposure) of independent and identical random variables. In that case the central limit theorem indicates that a normal approximation may be appropriate. The expected count (E_k) is the exposure times the estimated expected value for one exposure unit while the variance (V_k) is the exposure times the estimated variance for one exposure

Table 13.10 Automobile claims by year

Year	Exposure	Claims
1986	2,145	207
1987	2,452	227
1988	3,112	341
1989	3,458	335
1990	3,698	362
1991	3,872	359

unit. The test statistic is then

$$Q = \sum_k \frac{(n_k - E_k)^2}{V_k}$$

and has an approximate chi-square distribution with degrees of freedom equal to the number of data points less the number of estimated parameters. The expected count is $E_k = \lambda e_k$ and the variance is $V_k = \lambda e_k$ also. The test statistic is

$$
\begin{aligned}
Q &= \frac{(207 - 209.61)^2}{209.61} + \frac{(227 - 239.61)^2}{239.61} + \frac{(341 - 304.11)^2}{304.11} \\
&\quad + \frac{(335 - 337.92)^2}{337.92} + \frac{(362 - 361.37)^2}{361.37} + \frac{(359 - 378.38)^2}{378.38} \\
&= 6.19.
\end{aligned}
$$

With five degrees of freedom, the 5% critical value is 11.07 and the Poisson hypothesis is accepted. □

There is one important point to note about these tests. Suppose the sample size were to double but sampled values were not much different (imagine each number showing up twice instead of once). For the Kolmogorov–Smirnov test, the test statistic would be unchanged, but the critical value would be smaller. For the Anderson–Darling and chi-square tests, the test statistic would double while the critical value would be unchanged. As a result, for larger sample sizes, it is more likely that the null hypothesis (and thus the proposed model) will be rejected. This should not be surprising. We know that the null hypothesis is false (it is extremely unlikely that a simple distribution using a few parameters can explain the complex behavior that produced the observations) and with a large enough sample size we will have convincing evidence of that truth. When using these tests we must remember that, although all our models are wrong, some may be useful.

13.4.4   Likelihood ratio test

An alternative question to "Could the population have distribution A?" is "Is the population more likely to have distribution B than distribution A?" More formally:

H_0 : The data came from a population with distribution A.

H_1 : The data came from a population with distribution B.

In order to perform a formal hypothesis test distribution A must be a special case of distribution B, for example, exponential versus gamma. An easy way to complete this test is given below.

Definition 13.9 *The **likelihood ratio test** is conducted as follows. First, let the likelihood function be written as $L(\boldsymbol{\theta})$. Let $\boldsymbol{\theta}_0$ be the value of the parameters that maximizes the likelihood function. However, only values of the parameters that are within the null hypothesis may be considered. Let $L_0 = L(\boldsymbol{\theta}_0)$. Let $\boldsymbol{\theta}_1$ be the maximum likelihood estimator where the parameters can vary over all possible values from the alternative hypothesis and then let $L_1 = L(\boldsymbol{\theta}_1)$. The test statistic is $T = 2\ln(L_1/L_0) = 2(\ln L_1 - \ln L_0)$. The null hypothesis is rejected if $T > c$, where c is calculated from $\alpha = \Pr(T > c)$, where T has a chi-square distribution with degrees of freedom equal to the number of free parameters in the model from the alternative hypothesis less the number of free parameters in the model from the null hypothesis.*

This test makes some sense. When the alternative hypothesis is true, forcing the parameter to be selected from the null hypothesis should produce a likelihood value that is significantly smaller.

Example 13.10 *You want to test the hypothesis that the population that produced Data Set B (using the original largest observation) has a mean that is other than 1,200. Assume that the population has a gamma distribution and conduct the likelihood ratio test at a 5% significance level. Also, determine the p-value.*

The hypotheses are:

H_0 : gamma with $\mu = 1{,}200$.

H_1 : gamma with $\mu \neq 1{,}200$.

From earlier work the maximum likelihood estimates are $\hat{\alpha} = 0.55616$ and $\hat{\theta} = 2{,}561.1$. The loglikelihood at the maximum is $\ln L_1 = -162.293$. Next, the likelihood must be maximized, but only over those values α and θ for which $\alpha\theta = 1{,}200$. That means α can be free to range over all positive numbers but $\theta = 1{,}200/\alpha$. Thus, under the null hypothesis, there is only one free parameter. The likelihood function is maximized at $\hat{\alpha} = 0.54955$ and $\hat{\theta} = 2{,}183.6$. The loglikelihood at this maximum is $\ln L_0 = -162.466$.

Table 13.11   Six useful models for Example 13.11

Model	Number of parameters	Negative loglikelihood	χ^2	p-value
Negative binomial	2	5,348.04	8.77	0.0125
ZM logarithmic	2	5,343.79	4.92	0.1779
Poisson–inverse Gaussian	2	5,343.51	4.54	0.2091
ZM negative binomial	3	5,343.62	4.65	0.0979
Geometric–negative binomial	3	5,342.70	1.96	0.3754
Poisson–ETNB	3	5,342.51	2.75	0.2525

The test statistic is $T = 2(-162.293 + 162.466) = 0.346$. For a chi-square distribution with one degree of freedom, the critical value is 3.8415. Because $0.346 < 3.8415$, the null hypothesis is not rejected. The probability that a chi-square random variable with one degree of freedom exceeds 0.346 is 0.556, a p-value that indicates little support for the alternative hypothesis.   □

Example 13.11 (Example 4.42 continued) *Members of the $(a, b, 0)$ class were not sufficient to describe these data. Determine a suitable model.*

Thirteen different distributions were fit to the data. The results of that process revealed six models with p-values above 0.01 for the chi-square goodness-of-fit test. Information about those models is given in Table 13.11. The likelihood ratio test indicates that the three-parameter model with the smallest negative loglikelihood (Poisson–ETNB) is not significantly better than the two-parameter Poisson–inverse Gaussian model. The latter appears to be an excellent choice.   □

Example 13.12 *The estimated value of β_1 in Example 12.65 is small. Perform a likelihood ratio test using the beta model to see if age has a significant impact on losses.*

The parameters are reestimated forcing β_1 to be zero. When this is done, the estimates are $\hat{\beta}_2 = -0.79193$, $\hat{a} = 1.03118$, and $\hat{b} = 0.74249$. The value of the logarithm of the likelihood function is -4.2209. Adding age improves the likelihood by 0.0054, which is not significant.   □

It is tempting to use this test when the alternative distribution simply has more parameters than the null distribution. In such cases the test is not appropriate. For example, it is possible for a two-parameter lognormal model to have a higher loglikelihood value than a three-parameter Burr model. This produces a negative test statistic, indicating that a chi-square distribution is not appropriate. When the null distribution is a limiting (rather than special) case of the alternative distribution, the test may still be used, but the test statistic's distribution is now a mixture of chi-square distributions (see [120]). Regardless, it is still reasonable to use the "test" to make decisions in these cases, provided it is clearly understood that a formal hypothesis test was not conducted. Further examples and exercises using this test to make decisions appear in both the next section and the next chapter.

13.4.5   Exercises

13.4 Use the Kolmogorov–Smirnov test to see if a Weibull model is appropriate for the data used in Example 13.5.

13.5 (*) Five observations are made from a random variable. They are 1, 2, 3, 5, and 13. Determine the value of the Kolmogorov–Smirnov test statistic for the null hypothesis that $f(x) = 2x^{-2}e^{-2/x}$, $x > 0$.

13.6 (*) You are given the following five observations from a random sample: 0.1, 0.2, 0.5, 1.0, and 1.3. Calculate the Kolmogorov–Smirnov test statistic for the null hypothesis that the population density function is $f(x) = 2(1+x)^{-3}$, $x > 0$.

13.7 Perform the Anderson–Darling test of the Weibull distribution for Example 13.6.

13.8 Repeat Example 13.7 for the Weibull model.

13.9 (*) One hundred and fifty policyholders were observed from the time they arranged a viatical settlement until their death. No observations were censored. There were 21 deaths in the first year, 27 deaths in the second year, 39 deaths in the third year, and 63 deaths in the fourth year. The survival model

$$S(t) = 1 - \frac{t(t+1)}{20}, \ 0 \leq t \leq 4,$$

is being considered. At a 5% significance level, conduct the chi-square goodness-of-fit test.

13.10 (*) Each day, for 365 days, the number of claims is recorded. The results were 50 days with no claims, 122 days with one claim, 101 days with two claims, 92 days with three claims, and no days with four or more claims. For a Poisson model determine the maximum likelihood estimate of λ and then perform the chi-square goodness-of-fit test at a 2.5% significance level.

13.11 (*) During a one-year period, the number of accidents per day was distributed as given in Table 13.12. Test the hypothesis that the data are from a Poisson distribution with mean 0.6 using the maximum number of groups such that each group has at least five expected observations. Use a significance level of 5%.

Table 13.12 Data for Exercise 13.11

No. of accidents	Days
0	209
1	111
2	33
3	7
4	3
5	2

13.12 Redo Example 13.8 assuming that each exposure unit has a geometric distribution. Conduct the approximate chi-square goodness-of-fit test. Is the geometric preferable to the Poisson model?

13.13 Using Data Set B (with the original largest value), determine if a gamma model is more appropriate than an exponential model. Recall that an exponential model is a gamma model with $\alpha = 1$. Useful values were obtained in Example 12.8.

13.14 Use Data Set C to choose a model for the population that produced those numbers. Choose from the exponential, gamma, and transformed gamma models. Information for the first two distributions was obtained in Example 12.9 and Exercise 12.21, respectively.

13.15 Conduct the chi-square goodness-of-fit test for each of the models obtained in Exercise 12.96.

13.16 Conduct the chi-square goodness-of-fit test for each of the models obtained in Exercise 12.98.

13.17 Conduct the chi-square goodness-of-fit test for each of the models obtained in Exercise 12.99.

13.18 For the data in Table 13.20 determine the method of moments estimates of the parameters of the Poisson–Poisson distribution where the secondary distribution is the ordinary (not zero-truncated) Poisson distribution. Perform the chi-square goodness-of-fit test using this model.

13.19 You are given the data in Table 13.13 which represent results from 23,589 automobile insurance policies. The third column headed "fitted model" represents the expected number of losses for a fitted (by maximum likelihood) negative binomial distribution.

    (a) Perform the chi-squared goodness-of-fit test at a significance level of 5%.

Table 13.13   Data for Exercise 13.19

Number of losses, k	Number of policies, n_k	Fitted model
0	20,592	20,596.76
1	2,651	2,631.03
2	297	318.37
3	41	37.81
4	7	4.45
5	0	0.52
6	1	0.06
≥ 7	0	0.00

(b) Determine the maximum likelihood estimates of the negative binomial parameters r and β. This can be done from the given numbers without actually maximizing the likelihood function.

13.5   SELECTING A MODEL

13.5.1   Introduction

Almost all of the tools are in place for choosing a model. Before outlining a recommended approach, two important concepts must be introduced. The first is **parsimony**. The principle of parsimony states that unless there is considerable evidence to do otherwise a simpler model is preferred. The reason is that a complex model may do a great job of matching the data, but that is no guarantee the model matches the population from which the observations were sampled. For example, given any set of 10 (x, y) pairs with unique x values, there will always be a polynomial of degree 9 or less that goes through all 10 points. But if these points were a random sample, it is highly unlikely that the population values all lie on that polynomial. However, there may be a straight line that comes close to the sampled points as well as the other points in the population. This matches the spirit of most hypothesis tests. That is, do not reject the null hypothesis (and thus claim a more complex description of the population holds) unless there is strong evidence to do so.

The second concept does not have a name. It states that, if you try enough models, one will look good, even if it is not. Suppose I have 900 models at my disposal. For most data sets, it is likely that one of them will fit well, but this does not help us learn about the population.

Thus, in selecting models, there are two things to keep in mind:

1. Use a simple model if at all possible.

2. Restrict the universe of potential models.

The methods outlined in the remainder of this section will help with the first point. The second one requires some experience. Certain models make more sense in certain situations, but only experience can enhance the modeler's senses so that only a short list of quality candidates is considered.

The section is split into two types of selection criteria. The first set is based on the modeler's judgment while the second set is more formal in the sense that most of the time all analysts will reach the same conclusions. That is because the decisions are made based on numerical measurements rather than charts or graphs.

13.5.2   Judgment-based approaches

Using one's own judgment to select models involves one or more of the three concepts outlined below. In all cases, the analyst's experience is critical.

First, the decision can be based on the various graphs (or tables based on the graphs) presented in this chapter.[7] This allows the analyst to focus on aspects of the model that are important for the proposed application. For example, it may be more important to fit the tail well or it may be more important to match the mode or modes. Even if a score-based approach is used, it may be appropriate to present a convincing picture to support the chosen model.

Second, the decision can be influenced by the success of particular models in similar situations or the value of a particular model for its intended use. For example, the 1941 CSO mortality table follows a Makeham distribution for much of its range of ages. In a time of limited computing power, such a distribution allowed for easier calculation of joint life values. As long as the fit of this model was reasonable, this advantage outweighed the use of a different, but better fitting, model. Similarly, if the Pareto distribution has been used to model a particular line of liability insurance both by the analyst's company and by others, it may require more than the usual amount of evidence to change to an alternative distribution.

Third, the situation may completely determine the distribution. For example, suppose a dental insurance contract provides for at most two check-ups per year and suppose that individuals make two independent choices each year as to whether or not to have a check-up. If each time the probability is q, then the distribution must be binomial with $m = 2$.

Finally, it should be noted that the more algorithmic approaches outlined below do not always agree. In that case judgment is most definitely required, if only to decide which algorithmic approach to use.

---

[7] Besides the ones discussed here, there are other plots/tables that could be used. Other choices are a q-q plot and a comparison of model and empirical limited expected values or mean residual life functions.

13.5.3   Score-based approaches

Some analysts might prefer an automated process for selecting a model. An easy way to do that would be to assign a score to each model and the model with the best value wins. The following scores are worth considering:

1. Lowest value of the Kolmogorov–Smirnov test statistic.

2. Lowest value of the Anderson–Darling test statistic.

3. Lowest value of the chi-square goodness-of-fit test statistic.

4. Highest p-value for the chi-square goodness-of-fit test.

5. Highest value of the likelihood function at its maximum.

All but the chi-square p-value have a deficiency with respect to parsimony. First, consider the likelihood function. When comparing, say, an exponential to a Weibull model, the Weibull model must have a likelihood value that is at least as large as the exponential model. They would only be equal in the rare case that the maximum likelihood estimate of the Weibull parameter τ is equal to 1. Thus, the Weibull model would always win over the exponential model, a clear violation of the principle of parsimony. For the three test statistics, there is no assurance that the same relationship will hold, but it seems likely that, if a more complex model is selected, the fit measure is likely to be better. The only reason the p-value is immune from this problem is that with more complex models the test has fewer degrees of freedom. It is then possible that the more complex model will have a smaller p-value. There is no comparable adjustment for the first two test statistics listed.

With regard to the likelihood value, there are two ways to proceed. One is to perform the likelihood ratio test and the other is to extract a penalty for employing additional parameters. The likelihood ratio test is technically only available when one model is a special case of another (for example, Pareto vs generalized Pareto). The concept can be turned into an algorithm by using the test at a 5% significance level. Begin with the best one-parameter model (the one with the highest loglikelihood value). Add a second parameter only if the two-parameter model with the highest loglikelihood value shows an increase of at least 1.92 (so twice the difference exceeds the critical value of 3.84). Then move to three-parameter models. If the comparison is to a two-parameter model, a 1.92 increase is again needed. If the early comparison led to keeping the one-parameter model, an increase of 3.00 is needed (because the test has two degrees of freedom). To add three parameters requires a 3.91 increase, four parameters a 4.74 increase, and so on. In the spirit of this chapter, this algorithm can be used even for nonspecial cases. However, it would not be appropriate to claim that a likelihood ratio test was being conducted.

Aside from the issue of special cases, the likelihood ratio test has the same problem as the other hypothesis tests. Were the sample size to double, the loglikelihoods would also double, making it more likely that a model with a higher number of parameters will be selected. This tends to defeat the parsimony principle. On the other hand, it could be argued that, if we possess a lot of data, we have the right to consider and fit more complex models. A method that effects a compromise between these positions is the Schwarz Bayesian criterion (SBC) [121], which recommends that when ranking models a deduction of $(r/2)\ln n$ should be made from the loglikelihood value, where r is the number of estimated parameters and n is the sample size.[8] Thus, adding a parameter requires an increase of $0.5\ln n$ in the loglikelihood. For larger sample sizes, a greater increase is needed, but it is not proportional to the sample size itself.[9]

Example 13.13 *For the continuing example in this chapter, choose between the exponential and Weibull models for the data.*

Graphs were constructed in the various examples and exercises. Table 13.14 summarizes the numerical measures. For the truncated version of Data Set B, the SBC is calculated for a sample size of 19, while for the version censored at 1,000 there are 20 observations. For both versions of Data Set B, while the Weibull offers some improvement, it is not convincing. In particular, neither the likelihood ratio test nor the SBC indicates value in the second parameter. For Data Set C it is clear that the Weibull model is superior and provides an excellent fit.   □

Example 13.14 *In Example 4.57 an ad hoc method was used to demonstrate that the Poisson–ETNB distribution provided a good fit. Use the methods of this chapter to determine a good model.*

The data set is very large and, as a result, requires a very close correspondence of the model to the data. The results are given in Table 13.15.

From Table 13.15, it is seen that the negative binomial distribution does not fit well while the fit of the Poisson–inverse Gaussian is marginal at best ($p = 2.88\%$). The Poisson–inverse Gaussian is a special case ($r = -0.5$) of the Poisson–ETNB. Hence, a likelihood ratio test can be formally applied to determine if the additional parameter r is justified. Because the loglikelihood increases by 5, which is more than 1.92, the three-parameter model is a significantly better fit. The chi-square test shows that the Poisson-ETNB provides an adequate fit. On the other hand, the SBC favors the Poisson-inverse Gaussian distribution. Given the improved fit in the tail for the three parameter model, it seems to be the best choice.   □

---

[8] In the first edition not only was Schwarz' name misspelled, but the formula for the penalty was incorrect. This edition has the correct version.

[9] There are other information-based decision rules. Section 3 of Brockett [17] promotes the Akaike information criterion. In a discussion to that paper, Carlin provides support for the SBC.

Table 13.14 Results for Example 13.13

	B truncated at 50		B censored at 1,000	
Criterion	Exponential	Weibull	Exponential	Weibull
K-S*	0.1340	0.0887	0.0991	0.0991
A-D*	0.4292	0.1631	0.1713	0.1712
χ^2	1.4034	0.3615	0.5951	0.5947
p-value	0.8436	0.9481	0.8976	0.7428
Loglikelihood	-146.063	-145.683	-113.647	-113.647
SBC	-147.535	-148.628	-115.145	-116.643
	C			
χ^2	61.913	0.3698		
p-value	10^{-12}	0.9464		
Loglikelihood	-214.924	-202.077		
SBC	-217.350	-206.929		

*K-S and A-D refer to the Kolmogorov–Smirnov and Anderson–Darling test statistics, respectively.

Example 13.15 *The following example is taken from Douglas [29], p. 253. An insurance company's records for one year show the number of accidents per day which resulted in a claim to the insurance company for a particular insurance coverage. The results are in Table* 13.16. *Determine if a Poisson model is appropriate.*

A Poisson model is fitted to these data. The method of moments and the maximum likelihood method both lead to the estimate of the mean,

$$\hat{\lambda} = \frac{742}{365} = 2.0329.$$

The results of a chi-square goodness-of-fit test are in Table 13.17. Any time such a table is made, the expected count for the last group is

$$E_{k+} = n\hat{p}_{k+} = n(1 - \hat{p}_0 - \cdots - \hat{p}_{k-1}).$$

The last three groups were combined to ensure an expected count of at least one for each row. The test statistic is 9.93 with six degrees of freedom. The critical value at a 5% significance level is 12.59 and the p-value is 0.1277. By this test the Poisson distribution is an acceptable model; however, it should be noted that the fit is poorest at the large values, and with the model understating the observed values, this may be a risky choice.   □

Example 13.16 *The data set in Table* 12.13 *come from Beard et al. [12] and were previously analyzed in Example 12.58. Determine a model that adequately describes the data.*

Table 13.15 Results for Example 13.14

No. of claims	Observed frequency	Fitted distributions		
		Negative binomial	Poisson– inverse Gaussian	Poisson– ETNB
0	565,664	565,708.1	565,712.4	565,661.2
1	68,714	68,570.0	68,575.6	68,721.2
2	5,177	5,317.2	5,295.9	5,171.7
3	365	334.9	344.0	362.9
4	24	18.7	20.8	29.6
5	6	1.0	1.2	3.0
6+	0	0.0	0.1	0.4
Parameters		$\beta = 0.0350662$ $r = 3.57784$	$\lambda = 0.123304$ $\beta = 0.0712027$	$\lambda = 0.123395$ $\beta = 0.233862$ $r = -0.846872$
Chi square		12.13	7.09	0.29
Degrees of freedom		2	2	1
p-value		<1%	2.88%	58.9%
$-$Loglikelihood		251,117	251,114	251,109
SBC		$-251,130$	$-251,127$	$-251,129$

Table 13.16 Data for Example 13.15

No. of claims/day	Observed no. of days
0	47
1	97
2	109
3	62
4	25
5	16
6	4
7	3
8	2
9+	0

Parameter estimates from fitting four models are in Table 12.13. Various fit measures are given in Table 13.18. Only the zero-modified geometric distribution passes the goodness-of-fit test. It is also clearly superior according to the SBC. A likelihood ratio test against the geometric has a test statistic of $2(171,479 - 171,133) = 692$, which with one degree of freedom is clearly significant. This confirms the qualitative conclusion in Example 12.58.   □

Table 13.17   Chi-square goodness-of-fit test for Example 13.15

Claims/day	Observed	Expected	Chi square
0	47	47.8	0.01
1	97	97.2	0.00
2	109	98.8	1.06
3	62	66.9	0.36
4	25	34.0	2.39
5	16	13.8	0.34
6	4	4.7	0.10
7+	5	1.8	5.66
Totals	365	365	9.93

Table 13.18   Test results for Example 13.16

	Poisson	Geometric	ZM Poisson	ZM geometric
Chi square	543.0	643.4	64.8	0.58
Degrees of freedom	2	4	2	2
p-value	$< 1\%$	$< 1\%$	$< 1\%$	74.9%
Loglikelihood	$-171{,}373$	$-171{,}479$	$-171{,}160$	$-171{,}133$
SBC	$-171{,}379.5$	$-171{,}485.5$	$-171{,}173$	$-171{,}146$

Example 13.17 *The data in Table* 13.19, *from Simon* [122], *represent the observed number of claims per contract for* 298 *contracts. Determine an appropriate model.*

The Poisson, negative binomial, and Polya–Aeppli distributions are fitted to the data. The Polya–Aeppli and the negative binomial are both plausible distributions. The p-value of the chi-square statistic and the loglikelihood both indicate that the Polya–Aeppli is slightly better than the negative binomial. The SBC verifies that both models are superior to the Poisson distribution. The ultimate choice may depend on familiarity, prior use, and computational convenience of the negative binomial versus the Polya–Aeppli model.   □

Example 13.18 *Consider the data in Table* 13.20 *on automobile liability policies in Switzerland taken from Bühlmann* [19]. *Determine an appropriate model.*

Three models are considered in Table 13.20. The Poisson distribution is a very bad fit. Its tail is far too light compared with the actual experience. The negative binomial distribution appears to be much better but cannot be accepted because the p-value of the chi-square statistic is very small. The large sample size requires a better fit. The Poisson–inverse Gaussian distribution

Table 13.19 Fit of Simon data

Number of claims/contract	Number of contracts	Poisson	Negative binomial	Polya–Aeppli
0	99	54.0	95.9	98.7
1	65	92.2	75.8	70.6
2	57	78.8	50.4	50.2
3	35	44.9	31.3	32.6
4	20	19.2	18.8	20.0
5	10	6.5	11.0	11.7
6	4	1.9	6.4	6.6
7	0	0.5	3.7	3.6
8	3	0.1	2.1	2.0
9	4	0.0	1.2	1.0
10	0	0.0	0.7	0.5
11	1	0.0	0.4	0.3
12+	0	0.0	0.5	0.3
Parameters		$\lambda = 1.70805$	$\beta = 1.15907$ $r = 1.47364$	$\lambda = 1.10551$ $\beta = 0.545039$
Chi square		72.64	4.06	2.84
Degrees of freedom		4	5	5
p-Value		<1%	54.05%	72.39%
Loglikelihood		−577.0	−528.8	−528.5
SBC		−579.8	−534.5	−534.2

provides an almost perfect fit (p-value is large). Note that the Poisson–inverse Gaussian has two parameters, like the negative binomial. The SBC also favors this choice. This example shows that the Poisson–inverse Gaussian can have a much heavier right-hand tail than the negative binomial. □

Example 13.19 *Comprehensive medical claims were studied by Bevan* [15] *in 1963. Male* (955 *payments*) *and female* (1,291 *payments*) *claims were studied separately. The data appear in Table* 13.21 *where there was a deductible of 25. Can a common model be used?*

When using the combined data set the lognormal distribution is the best two-parameter model. Its negative loglikelihood (NLL) is 4,580.20. This is 19.09 better than the one-parameter inverse exponential model and 0.13 worse than the three-parameter Burr model. Because none of these models is a special case of the other, the likelihood ratio test (LRT) cannot be used, but it is clear that using the 1.92 difference as a standard, the lognormal is preferred. The SBC requires an improvement of $0.5 \ln(2{,}246) = 3.86$ and again

Table 13.20 Fit of Buhlmann data

No. of accidents	Observed frequency	Fitted distributions		
		Poisson	Negative binomial	P.–i.G.[a]
0	103,704	102,629.6	103,723.6	103,710.0
1	14,075	15,922.0	13,989.9	14,054.7
2	1,766	1,235.1	1,857.1	1,784.9
3	255	63.9	245.2	254.5
4	45	2.5	32.3	40.4
5	6	0.1	4.2	6.9
6	2	0.0	0.6	1.3
7+	0	0.0	0.1	0.3
Parameters		$\lambda = 0.155140$	$\beta = 0.150232$	$\lambda = 0.144667$
			$r = 1.03267$	$\beta = 0.310536$
Chi square		1,332.3	12.12	0.78
Degrees of freedom		2	2	3
p-Values		<1%	<1%	85.5%
Loglikelihood		−55,108.5	−54,615.3	−54,609.8
SBC		−55,114.3	−54,627.0	−54,621.5

[a]P.–i.G. stands for Poisson–inverse Gaussian.

the lognormal is preferred. The parameters are $\mu = 4.5237$ and $\sigma = 1.4950$. When separate lognormal models are fit to males ($\mu = 3.9686$ and $\sigma = 1.8432$) and females ($\mu = 4.7713$ and $\sigma = 1.2848$), the respective NLLs are 1,977.25 and 2,583.82 for a total of 4,561.07. This is an improvement of 19.13 over a common lognormal model, which is significant by both the LRT (3.00 needed) and SBC (7.72 needed). Sometimes it is useful to be able to use the same nonscale parameter in both models. When a common value of σ is used, the NLL is 4,579.77, which is significantly worse than using separate models. □

Example 13.20 *In 1958 Longley-Cook [86] examined employment patterns of casualty actuaries. One of his tables listed the number of members of the Casualty Actuarial Society employed by casualty companies in 1949 (55 actuaries) and 1957 (78 actuaries). Using the data in Table 13.22 determine a model for the number of actuaries per company which employs at least one actuary and find out whether the distribution has changed over the eight-year period.*

Because a value of zero is impossible, only zero-trucated distributions should be considered. In all three cases (1949 data only, 1957 data only, combined data) the ZT logarithmic and ZT (extended) negative binomial distributions have acceptable goodness-of-fit test values. The improvement in NLL is 0.52, 0.02, and 0.94. The LRT can be applied (except that the ZT

Table 13.21   Comprehensive medical losses for Example 13.19

Loss	Male	Female
25–50	184	199
50–100	270	310
100–200	160	262
200–300	88	163
300–400	63	103
400–500	47	69
500–1,000	61	124
1,000–2,000	35	40
2,000–3,000	18	12
3,000–4,000	13	4
4,000–5,000	2	1
5,000–6,667	5	2
6,667–7,500	3	1
7,500–10,000	6	1

Table 13.22   Number of actuaries per company for Example 13.20

Number of actuaries	Number of companies—1949	Number of companies—1957
1	17	23
2	7	7
3–4	3	3
5–9	2	3
10+	0	1

logarithmic distribution is a limiting case of the ZT negative binomial distribution with $r \to 0$), and the improvement is not significant in any of the cases. The same conclusions apply if the SBC is used. The parameter estimates (where β is the only parameter) are 2.0227, 2.8114, and 2.4479, respectively. The NLL for the combined data set is 74.35 while the total for the two separate models is 74.15. The improvement is only 0.20, which is not significant (there is one degree of freedom). Even though the estimated mean has increased from $2.0227/\ln(3.0227) = 1.8286$ to $2.8114/\ln(3.8114) = 2.1012$, there is not enough data to make a convincing case that the true mean has increased. □

13.5.4   Exercises

13.20 (*) One thousand policies were sampled and the number of accidents for each recorded. The results are in Table 13.23. Without doing any for-

Table 13.23 Data for Exercise 13.20

No. of accidents	No. of policies
0	100
1	267
2	311
3	208
4	87
5	23
6	4
Total	1,000

Table 13.24 Results for Exercise 13.23

Model	No. of parameters	Negative loglikelihood
Generalized Pareto	3	219.1
Burr	3	219.2
Pareto	2	221.2
Lognormal	2	221.4
Inverse exponential	1	224.3

mal tests, determine which of the following five models is most appropriate: binomial, Poisson, negative binomial, normal, gamma.

13.21 For Example 13.1, determine if a transformed gamma model is more appropriate than either the exponential model or the Weibull model for each of the three data sets.

13.22 (*) From the data in Exercise 13.11 the maximum likelihood estimates are $\hat{\lambda} = 0.60$ for the Poisson distribution and $\hat{r} = 2.9$ and $\hat{\beta} = 0.21$ for the negative binomial distribution. Conduct the likelihood ratio test for choosing between these two models.

13.23 (*) From a sample of size 100, five models are fit with the results given in Table 13.24. Use the Schwarz Bayesian criterion to select the best model.

13.24 This is a continuation of Exercise 12.38. Use both the likelihood ratio test (at a 5% significance level) and the Schwarz Bayesian criterion to decide if Sylvia's claim is true.

13.25 Using the results from Exercises 12.96 and 13.15, use the chi-square goodness-of-fit test, the likelihood ratio test, and the Schwarz Bayesian criterion to determine the best model from the members of the $(a, b, 0)$ class.

Table 13.25   Data for Exercise 13.28

No. of medical claims	No. of accidents
0	529
1	146
2	169
3	137
4	99
5	87
6	41
7	25
8+	0

13.26 Using the results from Exercises 12.98 and 13.16, use the chi-square goodness-of-fit test, the likelihood ratio test, and the Schwarz Bayesian criterion to determine the best model from the members of the $(a, b, 0)$ class.

13.27 Using the results from Exercises 12.99 and 13.17, use the chi-square goodness-of-fit test, the likelihood ratio test, and the Schwarz Bayesian criterion to determine the best model from the members of the $(a, b, 0)$ class.

13.28 Table 13.25 gives the number of medical claims per reported automobile accident.

   (a) Construct a plot similar to Figure 4.8. Does it appear that a member of the $(a, b, 0)$ class will provide a good model? If so, which one?

   (b) Determine the maximum likelihood estimates of the parameters for each member of the $(a, b, 0)$ class.

   (c) Based on the chi-square goodness-of-fit test, the likelihood ratio test, and the Schwarz Bayesian criterion, which member of the $(a, b, 0)$ class provides the best fit? Is this model acceptable?

13.29 For the four data sets introduced in Exercises 12.96, 12.98, 12.99, and 13.28, you have determined the best model from among members of the $(a, b, 0)$ class. For each data set determine the maximum likelihood estimates of the zero-modified Poisson, geometric, logarithmic, and negative binomial distributions. Use the chi-square goodness-of-fit test and likelihood ratio tests to determine the best of the eight models considered and state whether or not the selected model is acceptable.

13.30 A frequency model that has not been mentioned to this point is the **zeta distribution**. It is a zero-truncated distribution with $p_k^T = k^{-(\rho+1)}/\zeta(\rho+1)$, $k = 1, 2, \dots, \rho > 0$. The denominator is the zeta function, which must be

Table 13.26   Data for Excercise 13.32(a)

No. of claims	No. of policies
0	96,978
1	9,240
2	704
3	43
4	9
5+	0

evaluated numerically as $\zeta(\rho + 1) = \sum_{k=1}^{\infty} k^{-(\rho+1)}$. The zero-modified zeta distribution can be formed in the usual way. More information can be found in Luong and Doray [88].

(a) Determine the maximum likelihood estimates of the parameters of the zero-modified zeta distribution for the data in Example 12.58.

(b) Is the zero-modified zeta distribution acceptable?

13.31 In Exercise 13.29 the best model from among the members of the $(a, b, 0)$ and $(a, b, 1)$ classes was selected for the data sets in Exercises 12.96, 12.98, 12.99, and 13.28. Fit the Poisson–Poisson, Polya–Aeppli, Poisson–inverse Gaussian, and Poisson–ETNB distributions to these data and determine if any of these distributions should replace the one selected in Exercise 13.29. Is the current best model acceptable?

13.32 The five data sets presented in this problem are all taken from Lemaire [82]. For each data set compute the first three moments and then use the ideas in Section 4.6.8 to make a guess at an appropriate model from among the compound Poisson collection (Poisson, geometric, negative binomial, Poisson–binomial (with $m = 2$ and $m = 3$), Polya–Aeppli, Neyman Type A, Poisson–inverse Gaussian, and Poisson–ETNB). From the selected model (if any) and members of the $(a, b, 0)$ and $(a, b, 1)$ classes, determine the best model.

(a) The data in Table 13.26 represent counts from third-party automobile liability coverage in Belgium.

(b) The data in Table 13.27 represent the number of deaths due to horse kicks in the Prussian army between 1875 and 1894. The counts are the number of deaths in a corps (there were 10 of them) in a given year, and thus there are 200 observations. This data set is often cited as the inspiration for the Poisson distribution. For using any of our models, what additional assumption about the data must be made?

(c) The data in Table 13.28 represent the number of major international wars per year from 1500 through 1931.

Table 13.27   Data for Excercise 13.32(b)

No. of deaths	No. of corps
0	109
1	65
2	22
3	3
4	1
5+	0

Table 13.28   Data for Excercise 13.32(c)

No. of wars	No. of years
0	223
1	142
2	48
3	15
4	4
5+	0

Table 13.29   Data for Excercise 13.32(d)

No. of runs	No. of half innings
0	1,023
1	222
2	87
3	32
4	18
5	11
6	6
7+	3

(d) The data in Table 13.29 represent the number of runs scored in each half-inning of World Series baseball games played from 1947 through 1960.

(e) The data in Table 13.30 represent the number of goals per game per team in the 1966–1967 season of the National Hockey League.

13.33 Verify that the estimates presented in Example 4.64 are the maximum likelihood estimates. (Because only two decimals are presented, it is probably sufficient to observe that the likelihood function takes on smaller values at

Table 13.30 Data for Excercise 13.32(e)

No. of goals	No. of games
0	29
1	71
2	82
3	89
4	65
5	45
6	24
7	7
8	4
9	1
10+	3

each of the nearby points.) The negative binomial distribution was fit to these data in Example 12.56. Which of these two models is preferable?

14

Five examples

14.1 INTRODUCTION

In this chapter we present five examples that illustrate many of the concepts discussed to this point. The first is a model for the time to death. The second model is for the time from when a medical malpractice incident occurs to when it is reported. The third model is for the amount of a liability payment. This model is also continuous but most likely has a decreasing failure rate (typical of payment amount variables). On the other hand, time to event variables tend to have an increasing failure rate. The last two examples add aggregate loss calculations from Chapter 6 to the mix.

14.2 TIME TO DEATH

14.2.1 The data

A variety of mortality tables are available from the Society of Actuaries at www.soa.org. The typical mortality table provides values of the survival function at each whole-number age at death. Table 14.1 represents female mortality in 1900, with only some of the data points presented. It is followed by

Loss Models: From Data to Decisions, Second Edition.
By Stuart A. Klugman, Harry H. Panjer, and Gordon E. Willmot
ISBN 0-471-21577-5   Copyright © 2004 John Wiley & Sons, Inc.

Table 14.1   1900 female mortality

x	$S(x)$	x	$S(x)$	x	$S(x)$
0	1.000	35	0.681	75	0.233
1	0.880	40	0.650	80	0.140
5	0.814	45	0.617	85	0.062
10	0.796	50	0.580	90	0.020
15	0.783	55	0.534	95	0.003
20	0.766	60	0.478	100	0.000
25	0.739	65	0.410		
30	0.711	70	0.328		

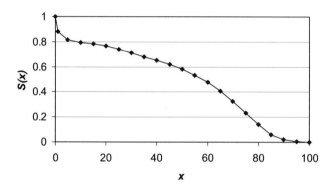

Fig. 14.1   Survival function for Society of Actuaries data.

Figure 14.1, a graph of the survival function obtained by connecting the given points with straight lines.

The mean residual life function can be obtained by assuming that the survival function is indeed a straight line connecting each of the available points. From (3.5) it can be computed as the area under the curve beyond the given age divided by the value of the survival function at that age. Figure 14.2 contains a plot of the mean residual life function. The slight increase shortly after birth indicates that in 1900 infant mortality was high. Surviving the first year after birth adds about five years to one's expected remaining lifetime. After that, the mean residual life steadily decreases, which is the effect of aging that we would have expected.

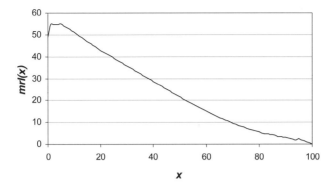

Fig. 14.2 Mean residual life function for Society of Actuaries data.

14.2.2 Some calculations

Items such as deductibles, limits, and coinsurances are not particularly in-teresting with regard to insurances on human lifetimes. We will consider the following two questions:

1. For a person age 65, determine the expected present value of providing 1,000 at the beginning of each year in which the person is alive. The interest rate is 6%.

2. For a person age 20, determine the expected present value of providing 1,000 at the moment of death. The interest rate is 6%.

For the first problem, the present value random variable Y can be written as $Y = 1,000(Y_0 + \cdots + Y_{34})$, where Y_j is the present value of that part of the benefit that pays 1 at age $65 + j$ if the person is alive at that time. Then,

$$Y_j = \begin{cases} 1.06^{-j} & \text{with probability } \dfrac{S(65+j)}{S(65)}, \\ 0 & \text{with probability } 1 - \dfrac{S(65+j)}{S(65)}. \end{cases}$$

The answer is then

$$\begin{aligned} \mathrm{E}(Y) &= 1,000 \sum_{j=0}^{34} \frac{1.06^{-j} S(65+j)}{0.410} \\ &= 8,408.07, \end{aligned}$$

where linear interpolation was used for intermediate values of the survival function.

For the second problem, let $Z = 1{,}000(1.06^{-T})$ be the present value random variable, where T is the time in years to death of the 20-year old. The calculation is

$$\mathrm{E}(Z) = 1{,}000 \int_0^{80} \frac{1.06^{-t} f(20 + t)}{S(20)} dt.$$

When linear interpolation is used to obtain the survival function at intermediate ages, the density function becomes the slope. That is, if x is a multiple of 5, then

$$f(t) = \frac{S(x) - S(x + 5)}{5}, \quad x < t < x + 5.$$

Breaking the range of integration into 16 pieces gives

$$\begin{aligned}
\mathrm{E}(Z) &= \frac{1000}{0.766} \sum_{j=0}^{15} \frac{S(20 + 5j) - S(25 + 5j)}{5} \int_{5j}^{5+5j} 1.06^{-t} dt \\
&= \frac{200}{0.766} \sum_{j=0}^{15} [S(20 + 5j) - S(25 + 5j)] \frac{1.06^{-5j} - 1.06^{-5-5j}}{\ln 1.06} \\
&= 155.10.
\end{aligned}$$

While it is unusual for a parametric model to be used, we will do so anyway. Consider the Makeham distribution with hazard rate function $h(x) = A + Bc^x$. Then

$$S(x) = \exp\left[-Ax - \frac{B(c^x - 1)}{\ln c} \right].$$

Maximum likelihood estimation cannot be used because no sample size is given. Because it is unlikely that this model will be effective below age 20, only information beyond that age will be used. Assume that that there were 1,000 lives at age 0 who died according to the survival function in Table 14.1. Then, for example, the contribution to the likelihood function for the interval from age 30 to 35 is $30 \ln\{[S(30) - S(35)]/S(20)\}$ with the survival function using the Makeham distribution. The sample size comes from $1{,}000(0.711 - 0.681)$ with these survival function values taken from the "data."[1] The values that maximize this likelihood function are $\hat{A} = 0.006698$, $\hat{B} = 0.00007976$, and $\hat{c} = 1.09563$. In Figure 14.3 the diamonds represent the "data" and the solid curve is the Makeham survival function (both have been conditioned on being alive at age 20). The fit is almost too good, suggesting that perhaps this mortality table was already smoothed to follow a Makeham distribution at adult ages.

The same calculations can be done. For the annuity, no interpolation is needed because the Makeham function provides the survival function values

---

[1] Aside from not knowing the sample size, the values in Table 14.1 are probably not random observations. It is possible the values in the table were smoothed using techniques of the kind discussed in Chapter 15.

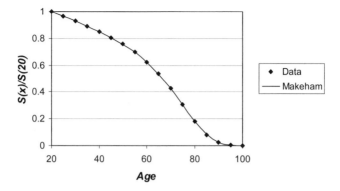

Fig. 14.3 Comparison of "data" and Makeham model.

at each age. The answer is 8,405.24. For the insurance, it is difficult to do the integral analytically. Linear interpolation was used between integral ages to produce an answer of 154.90. The agreement with the answers obtained earlier is not surprising.

14.2.3 Exercise

14.1 From ages 5 through 100 the mean residual life function is essentially linear. Because insurances are rarely sold under age 5, it would be reasonable to extend the graph linearly back to 0. Then a reasonable approximation is $e(x) = 60 - 0.6x$. From this, determine the density and survival function for the age at death and then use this function to solve the two problems.

14.3 TIME FROM INCIDENCE TO REPORT

Consider an insurance contract that provides payment when a certain event (such as death, disability, fire) occurs. There are three key dates. The first is when the event occurs, the second is when it is reported to the insurance company, and the third is when the claim is settled. The time between these dates is important because it affects the amount of interest that can be earned on the premium prior to paying the claim and because it provides a mechanism for estimating unreported claims. This example concerns the time from incidence to report. The particular example used here is based on a paper by Accomando and Weissner [4].

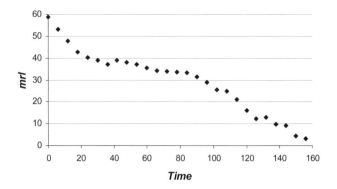

Fig. 14.4   Mean residual life function for report lag data.

14.3.1   The problem and some data

This example concerns medical malpractice claims that occurred in a particular year. One hundred sixty-eight months after the beginning of the year
under study, there have been 463 claims reported that were known to have
occurred in that year. The distribution of the times from occurrence to report
(by month in six month intervals) is given in Table 14.2. A graph of the mean
residual life function appears in Figure 14.4.[2]

Your task is to fit a model to these observations and then use the model to
estimate the total number of claims that occurred in the year under study. A
look at the mean residual life function indicates a decreasing pattern and so
a lighter than exponential tail is expected. A Weibull model can have such a
tail and so can be used here.

14.3.2   Analysis

Using maximum likelihood to estimate the Weibull parameters, the result is
$\hat{\tau} = 1.71268$ and $\hat{\theta} = 67.3002$. According to the Weibull distribution, the
probability that a claim is reported by time 168 is

$$F(168) = 1 - e^{-(168/\theta)^{\tau}}.$$

If N is the unknown total number of claims, the number observed by time
168 is the result of binomial sampling, and thus on an expected value basis

---

[2] Because of the right truncation of the data, there are some items missing for calculation
of the mean residual life. It is not clear from the data what the effect will be. This picture
gives a guide, but the model ultimately selected should both fit the data and be reasonable
based on the analyst's experience and judgment.

Table 14.2 Medical malpractice report lags

Lag in months	No. of claims	Lag in months	No. of claims
0–6	4	84–90	11
6–12	6	90–96	9
12–18	8	96–102	7
18–24	38	102–108	13
24–30	45	108–114	5
30–36	36	114–120	2
36–42	62	120–126	7
42–48	33	126–132	17
48–54	29	132–138	5
54–60	24	138–144	8
60–66	22	144–150	2
66–72	24	150–156	6
72–78	21	156–162	2
78–84	17	162–168	0

we obtain

Expected number of reported claims by time $168 = N[1 - e^{-(168/\theta)^\tau}]$.

Setting this expectation equal to the observed number reported of 463 and then solving for N yields

$$N = \frac{463}{1 - e^{-(168/\theta)^\tau}}.$$

Inserting the parameter estimates yields the value 466.88. Thus, after 14 years, we expect to have about four more claims reported.

The delta method (Theorem 12.17) can be used to produce a 95% confidence interval. It is 466.88 ± 2.90, indicating that there could reasonably be between one and seven additional claims reported.

14.4 PAYMENT AMOUNT

You are the consulting actuary for a reinsurer and have been asked to determine the expected cost and the risk (as measured by the coefficient of variation) for various coverages. To help you out, losses from 200 claims have been supplied. The reinsurer also estimates (and you may confidently rely on its estimate) that there will be 21 losses per year and the number of losses has a Poisson distribution. The coverages it is interested in are full coverage, 1 million excess of 250,000, and 2 million excess of 500,000. The phrase "z excess of y" is to be interpreted as $d = y$ and $u = y + z$ in the notation of Theorem 5.13.

Table 14.3 Losses up to 200 (thousand)

Loss range (thousands)	Number of losses	Loss range (thousands)	Number of losses
1–5	3	41–50	19
6–10	12	51–75	28
11–15	14	76–100	21
16–20	9	101–125	15
21–25	7	126–150	10
26–30	7	151–200	15
31–40	18		

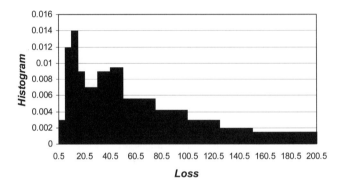

Fig. 14.5 Histogram of losses.

14.4.1 The data

One hundred seventy-eight losses that were 200,000 or below (all expressed in whole numbers of thousands of dollars) that were supplied are summarized in Table 14.3. In addition, there were 22 losses in excess of 200. They are listed below:

206	219	230	235	241	272	283	286	312	319	385
427	434	555	562	584	700	711	869	980	999	1506

Finally, the 178 losses in the table sum to 11,398 and their squares sum to 1,143,164.

To get a feel for the data in the table, the histogram in Figure 14.5 was constructed. Keep in mind that the height of a histogram bar is the count in the cell divided by the sample size (200) and then further divided by the interval width. Therefore, the first bar has a height of $3/[200(5)] = 0.003$.

Table 14.4 Mean residual life for losses above 200 (thousand)

Loss	Mean residual life
200	314
300	367
400	357
500	330
600	361
700	313
800	289
900	262

It can be seen from the histogram that the underlying distribution has a nonzero mode. To check the tail, we can compute the empirical mean residual life function at a number of values. They are presented in Table 14.4. The function appears to be fairly constant and so an exponential model seems reasonable.

14.4.2 The first model

A two-component spliced model was selected. The empirical model is used through 200 (thousand) and an exponential model thereafter. There are (at least) two ways to choose the exponential model. One is to restrict the parameter by forcing the distribution to place 11% (22 out of 200) of probability at points above 200. The other option is to estimate the exponential model independent of the 11% requirement and then multiply the density function to make the area above 200 be 0.11. The latter was selected and the resulting parameter estimate is $\theta = 314$. For values below 200, the empirical distribution places probability $1/200$ at each observed value. The resulting exponential density function (for $x > 200$) is

$$f(x) = 0.000662344e^{-x/314}.$$

For a coverage that pays all losses, the kth moment is (where the 200 losses in the sample have been ordered from smallest to largest)

$$E(X^k) = \frac{1}{200} \sum_{j=1}^{178} x_j^k + \int_{200}^{\infty} x^k f(x)dx.$$

Then,

$$E(X) \quad = \quad \frac{11{,}398}{200} + 0.000662344[314(200) + 314^2]e^{-200/314} = 113.53,$$

$$E(X^2) \quad = \quad \frac{1{,}143{,}164}{200}$$

$$+0.000662344[314(200)^2 + 2(314)^2(200) + 2(314)^3]e^{-200/314}$$

$$= \quad 45{,}622.93.$$

The variance is $45{,}622.93 - 113.53^2 = 32{,}733.87$ for a coefficient of variation of 1.59. However, these are for one loss only. The distribution of annual losses follows a compound Poisson distribution. The mean is

$$E(S) = E(N)E(X) = 21(113.53) = 2{,}384.13$$

and the variance is

$$\text{Var}(S) \quad = \quad E(N)\,\text{Var}(X) + \text{Var}(N)E(X)^2$$
$$= \quad 21(32{,}733.87) + 21(113.53)^2 = 958{,}081.53$$

for a coefficient of variation of 0.41.

For the other coverages we need general formulas for the first two limited expected moments. For $u > 200$,

$$E(X \wedge u) \quad = \quad 56.99 + \int_{200}^{u} x f(x)\,dx + \int_{u}^{\infty} u f(x)\,dx$$

$$= \quad 56.99 + c\int_{200}^{u} x e^{-x/314}\,dx + c\int_{u}^{\infty} u e^{-x/314}\,dx$$

$$= \quad 56.99 + c\left(-314x e^{-x/314} - 314^2 e^{-x/314}\right)\Big|_{200}^{u}$$

$$+ -cu314 e^{-x/314}\Big|_{u}^{\infty}$$

$$= \quad 56.99 + c\left(161{,}396 e^{-200/314} - 314^2 e^{-u/314}\right),$$

where $c = 0.000662344$ and similarly

$$E[(X \wedge u)^2] \quad = \quad 5{,}715.82 + c\int_{200}^{u} x^2 e^{-x/314}\,dx + c\int_{u}^{\infty} u^2 e^{-x/314}\,dx$$

$$5{,}715.82 + c\left[-314x^2 - 314^2(2x) - 314^3(2)\right]e^{-x/314}\Big|_{200}^{u}$$

$$- cu^2 314 e^{-x/314}\Big|_{u}^{\infty}$$

$$= \quad 5{,}715.82 + c\Big[113{,}916{,}688 e^{-200/314}$$

$$-(197{,}192u + 61{,}918{,}288)e^{-u/314}\Big].$$

Table 14.5   Limited moment calculations

u	$\mathrm{E}(X \wedge u)$	$\mathrm{E}[(X \wedge u)^2]$
250	84.07	12,397.08
500	100.24	23,993.47
1,250	112.31	41,809.37
2,500	113.51	45,494.83

Table 14.5 gives the quantities needed to complete the assignment.

The requested moments for the 1,000 excess of 250 coverage are, for one loss,

$$
\begin{aligned}
\text{Mean} &= 112.31 - 84.07 = 28.24, \\
\text{Second moment} &= 41,809.37 - 12,397.08 - 2(250)(28.24) \\
&= 15,292.29, \\
\text{Variance} &= 15,292.29 - 28.24^2 = 14,494.79, \\
\text{Coefficient of variation} &= \frac{\sqrt{14,494.79}}{28.24} = 4.26.
\end{aligned}
$$

It is interesting to note that while, as expected, the coverage limitations reduce the variance, the risk, as measured by the coefficient of variation, has increased considerably. For a full year, the mean is 593.04, the variance is 321,138.09, and the coefficient of variation is 0.96.

For the 2,000 excess of 500 coverage, we have, for one loss,

$$
\begin{aligned}
\text{Mean} &= 113.51 - 100.24 = 13.27, \\
\text{Second moment} &= 45,494.83 - 23,993.47 - 2(500)(13.27) \\
&= 8,231.36, \\
\text{Variance} &= 8,231.36 - 13.27^2 = 8,055.27, \\
\text{Coefficient of variation} &= \frac{\sqrt{8,055.27}}{13.27} = 6.76.
\end{aligned}
$$

Moving further into the tail increases our risk. For one year, the three items are 278.67, 172,858.56, and 1.49.

14.4.3   The second model

From Figure 14.5, if a single parametric distribution is to be used, one with a nonzero mode should be tried. Because the data were rounded to the nearest 1,000, the intervals should be treated as 0.5–5.5, 5.5–10.5, and so on. After considering lognormal, Weibull, gamma, and mixture models (adding an exponential distribution), the lognormal distribution is clearly superior (using the SBC). The parameters are $\hat{\mu} = 4.0626$ and $\hat{\sigma} = 1.1466$. The chi-square

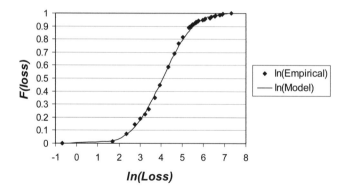

Fig. 14.6 Distribution function plot.

goodness-of-fit test (placing the observations above 200 into a single group) statistic is 7.77 for a *p*-value of 0.73. Figure 14.6 compares the lognormal model to the empirical model. The graph confirms the good fit.

14.5 AN AGGREGATE LOSS EXAMPLE

The example to be covered in this section summarizes many of the techniques introduced up to this point. The coverage is perhaps more complex than those found in practice, but that gives us a chance to work through a variety of tasks.

Example 14.1 *You are a consulting actuary and have been retained to assist in the pricing of a group hospitalization policy. Your task is to determine the expected payment to be made by the insurer. The terms of the policy (per covered employee) are as follows:*

1. *For each hospitalization of the employee or a member of the employee's family, the employee pays the first 500 plus any losses in excess of 50,500. On any one hospitalization, the insurance will pay at most 50,000.*

2. *In any calendar year, the employee will pay no more than 1,000 in deductibles, but there is no limit on how much the employee will pay in respect of losses exceeding 50,500.*

3. *Any particular hospitalization is assigned to the calendar year in which the individual entered the hospital. Even if hospitalization extends into subsequent years, all payments are made in respect to the policy year assigned.*

Table 14.6 Hospitalizations, per family member, per year

No. of hospitalizations per family member	No. of family members
0	2,659
1	244
2	19
3	2
4 or more	0
Total	2,924

Table 14.7 Number of family members per employee

No. of family members per employee	No. of employees
1	84
2	140
3	139
4	131
5	73
6	42
7	27
8 or more	33
Total	669

4. The premium is the same, regardless of the number of family members.

Experience studies have provided the data contained in Tables 14.6 and 14.8. The data in Table 14.7 represent the profile of the current set of employees.

The first step is to fit parametric models to each of the three data sets. For the data in Table 14.6, 12 distributions were fitted. The best one-parameter distribution is the geometric with a negative loglikelihood (NLL) of 969.251 and a chi-square goodness-of-fit p-value of 0.5325. The best two-parameter model is the zero-modified geometric. The NLL improves to 969.058, but by the likelihood ratio test, this is not sufficient to justify the second parameter. The best three-parameter distribution is the zero-modified negative binomial, which has an NLL of 969.056, again not enough to dislodge the geometric as our choice. For the two- and three-parameter models there were not enough degrees of freedom to conduct the chi-square test. We choose the geometric distribution with $\beta = 0.098495$.

Table 14.8 Losses per hospitalization

Loss per hospitalization	No. of hospitalizations
0–250	36
250–500	29
500–1,000	43
1,000–1,500	35
1,500–2,500	39
2,500–5,000	47
5,000–10,000	33
10,000–50,000	24
50,000–	2
Total	288

For the data in Table 14.7, only zero-truncated distributions should be considered. The best one-parameter model is the zero-truncated Poisson with an NLL of 1,298.725 and a p-value near zero. The two-parameter zero-truncated negative binomial has an NLL of 1,292.532, a significant improvement. The p-value is 0.2571, indicating that this is an acceptable choice. The parameters are $r = 13.207$ and $\beta = 0.25884$.

For the data in Table 14.8, 15 continuous distributions were fitted. The four best models for a given number of parameters are listed in Table 14.9. It should be clear that the best choice is the Pareto distribution. The parameters are $\alpha = 1.6693$ and $\theta = 3,053.0$.

The remaining calculations were done using the recursive method, but inversion or simulation would work equally well.

The first step is to determine the distribution of payments by the employee per family member with regard to the deductible. The frequency distribution is the geometric distribution while the individual loss distribution is the Pareto distribution, limited to the maximum deductible of 500. That is, any losses in excess of 500 are assigned to the value 500. With regard to discretization for recursion, the span should divide evenly into 500 and then all probability

Table 14.9 Four best models for loss per hospitalization

Name	No. of parameters	NLL	p-value
Inverse exponential	1	632.632	Near 0
Pareto	2	601.642	0.9818
Burr	3	601.612	0.9476
Transformed beta	4	601.553	0.8798

Table 14.10 Discretized Pareto distribution with 500 limit

Loss	Probability
0	0.000273
1	0.000546
2	0.000546
3	0.000545
⋮	⋮
498	0.000365
499	0.000365
500	0.776512

Table 14.11 Probabilities for aggregate deductibles per family member

Loss	Probability
0	0.910359
1	0.000045
2	0.000045
3	0.000045
⋮	⋮
499	0.000031
500	0.063386
501	0.000007
⋮	⋮
999	0.000004
1,000	0.004413
1,001	0.000001
⋮	⋮

not accounted for by the time 500 is reached is placed there. For this example a span of 1 was used. The first few and last few values of the discretized distribution appear in Table 14.10. After applying the recursive formula, it is clear that there is non-zero probability beyond 3,000. However, looking ahead, we know that, with regard to the employee aggregate deductible, payments beyond 1,000 have no impact. A few of these probabilities appear in Table 14.11.

We next must obtain the aggregate distribution of deductibles paid per employee per year. This is another compound distribution. The frequency distribution is the truncated negative binomial and the individual loss distribution is the one for losses per family member that was just obtained.

Table 14.12 Probabilities for aggregate deductibles per employee

Loss	Probability
0	0.725517
1	0.000116
2	0.000115
3	0.000115
⋮	⋮
499	0.000082
500	0.164284
501	0.000047
⋮	⋮
999	0.000031
1,000	0.042343

Recursions can again be used to obtain this distribution. Because there is a 1,000 limit on deductibles, all probability to the right of 1,000 will be placed at 1,000. Selected values from this aggregate distribution are given in Table 14.12. Note that the chance that more than 1,000 in deductibles will be paid is very small. The cost to the insurer of limiting the insured's costs is also small. Using this discrete distribution, it is easy to obtain the mean and standard deviation of aggregate deductibles. They are 150.02 and 274.42, respectively.

We next require the expected value of aggregate costs to the insurer for individual losses below the upper limit of 50,000. This can be found analytically. The expected payment per loss is $E(X \wedge 50,500) = 3,890.87$ for the Pareto distribution. The expected number of losses per family member is the mean of the geometric distribution which is the parameter, 0.098495. The expected number of family members per employee comes from the zero-truncated negative binomial distribution and is 3.59015. This implies that the expected number of losses per employee is $0.098495(3.59015) = 0.353612$. Then the expected aggregate dollars in payments up to the individual limit is $0.353612(3,890.87) = 1,375.86$.

Then the expected cost to the insurer is the difference $1,375.86 - 150.02 = 1,225.84$. As a final note, it is not possible to use any method other than simulation if the goal is to obtain the probability distribution of the insurer's payments. This situation is similar to that of Example 17.7, where it is easy to get the overall distribution, as well as the distribution for the insured (in this case, if payments for losses over 50,500 are ignored), but not for the insurer. □

14.6 ANOTHER AGGREGATE LOSS EXAMPLE

Careful modeling has revealed that individual losses have the lognormal distribution with $\mu = 10.5430$ and $\sigma = 2.31315$. It has also been determined that the number of losses has the Poisson distribution with $\lambda = 0.0154578$.

Begin by considering excess of loss reinsurance in which the reinsurance pays the excess over a deductible, d, up to a maximum payment $u - d$, where u is the limit established in the primary coverage. There are two approaches available to create the distribution of reinsurer payments. The first is to work with the distribution of payments per payment. On this basis, the severity distribution is mixed, with pdf

$$f_Y(x) = \frac{f_X(x + d)}{1 - F_X(d)}, \quad 0 \le x < u - d,$$

and discrete probability

$$\Pr(Y = u - d) = \frac{1 - F_X(u)}{1 - F_X(d)}.$$

This distribution would then be discretized for use with the recursive formula or the FFT or approximated by a histogram for use with the Heckman–Meyers method. Regardless, the frequency distribution must be adjusted to reflect the distribution of the number of payments as opposed to the number of losses. The new Poisson parameter will be $\lambda[1 - F_X(d)]$.

14.6.1 Distribution for a single policy

We consider the distribution of losses for a single policy for various combinations of d and u. We use the Poisson parameter for the combined group and have employed the recursive algorithm with a discretization interval of 10,000 and the method of rounding. In all cases the 90th and 99th percentiles are zero, indicating that most of the time the excess of loss reinsurance will involve no payments. This is not surprising because the probability there will be no losses is $\exp(-0.0154578) = 0.985$ and with the deductible this probability is even higher. The mean, standard deviation, and coefficient of variation for various combinations of d and u are given in Table 14.13.

It is not surprising that the risk (as measured by the coefficient of variation, C.V.) increases when either the deductible or the limit is increased. It is also clear that the risk of writing one policy is extreme.

14.6.2 One hundred policies—excess of loss

We next consider the possibility of reinsuring 100 policies. If we assume that the same deductible and limit apply to all of them, the aggregate distribution requires only that the frequency be changed. When 100 independent Poisson

Table 14.13   Excess of loss reinsurance, one policy

Deductible (10^6)	Limit (10^6)	Mean	Standard Deviation	C.V.
0.5	1	778	18,858	24.24
0.5	5	2,910	94,574	32.50
0.5	10	3,809	144,731	38.00
0.5	25	4,825	229,284	47.52
0.5	50	5,415	306,359	56.58
1.0	5	2,132	80,354	37.69
1.0	10	3,031	132,516	43.72
1.0	25	4,046	219,475	54.24
1.0	50	4,636	298,101	64.30
5.0	10	899	62,556	69.58
5.0	25	1,914	162,478	84.89
5.0	50	2,504	249,752	99.74
10.0	25	1,015	111,054	109.41
10.0	50	1,605	205,939	128.71

Table 14.14   Excess of loss reinsurance, 100 policies

Deductible (10^6)	Limit (10^6)	Mean (10^3)	Standard deviation (10^3)	C.V.	Percentiles (10^3) 90	99
0.5	5	291	946	3.250	708	4,503
0.5	10	381	1,447	3.800	708	9,498
0.5	25	482	2,293	4.752	708	11,674
1.0	5	213	804	3.769	190	4,002
1.0	10	303	1,325	4.372	190	8,997
1.0	25	405	2,195	5.424	190	11,085
5.0	10	90	626	6.958	0	4,997
5.0	25	191	1,625	8.489	0	6,886
10.0	25	102	1,111	10.941	0	1,854

random variables are added, the sum has a Poisson distribution with the original parameter multiplied by 100. The same process was repeated with the revised Poisson parameter. The results appear in Table 14.14.

As must be the case with independent policies, the mean is 100 times the mean for one policy and the standard deviation is 10 times the standard deviation for one policy. This implies that the coefficient of variation will be one-tenth of its previous value. In all cases, the 99th percentile is now above zero. This may make it appear that there is more risk, but in reality it just indicates that it is now more likely that a claim will be paid.

14.6.3   One hundred policies—aggregate stop-loss

We now turn to aggregate reinsurance. Assume policies have no individual deductible but do have a policy limit of u. There are again 100 policies and this time the reinsurer pays all aggregate losses in excess of an aggregate deductible of a. For a given limit, the severity distribution is modified as before, the Poisson parameter is multiplied by 100, and then some algorithm is used to obtain the aggregate distribution. Let this distribution have cdf $F_S(s)$ or, in the case of a discretized distribution (as will be the output from the recursive algorithm or the FFT), a pf $f_S(s_i)$ for $i = 1, \ldots, n$. For a deductible of a, the corresponding functions for the reinsurance distribution S_r are

$$
\begin{aligned}
F_{S_r}(s) &= F_S(s+a), \quad s \geq 0, \\
f_{S_r}(0) &= F_S(a) = \sum_{s_i \leq a} f_S(s_i), \\
f_{S_r}(r_i) &= f_S(r_i + a), \quad r_i = s_i - a, \ i = 1, \ldots, n.
\end{aligned}
$$

Moments and percentiles may be determined in the usual manner.

Using the recursive formula with an interval of 10,000, results for various stop-loss deductibles and individual limits are given in Table 14.15. The results are similar to those for the excess of loss coverage. For the most part, as either the individual limit or the aggregate deductible is increased, the risk, as measured by the coefficient of variation, increases. The exception is when both the limit and the deductible are 5,000,000. This is a risky setting because it is the only one in which two losses are required before the reinsurance will take effect.

Now suppose the 100 policies are known to have different Poisson parameters (but the same severity distribution). Assume 30 have $\lambda = 0.0162249$ and so the number of claims from this subgroup is Poisson with mean

$$30(0.0162249) = 0.486747.$$

For the second group (50 members) the parameter is $50(0.0174087) = 0.870435$ and for the third group (20 members) it is $20(0.0096121) = 0.192242$. There are three methods for obtaining the distribution of the sum of the three separate aggregate distributions.

1. Because the sum of independent Poisson random variables is still Poisson, the total number of losses has the Poisson distribution with parameter 1.549424. The common severity distribution remains the lognormal. This reduces to a single compound distribution which can be evaluated by any method.

2. Obtain the three aggregate distributions separately. If the recursive or FFT algorithms are used, the result will be three discrete distributions. The distribution of their sum can be obtained by using convolutions.

Table 14.15 Aggregate stop-loss reinsurance, 100 policies

Deductible (10^6)	Limit (10^6)	Mean (10^3)	Standard deviation (10^3)	C.V.	Percentiles (10^3) 90	99
0.5	5	322	1,003	3.11	863	4,711
0.5	10	412	1,496	3.63	863	9,504
0.5	25	513	2,331	4.54	863	11,895
1.0	5	241	879	3.64	363	4,211
1.0	10	331	1,389	4.19	363	9,004
1.0	25	433	2,245	5.19	363	11,395
2.5	5	114	556	4.86	0	2,711
2.5	10	204	1,104	5.40	0	7,504
2.5	25	306	2,013	6.58	0	9,895
5.0	5	13	181	13.73	0	211
5.0	10	103	714	6.93	0	5,004
5.0	25	205	1,690	8.26	0	7,395

3. If the FFT or Heckman–Meyers algorithms are used, the three transforms can be found and then multiplied. The inverse transform is then taken of the product.

Each of the methods has advantages and drawbacks. The first method is restricted to those frequency distributions for which the sum has a known form. If the severity distributions are not identical, it may not be possible to combine them to form a single model. The major advantage is that, if it is available, this method requires only one aggregate calculation.

The advantage of method 2 is that there is no restriction on the frequency and severity components of the components. The drawback is the expansion of computer storage. For example, if the first distribution requires 3,000 points, the second one 5,000 points, and the third one 2,000 points (with the same discretization interval being used for the three distributions), the combined distribution will require 10,000 points. More will be said about this at the end of this section.

The third method also has no restriction on the separate models. It has the same drawback as the second method, but here the expansion must be done in advance. That is, in the example, all three components must work with 10,000 points. There is no way to avoid this.

14.6.4 Numerical convolutions

The remaining problem is expansion of the number of points required when performing numerical convolutions. The problem arises when the individual distributions use a large number of discrete points, to the point where the storage capacity of the computer becomes an obstacle. The following example is a small-scale version of the problem and indicates a simple solution.

Example 14.2 *The probability functions for two discrete distributions are given below. Suppose the maximum vector allowed by the computer program being used is of length 6. Determine an approximation to the probability function for the sum of the two random variables.*

x	$f_1(x)$	$f_2(x)$
0	0.3	0.4
2	0.2	0.3
4	0.2	0.2
6	0.2	0.1
8	0.1	0.0

The maximum possible value for the sum of the two random variables is 14 and would require a vector of length 8 to store. Usual convolutions produce the answer as given below.

x	0	2	4	6	8	10	12	14
$f(x)$	0.12	0.17	0.20	0.21	0.16	0.09	0.04	0.01

With 6 points available, the span must be increased to $14/5 = 2.8$. We then do a sort of reverse interpolation, taking the probability at each point that is not a multiple of 2.8 and allocating it to the two nearest multiples of 2.8. For example, the probability of 0.16 at $x = 8$ is allocated to the points 5.6 and 8.4. Because 8 is 2.4/2.8 of the way from 5.6 to 8.4, six-sevenths of the probability is placed at 8.4 and the remaining one-seventh is placed at 5.6. The complete allocation process appears in Table 14.16. The probabilities allocated to each multiple of 2.8 are then combined to produce the approximation to the true distribution of the sum. The approximating distribution is given below.

x	0	2.8	5.6	8.4	11.2	14.0
$f(x)$	0.1686	0.2357	0.2886	0.2057	0.0800	0.0214

This method preserves both the total probability of one and the mean (both the true distribution and the approximating distribution have a mean of 5.2). □

One refinement that can eliminate some of the need for storage is to note that when a distribution requires a large vector the probabilities at the end are

Table 14.16   Allocation of probabilities for Example 14.2

x	$f(x)$	Lower point	Probabiity	Upper point	Probability
0	0.12	0	0.1200		
2	0.17	0	0.0486	2.8	0.1214
4	0.20	2.8	0.1143	5.6	0.0857
6	0.21	5.6	0.1800	8.4	0.0300
8	0.16	5.6	0.0229	8.4	0.1371
10	0.09	8.4	0.0386	11.2	0.0514
12	0.04	11.2	0.0286	14.0	0.0114
14	0.01	14.0	0.0100		

likely to be very small. When they are multiplied to create the convolution, the probabilities at the ends of the new, long vector may be so small that they can be ignored. Thus those cells need not be retained and do not add to the storage problem.

Many more refinements are possible. In the appendix to the article by Bailey [9] a method which preserves the first three moments is presented. He also provides guidance with regard to the elimination or combination of storage locations with exceptionally small probability.

14.7   COMPREHENSIVE EXERCISES

The exercises in this section are similar to the examples presented earlier in this chapter. They are based on questions that arose in published papers.

14.2 In New York there were special funds for some infrequent occurrences under workers compensation insurance. One was the event of a case being reopened. Hipp [57] collected data on the time from an accident to when the case was reopened. These covered cases reopened between April 24, 1933 and December 31, 1936. The data appear in Table 14.17. Determine a parametric model for the time from accident to reopening. By definition, at least seven years must elapse before a claim can qualify as a reopening, so the model should be conditioned on the time being at least seven years.

14.3 In the first of two papers by Arthur Bailey [6], written in 1942 and 1943, he observed on page 51 that "Another field where a knowledge of sampling distributions could be used to advantage is that of rating procedures for deductibles and excess coverages." In the second paper [7], he presented some data (Table 14.18) on the distribution of loss ratios. In that paper he made the statement that the popular lognormal model provided a good fit and passed the chi-square test. Does it? Is there a better model?

Table 14.17   Time to reopening of a workers compensation claim for Exercise 14.2

Years	No. reopened	Years	No. reopened
7–8	27	15–16	13
8–9	43	16–17	9
9–10	42	17–18	7
10–11	37	18–19	4
11–12	25	19–20	4
12–13	19	20–21	1
13–14	23	21+	0
14–15	10		
		Total	264

Table 14.18   Loss ratio data for Exercise 14.3

Loss ratio	Number
0.0–0.2	16
0.2–0.4	27
0.4–0.6	22
0.6–0.8	29
0.8–1.0	19
1.0–1.5	32
1.5–2.0	10
2.0–3.0	13
3.0+	5
Total	173

14.4 In 1979, Hewitt and Lefkowitz [56] looked at automobile bodily injury liability data (Table 14.19) and concluded that a two-point mixture of the gamma and loggamma distributions [If X has a gamma distribution, then $Y = \exp(X)$ has the loggamma distribution. Note that its support begins at 1] was superior to the lognormal. Do you agree? Also consider the gamma and loggamma distributions.

14.5 A 1980 paper by Patrik [102] contained many of the ideas recommended in this text. One of his examples was data supplied by the Insurance Services Office on Owners, Landlords, and Tenants bodily injury liability. Policies at two different limits were studied. Both were for policy year 1976 with losses developed to the end of 1978. The groupings in Table 14.20 have been condensed from those in the paper. Can the same model (with or without identical parameters) be used for the two limits?

Table 14.19   Automobile bodily injury liability losses for Exercise 14.4

Loss	Number	Loss	Number
0–50	27	750–1,000	8
50–100	4	1,000–1,500	16
100–150	1	1,500–2,000	8
150–200	2	2,000–2,500	11
200–250	3	2,500–3,000	6
250–300	4	3,000–4,000	12
300–400	5	4,000–5,000	9
400–500	6	5,000–7,500	14
500–750	13	7,500–	40
		Total	189

Table 14.20   OLT bodily injury liability losses for Exercise 14.5

Loss (10^3)	300 Limit	500 Limit	Loss (10^3)	300 Limit	500 Limit
0–0.2	10,075	3,977	11–12	56	22
0.2–0.5	3,049	1,095	12–13	47	23
0.5–1	3,263	1,152	13–14	20	6
1–2	2,690	991	14–15	151	51
2–3	1,498	594	15–20	151	54
3–4	964	339	20–25	109	44
4–5	794	307	25–50	154	53
5–6	261	103	50–75	24	14
6–7	191	79	75–100	19	5
7–8	406	141	100–200	22	6
8–9	114	52	200–300	6	9
9–10	279	89	300–500	10[a]	3
10–11	58	23	500–		0
			Totals	24,411	9,232

[a]losses for 300+

14.6 The data in Table 14.21 were collected by Fisher [37] on coal mining disasters in the United States over 25 years ending about 1910. This particular compilation counted the number of disasters per year that claimed the lives of five to nine miners. In the article, Fisher claimed that a Poisson distribution was a good model. Is it? Is there a better model?

14.7 Harwayne [49] was curious as to the relationship between driving record and number of accidents. His data on California drivers included the number of violations. For each of the six data sets represented by each column in

Table 14.21   Mining disasters per year for Exercise 14.6

No. of disasters	No. of years	No. of disasters	No. of years
0	1	7	3
1	1	8	1
2	3	9	0
3	4	10	1
4	5	11	1
5	2	12	1
6	2	13+	0

Table 14.22   Number of accidents by number of violations for Exercise 14.7

Number of Accidents	No. of violations					
	0	1	2	3	4	5+
0	51,365	17,081	6,729	3,098	1,548	1,893
1	3,997	3,131	1,711	963	570	934
2	357	353	266	221	138	287
3	34	41	44	31	34	66
4	4	6	6	6	4	14
5+	0	1	1	1	3	1

Table 14.23   Number of accidents per year for Exercise 14.8

No. of accidents	No. of stretches	No. of accidents	No. of stretches
0	99	6	4
1	65	7	0
2	57	8	3
3	35	9	4
4	20	10	0
5	10	11	1

Table 14.22, is a negative binomial distribution appropriate? If so, are the same parameters appropriate? Is it reasonable to conclude that the expected number of accidents increases with the number of violations?

14.8 In 1961, Simon [122] proposed using the zero-modified negative binomial distribution. His data set was the number of accidents in one year along various one-mile stretches of Oregon highway. The data appear in Table 14.23. Simon claimed that the zero-modified negative binomial distribution was superior to the negative binomial. Is he correct? Is there a better model?

Part V

Adjusted estimates and simulation

15

Interpolation and smoothing

15.1 INTRODUCTION

Methods of model building discussed to this point are based on ideas that came primarily from the fields of probability and statistics. Data are considered to be observations from a sample space associated with a probability distribution. The quantities to be estimated are functions of that probability distribution for example, pdf, cdf, hazard rate (force of mortality), mean, variance.

In contrast, the methods described in this chapter have their origins in the field of numerical analysis, without specific considerations of probabilistic statistical concepts.

In practice, many of these numerical methods have been subsequently adapted to a probability and statistics framework. Although the key ideas of the methods are easy to understand, most of these techniques are computationally demanding, thus requiring computer programs. The techniques described in this chapter are at the lowest end of the complexity scale.

The objective is to fit a smooth curve through a set of data according to some specified criteria. This has many applications in actuarial science as it has in many other fields. We begin with a set of distinct points in the plane. In practice these points represent a sequence of successive observations of some quantity, for example, a series of successive monthly inflation rates, a set of

Loss Models: From Data to Decisions, Second Edition.
By Stuart A. Klugman, Harry H. Panjer, and Gordon E. Willmot
ISBN 0-471-21577-5   Copyright © 2004 John Wiley & Sons, Inc.

successive average annual claim costs, or a set of successive observed mortality rates by age. The methods in this chapter are considered to be nonparametric in nature in the sense that the underlying model is not prespecified by a simple mathematical function with a small number of parameters. The methods in this chapter allow for great flexibility in the shape of the resulting curve. They are especially useful in situations where the shape is complex.

One such example is the curve representing the probabilities of death within a short period for humans, such as the function q_x. These probabilities decrease sharply at the youngest ages as a result of neonatal deaths, are relatively flat until the early teens, rise slowly during the teens, rise and then fall (especially for males) during the 18–25 age range (as a result of accidents), then continue to rise slowly but at an increasing rate for higher ages. This curve is not captured adequately by a simple function (although there are models with eight or more parameters available).

Historically, the process of smoothing a set of observed irregular points is called graduation. The set of points typically represents observed rates of mortality (probability of death within one year) or rates of some other contingency such as disablement, unemployment, or accident. The methods described in this chapter are not restricted to these kinds of applications. Indeed, they can be applied to any set of successive points.

In graduation theory, it is assumed that there is some underlying, but unobservable, true curve or function that is to be estimated or approximated. Graduation depends on a trade-off between the high degree of fit that is obtained by a "noisy" curve such as a high-degree polynomial that fits the data well and the high degree of smoothness that is obtained by a simple curve such as a straight line or an exponential curve.

There are a number of classical methods described in older actuarial textbooks such as Miller [94]. These include simple graphical methods using an engineering draftsman's French curve or a spline and weights. A French curve is a flat piece of wood with a smooth outside edge, with the diameter of the outside edge changing gradually. This could be used to draw curves through specified points. A spline was a thin rod of flexible metal or plastic that was anchored by attaching lead weights called *ducks* at specified points along the rod. By altering the position of the ducks on the rod and moving the rod relative to the drafting surface, smooth curves could be drawn through successive sets of points. The resulting shape of the rod is the one that minimizes the *energy of deflection* subject to the rod passing through the specified points. In that sense it is a very natural method for developing the shape of a structure so that it has maximal strength. Methods developed by actuaries included mathematical methods based on running averages, methods based on interpolation, and methods based directly on finding a balance between fit and smoothness. All these methods were developed in the early 1900s, some even earlier. They were developed using methods of finite differences, in which it was frequently assumed that fourth and higher differences should be set to zero, implicitly forcing the use of third-degree polynomials. Formulas involving differences were developed so that an actuary could develop smooth functions using only pencil and paper. Remember these formulas were developed long before calculators (mechanical or electronic!) and very long before computers were developed. A more recent summary of these methods along with some updated variations can be found in London [84].

With the advent of computers in the 1950s and 1960s, many computerized mathematical procedures were developed. Among them was the theory of splines, this time not mechanical in nature. As with graduation, the objective of splines is to find an appropriate balance between fit and smoothness. The solutions that were developed were in terms of linear systems of equations that could be easily solved on a computer. The modern theory of splines dates back to Schoenberg [117].

In this chapter, we focus only on the modern techniques of spline interpolation and smoothing. These techniques are so powerful and flexible that they have largely superseded the older methods.

15.2 POLYNOMIAL INTERPOLATION AND SMOOTHING

Consider $n + 1$ distinct points labeled $(x_0, y_0), (x_1, y_1), \ldots, (x_n, y_n)$ with $x_0 < x_1 < x_2 < \cdots < x_n$. A unique polynomial of degree n can be passed through these points. This polynomial is called a *collocation* polynomial and can be expressed as

$$f(x) = \sum_{j=0}^{n} a_j x^j, \tag{15.1}$$

where

$$f(x_j) = y_j, \quad j = 0, 1, \ldots, n. \tag{15.2}$$

Equations (15.2) form a system of $n + 1$ equations in $n + 1$ unknowns $\{a_j; j = 0, 1, \ldots, n\}$. However, when n is large, the numerical exercise of solving the system of equations may be difficult.

Fortunately, the solution can be explicitly written without solving the system of equations. The solution is known as Lagrange's formula:

$$
\begin{aligned}
f(x) &= y_0 \frac{(x - x_1)(x - x_2) \ldots (x - x_n)}{(x_0 - x_1)(x_0 - x_2) \ldots (x_0 - x_n)} \\
&\quad + y_1 \frac{(x - x_0)(x - x_2) \ldots (x - x_n)}{(x_1 - x_0)(x_1 - x_2) \ldots (x_1 - x_n)} \\
&\quad + \ldots \\
&\quad + y_n \frac{(x - x_0)(x - x_1) \ldots (x - x_{n-1})}{(x_n - x_0)(x_n - x_1) \ldots (x_n - x_{n-1})} \\
&= \sum_{j=0}^{n} y_j \frac{(x - x_0) \ldots (x - x_{j-1})(x - x_{j+1}) \ldots (x - x_n)}{(x_j - x_0) \ldots (x_j - x_{j-1})(x_j - x_{j+1}) \ldots (x_j - x_n)}. \tag{15.3}
\end{aligned}
$$

Table 15.1   Mortality rates for Example 15.1

j	Ages	Exposed to Risk	Actual Deaths	Estimated Mortality Rate Per 1,000
0	25-29	35,700	139	3.89
1	30-34	244,066	599	2.45
2	35-39	741,041	1,842	2.49
3	40-44	1,250,601	4,771	3.81
4	45-49	1,746,393	11,073	6.34
5	50-54	2,067,008	21,693	10.49
6	55-59	1,983,710	31,612	15.94
7	60-64	1,484,347	39,948	26.91
8	65-69	988,980	40,295	40.74
9	70-74	559,049	33,292	59.55
10	75-79	241,497	20,773	86.02
11	80-84	78,229	11,376	145.42
12	85-89	15,411	2,653	172.15
13	90-94	2,552	589	230.80
14	95-	162	44	271.60
	Total	11,438,746	220,699	

To verify that (15.3) is the collocation polynomial, note that each term is a polynomial of degree n and that when $x = x_j$ the right-hand side of (15.3) takes on value y_j for each of $j = 0, 1, 2, \ldots, n$.

The n-degree polynomial $f(x)$ provides interpolation between (x_0, y_0) and (x_n, y_n) and passes through all interior points $\{(x_j, y_j); j = 1, \ldots, n-1\}$. However, for large n, the function $f(x)$ can exhibit excessive oscillation; that is to say, it can be very "wiggly." This is particularly problematic when there is some "noise" in the original series $\{(x_j, y_j); j = 0, \ldots, n\}$. Such noise can be caused by measurement error or random fluctuation.

Example 15.1 *The data in Table* 15.1 *are from Miller* [94], *p.* 62. *They are observed mortality rates in five-year age groups. The estimated mortality rates are obtained as the ratio of the dollars of death claims paid to the total dollars exposed to death.*[1] *The rates are plotted in Figure* 15.1.

The estimates of mortality rates at each age are the maximum likelihood estimates of the true rates assuming mutually independent binomial models

[1]Deaths and exposures are in units of $1,000. It is common in mortality studies to count dollars rather than lives in order to give more weight to the larger policies. The mortality rates in the table are the ratios of the given deaths and exposures. The last entry differs from Miller's table due to rounding.

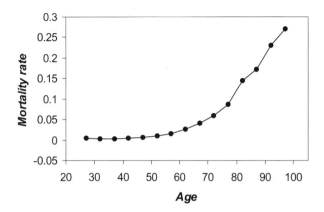

Fig. 15.1   Mortality rates for Example 15.1.

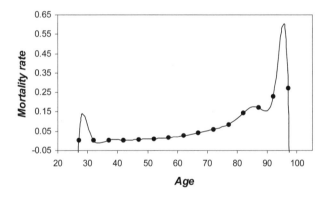

Fig. 15.2   Collocation polynomial for mortality data.

at each age. Note that there is considerable variability in successive estimates. Of course, mortality rates are expected to be relatively smooth from age to age. Figure 15.1 shows the observed mortality rates connected by straight lines while Figure 15.2 shows a collocation polynomial fitted through the observed rates. Notice its wiggly form and its extreme oscillation near the ends.   □

To avoid the excessive oscillatory behavior or wiggliness, lower order polynomials could be used for interpolation. For example, successive values could be joined by straight lines. However, the successive interpolating lines form a jagged series because of the "kinks" at the points of juncture.

Another method is to piece together a sequence of low-degree polynomials. For example, a quadratic function can be collocated with successive points at $(x_0, x_1, x_2), (x_2, x_3, x_4) \ldots$. However, there will not be smoothness at the points of juncture $x_2, x_4, \ldots$ in the sense that the interpolating function will have kinks at these points with slopes and curvature not matching. One way to get rid of the kinks is to force some left-hand and right-hand derivatives to be equal at these points. This creates apparent smoothness at the points of juncture of the successive polynomials. This is the key idea behind splines. Interpolating splines are piecewise polynomial functions that pass through the given data points but that have the added feature that they are smooth at the points of juncture of the successive pieces. The order of the polynomial is kept low to minimize "wiggly" behavior. Interpolation using cubic splines is introduced in Section 15.3.

An alternative to interpolation is *smoothing*, or, more precisely, fitting a smooth function to the observed data but not requiring that the function pass through each data point. Polynomials allow for great flexibility of shapes. However, this flexibility of shape also makes polynomials quite risky to use for extrapolation, especially for polynomials of high degree. This was the case in Figure 15.2, where the extrapolated values, even for one year, were completely unreliable. As with the fitting of other models earlier in this book, a fitting criterion needs to be selected in order to fit a model. We will illustrate the use of polynomial smoothing by using a least squares criterion. Figures 15.3–15.6 show the fits of polynomials of degree 2, 3, 4, and 5 to the data of Example 15.1. It should be noted that the fit improves with each increase in degree because there is one additional degree of freedom in carrying out the fit. However, it can be seen that as each degree is added the behavior of the extrapolated values for only a few years below age 27 and above age 97 changes quite significantly. Smoothing splines provide one solution to this dilemma. Smoothing splines are just like interpolating splines except that the spline is not required to pass through the data points but, rather, should be close to the data points. Cubic splines limit the degree of the polynomial to 3.

15.2.1   Exercises

15.1 Determine the equation of the polynomial that interpolates the points $(2, 50)$, $(4, 25)$, and $(5, 20)$.

15.2 Determine the equation of the straight line that best fits the data of Exercise 15.1 using the least squares criterion.

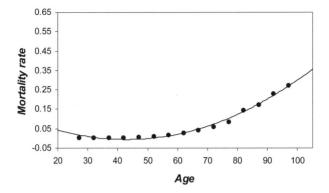

Fig. 15.3   Second-degree polynomial fit.

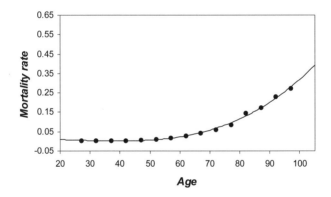

Fig. 15.4   Third-degree polynomial fit.

15.3   CUBIC SPLINE INTERPOLATION

Cubic splines are piecewise cubic functions that have the property that the first and second derivatives can be forced to be continuous, unlike the approach of successive polynomials with jagged points of juncture.

Cubic splines are used extensively in computer-aided design and manufacturing in creating surfaces that are smooth to the touch and to the eye. The cubic spline is fitted to a series of points, called **knots**, that give the basic shape of the object being designed or manufactured.

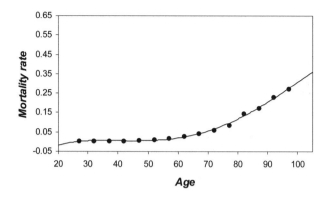

Fig. 15.5   Fourth-degree polynomial fit.

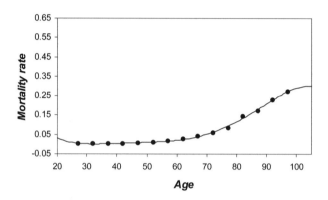

Fig. 15.6   Fifth-degree polynomial fit.

In the terminology of graduation theory as developed by actuaries in the early 1900s, cubic spline interpolation is called **osculatory interpolation.**[2]

Programs for cubic splines are included in many mathematical and engineering software packages. This makes them very easy to apply.

---

[2] The word **osculation** means "the act of kissing." Successive cubic polynomials exhibit osculatory behavior by "kissing" each other smoothly at the knots!

Definition 15.2 *Suppose that $\{(x_j, y_j); j = 0, \ldots, n\}$ are $n+1$ distinct knots with $x_0 < x_1 < x_2 < \cdots < x_n$. The function $f(x)$ is a **cubic spline** if there exist n cubic polynomials $f_j(x)$ with coefficients a_j, b_j, c_j, and d_j that satisfy:*

I. $f(x) = f_j(x) = a_j + b_j(x - x_j) + c_j(x - x_j)^2 + d_j(x - x_j)^3$ for $x_j \leq x \leq x_{j+1}$ and $j = 0, 1, \ldots, n-1$.

II. $f(x_j) = y_j$, $j = 0, 1, \ldots, n$.

III. $f_j(x_{j+1}) = f_{j+1}(x_{j+1})$, $j = 0, 1, 2, \ldots, n-2$.

IV. $f'_j(x_{j+1}) = f'_{j+1}(x_{j+1})$, $j = 0, 1, 2, \ldots, n-2$.

V. $f''_j(x_{j+1}) = f''_{j+1}(x_{j+1})$, $j = 0, 1, 2, \ldots, n-2$.

Property I states that $f(x)$ consists of piecewise cubics. Property II states that the piecewise cubics pass through the given set of data points. Property III requires the spline to be continuous at the interior data points. Properties IV and V provide smoothness at the interior data points by forcing the first and second derivatives to be continuous.

15.3.1   Construction of cubic splines

Each cubic polynomial has four unknown constants: a_j, b_j, c_j, and d_j. Because there are n such cubics, there are $4n$ coefficients to be determined. Properties II–V provide $n+1, n-1, n-1$, and $n-1$ conditions, respectively, for a total of $4n - 2$ conditions. In order to determine the $4n$ coefficients, we need exactly two more conditions. This can be done by adding two **endpoint constraints** involving some of $f'(x), f''(x)$, or $f'''(x)$ at x_0 and x_n. Different choices of endpoint constraints lead to different results. Various possible endpoint constraints are discussed in the next section.

In order to construct the cubic segments in the successive intervals, first consider the second derivative $f''_j(x)$. It is a linear function because $f_j(x)$ is cubic. Therefore, the Lagrangian representation of the second derivatives is

$$f''_j(x) = f''(x_j)\frac{x - x_{j+1}}{x_j - x_{j+1}} + f''(x_{j+1})\frac{x - x_j}{x_{j+1} - x_j}. \tag{15.4}$$

To simplify notation, let $m_j = f''(x_j)$ and $h_j = x_{j+1} - x_j$, so that

$$f''_j(x) = \frac{m_j}{h_j}(x_{j+1} - x) + \frac{m_{j+1}}{h_j}(x - x_j) \tag{15.5}$$

for $x_j \leq x \leq x_{j+1}$ and $j = 0, 1, \ldots, n-1$.

Integrating this twice leads to

$$f_j(x) = \frac{m_j}{6h_j}(x_{j+1} - x)^3 + \frac{m_{j+1}}{6h_j}(x - x_j)^3 + p_j(x_{j+1} - x) + q_j(x - x_j), \tag{15.6}$$

where p_j and q_j are undetermined constants of integration. [To check this, just differentiate (15.6) twice.]

Substituting x_j and x_{j+1} into (15.6) yields

$$y_j = \frac{m_j}{6} h_j^2 + p_j h_j \tag{15.7}$$

and

$$y_{j+1} = \frac{m_{j+1}}{6} h_j^2 + q_j h_j \tag{15.8}$$

because $f_j(x_j) = y_j$ and $f_j(x_{j+1}) = y_{j+1}$.

We now obtain the constants p_j and q_j from (15.7) and (15.8). When they are substituted into (15.6), we obtain

$$
\begin{aligned}
f_j(x) \;=\;& \frac{m_j}{6h_j}(x_{j+1} - x)^3 + \frac{m_{j+1}}{6h_j}(x - x_j)^3 \\
&+ \left(\frac{y_j}{h_j} - \frac{m_j h_j}{6} \right)(x_{j+1} - x) \\
&+ \left(\frac{y_{j+1}}{h_j} - \frac{m_{j+1} h_j}{6} \right)(x - x_j).
\end{aligned}
\tag{15.9}
$$

Note that the $m_j = f''(x_j)$ terms are still unknown. To obtain them, differentiate (15.9),

$$
\begin{aligned}
f_j'(x) \;=\;& -\frac{m_j}{2h_j}(x_{j+1} - x)^2 + \frac{m_{j+1}}{2h_j}(x - x_j)^2 \\
&- \left(\frac{y_j}{h_j} - \frac{m_j h_j}{6} \right) + \frac{y_{j+1}}{h_j} - \frac{m_{j+1} h_j}{6}.
\end{aligned}
\tag{15.10}
$$

Now setting $x = x_j$ yields, after simplification,

$$f_j'(x_j) = -\frac{m_j}{3} h_j - \frac{m_{j+1}}{6} h_j + \frac{y_{j+1} - y_j}{h_j}. \tag{15.11}$$

Replacing j by $j - 1$ in (15.10) and setting $x = x_j$,

$$f_{j-1}'(x_j) = \frac{m_j}{3} h_{j-1} + \frac{m_{j-1}}{6} h_{j-1} + \frac{y_j - y_{j-1}}{h_{j-1}}. \tag{15.12}$$

Now, Property IV forces the slopes to be equal at each knot. This requires us to equate the right-hand sides of (15.11) and (15.12), yielding the following relation between successive values m_{j-1}, m_j and m_{j+1}:

$$h_{j-1} m_{j-1} + 2(h_{j-1} + h_j) m_j + h_j m_{j+1} = 6 \left(\frac{y_{j+1} - y_j}{h_j} - \frac{y_j - y_{j-1}}{h_{j-1}} \right) \tag{15.13}$$

for $j = 1, 2, \ldots, n - 1$.

The system of equations (15.13) consists of $n-1$ equations in $n+1$ unknowns $m_0, m_1, \ldots, m_n$. Two endpoint constraints can be added to determine m_0

and m_n. Obtaining the $n-1$ remaining unknowns in (15.13) then allows for complete determination of the cubic (15.9) for $j = 0, 1, 2, \ldots, n-1$ and therefore the entire cubic spline.

For purpose of notational simplicity, we can rewrite (15.13) as

$$h_{j-1}m_{j-1} + g_j m_j + h_j m_{j+1} = u_j, \quad j = 1, 2, \ldots, n-1, \tag{15.14}$$

where

$$u_j = 6\left(\frac{y_{j+1} - y_j}{h_j} - \frac{y_j - y_{j-1}}{h_{j-1}}\right) \text{ and } g_j = 2(h_{j-1} + h_j). \tag{15.15}$$

When the endpoints m_0 and m_n are determined externally, the system (15.14) can be rewritten in matrix notation as

$$
\begin{bmatrix}
g_1 & h_1 & 0 & & \cdots & & 0 \\
h_1 & g_2 & h_2 & 0 & & \cdots & 0 \\
0 & h_2 & g_3 & h_3 & 0 & \cdots & 0 \\
& & 0 & & & & \vdots \\
& & \ddots & \ddots & & h_{n-3} & 0 \\
& & & h_{n-3} & g_{n-2} & h_{n-2} \\
0 & 0 & & \cdots & 0 & h_{n-2} & g_{n-1}
\end{bmatrix}_{(n-1)\times(n-1)}
\begin{bmatrix}
m_1 \\
m_2 \\
\vdots \\
\vdots \\
\vdots \\
m_{n-2} \\
m_{n-1}
\end{bmatrix}_{(n-1)\times 1}
=
\begin{bmatrix}
u_1 - h_0 m_0 \\
u_2 \\
\vdots \\
\vdots \\
\vdots \\
u_{n-2} \\
u_{n-1} - h_{n-1}m_n
\end{bmatrix}_{(n-1)\times 1}
\tag{15.16}
$$

or as

$$\mathbf{Hm} = \mathbf{v}. \tag{15.17}$$

The matrix $\mathbf{H}$ is tridiagonal and invertible. Thus the system (15.17) has a unique solution $\mathbf{m} = \mathbf{H}^{-1}\mathbf{v}$. Alternatively, the system can be solved manually using Gaussian elimination.

Once the values $m_1, m_2, \ldots, m_{n-1}$ are determined, the values of c_j are determined by

$$c_j = \frac{m_j}{2}, \quad j = 1, \ldots, n-1.$$

Property II specifies that

$$a_j = y_j, \quad j = 0, \ldots, n-1.$$

Property V specifies that

$$m_j + 6d_j h_j = m_{j+1}, \quad j = 0, \ldots, n-2,$$

yielding

$$d_j = \frac{m_{j+1} - m_j}{6h_j}, \quad j = 0, \ldots, n-2.$$

Property III specifies that

$$a_j + b_j h_j + c_j h_j^2 + d_j h_j^3 = y_{j+1}, \quad j = 0, \ldots, n-2.$$

Substituting for a_j, c_j, and d_j yields

$$b_j = \frac{y_{j+1} - y_j}{h_j} - \frac{h_j(2m_j + m_{j+1})}{6}, \quad j = 0, \ldots, n-2.$$

Summarizing, the spline coefficients for the first $n-1$ spline segments are computed as

$$
\begin{aligned}
a_j &= y_j, \\
b_j &= \frac{y_{j+1} - y_j}{h_j} - \frac{h_j(2m_j + m_{j+1})}{6}, \\
c_j &= \frac{m_j}{2}, \\
d_j &= \frac{m_{j+1} - m_j}{6h_j}, \quad j = 0, \ldots, n-2.
\end{aligned}
\tag{15.18}
$$

The only remaining issue in order to obtain the cubic spline is the choice of the two endpoint constraints. There are several possible choices. Once the two endpoint constraints are selected, the n cubics are fully specified. Thus the values of b_{n-1}, c_{n-1}, and d_{n-1} can also be obtained using (15.18).

Case 1: Natural Cubic Spline $(m_0 = m_n = 0)$

The natural spline is obtained by setting m_0 and m_n to zero in (15.16). Because m_0 and m_n are the second derivatives at the endpoints, the choice of zero minimizes the oscillatory behavior at both ends. It also makes the spline linear beyond the boundary knots, a property that minimizes oscillatory behavior beyond both ends of the data. This is probably safest for extrapolation beyond the data points in most applications. Note that the second-derivative endpoint constraints do not in themselves restrict the slopes at the endpoints.

Case 2: Curvature-Adjusted Cubic Spline $(m_0$ and m_n fixed)

It is similarly possible to fix the endpoint second derivatives m_0 and m_n to prespecified values $f''(x_0)$ and $f''(x_n)$, respectively. Then (15.16) can again be used directly to obtain the values of $m_1, m_2, \ldots, m_{n-1}$. However, in practice, this is difficult to do without some judgment. It is suggested that the natural spline is a good place to start. If more curvature at the ends is wanted, it can be added using this procedure.

Other endpoint constraints may be a bit more complicated and may require modification of the first and last of the system of equations (15.14), which will result in changes in the matrix $\mathbf{H}$ and the vector $\mathbf{v}$ in (15.17).

Case 3: Parabolic Runout Spline $(m_0 = m_1, m_n = m_{n-1})$

Reducing the cubic functions on the first and last intervals to quadratics adds two more constraints, $d_0 = 0$ and $d_n = 0$. This results in the second derivatives being identical at both ends of the first and last intervals; that is, $m_0 = m_1$ and $m_n = m_{n-1}$. As a result, the first and last equations of (15.14) are replaced by

$$
\begin{aligned}
(3h_0 + 2h_1)m_1 + h_1 m_2 &= u_1, \\
h_{n-2}m_{n-2} + (2h_{n-2} + 3h_{n-1})m_{n-1} &= u_{n-1}.
\end{aligned}
\tag{15.19}
$$

Case 4: Cubic Runout Spline

This method requires the cubic over $[x_0, x_1]$ to be an extension of that over $[x_1, x_2]$, thus imposing the same cubic function over the entire interval $[x_0, x_2]$. This is also known as the *not-a-knot* condition. A similar condition is imposed at the other end.

This can be achieved by requiring that the third derivatives at the endpoints also agree at x_1 and x_{n-1}; that is,

$$
f_0'''(x_1) = f_1'''(x_1)
$$

and

$$
f_{n-2}'''(x_{n-1}) = f_{n-1}'''(x_{n-1}).
$$

Because the third derivative is then constant throughout $[x_0, x_2]$ and also throughout $[x_{n-2}, x_n]$, the second derivative will be a linear function throughout the same two intervals. Hence, the slope of the second derivative will be the same in any subintervals within $[x_0, x_2]$ and within $[x_{n-2}, x_n]$. Thus, we can write

$$
\begin{aligned}
\frac{m_1 - m_0}{h_0} &= \frac{m_2 - m_1}{h_1}, \\
\frac{m_n - m_{n-1}}{h_{n-1}} &= \frac{m_{n-1} - m_{n-2}}{h_{n-2}},
\end{aligned}
$$

or equivalently

$$
\begin{aligned}
m_0 &= m_1 - \frac{h_0(m_2 - m_1)}{h_1}, \\
m_n &= m_{n-1} + \frac{h_{n-1}(m_{n-1} - m_{n-2})}{h_{n-2}}.
\end{aligned}
\tag{15.20}
$$

Then the first and last equations of (15.14) are replaced by

$$
\left(3h_0 + 2h_1 + \frac{h_0^2}{h_1} \right) m_1 + \left(h_1 - \frac{h_0^2}{h_1} \right) m_2 = u_1,
$$

$$
\left(h_{n-2} - \frac{h_{n-1}^2}{h_{n-2}} \right) m_{n-2} + \left(2h_{n-2} + 3h_{n-1} + \frac{h_{n-1}^2}{h_{n-2}} \right) m_{n-1} = u_{n-1}.
$$

$$
\tag{15.21}
$$

Case 5: Clamped Cubic Spline

This procedure fixes the slope $f_0'(x_0)$ and $f_{n-1}'(x_n)$ of the spline at each endpoint. In this case, from (15.11) and (15.12), the second derivatives are

$$m_0 = \frac{3}{h_0}\left(\frac{y_1 - y_0}{h_0} - f_0'(x_0)\right) - \frac{m_1}{2},$$

$$m_n = \frac{3}{h_{n-1}}\left(f_{n-1}'(x_n) - \frac{y_n - y_{n-1}}{h_{n-1}}\right) - \frac{m_{n-1}}{2}. \qquad (15.22)$$

As a result the first and last equations of (15.14) are replaced by

$$\left(\tfrac{3}{2}h_0 + 2h_1\right)m_1 + h_1 m_2 = u_1 - 3\left(\frac{y_1 - y_0}{h_0} - f_0'(x_0)\right),$$

and

$$h_{n-2}m_{n-2} + \left(2h_{n-2} + \tfrac{3}{2}h_{n-1}\right)m_{n-1} = u_{n-1} - 3\left(f_{n-1}'(x_n) - \frac{y_n - y_{n-1}}{h_{n-1}}\right)$$

respectively.

Example 15.3 *From first principles, using conditions I–V, obtain the cubic spline through the points $(2, 50), (4, 25)$, and $(5, 20)$ with the clamped boundary conditions $f'(2) = -25$ and $f'(5) = -4$.*

Let the cubic spline in the interval from $x_0 = 2$ to $x_1 = 4$ be the polynomial

$$f_0(x) = 50 + b_0(x - 2) + c_0(x - 2)^2 + d_0(x - 2)^3$$

and the spline in the interval from $x_1 = 4$ to $x_2 = 5$ be the polynomial

$$f_1(x) = 25 + b_1(x - 4) + c_1(x - 4)^2 + d_1(x - 4)^3.$$

The six coefficients $b_0, c_0, d_0, b_1, c_1, d_1$ are the unknowns that we need to determine. From the interpolation conditions

$$\begin{aligned} f_0(4) &= 50 + 2b_0 + 4c_0 + 8d_0 = 25, \\ f_1(5) &= 25 + b_1 + c_1 + d_1 = 20. \end{aligned}$$

From the smoothness conditions at $x = 4$

$$\begin{aligned} f_0'(4) &= b_0 + 2c_0(4 - 2) + 3d_0(4 - 2)^2 = f_1'(4) = b_1, \\ f_0''(4) &= 2c_0 + 6d_0(4 - 2) = f_1''(4) = 2c_1. \end{aligned}$$

Finally, from the boundary conditions, we get

$$\begin{aligned} f_0'(2) &= b_0 = -25, \\ f_1'(5) &= b_1 + 2c_1 + 3d_1 = -4. \end{aligned}$$

Thus, we have six linear equations to determine the six unknowns. In matrix form, the equations are

$$
\begin{bmatrix}
2 & 4 & 8 & 0 & 0 & 0 \\
0 & 0 & 0 & 1 & 1 & 1 \\
1 & 4 & 12 & -1 & 0 & 0 \\
0 & 2 & 12 & 0 & -2 & 0 \\
1 & 0 & 0 & 0 & 0 & 0 \\
0 & 0 & 0 & 1 & 2 & 3
\end{bmatrix}
\begin{bmatrix}
b_0 \\ c_0 \\ d_0 \\ b_1 \\ c_1 \\ d_1
\end{bmatrix}
=
\begin{bmatrix}
-25 \\ -5 \\ 0 \\ 0 \\ -25 \\ -4
\end{bmatrix}.
$$

The equations can be solved by successive elimination of unknowns. We get $b_0 = -25$, then

$$
\begin{bmatrix}
4 & 8 & 0 & 0 & 0 \\
0 & 0 & 1 & 1 & 1 \\
4 & 12 & -1 & 0 & 0 \\
2 & 12 & 0 & -2 & 0 \\
0 & 0 & 1 & 2 & 3
\end{bmatrix}
\begin{bmatrix}
c_0 \\ d_0 \\ b_1 \\ c_1 \\ d_1
\end{bmatrix}
=
\begin{bmatrix}
25 \\ -5 \\ 25 \\ 0 \\ -4
\end{bmatrix}.
$$

Take $c_0 = 6.25 - 2d_0$, then

$$
\begin{bmatrix}
0 & 1 & 1 & 1 \\
4 & -1 & 0 & 0 \\
8 & 0 & -2 & 0 \\
0 & 1 & 2 & 3
\end{bmatrix}
\begin{bmatrix}
d_0 \\ b_1 \\ c_1 \\ d_1
\end{bmatrix}
=
\begin{bmatrix}
-5 \\ 0 \\ -12.5 \\ -4
\end{bmatrix}.
$$

Take $d_0 = 0.25b_1$, then

$$
\begin{bmatrix}
1 & 1 & 1 \\
2 & -2 & 0 \\
1 & 2 & 3
\end{bmatrix}
\begin{bmatrix}
b_1 \\ c_1 \\ d_1
\end{bmatrix}
=
\begin{bmatrix}
-5 \\ -12.5 \\ -4
\end{bmatrix}.
$$

Take $b_1 = -6.25 + c_1$, then

$$
\begin{bmatrix}
2 & 1 \\
3 & 3
\end{bmatrix}
\begin{bmatrix}
c_1 \\ d_1
\end{bmatrix}
=
\begin{bmatrix}
1.25 \\ 2.25
\end{bmatrix}.
$$

Finally, take $c_1 = 0.625 - 0.5d_1$ and get $d_1 = 0.25$. The final answer is

$$
\begin{aligned}
b_0 &= -25 \\
c_0 &= 9.125 \\
d_0 &= -1.4375 \\
b_1 &= -5.75 \\
c_1 &= 0.5 \\
d_1 &= 0.25.
\end{aligned}
$$

Thus the final interpolating cubic spline is

$$
f(x) = \begin{cases}
50 - 25(x-2) + 9.125(x-2)^2 - 1.4375(x-2)^3, & 2 \le x \le 4, \\
25 - 5.75(x-4) + 0.5(x-4)^2 + 0.25(x-4)^3, & 4 \le x \le 5.
\end{cases}
$$

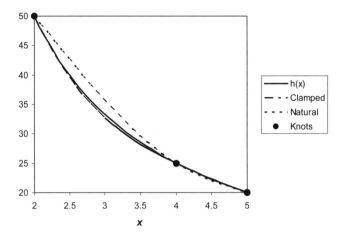

Fig. 15.7 Clamped and natural splines for Example 15.3.

Figure 15.7 shows the interpolating cubic spline and the corresponding natural cubic spline that is the solution of Exercise 15.3. It also shows the function $h(x) = 100/x$, which also passes through the same three knots. The slope of the clamped spline at the endpoints is the same as the slope of the function $h(x)$. These endpoint conditions force the clamped spline to be much closer to the function $h(x)$ than the natural spline. The natural spline has endpoint conditions that force the spline to look more like a straight line near the ends due to requiring the second derivative to be zero at the endpoints. □

The cubic splines in this section all pass through the knots. If smoothing is desired, that restriction may be lifted. Smoothing splines are introduced in Section 15.6.

Example 15.4 *The data in the last column of Table 15.1 are one-year mortality rates for the 15 five-year age intervals shown in the first column. The last interval is treated as 95–99. We have used a natural cubic spline to interpolate between these values as follows. The listed mortality rate is treated as the one-year mortality rate for the middle age within the five-year interval. The resulting values are treated as knots for a natural cubic spline. The fitted interpolating cubic spline is shown in Figure 15.8 on a logarithmic scale. The formula for the spline is given in Property I of Definition 15.2. The coefficients of the 14 cubic segments of the spline are given in Table 15.2.*

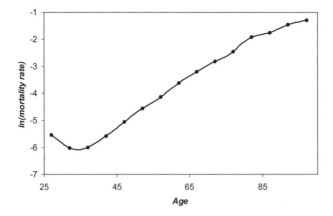

Fig. 15.8   Cubic spline fit to mortality data for Example 15.4.

Table 15.2   Spline coefficients for Example 15.4

j	x_j	a_j	b_j	c_j	d_j
0	27	3.8936×10^{-3}	-3.5093×10^{-4}	0	2.5230×10^{-6}
1	32	2.4543×10^{-3}	-1.6171×10^{-4}	3.7844×10^{-5}	-8.4886×10^{-7}
2	37	2.4857×10^{-3}	1.5307×10^{-4}	2.5112×10^{-5}	-5.1079×10^{-7}
3	42	3.8150×10^{-3}	3.6587×10^{-4}	1.7450×10^{-5}	2.0794×10^{-6}
4	47	6.3405×10^{-3}	6.9632×10^{-4}	4.8640×10^{-5}	-4.3460×10^{-6}
5	52	1.0495×10^{-2}	8.5678×10^{-4}	-1.6550×10^{-5}	1.2566×10^{-5}
6	57	1.5936×10^{-2}	1.6337×10^{-3}	1.7194×10^{-4}	-1.1922×10^{-5}
7	62	2.6913×10^{-2}	2.4590×10^{-3}	-6.8828×10^{-6}	1.3664×10^{-5}
8	67	4.0744×10^{-2}	3.4150×10^{-3}	1.9808×10^{-4}	-2.5761×10^{-5}
9	72	5.9551×10^{-2}	3.4638×10^{-3}	-1.8833×10^{-4}	1.1085×10^{-4}
10	77	8.6018×10^{-2}	9.8939×10^{-3}	1.4744×10^{-3}	-2.1542×10^{-4}
11	82	1.4542×10^{-1}	8.4813×10^{-3}	-1.7569×10^{-3}	2.2597×10^{-4}
12	87	1.7215×10^{-1}	7.8602×10^{-3}	1.6327×10^{-3}	-1.7174×10^{-4}
13	92	2.3080×10^{-1}	1.1306×10^{-2}	-9.4349×10^{-4}	6.2899×10^{-5}

15.3.2   Exercises

15.3 Repeat Example 15.3 for the natural cubic spline by removing the clamped spline boundary conditions.

15.4 Construct a natural cubic spline through the points $(-2, 0)$, $(-1, 1)$, $(0, 0)$, $(1, 1)$, and $(2, 0)$ by setting up the system of equations (15.16).

15.5 Determine if the following functions can be cubic splines:

(a)

$$f(x) = \begin{cases} x, & -4 \le x \le 0, \\ x^3 + x, & 0 \le x \le 1, \\ 3x^2 - 2x + 1, & 1 \le x \le 9. \end{cases}$$

(b)

$$f(x) = \begin{cases} x^3, & 0 \le x \le 1, \\ 3x^2 - 3x + 1, & 1 \le x \le 2, \\ x^3 - 4x^2 + 13x - 11, & 2 \le x \le 4. \end{cases}$$

(c)

$$f(x) = \begin{cases} x^3 + 2x, & -1 \le x \le 0, \\ 2x^2 + 2x, & 0 \le x \le 1, \\ x^3 - x^2 + 5x - 1, & 1 \le x \le 3. \end{cases}$$

15.6 Determine the coefficients a, b, and c so that

$$f(x) = \begin{cases} x^3 + 4, & 0 \le x \le 1, \\ a + b(x-1) + c(x-1)^2 + 4(x-1)^3, & 1 \le x \le 3. \end{cases}$$

is a cubic spline.

15.7 Determine the clamped cubic spline that agrees with $\sin(x\pi/2)$ at $x = -1, 0, 1$.

15.8 Consider the function

$$f(x) = \begin{cases} 28 + 25x + 9x^2 + x^3, & -3 \le x \le -1, \\ 26 + 19x + 3x^2 - x^3, & -1 \le x \le 0, \\ 26 + 19x + 3x^2 - 2x^3, & 0 \le x \le 3, \\ -163 + 208x - 60x^2 + 5x^3, & 3 \le x \le 4. \end{cases}$$

(a) Prove that $f(x)$ can be a cubic spline.

(b) Determine which of the five endpoint conditions could have been used in developing this spline.

15.4   APPROXIMATING FUNCTIONS WITH SPLINES

The natural and clamped cubic splines have a particularly desirable property when the spline is considered to be an approximation to some other continuous function. For example, consider the function

$$h(x) = \frac{100}{x}, \quad 2 \le x \le 5.$$

This function collocates with the knots at $x = 2, 4, 5$ in Example 15.3. Let us suppose the knots had indeed come from this function. Then, we could consider the interpolating cubic spline to be an approximation to the function $h(x)$. In many applications, such as computer graphics, where smooth images are needed, those smooth images can be represented very efficiently using a limited number of selected knots and a cubic spline interpolation algorithm.

Smoothness can be measured by the total curvature of a function. The most popular of such measures is the squared norm

$$S = \int_{x_0}^{x_n} [f''(x)]^2 dx, \tag{15.23}$$

representing the total squared second derivative.

Now consider any continuous function $h(x)$ that also has continuous first and second derivatives over some interval $[x_0, x_n]$. Suppose that we select $n-1$ interior knots $\{x_j, h(x_j)\}_{j=1}^{n-1}$ with $x_0 < x_1 < x_2 < \cdots < x_n$.

Let $f(x)$ be a cubic spline that collocates with these knots and has endpoint conditions either

$$f'(x_0) = h'(x_0) \text{ and } f'(x_n) = h'(x_n) \quad \text{(clamped spline)}$$

or

$$f''(x_0) = 0 \text{ and } f''(x_n) = 0. \quad \text{(natural spline)}.$$

The natural or clamped cubic spline $f(x)$ has less total curvature than any other function $h(x)$ passing through the $n+1$ knots, as shown in the following theorem.

Theorem 15.5 *Let $f(x)$ be the natural or clamped cubic spline passing through the $n+1$ given knots. Let $h(x)$ be any function with continuous first and second derivatives that passes through the same knots. Also, for the clamped cubic spline assume $h'(x_0) = f'(x_0)$ and $h'(x_n) = f'(x_n)$. Then*

$$\int_{x_0}^{x_n} [f''(x)]^2 dx \leq \int_{x_0}^{x_n} [h''(x)]^2 dx. \tag{15.24}$$

Proof: Let us form the difference $D(x) = h(x) - f(x)$. Then, $D''(x) = h''(x) - f''(x)$ and therefore

$$[h''(x)]^2 = [f''(x)]^2 + [D''(x)]^2 + 2f''(x)D''(x).$$

Integrating both sides produces

$$\int_{x_0}^{x_n} [h''(x)]^2 dx = \int_{x_0}^{x_n} [f''(x)]^2 dx + \int_{x_0}^{x_n} [D''(x)]^2 dx + 2\int_{x_0}^{x_n} f''(x)D''(x)dx.$$

The result will be proven if we can show that

$$\int_{x_0}^{x_n} f''(x)D''(x)dx = 0.$$

because the total curvature of the function $h(x)$,

$$\int_{x_0}^{x_n} [h''(x)]^2 dx,$$

will be equal to the total curvature of the spline,

$$\int_{x_0}^{x_n} [f''(x)]^2 dx$$

plus a nonnegative quantity

$$\int_{x_0}^{x_n} [D''(x)]^2 dx.$$

Applying integration by parts, we get

$$\int_{x_0}^{x_n} f''(x)D''(x)dx = f''(x)D'(x)\Big|_{x_0}^{x_n} - \int_{x_0}^{x_n} f'''(x)D'(x)dx.$$

For the clamped cubic spline, the first term is zero because the clamped boundary conditions imply that

$$\begin{aligned} D'(x_0) &= h'(x_0) - f'(x_0) = 0, \\ D'(x_n) &= h'(x_n) - f'(x_n) = 0. \end{aligned}$$

For the natural cubic spline $f''(x_0) = f''(x_n) = 0$, which also makes the first term zero.

The integral in the second term can be divided into subintervals as follows:

$$\int_{x_0}^{x_n} f'''(x)D'(x)dx = \sum_{j=0}^{n-1} \int_{x_j}^{x_{j+1}} f'''(x)D'(x)dx.$$

Integration by parts in each subinterval yields

$$\int_{x_j}^{x_{j+1}} f'''(x)D'(x)dx = f'''(x)D(x)\big|_{x_j}^{x_{j+1}} - \int_{x_j}^{x_{j+1}} f^{(4)}(x)D(x)dx.$$

The first term is zero because of the interpolation condition

$$D(x_j) = h(x_j) - f(x_j) = 0, \quad j = 0, 1, \ldots, n.$$

That is, we are only considering functions $h(x)$ that pass through the knots.

The second term is zero because the spline $f(x)$ in each subinterval is a cubic polynomial and has zero fourth derivative. Thus, for the clamped or natural cubic spline,

$$\int_{x_0}^{x_n} f''(x)D''(x)dx = 0,$$

which proves the result.   □

Thus the clamped cubic spline has great appeal if we want to produce a smooth set of successive values and if we have some knowledge of the slope of the function at each end of the interval. This is often the case in mortality table construction. At very early ages in the first few days and weeks of life, the force of mortality or hazard rate decreases sharply as a result of deaths of newborn lives with congenital and other conditions that contribute to neonatal deaths. At the highest ages, the force of mortality tends to flatten out at a level of between 0.3 and 0.4 at ages well over 100. Using a clamped cubic spline to graduate observed rates will result in obtaining the smoothest possible function that incorporates the desired properties at each end of the age spectrum. If the mortality data are only over some more limited age range (as is usually the case with life insurance or annuity data), either natural or clamped cubic splines can be used. Including a clamping condition controls the slope at the endpoints.

Example 15.6 *For the clamped cubic spline obtained in Example 15.3 calcu-late the value of the squared norm measure of curvature. Calculate the same quantity for the function $h(x) = 100/x$ which also passes through the given knots.*

The spline function is

$$f(x) = \begin{cases} 50 - 25(x-2) + 9.125(x-2)^2 - 1.4375(x-2)^3, & 2 \le x \le 4, \\ 25 - 5.75(x-4) + 0.5(x-4)^2 + 0.25(x-4)^3, & 4 \le x \le 5, \end{cases}$$

and the second derivative is

$$f''(x) = \begin{cases} 18.25 - 8.625(x-2) = 35.5 - 8.625x, & 2 \le x \le 4, \\ 1 + 1.5(x-4) = 1.5x - 5 & 4 \le x \le 5. \end{cases}$$

The total curvature of the spline is

$$\begin{aligned} \int_2^5 [f''(x)]^2 dx &= \int_2^4 (35.5 - 8.625x)^2 dx + \int_4^5 (1.5x - 5)^2 dx \\ &= \int_1^{18.25} y^2 \frac{1}{8.625} dy + \int_1^{2.5} y^2 \frac{1}{1.5} dy \\ &= \frac{y^3}{25.875}\Big|_1^{18.25} + \frac{y^3}{4.5}\Big|_1^{2.5} = 238.125. \end{aligned}$$

For $h(x)$, the second derivative is $h''(x) = 200x^{-3}$ and the curvature is

$$\begin{aligned} \int_2^5 (200x^{-3})^2 dx &= \int_2^5 40{,}000x^{-6} dx \\ &= -8{,}000x^{-5}\Big|_2^5 \\ &= 247.44. \end{aligned}$$

Notice how close the total curvature of the function $h(x)$ and the clamped spline are. Now look at Figure 15.7, which plots both functions. They are very similar in shape. Hence we would expect them to have similar curvature. Of course, as a result of Theorem 15.5, the curvature of the spline should be less, though in this case it is only slightly less. In Exercise 15.9 you are asked to calculate the total curvature of the corresponding natural spline (which also appears in Figure 15.7). Because it is much "straighter," you would expect its total curvature to be significantly less, which is confirmed in Exercise 15.9. □

15.4.1 Exercise

15.9 For the natural cubic spline obtained in Exercise 15.3 calculate the value of the squared norm measure of curvature.

15.5 EXTRAPOLATING WITH SPLINES

In many applications we may want to produce a model that can be faithful to a set of historical data but that can also be used to forecast into the future. For example, in determining liabilities of an insurer when future claim payments are subject to inflationary growth, the actuary may need to project the rate of future claims inflation for some 5 to 10 years into the future. One way to do this is by fitting a function, in this case a cubic spline, to historic claims inflation data.

Simply projecting the cubic in the last interval beyond x_n may result in excessive oscillatory behavior in the region beyond x_n. This could result in projected values that are wildly unreasonable. It makes much more sense to require projected values to form a simple pattern. In particular, a linear projection is likely to be reasonable in most practical situations. This is easily handled by cubic splines.

The natural cubic spline has endpoint conditions that require the second derivatives to be zero at the endpoints. The natural extrapolation is linear with the slope coming from the endpoints. Of course, the linear extrapolation function can be done for any spline using the first derivative at the end points. However, unless the second derivative is zero, as with the natural spline, the second derivative condition will be violated at the endpoints. The extrapolated values at each end are then

$$\begin{aligned} f(x) &= f(x_n) + f'(x_n)(x - x_n), \ x > x_n, \\ f(x) &= f(x_0) - f'(x_0)(x_0 - x), \ x < x_0. \end{aligned}$$

Example 15.7 *Obtain formulas for the extrapolated values for the clamped spline in Example 15.3 and determine the extrapolated values at $x = 0$ and $x = 7$.*

In the first interval, $f(x) = 50 - 25(x-2) + 9.125(x-2)^2 - 1.4375(x-2)^3$ and so $f(2) = 50$ and $f'(2) = -25$. Then, for $x < 2$, the extrapolation is $f(x) = 50 - (-25)(2-x) = 100 - 25x$. In the final interval, $f(x) = 25 - 5.75(x-4) + 0.5(x-4)^2 + 0.25(x-4)^3$ and so $f(5) = 20$ and $f'(5) = -4$. Then, for $x > 5$, the extrapolation is $f(x) = 20 - 4(x-5) = 40 - 4x$. At $x = 0$ the extrapolated value is $100 - 25(0) = 100$ and at $x = 7$ it is $40 - 4(7) = 12$. $\square$

15.5.1 Exercise

15.10 Obtain formulas for the extrapolated values for the natural spline in Exercise 15.3 and determine the extrapolated values at $x = 0$ and $x = 7$.

15.6 SMOOTHING SPLINES

In many actuarial applications, it may be desirable to do more than interpolate between observed data. If data include a random (or "noise") element, it is often best to allow the cubic spline or other smooth function to lie near the data points, rather than requiring the function to pass through each data point.

In the terminology of graduation theory as developed by actuaries in the early 1900s, this is called **modified osculatory interpolation**. The term *modified* is added to recognize that the points of intersection (or knots in the language of splines) are modified from the original data points.

The technical development of smoothing cubic splines is identical to interpolating cubic splines except that the original knots at each data point (x_i, y_i) are replaced by knots at (x_j, a_j) where the ordinate a_j is the constant term in the smoothing cubic spline

$$f_j(x) = a_j + b_j(x - x_j) + c_j(x - x_j)^2 + d_j(x - x_j)^3. \tag{15.25}$$

We first imagine that the ordinates of original data points are the outcomes of the model

$$y_j = g(x_j) + \epsilon_j,$$

where ϵ_j, $j = 0, 1, \ldots, n$, are independently distributed random variables with mean 0 and variance σ_j^2 and where $g(x)$ is a well-behaved function.[3]

Example 15.8 *Mortality rates q_j at each age j are estimated by the ratio of observed deaths to the number of life-years of exposure D_j/n_j, where D_j is a binomial (n_j, q_j) random variable. The estimator $\hat{q}_j = d_j/n_j$, where d_j is*

---

[3]Without specifying what "well-behaved" means in technical terms, we are simply trying to say that $g(x)$ is smooth in a general way. Typically we will require at least the first two derivatives to be continuous.

the observed number of deaths, has variance $\sigma_j^2 = q_j(1 - q_j)/n_j$, which can be estimated by $\hat{q}_j(1 - \hat{q}_j)/n_j$.

We attempt to find a smooth function $f(x)$, in this case a cubic spline, that will serve as an approximation to the "true" function $g(x)$. Because $g(x)$ is assumed to be well behaved, we will require the smoothing cubic spline $f(x)$ itself to be as smooth as possible. On the other hand, we want it to be faithful to the given data as much as possible. These are conflicting objectives. Therefore, a compromise will be necessary between fit and smoothness.

The degree of fit can be measured using the chi-square criterion

$$F = \sum_{j=0}^{n} \left(\frac{y_j - a_j}{\sigma_j} \right)^2 . \tag{15.26}$$

This is a standard statistical criterion for measuring the degree of fit and was discussed in that context in Section 13.4.3. It has a chi-square distribution with $n + 1$ degrees of freedom.[4]

The degree of smoothness can be measured by the overall smoothness of the cubic spline. The smoothness, or equivalently the total curvature, can be measured by the squared norm smoothness criterion

$$S = \int_{x_0}^{x_n} [f''(x)]^2 dx.$$

It was shown in Theorem 15.5 that within the broad class of functions with continuous first and second derivatives, the natural or clamped cubic spline minimizes the squared norm. This supports the choice of the cubic spline as the smoothing function.

In order to recognize the conflicting objectives of fit and smoothness, we construct a criterion which is a weighted average of the measures of fit and smoothness. Let

$$
\begin{aligned}
L &= pF + (1 - p)S \\
&= p\sum_{j=0}^{n} \left(\frac{y_j - a_j}{\sigma_j} \right)^2 + (1 - p) \int_{x_0}^{x_n} [f''(x)]^2 dx.
\end{aligned}
$$

The parameter p reflects the relative importance which we give to the conflicting objectives of remaining close to the data, on the one hand, and of obtaining a smooth curve, on the other hand. Notice that a linear function satisfies the equation

$$S = \int_{x_0}^{x_n} [f''(x)]^2 dx = 0,$$

---

[4]No degree of freedom is lost, because unlike with the goodness-of-fit test, if you know all but one of the terms of the sum, it is not possible to infer the remaining value.

which suggests that, in the limiting case, where $p = 0$ and thus smoothness is all that matters, the spline function $f(x)$ will become a straight line. At the other extreme, where $p = 1$ and thus the closeness of the spline to the data is all that matters, we will obtain an interpolating spline which passes exactly through the data points.

The spline is piecewise cubic and thus the smoothness criterion can be written

$$S = \int_{x_0}^{x_n} [f''(x)]^2 dx = \sum_{j=0}^{n-1} \int_{x_j}^{x_{j+1}} [f_j''(x)]^2 dx.$$

From (15.5),

$$f_j''(x) = \frac{m_j}{h_j}(x_{j+1} - x) + \frac{m_{j+1}}{h_j}(x - x_j),$$

and then

$$
\begin{aligned}
\int_{x_j}^{x_{j+1}} [f_j''(x)]^2 dx &= \int_{x_j}^{x_{j+1}} \left[\frac{m_j}{h_j}(x_{j+1} - x) + \frac{m_{j+1}}{h_j}(x - x_j) \right]^2 dx \\
&= \int_0^1 [m_j(1 - y) + m_{j+1}y]^2 h_j \, dy \\
&= h_j \int_0^1 [m_j + (m_{j+1} - m_j)y]^2 \, dy \\
&= h_j \left. \frac{[m_j + (m_{j+1} - m_j)y]^3}{3(m_{j+1} - m_j)} \right|_0^1 \\
&= \frac{h_j}{3}(m_j^2 + m_j m_{j+1} + m_{j+1}^2),
\end{aligned}
$$

where the substitution $y = (x - x_j)/h_j$ is used in the second line. The criterion function then becomes

$$L = p \sum_{j=0}^{n} \left(\frac{y_j - a_j}{\sigma_j} \right)^2 + (1 - p) \sum_{j=0}^{n-1} \frac{h_j}{3}(m_j^2 + m_j m_{j+1} + m_{j+1}^2).$$

We need to minimize this function with respect to the $2n + 2$ unknown quantities $\{a_j, m_j; j = 0, \ldots, n\}$. Note that when we have solved for these variables we will have four pieces of information $\{a_j, a_{j+1}, m_j, m_{j+1}\}$ for each interval $[x_j, x_{j+1}]$. This allows us to fully specify the interpolating cubic spline in each interval. We now address the issue of solving for these quantities.

We now consider the natural smoothing spline. The equations developed for interpolating splines apply to smoothing cubic splines except that the y_j's are replaced by a_j's to recognize that the abscissas $\{a_j; j = 0, \ldots, n\}$ of the smoothing splines do not pass through the abscissas of the data points $\{y_j; j = 0, \ldots, n\}$. From (15.16), we can write

$$\mathbf{Hm = u},$$

where $\mathbf{m} = (m_1, m_2, \ldots, m_{n-1})^T$ and $\mathbf{u} = (u_1, u_2, \ldots, u_{n-1})^T$ because $m_0 = m_n = 0$ from the natural spline condition. From (15.15), the vector $\mathbf{u}$ can be rewritten as

$$\mathbf{u} = \mathbf{R}\mathbf{a},$$

where $\mathbf{R}$ is the $(n-1) \times (n+1)$ matrix

$$\mathbf{R} = \begin{bmatrix} r_0 & -(r_0 + r_1) & r_1 & 0 & \cdots & \cdots & 0 \\ 0 & r_1 & -(r_1 + r_2) & r_2 & 0 & \cdots & 0 \\ \ddots & & \ddots & & \ddots & & \ddots \\ 0 & \cdots & & \cdots & 0 & r_{n-2} & -(r_{n-2} + r_{n-1}) & r_{n-1} \end{bmatrix}$$

and

$$\mathbf{a} = (a_0, a_1, \ldots, a_n)^T, \quad r_j = 6h_j^{-1}.$$

Then we have

$$\mathbf{H}\mathbf{m} = \mathbf{R}\mathbf{a}. \tag{15.27}$$

We can now rewrite the criterion L as

$$L = p(\mathbf{y} - \mathbf{a})^T \mathbf{\Sigma}^{-1} (\mathbf{y} - \mathbf{a}) + \tfrac{1}{6}(1 - p)\mathbf{m}^T \mathbf{H}\mathbf{m}$$

where $\mathbf{\Sigma} = \text{diag}\{\sigma_0^2, \sigma_1^2, \ldots, \sigma_n^2\}$. Because $\mathbf{m} = \mathbf{H}^{-1}\mathbf{R}\mathbf{a}$, we can rewrite the criterion as

$$L = p(\mathbf{y} - \mathbf{a})^T \mathbf{\Sigma}^{-1} (\mathbf{y} - \mathbf{a}) + \tfrac{1}{6}(1 - p)\mathbf{a}^T \mathbf{R}^T \mathbf{H}^{-1} \mathbf{R}\mathbf{a}.$$

We can differentiate the criterion L with respect to each of $a_0, a_1, \ldots, a_n$ successively to obtain the optimal values of the ordinates. In matrix notation, the result is (after dividing the derivative by 2)

$$-p(\mathbf{y} - \mathbf{a})^T \mathbf{\Sigma}^{-1} + \tfrac{1}{6}(1 - p)\mathbf{a}^T \mathbf{R}^T \mathbf{H}^{-1} \mathbf{R} = \mathbf{0},$$

where $\mathbf{0}$ is the $(n+1) \times 1$ vector of zeros, $(0, \ldots, 0)^T$. This yields, after transposition,

$$6p\mathbf{\Sigma}^{-1}(\mathbf{y} - \mathbf{a}) = (1 - p)\mathbf{R}^T \mathbf{H}^{-1} \mathbf{R}\mathbf{a}$$

or

$$6p\mathbf{\Sigma}^{-1}(\mathbf{y} - \mathbf{a}) = (1 - p)\mathbf{R}^T \mathbf{m}. \tag{15.28}$$

We now premultiply by $\mathbf{R}\mathbf{\Sigma}$, yielding

$$6p\mathbf{R}\mathbf{\Sigma}\mathbf{\Sigma}^{-1}(\mathbf{y} - \mathbf{a}) = (1 - p)\mathbf{R}\mathbf{\Sigma}\mathbf{R}^T \mathbf{m}$$

or

$$6p(\mathbf{R}\mathbf{y} - \mathbf{R}\mathbf{a}) = (1 - p)\mathbf{R}\mathbf{\Sigma}\mathbf{R}^T \mathbf{m}. \tag{15.29}$$

Because $\mathbf{H}\mathbf{m} = \mathbf{R}\mathbf{a}$, this reduces to

$$p\mathbf{R}\mathbf{y} - p\mathbf{H}\mathbf{m} = \tfrac{1}{6}(1 - p)\mathbf{R}\mathbf{\Sigma}\mathbf{R}^T \mathbf{m}$$

or

$$\left(p\mathbf{H} + \tfrac{1}{6}(1-p)\mathbf{R}\boldsymbol{\Sigma}\mathbf{R}^T\right)\mathbf{m} = p\mathbf{R}\mathbf{y}. \tag{15.30}$$

This is a system of $n-1$ equations in $n-1$ unknowns. The system of equations can be solved for $m_1, m_2, \ldots, m_{n-1}$. Using matrix methods, the solution can be obtained from (15.30) as

$$\mathbf{m} = \left(\mathbf{H} + \frac{1-p}{6p}\mathbf{R}\boldsymbol{\Sigma}\mathbf{R}^T\right)^{-1}\mathbf{R}\mathbf{y}. \tag{15.31}$$

Now, the values of $a_0, a_1, \ldots, a_n$ can be obtained by rewriting (15.28) as

$$\mathbf{a} = \mathbf{y} - \frac{1-p}{6p}\boldsymbol{\Sigma}\mathbf{R}^T\mathbf{m}. \tag{15.32}$$

Finally, substitution of (15.31) into (15.32) results in

$$\mathbf{a} = \mathbf{y} - \frac{1-p}{6p}\boldsymbol{\Sigma}\mathbf{R}^T\left(\mathbf{H} + \frac{1-p}{6p}\mathbf{R}\boldsymbol{\Sigma}\mathbf{R}^T\right)^{-1}\mathbf{R}\mathbf{y}. \tag{15.33}$$

Thus we have obtained the values of the intercepts of the n cubic spline segments of the smoothing spline. The values of the other coefficients of the spline segments can now be calculated in the same way as for the natural interpolating spline, as discussed in Section 15.3 using the knots $\{(x_j, a_j), j = 0, \ldots, n\}$ and setting $m_0 = m_n = 0$. It should be noted that the only additional calculation for the natural smoothing spline as compared with the natural interpolation spline is given by (15.33).

The magnitude of the values of the criteria for fit F and smoothness S may be very different. Therefore one should not place any significance on the specific choice of the value of p (unless it is 0 or 1). Smaller values of p result in more smoothing; larger values result in less. In some applications it may be necessary to make the value of p very small, for example, 0.001, to begin to get visual images with any significant amount of smoothing. This is, in part, due to the role of the variances which appear in the denominator of the fit criterion. Small variances can result in the fit term being much larger than the smoothness term. Therefore, it may be necessary to have a very small value for p to get any visible smoothing.

Example 15.9 *Construct natural cubic smoothing splines for the data in Table* 15.1. *The natural cubic interpolating spline through the mortality rates was shown in Figure* 15.8.

Natural cubic smoothing splines with $p = 0.5$ and $p = 0.1$ are shown in Figures 15.9 and 15.10. The coefficients for the smoothing spline with $p = 0.1$ are given in Table 15.3. Note that the resulting splines look much like the one in Figure 15.8 except near the upper end of the data where there are relatively fewer actual deaths and less smoothness in the successive observed

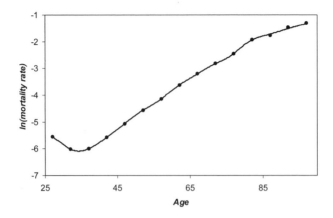

Fig. 15.9 Smoothing spline with $p = 0.5$ for Example 15.9.

values. Also observe the increased smoothness in the spline in Figure 15.10 resulting from the smaller emphasis on fit. The standard deviations were calculated as in Example 15.8 with the resulting values multiplied by 1,000 to make the numbers more reasonable.[5]   □

Example 15.9 illustrates how the smoothing splines can be used to carry out both interpolation and smoothing automatically. The knots at quinquennial ages were smoothed using (15.32). The modified knots were then used as knots for an interpolating spline. The interpolated values are the revised mortality rates at the intermediate ages. The smoothing effect was not visually dramatic in Example 15.9 because the original data series was already quite smooth. The next example illustrates how successive values in a very noisy series can be smoothed dramatically using a smoothing spline.

Example 15.10 *Table 15.4 gives successive observed mortality rates for a 15-year period. The data can be found in Miller [94], p. 11 and are shown in Figure 15.11. Fit smoothing splines changing p until smoothing appears reasonable and provide values of the revised mortality rates at each age.*

Unlike Example 15.9, the numbers represent numbers of persons, not dollar amounts, and can be used directly in the estimates of the variances of the

---

[5]Had the values not been multiplied by 1,000 the same answers could have been obtained by altering the value of p. This method of calculating the standard deviations does not consider the possible variation in sizes of the insurance policies. See Klugman [75] for a more detailed treatment. The method used here implicitly treats all policies as being of the same size. That size is not important because as with the factor of 1,000, a constant of proportionality can be absorbed into p.

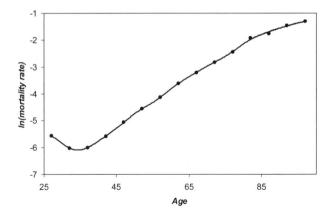

Fig. 15.10 Smoothing spline with $p = 0.1$ for Example 15.9.

Table 15.3 Spline coefficients for Example 15.9 with $p = 0.1$

j	x_j	a_j	b_j	c_j	d_j
0	27	3.8790×10^{-3}	-3.4670×10^{-4}	0	2.4846×10^{-6}
1	32	2.4560×10^{-3}	-1.6036×10^{-4}	3.7269×10^{-5}	-8.0257×10^{-7}
2	37	2.4856×10^{-3}	1.5214×10^{-4}	2.5230×10^{-5}	-5.0019×10^{-7}
3	42	3.8146×10^{-3}	3.6693×10^{-4}	1.7728×10^{-5}	1.9945×10^{-6}
4	47	6.3417×10^{-3}	6.9379×10^{-4}	4.7644×10^{-5}	-4.0893×10^{-6}
5	52	1.0491×10^{-2}	8.6353×10^{-4}	-1.3695×10^{-5}	1.1833×10^{-5}
6	57	1.5945×10^{-2}	1.6141×10^{-3}	1.6380×10^{-4}	-9.7024×10^{-6}
7	62	2.6898×10^{-2}	2.5244×10^{-3}	1.8268×10^{-5}	6.2633×10^{-6}
8	67	4.0759×10^{-2}	3.1769×10^{-3}	1.1222×10^{-4}	-9.4435×10^{-7}
9	72	5.9331×10^{-2}	4.2282×10^{-3}	9.8052×10^{-5}	3.9737×10^{-5}
10	77	8.7891×10^{-2}	8.1890×10^{-3}	6.9411×10^{-4}	-6.6804×10^{-5}
11	82	1.3784×10^{-1}	1.0120×10^{-2}	-3.0794×10^{-4}	2.1572×10^{-5}
12	87	1.8344×10^{-1}	8.6583×10^{-3}	1.5633×10^{-5}	-1.0282×10^{-6}
13	92	2.2699×10^{-1}	8.7376×10^{-3}	2.1021×10^{-7}	-1.4014×10^{-8}

mortality rates (see Example 15.8). The standard deviations are multiplied by a factor of 10 for convenience. For insurance purposes, we are more interested in the spline values at the knots, that is, the a_j. The interpolated values are given in Table 15.4 and the spline values are plotted in Figures 15.12–15.14 for $p = 0.5, 0.1, 0.05$. Note that for $p = 0.5$ there is significant smoothing but that some points still have a lot of influence on the result. For example the large number of actual deaths at age 76 causes the curve to be pulled upward.

Table 15.4 Mortality rates and interpolated values for Example 15.10

j	Age x_j	Exposed to risk	Observed deaths	Estimated mort. rate	Smoothed $p = 0.5$	$p = 0.1$	$p = 0.05$
0	70	135	6	0.044	0.046	0.050	0.052
1	71	143	12	0.084	0.078	0.069	0.065
2	72	140	10	0.071	0.077	0.071	0.069
3	73	144	11	0.076	0.066	0.064	0.065
4	74	149	6	0.040	0.049	0.062	0.066
5	75	154	16	0.104	0.100	0.084	0.080
6	76	150	24	0.160	0.126	0.096	0.089
7	77	139	8	0.058	0.076	0.087	0.088
8	78	145	16	0.110	0.091	0.091	0.093
9	79	140	13	0.093	0.102	0.105	0.107
10	80	137	19	0.139	0.131	0.128	0.128
11	81	136	21	0.154	0.157	0.155	0.154
12	82	126	23	0.183	0.182	0.181	0.181
13	83	126	26	0.206	0.208	0.209	0.208
14	84	109	26	0.239	0.238	0.237	0.236
Total		2,073	237				

More smoothing can be obtained by reducing p, as can be observed from the three figures. □

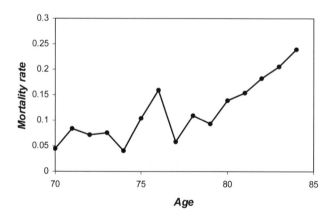

Fig. 15.11 Mortality data for Example 15.10.

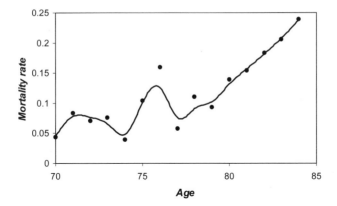

Fig. 15.12   Smoothing spline for mortality data with $p = 0.5$.

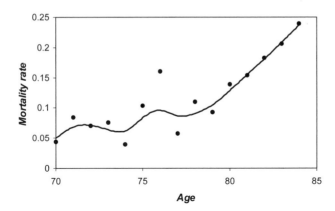

Fig. 15.13   Smoothing spline for mortality data with $p = 0.1$.

Example 15.10 demonstrated the smoothing capability of splines. However, one still needs to choose a value of p. In practice, this is done using professional judgment and visual inspection. If, as with Example 15.9, data sets are large and there is already some degree of smoothness in the observed data, then a fitted curve which closely follows the data is likely highly desirable. If the available data set is more limited, as with Example 15.10, considerable smoothing is needed and judgment plays a large role. For data sets of any size, formal tests of fit can be conducted. The fit criterion F has a chi-square distribution with $n + 1$ degrees of freedom. This can provide some guidance.

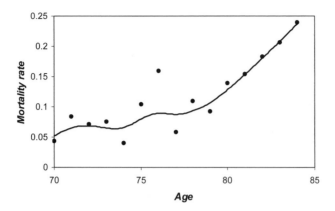

Fig. 15.14   Smoothing spline for mortality data with $p = 0.05$.

The choice of other tests of fit such as the runs test can be employed to identify specific anomalies of the fitted spline.

15.6.1   Exercise

15.11 Consider the natural cubic smoothing spline that smooths the points $(0, 0)$, $(1, 2)$, $(2, 1)$, $(3, 3)$ using $p = 0.9$ and standard deviations of 0.5. (Use a spreadsheet for the calculations.)

    (a) Obtain the values of the intercepts of the nodes by using (15.33).

    (b) Obtain the natural cubic smoothing spline as the natural interpolating spline through the nodes using (15.16) and (15.18).

    (c) Graph the resulting spline from $x = -0.5$ to $x = 2.5$.

16

Credibility

16.1 INTRODUCTION

Credibility theory is a set of quantitative tools which allows an insurer to perform prospective experience rating (adjust future premiums based on past experience) on a risk or group of risks. If the experience of a policyholder is consistently better than that assumed in the underlying manual rate (sometimes called the **pure premium**), then the policyholder may demand a rate reduction.

The policyholder's argument is as follows: The manual rate is designed to reflect the expected experience of the entire rating class and implicitly assumes that the risks are homogeneous. However, no rating system is perfect, and there always remains some heterogeneity in the risk levels after all the underwriting criteria are accounted for. Consequently, some policyholders will be better risks than that assumed in the underlying manual rate. Of course, the same logic dictates that a rate increase should be applied to a poor risk, but the policyholder in this situation is certainly not going to ask for a rate increase! Nevertheless, an increase may be necessary, due to considerations of equity and the economics of the situation.

The insurer is then forced to answer the following question: How much of the difference in experience of a given policyholder is due to random variation

Loss Models: From Data to Decisions, Second Edition.
By Stuart A. Klugman, Harry H. Panjer, and Gordon E. Willmot
ISBN 0-471-21577-5   Copyright © 2004 John Wiley & Sons, Inc.

in the underlying claims experience and how much is due to the fact that the policyholder really is a better or worse risk than average for the given rating class? In other words, how credible is the policyholder's own experience? Two facts must be considered in this regard:

1. The more past information the insurer has on a given policyholder, the more *credible* the policyholder's own experience, all else being equal. In the same vein, in group insurance the experience of larger groups is more credible than that of smaller groups.

2. Competitive considerations may force the insurer to give full (using the past experience of the policyholder only and not the manual rate) or nearly full credibility to a given policyholder in order to retain the business.

Another use for credibility is in the setting of rates for classification systems. For example, in workers compensation insurance there may be hundreds of occupational classes, some of which may provide very little data. In order to accurately estimate the expected cost for insuring these classes, it may be appropriate to combine the limited actual experience with some other information, such as past rates, or the experience of occupations that are closely related.

From a statistical perspective, credibility theory leads to a result that would appear to be counterintuitive. If experience from an insured or group of insureds is available, our statistical training may convince us to use the sample mean or some other unbiased estimator. But credibility theory tells us that it is optimal to give only partial weight to this experience and give the remaining weight to an estimator produced from other information. We will discover that what we sacrifice in terms of bias we gain in terms of reducing the average (squared) error.

Credibility theory allows an insurer to quantitatively formulate the above problem, and this chapter provides an introduction to this theory. A few relevant statistical concepts are reviewed in the next section. Some topics were covered in Sections 9.2 and 12.4 are repeated and there are some new formulas and concepts as well.

Section 16.3 deals with **limited fluctuation credibility theory**, a subject developed in the early part of the twentieth century. This provides a mechanism for assigning full (Section 16.3.1) or partial (Section 16.3.2) credibility to a policyholder's experience. The difficulty with this approach is the lack of a sound underlying mathematical theory justifying the use of these methods. Nevertheless, this approach provided the original treatment of the subject and is still in use today.

A classic paper by Bühlmann in 1967 [18] provided a statistical framework within which credibility theory has developed and flourished. While this approach, termed **greatest accuracy credibility theory**,[1] was formalized by Bühlmann, the basic ideas were around for some time. This approach is introduced in Section 16.4. The simplest model, that of Bühlmann [18], is discussed in Section 16.4.4. Practical improvements were made by Bühlmann and Straub in 1970 [20]. Their model is discussed in Section 16.4.5. The concept of exact credibility is presented in Section 16.4.6.

Practical use of the theory requires that unknown model parameters be estimated from data. Nonparametric estimation (where the problem is somewhat model free and the parameters are generic, such as the mean and variance) is considered in Section 16.5.1, semiparametric estimation (where some of the parameters are based on assuming particular distributions) in Section 16.5.2, and finally the fully parametric situation (where all parameters come from assumed distributions) in Section 16.5.3.

We close with a quote from Arthur Bailey in 1950 [8], p. 8, that aptly summarizes much of the history of credibility. We, too, must tip our hats to the early actuaries, who, with unsophisticated mathematical tools at their disposal, were able to come up with formulas that not only worked but also were very similar to those we carefully develop in this chapter.

> It is at this point in the discussion that the ordinary individual has to admit that, while there seems to be some hazy logic behind the actuaries' contentions, it is too obscure for him to understand. The trained statistician cries "Absurd! Directly contrary to any of the accepted theories of statistical estimation." The actuaries themselves have to admit that they have gone beyond anything that has been proven mathematically, that all of the values involved are still selected on the basis of judgment, and that the only demonstration they can make is that, in actual practice, it works. Let us not forget, however, that they have made this demonstration many times. It does work!

16.2   STATISTICAL CONCEPTS

In this section various statistical concepts relevant to credibility theory are presented. Much of the material is of a review nature and hence may be quickly glossed over by a reader with a good background in statistics. Nevertheless, there may be some material which may not have been seen before, and so this section should not be completely ignored. Subsequent sections will refer back to this material.

---

[1] The terms *limited fluctuation* and *greatest accuracy* go back at least as far as a 1943 paper by Arthur Bailey [7].

16.2.1 Conditional distributions

Suppose that X and Y are two random variables with joint probability function (pf) or probability density function (pdf)[2] $f_{X,Y}(x,y)$ and marginal pfs $f_X(x)$ and $f_Y(y)$, respectively. The conditional pf of X given that $Y = y$ is

$$f_{X|Y}(x|y) = \frac{f_{X,Y}(x,y)}{f_Y(y)}. \tag{16.1}$$

If X and Y are discrete random variables, then (16.1) is the conditional probability of the event $X = x$ under the hypothesis that $Y = y$. If X and Y are continuous, then (16.1) may be interpreted as a definition. When X and Y are independent random variables,

$$f_{X,Y}(x,y) = f_X(x)f_Y(y),$$

and in this case, (16.1) yields

$$f_{X|Y}(x|y) = f_X(x),.$$

We observe that the conditional and marginal distributions of X are identical.

Example 16.1 *Suppose X and Z are independent Poisson random variables with means λ_1 and λ_2, respectively. Let $Y = X + Z$. Demonstrate that $X|Y = y$ is binomial with parameters $m = y$ and $q = \lambda_1/(\lambda_1 + \lambda_2)$ (see, for example, [58], p. 131).*

The conditional distribution of X given that $Y = y$ is

---

[2]When it is unclear, or when the random variable may be continuous, discrete, or a mixture of the two, the term **probability function** and abbreviation pf will be used. The term **probability density function** and the abbreviation pdf will be used only when the random variable is known to be continuous.

$$
\begin{aligned}
f_{X|Y}(x|y) &= \frac{f_{X,Y}(x,y)}{f_Y(y)} \\
&= \frac{\Pr(X = x, Y = y)}{\Pr(Y = y)} \\
&= \frac{\Pr(X = x, Z = y - x)}{\Pr(Y = y)} \\
&= \frac{\Pr(X = x)\Pr(Z = y - x)}{\Pr(Y = y)} \\
&= \frac{\dfrac{\lambda_1^x e^{-\lambda_1}}{x!} \dfrac{\lambda_2^{y-x} e^{-\lambda_2}}{(y - x)!}}{\dfrac{(\lambda_1 + \lambda_2)^y e^{-\lambda_1 - \lambda_2}}{y!}} \\
&= \frac{y!}{x!(y - x)!} \left(\frac{\lambda_1}{\lambda_1 + \lambda_2}\right)^x \left(\frac{\lambda_2}{\lambda_1 + \lambda_2}\right)^{y-x}
\end{aligned}
$$

for $x = 0, 1, 2, \cdots, y$. This is a binomial distribution with parameters $m = y$ and $q = \lambda_1/(\lambda_1 + \lambda_2)$.   □

Note that (16.1) may be rewritten as

$$
f_{X,Y}(x, y) = f_{X|Y}(x|y)f_Y(y), \tag{16.2}
$$

demonstrating that joint distributions may be constructed from products of conditional and marginal distributions. Because the marginal distribution of X may be obtained by integrating (or summing) y out of the joint distribution,

$$
f_X(x) = \int f_{X,Y}(x, y)\, dy,
$$

we find using (16.2) that

$$
f_X(x) = \int f_{X|Y}(x|y)f_Y(y)\, dy. \tag{16.3}
$$

Formula (16.3) has an interesting interpretation as a mixed distribution (see Section 4.4.5). To see this, assume that the conditional distribution $f_{X|Y}(x|y)$ is one of the usual parametric distributions where y is the realization of a random parameter Y with distribution $f_Y(y)$. In Section 4.6.3 it was shown that if, given $\Theta = \theta$, X has a Poisson distribution with mean θ and Θ has a gamma distribution, then the marginal distribution of X will be negative binomial. Also, Example 4.30 showed that, if $X|\Theta$ has a normal distribution with mean Θ and variance v and Θ has a normal distribution with mean μ

and variance a, then the marginal distribution of X is normal with mean μ and variance $a + v$.

Note that the roles of X and Y in (16.2) can be interchanged, yielding

$$f_{X|Y}(x|y)f_Y(y) = f_{Y|X}(y|x)f_X(x),$$

because both sides of this equation equal the joint distribution of X and Y. Division by $f_Y(y)$ yields Bayes' theorem, namely,

$$f_{X|Y}(x|y) = \frac{f_{Y|X}(y|x)f_X(x)}{f_Y(y)}.$$

16.2.2   Conditional expectation

As in the previous subsection, assume that X and Y are two random variables and the conditional pf of X given that $Y = y$ is $f_{X|Y}(x|y)$. Clearly, this is a valid probability distribution, and its mean is denoted by

$$E(X|Y = y) = \int x \, f_{X|Y}(x|y) \, dx \tag{16.4}$$

with the integral replaced by a sum in the discrete case. Clearly, (16.4) is a function of y, and it is often of interest to view this conditional expectation as a random variable obtained by replacing y by Y in the right-hand side of (16.4). Thus we can write $E(X|Y)$ instead of the left-hand side of (16.4), and so $E(X|Y)$ is itself a random variable because it is a function of the random variable Y. The expectation of $E(X|Y)$ is given by

$$E[E(X|Y)] = E(X). \tag{16.5}$$

To see this, note that from (16.3) and (16.4)

$$
\begin{aligned}
E[E(X|Y)] &= \int E(X|Y = y)f_Y(y) \, dy \\
&= \int \int x f_{X|Y}(x|y) dx f_Y(y) \, dy \\
&= \int x \int f_{X|Y}(x|y) f_Y(y) \, dy \, dx \\
&= \int x f_X(x) \, dx \\
&= E(X)
\end{aligned}
$$

with a similar proof in the discrete case.

Example 16.2 *Derive the mean of the negative binomial distribution by conditional expectation, recalling that, if $X|\Theta \sim Poisson(\Theta)$ and $\Theta \sim gamma(\alpha, \beta)$, then $X \sim$ negative binomial with $r = \alpha$ and $\beta = \beta$.*

We have
$$E(X|\Theta) = \Theta$$
and so
$$E(X) = E[E(X|\Theta)] = E(\Theta).$$
From Appendix A the mean of the gamma distribution of Θ is $\alpha\beta$, and so $E(X) = \alpha\beta$. $\qquad\qquad\qquad\qquad\qquad\qquad\qquad\qquad\qquad\qquad\qquad\square$

It is often convenient to replace X by an arbitrary function $h(X,Y)$ in (16.4), yielding the more general definition

$$E[h(X,Y)|Y=y] = \int h(x,y)f_{X|Y}(x|y)\,dx.$$

Similarly, $E[h(X,Y)|Y]$ is the conditional expectation viewed as a random variable which is a function of Y. Then, (16.5) generalizes to

$$E\{E[h(X,Y)|Y]\} = E[h(X,Y)]. \qquad\qquad (16.6)$$

To see (16.6), note that

$$
\begin{aligned}
E\{E[h(X,Y)|Y]\} &= \int E[h(X,Y)|Y=y]f_Y(y)\,dy \\
&= \int\int h(x,y)f_{X|Y}(x|y)\,dx f_Y(y)\,dy \\
&= \int\int h(x,y)[f_{X|Y}(x|y)f_Y(y)]\,dx\,dy \\
&= \int\int h(x,y)f_{X,Y}(x,y)\,dx\,dy \\
&= E[h(X,Y)]
\end{aligned}
$$

from (16.2).

If we choose $h(X,Y) = [X - E(X|Y)]^2$, then its expected value, based on the conditional distribution of X given Y, is the variance of this conditional distribution,

$$\mathrm{Var}(X|Y) = E\{[X - E(X|Y)]^2|Y\}. \qquad\qquad (16.7)$$

Clearly, (16.7) is still a function of the random variable Y.

It is instructive now to analyze the variance of X where X and Y are two random variables. To begin, note that (16.7) may be written as

$$\mathrm{Var}(X|Y) = E(X^2|Y) - [E(X|Y)]^2.$$

Thus,

$$
\begin{aligned}
E[\mathrm{Var}(X|Y)] &= E\{E(X^2|Y) - [E(X|Y)]^2\} \\
&= E[E(X^2|Y)] - E\{[E(X|Y)]^2\} \\
&= E(X^2) - E\{[E(X|Y)]^2\}.
\end{aligned}
$$

Also, because $\text{Var}[h(Y)] = \text{E}\{[h(Y)]^2\} - \{\text{E}[h(Y)]\}^2$, we may use $h(Y) = \text{E}(X|Y)$ to obtain

$$\begin{aligned} \text{Var}[\text{E}(X|Y)] &= \text{E}\{[\text{E}(X|Y)]^2\} - \{\text{E}[\text{E}(X|Y)]\}^2 \\ &= \text{E}\{[\text{E}(X|Y)]^2\} - [\text{E}(X)]^2. \end{aligned}$$

Thus,

$$\begin{aligned} \text{E}[\text{Var}(X|Y)] + \text{Var}[\text{E}(X|Y)] &= \text{E}(X^2) - \text{E}\{[\text{E}(X|Y)]^2\} \\ &\quad + \text{E}\{[\text{E}(X|Y)]^2\} - [\text{E}(X)]^2 \\ &= \text{E}(X^2) - [\text{E}(X)]^2 \\ &= \text{Var}(X). \end{aligned}$$

Thus, we have established the important formula

$$\text{Var}(X) = \text{E}[\text{Var}(X|Y)] + \text{Var}[\text{E}(X|Y)]. \tag{16.8}$$

Formula (16.8) states that the variance of X is composed of the sum of two parts: the mean of the conditional variance plus the variance of the conditional mean.

Example 16.3 *Derive the variance of the negative binomial distribution.*

The Poisson distribution has equal mean and variance, that is,

$$\text{E}(X|\Theta) = \text{Var}(X|\Theta) = \Theta,$$

and so, from (16.8),

$$\begin{aligned} \text{Var}(X) &= \text{E}[Var(X|\Theta)] + \text{Var}[\text{E}(X|\Theta)] \\ &= \text{E}(\Theta) + \text{Var}(\Theta). \end{aligned}$$

Because Θ itself has a gamma distribution with parameters α and β, $\text{E}(\Theta) = \alpha\beta$ and $\text{Var}(\Theta) = \alpha\beta^2$. Thus the variance of the negative binomial distribution is

$$\begin{aligned} \text{Var}(X) &= \text{E}(\Theta) + \text{Var}(\Theta) \\ &= \alpha\beta + \alpha\beta^2 \\ &= \alpha\beta(1 + \beta). \end{aligned} \qquad \square$$

Example 16.4 *It was shown in Example 4.30 that, if $X|\Theta$ is normally distributed with mean Θ and variance v where Θ is itself normally distributed with mean μ and variance a, then X (unconditionally) is normally distributed with mean μ and variance $a + v$. Use (16.5) and (16.8) to obtain the mean and variance of X directly.*

For the mean we have

$$E(X) = E[E(X|\Theta)] = E(\Theta) = \mu$$

and for the variance we obtain

$$
\begin{aligned}
\text{Var}(X) &= E[\text{Var}(X|\Theta)] + \text{Var}[E(X|\Theta)] \\
&= E(v) + \text{Var}(\Theta) \\
&= v + a
\end{aligned}
$$

because v is a constant. □

Example 16.5 *Consider a compound Poisson distribution with Poisson mean* λ, *where* $X = Y_1 + \cdots + Y_N$ *with* $E(Y_i) = \mu_Y$ *and* $\text{Var}(Y_i) = \sigma_Y^2$. *Determine the mean and variance of* X.

Formula (16.8) was used in Chapter 6 to obtain the answers:

$$E(X) = \lambda\mu_Y \text{ and } \text{Var}(X) = \lambda(\mu_Y^2 + \sigma_Y^2).$$
□

16.2.3   Nonparametric unbiased estimators

Unbiased estimation was covered in Section 9.2.2. It plays an important role in the development of credibility formulas. We begin by showing that two commonly used estimators are unbiased.

Theorem 16.6 *If* $X_1, \ldots, X_n$ *are independent but not necessarily identically distributed with common mean* $\mu = E(X_j)$ *and common variance* $v = \text{Var}(X_j)$, *then*

$$\bar{X} = \frac{1}{n}\sum_{j=1}^{n} X_j$$

is an unbiased estimator of μ *and*

$$\hat{v} = \frac{1}{n-1}\sum_{j=1}^{n}(X_j - \bar{X})^2 \tag{16.9}$$

is an unbiased estimator of v.

Proof: For $\bar{X}$, we have

$$E(\bar{X}) = E\left(\frac{1}{n}\sum_{j=1}^{n} X_j\right) = \frac{1}{n}\sum_{j=1}^{n} E(X_j) = \mu.$$

For the variance estimator, begin with the following result, which will be used later:

$$
\begin{aligned}
\sum_{j=1}^{n}(X_j - \bar{X})^2 &= \sum_{j=1}^{n}(X_j - \mu + \mu - \bar{X})^2 \\
&= \sum_{j=1}^{n}(X_j - \mu)^2 + 2\sum_{j=1}^{n}(X_j - \mu)(\mu - \bar{X}) + \sum_{j=1}^{n}(\mu - \bar{X})^2 \\
&= \sum_{j=1}^{n}(X_j - \mu)^2 + 2(\mu - \bar{X})\sum_{j=1}^{n}(X_j - \mu) + n(\mu - \bar{X})^2 \\
&= \sum_{j=1}^{n}(X_j - \mu)^2 + 2(\mu - \bar{X})n(\bar{X} - \mu) + n(\mu - \bar{X})^2 \\
&= \sum_{j=1}^{n}(X_j - \mu)^2 - n(\bar{X} - \mu)^2. \qquad (16.10)
\end{aligned}
$$

We also have (from the independence of $X_1, \ldots, X_n$),

$$
\begin{aligned}
\mathrm{Var}(\bar{X}) &= \mathrm{Var}\left(\frac{1}{n}\sum_{j=1}^{n} X_j\right) \\
&= \frac{1}{n^2}\sum_{j=1}^{n}\mathrm{Var}(X_j) \\
&= \frac{1}{n^2}\sum_{j=1}^{n} v \\
&= \frac{v}{n}.
\end{aligned}
$$

Take expectations in (16.10) to obtain

$$
\begin{aligned}
\mathrm{E}\left[\sum_{j=1}^{n}(X_j - \bar{X})^2\right] &= \mathrm{E}\left[\sum_{j=1}^{n}(X_j - \mu)^2\right] - n\mathrm{E}[(\bar{X} - \mu)^2] \\
&= \sum_{j=1}^{n}\mathrm{E}[(X_j - \mu)^2] - n\,\mathrm{Var}(\bar{X}) \\
&= \sum_{j=1}^{n}\mathrm{Var}(X_j) - n\frac{v}{n} \\
&= \left(\sum_{j=1}^{n} v\right) - v \\
&= (n-1)v.
\end{aligned}
$$

Dividing both sides by $n-1$ demonstrates that $\hat{v}$ is an unbiased estimator of v. $\qquad\qquad\qquad\qquad\qquad\qquad\qquad\qquad\qquad\qquad\qquad\qquad\qquad\quad\square$

The following example generalizing these results may appear somewhat artificial at this point, but is important in connection with the Bühlmann–Straub model of Section 16.4.5.

Example 16.7 *Suppose $X_1, \ldots, X_n$ are independent with common mean $\mu = \mathrm{E}(X_j)$ and variance $\mathrm{Var}(X_j) = \beta + \alpha/m_j$, $\alpha, \beta > 0$ and all $m_j \geq 1$. Let $m = \sum_{j=1}^{n} m_j$ and consider the three estimators*

$$\bar{X} = \frac{1}{m}\sum_{j=1}^{n} m_j X_j, \quad \hat{\mu}_1 = \frac{1}{n}\sum_{j=1}^{n} X_j,$$

and

$$\hat{\mu}_2 = \frac{\sum_{j=1}^{n} \dfrac{m_j X_j}{m_j \beta + \alpha}}{\sum_{j=1}^{n} \dfrac{m_j}{m_j \beta + \alpha}}.$$

Show that all three estimators are unbiased for μ and then rank them in order by mean-squared error. Also obtain the expected value of a sum of squares that may be useful for estimating α and β.

First consider $\bar{X}$.

$$\begin{aligned}
\mathrm{E}(\bar{X}) &= m^{-1}\sum_{j=1}^{n} m_j \mathrm{E}(X_j) = m^{-1}\sum_{j=1}^{n} m_j \mu = \mu,\\
\mathrm{Var}(\bar{X}) &= m^{-2}\sum_{j=1}^{n} m_j^2 \, \mathrm{Var}(X_j)\\
&= m^{-2}\sum_{j=1}^{n} m_j^2 \left(\beta + \frac{\alpha}{m_j}\right)\\
&= \alpha m^{-1} + \beta m^{-2}\sum_{j=1}^{n} m_j^2.
\end{aligned}$$

The estimator $\hat{\mu}_1$ is the one defined in Theorem 16.6 and has already been shown to be unbiased. We also have

$$
\begin{aligned}
\mathrm{Var}(\hat{\mu}_1) &= n^{-2} \sum_{j=1}^{n} \mathrm{Var}(X_j) \\
&= n^{-2} \sum_{j=1}^{n} \left(\beta + \frac{\alpha}{m_j} \right) \\
&= \beta n^{-1} + n^{-2} \alpha \sum_{j=1}^{n} m_j^{-1}.
\end{aligned}
$$

With regard to $\hat{\mu}_2$,

$$
\mathrm{E}(\hat{\mu}_2) = \frac{\sum_{j=1}^{n} \dfrac{m_j}{m_j \beta + \alpha} \mathrm{E}(X_j)}{\sum_{j=1}^{n} \dfrac{m_j}{m_j \beta + \alpha}} = \frac{\sum_{j=1}^{n} \dfrac{m_j}{m_j \beta + \alpha} \mu}{\sum_{j=1}^{n} \dfrac{m_j}{m_j \beta + \alpha}} = \mu
$$

and

$$
\begin{aligned}
\mathrm{Var}(\hat{\mu}_2) &= \frac{\sum_{j=1}^{n} \left(\dfrac{m_j}{m_j \beta + \alpha} \right)^2 \left(\beta + \dfrac{\alpha}{m_j} \right)}{\left(\sum_{j=1}^{n} \dfrac{m_j}{m_j \beta + \alpha} \right)^2} \\
&= \frac{\sum_{j=1}^{n} \left(\dfrac{m_j}{m_j \beta + \alpha} \right)}{\left(\sum_{j=1}^{n} \dfrac{m_j}{m_j \beta + \alpha} \right)^2} \\
&= \left(\sum_{j=1}^{n} \dfrac{m_j}{m_j \beta + \alpha} \right)^{-1}.
\end{aligned}
$$

We now consider the relative ranking of these variances (because all three estimators are unbiased, their mean-squared errors equal their variances, so it is sufficient to rank the variances). To show that it is not possible to order $\mathrm{Var}(\hat{\mu}_1)$ and $\mathrm{Var}(\bar{X})$, examine their difference:

$$
\mathrm{Var}(\bar{X}) - \mathrm{Var}(\hat{\mu}_1) = \alpha \left(m^{-1} - n^{-2} \sum_{j=1}^{n} m_j^{-1} \right) + \beta \left(m^{-2} \sum_{j=1}^{n} m_j^2 - n^{-1} \right).
$$

The coefficient of β must be nonnegative. To see this, note that

$$
\frac{1}{n} \sum_{j=1}^{n} m_j^2 \geq \left(\frac{1}{n} \sum_{j=1}^{n} m_j \right)^2 = \frac{m^2}{n^2}
$$

(the left-hand side is like a sample second moment and the right-hand side is like the square of the sample mean) and then multiply both sides by nm^{-2}. To show that the coefficient of α must be nonpositive, note that

$$\frac{n}{\sum_{j=1}^{n} m_j^{-1}} \leq \frac{1}{n} \sum_{j=1}^{n} m_j = \frac{m}{n}$$

(the harmonic mean is always less than or equal to the arithmetic mean) and then multiply both sides by n and then invert both sides. Therefore, by suitable choice of α and β, the difference in the variances can be made positive or negative.

We can do more than just show that $\hat{\mu}_2$ has the smallest variance of the three. Consider an arbitrary estimator of the form $\hat{\mu} = \sum_{j=1}^{n} a_j X_j$, where $\sum_{j=1}^{n} a_j = 1$ (needed to ensure that $\hat{\mu}$ is unbiased). All three estimators are of this type. Incorporating the constraint by using Lagrange multipliers, the smallest variance is found by minimizing

$$\sum_{j=1}^{n} a_j^2 \operatorname{Var}(X_j) + \lambda \left(\sum_{j=1}^{n} a_j - 1 \right).$$

The derivative with regard to a_i is

$$2a_i \operatorname{Var}(X_i) + \lambda,$$

and setting it equal to zero gives $a_i = -\lambda[2\operatorname{Var}(X_i)]^{-1}$. In other words, the weights should be proportional to the reciprocal of the variance. These are precisely the weights used in $\hat{\mu}_2$, and therefore it must have the smallest variance of all linear estimators.

With regard to a sum of squares, consider

$$\sum_{j=1}^{n} m_j(X_j - \bar{X})^2 = \sum_{j=1}^{n} m_j(X_j - \mu + \mu - \bar{X})^2$$

$$= \sum_{j=1}^{n} m_j(X_j - \mu)^2 + 2\sum_{j=1}^{n} m_j(X_j - \mu)(\mu - \bar{X})$$

$$+ \sum_{j=1}^{n} m_j(\mu - \bar{X})^2$$

$$= \sum_{j=1}^{n} m_j(X_j - \mu)^2 + 2(\mu - \bar{X})\sum_{j=1}^{n} m_j(X_j - \mu)$$

$$+ m(\mu - \bar{X})^2$$

$$= \sum_{j=1}^{n} m_j(X_j - \mu)^2 + 2(\mu - \bar{X})m(\bar{X} - \mu) + m(\mu - \bar{X})^2$$

$$= \sum_{j=1}^{n} m_j(X_j - \mu)^2 - m(\bar{X} - \mu)^2. \qquad (16.11)$$

Taking expectations yields

$$\mathrm{E}\left[\sum_{j=1}^{n} m_j(X_j - \bar{X})^2\right] = \sum_{j=1}^{n} m_j\mathrm{E}[(X_j - \mu)^2] - m\mathrm{E}[(\bar{X} - \mu)^2]$$

$$= \sum_{j=1}^{n} m_j \,\mathrm{Var}(X_j) - m\,\mathrm{Var}(\bar{X})$$

$$= \sum_{j=1}^{n} m_j\left(\beta + \frac{\alpha}{m_j}\right) - \beta\left(m^{-1}\sum_{j=1}^{n} m_j^2\right) - \alpha$$

and thus

$$\mathrm{E}\left[\sum_{j=1}^{n} m_j(X_j - \bar{X})^2\right] = \beta\left(m - m^{-1}\sum_{j=1}^{n} m_j^2\right) + \alpha(n - 1). \qquad (16.12)$$

In addition to being of interest in its own right, (16.12) provides an unbiased estimator in situations more general than (16.9). The latter is recovered with the choice $\alpha = 0$ and $m_j = 1$ for $j = 1, 2, \cdots, n$, implying that $m = n$. Also, if $\beta = 0$, (16.12) allows us to derive an estimator of α when each X_j is the average of m_j independent observations each with mean μ and variance α. In any event, it is usually the case that the m_js (and hence m) are known. □

16.2.4   Exercises

16.1 Suppose X is binomially distributed with parameters n_1 and p, that is,

$$f_X(x) = \binom{n_1}{x} p^x (1-p)^{n_1-x}, \quad x = 0, 1, 2, \ldots, n_1.$$

Suppose also that Z is binomially distributed with parameters n_2 and p independently of X. Then $Y = X + Z$ is binomially distributed with parameters $n_1 + n_2$ and p. Find the conditional distribution of X given that $Y = y$.

16.2 Let X and Y have joint probability distribution as follows:

		y	
x	0	1	2
0	0.20	0	0.10
1	0	0.15	0.25
2	0.05	0.15	0.10

(a) Compute the marginal distributions of X and Y.

(b) Compute the conditional distribution of X given $Y = y$ for $y = 0, 1, 2$.

(c) Compute $E(X|y)$, $E(X^2|y)$, and $Var(X|y)$ for $y = 0, 1, 2$.

(d) Compute $E(X)$ and $Var(X)$ using (16.5), (16.8), and (c).

16.3 Suppose that X and Y are two random variables with bivariate normal joint density function

$$
\begin{aligned}
f_{X,Y}(x,y) \quad = \quad & \frac{1}{2\pi\sigma_1\sigma_2\sqrt{1-\rho^2}} \\
& \times \exp\left\{ -\frac{1}{2(1-\rho^2)} \left[\left(\frac{x-\mu_1}{\sigma_1}\right)^2 - 2\rho\left(\frac{x-\mu_1}{\sigma_1}\right)\left(\frac{y-\mu_2}{\sigma_2}\right) \right.\right. \\
& \left.\left. + \left(\frac{y-\mu_2}{\sigma_2}\right)^2 \right] \right\}.
\end{aligned}
$$

Show that:

(a) The conditional density function is

$$
f_{X|Y}(x|y) = \frac{1}{\sqrt{2\pi}\sigma_1\sqrt{1-\rho^2}} \exp\left\{ -\frac{1}{2}\left[\frac{x - \mu_1 - \rho\frac{\sigma_1}{\sigma_2}(y-\mu_2)}{\sigma_1\sqrt{1-\rho^2}} \right]^2 \right\}.
$$

Hence,

$$E(X|Y = y) = \mu_1 + \rho\frac{\sigma_1}{\sigma_2}(y - \mu_2).$$

(b) The marginal pdf is

$$f_X(x) = \frac{1}{\sqrt{2\pi}\sigma_1} \exp\left[-\frac{1}{2}\left(\frac{x - \mu_1}{\sigma_1}\right)^2\right].$$

(c) The variables X and Y are independent if and only if $\rho = 0$.

16.4 Suppose that the random variables $Y_1, \cdots, Y_n$ are independent with

$$E(Y_j) = \gamma \quad \text{and} \quad \text{Var}(Y_j) = a_j + \sigma^2/b_j, \quad j = 1, 2, \ldots, n.$$

Define $b = b_1 + b_2 + \cdots + b_n$ and $\bar{Y} = \sum_{j=1}^n \frac{b_j}{b}Y_j$. Prove that

$$E\left[\sum_{j=1}^n b_j(Y_j - \bar{Y})^2\right] = (n-1)\sigma^2 + \sum_{j=1}^n a_j\left(b_j - \frac{b_j^2}{b}\right).$$

16.5 Suppose that given $\Theta = (\Theta_1, \Theta_2)$ the random variable X is normally distributed with mean Θ_1 and variance Θ_2.

(a) Show that $E(X) = E(\Theta_1)$ and $\text{Var}(X) = E(\Theta_2) + \text{Var}(\Theta_1)$.

(b) If Θ_1 and Θ_2 are independent, show that X has the same distribution as $\Theta_1 + Y$, where Θ_1 and Y are independent and Y conditional on Θ_2 is normally distributed with mean 0 and variance Θ_2.

16.6 Suppose that Θ has pdf $\pi(\theta)$, $\theta > 0$, and Θ_1 has pdf $\pi_1(\theta) = \pi(\theta - \alpha)$, $\theta > \alpha > 0$. If, given Θ_1, X is Poisson distributed with mean Θ_1, show that X has the same distribution as $Y + Z$, where Y and Z are independent, Y is Poisson distributed with mean α, and $Z|\Theta$ is Poisson distributed with mean Θ.

16.3   LIMITED FLUCTUATION CREDIBILITY THEORY

This branch of credibility theory represents the first attempt to quantify the credibility problem. This approach was suggested in the early nineteen hundreds in connection with workers compensation insurance. The original paper on the subject was by Mowbray in 1914 [96]. The problem may be formulated as follows. Suppose that a policyholder has experienced X_j claims or losses[3] in

---

[3] "Claims" will refer to the number of claims and "losses" will refer to payment amounts. In many cases, such as in this introductory paragraph, the ideas apply equally whether we are counting claims or losses.

past experience period j, where $j \in \{1, 2, 3, \ldots, n\}$. Another view is that X_j is the experience from the jth policy in a group or from the jth member of a particular class in a rating scheme. Suppose that $\mathrm{E}(X_j) = \xi$, that is, the mean is stable over time or across the members of a group or class.[4] This quantity would be the premium to charge (net of expenses, profits, and a provision for adverse experience) if only we knew its value. Also suppose $\mathrm{Var}(X_j) = \sigma^2$, again, the same for all j. The past experience may be summarized by the average $\bar{X} = n^{-1}(X_1 + \cdots + X_n)$. We know that $\mathrm{E}(\bar{X}) = \xi$, and if the X_j are independent, $\mathrm{Var}(\bar{X}) = \sigma^2/n$. The insurer's goal is to decide on the value of ξ. One possibility is to ignore the past data (no credibility) and simply charge M a value obtained from experience on other similar but not identical policyholders. This quantity is often called the **manual premium** because it would come from a book (manual) of premiums. Another possibility is to ignore M and charge $\bar{X}$ (full credibility). A third possibility is to choose some combination of M and $\bar{X}$ (partial credibility).

From the insurer's standpoint, it seems sensible to "lean toward" the choice $\bar{X}$ if the experience is more "stable" (less variable, σ^2 small). This implies that $\bar{X}$ is of more use as a predictor of next year's results. Conversely, if the experience is more volatile (variable), then $\bar{X}$ is of less use as a predictor of next year's results and the choice M makes more sense.

Also, if we have an a priori reason to believe that the chances are great that this policyholder is unlike those who produced the manual premium M, then more weight should be given to $\bar{X}$. This is because as an unbiased estimator $\bar{X}$ tells us something useful about ξ while M is likely to be of little value. On the other hand, if all of our other policyholders have similar values of ξ there is no point in relying on the (perhaps limited) experience of any one of them when M is likely to provide an excellent description of the propensity for claims or losses.

While reference is made to policyholders, the entity contributing to each X_j could arise from a single policyholder, a class of policyholders possessing similar underwriting characteristics, or a group of insureds assembled for some other reason. For example, for a given year j, X_j could be the number of claims filed in respect of a single automobile policy in one year, the average number of claims filed by all policyholders in a certain ratings class (e.g., single, male, under age 25, living in an urban area, driving over 7,500 miles per year), or the average amount of losses per vehicle for a fleet of delivery trucks owned by a food wholesaler.

We first present one approach to decide whether to assign full credibility (charge $\bar{X}$), and then we present an approach to assign partial credibility if it is felt that full credibility is inappropriate.

---

[4]The customary symbol for the mean, μ, is not used here because that symbol is used for a different but related mean in the next section. We have chosen this particular symbol ("Xi") because it is the most difficult Greek letter to write and pronounce. It is an unwritten rule of textbook writing that it appear at least once.

16.3.1   Full credibility

One method of quantifying the stability of $\bar{X}$ is to infer that $\bar{X}$ is stable if the difference between $\bar{X}$ and ξ is small relative to ξ with high probability. In statistical terms, this means that we should select two numbers $r > 0$ and $0 < p < 1$ (with r close to 0 and p close to 1, common choices being $r = 0.05$ and $p = 0.9$) and assign full credibility if

$$\Pr(-r\xi \le \bar{X} - \xi \le r\xi) \ge p. \qquad (16.13)$$

It is convenient to restate (16.13) as

$$\Pr\left(\left|\frac{\bar{X} - \xi}{\sigma/\sqrt{n}}\right| \le \frac{r\xi\sqrt{n}}{\sigma}\right) \ge p.$$

Now let y_p be defined by

$$y_p = \inf_y \left\{ \Pr\left(\left|\frac{\bar{X} - \xi}{\sigma/\sqrt{n}}\right| \le y\right) \ge p \right\}. \qquad (16.14)$$

That is, y_p is the smallest value of y which satisfies the probability statement in braces in (16.14). If $\bar{X}$ has a continuous distribution, the "$\ge$" sign in (16.14) may be replaced by an "$=$" sign and y_p satisfies

$$\Pr\left(\left|\frac{\bar{X} - \xi}{\sigma/\sqrt{n}}\right| \le y_p\right) = p. \qquad (16.15)$$

Then the condition for full credibility is $r\xi\sqrt{n}/\sigma \ge y_p$,

$$\frac{\sigma}{\xi} \le \frac{r}{y_p}\sqrt{n} = \sqrt{\frac{n}{\lambda_0}}, \qquad (16.16)$$

where $\lambda_0 = (y_p/r)^2$. Condition (16.16) states that full credibility is assigned if the coefficient of variation σ/ξ is no larger than $\sqrt{n/\lambda_0}$, an intuitively reasonable result.

Also of interest is that (16.16) can be rewritten to show that full credibility occurs when

$$\mathrm{Var}(\bar{X}) = \frac{\sigma^2}{n} \le \frac{\xi^2}{\lambda_0}. \qquad (16.17)$$

Alternatively, solving (16.16) for n gives the number of exposure units required for full credibility, namely

$$n \ge \lambda_0 \left(\frac{\sigma}{\xi}\right)^2. \qquad (16.18)$$

In many situations it is reasonable to approximate the distribution of $\bar{X}$ by a normal distribution with mean ξ and variance σ^2/n. For example, central limit theorem arguments may be applicable if n is large. In that case $(\bar{X} - \xi)/(\sigma/\sqrt{n})$ has a standard normal distribution. Then (16.15) becomes (where Z has a standard normal distribution and $\Phi(y)$ is its cdf)

$$
\begin{aligned}
p &= \Pr(|Z| \le y_p) \\
&= \Pr(-y_p \le Z \le y_p) \\
&= \Phi(y_p) - \Phi(-y_p) \\
&= \Phi(y_p) - 1 + \Phi(y_p) \\
&= 2\Phi(y_p) - 1.
\end{aligned}
$$

Therefore $\Phi(y_p) = (1+p)/2$ and therefore y_p is the $(1+p)/2$ percentile of the standard normal distribution.

For example, if $p = 0.9$, then standard normal tables give $y_{0.9} = 1.645$. If, in addition, $r = 0.05$, then $\lambda_0 = (32.9)^2 = 1{,}082.41$ and (16.18) yields $n \ge 1{,}082.41\sigma^2/\xi^2$. Note that this answer assumes we know the coefficient of variation of X_j. It is possible we have some idea of its value, even though we do not know the value of ξ (remember, that is the quantity we want to estimate).

The important thing to note when using (16.18) is that the coefficient of variation is for the estimator of the quantity to be estimated. The right-hand side gives the standard for full credibility when measuring it in terms of exposure units. If some other unit is desired, it is usually sufficient to multiply both sides by an appropriate quantity. Finally, any unknown quantities will have be to estimated from the data. This implies that the credibility question can be posed in a variety of ways. The following examples cover the most common cases.

Example 16.8 *Suppose past losses $X_1, \dots, X_n$ are available for a particular policyholder. The sample mean is to be used to estimate $\xi = E(X_j)$. Determine the standard for full credibility. Then suppose there were 10 observations with 6 being zero and the others being 253, 398, 439, and 756. Determine the full-credibility standard for this case with $r = 0.05$ and $p = 0.9$.*

The solution is available directly from (16.18) as

$$
n \ge \lambda_0 \left(\frac{\sigma}{\xi} \right)^2.
$$

For this specific case, the mean and standard deviation can be estimated from the data as 184.6 and 267.89 (where the variance estimate is the unbiased version using $n - 1$). With $\lambda_0 = 1082.41$, the standard is

$$
n \ge 1082.41 \left(\frac{267.89}{184.6} \right)^2 = 2279.51
$$

and the 10 observations do not deserve full credibility. $\square$

In the next example it is further assumed that the observations are from a particular type of distribution.

Example 16.9 *Suppose that past losses $X_1, \ldots, X_n$ are available for a particular policyholder and it is reasonable to assume that the X_js are independent and compound Poisson distributed, that is, $X_j = Y_{j1} + \cdots + Y_{jN_j}$, where each N_j is Poisson with parameter λ and the claim size distribution Y has mean θ_Y and variance σ_Y^2. Determine the standard for full credibility when estimating the expected number of claims per policy and then when estimating the expected dollars of claims per policy. Then determine if these standards are met for the data in Example 16.8, where it is now known that the first three nonzero payments came from a single claim but the final one was from two claims, one for 129 and the other for 627.*

Case 1: Accuracy is to be measured with regard to the average number of claims. Then, using the N_js rather than the X_js, we have $\xi = \mathrm{E}(N_j) = \lambda$ and $\sigma^2 = \mathrm{Var}(N_j) = \lambda$, implying from (16.18) that

$$n \geq \lambda_0 \left(\frac{\lambda^{1/2}}{\lambda} \right)^2 = \frac{\lambda_0}{\lambda}.$$

Thus, if the standard is in terms of the number of policies, it will have to exceed λ_0/λ for full credibility and λ will have to be estimated from the data. If the standard is in terms of the number of expected claims, that is, $n\lambda$, we must multiply both sides by λ. This sets the standard as

$$n\lambda \geq \lambda_0.$$

While it appears that no estimation is needed for this standard, it is in terms of the expected number of claims needed. In practice, the standard is set in terms of the actual number of claims experienced, effectively replacing $n\lambda$ on the left by its estimate $N_1 + \cdots + N_n$.

For the given data, there were 5 claims, for an estimate of λ of 0.5 per policy. The standard is then

$$n \geq \frac{1,082.41}{0.5} = 2,164.82$$

and the 10 policies are far short of this standard. Or the 5 actual claims could be compared to $\lambda_0 = 1,082.41$, which leads to the same result.

Case 2: When accuracy is with regard to the average total payment, we have $\xi = \mathrm{E}(X_j) = \lambda\theta_Y$ and $\mathrm{Var}(Y_j) = \lambda(\theta_Y^2 + \sigma_Y^2)$, formulas developed in Chapter 6. In terms of the sample size, the standard is

$$n \geq \lambda_0 \frac{\lambda(\theta_Y^2 + \sigma_Y^2)}{\lambda^2\theta_Y^2} = \frac{\lambda_0}{\lambda} \left[1 + \left(\frac{\sigma_Y}{\theta_Y} \right)^2 \right].$$

If the standard is in terms of the expected number of claims, multiply both sides by λ to obtain

$$n\lambda \geq \lambda_0 \left[1 + \left(\frac{\sigma_Y}{\theta_Y} \right)^2 \right].$$

Finally, if the standard is in terms of the expected total dollars of claims, multiply both sides by θ_Y to obtain

$$n\lambda\theta_Y \geq \lambda_0 \left(\theta_Y + \frac{\sigma_Y^2}{\theta_Y} \right).$$

For the given data, the five claims have mean 369.2 and standard deviation 189.315 and thus

$$n \geq \frac{\lambda_0}{\lambda} \left[1 + \left(\frac{\sigma_Y}{\theta_Y} \right)^2 \right] = \frac{1,082.41}{0.5} \left[1 + \left(\frac{189.315}{369.2} \right)^2 \right] = 2,734.02$$

and again the 10 observations are far short of what is needed. If the standard is to be set in terms of claims (of which there are 5), multiply both sides by 0.5 to obtain a standard of 1,367.01. Finally, the standard could be set in terms of total dollars of claims. To do so, multiply both sides by 369.2 to obtain 504,701. Note that in all three cases the ratio of the observed quantity to the corresponding standard is unchanged:

$$\frac{10}{2,734.02} = \frac{5}{1,367.01} = \frac{1,846}{504,701} = 0.003658. \qquad \square$$

In these examples, the standard for full credibility is not met and so the sample means are not sufficiently accurate to be used as estimates of the expected value. We need a method for dealing with this situation.

16.3.2   Partial credibility

If it is decided that full credibility is inappropriate, then for competitive reasons (or otherwise) it may be desirable to reflect the past experience $\bar{X}$ in the net premium as well as the externally obtained mean, M. An intuitively appealing method for doing this is through a weighted average, that is, through the credibility premium

$$P_c = Z\bar{X} + (1 - Z)M, \qquad (16.19)$$

where the credibility factor $Z \in [0, 1]$ needs to be chosen. There are many formulas for Z which have been suggested in the actuarial literature, usually justified on intuitive rather than theoretical grounds. (We remark that Mowbray [96] considered full, but not partial credibility.) One important choice is

$$Z = \frac{n}{n + k}, \qquad (16.20)$$

where k needs to be determined. This particular choice will be shown to be theoretically justified on the basis of a statistical model to be presented in the next section. Another choice, based on the same idea as full credibility (and including the full-credibility case $Z = 1$), will now be discussed.

A variety of arguments have been used for developing the value of Z, many of which lead to the same answer. All of them are flawed in one way or another. The development we have chosen to present is also flawed but is at least simple. Recall that the goal of the full-credibility standard was to ensure that the difference between the net premium we are considering ($\bar{X}$) and what we should be using (ξ) is small with high probability. Because $\bar{X}$ is unbiased, this is essentially (and exactly if $\bar{X}$ has the normal distribution) equivalent to controlling the variance of the proposed net premium, $\bar{X}$, in this case. We see from (16.17) that there is no assurance that the variance of $\bar{X}$ will be small enough. However, it is possible to control the variance of the credibility premium, P_c, as follows:

$$
\begin{aligned}
\frac{\xi^2}{\lambda_0} &= \text{Var}(P_c) \\
&= \text{Var}[Z\bar{X} + (1 - Z)M] \\
&= Z^2 \text{Var}(\bar{X}) \\
&= Z^2 \frac{\sigma^2}{n}.
\end{aligned}
$$

Thus $Z = (\xi/\sigma)\sqrt{n/\lambda_0}$, provided it is less than 1. This can be written using the single formula

$$
Z = \min\left\{ \frac{\xi}{\sigma}\sqrt{\frac{n}{\lambda_0}}, 1 \right\}. \tag{16.21}
$$

One interpretation of (16.21) is that the credibility factor Z is the ratio of the coefficient of variation required for full credibility ($\sqrt{n/\lambda_0}$) to the actual coefficient of variation. For obvious reasons this is often called the square root rule for partial credibility.

While we could do the algebra with regard to (16.21), it is sufficient to note that it always turns out that Z is the square root of the ratio of the actual count to the count required for full credibility.

Example 16.10 *Suppose in Example* 16.8 *that the manual premium M is* 225. *Determine the credibility estimate.*

The average of the payments is 184.6. With the square root rule the credibility factor is

$$
Z = \sqrt{\frac{10}{2,279.51}} = 0.06623.
$$

Then the credibility premium is

$$
P_c = 0.06623(184.6) + 0.93377(225) = 222.32. \qquad \square
$$

Example 16.11 *Suppose in Example 16.9 that the manual premium M is 225. Determine the credibility estimate using both cases.*

For the first case, the credibility factor is

$$Z = \sqrt{\frac{5}{1,082.41}} = 0.06797$$

and applying it yields

$$P_c = 0.06797(184.6) + 0.93203(225) = 222.25.$$

At first glance this may appear inappropriate. The standard was set in terms of estimating the frequency but was applied to the aggregate claims. Often, individuals are distinguished more by differences in the frequency with which they have claims rather than by differences in the cost per claim. So this factor captures the most important feature.

For the second case, we can use any of the three calculations:

$$Z = \sqrt{\frac{10}{2,734.02}} = \sqrt{\frac{5}{1,367.01}} = \sqrt{\frac{1,846}{504,701}} = 0.06048.$$

Then,

$$P_c = 0.06048(184.6) + 0.93952(225) = 222.56. \qquad \square$$

Earlier we mentioned a flaw in the approach. Other than assuming that the variance captures the variability of $\bar{X}$ in the right way, all of the mathematics is correct. The flaw is in the goal. Unlike $\bar{X}$, P_c is not an unbiased estimator of ξ. In fact, one of the qualities that allows credibility to work is its use of biased estimators. But that means that the appropriate measure of the quality of P_c is not its variance, but its mean-squared error. However, the mean-squared error requires knowledge of the bias, and, in turn, that requires knowledge of the relationship of ξ and M. However, we know nothing about that relationship, and the data we have collected are of little help. As noted in the next subsection, this is not only a problem with our determination of Z, it is a problem that is characteristic of the limited fluctuation approach. A model for this relationship is introduced in the next section.

This section closes with a few additional examples. In each of the first two examples $\lambda_0 = 1,082.41$ is used.

Example 16.12 *For group dental insurance, historical experience on many groups has revealed that annual losses per life insured have a mean of 175 and a standard deviation of 140. A particular group has been covered for two years with 100 lives insured in year 1 and 110 in year 2 and has experienced average claims of 150 over that period. Determine if full or partial credibility is appropriate, and determine the credibility premium for next year's losses if there will be 125 lives insured.*

We will apply the credibility on a per-life-insured basis. We have observed $100+110 = 210$ exposure units (assume experience is independent for different lives and years), and $\bar{X} = 150$. Now $M = 175$ and we assume that σ will be 140 for this group. Because we are trying to estimate the average cost per person, the calculations done in Example 16.11 for Case 2 apply. Thus, with $n = 210$ and $\lambda_0 = 1{,}082.41$ we estimate θ_Y with the sample mean of 150 to obtain the standard for full credibility as

$$n \geq 1{,}082.41 \left(\frac{140}{150}\right)^2 = 942.90$$

and then calculate

$$Z = \sqrt{\frac{210}{942.90}} = 0.472$$

(note that $\bar{X}$ is the average of 210 claims, so approximate normality is assumed by the central limit theorem). Thus, the net premium per life insured is

$$P_c = 0.472(150) + 0.528(175) = 163.2.$$

The net premium for the whole group is $125(163.2) = 20{,}400$. $\qquad\square$

Example 16.13 *An insurance coverage involves credibility based on number of claims only. For a particular group, 715 claims have been observed. Determine an appropriate credibility factor, assuming that the number of claims is Poisson distributed.*

This is Case 1 from Example 16.11 and the standard for full credibility with regard to the number of claims is $n\lambda \geq \lambda_0 = 1082.41$. Then

$$Z = \sqrt{\frac{715}{1{,}082.41}} = 0.813.$$

$\qquad\square$

Example 16.14 *Past data on a particular group are $\mathbf{X} = (X_1, X_2, \ldots, X_n)^T$, where the X_j are independent and identically distributed compound Poisson random variables with exponentially distributed claim sizes. If the credibility factor based on claim numbers is 0.8, determine the appropriate credibility factor based on total claims.*

When based on Poisson claim numbers, from Example 16.9, $Z = 0.8$ implies that $\lambda n/\lambda_0 = (0.8)^2 = 0.64$, where λn is the observed number of claims. For exponentially distributed claim sizes $\sigma_Y^2 = \theta_Y^2$. From Case 2 of Example 16.9, the standard for full credibility in terms of the number of claims is

$$n\lambda \geq \lambda_0 \left[1 + \left(\frac{\sigma_Y}{\theta_Y}\right)^2\right] = 2\lambda_0.$$

Then

$$Z = \sqrt{\frac{\lambda n}{2\lambda_0}} = \sqrt{0.32} = 0.566.$$

$\qquad\square$

16.3.3   Problems with the approach

While the limited fluctuation approach yields simple solutions to the problem, there are theoretical difficulties. First, there is no underlying theoretical model for the distribution of the X_js and thus no reason why a premium of the form (16.19) is appropriate and preferable to M. Why not just estimate ξ from a collection of homogeneous policyholders and charge all policyholders the same rate? While there is a practical reason for using (16.19), no model has been presented to suggest that this may be appropriate. Consequently, the choice of Z (and hence P_c) is completely arbitrary.

Second, even if (16.19) were appropriate for a particular model, there is no guidance for the selection of r and p.

Finally, the limited fluctuation approach does not examine the difference between ξ and M. When (16.19) is employed, we are essentially stating that the value of M is accurate as a representation of the expected value given no information about this particular policyholder. However, it is usually the case that M is also an estimate and therefore unreliable in itself. The correct credibility question should be "how much more reliable is $\bar{X}$ compared to M?" and not "how reliable is $\bar{X}$?"

In the remainder of this chapter, a systematic modeling approach is presented for the claims experience of a particular policyholder which suggests that the past experience of the policyholder is relevant for prospective rate making. Furthermore, the intuitively appealing formula (16.19) is a consequence of this approach, and Z is often obtained from relations of the form (16.20).

16.3.4   Notes and References

The limited fluctuation approach is discussed by Herzog [52] and Longley-Cook [87]. See also Norberg [100].

16.3.5   Exercises

16.7 An insurance company has decided to establish its full-credibility requirements for an individual state rate filing. The full-credibility standard is to be set so that the observed total amount of claims underlying the rate filing would be within 5% of the true value with probability 0.95. The claim frequency follows a Poisson distribution and the severity distribution has pdf

$$f(x) = \frac{100 - x}{5{,}000}, \quad 0 \le x \le 100.$$

Determine the expected number of claims necessary to obtain full credibility using the normal approximation.

16.8 For a particular policyholder, the past total claims experience is given by $X_1, \ldots, X_n$, where the X_js are independent and identically distributed

Table 16.1   Data for Exercise 16.9

Year	1	2	3
Claims	475	550	400

compound random variables with Poisson parameter λ and gamma claim size distribution with pdf

$$f_Y(y) = \frac{y^{\alpha-1}e^{-y/\beta}}{\Gamma(\alpha)\beta^\alpha}, \quad y > 0.$$

You also know the following:

1. The credibility factor based on numbers of claims is 0.9.

2. The expected claim size $\alpha\beta = 100$.

3. The credibility factor based on total claims is 0.8.

Determine α and β.

16.9 For a particular policyholder, the manual premium is 600 per year. The past claims experience is given in Table 16.1. Assess whether full or partial credibility is appropriate and determine the net premium for next year's claims assuming the normal approximation. Use $r = 0.05$ and $p = 0.9$.

16.10 Redo Example 16.9 assuming that X_j is a compound negative binomial distribution rather than compound Poisson.

16.11 (*) The total number of claims for a group of insureds is Poisson with mean λ. Determine the value of λ such that the observed number of claims will be within 3% of λ with a probability of 0.975 using the normal approximation.

16.12 (*) An insurance company is revising rates based on old data. The expected number of claims for full credibility is selected so that observed total claims will be within 5% of the true value 90% of the time. Individual claim amounts have pdf $f(x) = 1/200,000$, $0 < x < 200,000$, and the number of claims has the Poisson distribution. The recent experience consists of 1,082 claims. Determine the credibility, Z, to be assigned to the recent experience. Use the normal approximation.

16.13 (*) The average claim size for a group of insureds is 1,500 with a standard deviation of 7,500. Assume that claim counts have the Poisson distribution. Determine the expected number of claims so that the total loss will be within 6% of the expected total loss with probability 0.90.

16.14 (*) A group of insureds had 6,000 claims and a total loss of 15,600,000. The prior estimate of the total loss was 16,500,000. Determine the limited fluctuation credibility estimate of the total loss for the group. Use the standard for full credibility determined in Exercise 16.13.

16.15 (*) The full-credibility standard is set so that the total number of claims is within 5% of the true value with probability p. This standard is 800 claims. The standard is then altered so that the total cost of claims is to be within 10% of the true value with probability p. The claim frequency has a Poisson distribution and the claim severity distribution has pdf $f(x) = 0.0002(100 - x)$, $0 < x < 100$. Determine the expected number of claims necessary to obtain full credibility under the new standard.

16.16 (*) A standard for full credibility of 1,000 claims has been selected so that the actual pure premium will be within 10% of the expected pure premium 95% of the time. The number of claims has the Poisson distribution. Determine the coefficient of variation of the severity distribution.

16.17 (*) For a group of insureds you are given the following information:

1. The prior estimate of expected total losses is 20,000,000.

2. The observed total losses are 25,000,000.

3. The observed number of claims is 10,000.

4. The number of claims required for full credibility is 17,500.

Determine the credibility estimate of the group's expected total losses based upon all the above information. Use the credibility factor that is appropriate if the goal is to estimate the expected number of losses.

16.18 (*) A full-credibility standard is determined so that the total number of claims is within 5% of the expected number with probability 98%. If the same expected number of claims for full credibility is applied to the total cost of claims, the actual total cost would be within $100K\%$ of the expected cost with 95% probability. Individual claims have severity pdf $f(x) = 2.5x^{-3.5}$, $x > 1$ and the number of claims has the Poisson distribution. Determine K.

16.19 (*) The number of claims has the Poisson distribution. The number of claims and the claim severity are independent. Individual claim amounts can be for 1, 2, or 10 with probabilities 0.5, 0.3, and 0.2, respectively. Determine the expected number of claims needed so that the total cost of claims is within 10% of the expected cost with 90% probability.

16.20 (*) The number of claims has the Poisson distribution. The coefficient of variation of the severity distribution is 2. The standard for full credibility in estimating total claims is 3,415. With this standard the observed pure

3415

premium will be within $k\%$ of the expected pure premium 95% of the time. Determine k.

⤳**16.21** (*) You are given the following:

1. P = Prior estimate of pure premium for a particular class of business.

2. O = Observed pure premium during the latest experience period for the same class of business.

3. R = Revised estimate of pure premium for the same class following the observations.

4. F = Number of claims required for full credibility of the pure premium.

Express the observed number of claims as a function of these four items.

16.4   GREATEST ACCURACY CREDIBILITY THEORY

16.4.1   Introduction

In this and the following section, we consider a model-based approach to the solution of the credibility problem. This approach, referred to as greatest accuracy credibility theory, is the outgrowth of a classic 1967 paper by Bühlmann [18]. Many of the ideas are also found in Whitney [136] and Bailey [8].

We return to the basic problem. For a particular policyholder, we have observed n exposure units of past claims $\mathbf{X} = (X_1, \ldots, X_n)^T$. We have a manual rate μ (we no longer use M for the manual rate) which is applicable to this policyholder, but the past experience indicates that this may not be appropriate $[\bar{X} = n^{-1}(X_1 + \cdots + X_n)$, as well as $\mathrm{E}(X)$, could be quite different from $\mu]$. This raises the question of whether next year's net premium (per exposure unit) should be based on μ, on $\bar{X}$, or on a combination of the two.

The insurer needs to consider the following question: Is the policyholder really different from what has been assumed in the calculation of μ or has it just been random chance which has been responsible for the differences between μ and $\bar{X}$?

While it is difficult to definitively answer the above question, it is clear that no underwriting system is perfect. The manual rate μ has presumably been obtained by (a) evaluation of the underwriting characteristics of the policyholder and (b) assignment of the rate on the basis of inclusion of the policyholder in a rating class. Such a class should include risks with similar underwriting characteristics. In other words, the rating class is viewed as homogeneous with respect to the underwriting characteristics used. Surely, not all risks in the class are truly homogeneous, however. No matter how detailed the underwriting procedure, there still remains some heterogeneity with respect to risk characteristics within the rating class (good and bad risks, relatively speaking).

Thus, it is possible that the given policyholder may be different from what has been assumed. If this is the case, how should one choose an appropriate rate for the policyholder?

To proceed, let us assume that the risk level of each policyholder in the rating class may be characterized by a risk parameter θ (possibly vector valued), but the value of θ varies by policyholder. This allows us to quantify the differences between policyholders with respect to the risk characteristics. Because all observable underwriting characteristics have already been used, θ may be viewed as representative of the residual, unobserved factors which affect the risk level. Consequently, we shall assume the existence of θ, but we shall further assume that it is not observable and that we can never know its true value.

Because θ varies by policyholder, there is a probability distribution with pf $\pi(\theta)$ of these values across the rating class. Thus, if θ is a scalar parameter, the cumulative distribution function $\Pi(\theta)$ may be interpreted as the proportion of policyholders in the rating class with risk parameter Θ less than or equal to θ. [In statistical terms, Θ is a random variable with distribution function $\Pi(\theta) = \Pr(\Theta \leq \theta)$.] Stated another way, $\Pi(\theta)$ represents the probability that a policyholder picked at random from the rating class has a risk parameter less than or equal to θ (to accommodate the possibility of new insureds, we slightly generalize the "rating class" interpretation to include the population of all potential risks, whether insured or not).

While the θ value associated with an individual policyholder is not (and cannot be) known, we assume (for this section) that $\pi(\theta)$ is known. That is, the structure of the risk characteristics within the population is known. This assumption can be relaxed, and we shall decide later how to estimate the relevant characteristics of $\pi(\theta)$ because this is needed in order to implement the theory.

Because risk levels vary within the population, it is clear that the experience of the policyholder varies in a systematic way with θ. Imagine that the experience of a policyholder picked (at random) from the population arises from a two-stage process. First, the risk parameter θ is selected from the distribution $\pi(\theta)$. Then the claims or losses X arise from the conditional distribution of X given θ, $f_{X|\Theta}(x|\theta)$. Thus the experience varies with θ via the distribution given the risk parameter θ. The distribution of claims thus differs from policyholder to policyholder to reflect the differences in the risk parameters.

Example 16.15 *Consider a rating class for automobile insurance, where θ represents the expected number of claims for a policyholder with risk parameter θ. To accommodate the variability in claims incidence, we assume that the values of θ vary across the rating class. Relatively speaking, the good*

Table 16.2   Probabilities for Example 16.16

x	$\Pr(X = x \mid \Theta = G)$	$\Pr(X = x \mid \Theta = B)$	θ	$\Pr(\Theta = \theta)$
0	0.7	0.5	G	0.75
1	0.2	0.3	B	0.25
2	0.1	0.2		

drivers are those with small values of θ, whereas the poor drivers are those with larger values of θ. It is convenient mathematically in this case to assume that the number of claims for a policyholder with risk parameter θ is Poisson distributed with mean θ. The random variable Θ may also be assumed to be gamma distributed with parameters α and β. Suppose it is known that the average number of expected claims for this rating class is 0.15 $[\mathrm{E}(\Theta) = 0.15]$, and 95% of the policyholders have expected claims between 0.10 and 0.20. Determine α and β.

Assuming the normal approximation to the gamma, where it is known that 95% of the probability lies within about two standard deviations of the mean, it follows that Θ has standard deviation 0.025. Thus $\mathrm{E}(\Theta) = \alpha\beta = 0.15$ and $\mathrm{Var}(\Theta) = \alpha\beta^2 = (0.025)^2$. Solving for α and β yields $\beta = 1/240$ and $\alpha = 36$.□

Example 16.16 *There are two types of driver. Good drivers make up 75% of the population and in one year have zero claims with probability 0.7, one claim with probability 0.2, and two claims with probability 0.1. Bad drivers make up the other 25% of the population and have zero, one, or two claims with probabilities 0.5, 0.3, and 0.2, respectively. Describe this process and how it relates to an unknown risk parameter.*

When a driver buys our insurance, we do not know if the individual is a good or bad driver. So the risk parameter Θ can be one of two values. We can set $\Theta = G$ for good drivers and $\Theta = B$ for bad drivers. The probability model for the number of claims, X, and risk parameter Θ is given in Table 16.2. □

Example 16.17 *The amount of a claim has the exponential distribution with mean $1/\Theta$. Among the class of insureds and potential insureds, the parameter Θ varies according to the gamma distribution with $\alpha = 4$ and scale parameter $\beta = 0.001$. Provide a mathematical description of this model.*

For claims,

$$f_{X|\Theta}(x|\theta) = \theta e^{-\theta x}, \quad x, \theta > 0,$$

and for the risk parameter,

$$\pi_{\Theta}(\theta) = \frac{\theta^3 e^{-1,000\theta} 1,000^4}{6}, \quad \theta > 0.$$

□

16.4.2   The Bayesian methodology

Continue to assume that the distribution of the risk characteristics in the population may be represented by $\pi(\theta)$, and the experience of a particular policyholder with risk parameter θ arises from the conditional distribution $f_{X|\Theta}(x|\theta)$ of claims or losses given θ.

We now return to the problem introduced in Section 16.3. That is, for a particular policyholder, we have observed $\mathbf{X} = \mathbf{x}$, where $\mathbf{X} = (X_1, \ldots, X_n)^T$ and $\mathbf{x} = (x_1, \ldots, x_n)^T$, and are interested in setting a rate to cover X_{n+1}. We assume that the risk parameter associated with the policyholder is θ (which is unknown). Furthermore, the experience of the policyholder corresponding to different exposure periods is assumed to be independent. In statistical terms, conditional on θ, the claims or losses $X_1, \ldots, X_n, X_{n+1}$ are independent (although not necessarily identically distributed).

Let X_j have conditional pf

$$f_{X_j|\Theta}(x_j|\theta), \quad j = 1, \ldots, n, n+1.$$

Note that, if the X_j are identically distributed (conditional on $\Theta = \theta$), then $f_{X_j|\Theta}(x_j|\theta)$ does not depend on j. Ideally, we are interested in the conditional distribution of X_{n+1} given $\Theta = \theta$ in order to predict the claims experience X_{n+1} of the same policyholder (whose value of θ has been assumed not to have changed). If we knew θ, we could use $f_{X_{n+1}|\Theta}(x_{n+1}|\theta)$. Unfortunately, we do not know θ, but we do know $\mathbf{x}$ for the same policyholder. The obvious next step is to condition on $\mathbf{x}$ rather than θ. Consequently, we will calculate the conditional distribution of X_{n+1} given $\mathbf{X} = \mathbf{x}$, termed the **predictive distribution** as defined in Section 12.4.

The predictive distribution of X_{n+1} given $\mathbf{X} = \mathbf{x}$ is the relevant distribution for risk analysis, management, and decision making. It combines the uncertainty about the claims losses with that of the parameters associated with the risk process.

Here we repeat the development in Section 12.4, noting that if Θ has a discrete distribution the integrals are replaced by sums. Because the X_js are independent conditional on $\Theta = \theta$, we have

$$f_{\mathbf{X},\Theta}(\mathbf{x}, \theta) = f(x_1, \ldots, x_n|\theta)\pi(\theta) = \left[\prod_{j=1}^{n} f_{X_j|\Theta}(x_j|\theta)\right]\pi(\theta).$$

The joint distribution of $\mathbf{X}$ is thus the marginal distribution obtained by integrating θ out, that is,

$$f_{\mathbf{X}}(\mathbf{x}) = \int \left[\prod_{j=1}^{n} f_{X_j|\Theta}(x_j|\theta)\right]\pi(\theta)\,d\theta. \tag{16.22}$$

Similarly, the joint distribution of $X_1, \ldots, X_{n+1}$ is the right-hand side of (16.22) with n replaced by $n+1$ in the product. Finally, the conditional density of X_{n+1} given $\mathbf{X} = \mathbf{x}$ is the joint density of $(X_1, \ldots, X_{n+1})$ divided by that of $\mathbf{X}$, namely,

$$f_{X_{n+1}|\mathbf{X}}(x_{n+1}|\mathbf{x}) = \frac{1}{f_{\mathbf{X}}(\mathbf{x})} \int \left[\prod_{j=1}^{n+1} f_{X_j|\Theta}(x_j|\theta) \right] \pi(\theta)\, d\theta. \qquad (16.23)$$

There is a hidden mathematical structure underlying (16.23) which may often be exploited. The posterior density of Θ given $\mathbf{X}$ is

$$\pi_{\Theta|\mathbf{X}}(\theta|\mathbf{x}) = \frac{f_{\mathbf{X},\Theta}(\mathbf{x},\theta)}{f_{\mathbf{X}}(\mathbf{x})} = \frac{1}{f_{\mathbf{X}}(\mathbf{x})} \left[\prod_{j=1}^{n} f_{X_j|\Theta}(x_j|\theta) \right] \pi(\theta). \qquad (16.24)$$

In other words, $\left[\prod_{j=1}^{n} f_{X_j|\Theta}(x_j|\theta) \right] \pi(\theta) = \pi_{\Theta|\mathbf{X}}(\theta|\mathbf{x}) f_{\mathbf{X}}(\mathbf{x})$, and substitution in the numerator of (16.23) yields

$$f_{X_{n+1}|\mathbf{X}}(x_{n+1}|\mathbf{x}) = \int f_{X_{n+1}|\Theta}(x_{n+1}|\theta) \pi_{\Theta|\mathbf{X}}(\theta|\mathbf{x})\, d\theta. \qquad (16.25)$$

Equation (16.25) provides the additional insight that the conditional distribution of X_{n+1} given $\mathbf{X}$ may be viewed as a mixture distribution, with the mixing distribution the posterior distribution $\pi_{\Theta|\mathbf{X}}(\theta|\mathbf{x})$.

The posterior distribution combines and summarizes the information about θ contained in the prior distribution and the likelihood and consequently (16.25) reflects this information. As noted in Theorem 12.49, the posterior distribution admits a convenient form when the likelihood is derived from the linear exponential family and $\pi(\theta)$ is the natural conjugate prior. This provides an easy method to evaluate the conditional distribution of X_{n+1} given $\mathbf{X}$ in these cases.

Example 16.18 (Example 16.16 continued) *For a particular policyholder suppose we have observed $x_1 = 0$ and $x_2 = 1$. Determine the predictive distribution of $X_3|X_1 = 0, X_2 = 1$ and the posterior distribution of $\Theta|X_1 = 0, X_2 = 1$.*

From (16.22), the marginal probability is

$$\begin{aligned} f_{\mathbf{X}}(0,1) &= \sum_{\theta} f_{X_1|\Theta}(0|\theta) f_{X_2|\Theta}(1|\theta) \pi(\theta) \\ &= 0.7(0.2)(0.75) + 0.5(0.3)(0.25) \\ &= 0.1425. \end{aligned}$$

Similarly, the joint probability of all three variables is

$$f_{\mathbf{X},X_3}(0,1,x_3) = \sum_{\theta} f_{X_1|\Theta}(0|\theta) f_{X_2|\Theta}(1|\theta) f_{X_3|\Theta}(x_3|\theta) \pi(\theta).$$

Thus,

$$
\begin{aligned}
f_{\mathbf{X}, X_3}(0, 1, 0) &= 0.7(0.2)(0.7)(0.75) + 0.5(0.3)(0.5)(0.25) = 0.09225, \\
f_{\mathbf{X}, X_3}(0, 1, 1) &= 0.7(0.2)(0.2)(0.75) + 0.5(0.3)(0.3)(0.25) = 0.03225, \\
f_{\mathbf{X}, X_3}(0, 1, 2) &= 0.7(0.2)(0.1)(0.75) + 0.5(0.3)(0.2)(0.25) = 0.01800.
\end{aligned}
$$

The predictive distribution is then

$$
\begin{aligned}
f_{X_3|\mathbf{X}}(0|0, 1) &= \frac{0.09225}{0.1425} = 0.647368, \\
f_{X_3|\mathbf{X}}(1|0, 1) &= \frac{0.03225}{0.1425} = 0.226316, \\
f_{X_3|\mathbf{X}}(2|0, 1) &= \frac{0.01800}{0.1425} = 0.126316.
\end{aligned}
$$

The posterior probabilities are, from (16.24),

$$
\begin{aligned}
\pi(G|0, 1) &= \frac{f(0|G)f(1|G)\pi(G)}{f(0, 1)} = \frac{0.7(0.2)(0.75)}{0.1425} = 0.736842, \\
\pi(B|0, 1) &= \frac{f(0|B)f(1|B)\pi(B)}{f(0, 1)} = \frac{0.5(0.3)(0.25)}{0.1425} = 0.263158.
\end{aligned}
$$

From this point forward the subscripts on f and π will be dropped unless needed for clarity. The predictive probabilities could also have been obtained using (16.25). This method is often simpler from a computation viewpoint.

$$
\begin{aligned}
f(0|0, 1) &= \sum_{\theta} f(0|\theta)\pi(\theta|0, 1) \\
&= 0.7(0.736842) + 0.5(0.263158) = 0.647368, \\
f(1|0, 1) &= 0.2(0.736842) + 0.3(0.263158) = 0.226316, \\
f(2|0, 1) &= 0.1(0.736842) + 0.2(0.263158) = 0.126316,
\end{aligned}
$$

which matches the previous calculations.   □

Example 16.19 (Example 16.17 continued) *Suppose a person had claims of 100, 950, and 450. Determine the predictive distribution of the fourth claim and the posterior distribution of Θ.*

The marginal density at the observed values is

$$
\begin{aligned}
f(100, 950, 450) &= \int_0^{\infty} \theta e^{-100\theta} \theta e^{-950\theta} \theta e^{-450\theta} \frac{1{,}000^4}{6} \theta^3 e^{-1{,}000\theta} d\theta \\
&= \frac{1{,}000^4}{6} \int_0^{\infty} \theta^6 e^{-2{,}500\theta} d\theta = \frac{1{,}000^4}{6} \frac{720}{2{,}500^7}.
\end{aligned}
$$

Similarly,

$$
\begin{aligned}
f(100, 950, 450, x_4) &= \int_0^\infty \theta e^{-100\theta}\theta e^{-950\theta}\theta e^{-450\theta}\theta^{-\theta x_4}\frac{1{,}000^4}{6}\theta^3 e^{-1{,}000\theta}\,d\theta \\
&= \frac{1{,}000^4}{6}\int_0^\infty \theta^7 e^{-(2{,}500+x_4)\theta}\,d\theta \\
&= \frac{1{,}000^4}{6}\frac{5{,}040}{(2{,}500+x_4)^8}.
\end{aligned}
$$

Then the predictive density is

$$
f(x_4|100, 950, 450) = \frac{\dfrac{1{,}000^4}{6}\dfrac{5{,}040}{(2{,}500+x_4)^8}}{\dfrac{1{,}000^4}{6}\dfrac{720}{2{,}500^7}} = \frac{7(2{,}500)^7}{(2{,}500+x_4)^8}
$$

which is a Pareto density with parameters 7 and 2,500.

For the posterior distribution we take a shortcut. The denominator is an integral that produces a number and can be ignored for now. The numerator can be written

$$
\pi(\theta|100, 950, 450) \propto \theta e^{-100\theta}\theta e^{-950\theta}\theta e^{-450\theta}\frac{1{,}000^4}{6}\theta^3 e^{-1{,}000\theta},
$$

which was the term to be integrated in the calculation of the marginal density. Because there are constants in the denominator that have been ignored, we might as well ignore constants in the numerator. Only multiplicative terms involving the variable (θ in this case) need to be retained. Then

$$
\pi(\theta|100, 950, 450) \propto \theta^6 e^{-2{,}500\theta}.
$$

We could integrate this expression in order to determine the constant needed to make this a density function (that is, make the integral equal 1). But we recognize this function as that of a gamma distribution with parameters 7 and $1/2{,}500$. Therefore,

$$
\pi(\theta|100, 950, 450) = \frac{\theta^6 e^{-2{,}500\theta}2{,}500^7}{\Gamma(7)}.
$$

Then the predictive density can be alternatively calculated from

$$
\begin{aligned}
f(x_4|100, 950, 450) &= \int_0^\infty \theta e^{-\theta x_4}\frac{\theta^6 e^{-2{,}500\theta}2{,}500^7}{\Gamma(7)}\,d\theta \\
&= \frac{2{,}500^7}{6!}\int_0^\infty \theta^7 e^{-(2{,}500+x_4)\theta}\,d\theta \\
&= \frac{2{,}500^7}{6!}\frac{7!}{(2{,}500+x_4)^8},
\end{aligned}
$$

matching the answer previously obtained.   □

Note that the posterior distribution is of the same type (gamma) as the prior distribution. The concept of a conjugate prior distribution was introduced in Section 12.4.3. This also implies that $X_{n+1}|\mathbf{x}$ is a mixture distribution with a simple mixing distribution, facilitating evaluation of the density of $X_{n+1}|\mathbf{x}$. Further examples of this idea are found in the exercises.

To return to the original problem, we have observed $\mathbf{X} = \mathbf{x}$ for a particular policyholder and we wish to predict X_{n+1} (or its mean). An obvious choice would be the hypothetical mean (or individual premium)

$$\mu_{n+1}(\theta) = \mathrm{E}(X_{n+1}|\Theta = \theta) = \int x_{n+1} f_{X_{n+1}|\Theta}(x_{n+1}|\theta)\,dx_{n+1} \qquad (16.26)$$

if we knew θ. Note that replacement of θ by Θ in (16.26) yields, upon taking the expectation,

$$\mu_{n+1} = \mathrm{E}(X_{n+1}) = \mathrm{E}[\mathrm{E}(X_{n+1}|\Theta)] = \mathrm{E}[\mu_{n+1}(\Theta)]$$

so that the pure, or collective, premium is the mean of the hypothetical means. This is the premium we would use if we knew nothing about the individual. It does not depend on the individual's risk parameter, θ, nor does it use $\mathbf{x}$, the data collected from the individual. Because θ is unknown, the best we can do is try to use the data. This suggests the use of the Bayesian premium (the mean of the predictive distribution)

$$\mathrm{E}(X_{n+1}|\mathbf{X} = \mathbf{x}) = \int x_{n+1} f_{X_{n+1}|\mathbf{X}}(x_{n+1}|\mathbf{x})\,dx_{n+1}. \qquad (16.27)$$

A computationally more convenient form is

$$\mathrm{E}(X_{n+1}|\mathbf{X} = \mathbf{x}) = \int \mu_{n+1}(\theta)\pi_{\Theta|\mathbf{X}}(\theta|\mathbf{x})\,d\theta. \qquad (16.28)$$

In other words, the Bayesian premium is the expected value of the hypothetical means, with expectation taken over the posterior distribution $\pi_{\Theta|\mathbf{X}}(\theta|\mathbf{x})$. We remind the reader that the integrals are replaced by sums in the discrete case. To prove (16.28), we see from (16.25) that

$$
\begin{aligned}
\mathrm{E}(X_{n+1}|\mathbf{X} = \mathbf{x}) &= \int x_{n+1} f_{X_{n+1}|\mathbf{X}}(x_{n+1}|\mathbf{x})\,dx_{n+1} \\
&= \int x_{n+1} \left[\int f_{X_{n+1}|\Theta}(x_{n+1}|\theta)\pi_{\Theta|\mathbf{X}}(\theta|\mathbf{x})d\theta\right]dx_{n+1} \\
&= \int \left[\int x_{n+1} f_{X_{n+1}|\Theta}(x_{n+1}|\theta)dx_{n+1}\right]\pi_{\Theta|\mathbf{X}}(\theta|\mathbf{x})\,d\theta \\
&= \int \mu_{n+1}(\theta)\pi_{\Theta|\mathbf{X}}(\theta|\mathbf{x})\,d\theta.
\end{aligned}
$$

Example 16.20 (Example 16.18 continued) *Determine the Bayesian premium using both (16.27) and (16.28).*

The (unobservable) hypothetical means are

$$
\begin{aligned}
\mu_3(G) &= (0)(0.7) + 1(0.2) + 2(0.1) = 0.4, \\
\mu_3(B) &= (0)(0.5) + 1(0.3) + 2(0.2) = 0.7.
\end{aligned}
$$

If, as in Example 16.18, we have observed $x_1 = 0$ and $x_2 = 1$, we have the Bayesian premiums obtained directly from (16.27):

$$
E(X_3|0, 1) = 0(0.647368) + 1(0.226316) + 2(0.126316) = 0.478948.
$$

The (unconditional) pure premium is

$$
\mu_3 = E(X_3) = \sum_\theta \mu_3(\theta)\pi(\theta) = (0.4)(0.75) + (0.7)(0.25) = 0.475.
$$

To verify (16.28) with $x_1 = 0$ and $x_2 = 1$, we have the posterior distribution $\pi(\theta|0, 1)$ from Example 16.18.

Thus, (16.28) yields

$$
E(X_3|0, 1) = 0.4(0.736842) + 0.7(0.263158) = 0.478947
$$

with the difference due to rounding. In general, the latter approach utilizing (16.28) is simpler than the direct approach using the conditional distribution of $X_{n+1}|\mathbf{X} = \mathbf{x}$.   □

As expected, the revised value based on two observations is between the prior value (0.475) based on no data and the value based only on the data (0.5).

Example 16.21 (Example 16.19 continued) *Determine the Bayesian premium.*

From Example 16.19, we have $\mu_4(\theta) = \theta^{-1}$. Then, (16.28) yields

$$
\begin{aligned}
E(X_4|100, 950, 450) &= \int_0^\infty \theta^{-1} \frac{\theta^6 e^{-2,500\theta} 2,500^7}{720} d\theta \\
&= \frac{2,500^7}{720} \frac{120}{2,500^6} = 416.67.
\end{aligned}
$$

This could also have been obtained from the formula for the moments of the gamma distribution in Appendix A. From the prior distribution,

$$
\mu = E(\Theta^{-1}) = \frac{1,000}{3} = 333.33
$$

and once again the Bayesian estimate is between the prior estimate and one based solely on the data (the sample mean of 500).

From (16.27),

$$E(X_4|100, 950, 450) = \frac{2,500}{6} = 416.67,$$

the mean of the predictive Pareto distribution. □

Example 16.22 *Generalize the result of Example 16.21 for an arbitrary sample size of n and an arbitrary prior gamma distribution with parameters α and β, where β is the reciprocal of the usual scale parameter.*

The posterior distribution can be determined from

$$\pi(\theta|\mathbf{x}) \quad \propto \quad \left(\prod_{j=1}^{n} \theta e^{-\theta x_j} \right) \frac{\theta^{\alpha-1} e^{-\beta\theta} \beta^{\alpha}}{\Gamma(\alpha)}$$

$$\propto \quad \theta^{n+\alpha-1} e^{-(\Sigma x_j + \beta)\theta}.$$

The second line follows because the posterior density is a function of θ and thus all multiplicative terms not involving θ may be dropped. Rather than perform the integral to determine the constant, we recognize that the posterior distribution is gamma with first parameter $n + \alpha$ and scale parameter $(\Sigma x_j + \beta)^{-1}$. The Bayes estimate of X_{n+1} is the expected value of Θ^{-1} using the posterior distribution. It is

$$\frac{\Sigma x_j + \beta}{n + \alpha - 1} = \frac{n}{n + \alpha - 1} \bar{x} + \frac{\alpha - 1}{n + \alpha - 1} \frac{\beta}{\alpha - 1}.$$

Note that the estimate is a weighted average of the observed values and the unconditional mean. This formula is of the credibility weighted type (16.19). □

Here is an example where the random variables do not have identical distributions.

Example 16.23 *Suppose that the number of claims N_j in year j for a group policyholder with (unknown) risk parameter θ and m_j individuals in the group is Poisson distributed with mean $m_j\theta$, that is, for $j = 1, \ldots, n$,*

$$\Pr(N_j = x|\Theta = \theta) = \frac{(m_j\theta)^x e^{-m_j\theta}}{x!}, \quad x = 0, 1, 2, \ldots .$$

This would be the case if, per individual, the number of claims were independently Poisson distributed with mean θ. Determine the Bayesian expected number of claims for the m_{n+1} individuals to be insured in year $n + 1$.

With these assumptions, the average number of claims per individual in year j is

$$X_j = \frac{N_j}{m_j}, \quad j = 1, \ldots, n.$$

Therefore,

$$f_{X_j|\Theta}(x_j|\theta) = \Pr[N_j = m_j x_j|\Theta = \theta].$$

Assume Θ is gamma distributed with parameters α and β,

$$\pi(\theta) = \frac{\theta^{\alpha-1} e^{-\theta/\beta}}{\Gamma(\alpha)\beta^\alpha}, \quad \theta > 0;$$

then the posterior distribution $\pi_{\Theta|\mathbf{X}}(\theta|\mathbf{x})$ is proportional (as a function of θ) to

$$\left[\prod_{j=1}^{n} f_{X_j|\Theta}(x_j|\theta) \right] \pi(\theta),$$

which is itself proportional to

$$\left[\prod_{j=1}^{n} \theta^{m_j x_j} e^{-m_j \theta} \right] \theta^{\alpha-1} e^{-\theta/\beta} = \theta^{\alpha + \sum_{j=1}^{n} m_j x_j - 1} e^{-\theta\left(\beta^{-1} + \sum_{j=1}^{n} m_j\right)}.$$

This is proportional to a gamma density with parameters $\alpha_* = \alpha + \sum_{j=1}^{n} m_j x_j$ and $\beta_* = (1/\beta + \sum_{j=1}^{n} m_j)^{-1}$, and so $\Theta|\mathbf{X}$ is also gamma, but with α and β replaced by α_* and β_*, respectively.

Now,

$$\mathrm{E}(X_j|\Theta = \theta) = \mathrm{E}\left(\frac{1}{m_j} N_j|\Theta = \theta\right) = \frac{1}{m_j}\mathrm{E}(N_j|\Theta = \theta) = \theta.$$

Thus $\mu_{n+1}(\theta) = \mathrm{E}(X_{n+1}|\Theta = \theta) = \theta$ and $\mu_{n+1} = \mathrm{E}(X_{n+1}) = \mathrm{E}[\mu_{n+1}(\Theta)] = \alpha\beta$ because Θ is gamma distributed with parameters α and β. From (16.28) and because $\Theta|\mathbf{X}$ is also gamma distributed with parameters α_* and β_*,

$$\begin{aligned}
\mathrm{E}(X_{n+1}|\mathbf{X} = \mathbf{x}) &= \int_0^\infty \mu_{n+1}(\theta) \pi_{\Theta|\mathbf{X}}(\theta|\mathbf{x}) \, d\theta \\
&= \mathrm{E}[\mu_{n+1}(\Theta)|\mathbf{X} = \mathbf{x}] \\
&= \mathrm{E}(\Theta|\mathbf{X} = \mathbf{x}) \\
&= \alpha_* \beta_*.
\end{aligned}$$

Define the total number of lives observed to be $m = \sum_{j=1}^{n} m_j$.
Then,

$$\mathrm{E}(X_{n+1}|\mathbf{X} = \mathbf{x}) = Z\bar{x} + (1 - Z)\mu_{n+1},$$

where $Z = m/(m + \beta^{-1})$ and $\bar{x} = m^{-1} \sum_{j=1}^{n} m_j x_j$, and $\mu = \alpha\beta$, again an expression of the form (16.19).

The total Bayesian expected number of claims for m_{n+1} individuals in the group for the next year would be $m_{n+1}\mathrm{E}(X_{n+1}|\mathbf{X}=\mathbf{x})$.

The analysis based on independent and identically distributed Poisson claim counts is obtained with $m_j = 1$. Then $X_j \equiv N_j$ for $j = 1,2,\ldots,n$ are independent (given θ) Poisson random variables with mean θ. In this case

$$\mathrm{E}(X_{n+1}|\mathbf{X}=\mathbf{x}) = Z\bar{x} + (1-Z)\mu,$$

where $Z = n/(n+\beta^{-1})$, $\bar{x} = n^{-1}\sum_{j=1}^{n} x_j$, and $\mu = \alpha\beta$. $\square$

In each of Examples 16.22 and 16.23 the Bayesian estimate was a weighted average of the sample mean $\bar{x}$ and the pure premium μ_{n+1}. This is appealing from a credibility standpoint. Furthermore, the credibility factor Z in each case is an increasing function of the number of exposure units. The greater the amount of past data observed, the closer Z is to 1, consistent with our intuition.

16.4.3   The credibility premium

In the previous section a systematic approach was suggested for treatment of the past data of a particular policyholder. Ideally, rather than the pure premium $\mu_{n+1} = \mathrm{E}(X_{n+1})$, one would like to charge the individual premium (or hypothetical mean) $\mu_{n+1}(\theta)$, where θ is the (hypothetical) parameter associated with the policyholder. Because θ is unknown, this is impossible, but we could instead condition on $\mathbf{x}$, the past data from the policyholder. This leads to the Bayesian premium $\mathrm{E}(X_{n+1}|\mathbf{x})$.

The major challenge with this approach is that it may be difficult to evaluate the Bayesian premium. Of course, in simple examples such as in the previous subsection, the Bayesian premium is not difficult to evaluate numerically. But these examples can hardly be expected to capture the essential features of a realistic insurance scenario. More realistic models may well introduce analytic difficulties with respect to evaluation of $\mathrm{E}(X_{n+1}|\mathbf{x})$, whether one uses (16.27) or (16.28). Often, numerical integration may be required. There are exceptions such as Examples 16.22 and 16.23.

We now present an alternative suggested by Bühlmann [18] in 1967. Recall the basic problem: We wish to use the conditional distribution $f_{X_{n+1}|\Theta}(x_{n+1}|\theta)$ or the hypothetical mean $\mu_{n+1}(\theta)$ for estimation of next year's claims. Because we have observed $\mathbf{x}$, one suggestion is to approximate $\mu_{n+1}(\theta)$ by a linear function of the past data. [After all, the formula $Z\overline{X} + (1-Z)\mu$ is of this form.] Thus, let us restrict ourselves to estimators of the form $\alpha_0 + \sum_{j=1}^{n}\alpha_j X_j$, where $\alpha_0, \alpha_1, \ldots, \alpha_n$ need to be chosen. To this end, we will choose the αs to minimize squared error loss, that is,

$$Q = \mathrm{E}\left\{\left[\mu_{n+1}(\Theta) - \alpha_0 - \sum_{j=1}^{n}\alpha_j X_j\right]^2\right\} \tag{16.29}$$

and the expectation is over the joint distribution of $X_1,\ldots,X_n$ and Θ. That is, the squared error is averaged over all possible values of Θ and all possible observations. To minimize Q, we take derivatives. Thus,

$$\frac{\partial Q}{\partial \alpha_0} = \mathrm{E}\left\{2\left[\mu_{n+1}(\Theta) - \alpha_0 - \sum_{j=1}^{n}\alpha_j X_j\right](-1)\right\}.$$

We shall denote by $\tilde{\alpha}_0, \tilde{\alpha}_1, \ldots, \tilde{\alpha}_n$ the values of $\alpha_0, \alpha_1, \ldots, \alpha_n$ which minimize (16.29). Then equating $\partial Q/\partial \alpha_0$ to 0 yields

$$\mathrm{E}[\mu_{n+1}(\Theta)] = \tilde{\alpha}_0 + \sum_{j=1}^{n}\tilde{\alpha}_j \mathrm{E}(X_j).$$

But $\mathrm{E}(X_{n+1}) = \mathrm{E}[\mathrm{E}(X_{n+1}|\Theta)] = \mathrm{E}[\mu_{n+1}(\Theta)]$, and so $\partial Q/\partial \alpha_0 = 0$ implies that

$$\mathrm{E}(X_{n+1}) = \tilde{\alpha}_0 + \sum_{j=1}^{n}\tilde{\alpha}_j \mathrm{E}(X_j). \tag{16.30}$$

Equation (16.30) may be termed the **unbiasedness equation** because it requires that the estimate $\tilde{\alpha}_0 + \sum_{j=1}^{n}\tilde{\alpha}_j X_j$ be unbiased for $\mathrm{E}(X_{n+1})$. However, the credibility estimate may be biased as an estimator of $\mu_{n+1}(\theta) = \mathrm{E}(X_{n+1}|\theta)$, the quantity we are trying to estimate. This bias will average out over the members of Θ. By accepting this bias we are able to reduce the overall mean-squared error. For $i = 1, \ldots, n$, we have

$$\frac{\partial Q}{\partial \alpha_i} = \mathrm{E}\left\{2\left[\mu_{n+1}(\Theta) - \alpha_0 - \sum_{j=1}^{n}\alpha_j X_j\right](-X_i)\right\}$$

and setting this equal to 0 yields

$$\mathrm{E}[\mu_{n+1}(\Theta)X_i] = \tilde{\alpha}_0 \mathrm{E}(X_i) + \sum_{j=1}^{n}\tilde{\alpha}_j \mathrm{E}(X_i X_j).$$

The left-hand side of this equation may be reexpressed as

$$\begin{aligned}
\mathrm{E}[\mu_{n+1}(\Theta)X_i] &= \mathrm{E}\{\mathrm{E}[X_i \mu_{n+1}(\Theta)|\Theta]\}\\
&= \mathrm{E}\{\mu_{n+1}(\Theta)\mathrm{E}[X_i|\Theta]\}\\
&= \mathrm{E}[\mathrm{E}(X_{n+1}|\Theta)\mathrm{E}(X_i|\Theta)]\\
&= \mathrm{E}[\mathrm{E}(X_{n+1}X_i|\Theta)]\\
&= \mathrm{E}(X_i X_{n+1}),
\end{aligned}$$

where the second from the last step follows by independence of X_i and X_{n+1} conditional on Θ. Thus $\partial Q / \partial \alpha_i = 0$ implies

$$E(X_i X_{n+1}) = \tilde{\alpha}_0 E(X_i) + \sum_{j=1}^{n} \tilde{\alpha}_j E(X_i X_j). \tag{16.31}$$

Next multiply (16.30) by $E(X_i)$ and subtract from (16.31) to obtain

$$\operatorname{Cov}(X_i, X_{n+1}) = \sum_{j=1}^{n} \tilde{\alpha}_j \operatorname{Cov}(X_i, X_j), \quad i = 1, \ldots, n. \tag{16.32}$$

Equation (16.30) and the n equations (16.32) together are called the **normal equations**. These equations may be solved for $\tilde{\alpha}_0, \tilde{\alpha}_1, \ldots, \tilde{\alpha}_n$ to yield the credibility premium

$$\tilde{\alpha}_0 + \sum_{j=1}^{n} \tilde{\alpha}_j X_j. \tag{16.33}$$

While it is straightforward to express the solution $\tilde{\alpha}_0, \tilde{\alpha}_1, \ldots, \tilde{\alpha}_n$ to the normal equations in matrix notation (if the covariance matrix of the X_js is non-singular), we shall be content with solutions for some special cases.

Note that exactly one of the terms on the right-hand side of (16.32) is a variance term, that is, $\operatorname{Cov}(X_i, X_i) = \operatorname{Var}(X_i)$. The other $n - 1$ terms are true covariance terms.

As an added bonus, the values $\tilde{\alpha}_0, \tilde{\alpha}_1, \ldots, \tilde{\alpha}_n$ also minimize

$$Q_1 = E \left\{ \left[E(X_{n+1} | \mathbf{X}) - \alpha_0 - \sum_{j=1}^{n} \alpha_j X_j \right]^2 \right\} \tag{16.34}$$

and

$$Q_2 = E \left[\left(X_{n+1} - \alpha_0 - \sum_{j=1}^{n} \alpha_j X_j \right)^2 \right]. \tag{16.35}$$

To see this, differentiate (16.34) or (16.35) with respect to $\alpha_0, \alpha_1, \ldots, \alpha_n$ and observe that the solutions still satisfy the normal equations (16.30) and (16.32). Thus the credibility premium (16.33) is the best linear estimator of each of the hypothetical mean $E(X_{n+1} | \Theta)$, the Bayesian premium $E(X_{n+1} | \mathbf{X})$, and X_{n+1}.

Example 16.24 *If $E(X_j) = \mu$, $\operatorname{Var}(X_j) = \sigma^2$, and, for $i \neq j$, $\operatorname{Cov}(X_i, X_j) = \rho\sigma^2$, where the correlation coefficient ρ satisfies $-1 < \rho < 1$, determine the credibility premium $\tilde{\alpha}_0 + \sum_{j=1}^{n} \tilde{\alpha}_j X_j$.*

The unbiasedness equation (16.30) yields

$$\mu = \tilde{\alpha}_0 + \mu \sum_{j=1}^{n} \tilde{\alpha}_j$$

or

$$\sum_{j=1}^{n} \tilde{\alpha}_j = 1 - \frac{\tilde{\alpha}_0}{\mu}.$$

The n equations (16.32) become, for $i = 1, \ldots, n$,

$$\rho = \sum_{\substack{j=1 \\ j \neq i}}^{n} \tilde{\alpha}_j \rho + \tilde{\alpha}_i$$

or, stated another way,

$$\rho = \sum_{j=1}^{n} \tilde{\alpha}_j \rho + \tilde{\alpha}_i(1 - \rho), \quad i = 1, \ldots, n.$$

Thus

$$\tilde{\alpha}_i = \frac{\rho \left(1 - \sum_{j=1}^{n} \tilde{\alpha}_j \right)}{1 - \rho} = \frac{\rho \tilde{\alpha}_0}{\mu(1 - \rho)}$$

using the unbiasedness equation. Summation over i from 1 to n yields

$$\sum_{i=1}^{n} \tilde{\alpha}_i = \sum_{j=1}^{n} \tilde{\alpha}_j = \frac{n\rho \tilde{\alpha}_0}{\mu(1 - \rho)},$$

which combined with the unbiasedness equation gives an equation for $\tilde{\alpha}_0$, namely

$$1 - \frac{\tilde{\alpha}_0}{\mu} = \frac{n\rho \tilde{\alpha}_0}{\mu(1 - \rho)}.$$

Solving for $\tilde{\alpha}_0$ yields

$$\tilde{\alpha}_0 = \frac{(1 - \rho)\mu}{1 - \rho + n\rho}.$$

Thus,

$$\tilde{\alpha}_j = \frac{\rho \tilde{\alpha}_0}{\mu(1 - \rho)} = \frac{\rho}{1 - \rho + n\rho}.$$

The credibility premium is then

$$\tilde{\alpha}_0 + \sum_{j=1}^{n} \tilde{\alpha}_j X_j = \frac{(1 - \rho)\mu}{1 - \rho + n\rho} + \sum_{j=1}^{n} \frac{\rho X_j}{1 - \rho + n\rho}$$

$$= (1 - Z)\mu + Z\bar{X},$$

where $Z = n\rho/(1 - \rho + n\rho)$ and $\bar{X} = n^{-1} \sum_{j=1}^{n} X_j$. Thus, if $0 < \rho < 1$, then $0 < Z < 1$ and the credibility premium is a weighted average of $\mu = \mathrm{E}(X_{n+1})$ and $\bar{X}$, that is, is of the form (16.19). $\square$

We now turn to some models which specify the conditional means and variances of $X_j | \Theta$ and hence the means $\mathrm{E}(X_j)$, variances $\mathrm{Var}(X_j)$, and covariances $\mathrm{Cov}(X_i, X_j)$.

16.4.4   The Buhlmann model

This, the first and simplest credibility model, specifies that for each policy-holder (conditional on Θ) past losses $X_1, \ldots, X_n$ have the same mean and variance and are independent and identically distributed conditional on Θ.

Thus, define

$$\mu(\theta) = E(X_j | \Theta = \theta)$$

and

$$v(\theta) = \text{Var}(X_j | \Theta = \theta).$$

As discussed previously, $\mu(\theta)$ is referred to as the **hypothetical mean** whereas $v(\theta)$ is called the **process variance**. Define

$$\mu = E[\mu(\Theta)], \tag{16.36}$$
$$v = E[v(\Theta)], \tag{16.37}$$

and

$$a = \text{Var}[\mu(\Theta)]. \tag{16.38}$$

The quantity μ in (16.36) is the **expected value of the hypothetical means**, v in (16.37) is the **expected value of the process variance**, and a in (16.38) is the **variance of the hypothetical means**. Note that μ is the estimate to use if we have no information about θ [and thus no information about $\mu(\theta)$]. It will also be referred to as the **collective premium**.

The mean, variance, and covariance of the X_js may now be obtained. First,

$$E(X_j) = E[E(X_j | \Theta)] = E[\mu(\Theta)] = \mu. \tag{16.39}$$

Second,

$$\begin{aligned}
\text{Var}(X_j) &= E[\text{Var}(X_j | \Theta)] + \text{Var}[E(X_j | \Theta)] \\
&= E[v(\Theta)] + \text{Var}[\mu(\Theta)] \\
&= v + a. \tag{16.40}
\end{aligned}$$

Finally, for $i \neq j$,

$$\begin{aligned}
\text{Cov}(X_i, X_j) &= E(X_i X_j) - E(X_i)E(X_j) \\
&= E[E(X_i X_j | \Theta)] - \mu^2 \\
&= E[E(X_i | \Theta)E(X_j | \Theta)] - \{E[\mu(\Theta)]\}^2 \\
&= E\{[\mu(\Theta)]^2\} - \{E[\mu(\Theta)]\}^2 \\
&= \text{Var}[\mu(\Theta)] \\
&= a. \tag{16.41}
\end{aligned}$$

This is exactly of the form of Example 16.24 with parameters $\mu, \sigma^2 = v + a$, and $\rho = a/(v + a)$. Thus the credibility premium is

$$\tilde{\alpha}_0 + \sum_{j=1}^{n} \tilde{\alpha}_j X_j = Z\bar{X} + (1 - Z)\mu, \tag{16.42}$$

where
$$Z = \frac{n}{n+k} \qquad (16.43)$$

and
$$k = \frac{v}{a} = \frac{\mathrm{E}[\mathrm{Var}(X_j|\Theta)]}{\mathrm{Var}[\mathrm{E}(X_j|\Theta)]}. \qquad (16.44)$$

The credibility factor Z in (16.43) with k given by (16.44) is referred to as the **Bühlmann credibility factor**. Note that (16.42) is of the form (16.19), and (16.43) is exactly (16.20). Now, however, we know how to obtain k, namely from (16.44).

Formula (16.42) has many appealing features. First, the credibility premium (16.42) is a weighted average of the sample mean $\bar{X}$ and the collective premium μ, a formula which we find desirable. Furthermore, Z approaches 1 as n increases, giving more credit to $\bar{X}$ rather than μ as more past data accumulates, a feature which agrees with intuition. Also, if the population is fairly homogeneous with respect to the risk parameter Θ, then (relatively speaking) the hypothetical means $\mu(\Theta) = \mathrm{E}(X_j|\Theta)$ do not vary greatly with Θ (i.e., they are close in value) and hence have small variability. Thus a is small relative to v, that is, k is large and Z is closer to 0. But this agrees with intuition because for a homogeneous population the overall mean μ is of more value in helping to predict next year's claims for a particular policyholder. Conversely, for a heterogeneous population, the hypothetical means $\mathrm{E}(X_j|\Theta)$ are more variable, that is, a is large and k is small, and so Z is closer to 1. Again this makes sense because in a heterogeneous population the experience of other policyholders is of less value in predicting the future experience of a particular policyholder than is the past experience of that policyholder.

We now present some examples.

Example 16.25 (Example 16.20 continued) *Determine the Bühlmann estimate of* $\mathrm{E}(X_3|0,1)$.

From earlier work,
$$\mu(G) = \mathrm{E}(X_j|G) = 0.4, \quad \mu(B) = \mathrm{E}(X_j|B) = 0.7,$$
$$\pi(G) = 0.75, \qquad\qquad \pi(B) = 0.25,$$

and therefore,
$$\mu = \sum_{\theta} \mu(\theta)\pi(\theta) = 0.4(0.75) + 0.7(0.25) = 0.475,$$

$$a = \sum_{\theta} \mu(\theta)^2 \pi(\theta) - \mu^2 = 0.16(0.75) + 0.49(0.25) - 0.475^2 = 0.016875.$$

For the process variance,
$$v(G) = \mathrm{Var}(X_j|G) = 0^2(0.7) + 1^2(0.2) + 2^2(0.1) - 0.4^2 = 0.44,$$
$$v(B) = \mathrm{Var}(X_j|B) = 0^2(0.5) + 1^2(0.3) + 2^2(0.2) - 0.7^2 = 0.61,$$
$$v = \sum_{\theta} v(\theta)\pi(\theta) = 0.44(0.75) + 0.61(0.25) = 0.4825.$$

Then (16.44) gives

$$k = \frac{v}{a} = \frac{0.4825}{0.016875} = 28.5926$$

and (16.43) gives

$$Z = \frac{2}{2 + 28.5926} = 0.0654.$$

The expected next value is then $0.0654(0.5) + 0.9346(0.475) = 0.4766$. This is the best linear approximation to the Bayesian premium (given in Example 16.20). □

Example 16.26 *Suppose as in Example 16.23 (with $m_j = 1$) that $X_j|\Theta$, $j = 1, \ldots, n$, are independently and identically Poisson distributed with (given) mean Θ and Θ is gamma distributed with parameters α and β. Determine the Bühlmann premium.*

We have

$$\mu(\theta) = \mathrm{E}(X_j|\Theta = \theta) = \theta, \quad v(\theta) = \mathrm{Var}(X_j|\Theta = \theta) = \theta,$$

and so

$$\mu = \mathrm{E}[\mu(\Theta)] = \mathrm{E}(\Theta) = \alpha\beta, \quad v = \mathrm{E}[v(\Theta)] = \mathrm{E}(\Theta) = \alpha\beta,$$

and

$$a = \mathrm{Var}[\mu(\Theta)] = \mathrm{Var}(\Theta) = \alpha\beta^2.$$

Then

$$k = \frac{v}{a} = \frac{\alpha\beta}{\alpha\beta^2} = \frac{1}{\beta}, \quad Z = \frac{n}{n+k} = \frac{n}{n+1/\beta} = \frac{n\beta}{n\beta+1},$$

and the credibility premium is

$$Z\bar{X} + (1-Z)\mu = \frac{n\beta}{n\beta+1}\bar{X} + \frac{1}{n\beta+1}\alpha\beta.$$

But, as shown at the end of Example 16.23, this is also the Bayesian estimate $\mathrm{E}(X_{n+1}|\mathbf{X})$. Thus, the credibility premium equals the Bayesian estimate in this case. □

Example 16.27 *Determine the Bühlmann estimate for the setting in Example 16.22.*

For this model,

$$\mu(\Theta) = \Theta^{-1}, \mu = E(\Theta^{-1}) = \frac{\beta}{\alpha - 1},$$

$$v(\Theta) = \Theta^{-2}, v = E(\Theta^{-2}) = \frac{\beta^2}{(\alpha - 1)(\alpha - 2)},$$

$$a = \text{Var}(\Theta^{-1}) = \frac{\beta^2}{(\alpha - 1)(\alpha - 2)} - \left(\frac{\beta}{\alpha - 1}\right)^2 = \frac{\beta^2}{(\alpha - 1)^2(\alpha - 2)},$$

$$k = \frac{v}{a} = \alpha - 1,$$

$$Z = \frac{n}{n + k} = \frac{n}{n + \alpha - 1},$$

$$P_c = \frac{n}{n + \alpha - 1}\bar{X} + \frac{\alpha - 1}{n + \alpha - 1}\frac{\beta}{\alpha - 1},$$

which again matches the Bayesian estimate.

An alternative analysis for this problem could have started with a single observation of $S = X_1 + \cdots + X_n$. From the assumptions of the problem, S has a mean of $n\Theta^{-1}$ and a variance of $n\Theta^{-2}$. While it is true that S has a gamma distribution, that information is not needed because the Bühlmann approximation requires only moments. Following the above calculations,

$$\mu = \frac{n\beta}{\alpha - 1}, v = \frac{n\beta^2}{(\alpha - 1)(\alpha - 2)}, a = \frac{n^2\beta^2}{(\alpha - 1)^2(\alpha - 2)},$$

$$k = \frac{\alpha - 1}{n}, Z = \frac{1}{1 + k} = \frac{n}{n + \alpha - 1}.$$

The key is to note that in calculating Z the sample size is now 1, reflecting the single observation of S. Because $S = n\bar{X}$, the Bühlmann estimate is

$$P_c = \frac{n}{n + \alpha - 1}n\bar{X} + \frac{\alpha - 1}{n + \alpha - 1}\frac{n\beta}{\alpha - 1},$$

which is n times the previous answer. That is because we are now estimating the next value of S rather than the next value of X. However, the credibility factor itself (that is, Z) is the same whether we are predicting X_{n+1} or the next value of S. □

16.4.5 The Buhlmann–Straub model

The Bühlmann model of the previous section is the simplest of the credibility models because it effectively requires that the past claims experience of a policyholder comprise independent and identically distributed components with respect to each past year. An important practical difficulty with this assumption is that it does not allow for variations in exposure or size.

For example, what if the first year's claims experience of a policyholder reflected only a portion of a year due to an unusual policyholder anniversary?

What if a benefit change occurred part way through a policy year? For group insurance, what if the size of the group changed over time?

To handle these variations, we consider the following generalization of the Bühlmann model. Assume that $X_1, \ldots, X_n$ are independent, conditional on Θ, with common mean (as before)

$$\mu(\theta) = E(X_j | \Theta = \theta)$$

but with conditional variances

$$\text{Var}(X_j | \Theta = \theta) = \frac{v(\theta)}{m_j},$$

where m_j is a known constant measuring exposure. Note that m_j need only be proportional to the size of the risk. This model would be appropriate if each X_j were the average of m_j independent (conditional on Θ) random variables each with mean $\mu(\theta)$ and variance $v(\theta)$. In the above situations, m_j could be the number of months the policy was in force in past year j, or the number of individuals in the group in past year j, or the amount of premium income for the policy in past year j.

As in the Bühlmann model, let

$$\mu = E[\mu(\Theta)], \quad v = E[v(\Theta)],$$

and

$$a = \text{Var}[\mu(\Theta)].$$

Then, for the unconditional moments, from (16.39) $E(X_j) = \mu$, and from (16.41) $\text{Cov}(X_i, X_j) = a$, but

$$
\begin{aligned}
\text{Var}(X_j) &= E[\text{Var}(X_j | \Theta)] + \text{Var}[E(X_j | \Theta)] \\
&= E\left[\frac{v(\Theta)}{m_j}\right] + \text{Var}[\mu(\Theta)] \\
&= \frac{v}{m_j} + a.
\end{aligned}
$$

To obtain the credibility premium (16.33), we will solve the normal equations (16.30) and (16.32) to obtain $\tilde{\alpha}_0, \tilde{\alpha}_1, \ldots, \tilde{\alpha}_n$. For notational convenience, define

$$m = m_1 + m_2 + \cdots + m_n$$

to be the total exposure. Then using (16.39) the unbiasedness equation (16.30) becomes

$$\mu = \tilde{\alpha}_0 + \sum_{j=1}^{n} \tilde{\alpha}_j \mu$$

which implies

$$\sum_{j=1}^{n} \tilde{\alpha}_j = 1 - \frac{\tilde{\alpha}_0}{\mu}. \tag{16.45}$$

For $i = 1, \ldots, n$, (16.32) becomes

$$a = \sum_{\substack{j=1 \\ j \neq i}}^{n} \tilde{\alpha}_j a + \tilde{\alpha}_i \left(a + \frac{v}{m_i} \right) = \sum_{j=1}^{n} \tilde{\alpha}_j a + \frac{v \tilde{\alpha}_i}{m_i},$$

which may be rewritten as

$$\tilde{\alpha}_i = \frac{a}{v} m_i \left(1 - \sum_{j=1}^{n} \tilde{\alpha}_j \right) = \frac{a}{v} \frac{\tilde{\alpha}_0}{\mu} m_i, \quad i = 1, \ldots, n. \tag{16.46}$$

Then, using (16.45) and (16.46),

$$1 - \frac{\tilde{\alpha}_0}{\mu} = \sum_{j=1}^{n} \tilde{\alpha}_j = \sum_{i=1}^{n} \tilde{\alpha}_i = \frac{a}{v} \frac{\tilde{\alpha}_0}{\mu} \sum_{i=1}^{n} m_i = \frac{a \tilde{\alpha}_0 m}{\mu v},$$

and so

$$\tilde{\alpha}_0 = \frac{\mu}{1 + am/v} = \frac{v/a}{m + v/a} \mu.$$

But this means that

$$\tilde{\alpha}_j = \frac{a \tilde{\alpha}_0}{\mu v} \cdot m_j = \frac{m_j}{m + v/a}.$$

The credibility premium (16.33) becomes

$$\tilde{\alpha}_0 + \sum_{j=1}^{n} \tilde{\alpha}_j X_j = Z \bar{X} + (1 - Z) \mu, \tag{16.47}$$

where with $k = v/a$ from (16.44)

$$Z = \frac{m}{m + k}$$

and

$$\bar{X} = \sum_{j=1}^{n} \frac{m_j}{m} X_j. \tag{16.48}$$

Clearly, the credibility premium (16.47) is still of the form (16.19). In this case, m is the total exposure associated with the policyholder, and the Bühlmann–Straub credibility factor Z depends on m. Furthermore, $\bar{X}$ is a weighted average of the X_j, with weights proportional to m_j. Following the group interpretation, X_j is the average loss of the m_j group members in year j and so $m_j X_j$ is the total loss of the group in year j. Then $\bar{X}$ is the overall average loss per group member over the n years. The credibility premium to be charged to the group in year $n + 1$ would thus be $m_{n+1}[Z\bar{X} + (1 - Z)\mu]$ for m_{n+1} members in the next year.

Had we known that (16.48) would be the correct weighting of the X_j to receive the credibility weight Z, the rest would have been easy. For the single observation $\bar{X}$ the process variance is

$$\text{Var}(\bar{X}|\theta) = \sum_{j=1}^{n} \frac{m_j^2}{m^2} \frac{v(\theta)}{m_j} = \frac{v(\theta)}{m}$$

and so the expected process variance is v/m. The variance of the hypothetical means is still a and therefore $k = v/(am)$. There is only one observation of $\bar{X}$ and so the credibility factor is

$$Z = \frac{1}{1 + v/(am)} = \frac{m}{m + v/a} \tag{16.49}$$

as before. Equation (16.48) should not have been surprising because the weights are simply inversely proportional to the (conditional) variance of each X_j.

Example 16.28 *As in Example 16.23, assume that in year j there are N_j claims from m_j policies, $j = 1, \ldots, n$. An individual policy has the Poisson distribution with parameter Θ and the parameter itself has the gamma distribution with parameters α and β. Determine the Bühlmann–Straub estimate of the number of claims in year $n+1$ if there will be m_{n+1} policies.*

In order to meet the conditions of this model, let $X_j = N_j/m_j$. Because N_j has the Poisson distribution with mean $m_j\Theta$, $\text{E}(X_j|\Theta) = \Theta = \mu(\Theta)$ and $\text{Var}(X_j|\Theta) = \Theta/m_j = v(\Theta)/m_j$. Then,

$$\mu = \text{E}(\Theta) = \alpha\beta, \quad a = \text{Var}(\Theta) = \alpha\beta^2, \quad v = \text{E}(\Theta) = \alpha\beta,$$

$$k = \frac{1}{\beta}, \quad Z = \frac{m}{m + 1/\beta} = \frac{m\beta}{m\beta + 1},$$

and the estimate for one policyholder is

$$P_c = \frac{m\beta}{m\beta + 1}\bar{X} + \frac{1}{m\beta + 1}\alpha\beta,$$

where $\bar{X} = m^{-1}\sum_{j=1}^{n} m_j X_j$. For year $n+1$, the estimate is $m_{n+1}P_c$, matching the answer to Example 16.23. $\square$

The assumptions underlying the Bühlmann–Straub model may be too restrictive to represent reality. In a 1967 paper, Hewitt [55] observed that large risks do not behave the same as an independent aggregation of small risks and, in fact, are more variable than would be indicated by independence. A model that reflects this observation is created in the following example.

Example 16.29 *Let the conditional mean be* $E(X_j|\Theta) = \mu(\Theta)$ *and the conditional variance be* $Var(X_j|\Theta) = w(\Theta) + v(\Theta)/m_j$. *Further assume that* $X_1, \ldots, X_n$ *are conditionally independent given* Θ. *Show that this model supports Hewitt's observation and determine the credibility premium.*

Consider independent risks i and j with exposures m_i and m_j and with a common value of Θ. When aggregated, the variance of the average loss is

$$
\begin{aligned}
\mathrm{Var}\left(\frac{m_iX_i + m_jX_j}{m_i + m_j}\Big|\Theta\right) &= \left(\frac{m_i}{m_i + m_j}\right)^2 \mathrm{Var}(X_i|\Theta) \\
&\quad + \left(\frac{m_j}{m_i + m_j}\right)^2 \mathrm{Var}(X_j|\Theta) \\
&= \frac{m_i^2 + m_j^2}{(m_i + m_j)^2}w(\Theta) + \frac{1}{m_i + m_j}v(\Theta)
\end{aligned}
$$

while a single risk with exposure $m_i + m_j$ has variance $w(\Theta) + v(\Theta)/(m_i + m_j)$, which is larger.

With regard to the credibility premium, we have

$$
\begin{aligned}
E(X_j) &= E[E(X_j|\Theta)] = E[\mu(\Theta)] = \mu \\
\mathrm{Var}(X_j) &= E[\mathrm{Var}(X_j|\Theta)] + \mathrm{Var}[E(X_j|\Theta)] \\
&= E\left[w(\Theta) + \frac{v(\Theta)}{m_j}\right] + \mathrm{Var}[\mu(\Theta)] \\
&= w + \frac{v}{m_j} + a,
\end{aligned}
$$

and for $i \neq j$, $\mathrm{Cov}(X_i, X_j) = a$ as in (16.41). The unbiasedness equation is still

$$
\mu = \tilde{\alpha}_0 + \sum_{j=1}^{n} \tilde{\alpha}_j \mu
$$

and so

$$
\sum_{j=1}^{n} \tilde{\alpha}_j = 1 - \frac{\tilde{\alpha}_0}{\mu}.
$$

Equation (16.32) becomes

$$
\begin{aligned}
a &= \sum_{j=1}^{n} \tilde{\alpha}_j a + \tilde{\alpha}_i\left(w + \frac{v}{m_i}\right) \\
&= a\left(1 - \frac{\tilde{\alpha}_0}{\mu}\right) + \tilde{\alpha}_i\left(w + \frac{v}{m_i}\right), \quad i = 1, \ldots, n.
\end{aligned}
$$

Therefore,

$$
\tilde{\alpha}_i = \frac{a\tilde{\alpha}_0/\mu}{w + v/m_i}.
$$

Summing both sides yields

$$\frac{a\tilde{\alpha}_0}{\mu} \sum_{j=1}^{n} \frac{m_j}{v + wm_j} = \sum_{j=1}^{n} \tilde{\alpha}_j = 1 - \frac{\tilde{\alpha}_0}{\mu}$$

and so

$$\tilde{\alpha}_0 = \frac{1}{(a/\mu) \sum_{j=1}^{n} \dfrac{m_j}{v + wm_j} + \dfrac{1}{\mu}} = \frac{\mu}{1 + am^*}$$

where

$$m^* = \sum_{j=1}^{n} \frac{m_j}{v + wm_j}.$$

Then

$$\tilde{\alpha}_j = \frac{am_j}{v + wm_j} \frac{1}{1 + am^*}.$$

The credibility premium is

$$\frac{\mu}{1 + am^*} + \frac{a}{1 + am^*} \sum_{j=1}^{n} \frac{m_j X_j}{v + wm_j}.$$

The sum can be made to define a weighted average of the observations by letting

$$\bar{X} = \frac{\sum_{j=1}^{n} \dfrac{m_j}{v + wm_j} X_j}{\sum_{j=1}^{n} \dfrac{m_j}{v + wm_j}} = \frac{1}{m^*} \sum_{j=1}^{n} \frac{m_j}{v + wm_j} X_j.$$

If we now set

$$Z = \frac{am^*}{1 + am^*},$$

the credibility premium is

$$Z\bar{X} + (1 - Z)\mu.$$

Observe what happens as the exposures m_j go to infinity. The credibility factor becomes

$$Z \to \frac{an/w}{1 + an/w} < 1.$$

Contrast this to the Bühlmann–Straub model where the limit is 1. Thus, no matter how large the risk, there is a limit to its credibility. A further generalization of this result is provided in Exercise 16.26. □

Another generalization is provided by letting the variance of $\mu(\Theta)$ depend on the exposure. This may be reasonable if we believe that the extent to which a given risk's propensity to produce claims that differ from the mean is related to its size. For example, larger risks may be underwritten more carefully. In this case, extreme variations from the mean are less likely because we ensure that the risk not only meets the underwriting requirements but also appears to be exactly what it claims to be.

Example 16.30 (Example 16.29 continued) *In addition to the specification presented in Example 16.29, let* $\mathrm{Var}[\mu(\Theta)] = a + b/m$, *where* $m = \sum_{j=1}^{n} m_j$ *is the total exposure for the group. Develop the credibility formula.*

We now have

$$
\begin{aligned}
\mathrm{E}(X_j) &= \mathrm{E}[\mathrm{E}(X_j|\Theta)] = \mathrm{E}[\mu(\Theta)] = \mu \\
\mathrm{Var}(X_j) &= \mathrm{E}[\mathrm{Var}(X_j|\Theta)] + \mathrm{Var}[\mathrm{E}(X_j|\Theta)] \\
&= \mathrm{E}\left[w(\Theta) + \frac{v(\Theta)}{m_j}\right] + \mathrm{Var}[\mu(\Theta)] \\
&= w + \frac{v}{m_j} + a + \frac{b}{m}
\end{aligned}
$$

and for $i \neq j$

$$
\begin{aligned}
\mathrm{Cov}(X_i, X_j) &= \mathrm{E}[\mathrm{E}(X_i X_j|\Theta)] - \mu^2 \\
&= \mathrm{E}[\mu(\Theta)^2] - \mu^2 \\
&= a + \frac{b}{m}.
\end{aligned}
$$

It can be seen that all the calculations used in Example 16.29 apply here with a replaced by $a + b/m$. The credibility factor is

$$
Z = \frac{(a + b/m)m^*}{1 + (a + b/m)m^*}
$$

and the credibility premium is

$$
Z\bar{X} + (1 - Z)\mu
$$

with $\bar{X}$ and m^* defined as in Example 16.29. This particular credibility formula has been used in workers compensation experience rating. One example of this is presented in detail in [45].   □

⬥

16.4.6   Exact credibility

In Examples 16.26–16.28 we found that the credibility premium and the Bayesian premium were equal. From (16.34), one may view the credibility premium as the best linear approximation to the Bayesian premium in the sense of squared error loss. In these examples the approximation is exact because the two premiums are equal. The term **exact credibility** is used to describe the situation when the credibility premium equals the Bayesian premium.

In fact, it is not hard to see that one can ascertain whether credibility is exact without even calculating the credibility premium. If the Bayesian premium is a linear function of $X_1, \ldots, X_n$,

$$E(X_{n+1}|\mathbf{X}) = a_0 + \sum_{j=1}^{n} a_j X_j,$$

then it is clear that in (16.34) the quantity Q_1 attains its minimum value of zero with $\tilde{\alpha}_j = a_j$ for $j = 0, 1, \ldots, n$. Thus the credibility premium is $\tilde{\alpha}_0 + \sum_{j=1}^{n} \tilde{\alpha}_j X_j = a_0 + \sum_{j=1}^{n} a_j X_j = E(X_{n+1}|\mathbf{X})$ and credibility is exact.

This phenomenon occurs fairly generally in connection with linear exponential family members (Section 12.4.3) and their conjugate priors. We parameterize such that $X_j|\Theta = \theta$ is independently (conditional on $\Theta = \theta$) distributed with pf for $j = 1, \ldots, n + 1$,

$$f_{X_j|\Theta}(x_j|\theta) = \frac{p(x_j)e^{-\theta x_j}}{q(\theta)},$$

and Θ has pdf

$$\pi(\theta) = \frac{[q(\theta)]^{-k}e^{-\mu k\theta}}{c(\mu, k)}, \qquad \theta_0 < \theta < \theta_1, \tag{16.50}$$

where $-\infty \leq \theta_0 < \theta_1 \leq \infty$. It is also assumed that $\pi(\theta_0) = \pi(\theta_1) = 0$. For the moment, μ and k are simply parameters of $\pi(\theta)$. We will now demonstrate that the choice of symbols was no coincidence.

In Section 12.4.3 it was shown that

$$\mu(\theta) = E(X_j|\Theta = \theta) = -\frac{q'(\theta)}{q(\theta)}.$$

We wish to find $E[\mu(\Theta)]$. From (16.50),

$$\ln \pi(\theta) = -k \ln q(\theta) - \mu k\theta - \ln c(\mu, k)$$

and differentiating with respect to θ gives

$$\frac{\pi'(\theta)}{\pi(\theta)} = -\frac{kq'(\theta)}{q(\theta)} - \mu k.$$

In other words,

$$\pi'(\theta) = k[\mu(\theta) - \mu]\pi(\theta) \tag{16.51}$$

and integrating from θ_0 to θ_1 gives

$$\pi(\theta_1) - \pi(\theta_0) = k \int_{\theta_0}^{\theta_1} \mu(\theta)\pi(\theta)\,d\theta - k\mu \int_{\theta_0}^{\theta_1} \pi(\theta)\,d\theta.$$

This implies that $0 = kE[\mu(\Theta)] - k\mu$, or equivalently,

$$E[\mu(\Theta)] = \mu. \tag{16.52}$$

Now consider the posterior distribution $\pi_{\Theta|\mathbf{X}}(\theta|\mathbf{x})$. It is proportional to

$$\left[\prod_{j=1}^{n} f_{X_j|\Theta}(x_j|\theta)\right]\pi(\theta),$$

itself proportional to

$$\left[\prod_{j=1}^{n}\frac{e^{-\theta x_j}}{q(\theta)}\right][q(\theta)]^{-k}e^{-\mu k\theta}$$

$$= [q(\theta)]^{-(n+k)}e^{-\theta(\mu k+n\bar{x})}$$

$$= [q(\theta)]^{-k_*}e^{-\mu_* k_*\theta}, \tag{16.53}$$

where

$$k_* = n + k$$

and

$$\mu_* = \frac{\mu k + n\bar{x}}{k + n} = \frac{n}{n+k}\bar{x} + \frac{k}{n+k}\mu.$$

Observe that (16.53) is proportional to a density of the form (16.50) with μ and k replaced by μ_* and k_*, respectively. Hence

$$\pi_{\Theta|\mathbf{X}}(\theta|\mathbf{x}) = \frac{[q(\theta)]^{-k_*}e^{-\mu_* k_*\theta}}{c(\mu_*,k_*)}, \qquad \theta_0 < \theta < \theta_1.$$

From (16.28) and using the same development that led to (16.52), the Bayesian premium is

$$E(X_{n+1}|\mathbf{x}) = \int_{\theta_0}^{\theta_1}\mu(\theta)\pi_{\Theta|\mathbf{X}}(\theta|\mathbf{x})\,d\theta$$

$$= \mu_*$$

$$= Z\bar{x} + (1-Z)\mu,$$

where $Z = n/(n+k)$. This is of the form (16.19), and because it is a linear function of the x_js, credibility must be exact, that is, the credibility premium is

$$\tilde{\alpha}_0 + \sum_{j=1}^{n}\tilde{\alpha}_j X_j = Z\bar{X} + (1-Z)\mu = E(X_{n+1}|\mathbf{x}).$$

Because the $X_j|\Theta$ are also identically distributed for $j = 1,\ldots,n$, the Bühlmann model applies and so (16.42) also applies; that is, k must also satisfy (16.44). To see this directly, recall from Section 12.4.3 that

$$v(\theta) = \text{Var}(X_j|\Theta = \theta) = -\mu'(\theta).$$

Differentiation of (16.51) yields

$$
\begin{aligned}
\pi''(\theta) &= k\mu'(\theta)\pi(\theta) + k^2[\mu(\theta) - \mu]^2\pi(\theta) \\
&= -kv(\theta)\pi(\theta) + k^2[\mu(\theta) - \mu]^2\pi(\theta).
\end{aligned}
$$

Integration with respect to θ from θ_0 to θ_1 yields

$$
\begin{aligned}
\pi'(\theta_1) - \pi'(\theta_0) &= -kE[v(\Theta)] + k^2E\{[\mu(\Theta) - \mu]^2\} \\
&= -kv + k^2a
\end{aligned}
$$

because $\mu(\Theta)$ has mean μ and $E\{[\mu(\Theta) - \mu]^2\} = \mathrm{Var}[\mu(\Theta)] = a$. If $\pi'(\theta_1) = \pi'(\theta_0) = 0$, this implies that $k = v/a$, and so (16.44) is satisfied.

16.4.7   Linear versus Bayesian versus no credibility

In Section 16.4.3 it was demonstrated that the credibility premium is the best linear estimator in the sense of minimizing the expected squared error with respect to the next observation, X_{n+1}. In Exercise 16.59 you are asked to demonstrate that the Bayesian premium is the best estimator with no restrictions, in the same least squares sense. It was also demonstrated in Section 16.4.3 that the credibility premium is the linear estimator that is closest to the Bayesian estimator, again in the mean squared error sense. Finally, we have seen that in a number of cases the credibility and Bayesian premiums are the same. This leaves two questions. Is the additional error caused by using the credibility premium in place of the Bayesian premium worth worrying about? Is it worthwhile to go through the bother of using credibility in the first place? While the exact answer to these questions depends on the underlying distributions, we can obtain some feel for the answers by considering two examples.

We begin with the second question and use a common situation that has already been discussed. What makes credibility work is that we expect to perform numerous estimations. As a result, we are willing to be biased in any one estimation provided that the biases cancel out over the numerous estimations. This allows us to reduce variability and, therefore, squared error. The following example shows the power of credibility in this setting.

Example 16.31 *Suppose there are* 50 *occasions on which we obtain a random sample of size* 10 *from a Poisson distribution with unknown mean. The samples are from different Poisson populations and therefore may involve different means. Let the true means be* $\theta_1, \ldots, \theta_{50}$. *Further assume that the Poisson parameters are drawn from a gamma distribution with parameters* $\alpha = 50$ *and* $\beta = 0.1$. *Compare the maximum likelihood estimates* $\bar{X}_j, j = 1, \ldots, 50$, *to the credibility estimates* $C_j = (\bar{X}_j + 5)/2$. *Note that this is the Bühlmann credibility estimate.*

We will first analyze the two estimates by determining their respective mean-squared errors. Using the sample mean the total squared error is, where

$$\Theta = (\Theta_1, \dots, \Theta_{50}),$$

$$S_1 = \sum_{j=1}^{50} (\bar{X}_j - \Theta_j)^2,$$

and the mean-squared error is

$$E(S_1) = E[E(S_1|\Theta)] = E\left[\sum_{j=1}^{50} \text{Var}(\bar{X}_j|\Theta_j)\right] = E\left(\sum_{j=1}^{50} \frac{\Theta_j}{10}\right) = 25.$$

Using the credibility estimator, the squared error is

$$S_2 = \sum_{j=1}^{50} (0.5\bar{X}_j + 2.5 - \Theta_j)^2$$

and the mean-squared error is

$$
\begin{aligned}
E(S_2) &= E[E(S_2|\Theta)] \\
&= E\left[\sum_{j=1}^{50} E(0.25\bar{X}_j^2 + 6.25 + \Theta_j^2 + 2.5\bar{X}_j - 5\Theta_j - \bar{X}_j\Theta_j|\Theta_j)\right] \\
&= E\left\{\sum_{j=1}^{50}\left[0.25\left(\frac{\Theta_j}{10} + \Theta_j^2\right) + 6.25 + \Theta_j^2 + 2.5\Theta_j - 5\Theta_j - \Theta_j^2\right]\right\} \\
&= \sum_{j=1}^{50} [0.25(0.5 + 25.5) + 6.25 + 25.5 + 2.5(5) - 5(5) - 25.5] \\
&= 12.5.
\end{aligned}
$$

Of course, we "cheated" a bit. We used squared error as our criterion and so knew in advance that the Bühlmann estimate would have the smaller value given that it is competing against another linear estimator. The interesting part is the significant improvement that resulted. This means that, even if the components of the credibility formula Z and μ were not set at their optimal values, the credibility formula is still likely to result in an improvement.

To get a feel for how this improvement comes about, consider a specific set of 50 values of θ_j. The ones presented in Table 16.3 are a random sample from the prior gamma distribution sorted in increasing order. The next column provides the mean-squared error of the sample mean ($\theta_j/10$). The final three columns provide the bias, variance, and mean-squared error for the credibility estimator based on $Z = 0.5$ and $\mu = 5$. The sample mean is always unbiased and therefore the variance matches the mean-squared error and so these two

Table 16.3   A comparison of the sample mean and the credibility estimator

θ	$\bar{X}$ MSE	$0.5\bar{X}+2.5$ Bias	Var.	MSE	θ	$\bar{X}$ MSE	$0.5\bar{X}+2.5$ Bias	Var.	MSE
3.510	.351	.745	.088	.643	4.875	.488	.062	.122	.126
3.637	.364	.681	.091	.555	4.894	.489	.053	.122	.125
3.742	.374	.629	.094	.489	4.900	.490	.050	.123	.125
3.764	.376	.618	.094	.476	4.943	.494	.028	.124	.124
3.793	.379	.604	.095	.459	4.977	.498	.012	.124	.125
4.000	.400	.500	.100	.350	5.002	.500	−.001	.125	.125
4.151	.415	.424	.104	.284	5.013	.501	−.006	.125	.125
4.153	.415	.424	.104	.283	5.108	.511	−.054	.128	.131
4.291	.429	.354	.107	.233	5.172	.517	−.086	.129	.137
4.405	.440	.298	.110	.199	5.198	.520	−.099	.130	.140
4.410	.441	.295	.110	.197	5.231	.523	−.116	.131	.144
4.413	.441	.293	.110	.196	5.239	.524	−.120	.131	.145
4.430	.443	.285	.111	.192	5.263	.526	−.132	.132	.149
4.438	.444	.281	.111	.190	5.300	.530	−.150	.132	.155
4.471	.447	.264	.112	.182	5.338	.534	−.169	.133	.162
4.491	.449	.254	.112	.177	5.400	.540	−.200	.135	.175
4.495	.449	.253	.112	.176	5.407	.541	−.203	.135	.176
4.505	.451	.247	.113	.174	5.431	.543	−.215	.136	.182
4.547	.455	.227	.114	.165	5.459	.546	−.229	.136	.189
4.606	.461	.197	.115	.154	5.510	.551	−.255	.138	.203
4.654	.465	.173	.116	.146	5.538	.554	−.269	.138	.211
4.758	.476	.121	.119	.134	5.646	.565	−.323	.141	.246
4.763	.476	.118	.119	.133	5.837	.584	−.419	.146	.321
4.766	.477	.117	.119	.133	5.937	.594	−.468	.148	.368
4.796	.480	.102	.120	.130	6.263	.626	−.631	.157	.555
					Mean	.482	.091	.120	.222

quantities are not presented. For the credibility estimator,

$$\text{Bias} = E(0.5\bar{X}_j + 2.5 - \theta_j) = 2.5 - 0.5\theta_j,$$

$$\text{Variance} = \text{Var}(0.5\bar{X}_j + 2.5) = \frac{0.25\theta_j}{10} = 0.025\theta_j,$$

$$\text{Mean-squared error} = \text{bias}^2 + \text{variance} = 0.25\theta_j^2 - 2.475\theta_j + 6.25.$$

We see that, as expected, the average mean-squared error is much lower for the credibility estimator, and this is achieved by allowing for some bias in the individual estimators. Further note that the credibility estimator is at its best near the mean of the prior distribution (5).   □

We have seen that there is real value in using credibility. Our next task is to compare the linear credibility estimator to the Bayesian estimator. In most examples, this is difficult because the Bayesian estimates must be obtained by approximate integration. An alternative would be to explore the mean squared errors by simulation. This approach is taken in an illustration presented in *Foundations of Casualty Actuarial Science* [24], p. 467. In the following example we use the same illustration but employ an approximation that avoids approximate integration. It should also be noted that the linear credibility approach requires only assumptions or estimation of the first two moments while the Bayesian approach requires the distributions to be completely specified. This nonparametric feature makes the linear approach more robust, which may compensate for any loss of accuracy.

Example 16.32 *Individual observations are samples of size 25 from an inverse gamma distribution with $\alpha = 4$ and unknown scale parameter Θ. The prior distribution for Θ is gamma with mean 50 and variance 5,000. Compare the linear credibility and Bayesian estimators.*

For the Bühlmann linear credibility estimator we have

$$\mu = \mathrm{E}[\mu(\Theta)] = \mathrm{E}\left(\frac{\Theta}{3}\right) = \frac{50}{3},$$

$$a = \mathrm{Var}[\mu(\Theta)] = \mathrm{Var}\left(\frac{\Theta}{3}\right) = \frac{5,000}{9},$$

$$v = \mathrm{E}[v(\Theta)] = \mathrm{E}\left(\frac{\Theta^2}{18}\right) = \frac{5,000 + 50^2}{18} = \frac{7,500}{18},$$

and so

$$Z = \frac{25}{25 + \dfrac{7,500/18}{5,000/9}} = \frac{100}{103}$$

and the credibility estimator is $\hat{\mu}_{\mathrm{cred}} = (100\bar{X} + 50)/103$.

For the Bayesian estimator, the posterior density is

$$\pi_{\Theta|\mathbf{x}}(\theta|\mathbf{x}) \propto e^{-\theta \sum_{j=1}^{25} x_j^{-1}} \theta^{100} \theta^{-0.5} e^{-\theta/100}$$

$$\propto \theta^{99.5} e^{-\theta(0.01 + \sum_{j=1}^{25} x_j^{-1})},$$

which is a gamma density with parameters 100.5 and $\left(0.01 + \sum_{j=1}^{25} x_j^{-1}\right)^{-1}$. The posterior mean is

$$\hat{\theta}_{\mathrm{Bayes}} = \frac{100.5}{0.01 + \sum_{j=1}^{25} x_j^{-1}} \quad \text{and so} \quad \hat{\mu}_{\mathrm{Bayes}} = \frac{33.5}{0.01 + \sum_{j=1}^{25} x_j^{-1}},$$

which is clearly a nonlinear estimator.

With regard to accuracy, we can also consider the sample mean. Given the value of θ, the sample mean is unbiased with variance and mean squared error

$\theta^2/(18 \times 25) = \theta^2/450$. For the credibility estimator the bias is

$$\begin{aligned}
\text{bias}_\theta(\hat{\mu}_{\text{cred}}) &= \text{E}\left(\frac{100\bar{X}}{103} + \frac{50}{103} - \frac{\theta}{3}\right) \\
&= \frac{100\theta}{309} + \frac{50}{103} - \frac{\theta}{3} \\
&= \frac{50}{103} - \frac{\theta}{103},
\end{aligned}$$

the variance is

$$\text{Var}_\theta(\hat{\mu}_{\text{cred}}) = \frac{(100/103)^2\theta^2}{450},$$

and the mean-squared error is

$$\text{MSE}_\theta(\hat{\mu}_{\text{cred}}) = \frac{1}{103^2}\left(2{,}500 - 100\theta + \frac{10{,}450\theta^2}{450}\right).$$

For the Bayes estimate we observe that, given θ, $1/X$ has a gamma distribution with parameters 4 and $1/\theta$. Therefore, $\sum_{j=1}^{25} X_j^{-1}$ has a gamma distribution with parameters 100 and $1/\theta$. We note that in the denominator of $\hat{\mu}_{\text{Bayes}}$, the term 0.01 will usually be small relative to the sum. An approximation can be created by ignoring this term, in which case $\hat{\mu}_{\text{Bayes}}$ has approximately an inverse gamma distribution with parameters 100 and 33.5θ. Then

$$\begin{aligned}
\text{Bias}_\theta(\hat{\mu}_{\text{Bayes}}) &= \frac{33.5\theta}{99} - \frac{\theta}{3} = \frac{0.5\theta}{99}, \\
\text{Var}_\theta(\hat{\mu}_{\text{Bayes}}) &= \frac{33.5^2\theta^2}{99^2(98)}, \\
\text{MSE}_\theta(\hat{\mu}_{\text{Bayes}}) &= \frac{33.5^2 + 49/2}{99^2(98)}\theta^2 = 0.0011939\theta^2.
\end{aligned}$$

If we compare the coefficients of θ^2 in the MSE for the three estimators, we see that they are 0.00222 for the sample mean, 0.00219 for the credibility estimator, and 0.00119 for the Bayesian estimator. Thus for large θ the credibility estimator is not much of an improvement over the sample mean, but the Bayesian estimator cuts the mean squared error about in half. Calculated values of these quantities for various percentiles from the gamma prior distribution appear in Table 16.4. □

The inferior behavior of the credibility estimator when compared with the Bayes estimator is due to the heavy tails of the two distributions. One way to lighten the tail is to work with the logarithm of the data. This idea was proposed in *Foundations of Casualty Actuarial Science* [24] and evaluated for the above example. The idea is to work with the logarithms of the data and

Table 16.4   A comparison of the sample mean, credibility, and Bayes estimators

Percentile	θ	$\bar{X}$ MSE	$\hat{\mu}_{\text{cred}}$ Bias	MSE	$\hat{\mu}_{\text{Bayes}}$ Bias	MSE
1	0.008	0.000	0.485	0.236	0.000	0.000
5	0.197	0.000	0.484	0.234	0.001	0.000
10	0.790	0.001	0.478	0.230	0.004	0.001
25	5.077	0.057	0.436	0.244	0.026	0.031
50	22.747	1.150	0.265	1.154	0.115	0.618
75	66.165	9.729	−0.157	9.195	0.334	5.227
90	135.277	40.667	−0.828	39.018	0.683	21.849
95	192.072	81.982	−1.379	79.178	0.970	44.046
99	331.746	244.568	−2.735	238.011	1.675	131.397

use linear credibility to estimate the mean of the distribution of logarithms. The result is then exponentiated. Because this procedure is sure to introduce bias,[5] a multiplicative adjustment is made. The results are presented in the following example with many of the details left for Exercise 16.57.

Example 16.33 (Example 16.32 continued) *Obtain the log-credibility estimator and evaluate its bias and mean-squared error.*

Let $W_j = \ln X_j$. Then for the credibility on the logarithms

$$
\begin{aligned}
\mu(\Theta) &= \mathrm{E}(W|\Theta) \\
&= \int_0^\infty (\ln x)\Theta^4 x^{-5} e^{-\Theta/x} \tfrac{1}{6}\, dx \\
&= \int_0^\infty (\ln \Theta - \ln y) y^3 e^{-y} \tfrac{1}{6}\, dy \\
&= \ln \Theta - \Psi(4),
\end{aligned}
$$

where the second integral was obtained using the substitution $y = \Theta/x$. The last line follows from observing that the term $y^3 e^{-y}/6$ is a gamma density and thus integrates to 1 while the second term is the **digamma** function (see Exercise 16.57) and using tables in [3] we have $\Psi(4) = 1.25612$. The next

---

[5] By Jensen's inequality, $\mathrm{E}[\ln X] < \ln \mathrm{E}(X)$, and therefore this procedure will underestimate the true value.

required quantity is

$$
\begin{aligned}
v(\Theta) &= \mathrm{E}(W^2|\theta) - \mu(\Theta)^2 \\
&= \int_0^\infty (\ln x)^2 \Theta^4 x^{-5} e^{-\Theta/x} \tfrac{1}{6}\, dx - [\ln\Theta - \Psi(4)]^2 \\
&= \int_0^\infty (\ln\Theta - \ln y)^2 y^3 e^{-y} \tfrac{1}{6}\, dy - [\ln\Theta - \Psi(4)]^2 \\
&= \Psi'(4),
\end{aligned}
$$

where $\Psi'(4) = 0.283823$ is the **trigamma** function (see Exercise 16.57). Then

$$
\begin{aligned}
\mu &= \mathrm{E}[\ln\Theta - \Psi(4)] \\
&= \int_0^\infty (\ln\theta)\theta^{-0.5} e^{-\theta/100} 100^{-0.5} \frac{1}{\Gamma(0.5)}\, d\theta - \Psi(4) \\
&= \int_0^\infty (\ln 100 + \ln\lambda)\lambda^{-0.5} e^{-\lambda} \frac{1}{\Gamma(0.5)}\, d\lambda - \Psi(4) \\
&= \ln 100 + \Psi(0.5) - \Psi(4) = 1.38554.
\end{aligned}
$$

Also,

$$
\begin{aligned}
v &= \mathrm{E}[\Psi'(4)] = \Psi'(4) = 0.283823 \\
a &= \mathrm{Var}[\ln\Theta - \Psi(4)] \\
&= \Psi'(0.5) = 4.934802 \\
Z &= \frac{25}{25 + \dfrac{0.283823}{4.934802}} = 0.997705.
\end{aligned}
$$

The log-credibility estimate is

$$
\hat\mu_{\text{log-cred}} = c\exp(0.997705\bar{W} + 0.00318024).
$$

The value of c is obtained by setting

$$
\begin{aligned}
\mathrm{E}(X) = \tfrac{50}{3} &= c\mathrm{E}[\exp(0.997705\bar{W} + 0.00318024)] \\
&= ce^{0.00318024}\mathrm{E}\left[\exp\left(\frac{0.997705}{25}\sum_{j=1}^{25}\ln X_j\right)\right] \\
&= ce^{0.00318024}\mathrm{E}\left[\mathrm{E}\left(\prod_{j=1}^{25} X_j^{0.997705/25}\Big|\Theta\right)\right].
\end{aligned}
$$

Given Θ, the X_js are independent and so the expected product is the product of the expected values. From Appendix A, the kth moment of the inverse gamma distribution produces

$$
\frac{50}{3} = ce^{0.00318024} E\left\{\left[\tfrac{1}{6}\Theta^{0.997705/25}\Gamma\left(4 - \frac{0.997705}{25}\right)\right]^{25}\right\}
$$

$$
= ce^{0.00318024}\left[\tfrac{1}{6}\Gamma\left(4 - \frac{0.997705}{25}\right)\right]^{25}\frac{100^{0.997705}\Gamma(0.5 + 0.997705)}{\Gamma(0.5)},
$$

which produces $c = 1.169318$ and

$$
\hat{\mu}_{\text{log-cred}} = 1.173043(2.712051)^{\bar{W}}.
$$

In order to evaluate the bias and mean-squared error for a given value of Θ, we must obtain

$$
\begin{aligned}
\mathrm{E}(\hat{\mu}_{\text{log-cred}}|\Theta = \theta) &= 1.173043\mathrm{E}\left(e^{\bar{W}\ln 2.712051}|\Theta = \theta\right)\\[2mm]
&= 1.173043\mathrm{E}\left[\prod_{j=1}^{25} X_j^{(\ln 2.712051)/25}|\Theta = \theta\right]\\[2mm]
&= 1.173043\left[\tfrac{1}{6}\theta^{(\ln 2.712051)/25}\Gamma\left(4 - \frac{\ln 2.712051}{25}\right)\right]^{25}
\end{aligned}
$$

and

$$
\begin{aligned}
\mathrm{E}(\hat{\mu}^2_{\text{log-cred}}|\Theta = \theta) &= 1.173043^2\mathrm{E}\left(e^{2\bar{W}\ln 2.712051}|\Theta = \theta\right)\\[2mm]
&= 1.173043^2\left[\tfrac{1}{6}\theta^{(2\ln 2.712051)/25}\Gamma\left(4 - \frac{2\ln 2.712051}{25}\right)\right]^{25}.
\end{aligned}
$$

The measures of quality are then

$$
\begin{aligned}
\mathrm{Bias}_\theta(\hat{\mu}_{\text{log-cred}}) &= \mathrm{E}(\hat{\mu}_{\text{log-cred}}|\Theta = \theta) - \tfrac{1}{3}\theta,\\
\mathrm{MSE}_\theta(\hat{\mu}_{\text{log-cred}}) &= \mathrm{E}(\hat{\mu}^2_{\text{log-cred}}|\Theta = \theta) - [\mathrm{E}(\hat{\mu}_{\text{log-cred}}|\Theta = \theta)]^2\\
&\quad + [\mathrm{bias}_\theta(\hat{\mu}_{\text{log-cred}})]^2.
\end{aligned}
$$

Values of these quantities are calculated for various values of θ in Table 16.5. A comparison with Table 16.4 indicates that the log-credibility estimator is almost as good as the Bayes estimator.   □

In practice, log-credibility is as easy to use as ordinary credibility. In either case, one of the computational methods of the next section would be used. For log-credibility, the logarithms of the observations are substituted for the observed values and then the final estimate is exponentiated. The bias is corrected by multiplying all the estimates by a constant such that the sample mean of the estimates matches the sample mean of the original data.

Table 16.5 Bias and mean squared error for the log-credibility estimator

Percentile	θ	Bias	MSE
1	0.008	0.000	0.000
5	0.197	0.001	0.000
10	0.790	0.003	0.001
25	5.077	0.012	0.034
50	22.747	0.026	0.666
75	66.165	0.023	5.604
90	135.277	−0.028	23.346
95	192.072	−0.091	46.995
99	331.746	−0.295	139.908

16.4.8 Notes and References

In this section, one of the two major criticisms of limited fluctuation credibility has been addressed. Through the use of the variance of the hypothetical means, we now have a means of relating the mean of the group of interest, $\mu(\theta)$, to the manual, or collective, premium, μ. The development was also mathematically sound in that the results followed directly from a specific model and objective. We have also seen that the additional restriction of a linear solution was not as bad as it might be in that often we still obtain the exact Bayesian solution. There has subsequently been a great deal of effort expended to generalize the model. With a sound basis for obtaining a credibility premium, we have but one remaining obstacle: how to numerically estimate the quantities a and v in the Bühlmann formulation, or how to specify the prior distribution in the Bayesian formulation. Those matters are addressed in the final section of this chapter.

A historical review of credibility theory including a description of the limited fluctuation and greatest accuracy approaches is provided by Norberg [100]. Since the classic paper of Bühlmann [18], there has developed a vast literature on credibility theory in the actuarial literature. Other elementary introductions are given by Herzog [52] and Waters [135]. Other more advanced treatments are Goovaerts and Hoogstad [46] and Sundt [127]. An important generalization of the Bühlmann–Straub model is the Hachemeister [48] regression model, which was not discussed here. See also Klugman [76]. The material on exact credibility is taken from Jewell [66]. See also Ericson [34]. A special issue of *Insurance: Abstracts and Reviews* (Sundt [126]) contains an extensive list of papers on credibility.

16.4.9   Exercises

16.22 Consider a die–spinner model. The first die has one "marked" face and five "unmarked" faces whereas the second die has four "marked" faces and two "unmarked" faces. There are three spinners, each with five equally spaced sectors marked 3 or 8. The first spinner has one sector marked 3 and four marked 8, the second has two marked 3 and three marked 8, and the third has four marked 3 and one marked 8. One die and one spinner are selected at random. If rolling the die produces an unmarked face, no claim occurs. If a marked face occurs, there is a claim and then the spinner is spun once to determine the amount of the claim.

(a) Determine $\pi(\theta)$ for each of the six die–spinner combinations.

(b) Determine the conditional distributions $f_{X|\Theta}(x|\theta)$ for the claim sizes for each die–spinner combination.

(c) Determine the hypothetical means $\mu(\theta)$ and the process variances $v(\theta)$ for each θ.

(d) Determine the marginal probability that the claim X_1 on the first iteration equals 3.

(e) Determine the posterior distribution $\pi_{\Theta|X_1}(\theta|3)$ of Θ using Bayes' theorem.

(f) Use (16.25) to determine the conditional distribution $f_{X_2|X_1}(x_2|3)$ of the claims X_2 on the second iteration given that $X_1 = 3$ was observed on the first iteration.

(g) Use (16.28) to determine the Bayesian premium $E(X_2|X_1 = 3)$.

(h) Determine the joint probability that $X_2 = x_2$ and $X_1 = 3$ for $x_2 = 0, 3, 8$.

(i) Determine the conditional distribution $f_{X_2|X_1}(x_2|3)$ directly using (16.23) and compare your answer to that of (f).

(j) Determine the Bayesian premium directly using (16.27) and compare your answer to that of (g).

(k) Determine the structural parameters μ, v, and a.

(l) Compute the Bühlmann credibility factor and the Bühlmann credibility premium to approximate the Bayesian premium $E(X_2|X_1 = 3)$.

16.23 Three urns have balls marked 0, 1, and 2 in the proportions given in Table 16.6. An urn is selected at random, and two balls are drawn from that urn with replacement. A total of 2 on the two balls is observed. Two more balls are then drawn with replacement from the same urn, and it is of interest to predict the total on these next two balls.

(a) Determine $\pi(\theta)$.

Table 16.6   Data for Exercise 16.23

Urn	0s	1s	2s
1	0.40	0.35	0.25
2	0.25	0.10	0.65
3	0.50	0.15	0.35

(b) Determine the conditional distributions $f_{X|\Theta}(x|\theta)$ for the totals on the two balls for each urn.

(c) Determine the hypothetical means $\mu(\theta)$ and the process variances $v(\theta)$ for each θ.

(d) Determine the marginal probability that the total X_1 on the first two balls equals 2.

(e) Determine the posterior distribution $\pi_{\Theta|X_1}(\theta|2)$ using Bayes' theorem.

(f) Use (16.25) to determine the conditional distribution $f_{X_2|X_1}(x_2|2)$ of the total X_2 on the next two balls drawn given that $X_1 = 2$ was observed on the first two draws.

(g) Use (16.28) to determine the Bayesian premium $E(X_2|X_1 = 2)$.

(h) Determine the joint probability that the total X_2 on the next two balls equals x_2 and the total X_1 on the first two balls equals 2 for $x_2 = 0, 1, 2, 3, 4$.

(i) Determine the conditional distribution $f_{X_2|X_1}(x_2|2)$ directly using (16.23) and compare your answer to that of (f).

(j) Determine the Bayesian premium directly using (16.27) and compare your answer to that of (g).

(k) Determine the structural parameters μ, v, and a.

(l) Determine the Bühlmann credibility factor and the Bühlmann credibility premium.

(m) Show that the Bühlmann credibility factor is the same if each "exposure unit" consists of one draw from the urn rather than two draws.

16.24 Suppose that there are two types of policyholder: type A and type B. Two-thirds of the total number of the policyholders are of type A and one-third are of type B. For each type, the information on annual claim numbers and severity are given as follows:

A policyholder has a total claim amount of 500 in the last four years. Determine the credibility factor Z and the credibility premium for next year for this policyholder.

Type	Number of claims Mean	Number of claims Variance	Severity Mean	Severity Variance
A	0.2	0.2	200	4,000
B	0.7	0.3	100	1,500

16.25 Let Θ_1 represent the risk factor for claim numbers and let Θ_2 represent the risk factor for the claim severity for a line of insurance. Suppose that Θ_1 and Θ_2 are independent. Suppose also that given $\Theta_1 = \theta_1$ the claim number N is Poisson distributed and given $\Theta_2 = \theta_2$ the severity Y is exponentially distributed. The expectations of the hypothetical means and process variances for the claim number and severity as well as the variance of the hypothetical means for frequency are respectively

$$\mu_N = 0.1, \qquad v_N = 0.1, \qquad a_N = 0.05,$$
$$\mu_Y = 100, \qquad v_Y = 25,000.$$

Three observations are made on a particular policyholder and we observe total claims of 200. Determine the Bühlmann credibility factor and the Bühlmann premium for this policyholder.

16.26 Suppose that $X_1, \ldots, X_n$ are independent (conditional on Θ) and that

$$E(X_j|\Theta) = \beta_j \mu(\Theta) \quad \text{and} \quad \text{Var}(X_j|\Theta) = \tau_j(\Theta) + \psi_j v(\Theta), \quad j = 1, \ldots, n.$$

Let

$$\mu = E[\mu(\Theta)], \quad v = E[v(\Theta)], \quad \tau_j = E[\tau_j(\Theta)], \quad a = \text{Var}[\mu(\Theta)].$$

(a) Show that

$$E(X_j) = \beta_j \mu, \quad \text{Var}(X_j) = \tau_j + \psi_j v + \beta_j^2 a,$$

and

$$\text{Cov}(X_i, X_j) = \beta_i \beta_j a, \quad i \neq j.$$

(b) Solve the normal equations for $\tilde{\alpha}_0, \tilde{\alpha}_1, \ldots, \tilde{\alpha}_n$ to show that the credibility premium satisfies

$$\tilde{\alpha}_0 + \sum_{j=1}^{n} \tilde{\alpha}_j X_j = (1 - Z) E(X_{n+1}) + Z\beta_{n+1}\bar{X},$$

where

$$m_j = \beta_j^2(\tau_j + \psi_j v)^{-1}, \quad j = 1, \ldots, n,$$
$$m = m_1 + \cdots + m_n,$$
$$Z = am(1 + am)^{-1},$$
$$\bar{X} = \sum_{j=1}^{n} \frac{m_j}{m} \frac{X_j}{\beta_j}.$$

16.27 For the situation described in Exercise 12.72 determine $\mu(\theta)$ and the Bayesian premium $E(X_{n+1}|\mathbf{x})$. Why is the Bayesian premium equal to the credibility premium?

16.28 For the situation described in Exercise 12.73 determine $\mu(\theta)$ and the Bayesian premium $E(X_{n+1}|\mathbf{x})$ and verify directly that the credibility premium equals the Bayesian premium.

16.29 For the situation described in Exercise 12.74 determine $\mu(\theta)$ and the Bayesian premium $E(X_{n+1}|\mathbf{x})$ and verify directly that the credibility premium equals the Bayesian premium.

16.30 Consider the generalization of the linear exponential family given by

$$f(x;\theta,m) = \frac{p(m,x)e^{-m\theta x}}{[q(\theta)]^m}.$$

If m is a parameter, this is called the **exponential dispersion family**. In Exercise 12.79 it was shown that the mean of this random variable is $-q'(\theta)/q(\theta)$. For this exercise, assume that m is known.

(a) Consider the prior distribution

$$\pi(\theta) = \frac{[q(\theta)]^{-k}\exp(-\theta\mu k)}{c(\mu,k)}, \quad \theta_0 < \theta < \theta_1 \text{ with } \pi(\theta_0) = \pi(\theta_1).$$

Determine the Bayesian premium.

(b) Using the same prior, determine the Bühlmann premium.

(c) Show that the inverse Gaussian distribution is a member of the exponential dispersion family.

16.31 Suppose that $X_1 \ldots, X_n$ are independent (conditional on Θ) and

$$E(X_j|\Theta) = \tau^j\mu(\Theta) \quad \text{and} \quad \text{Var}(X_j|\Theta) = \frac{\tau^{2j}v(\Theta)}{m_j}, \quad j = 1,\ldots,n.$$

Let $\mu = E[\mu(\Theta)]$, $v = E[v(\Theta)]$, $a = \text{Var}[\mu(\Theta)]$, $k = v/a$, and $m = m_1 + \cdots + m_n$.

(a) Discuss when these assumptions may be appropriate.

(b) Show that

$$E(X_j) = \tau^j\mu, \quad \text{Var}(X_j) = \tau^{2j}(a + v/m_j),$$

and

$$\text{Cov}(X_i, X_j) = \tau^{i+j}a, \quad i \neq j.$$

(c) Solve the normal equations for $\tilde{\alpha}_0, \tilde{\alpha}_1, \ldots, \tilde{\alpha}_n$ to show that the credibility premium satisfies

$$\tilde{\alpha}_0 + \sum_{j=1}^{n} \tilde{\alpha}_j X_j = \frac{k}{k+m} \tau^{n+1} \mu + \frac{m}{k+m} \sum_{j=1}^{n} \frac{m_j}{m} \tau^{n+1-j} X_j.$$

(d) Give a verbal interpretation of the formula in (c).

(e) Suppose that

$$f_{X_j|\Theta}(x_j|\theta) = \frac{p(x_j, m_j, \tau)e^{-m_j\tau^{-j}x_j\theta}}{[q(\theta)]^{m_j}}.$$

Show that $E(X_j|\Theta) = \tau^j \mu(\Theta)$ and that $\operatorname{Var}(X_j|\Theta) = \tau^{2j} v(\Theta)/m_j$, where $\mu(\theta) = -\frac{d}{d\theta} \ln q(\theta)$ and $v(\theta) = -\mu'(\theta)$.

(f) Prove that credibility is exact if Θ has pdf

$$\pi(\theta) = \frac{[q(\theta)]^{-k}e^{-\theta\mu k}}{c(\mu, k)}, \qquad \theta_0 < \theta < \theta_1,$$

which satisfies $\pi(\theta_0) = \pi(\theta_1) = 0$.

16.32 Suppose that given $\Theta = \theta$ the random variables $X_1, \cdots, X_n$ are independent with Poisson pf

$$f_{X_j|\Theta}(x_j|\theta) = \frac{\theta^{x_j} e^{-\theta}}{x_j!}, \qquad x_j = 0, 1, 2, \ldots .$$

(a) Let $S = X_1 + \cdots + X_n$. Show that S has pf

$$f_S(s) = \int_0^\infty \frac{(n\theta)^s e^{-n\theta}}{s!} \pi(\theta)\, d\theta, \qquad s = 0, 1, 2, \ldots,$$

where Θ has pdf $\pi(\theta)$.

(b) Show that the Bayesian premium is

$$E(X_{n+1}|X_1 + \cdots + X_n = s) = \frac{s+1}{n} \frac{f_S(s+1)}{f_S(s)},$$

where $s = \sum_{j=1}^{n} x_j$.

(c) Evaluate the distribution of S in (a) when $\pi(\theta)$ is a gamma distribution. What type of distribution is this?

16.33 Suppose $X_j|\Theta$ is normally distributed with mean Θ and variance v for $j = 1, 2, \ldots, n+1$. Further suppose Θ is normally distributed with mean μ and variance a. Thus,

$$f_{X_j|\Theta}(x_j|\theta) = (2\pi v)^{-1/2} \exp\left[-\frac{1}{2v}(x_j - \theta)^2\right], \qquad -\infty < x_j < \infty,$$

and

$$\pi(\theta) = (2\pi a)^{-1/2} \exp\left[-\frac{1}{2a}(\theta - \mu)^2\right], \quad -\infty < \theta < \infty.$$

Determine the posterior distribution of $\Theta|\mathbf{X}$ and the predictive distribution of $X_{n+1}|\mathbf{X}$. Then determine the Bayesian estimate of $E(X_{n+1}|\mathbf{X})$. Finally, show that the Bayesian and Bühlmann estimates are equal.

16.34 (*) Your friend selected at random one of two urns and then she pulled a ball with number 4 on it from the urn. Then she replaced the ball in the urn. One of the urns contains four balls, numbered 1–4. The other urn contains six balls, numbered 1–6. Your friend will make another random selection from the same urn.

(a) Estimate the expected value of the number on the next ball using the Bayesian method.

(b) Estimate the expected number on the next ball using Bühlmann credibility.

16.35 The number of claims for a randomly selected insured has the Poisson distribution with parameter θ. The parameter θ is distributed across the population with pdf $\pi(\theta) = 3\theta^{-4}$, $\theta > 1$. For an individual, the parameter does not change over time. A particular insured experienced a total of 20 claims in the previous two years.

(a) (*) Determine the Bühlmann credibility estimate for the future expected claim frequency for this particular insured.

(b) Determine the Bayesian credibility estimate for the future expected claim frequency for this particular insured.

16.36 (*) The distribution of payments to an insured is constant over time. If the Bühlmann credibility assigned for one-half year of observation is 0.5, determine the Bühlmann credibility to be assigned for three years.

16.37 (*) Three urns contain balls marked either 0 or 1. In urn A, 10% are marked 0; in urn B, 60% are marked 0; and in urn C, 80% are marked 0. An urn is selected at random and three balls selected with replacement. The total of the values is 1. Three more balls are selected with replacement from the same urn.

(a) Determine the expected total of the three balls using Bayes' theorem.

(b) Determine the expected total of the three balls using Bühlmann credibility.

16.38 (*) The number of claims follows the Poisson distribution with parameter λ. A particular insured had three claims in the past three years.

(a) The value of λ has pdf $f(\lambda) = 4\lambda^{-5}$, $\lambda > 1$. Determine the value of K used in Bühlmann's credibility formula. Then use Bühlmann credibility to estimate the claim frequency for this insured.

(b) The value of λ has pdf $f(\lambda) = 1$, $0 < \lambda < 1$. Determine the value of K used in Bühlmann's credibility formula. Then use Bühlmann credibility to estimate the claim frequency for this insured.

16.39 (*) The number of claims follows the Poisson distribution with parameter h. The value of h has the gamma distribution with pdf $f(h) = he^{-h}$, $h > 0$. Determine the Bühlmann credibility to be assigned to a single observation. (The Bayes solution was obtained in Exercise 12.86.)

16.40 Consider the situation of Exercise 12.88.

(a) Determine the expected number of claims in the second year using Bayesian credibility.

(b) (*) Determine the expected number of claims in the second year using Bühlmann credibility.

16.41 (*) One spinner is selected at random from a group of three spinners. Each spinner is divided into six equally likely sectors. The number of sectors marked 0, 12, and 48, respectively, on each spinner is as follows: spinner A: 2,2,2; spinner B: 3,2,1; spinner C: 4,1,1. A spinner is selected at random and a zero is obtained on the first spin.

(a) Determine the Bühlmann credibility estimate of the expected value of the second spin using the same spinner.

(b) Determine the Bayesian credibility estimate of the expected value of the second spin using the same spinner.

16.42 The number of claims in a year has the Poisson distribution with mean λ. The parameter λ has the uniform distribution over the interval $(1, 3)$.

(a) (*) Determine the probability that a randomly selected individual will have no claims.

(b) (*) If an insured had one claim during the first year, estimate the expected number of claims for the second year using Bühlmann credibility.

(c) If an insured had one claim during the first year, estimate the expected number of claims for the second year using Bayesian credibility.

16.43 (*) Each of two classes, A and B, has the same number of risks. In class A the number of claims per risk per year has mean $\frac{1}{6}$ and variance $\frac{5}{36}$ while the amount of a single claim has mean 4 and variance 20. In class B the number of claims per risk per year has mean $\frac{5}{6}$ and variance $\frac{5}{36}$ while the amount of a single claim has mean 2 and variance 5. A risk is selected at random from one of the two classes and is observed for four years.

(a) Determine the value of Z for Bühlmann credibility for the observed pure premium.

(b) Suppose the pure premium calculated from the four observations is 0.25. Determine the Bühlmann credibility estimate for the risk's pure premium.

16.44 (*) Let X_1 be the outcome of a single trial and let $E(X_2|X_1)$ be the expected value of the outcome of a second trial. You are given the following information:

Outcome, T	$\Pr(X_1 = T)$	Bühlmann estimate of $E(X_2\|X_1 = T)$	Bayesian estimate of $E(X_2\|X_1 = T)$
1	1/3	2.72	2.6
8	1/3	7.71	7.8
12	1/3	10.57	–

Determine the Bayesian estimate for $E(X_2|X_1 = 12)$.

16.45 Consider the situation of Exercise 12.90.

(a) Determine the expected number of claims in the second year using Bayesian credibility.

(b) (*) Determine the expected number of claims in the second year using Bühlmann credibility.

16.46 Consider the situation of Exercise 12.91.

(a) Determine the expected number of claims in the second year using Bayesian credibility.

(b) Determine the expected number of claims in the second year using Bühlmann credibility.

16.47 Two spinners, A_1 and A_2, are used to determine the number of claims. For spinner A_1 there is a 0.15 probability of one claim and 0.85 of no claim. For spinner A_2 there is a 0.05 probability of one claim and 0.95 of no claim. If there is a claim, one of two spinners, B_1 and B_2, is used to determine the amount. Spinner B_1 produces a claim of 20 with probability 0.8 and 40 with probability 0.2. Spinner B_2 produces a claim of 20 with probability 0.3 and 40 with probability 0.7. A spinner is selected at random from each of A_1, A_2 and from B_1, B_2. Three observations from the selected pair yields claims amounts of 0, 20, and 0.

(a) (*) Use Bühlmann credibility to separately estimate the expected number of claims and the expected severity. Use these estimates to estimate the expected value of the next observation from the same pair of spinners.

(b) Use Bühlmann credibility once on the three observations to estimate the expected value of the next observation from the same pair of spinners.

(c) (*) Repeat parts (a) and (b) using Bayesian estimation.

(d) (*) For the same selected pair of spinners, determine

$$\lim_{n \to \infty} E(X_n | X_1 = X_2 = \cdots = X_{n-1} = 0).$$

16.48 (*) A portfolio of risks is such that all risks are normally distributed. Those of type A have a mean of 0.1 and a standard deviation of 0.03. Those of type B have a mean of 0.5 and a standard deviation of 0.05. Those of type C have a mean of 0.9 and a standard deviation of 0.01. There are an equal number of each type of risk. The observed value for a single risk is 0.12. Determine the Bayesian estimate of the same risk's expected value.

16.49 (*) You are given the following:

1. The conditional distribution $f_{X|\Theta}(x|\theta)$ is a member of the linear exponential family.

2. The prior distribution $\pi(\theta)$ is a conjugate prior for $f_{X|\Theta}(x|\theta)$.

3. $E(X) = 1$.

4. $E(X|X_1 = 4) = 2$, where X_1 is the value of a single observation.

5. The expected value of the process variance $E[\text{Var}(X|\Theta)] = 3$

Determine the variance of the hypothetical means $\text{Var}[E(X|\Theta)]$.

16.50 (*) You are given the following:

1. X is a random variable with mean μ and variance v.

2. μ is a random variable with mean 2 and variance 4.

3. v is a random variable with mean 8 and variance 32.

Determine the value of the Bühlmann credibility factor Z after three observations of X.

16.51 The amount of an individual claim has the exponential distribution with pdf $f_{Y|\Lambda}(y|\lambda) = \lambda^{-1}e^{-y/\lambda}$, $y, \lambda > 0$. The parameter λ has the inverse gamma distribution with pdf $\pi(\lambda) = 400\lambda^{-3}e^{-20/\lambda}$.

    (a) (*) Determine the unconditional expected value, $E(X)$.

    (b) Suppose two claims were observed with values 15 and 25. Determine the Bühlmann credibility estimate of the expected value of the next claim from the same insured.

    (c) Repeat part (b), but determine the Bayesian credibility estimate.

16.52 The distribution of the number of claims is binomial with $n = 1$ and θ unknown. The parameter θ is distributed with mean 0.25 and variance 0.07. Determine the value of Z for a single observation using Bühlmann's credibility formula.

16.53 (*) Consider four marksmen. Each is firing at a target that is 100 feet away. The four targets are 2 feet apart (that is, they lie on a straight line at positions 0, 2, 4, and 6 in feet). The marksmen miss to the left or right, never high or low. Each marksman's shot follows a normal distribution with mean at his target and a standard deviation that is a constant times the distance to the target. At 100 feet the standard deviation is 3 feet. By observing where an unknown marksman's shot hits the straight line, you are to estimate the location of the next shot by the same marksman.

    (a) Determine the Bühlmann credibility assigned to a single shot of a randomly selected marksman.

    (b) Which of the following will increase Bühlmann credibility the most?

        i. Revise the targets to 0, 4, 8, and 12.

        ii. Move the marksmen to 60 feet from the targets.

        iii. Revise targets to 2, 2, 10, 10.

        iv. Increase the number of observations from the same marksman to three.

        v. Move two of the marksmen to 50 feet from the targets and increase the number of observations from the same marksman to two.

16.54 (*) Risk 1 produces claims of amounts 100, 1,000, and 20,000 with probabilities 0.5, 0.3, and 0.2, respectively. For risk 2 the probabilities are 0.7, 0.2, and 0.1. Risk 1 is twice as likely as risk 2 of being observed. A claim of 100 is observed, but the observed risk is unknown.

    (a) Determine the Bayesian credibility estimate of the expected value of the second claim amount from the same risk.

    (b) Determine the Bühlmann credibility estimate of the expected value of the second claim amount from the same risk.

16.55 (*) You are given the following:

1. The number of claims for a single insured follows a Poisson distribution with mean M.

2. The amount of a single claim has an exponential distribution with pdf $f_{X|\Lambda}(x|\lambda) = \lambda^{-1}e^{-x/\lambda}$, $x, \lambda > 0$.

3. M and Λ are independent.

4. $E(M) = 0.10$ and $\text{Var}(M) = 0.0025$.

5. $E(\Lambda) = 1,000$ and $\text{Var}(\Lambda) = 640,000$.

6. The number of claims and the claim amounts are independent.

   (a) Determine the expected value of the pure premium's process variance for a single risk.

   (b) Determine the variance of the hypothetical means for the pure premium.

16.56 In Example 16.24, if $\rho = 0$, then $Z = 0$, and the estimator is μ. That is, the data should be ignored. However, as ρ increases toward 1, Z increases to 1, and the sample mean becomes the preferred predictor of X_{n+1}. Explain why this is a reasonable result.

16.57 In this exercise you are asked to derive a number of the items from Example 16.33.

   (a) The **digamma function** is formally defined as $\Psi(\alpha) = \Gamma'(\alpha)/\Gamma(\alpha)$. From this definition, show that

   $$\Psi(\alpha) = \frac{1}{\Gamma(\alpha)} \int_0^\infty (\ln x)x^{\alpha-1}e^{-x}\, dx.$$

   (b) The **trigamma function** is formally defined as $\Psi'(\alpha)$. Derive an expression for

   $$\int_0^\infty (\ln x)^2 x^{\alpha-1}e^{-x}\, dx$$

   in terms of trigamma, digamma, and gamma functions.

16.58 Consider the following situation, which is similar to Examples 16.32 and 16.33. Individual observations are samples of size 25 from a lognormal distribution with μ unknown and $\sigma = 2$. The prior distribution for Θ (using Θ to represent the unknown value of μ) is normal with mean 5 and standard deviation 1. Determine the Bayes, credibility, and log-credibility estimators and compare their mean-squared errors, evaluating them at the same percentiles as used in Examples 16.32 and 16.33.

16.59 In the following, let the random vector $\mathbf{X}$ represent all the past data and let X_{n+1} represent the next observation. Let $g(\mathbf{X})$ be any function of the past data.

(a) Prove that the following is true.

$$
\begin{aligned}
\mathrm{E}\left\{[X_{n+1} - g(\mathbf{X})]^2\right\} &= \mathrm{E}\{[X_{n+1} - \mathrm{E}(X_{n+1}|\mathbf{X})]^2\} \\
&\quad + \mathrm{E}\{[\mathrm{E}(X_{n+1}|\mathbf{X}) - g(\mathbf{X})]^2\},
\end{aligned}
$$

where the expectation is taken over $(X_{n+1}, \mathbf{X})$.

(b) Show that setting $g(\mathbf{X})$ equal to the Bayesian premium (the mean of the predictive distribution) minimizes the expected squared error, $\mathrm{E}\left\{[X_{n+1} - g(\mathbf{X})]^2\right\}$.

(c) Show that, if $g(\mathbf{X})$ is restricted to be a linear function of the past data, then the expected squared error is minimized by the credibility premium.

16.5   EMPIRICAL BAYES PARAMETER ESTIMATION

In the previous section a modeling methodology was proposed which suggested the use of either the Bayesian or credibility premium as a way to incorporate past data into the prospective rate. There is a practical problem associated with the use of these models which has not yet been addressed.

In the examples, we were able to obtain numerical values for the quantities of interest because the input distributions $f_{X_j|\Theta}(x_j|\theta)$ and $\pi(\theta)$ were assumed to be known. These examples, while useful for illustration of the methodology, can hardly be expected to accurately represent the business of an insurance portfolio. More practical models of necessity involve the use of parameters which must be chosen to ensure a close agreement between the model and reality. Examples of this include: the Poisson–gamma model (Example 16.15), where the gamma parameters α and β need to be selected or the Bühlmann or Bühlmann–Straub parameters μ, v, and a. Assignment of numerical values to the Bayesian or credibility premium requires that these parameters be replaced by numerical values.

In general, the unknown parameters are those associated with the structure density $\pi(\theta)$, and hence we refer to these as **structural parameters**. The terminology we use follows the Bayesian framework of the previous section. Strictly speaking, in the Bayesian context all structural parameters are assumed known and there is no need for estimation. An example of this is the Poisson–gamma where our prior information about the structural density was quantified by the choice of $\alpha = 36$ and $\beta = \frac{1}{240}$. For our purposes, this fully Bayesian approach is often unsatisfactory (e.g., when there is little or no prior information available, such as with a new line of insurance) and we may need to use the data at hand to estimate the structural (prior) parameters. This approach is called **empirical Bayes estimation**.

We refer to the situation where $\pi(\theta)$ and $f_{X_j|\Theta}(x_j|\theta)$ are left largely unspecified (for example, in the Bühlmann or Bühlmann–Straub models where only the first two moments need be known) as the nonparametric case. This situation is dealt with in Section 16.5.1. If $f_{X_j|\Theta}(x_j|\theta)$ is assumed to be of parametric form (e.g., Poisson, normal, etc.) but not $\pi(\theta)$, then we refer to the problem as being of a semiparametric nature, and this is considered in Section 16.5.2. Finally, the (technically more difficult) fully parametric case where both $f_{X_j|\Theta}(x_j|\theta)$ and $\pi(\theta)$ are assumed to be of parametric form is briefly discussed in Section 16.5.3.

This decision as to whether to select a parametric model or not depends partially on the situation at hand and partially on the judgment and knowledge of the person doing the analysis. For example, an analysis based on claim counts might involve the assumption that $f_{X_j|\Theta}(x_j|\theta)$ is of Poisson form, whereas the choice of a parametric model for $\pi(\theta)$ may not be reasonable.

Any parametric assumptions should be reflected (as far as possible) in parametric estimation. For example, in the Poisson case, because the mean and variance are equal, the same estimate would normally be used for both. Nonparametric estimators would normally be no more efficient than estimators appropriate for the parametric model selected, assuming that the model selected is appropriate. This notion is relevant for the decision as to whether to select a parametric model.

Finally, nonparametric models have the advantage of being appropriate for a wide variety of situations, a fact which may well eliminate the extra burden of a parametric assumption (often a stronger assumption than is reasonable).

In this section the data are assumed to be of the following form. For each of $r \geq 1$ policyholders we have the observed losses per unit of exposure $\mathbf{X}_i = (X_{i1}, \ldots, X_{in_i})^T$ for $i = 1, \ldots, r$. The random vectors $\{\mathbf{X}_i, i = 1, \ldots, r\}$ are assumed to be statistically independent (experience of different policyholders is assumed to be independent). The (unknown) risk parameter for the ith policyholder is θ_i, $i = 1, \ldots, r$, and it is assumed further that $\theta_1, \ldots, \theta_r$ are realizations of the independent and identically distributed random variables Θ_i with structural density $\pi(\theta_i)$. For fixed i, the (conditional) random variables $X_{ij}|\Theta_i$ are assumed to be independent with pf $f_{X_{ij}|\Theta}(x_{ij}|\theta_i)$, $j = 1, \ldots, n_i$.

Two particularly common cases produce this data format. The first is classification rate making or experience rating. In either, i indexes the classes or groups and j indexes the individual members. The second case is like the first where i continues to index the class or group, but now j is the year and the observation is the average loss for that year. An example of the second setting is Meyers [91], where $i = 1, \ldots, 319$ employment classifications are studied over $j = 1, 2, 3$ years. Regardless of the potential settings, we will refer to the r entities as policyholders.

There may also be a known exposure vector $\mathbf{m}_i = (m_{i1}, m_{i2}, \cdots, m_{in_i})^T$ for policyholder i, where $i = 1, \ldots, r$. If not (and if it is appropriate) one may set $m_{ij} = 1$ in what follows for all i and j. For notational convenience let

$$m_i = \sum_{j=1}^{n_i} m_{ij}, \quad i = 1, \dots, r,$$

be the total past exposure for policyholder i, and let

$$\bar{X}_i = \frac{1}{m_i} \sum_{j=1}^{n_i} m_{ij} X_{ij}, \quad i = 1, \dots, r,$$

be the past average loss experience. Furthermore, the total exposure is

$$m = \sum_{i=1}^{r} m_i = \sum_{i=1}^{r} \sum_{j=1}^{n_i} m_{ij}$$

and the overall average losses are

$$\bar{X} = \frac{1}{m} \sum_{i=1}^{r} m_i \bar{X}_i = \frac{1}{m} \sum_{i=1}^{r} \sum_{j=1}^{n_i} m_{ij} X_{ij}. \tag{16.54}$$

The parameters which need to be estimated depend on what is assumed about the distributions $f_{X_{ij}|\Theta}(x_{ij}|\theta_i)$ and $\pi(\theta)$.

For the Bühlmann–Straub formulation there are additional quantities of interest. The hypothetical mean (assumed not to depend on j) is

$$E(X_{ij}|\Theta_i = \theta_i) = \mu(\theta_i)$$

and the process variance is

$$\mathrm{Var}(X_{ij}|\Theta_i = \theta_i) = \frac{v(\theta_i)}{m_{ij}}.$$

The structural parameters are

$$\mu = E[\mu(\Theta_i)], \quad v = E[v(\Theta_i)],$$

and

$$a = \mathrm{Var}[\mu(\Theta_i)].$$

The approach to be followed in this section is to estimate μ, v, and a (when unknown) from the data. The credibility premium for next year's losses (per exposure unit) for policyholder i is

$$Z_i \bar{X}_i + (1 - Z_i) \mu, \quad i = 1, \dots, r, \tag{16.55}$$

where

$$Z_i = \frac{m_i}{m_i + k}, \quad k = \frac{v}{a}.$$

If estimators of μ, v, and a are denoted by $\hat{\mu}, \hat{v}$, and $\hat{a}$, respectively, then one would replace the credibility premium (16.55) by its estimator

$$\hat{Z}_i \bar{X}_i + (1 - \hat{Z}_i)\hat{\mu}, \tag{16.56}$$

where

$$\hat{Z}_i = \frac{m_i}{m_i + \hat{k}}, \quad \hat{k} = \frac{\hat{v}}{\hat{a}}.$$

Note that, even if $\hat{v}$ and $\hat{a}$ are unbiased estimators of v and a, the same cannot be said of $\hat{k}$ and $\hat{Z}_i$. Finally, the credibility premium to cover all m_{i,n_i+1} exposure units for policyholder i in the next year would be (16.56) multiplied by m_{i,n_i+1}.

16.5.1 Nonparametric estimation

In this section we consider unbiased estimation of μ, v, and a. To illustrate the ideas, let us begin with the following simple Bühlmann-type example.

Example 16.34 *Suppose that $n_i = n > 1$ for all i and $m_{ij} = 1$ for all i and j. That is, for policyholder i, we have the loss vector*

$$\mathbf{X}_i = (X_{i1}, \ldots, X_{in})^T, \quad i = 1, \ldots, r.$$

Furthermore, conditional on $\Theta_i = \theta_i$, X_{ij} has mean

$$\mu(\theta_i) = E(X_{ij}|\Theta_i = \theta_i)$$

and variance

$$v(\theta_i) = \text{Var}(X_{ij}|\Theta_i = \theta_i),$$

and $X_{i1}, \ldots, X_{in}$ are independent (conditionally). Also, different policyholders' past data are independent, so that if $i \neq s$, then X_{ij} and X_{st} are independent. In this case

$$\bar{X}_i = n^{-1} \sum_{j=1}^{n} X_{ij} \text{ and } \bar{X} = r^{-1} \sum_{i=1}^{r} \bar{X}_i = (rn)^{-1} \sum_{i=1}^{r} \sum_{j=1}^{n} X_{ij}.$$

Determine unbiased estimators of the Bühlmann quantities.

An unbiased estimator of μ is

$$\hat{\mu} = \bar{X}$$

because

$$\begin{aligned} E(\hat{\mu}) &= (rn)^{-1} \sum_{i=1}^{r} \sum_{j=1}^{n} E(X_{ij}) = (rn)^{-1} \sum_{i=1}^{r} \sum_{j=1}^{n} E[E(X_{ij}|\Theta_i)] \\ &= (rn)^{-1} \sum_{i=1}^{r} \sum_{j=1}^{n} E[\mu(\Theta_i)] = (rn)^{-1} \sum_{i=1}^{r} \sum_{j=1}^{n} \mu = \mu. \end{aligned}$$

To estimate v, consider

$$\hat{v}_i = \frac{1}{n-1} \sum_{j=1}^{n} (X_{ij} - \bar{X}_i)^2.$$

Recall that for fixed i the random variables $X_{i1}, \ldots, X_{in}$ are independent, conditional on $\Theta_i = \theta_i$. Thus, $\hat{v}_i$ is an unbiased estimate of $\mathrm{Var}(X_{ij}|\Theta_i = \theta_i) = v(\theta_i)$. Unconditionally,

$$\mathrm{E}(\hat{v}_i) = \mathrm{E}[\mathrm{E}(\hat{v}_i|\Theta_i)] = \mathrm{E}[v(\Theta_i)] = v$$

and $\hat{v}_i$ is unbiased for v. Hence an unbiased estimator of v is

$$\hat{v} = \frac{1}{r} \sum_{i=1}^{r} \hat{v}_i = \frac{1}{r(n-1)} \sum_{i=1}^{r} \sum_{j=1}^{n} (X_{ij} - \bar{X}_i)^2. \tag{16.57}$$

We now turn to estimation of the parameter a. Begin with

$$\mathrm{E}(\bar{X}_i|\Theta_i = \theta_i) = n^{-1} \sum_{j=1}^{n} \mathrm{E}(X_{ij}|\Theta_i = \theta_i) = n^{-1} \sum_{j=1}^{n} \mu(\theta_i) = \mu(\theta_i).$$

Thus,

$$\mathrm{E}(\bar{X}_i) = \mathrm{E}[\mathrm{E}(\bar{X}_i|\Theta_i)] = \mathrm{E}[\mu(\Theta_i)] = \mu$$

and

$$\begin{aligned}
\mathrm{Var}(\bar{X}_i) &= \mathrm{Var}[\mathrm{E}(\bar{X}_i|\Theta_i)] + \mathrm{E}[\mathrm{Var}(\bar{X}_i|\Theta_i)] \\
&= \mathrm{Var}[\mu(\Theta_i)] + \mathrm{E}\left[\frac{v(\Theta_i)}{n}\right] = a + \frac{v}{n}.
\end{aligned}$$

Therefore, $\bar{X}_1, \ldots, \bar{X}_r$ are independent with common mean μ and common variance $a + v/n$. Their sample average is $\bar{X} = r^{-1} \sum_{i=1}^{r} \bar{X}_i$. Consequently, an unbiased estimator of $a + v/n$ is $(r-1)^{-1} \sum_{i=1}^{r} (\bar{X}_i - \bar{X})^2$. Because we already have an unbiased estimator of v given above, an unbiased estimator of a is given by

$$\begin{aligned}
\hat{a} &= \frac{1}{r-1} \sum_{i=1}^{r} (\bar{X}_i - \bar{X})^2 - \frac{\hat{v}}{n} \\
&= \frac{1}{r-1} \sum_{i=1}^{r} (\bar{X}_i - \bar{X})^2 - \frac{1}{rn(n-1)} \sum_{i=1}^{r} \sum_{j=1}^{n} (X_{ij} - \bar{X}_i)^2. \tag{16.58}
\end{aligned}$$

$\square$

These estimators might look familiar. Consider a one-factor analysis of variance in which each policyholder represents a treatment. The estimator for v (16.57) is the within (also called the error) mean square. The first term in the estimator for a (16.58) is the between (also called the treatment) mean square divided by n. The hypothesis that all treatments have the same mean is accepted when the between mean square is small relative to the within mean square—that is, when $\hat{a}$ is small relative to $\hat{v}$. But that implies $\hat{Z}$ will be near zero and little credibility will be given to each $\bar{X}_i$. This is as it should be when the policyholders are essentially identical.

Due to the subtraction in (16.58), it is possible that $\hat{a}$ could be negative. When that happens, it is customary to set $\hat{a} = \hat{Z} = 0$. This case is equivalent to the F test statistic in the analysis of variance being less than 1, a case that always leads to an acceptance of the hypothesis of equal means.

Example 16.35 (Example 16.34 continued) *As a numerical illustration, suppose we have $r = 2$ policyholders with $n = 3$ years experience for each. Let the losses be $\mathbf{x}_1 = (3, 5, 7)^T$ and $\mathbf{x}_2 = (6, 12, 9)^T$. Estimate the Bühlmann credibility premiums for each policyholder.*

We have

$$\bar{X}_1 = \tfrac{1}{3}(3 + 5 + 7) = 5, \ \ \bar{X}_2 = \tfrac{1}{3}(6 + 12 + 9) = 9$$

and so $\bar{X} = \tfrac{1}{2}(5 + 9) = 7$. Then $\hat{\mu} = 7$. We next have

$$\hat{v}_1 = \tfrac{1}{2}[(3 - 5)^2 + (5 - 5)^2 + (7 - 5)^2] = 4,$$
$$\hat{v}_2 = \tfrac{1}{2}[(6 - 9)^2 + (12 - 9)^2 + (9 - 9)^2] = 9,$$

and so $\hat{v} = \tfrac{1}{2}(4 + 9) = \tfrac{13}{2}$. Then

$$\hat{a} = [(5 - 7)^2 + (9 - 7)^2] - \tfrac{1}{3}\hat{v} = \tfrac{35}{6}.$$

Next, $\hat{k} = \hat{v}/\hat{a} = \tfrac{39}{35}$ and the estimated credibility factor is $\hat{Z} = 3/(3+\hat{k}) = \tfrac{35}{48}$. The estimated credibility premiums are

$$\hat{Z}\bar{X}_1 + (1 - \hat{Z})\hat{\mu} = \left(\tfrac{35}{48}\right)(5) + \left(\tfrac{13}{48}\right)(7) = \tfrac{133}{24},$$
$$\hat{Z}\bar{X}_2 + (1 - \hat{Z})\hat{\mu} = \left(\tfrac{35}{48}\right)(9) + \left(\tfrac{13}{48}\right)(7) = \tfrac{203}{24}$$

for policyholders 1 and 2 respectively.   □

We now turn to the more general Bühlmann–Straub setup described earlier in this section. We have $E(X_{ij}) = E[E(X_{ij}|\Theta_i)] = E[\mu(\Theta_i)] = \mu$. Thus,

$$E(\bar{X}_i|\Theta_i) = \sum_{j=1}^{n_i} \frac{m_{ij}}{m_i} E(X_{ij}|\Theta_i) = \sum_{j=1}^{n_i} \frac{m_{ij}}{m_i} \mu(\Theta_i) = \mu(\Theta_i),$$

implying that

$$E(\bar{X}_i) = E[E(\bar{X}_i|\Theta_i)] = E[\mu(\Theta_i)] = \mu.$$

Finally,

$$E(\bar{X}) = \frac{1}{m}\sum_{i=1}^{r} m_i E(\bar{X}_i) = \frac{1}{m}\sum_{i=1}^{r} m_i \mu = \mu$$

and so an obvious unbiased estimator of μ is

$$\hat{\mu} = \bar{X}. \tag{16.59}$$

Now, $E(X_{ij}|\Theta_i) = \mu(\Theta_i)$ and $Var(X_{ij}|\Theta_i) = v(\Theta_i)/m_{ij}$ for $j = 1,\dots,n_i$. Consider

$$\hat{v}_i = \frac{\sum_{j=1}^{n_i} m_{ij}(X_{ij}-\bar{X}_i)^2}{n_i - 1}, \quad i = 1,\dots,r. \tag{16.60}$$

Condition on Θ_i and use (16.12) with $\beta = 0$ and $\alpha = v(\Theta_i)$. Then $E(\hat{v}_i|\Theta_i) = v(\Theta_i)$. But this means that, unconditionally,

$$E(\hat{v}_i) = E[E(\hat{v}_i|\Theta_i)] = E[v(\Theta_i)] = v$$

and so $\hat{v}_i$ is unbiased for v for $i = 1,\dots,r$. Another unbiased estimator for v is then the weighted average $\hat{v} = \sum_{i=1}^{r} w_i \hat{v}_i$, where $\sum_{i=1}^{r} w_i = 1$. If we choose weights proportional to $n_i - 1$, we weight the original X_{ij}s by m_{ij}. That is, with $w_i = (n_i - 1)/\sum_{i=1}^{r}(n_i - 1)$, we obtain an unbiased estimator of v, namely,

$$\hat{v} = \frac{\sum_{i=1}^{r}\sum_{j=1}^{n_i} m_{ij}(X_{ij}-\bar{X}_i)^2}{\sum_{i=1}^{r}(n_i - 1)}. \tag{16.61}$$

We now turn to estimation of a. Recall that for fixed i the random variables $X_{i1},\dots,X_{in_i}$ are independent, conditional on Θ_i. Thus,

$$
\begin{aligned}
Var(\bar{X}_i|\Theta_i) &= \sum_{j=1}^{n_i}\left(\frac{m_{ij}}{m_i}\right)^2 Var(X_{ij}|\Theta_i) = \sum_{j=1}^{n_i}\left(\frac{m_{ij}}{m_i}\right)^2 \frac{v(\Theta_i)}{m_{ij}} \\
&= \frac{v(\Theta_i)}{m_i^2}\sum_{j=1}^{n_i} m_{ij} = \frac{v(\Theta_i)}{m_i}.
\end{aligned}
$$

But this means that, unconditionally,

$$
\begin{aligned}
Var(\bar{X}_i) &= Var[E(\bar{X}_i|\Theta_i)] + E[Var(\bar{X}_i|\Theta_i)] \\
&= Var[\mu(\Theta_i)] + E\left[\frac{v(\Theta_i)}{m_i}\right] = a + \frac{v}{m_i}. \tag{16.62}
\end{aligned}
$$

To summarize, $\bar{X}_1,\dots,\bar{X}_r$ are independent with common mean μ and variances $Var(\bar{X}_i) = a + v/m_i$. Furthermore, $\bar{X} = m^{-1}\sum_{i=1}^{r} m_i \bar{X}_i$. Now, (16.12) may again be used with $\beta = a$ and $\alpha = v$ to yield

$$E\left[\sum_{i=1}^{r} m_i(\bar{X}_i - \bar{X})^2\right] = a\left(m - m^{-1}\sum_{i=1}^{r} m_i^2\right) + v(r - 1).$$

An unbiased estimator for a may be obtained by replacing v by an unbiased estimator $\hat{v}$ and "solving" for a. That is, an unbiased estimator of a is

$$\hat{a} = \left(m - m^{-1} \sum_{i=1}^{r} m_i^2 \right)^{-1} \left[\sum_{i=1}^{r} m_i(\bar{X}_i - \bar{X})^2 - \hat{v}(r-1) \right] \qquad (16.63)$$

with $\hat{v}$ given by (16.61). An alternative form of (16.63) is given in Exercise 16.67.

Some remarks are in order at this point. Equations (16.59), (16.61), and (16.63) provide unbiased estimators for μ, v, and a, respectively. They are nonparametric, requiring no distributional assumptions. They are certainly not the only (unbiased) estimators which could be used, and it is possible that $\hat{a} < 0$. In this case, a is likely to be close to 0, and it makes sense to set $\hat{Z} = 0$. Furthermore, the ordinary Bühlmann estimators of Example 16.34 are recovered with $m_{ij} = 1$ and $n_i = n$. Furthermore, as may be seen from Example 16.41, these estimators are essentially maximum likelihood estimators in the case where $X_{ij}|\Theta_i$ and Θ_i are both normally distributed, and thus the estimators have good statistical properties.

There is one problem using the formulas developed above. In the past, the data from the ith policyholder was collected on an exposure of m_i. Total losses on all policyholders was $TL = \sum_{i=1}^{r} m_i \bar{X}_i$. If we had charged the credibility premium as given above, the total premium would have been

$$
\begin{aligned}
TP &= \sum_{i=1}^{r} m_i[\hat{Z}_i \bar{X}_i + (1 - \hat{Z}_i)\hat{\mu}] \\
&= \sum_{i=1}^{r} m_i(1 - \hat{Z}_i)(\hat{\mu} - \bar{X}_i) + \sum_{i=1}^{r} m_i \bar{X}_i \\
&= \sum_{i=1}^{r} m_i \frac{\hat{k}}{m_i + \hat{k}}(\hat{\mu} - \bar{X}_i) + \sum_{i=1}^{r} m_i \bar{X}_i.
\end{aligned}
$$

It is often desirable for TL to equal TP. The reason is that any premium increases that will meet the approval of regulators will be based on the total claim level from past experience. While credibility adjustments make both practical and theoretical sense, it is usually a good idea to keep the total unchanged. For this to happen, we need

$$0 = \sum_{i=1}^{r} m_i \frac{\hat{k}}{m_i + \hat{k}}(\hat{\mu} - \bar{X}_i)$$

or

$$\hat{\mu} \sum_{i=1}^{r} \hat{Z}_i = \sum_{i=1}^{r} \hat{Z}_i \bar{X}_i$$

or

$$\hat{\mu} = \frac{\sum_{i=1}^{r} \hat{Z}_i \bar{X}_i}{\sum_{i=1}^{r} \hat{Z}_i}. \qquad (16.64)$$

Table 16.7   Data for Example 16.36

	Policyholder	Year 1	Year 2	Year 3	Year 4
Total claims	1	–	10,000	13,000	–
No. in group		–	50	60	75
Total claims	2	18,000	21,000	17,000	–
No. in group		100	110	105	90

That is, rather than using (16.59) to compute $\hat{\mu}$, use a credibility-weighted average of the individual sample means. Either method provides an unbiased estimator (given the $\hat{Z}_i$s), but this latter one has the advantage of preserving total claims. It should be noted that when using (16.63), the value of $\bar{X}$ from (16.54) should still be used. It can also be derived by least squares arguments. Finally, from Example 16.7 and noting the form of $\text{Var}(\bar{X}_j)$ in (16.62), the weights in (16.64) provide the smallest unconditional variance for $\hat{\mu}$.

Example 16.36 *Past data on two group policyholders are available and are given in Table 16.7. Determine the estimated credibility premium to be charged to each group in year 4.*

We first need to determine the average claims per person for each group in each past year. We have $n_1 = 2$ years experience for group 1 and $n_2 = 3$ for group 2. It is immaterial which past years' data we have for policyholder 1, so for notational purposes we will choose

$$m_{11} = 50 \text{ and } X_{11} = \frac{10,000}{50} = 200.$$

Similarly,

$$m_{12} = 60 \text{ and } X_{12} = \frac{13,000}{60} = 216.67.$$

Then

$$m_1 = m_{11} + m_{12} = 50 + 60 = 110,$$
$$\bar{X}_1 = \frac{10,000 + 13,000}{110} = 209.09.$$

For policyholder 2,

$$m_{21} = 100, \ X_{21} = \frac{18,000}{100} = 180,$$
$$m_{22} = 110, \ X_{22} = \frac{21,000}{110} = 190.91,$$
$$m_{23} = 105, \ X_{23} = \frac{17,000}{105} = 161.90.$$

Then

$$m_2 = m_{21} + m_{22} + m_{23} = 100 + 110 + 105 = 315,$$
$$\bar{X}_2 = \frac{18,000 + 21,000 + 17,000}{315} = 177.78.$$

Now, $m = m_1 + m_2 = 110 + 315 = 425$. The overall mean is

$$\hat{\mu} = \bar{X} = \frac{10,000 + 13,000 + 18,000 + 21,000 + 17,000}{425} = 185.88.$$

The alternative estimate of μ (16.64) cannot be computed until later.
    Now,

$$\hat{v} = \frac{\begin{array}{c}50(200 - 209.09)^2 + 60(216.67 - 209.09)^2 + 100(180 - 177.78)^2 \\ +110(190.91 - 177.78)^2 + 105(161.90 - 177.78)^2\end{array}}{(2-1) + (3-1)}$$
$$= 17,837.87$$

and so

$$\hat{a} = \frac{110(209.09 - 185.88)^2 + 315(177.78 - 185.88)^2 - (17,837.87)(1)}{425 - (110^2 + 315^2)/425}$$
$$= 380.76.$$

Then $\hat{k} = \hat{v}/\hat{a} = 46.85$. The estimated credibility factors for the two policy-holders are

$$\hat{Z}_1 = \frac{110}{110 + 46.85} = 0.70, \quad \hat{Z}_2 = \frac{315}{315 + 46.85} = 0.87.$$

Per individual the estimated credibility premium for policyholder 1 is

$$\hat{Z}_1 \bar{X}_1 + (1 - \hat{Z}_1)\hat{\mu} = (0.70)(209.09) + (0.30)(185.88) = 202.13$$

and so the total estimated credibility premium for the whole group is

$$75(202.13) = 15,159.75.$$

For policyholder 2,

$$\hat{Z}_2 \bar{X}_2 + (1 - \hat{Z}_2)\hat{\mu} = (0.87)(177.78) + (0.13)(185.88) = 178.83$$

and the total estimated credibility premium is

$$90(178.83) = 16,094.70.$$

For the alternative estimator we would use

$$\hat{\mu} = \frac{0.70(209.09) + 0.87(177.78)}{0.70 + 0.87} = 191.74.$$

The credibility premiums are

$$0.70(209.09) + 0.30(191.74) = 203.89, \quad 0.87(177.78) + 0.13(191.74) = 179.59.$$

The total past credibility premium is $110(203.89) + 315(179.59) = 78{,}998.75$. Except for rounding error, this matches the actual total losses of 79,000. □

The above analysis assumes that the parameters μ, v, and a are all unknown and need to be estimated, and this may not always be the case. Also, it is assumed that $n_i > 1$ and $r > 1$. If $n_i = 1$, so that there is only one exposure unit's experience for policyholder i, it is difficult to obtain information on the process variance $v(\Theta_i)$ and thus v. Similarly, if $r = 1$, there is only one policyholder and it is difficult to obtain information on the variance of the hypothetical means a. In these situations, stronger assumptions are needed such as knowledge of one or more of the parameters (e.g., the pure premium or manual rate μ, discussed below) or parametric assumptions which imply functional relationships between the parameters (discussed in Sections 16.5.2 and 16.5.3).

To illustrate these ideas, suppose, for example, that the manual rate μ may be already known, but estimates of a and v may be needed. In that case, (16.61) can still be used to estimate v as it is unbiased whether μ is known or not. (Why is $\left[\sum_{j=1}^{n_i} m_{ij}(X_{ij} - \mu)^2\right]/n_i$ not unbiased for v in this case?) Similarly, (16.63) is still an unbiased estimator for a. However, if μ is known, an alternative unbiased estimator for a is

$$\tilde{a} = \sum_{i=1}^{r} \frac{m_i}{m}(\bar{X}_i - \mu)^2 - \frac{r}{m}\hat{v},$$

where $\hat{v}$ is given by (16.61). To see this, note that

$$
\begin{aligned}
\mathrm{E}(\tilde{a}) &= \sum_{i=1}^{r} \frac{m_i}{m} E[(\bar{X}_i - \mu)^2] - \frac{r}{m}E(\hat{v}) \\
&= \sum_{i=1}^{r} \frac{m_i}{m} \mathrm{Var}(\bar{X}_i) - \frac{r}{m}v \\
&= \sum_{i=1}^{r} \frac{m_i}{m}\left(a + \frac{v}{m_i}\right) - \frac{r}{m}v = a.
\end{aligned}
$$

If there are data on only one policyholder, an approach like this is necessary. Clearly, (16.60) provides an estimator for v based on data from policyholder i alone, and an unbiased estimator for a based on data from policyholder i alone is

$$\tilde{a}_i = (\bar{X}_i - \mu)^2 - \frac{\hat{v}_i}{m_i} = (\bar{X}_i - \mu)^2 - \frac{\sum_{j=1}^{n_i} m_{ij}(X_{ij} - \bar{X}_i)^2}{m_i(n_i - 1)},$$

which is unbiased because $E[(\bar{X}_i - \mu)^2] = Var(\bar{X}_i) = a + v/m_i$ and $E(\hat{v}_i) = v$.

Example 16.37 *For a group policyholder, we have the following data available:*

	Year 1	Year 2	Year 3
Total claims	60,000	70,000	–
No. in group	125	150	200

If the manual rate per person is 500 per year, estimate the total credibility premium for year 3.

In the above notation, we have (assuming for notational purposes that this group is policyholder i) $m_{i1} = 125$, $X_{i1} = 60,000/125 = 480$, $m_{i2} = 150$, $X_{i2} = 70,000/150 = 466.67$, $m_i = m_{i1} + m_{i2} = 275$, and $\bar{X}_i = (60,000 + 70,000)/275 = 472.73$. Then

$$\hat{v}_i = \frac{125(480 - 472.73)^2 + 150(466.67 - 472.73)^2}{2 - 1} = 12,115.15,$$

and with $\mu = 500$, $\tilde{a}_i = (472.73 - 500)^2 - (12,115.15/275) = 699.60$. We then estimate k by $\hat{v}_i/\tilde{a}_i = 17.32$. The estimated credibility factor is $m_i/(m_i + \hat{v}_i/\tilde{a}_i) = 275/(275 + 17.32) = 0.94$. The estimated credibility premium per person is then $0.94(472.73) + 0.06(500) = 474.37$ and the estimated total credibility premium for year 3 is $200(474.37) = 94,874$. □

It is instructive to note that estimation of the parameters a and v based on data from a single policyholder (as in the example above) is not advised unless there is no alternative because the estimators $\hat{v}_i$ and $\tilde{a}_i$ have high variability. In particular, we are effectively estimating a from one observation $(\bar{X}_i)$. It is strongly suggested that an attempt be made to obtain more data.

16.5.2 Semiparametric estimation

In some situations it may be reasonable to assume a parametric form for the conditional distribution $f_{X_{ij}|\Theta}(x_{ij}|\theta_i)$. The situation at hand may suggest that such an assumption is reasonable or prior information may imply its appropriateness.

For example, in dealing with numbers of claims, it may be reasonable to assume that the number of claims $m_{ij}X_{ij}$ for policyholder i in year j is Poisson distributed with mean $m_{ij}\theta_i$ given $\Theta_i = \theta_i$. Thus $E(m_{ij}X_{ij}|\Theta_i) = Var(m_{ij}X_{ij}|\Theta_i) = m_{ij}\Theta_i$, implying that $\mu(\Theta_i) = v(\Theta_i) = \Theta_i$ and so $\mu = v$ in this case. Rather than use (16.61) to estimate v, we could use $\hat{\mu} = \bar{X}$ to estimate v.

Example 16.38 *In the past year, the distribution of automobile insurance policyholders by number of claims is given below.*

No. of claims	No. of insureds
0	1,563
1	271
2	32
3	7
4	2
Total	1,875

For each policyholder, obtain a credibility estimate for the number of claims next year based on the past year's experience, assuming a (conditional) Poisson distribution of number of claims for each policyholder.

Assume that we have $r = 1{,}875$ policyholders, $n_i = 1$ year experience on each, and exposures $m_{ij} = 1$. For policyholder i (where $i = 1, \ldots, 1{,}875$) assume that $X_{i1}|\Theta_i = \theta_i$ is Poisson distributed with mean θ_i so that $\mu(\theta_i) = v(\theta_i) = \theta_i$ and $\mu = v$. As in Example 16.34,

$$
\begin{aligned}
\bar{X} &= \frac{1}{1{,}875}\left(\sum_{i=1}^{1{,}875} X_{i1}\right) \\
&= \frac{0(1{,}563) + 1(271) + 2(32) + 3(7) + 4(2)}{1{,}875} = 0.194.
\end{aligned}
$$

Now,

$$
\begin{aligned}
\operatorname{Var}(X_{i1}) &= \operatorname{Var}[\operatorname{E}(X_{i1}|\Theta_i)] + \operatorname{E}[\operatorname{Var}(X_{i1}|\Theta_i)] \\
&= \operatorname{Var}[\mu(\Theta_i)] + \operatorname{E}[v(\Theta_i)] = a + v = a + \mu.
\end{aligned}
$$

Thus an unbiased estimator of $a + v$ is the sample variance

$$
\frac{\sum_{i=1}^{1{,}875}(X_{i1} - \bar{X})^2}{1{,}874} = \frac{\begin{array}{c}1{,}563(0 - 0.194)^2 + 271(1 - 0.194)^2 \\ +32(2 - 0.194)^2 + 7(3 - 0.194)^2 + 2(4 - 0.194)^2\end{array}}{1{,}874}
$$

$$
= 0.226.
$$

Thus $\hat{a} = 0.226 - 0.194 = 0.032$ and $\hat{k} = 0.194/0.032 = 6.06$ and the credibility factor Z is $1/(1 + 6.06) = 0.14$. The estimated credibility premium for the number of claims for each policyholder is $(0.14)X_{i1} + (0.86)(0.194)$, where X_{i1} is 0, 1, 2, 3, or 4, depending on the policyholder. □

Note that in this case $v = \mu$ identically, so that only one year's experience per policyholder is needed.

Example 16.39 *Suppose we are interested in the probability that an individ- ual in a group makes a claim (e.g., group life insurance), and the probability is believed to vary by policyholder. Then $m_{ij}X_{ij}$ could represent the number of the m_{ij} individuals in year j for policyholder i who made a claim. Develop a credibility model for this situation.*

If the claim probability is θ_i for policyholder i, then a reasonable model to describe this effect is that $m_{ij}X_{ij}$ is binomially distributed with parameters m_{ij} and θ_i, given $\Theta_i = \theta_i$. Then

$$\mathrm{E}(m_{ij}X_{ij}|\Theta_i) = m_{ij}\Theta_i \quad \text{and} \quad \mathrm{Var}(m_{ij}X_{ij}|\Theta_i) = m_{ij}\Theta_i(1 - \Theta_i)$$

and so $\mu(\Theta_i) = \Theta_i$ with $v(\Theta_i) = \Theta_i(1 - \Theta_i)$. Thus

$$
\begin{aligned}
\mu &= \mathrm{E}(\Theta_i), \quad v = \mu - \mathrm{E}[(\Theta_i)^2], \\
a &= \mathrm{Var}(\Theta_i) = \mathrm{E}[(\Theta_i)^2] - \mu^2 = \mu - v - \mu^2. \qquad \square
\end{aligned}
$$

In these examples there is a functional relationship between the parameters μ, v, and a which follows from the parametric assumptions made, and this often facilitates estimation of parameters.

16.5.3   Parametric estimation

If fully parametric assumptions are made with respect to $f_{X_{ij}|\Theta}(x_{ij}|\theta_i)$ and $\pi(\theta_i)$ for $i = 1,\ldots,r$ and $j = 1,\ldots,n_i$, then the full battery of parametric estimation techniques are available in addition to the nonparametric methods discussed earlier. In particular, maximum likelihood estimation is straight- forward (at least in principle) and is now discussed. For policyholder i, the joint density of $\mathbf{X}_i = (X_{i1},\ldots,X_{in_i})^T$ is, by conditioning on Θ_i, given for $i = 1,\ldots,r$ by

$$f_{\mathbf{X}_i}(\mathbf{x}_i) = \int \left[\prod_{j=1}^{n_i} f_{X_{ij}|\Theta}(x_{ij}|\theta_i)\right] \pi(\theta_i)\, d\theta_i. \qquad (16.65)$$

The likelihood function is given by

$$L = \prod_{i=1}^{r} f_{\mathbf{X}_i}(\mathbf{x}_i). \qquad (16.66)$$

Maximum likelihood estimators of the parameters are then chosen to maximize L or equivalently $\ln L$.

Example 16.40 *As a simple example, suppose that $n_i = n$ for $i = 1,\ldots,r$ and $m_{ij} = 1$. Let $X_{ij}|\Theta_i$ be Poisson distributed with mean Θ_i, that is,*

$$f_{X_{ij}|\Theta}(x_{ij}|\theta_i) = \frac{\theta_i^{x_{ij}} e^{-\theta_i}}{x_{ij}!}, \quad x_{ij} = 0, 1, \ldots,$$

and let Θ_i *be exponentially distributed with mean* μ,

$$\pi(\theta_i) = \frac{1}{\mu} e^{-\theta_i/\mu}, \quad \theta_i > 0.$$

Determine the maximum likelihood estimator of μ.

Equation (16.65) becomes

$$
\begin{aligned}
f_{\mathbf{X}_i}(\mathbf{x}_i) &= \int_0^\infty \left(\prod_{j=1}^n \frac{\theta_i^{x_{ij}} e^{-\theta_i}}{x_{ij}!} \right) \frac{1}{\mu} e^{-\theta_i/\mu} \, d\theta_i \\
&= \left(\prod_{j=1}^n x_{ij}! \right)^{-1} \frac{1}{\mu} \int_0^\infty \theta_i^{\sum_{j=1}^n x_{ij}} e^{-\theta_i(n+1/\mu)} \, d\theta_i \\
&= C(\mathbf{x}_i)\mu^{-1} \left(n + \frac{1}{\mu} \right)^{-\sum_{j=1}^n x_{ij}-1} \int_0^\infty \frac{\beta(\beta\theta_i)^{\alpha-1} e^{-\beta\theta_i}}{\Gamma(\alpha)} \, d\theta_i,
\end{aligned}
$$

where $C(\mathbf{x}_i)$ may be expressed in combinatorial notation as

$$C(\mathbf{x}_i) = \left(\begin{array}{c} \sum_{j=1}^n x_{ij} \\ x_{i1} \; x_{i2} \; \cdots \; x_{in} \end{array} \right);$$

$$\beta = n + \frac{1}{\mu},$$

and

$$\alpha = \sum_{j=1}^n x_{ij} + 1.$$

The integral is that of a gamma density with parameters α and $1/\beta$ and therefore equals 1, and so

$$f(\mathbf{x}_i) = C(\mathbf{x}_i)\mu^{-1} \left(n + \frac{1}{\mu} \right)^{-\sum_{j=1}^n x_{ij}-1}.$$

Substitution into (16.66) yields

$$L(\mu) \propto \mu^{-r} \left(n + \frac{1}{\mu} \right)^{-\sum_{i=1}^r \sum_{j=1}^n x_{ij}-r}.$$

Thus

$$l(\mu) = \ln L(\mu) = -r \ln \mu - \left(r + \sum_{i=1}^r \sum_{j=1}^n x_{ij} \right) \ln \left(n + \frac{1}{\mu} \right) + c,$$

where c is a constant which does not depend on μ. Differentiating yields

$$l'(\mu) = -\frac{r}{\mu} - \frac{r + \sum_{i=1}^{r}\sum_{j=1}^{n} x_{ij}}{n + \frac{1}{\mu}}\left(-\frac{1}{\mu^2}\right).$$

The maximum likelihood estimator $\hat{\mu}$ of μ is found by setting $l'(\hat{\mu}) = 0$, which yields

$$\frac{r}{\hat{\mu}} = \frac{r + \sum_{i=1}^{r}\sum_{j=1}^{n} x_{ij}}{\hat{\mu}(\hat{\mu}n + 1)}$$

and so

$$\hat{\mu}n + 1 = 1 + \frac{1}{r}\sum_{i=1}^{r}\sum_{j=1}^{n} x_{ij}$$

or

$$\hat{\mu} = \frac{1}{nr}\sum_{i=1}^{r}\sum_{j=1}^{n} x_{ij}.$$

But this is the same as the nonparametric estimate obtained in Example 16.34. An explanation is in order. We have $\mu(\theta_i) = \theta_i$ by the Poisson assumption and so $\mathrm{E}[\mu(\Theta_i)] = \mathrm{E}(\Theta_i)$, which is the same μ as was used in the exponential distribution $\pi(\theta_i)$.

Furthermore, $v(\theta_i) = \theta_i$ as well (by the Poisson assumption), and so $v = \mathrm{E}[v(\Theta_i)] = \mu$. Also, $a = \mathrm{Var}[\mu(\Theta_i)] = \mathrm{Var}(\Theta_i) = \mu^2$ by the exponential assumption for $\pi(\theta_i)$. Thus the maximum likelihood estimators of v and a are $\hat{\mu}$ and $\hat{\mu}^2$ by the invariance of maximum likelihood estimation under a parameter transformation. Similarly, the maximum likelihood estimators of $k = v/a$, the credibility factor Z, and the credibility premium $Z\bar{X}_i + (1 - Z)\mu$ are $\hat{k} = \hat{\mu}^{-1} = \bar{X}^{-1}$, $\hat{Z} = n/(n + \hat{\mu}^{-1})$, and $\hat{Z}\bar{X}_i + (1 - \hat{Z})\hat{\mu}$, respectively. We mention also that credibility is exact in this model so that the Bayesian premium is equal to the credibility premium. □

Example 16.41 *Suppose that $n_i = n$ for all i and $m_{ij} = 1$. Assume that $X_{ij}|\Theta_i \sim N(\Theta_i, v)$,*

$$f_{X_{ij}|\Theta}(x_{ij}|\theta_i) = (2\pi v)^{-1/2}\exp\left[-\frac{1}{2v}(x_{ij} - \theta_i)^2\right], \quad -\infty < x_{ij} < \infty,$$

and $\Theta_i \sim N(\mu, a)$, so that

$$\pi(\theta_i) = (2\pi a)^{-1/2}\exp\left[-\frac{1}{2a}(\theta_i - \mu)^2\right], \quad -\infty < \theta_i < \infty.$$

Determine the maximum likelihood estimators of the parameters.

We have $\mu(\theta_i) = \theta_i$ and $v(\theta_i) = v$. Thus $\mu = \mathrm{E}[\mu(\Theta_i)]$, $v = \mathrm{E}[v(\Theta_i)]$, and $a = \mathrm{Var}[\mu(\Theta_i)]$, consistent with previous use of μ, v, and a. We shall now derive maximum likelihood estimators of μ, v, and a. To begin with, consider $\bar{X}_i = n^{-1} \sum_{j=1}^n X_{ij}$. Conditional on Θ_i, the X_{ij} are independent $N(\Theta_i, v)$ random variables, implying that $\bar{X}_i | \Theta_i \sim N(\Theta_i, v/n)$. Because $\Theta_i \sim N(\mu, a)$, it follows from Example 4.30 that unconditionally $\bar{X}_i \sim N(\mu, a+v/n)$. Hence the density of $\bar{X}_i$ is, with $w = a + v/n$,

$$f(\bar{x}_i) = (2\pi w)^{-1/2} \exp\left[-\frac{1}{2w}(\bar{x}_i - \mu)^2\right], \quad -\infty < \bar{x}_i < \infty.$$

On the other hand, by conditioning on Θ_i, we have

$$\begin{aligned} f(\bar{x}_i) &= \int_{-\infty}^{\infty} (2\pi v/n)^{-1/2} \exp\left[-\frac{n}{2v}(\bar{x}_i - \theta_i)^2\right] \\ &\quad \times (2\pi a)^{-1/2} \exp\left[-\frac{1}{2a}(\theta_i - \mu)^2\right] d\theta_i. \end{aligned}$$

Ignoring terms not involving μ, v, or a, this means that $f(\bar{x}_i)$ is proportional to

$$v^{-1/2} a^{-1/2} \int_{-\infty}^{\infty} \exp\left[-\frac{n}{2v}(\bar{x}_i - \theta_i)^2 - \frac{1}{2a}(\theta_i - \mu)^2\right] d\theta_i.$$

Now (16.65) yields

$$\begin{aligned} f(\mathbf{x}_i) &= \int_{-\infty}^{\infty} \left\{\prod_{j=1}^{n}(2\pi v)^{-1/2}\exp\left[-\frac{1}{2v}(x_{ij} - \theta_i)^2\right]\right\}(2\pi a)^{-1/2} \\ &\quad \times \exp\left[-\frac{1}{2a}(\theta_i - \mu)^2\right] d\theta_i, \end{aligned}$$

which is proportional to

$$v^{-n/2} a^{-1/2} \int_{-\infty}^{\infty} \exp\left[-\frac{1}{2v}\sum_{j=1}^{n}(x_{ij} - \theta_i)^2 - \frac{1}{2a}(\theta_i - \mu)^2\right] d\theta_i.$$

Now use the identity (16.10) restated as

$$\sum_{j=1}^{n}(x_{ij} - \theta_i)^2 = \sum_{j=1}^{n}(x_{ij} - \bar{x}_i)^2 + n(\bar{x}_i - \theta_i)^2,$$

which means that $f(\mathbf{x}_i)$ is proportional to

$$v^{-n/2} a^{-1/2} \int_{-\infty}^{\infty} \exp\left\{-\frac{1}{2v}\left[\sum_{j=1}^{n}(x_{ij} - \bar{x}_i)^2 + n(\bar{x}_i - \theta_i)^2\right] - \frac{1}{2a}(\theta_i - \mu)^2\right\} d\theta_i,$$

itself proportional to

$$v^{-(n-1)/2} \exp\left[-\frac{1}{2v}\sum_{j=1}^{n}(x_{ij}-\bar{x}_i)^2\right] f(\bar{x}_i)$$

using the second expression for the density $f(\bar{x}_i)$ of $\bar{X}_i$ given above. Then (16.66) yields

$$L \propto v^{-r(n-1)/2} \exp\left[-\frac{1}{2v}\sum_{i=1}^{r}\sum_{j=1}^{n}(x_{ij}-\bar{x}_i)^2\right]\prod_{i=1}^{r} f(\bar{x}_i).$$

Let us now invoke the invariance of maximum likelihood estimators under a parameter transformation and use μ, v, and $w = a + v/n$ rather than μ, v, and a. This means that

$$L \propto L_1(v)L_2(\mu, w),$$

where

$$L_1(v) = v^{-r(n-1)/2} \exp\left[-\frac{1}{2v}\sum_{i=1}^{r}\sum_{j=1}^{n}(x_{ij}-\bar{x}_i)^2\right]$$

and

$$L_2(\mu, w) = \prod_{i=1}^{r} f(\bar{x}_i) = \prod_{i=1}^{r}\left\{(2\pi w)^{-1/2}\exp\left[-\frac{1}{2w}(\bar{x}_i-\mu)^2\right]\right\}.$$

The maximum likelihood estimator $\hat{v}$ of v can be found by maximizing $L_1(v)$ alone and the mle $(\hat{\mu}, \hat{w})$ of (μ, w) can be found by maximizing $L_2(\mu, w)$. Taking logarithms, we obtain

$$l_1(v) = -\frac{r(n-1)}{2}\ln v - \frac{1}{2v}\sum_{i=1}^{r}\sum_{j=1}^{n}(x_{ij}-\bar{x}_i)^2,$$

$$l_1'(v) = -\frac{r(n-1)}{2v} + \frac{1}{2v^2}\sum_{i=1}^{r}\sum_{j=1}^{n}(x_{ij}-\bar{x}_i)^2,$$

and with $l'(\hat{v}) = 0$ we have

$$\hat{v} = \frac{\sum_{i=1}^{r}\sum_{j=1}^{n}(X_{ij}-\bar{X}_i)^2}{r(n-1)}.$$

Because $L_2(\mu, w)$ is the usual normal likelihood, the mles are simply the empirical mean and variance. That is,

$$\hat{\mu} = \frac{1}{r}\sum_{i=1}^{r}\bar{X}_i = \frac{1}{nr}\sum_{i=1}^{r}\sum_{j=1}^{n}X_{ij} = \bar{X}$$

and

$$\hat{w} = \frac{1}{r} \sum_{i=1}^{r} (\bar{X}_i - \bar{X})^2.$$

But $a = w - v/n$ and so the maximum likelihood estimator of a is

$$\hat{a} = \frac{1}{r} \sum_{i=1}^{r} (\bar{X}_i - \bar{X})^2 - \frac{1}{rn(n-1)} \sum_{i=1}^{r} \sum_{j=1}^{n} (X_{ij} - \bar{X}_i)^2.$$

It is instructive to note that the maximum likelihood estimators $\hat{\mu}$ and $\hat{v}$ are exactly the nonparametric unbiased estimators in the Bühlmann model of Example 16.34. The maximum likelihood estimator $\hat{a}$ is almost the same as the nonparametric unbiased estimator, the only difference being the divisor r rather than $r - 1$ in the first term. ☐

16.5.4 Notes and References

In this section a simple approach was employed to find parameter estimates. No attempt was made to find optimum estimators in the sense of minimum variance. A good deal of research has been done on this problem. See Goovaerts and Hoogstad [46] for more details and further references.

16.5.5 Exercises

16.60 Past claims data on a portfolio of policyholders are given in Table 16.8. Estimate the Bühlmann credibility premium for each of the three policyholders for year 4.

16.61 Past data on a portfolio of group policyholders are given in Table 16.9. Estimate the Bühlmann–Straub credibility premiums to be charged to each group in year 4.

16.62 For the situation in Exercise 16.9, estimate the Bühlmann credibility premium for the next year for the policyholder.

Table 16.8 Data for Exercise 16.60

	Year		
Policyholder	1	2	3
1	750	800	650
2	625	600	675
3	900	950	850

Table 16.9   Data for Exercise 16.61

Policyholder		Year			
		1	2	3	4
Claims	1	–	20,000	25,000	–
No. in group		–	100	120	110
Claims	2	19,000	18,000	17,000	–
No. in group		90	75	70	60
Claims	3	26,000	30,000	35,000	–
No. in group		150	175	180	200

16.63 Consider the Bühlmann model in Example 16.34.

(a) Prove that $\text{Var}(X_{ij}) = a + v$.

(b) If $\{X_{ij} : \ i = 1, \ldots, r \text{ and } j = 1, \ldots, n\}$ are unconditionally independent for all i and j, argue that an unbiased estimator of $a + v$ is

$$\frac{1}{nr - 1} \sum_{i=1}^{r} \sum_{j=1}^{n} (X_{ij} - \bar{X})^2.$$

(c) Prove the algebraic identity

$$\sum_{i=1}^{r} \sum_{j=1}^{n} (X_{ij} - \bar{X})^2 = \sum_{i=1}^{r} \sum_{j=1}^{n} (X_{ij} - \bar{X}_i)^2 + n \sum_{i=1}^{r} (\bar{X}_i - \bar{X})^2.$$

(d) Show that, conditionally,

$$E\left[\frac{1}{nr - 1} \sum_{i=1}^{r} \sum_{j=1}^{n} (X_{ij} - \bar{X})^2 \right] = (v + a) - \frac{n - 1}{nr - 1} a.$$

(e) Comment on the implications of (b) and (d).

16.64 The distribution of automobile insurance policyholders by number of claims is given in Table 16.10.

Assuming a (conditional) Poisson distribution for the number of claims per policyholder, estimate the Bühlmann credibility premiums for the number of claims next year.

16.65 Suppose that, given Θ, $X_1, \ldots, X_n$ are independently geometrically distributed with pf

$$f_{X_j|\Theta}(x_j|\theta) = \frac{1}{1 + \theta} \left(\frac{\theta}{1 + \theta} \right)^{x_j}, \quad x_j = 0, 1, \ldots .$$

Table 16.10   Data for Exercise 16.64

No. of claims	No. of insureds
0	2,500
1	250
2	30
3	5
4	2
Total	2,787

(a) Show that $\mu(\theta) = \theta$ and $v(\theta) = \theta(1 + \theta)$.

(b) Prove that $a = v - \mu - \mu^2$.

(c) Rework Exercise 16.64 assuming a (conditional) geometric distribution.

16.66 Suppose that

$$\Pr(m_{ij} X_{ij} = t_{ij} | \Theta_i = \theta_i) = \frac{(m_{ij}\theta_i)^{t_{ij}} e^{-m_{ij}\theta_i}}{t_{ij}!}$$

and

$$\pi(\theta_i) = \frac{1}{\mu} e^{-\theta_i/\mu}, \quad \theta_i > 0.$$

Write down the equation satisfied by the maximum likelihood estimator $\hat{\mu}$ of μ for Bühlmann–Straub-type data.

16.67   (a) Prove the algebraic identity

$$\sum_{i=1}^{r} \sum_{j=1}^{n_i} m_{ij}(X_{ij} - \bar{X})^2 = \sum_{i=1}^{r} \sum_{j=1}^{n_i} m_{ij}(X_{ij} - \bar{X}_i)^2 + \sum_{i=1}^{r} m_i(\bar{X}_i - \bar{X})^2.$$

(b) Use part (a) and (16.61) to show that (16.63) may be expressed as

$$\hat{a} = m_*^{-1} \left[\frac{\sum_{i=1}^{r} \sum_{j=1}^{n_i} m_{ij}(X_{ij} - \bar{X})^2}{\sum_{i=1}^{r} n_i - 1} - \hat{v} \right]$$

where

$$m_* = \frac{\sum_{i=1}^{r} m_i \left(1 - \dfrac{m_i}{m}\right)}{\sum_{i=1}^{r} n_i - 1}.$$

16.68 (*) A group of 340 insureds in a high-crime area submit the 210 theft claims in a one-year period as given in Table 16.11.

Table 16.11 Data for Exercise 16.68

Number of claims	Number of insureds
0	200
1	80
2	50
3	10

Each insured is assumed to have a Poisson distribution for the number of thefts, but the mean of such a distribution may vary from one insured to another. If a particular insured experienced two claims in the observation period, determine the Bühlmann credibility estimate for the number of claims for this insured in the next period.

17

Simulation

17.1 BASICS OF SIMULATION

Simulation has had an on-again, off-again history in actuarial practice. For example, in the 1970s, aggregate loss calculations were commonly done by simulation because the analytical methods available at the time were not adequate. However, the typical simulation often took a full day on the company's mainframe computer, a serious drag on resources. In the 1980s analytic methods such as Heckman–Meyers and the recursive formula were developed and were found to be significantly faster and more accurate. Today, desktop computers have sufficient power to run complex simulations that allow for the analysis of models not suitable for current analytic approaches.

In a similar vein, as investment vehicles become more complex, contracts have interest-sensitive components, and market fluctuations seem to be more pronounced, analysis of future cash flows must be done on a stochastic basis. In order to accommodate the complexities of the products and interest rate models, simulation has become the technique of choice.

In this chapter we will provide some illustrations of how simulation can solve problems such as those mentioned above. It is not our intention to cover the subject in great detail, but rather to give the reader an idea of how simulation can help. Study of simulation texts such as Herzog and Lord [53],

Loss Models: From Data to Decisions, Second Edition.
By Stuart A. Klugman, Harry H. Panjer, and Gordon E. Willmot
ISBN 0-471-21577-5   Copyright © 2004 John Wiley & Sons, Inc.

Ripley [110], and Ross [115] will provide many important additional insights. In addition, simulation can also be an aid in evaluating some of the statistical techniques covered in earlier chapters. This will also be covered here with an emphasis on the bootstrap method.

17.1.1   The simulation approach

The beauty of simulation is that once the model is created little additional creative thought is required.[1] The entire process can be summarized in four steps, where the goal is to determine values relating to the distribution of a random variable S.

1. Build a model for S which depends on random variables $X, Y, Z, \ldots$, where their distributions and any dependencies are known.

2. For $j = 1, \ldots, n$ generate pseudorandom values $x_j, y_j, z_j, \ldots$ and then compute s_j using the model from step 1.

3. The cdf of S may be approximated by $F_n(s)$, the empirical cdf based on the pseudorandom sample $s_1, \ldots, s_n$.

4. Compute quantities of interest, such as the mean, variance, percentiles, or probabilities, using the empirical cdf.

Two questions remain. First, what does it mean to generate a pseudorandom variable? Consider a random variable X with cdf $F_X(x)$. This is the real random variable produced by some phenomenon of interest. For example, it may be the result of the experiment "collect one automobile bodily injury medical payment at random and record its value." We assume that the cdf is known. For example, it may be the Pareto cdf, $F_X(x) = 1 - \left(\frac{1,000}{1,000+x} \right)^3$. Now consider a second random variable, X^*, resulting from some other process, but with the same Pareto distribution. A random sample from X^*, say $x_1^*, \ldots, x_n^*$, would be impossible to distinguish from one taken from X. That is, given the n numbers, we could not tell if they arose from automobile claims or something else. This means that, instead of learning about X by observing automobile claims, we could learn about it by observing X^*. Obtaining a random sample from a Pareto distribution is still probably difficult, so we have not yet accomplished much.

We can make some progress by making a concession. Let us accept as a replacement for a random sample from X^* a sequence of numbers $x_1^{**}, \ldots, x_n^{**}$ which is not a random sample at all, but simply a sequence of numbers which

---

[1] This is not entirely true. A great deal of creativity may be employed in designing an efficient simulation. The brute force approach used here will work; it just may take your computer longer to produce the answer.

may not be independent, or even random, but was generated by some known process that is related to the random variable X^*. Such a sequence is called a pseudorandom sequence because anyone who did not know its origin could not distinguish it from a random sample from X^* (and therefore from X). Such a sequence will be satisfactory for our purposes.

The field of developing processes for generating pseudorandom sequences of numbers has been well developed. One fact that makes it easier to do this is that it is sufficient to be able to generate such sequences for the uniform distribution on the interval $(0, 1)$. That is because, if U has the uniform$(0, 1)$ distribution, then $X = F_X^{-1}(U)$ will have $F_X(x)$ as its cdf. Therefore, we simply obtain uniform pseudorandom numbers $u_1^{**}, \ldots, u_n^{**}$ and then let $x_j^{**} = F_X^{-1}(u_j^{**})$. This is called the inversion method of generating random variates. Specific methods for particular distributions have been developed but will not be discussed here. There is a considerable literature on the best ways to generate pseudorandom uniform numbers and a variety of tests proposed to evaluate them. Readers are cautioned to ensure that one being used is a good one.

Example 17.1 *Generate* 10,000 *pseudo-Pareto* (*with* $\alpha = 3$, *and* $\theta = 1,000$) *variates and verify that they are indistinguishable from real Pareto observations.*

The pseudouniform values were obtained using the built-in generator supplied with a commercial programming language. The pseudo-Pareto values are calculated from

$$u^{**} = 1 - \left(\frac{1,000}{1,000 + x^{**}} \right)^3.$$

That is,

$$x^{**} = 1,000[(1 - u^{**})^{-1/3} - 1].$$

So, for example, if the first value generated is $u_1^{**} = 0.54246$, we have $x_1^{**} = 297.75$. This was repeated 10,000 times. The results are displayed in Table 17.1, where a chi-square goodness-of-fit test is conducted. The expected counts are calculated using the Pareto distribution with $\alpha = 3$ and $\theta = 1,000$. Because the parameters are known, there are nine degrees of freedom. At a significance level of 5% the critical value is 16.92, and we conclude that the pseudorandom sample could have been a random sample from this Pareto distribution. □

When the distribution function of X is continuous and strictly increasing, the equation $u = F_X(x)$ will have a unique solution for any u. In that case the inversion method reduces to solving the equation. In other cases some care must be taken. Suppose $F_X(x)$ jumps at $x = c$ so that $F_X(c-) = a$ and $F_X(c) = b > a$. If the uniform number is such that $a \le u < b$, the equation has no solution. In that situation choose c as the simulated value.

Table 17.1   Chi-square test of simulated Pareto observations

Interval	Observed	Expected	Chi square
0–100	2,519	2,486.85	0.42
100–250	2,348	2,393.15	0.85
250–500	2,196	2,157.04	0.70
500–750	1,071	1,097.07	0.62
750–1,000	635	615.89	0.59
1,000–1,500	589	610.00	0.72
1,500–2,500	409	406.76	0.01
2,500–5,000	192	186.94	0.14
5,000–10,000	36	38.78	0.20
10,000–	5	7.51	0.84
Total	10,000	10,000	5.10

Example 17.2 *Suppose*

$$F_X(x) = \begin{cases} 0.5x, & 0 \le x < 1, \\ 0.5 + 0.25x & 1 \le x \le 2. \end{cases}$$

Determine the simulated values of x resulting from the uniform numbers 0.3, 0.6, and 0.9.

In the first interval, the distribution function ranges from 0 to 0.5 and in the second interval from 0.75 to 1. With $u = 0.3$ in the first interval, solve $0.3 = 0.5x$ for $x = 0.6$. With the distribution function jumping from 0.5 to 0.75 at $x = 1$, any u in that interval will lead to a simulated value of 1, so for $u = 0.6$, the simulated value is $x = 1$. Note that $\Pr(0.5 \le U < 0.75) = 0.25$, so the value of $x = 1$ will be simulated 25% of the time, matching its true probability. Finally, with 0.9 in the second interval, solve $0.9 = 0.5 + 0.25x$ for $x = 1.6$. Figure 17.1 illustrates this process, showing how drawing vertical bars on the function makes the inversion obvious.   □

It is also possible for the distribution function to be constant over some interval. In that case the equation $u = F_X(x)$ will have multiple solutions over that interval. Our convention (to be justified shortly) is to choose the largest possible value in the interval.

Example 17.3 *Suppose*

$$F_X(x) = \begin{cases} 0.5x, & 0 \le x < 1, \\ 0.5, & 1 \le x < 2, \\ 0.5x - 0.5 & 2 \le x < 3. \end{cases}$$

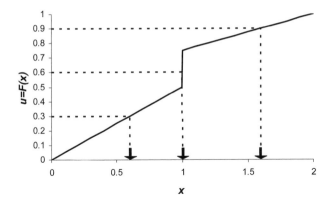

Fig. 17.1 Inversion of the distribution function for Example 17.2

Determine the simulated values of x resulting from the uniform numbers 0.3, 0.5, and 0.9.

The first interval covers values of the distribution function from 0 to 0.5 and the final interval covers the range 0.5 to 1. For $u = 0.3$, use the first interval and solve $0.3 = 0.5x$ for $x = 0.6$. The function is constant at 0.5 from 1 to 2 and so for $u = 0.5$ choose the largest value, $x = 2$. For $u = 0.9$ use the final interval and solve $0.9 = 0.5x - 0.5$ for $x = 2.8$. □

Discrete distributions have both features. The distribution function jumps at the possible values of the variable and is constant in between.

Example 17.4 *Simulate values from a binomial distribution with $m = 4$ and $q = 0.5$ using the uniform numbers 0.3, 0.6875, and 0.95.*

The distribution function is

$$F_X(x) = \begin{cases} 0, & x < 0, \\ 0.0625, & 0 \le x < 1, \\ 0.3125, & 1 \le x < 2, \\ 0.6875, & 2 \le x < 3, \\ 0.9375, & 3 \le x < 4, \\ 1, & x \ge 4. \end{cases}$$

For $u = 0.3$, the function is jumping at $x = 1$. For $u = 0.6875$, the function is constant from 2 to 3 (as the limiting value of the interval) and so $x = 3$. For $u = 0.95$ the function is jumping at $x = 4$. It is usually easier to present the simulation algorithm using a table based on the distribution function. Then a simple table lookup function (such as the VLOOKUP function in Excel®) can be used to obtain simulated values. For this example, the table is as follows.

For u in this range,	the simulated value is
$0 \leq u < 0.0625,$	0
$0.0625 \leq u < 0.3125,$	1
$0.3125 \leq u < 0.6875,$	2
$0.6875 \leq u < 0.9375,$	3
$0.9375 \leq u < 1,$	4

Many random number generators can produce a value of 0 but not a value of 1 (though some produce neither one). This is the motivation for choosing the largest value in an interval where the cdf is constant.   □

The second question is: What value of n should be used? We know that any consistent estimator will be arbitrarily close to the true value with high probability as the sample size is increased. In particular, empirical estimators have this attribute. With a little effort we should be able to determine the value of n that will get us as close as we want with a specified probability. Often, the central limit theorem will help, as in the following example.

Example 17.5 (Example 17.1 continued) *Use simulation to estimate the mean, $F_X(1,000)$, and $\pi_{0.9}$, the 90th percentile of the Pareto distribution with $\alpha = 3$ and $\theta = 1,000$. In each case, stop the simulations when you are 95% confident that the answer is within $\pm 1\%$ of the true value.*

In this example we know the values. Here, $\mu = 500$, $F_X(1,000) = 0.875$, and $\pi_{0.9} = 1,154.43$. For instructional purposes we will behave as if we do not know these values.

The empirical estimate of μ is $\bar{x}$. The central limit theorem tells us that for a sample of size n

$$
\begin{aligned}
0.95 &= \Pr(0.99\mu \leq \bar{X}_n \leq 1.01\mu) \\
&= \Pr\left(-\frac{0.01\mu}{\sigma/\sqrt{n}} \leq \frac{\bar{X}_n - \mu}{\sigma/\sqrt{n}} \leq \frac{0.01\mu}{\sigma/\sqrt{n}}\right) \\
&\doteq \Pr\left(-\frac{0.01\mu}{\sigma/\sqrt{n}} \leq Z \leq \frac{0.01\mu}{\sigma/\sqrt{n}}\right),
\end{aligned}
$$

where Z has the standard normal distribution. Our goal is achieved when

$$
\frac{0.01\mu}{\sigma/\sqrt{n}} = 1.96, \tag{17.1}
$$

which means $n = 38{,}416(\sigma/\mu)^2$. Because we do not know the values of σ and μ, we estimate them with the sample standard deviation and mean. The estimates improve with n, so our stopping rule is to cease simulating when

$$n \geq \frac{38{,}416s^2}{\bar{x}^2}.$$

For a particular simulation conducted by the authors, the criterion was met when $n = 106{,}934$, at which point $\bar{x} = 501.15$, a relative error of 0.23%, well within our goal.

We now turn to the estimation of $F_X(1{,}000)$. The empirical estimator is the sample proportion below 1,000, say P_n/n, where P_n is the number below 1,000 after n simulations. The central limit theorem tells us that P_n/n is approximately normal with mean $F_X(1{,}000)$ and variance $F_X(1{,}000)[1 - F_X(1{,}000)]/n$. Arguing as above, the requirement will be met when

$$n \geq 38{,}416\frac{n - P_n}{P_n}.$$

For our simulation, the criterion was met at $n = 5{,}548$, at which point the estimate was $4{,}848/5{,}548 = 0.87383$, which has a relative error of 0.13%.

Finally, for $\pi_{0.9}$, begin with

$$0.95 = \Pr(Y_a \leq \pi_{0.9} \leq Y_b),$$

where $Y_1 \leq Y_2 \leq \cdots \leq Y_n$ are the order statistics from the simulated sample, a is the greatest integer less than or equal to $0.9n + 0.5 - 1.96\sqrt{0.9(0.1)n}$, b is the smallest integer greater than or equal to $0.9n + 0.5 + 1.96\sqrt{0.9(0.1)n}$, and the process terminates when both

$$\hat{\pi}_{0.9} - Y_a \leq 0.01\hat{\pi}_{0.9}$$

and

$$Y_b - \hat{\pi}_{0.9} \leq 0.01\hat{\pi}_{0.9}.$$

For the example, this occurred when $n = 126{,}364$, and the estimated 90th percentile is 1,153.97, with a relative error of 0.04%. □

17.1.2 Exercises

17.1 Use the inversion method to simulate three values from the Poisson(3) distribution. Use 0.1247, 0.9321, and 0.6873 for the uniform random numbers.

17.2 Use the uniform random numbers 0.2, 0.5, and 0.7 to simulate values from

$$f_X(x) = \begin{cases} 0.25, & 0 \leq x \leq 2, \\ 0.1, & 4 \leq x \leq 9, \\ 0, & \text{otherwise.} \end{cases}$$

17.3 Demonstrate that $0.95 = \Pr(Y_a \leq \pi_{0.9} \leq Y_b)$ for Y_a and Y_b as defined in Example 17.5.

17.4 You are simulating observations from an exponential distribution with $\theta = 100$. How many simulations are needed to be 90% certain of being within 2% of each of the mean and the probability of being below 200? Conduct the required number of simulations and note if the 2% goal has been reached.

17.5 Simulate 1,000 observations from a gamma distribution with $\alpha = 2$ and $\theta = 500$. Perform the chi-square goodness-of-fit and Kolmogorov–Smirnov tests to see if the simulated values were actually from that distribution.

17.6 (*) To estimate $E(X)$, you have simulated five observations from the random variable X. The values are 1, 2, 3, 4, and 5. Your goal is to have the standard deviation of the estimate of $E(X)$ be less than 0.05. Estimate the total number of simulations needed.

17.2 EXAMPLES OF SIMULATION IN ACTUARIAL MODELING

17.2.1 Aggregate loss calculations

The analytic methods presented in Chapter 6 have two features in common. First, they are exact up to the level of the approximation introduced. For recursion and the FFT, that involves replacing the true severity distribution with an arithmetized approximation. For Heckman–Meyers a histogram approximation is required. Furthermore, Heckman–Meyers requires a numerical integration. In each case, the errors can be reduced to near zero by increasing the number of points used. Second, both recursion and inversion assume that aggregate claims can be written as $S = X_1 + \cdots + X_N$ with $N, X_1, X_2, \ldots$ independent and the X_js identically distributed.

There is no need to be concerned about the first feature because the approximation error can be made as small as desired. However, the second restriction may prevent the model from reflecting reality. In this section we indicate some common ways in which the independence or identical distribution assumptions may fail to hold and then demonstrate how simulation can lead to a solution. When the X_js are i.i.d. it does not matter how we go about labeling the losses—that is, which loss is called X_1, which one X_2, and so on. With the assumption removed, the labels become important. Because S is the aggregate loss for one year, time is a factor. One way of identifying the losses is to let X_1 be the first loss, X_2 be the second loss, and so on. Then let T_j be the random variable that records the time of the jth loss. Without going into much detail about the claims-paying process, we do want to note that T_j may be the time at which the loss occurred, the time it was reported, or the time payment was made. In the latter two cases it may be that $T_j > 1$, which occurs when the report of the loss or the payment of the claim takes place at a time subsequent to the end of the time period of the coverage, usually one year. If the timing of the losses is important, we will need to know the joint distribution of $(T_1, T_2, \ldots, X_1, X_2, \ldots)$.

17.2.2 Examples of lack of independence or identical distributions

There are two common ways to have the assumption fail to hold. One is through accounting for time (and in particular the time value of money) and the other is through coverage modifications. The latter may have a time factor as well. The following examples provide some illustrations.

Example 17.6 (Time value of loss payments) *Suppose the quantity of interest, S, is the present value of all payments made in respect of a policy issued today and covering loss events that occur in the next year. Develop a model for S.*

Let T_j be the time of the payment of the jth loss. While T_j records the time of the payment, the subscripts are selected in order of the loss events. Let $T_j = C_j + L_j$ where C_j is the time of the event and L_j is the time from occurrence to payment. Assume they are independent and the L_js are independent of each other. Let the time between events, $C_j - C_{j-1}$ (where $C_0 = 0$), be i.i.d. with an exponential distribution with mean 0.2 years.

Let X_j be the amount paid at time T_j on the loss that occurred at time C_j. Assume that X_j and C_j are independent (the amount of the claim does not depend on when in the year it occurred) but X_j and L_j are positively correlated (a specific distributional model will be specified when the example is continued). This is reasonable because the more expensive losses may take longer to settle.

Finally, let V_t be a random variable that represents the value, which, if invested today, will accumulate to 1 in t years. It is independent of all X_j, C_j, and L_j. But clearly, for $s \neq t$, V_s and V_t are dependent. We then have

$$S = \sum_{j=1}^{N} X_j V_{T_j}$$

where $N = \max_{C_j < 1}\{j\}$. The various dependencies were established in the development of the random variables. □

Example 17.7 (Out-of-pocket maximum) *Suppose there is a deductible, d, on individual losses. However, in the course of a year, the policyholder will pay no more than u. Develop a model for the insurer's aggregate payments.*

Let X_j be the amount of the jth loss. Here the assignment of j does not matter. Let $W_j = X_j \wedge d$ be the amount paid by the policyholder due to the deductible and let $Y_j = X_j - W_j$ be the amount paid by the insurer. Then $R = W_1 + \cdots + W_N$ is the total amount paid by the policyholder prior to imposing the out-of-pocket maximum. Then the amount actually paid by the policyholder is $R_u = R \wedge u$. Let $S = X_1 + \cdots + X_N$ be the total losses, and then the aggregate amount paid by the insurer is $T = S - R_u$. Note that the distributions of S and R_u are based on i.i.d. severity distributions. The analytic methods described earlier can be used to obtain their distributions. But because they are dependent, their individual distributions cannot be combined to produce the distribution of T. There is also no way to write T as a random sum of i.i.d. variables. At the beginning of the year, it appears that T will be the sum of i.i.d. Y_js, but at some point the Y_js may be replaced by X_js as the out-of-pocket maximum is reached.   □

17.2.3   Simulation analysis of the two examples

We now complete the two examples using the simulation approach. The models have been selected arbitrarily, but we should assume they were determined by a careful estimation process using the techniques presented earlier in this text.

Example 17.8 (Example 17.6 continued) *The model is completed with the following specifications. The amount of a payment* (X_j) *has the Pareto distribution with parameters* $\alpha = 3$ *and* $\theta = 1,000$. *The time from the occurrence of a claim to its payment* (L_j) *has a Weibull distribution with* $\tau = 1.5$ *and* $\theta = \ln(X_j)/6$. *This models the dependence by having the scale parameter depend on the size of the loss. The discount factor will be modeled by assuming that, for* $t > s$, $[\ln(V_s/V_t)]/(t - s)$ *has a normal distribution with mean 0.06 and variance* $0.0004(t - s)$. *We do not need to specify a model for the number of losses. Instead, we use the model given earlier for the time between losses. Use simulation to determine the expected present value of aggregate payments.*

The mechanics of a single simulation will be done in detail, and that should indicate how the process is to be done. Begin by generating i.i.d. exponential interloss times until their sum exceeds 1 (in order to obtain one year's worth of claims). The individual variates are generated from pseudouniform numbers using

$$u = 1 - e^{-5x},$$

which yields

$$x = -0.2 \ln(1 - u).$$

For the first simulation, the uniform pseudorandom numbers and the corresponding x values are $(0.25373, 0.0585)$, $(0.46750, 0.1260)$, $(0.23709, 0.0541)$, $(0.75780, 0.2836)$, and $(0.96642, 0.6788)$. At this point the simulated xs total 1.2010 and therefore there are four loss events, occurring at times $c_1 = 0.0585$, $c_2 = 0.1845$, $c_3 = 0.2386$, and $c_4 = 0.5222$.

The four loss amounts are found from inverting the Pareto cdf. That is,

$$x = 1,000[(1 - u)^{-1/3} - 1].$$

The four pseudouniform numbers are 0.71786, 0.47779, 0.61084, and 0.68579. This produces the four losses $x_1 = 524.68$, $x_2 = 241.80$, $x_3 = 369.70$, and $x_4 = 470.93$.

The times from occurrence to payment have a Weibull distribution. The equation to solve is

$$u = 1 - e^{-[6l/\ln(x)]^{1.5}},$$

where x is the loss. Solving for the lag time l yields

$$l = \tfrac{1}{6}\ln(x)[-\ln(1-u)]^{2/3}.$$

For the first lag we have $u = 0.23376$ and so

$$l_1 = \tfrac{1}{6}\ln(524.68)[-\ln 0.76624]^{2/3} = 0.4320.$$

Similarly, with the next three values of u being 0.85799, 0.12951, and 0.72085, we have $l_2 = 1.4286$, $l_3 = 0.2640$, and $l_4 = 1.2068$. The payment times of the four losses are the sum of c_j and l_j, namely $t_1 = 0.4905$, $t_2 = 1.6131$, $t_3 = 0.5026$, and $t_4 = 1.7290$.

Finally, we generate the discount factors. They must be generated in order of increasing t_j so we first obtain $v_{0.4905}$. We begin with a normal variate with mean 0.06 and variance $0.0004(0.4905) = 0.0001962$. Using inversion, the simulated value is $0.0592 = [\ln(1/v_{0.4905})]/0.4905$ and so $v_{0.4905} = 0.9714$. Note that for the first value we have $s = 0$, and $v_0 = 1$. For the second value we require a normal variate with mean 0.06 and variance $(0.5026 - 0.4905)(0.0004) = 0.00000484$. The simulated value is

$$0.0604 = \frac{\ln(0.9714/v_{0.5026})}{0.0121} \text{ for } v_{0.5026} = 0.9707.$$

For the next two payments, we have

$$0.0768 = \frac{\ln(0.9707/v_{1.6131})}{1.1105} \text{ for } v_{1.6131} = 0.8913,$$

$$0.0628 = \frac{\ln(0.8913/v_{1.7290})}{0.1159} \text{ for } v_{1.7290} = 0.8848.$$

We are now ready to determine the first simulated value of the aggregate present value. It is

$$
\begin{aligned}
s_1 &= 524.68(0.9714) + 241.80(0.8913) + 369.70(0.9707) + 470.93(0.8848) \\
&= 1{,}500.74.
\end{aligned}
$$

The process was then repeated until there was 95% confidence that the estimated mean was within 1% of the true mean. This took 26,944 simulations, producing a sample mean of 2,299.16. $\qquad\square$

Example 17.9 (Example 17.7 continued) *For this example, set the deductible d at 250 and the out-of-pocket maximum at $u = 1,000$. Assume that the*

Table 17.2   Negative binomial cumulative probabilities

n	$F_N(n)$	n	$F_N(n)$
0	0.03704	8	0.76589
1	0.11111	9	0.81888
2	0.20988	10	0.86127
3	0.31962	11	0.89467
4	0.42936	12	0.92064
5	0.53178	13	0.94062
6	0.62282	14	0.95585
7	0.70086	15	0.96735

number of losses has the negative binomial distribution with $r = 3$ and $\beta = 2$. Further assume that individual losses have the Weibull distribution with $\tau = 2$ and $\theta = 600$. Determine the 95th percentile of the insurer's losses.

In order to simulate the negative binomial claim counts, we require the cdf of the negative binomial distribution. There is no closed form, but a table can be constructed, and one appears here as Table 17.2. The number of losses for the year is generated by obtaining one pseudouniform value—for example, $u = 0.47515$—and then determining the smallest entry in the table that is larger than 0.47515. The simulated value appears to its left. In this case our first simulation produced $n = 5$ losses.

The amounts of the five losses are obtained from the Weibull distribution. Inversion of the cdf produces

$$x = 600[-\ln(1 - u)]^{1/2}.$$

The five simulated values are 544.04, 453.67, 217.87, 681.98, and 449.83. The total loss is 2,347.39. The policyholder pays $250.00+250.00+217.87+250.00+250.00 = 1,217.87$, but the out-of-pocket maximum limits this to 1,000. Thus our first simulated value has the insurer paying 1,347.39.

The goal was set to be 95% confident that the estimated 95th percentile would be within 2% of the true value. This required 11,476 simulations, producing an estimated 95th percentile of 6,668.18.   □

17.2.4   Statistical analyses

Simulation can help in a variety of ways when analyzing data. Two will be discussed here, both of which have to do with evaluating a statistical procedure. The first is the determination of the p-value (or critical value) for a hypothesis test. The second is to evaluate the mean-squared error of an estimator. We begin with the hypothesis testing situation.

Example 17.10 *It is conjectured that losses have a lognormal distribution. One hundred observations have been collected and the Kolmogorov–Smirnov test statistic is* 0.06272. *Determine the p-value for this test, first with the null hypothesis being that the distribution is lognormal with* $\mu = 7$ *and* $\sigma = 1$ *and then with the parameters unspecified.*

For the null hypothesis with each parameter specified, one simulation involves first simulating 100 lognormal observations from the specified lognormal distribution. Then the Kolmogorov–Smirnov test statistic is calculated. The estimated p-value is the proportion of simulations for which the test statistic exceeds 0.06272. After 1000 simulations, the estimate of the p-value is 0.836.

With the parameters unspecified, it is not clear which lognormal distribution should be used. It turned out that for the observations actually collected $\hat{\mu} = 7.2201$ and $\hat{\sigma} = 0.80893$. These were used as the basis for each simulation. The only change is that after the simulated observations have been obtained, the results are compared to a lognormal distribution with parameters estimated (by maximum likelihood) from the simulated data set. For 1,000 simulations, the test statistic exceeded 0.06272 491 times, for an estimated p-value of 0.491.

As indicated in Section 13.4.1, not specifying the parameters makes a considerable difference in the interpretation of the test statistic. $\square$

When testing hypotheses, p-values and significance levels are calculated assuming the null hypothesis to be true. In other situations, there is no known population distribution from which to simulate. For such situations, a technique called the bootstrap (see [33] for thorough coverage of this subject) may help. The key is to use the empirical distribution from the data as the population from which to simulate values. Theoretical arguments show that at least asymptotically the bootstrap estimate will converge to the true value. This is reasonable because as the sample size increases the empirical distribution becomes more and more like the true distribution. The following example shows how the bootstrap works and also indicates that, at least in the case illustrated, it gives a reasonable answer.

Example 17.11 *A sample (with replacement) of size* 3 *from a population produced the values* 2, 3, *and* 7. *Determine the bootstrap estimate of the mean-squared error of the sample mean as an estimator of the population mean.*

The bootstrap approach assumes that the population places probability $\frac{1}{3}$ on each of the three values 2, 3, and 7. The mean of this distribution is 4. From this population there are 27 samples of size 3 that might be drawn. Sample means can be 2 (sample values $2, 2, 2$, with probability $\frac{1}{27}$), $\frac{7}{3}$ (sample values $2, 2, 3$, $2, 3, 2$, and $3, 2, 2$, with probability $\frac{3}{27}$), and so on, up to 7 with probability $\frac{1}{27}$. The mean-squared error is

$$(2-4)^2(1/27) + \left(\frac{7}{3} - 4\right)^2 (3/27) + \cdots + (7-4)^2(1/27) = \frac{14}{9}.$$

The usual approach is to note that the sample mean is unbiased and therefore

$$\text{MSE}(\bar{X}) = \text{Var}(\bar{X}) = \sigma^2/n.$$

With the variance unknown, a reasonable choice is to use the sample variance. With a denominator of n, for this example, the estimated mean-squared error is

$$\frac{\frac{1}{3}[(2-4)^2 + (3-4)^2 + (7-4)^2]}{3} = \frac{14}{9},$$

the same as the bootstrap estimate. $\qquad\square$

In many situations, determination of the mean-squared error is not so easy, and then the bootstrap becomes an extremely useful tool. While simulation was not needed for the example, note that an original sample size of 3 led to 27 possible bootstrap values. Once the sample size gets beyond 6, it becomes impractical to enumerate all the cases. In that case, simulating observations from the empirical distribution becomes the only feasible choice.

Example 17.12 *In Example* 11.3 *an empirical model for time to death was obtained. The empirical probabilities are 0.0333, 0.0744, 0.0343, 0.0660, 0.0344, and 0.0361 that death is at times 0.8, 2.9, 3.1, 4.0, 4.1, and 4.8 respectively. The remaining 0.7215 probability is that the person will be alive five years from now. The expected present value for a five-year term insurance policy that pays 1,000 at the moment of death is estimated as*

$$1000(0.0333v^{0.8} + \cdots + 0.0361v^{4.8}) = 223.01,$$

where $v = 1.07^{-1}$. *Simulate* 10,000 *bootstrap samples to estimate the mean-squared error of this estimator.*

A method for conducting a bootstrap simulation with the Kaplan–Meier estimate is given by Efron [31]. Rather than simulate from the empirical distribution (as given by the Kaplan–Meier estimate), simulate from the original sample. In this example, that means assigning probability $\frac{1}{40}$ to each of the original observations. Then each bootstrap observation is a left-truncation point along with the accompanying censored or uncensored value. After 40 such observations are recorded, the Kaplan–Meier estimate is constructed from the bootstrap sample and then the quantity of interest computed. This is relatively easy because the bootstrap estimate can place probability only at the six original points. Ten thousand simulations were quickly done. The mean was 222.05 and the mean-squared error was 4,119. Efron also noted that the bootstrap estimate of the variance of $\hat{S}(t)$ is asymptotically equal to Greenwood's estimate, thus giving credence to both methods. $\qquad\square$

17.2.5   Exercises

17.7 (*) Insurance for a city's snow removal costs covers four winter months. There is a deductible of 10,000 per month. Monthly costs are independent and normally distributed with $\mu = 15,000$ and $\sigma = 2,000$. Monthly costs are simulated using the inversion method. For one simulation of a year's payments the four uniform pseudorandom numbers are 0.5398, 0.1151, 0.0013, and 0.7881. Calculate the insurer's cost for this simulated year.

17.8 (*) After one period, the price of a stock is X times its price at the beginning of the period, where X has a lognormal distribution with $\mu = 0.01$ and $\sigma = 0.02$. The price at time 0 is 100. The inversion method is used to simulate price movements. The pseudouniform random numbers are 0.1587 and 0.9332 for periods 1 and 2. Determine the simulated prices at the end of each of the first two periods.

17.9 (*) You have insured 100 people, each age 70. Each person has probability 0.03318 of dying in the next year and the deaths are independent. Therefore, the number of deaths has a binomial distribution with $m = 100$ and $q = 0.03318$. Use the inversion method to determine the simulated number of deaths in the next year based on $u = 0.18$.

17.10 (*) For a surplus process, claims occur according to a Poisson process at the rate of two per year. Thus the time between claims has the exponential distribution with $\theta = 2$. Claims have a Pareto distribution with $\alpha = 2$ and $\theta = 1,000$. The initial surplus is 2,000 and premiums are collected at a rate of 2,200. Ruin occurs any time the surplus is negative, at which time no further premiums are collected or claims paid. All simulations are done with the inversion method. For the time between claims, use 0.83, 0.54, 0.48, and 0.14 as the pseudorandom numbers. For claim amounts use 0.89, 0.36, 0.70, and 0.61. Determine the surplus at time 1.

17.11 (*) You are given a random sample of size 2 from some distribution. The values are 1 and 3. You plan to estimate the population variance with the estimator $[(X_1 - \bar{X})^2 + (X_2 - \bar{X})^2]/2$. Determine the bootstrap estimate of the mean-squared error of this estimator.

17.12 A sample of three items from the uniform(0,10) distribution produced the following values: 2, 4, and 7.

    (a) Calculate the Kolmogorov–Smirnov test statistic for the null hypothesis that the data came from the uniform(0,10) distribution.

    (b) Simulate 10,000 samples of size 3 from the uniform(0,10) distribution and compute the Kolmogorov–Smirnov test statistic for each. The proportion of times the value equals or exceeds your answer to part (a) is an estimate of the p-value.

17.13 A sample of three items from the uniform$(0, \theta)$ distribution produced the following values: 2, 4, and 7. Consider the estimator of θ,

$$\hat{\theta} = \tfrac{4}{3}\max(x_1, x_2, x_3).$$

From example 9.15 the mean-squared error of this unbiased estimator was shown to be $\theta^2/15$.

  (a) Estimate the mean-squared error by replacing θ with its estimate.

  (b) Obtain the bootstrap estimate of the variance of the estimator. (It is not possible to use the bootstrap to estimate the mean-squared error because you cannot obtain the true value of θ from the empirical distribution, but you can obtain the expected value of the estimator.)

Appendix A
An inventory of
continuous distributions

A.1 INTRODUCTION

Descriptions of the models are given below. First a few mathematical prelimi-
naries are presented that indicate how the various quantities can be computed.
   The incomplete gamma function[1] is given by

$$\Gamma(\alpha; x) = \frac{1}{\Gamma(\alpha)} \int_0^x t^{\alpha-1} e^{-t} \, dt, \quad \alpha > 0, \; x > 0$$

$$\text{with } \Gamma(\alpha) = \int_0^\infty t^{\alpha-1} e^{-t} \, dt, \quad \alpha > 0.$$

---

[1] Some references, such as [3], denote this integral $P(\alpha, x)$ and define $\Gamma(\alpha, x) = \int_x^\infty t^{\alpha-1} e^{-t} \, dt$. Note that this definition does not normalize by dividing by $\Gamma(\alpha)$. When using software to evaluate the incomplete gamma function, be sure to note how it is defined.

Loss Models: From Data to Decisions, Second Edition.
By Stuart A. Klugman, Harry H. Panjer, and Gordon E. Willmot
ISBN 0-471-21577-5   Copyright © 2004 John Wiley & Sons, Inc.

Also, define

$$G(\alpha; x) = \int_x^\infty t^{\alpha-1} e^{-t}\, dt, \quad x > 0.$$

At times we will need this integral for nonpositive values of α. Integration by parts produces the relationship

$$G(\alpha; x) = -\frac{x^\alpha e^{-x}}{\alpha} + \frac{1}{\alpha} G(\alpha + 1; x).$$

This can be repeated until the first argument of G is $\alpha + k$, a positive number. Then it can be evaluated from

$$G(\alpha + k; x) = \Gamma(\alpha + k)[1 - \Gamma(\alpha + k; x)].$$

However, if α is a negative integer or zero, the value of $G(0; x)$ is needed. It is

$$G(0; x) = \int_x^\infty t^{-1} e^{-t}\, dt = E_1(x),$$

which is called the **exponential integral**. A series expansion for this integral is

$$E_1(x) = -0.57721566490153 - \ln x - \sum_{n=1}^\infty \frac{(-1)^n x^n}{n(n!)}.$$

When α is a positive integer, the incomplete gamma function can be evaluated exactly as given in the following theorem.

Theorem A.1 *For integer α,*

$$\Gamma(\alpha; x) = 1 - \sum_{j=0}^{\alpha-1} \frac{x^j e^{-x}}{j!}.$$

Proof: For $\alpha = 1$, $\Gamma(1; x) = \int_0^x e^{-t}\, dt = 1 - e^{-x}$, and so the theorem is true for this case. The proof is completed by induction. Assume it is true for $\alpha = 1, \ldots, n$. Then

$$
\begin{aligned}
\Gamma(n + 1; x) &= \frac{1}{n!} \int_0^x t^n e^{-t}\, dt \\
&= \frac{1}{n!} \left(-t^n e^{-t} \Big|_0^x + \int_0^x n t^{n-1} e^{-t}\, dt \right) \\
&= \frac{1}{n!} \left(-x^n e^{-x} \right) + \Gamma(n; x) \\
&= -\frac{x^n e^{-x}}{n!} + 1 - \sum_{j=0}^{n-1} \frac{x^j e^{-x}}{j!} \\
&= 1 - \sum_{j=0}^{n} \frac{x^j e^{-x}}{j!}.
\end{aligned}
$$

The incomplete beta function is given by

$$\beta(a, b; x) = \frac{\Gamma(a+b)}{\Gamma(a)\Gamma(b)} \int_0^x t^{a-1}(1-t)^{b-1}\, dt, \quad a > 0,\ b > 0,\ 0 < x < 1,$$

and when $b < 0$ (but $a > 1 + \lfloor -b \rfloor$), repeated integration by parts produces

$$
\begin{aligned}
\Gamma(a)\Gamma(b)\beta(a, b; x) \;=\; & -\Gamma(a+b) \left[\frac{x^{a-1}(1-x)^b}{b} \right. \\
& + \frac{(a-1)x^{a-2}(1-x)^{b+1}}{b(b+1)} + \cdots \\
& \left. + \frac{(a-1)\cdots(a-r)x^{a-r-1}(1-x)^{b+r}}{b(b+1)\cdots(b+r)} \right] \\
& + \frac{(a-1)\cdots(a-r-1)}{b(b+1)\cdots(b+r)}\Gamma(a-r-1) \\
& \times \Gamma(b+r+1)\beta(a-r-1, b+r+1; x),
\end{aligned}
$$

where r is the smallest integer such that $b + r + 1 > 0$. The first argument must be positive (that is, $a - r - 1 > 0$).

Numerical approximations for both the incomplete gamma and the incomplete beta function are available in many statistical computing packages as well as in many spreadsheets because they are just the distribution functions of the gamma and beta distributions. The following approximations are taken from [3]. The suggestion regarding using different formulas for small and large x when evaluating the incomplete gamma function is from [107]. That reference also contains computer subroutines for evaluating these expressions. In particular, it provides an effective way of evaluating continued fractions.

For $x \le \alpha + 1$ use the series expansion

$$\Gamma(\alpha; x) = \frac{x^\alpha e^{-x}}{\Gamma(\alpha)} \sum_{n=0}^{\infty} \frac{x^n}{\alpha(\alpha+1)\cdots(\alpha+n)}$$

while for $x > \alpha + 1$ use the continued-fraction expansion

$$1 - \Gamma(\alpha; x) = \frac{x^\alpha e^{-x}}{\Gamma(\alpha)} \cfrac{1}{x + \cfrac{1-\alpha}{1 + \cfrac{1}{x + \cfrac{2-\alpha}{1 + \cfrac{2}{x + \cdots}}}}}.$$

The incomplete gamma function can also be used to produce cumulative probabilities from the standard normal distribution. Let $\Phi(z) = \Pr(Z \le z)$, where Z has the standard normal distribution. Then, for $z \geq 0$, $\Phi(z) = 0.5 + \Gamma(0.5; z^2/2)/2$ while, for $z < 0$, $\Phi(z) = 1 - \Phi(-z)$.

The incomplete beta function can be evaluated by the series expansion

$$\beta(a, b; x) = \frac{\Gamma(a + b)x^a(1 - x)^b}{a\Gamma(a)\Gamma(b)}$$

$$\times \left[1 + \sum_{n=0}^{\infty} \frac{(a + b)(a + b + 1) \cdots (a + b + n)}{(a + 1)(a + 2) \cdots (a + n + 1)} x^{n+1}\right].$$

The gamma function itself can be found from

$$\ln \Gamma(\alpha) \doteq (\alpha - \tfrac{1}{2}) \ln \alpha - \alpha + \frac{\ln(2\pi)}{2}$$

$$+ \frac{1}{12\alpha} - \frac{1}{360\alpha^3} + \frac{1}{1,260\alpha^5} - \frac{1}{1,680\alpha^7} + \frac{1}{1,188\alpha^9} - \frac{691}{360,360\alpha^{11}}$$

$$+ \frac{1}{156\alpha^{13}} - \frac{3,617}{122,400\alpha^{15}} + \frac{43,867}{244,188\alpha^{17}} - \frac{174,611}{125,400\alpha^{19}}.$$

For values of α above 10 the error is less than 10^{-19}. For values below 10 use the relationship

$$\ln \Gamma(\alpha) = \ln \Gamma(\alpha + 1) - \ln \alpha.$$

The distributions are presented in the following way. First the name is given along with the parameters. Many of the distributions have other names, which are noted in parentheses. Next the density function $f(x)$ and distribution function $F(x)$ are given. For some distributions, formulas for starting values are given. Within each family the distributions are presented in decreasing order with regard to the number of parameters. The Greek letters used are selected to be consistent. Any Greek letter that is not used in the distribution means that that distribution is a special case of one with more parameters but with the missing parameters set equal to 1. Unless specifically indicated, all parameters must be positive.

Except for two distributions, inflation can be recognized by simply inflating the scale parameter θ. That is, if X has a particular distribution, then cX has the same distribution type, with all parameters unchanged except θ is changed to $c\theta$. For the lognormal distribution, μ changes to $\mu + \ln(c)$ with σ unchanged, while for the inverse Gaussian both μ and θ are multiplied by c.

For several of the distributions, starting values are suggested. They are not necessarily good estimators, just places from which to start an iterative procedure to maximize the likelihood or other objective function. These are found by either the methods of moments or percentile matching. The quantities used are:

$$\text{Moments:} \quad m = \frac{1}{n} \sum_{i=1}^{n} x_i, \quad t = \frac{1}{n} \sum_{i=1}^{n} x_i^2,$$

Percentile matching: $p =$ 25th percentile, $q =$ 75th percentile.

For grouped data or data that have been truncated or censored, these quantities may have to be approximated. Because the purpose is to obtain starting values and not a useful estimate, it is often sufficient to just ignore modifications. For three- and four-parameter distributions, starting values can be obtained by using estimates from a special case, then making the new parameters equal to 1. An all-purpose starting value rule (for when all else fails) is to set the scale parameter (θ) equal to the mean and set all other parameters equal to 2.

All the distributions listed here (and many more) are discussed in great detail in [73]. In many cases, alternatives to maximum likelihood estimators are presented.

A.2   TRANSFORMED BETA FAMILY

A.2.1   Four-parameter distribution

A.2.1.1   Transformed beta—$\alpha, \theta, \gamma, \tau$ (generalized beta of the second kind, Pearson Type VI)

$$f(x) = \frac{\Gamma(\alpha+\tau)}{\Gamma(\alpha)\Gamma(\tau)} \frac{\gamma(x/\theta)^{\gamma\tau}}{x[1+(x/\theta)^\gamma]^{\alpha+\tau}},$$

$$F(x) = \beta(\tau,\alpha;u), \quad u = \frac{(x/\theta)^\gamma}{1+(x/\theta)^\gamma},$$

$$E[X^k] = \frac{\theta^k\Gamma(\tau+k/\gamma)\Gamma(\alpha-k/\gamma)}{\Gamma(\alpha)\Gamma(\tau)}, \quad -\tau\gamma < k < \alpha\gamma,$$

$$E[(X \wedge x)^k] = \frac{\theta^k\Gamma(\tau+k/\gamma)\Gamma(\alpha-k/\gamma)}{\Gamma(\alpha)\Gamma(\tau)}\beta(\tau+k/\gamma,\alpha-k/\gamma;u)$$
$$+x^k[1-F(x)], \quad k > -\tau\gamma,$$

$$\text{Mode} = \theta\left(\frac{\tau\gamma-1}{\alpha\gamma+1}\right)^{1/\gamma}, \quad \tau\gamma > 1, \text{ else } 0.$$

A.2.2   Three-parameter distributions

A.2.2.1   Generalized Pareto—α, θ, τ (beta of the second kind)

$$f(x) = \frac{\Gamma(\alpha+\tau)}{\Gamma(\alpha)\Gamma(\tau)} \frac{\theta^\alpha x^{\tau-1}}{(x+\theta)^{\alpha+\tau}},$$

$$F(x) = \beta(\tau,\alpha;u), \quad u = \frac{x}{x+\theta},$$

$$\mathrm{E}[X^k] = \frac{\theta^k \Gamma(\tau+k)\Gamma(\alpha-k)}{\Gamma(\alpha)\Gamma(\tau)}, \quad -\tau < k < \alpha,$$

$$\mathrm{E}[X^k] = \frac{\theta^k \tau(\tau+1)\cdots(\tau+k-1)}{(\alpha-1)\cdots(\alpha-k)} \quad \text{if } k \text{ is an integer},$$

$$\mathrm{E}[(X \wedge x)^k] = \frac{\theta^k \Gamma(\tau+k)\Gamma(\alpha-k)}{\Gamma(\alpha)\Gamma(\tau)}\beta(\tau+k, \alpha-k; u),$$
$$+ x^k[1 - F(x)], \quad k > -\tau,$$

$$\text{Mode} = \theta\frac{\tau-1}{\alpha+1}, \quad \tau > 1, \text{ else } 0.$$

A.2.2.2 Burr—α, θ, γ (Burr Type XII, Singh–Maddala)

$$f(x) = \frac{\alpha\gamma(x/\theta)^\gamma}{x[1+(x/\theta)^\gamma]^{\alpha+1}},$$

$$F(x) = 1 - u^\alpha, \quad u = \frac{1}{1+(x/\theta)^\gamma},$$

$$\mathrm{E}[X^k] = \frac{\theta^k \Gamma(1+k/\gamma)\Gamma(\alpha-k/\gamma)}{\Gamma(\alpha)}, \quad -\gamma < k < \alpha\gamma,$$

$$\mathrm{E}[(X \wedge x)^k] = \frac{\theta^k \Gamma(1+k/\gamma)\Gamma(\alpha-k/\gamma)}{\Gamma(\alpha)}\beta(1+k/\gamma, \alpha-k/\gamma; 1-u)$$
$$+ x^k u^\alpha, \quad k > -\gamma,$$

$$\text{Mode} = \theta\left(\frac{\gamma-1}{\alpha\gamma+1}\right)^{1/\gamma}, \quad \gamma > 1, \text{ else } 0.$$

A.2.2.3 Inverse Burr—τ, θ, γ (Dagum)

$$f(x) = \frac{\tau\gamma(x/\theta)^{\gamma\tau}}{x[1+(x/\theta)^\gamma]^{\tau+1}},$$

$$F(x) = u^\tau, \quad u = \frac{(x/\theta)^\gamma}{1+(x/\theta)^\gamma},$$

$$\mathrm{E}[X^k] = \frac{\theta^k \Gamma(\tau+k/\gamma)\Gamma(1-k/\gamma)}{\Gamma(\tau)}, \quad -\tau\gamma < k < \gamma,$$

$$\mathrm{E}[(X \wedge x)^k] = \frac{\theta^k \Gamma(\tau+k/\gamma)\Gamma(1-k/\gamma)}{\Gamma(\tau)}\beta(\tau+k/\gamma, 1-k/\gamma; u)$$
$$+ x^k[1 - u^\tau], \quad k > -\tau\gamma,$$

$$\text{Mode} = \theta\left(\frac{\tau\gamma-1}{\gamma+1}\right)^{1/\gamma}, \quad \tau\gamma > 1, \text{ else } 0.$$

A.2.3   Two-parameter distributions

A.2.3.1   Pareto—α, θ   (Pareto Type II, Lomax)

$$f(x) = \frac{\alpha\theta^\alpha}{(x+\theta)^{\alpha+1}},$$

$$F(x) = 1 - \left(\frac{\theta}{x+\theta}\right)^\alpha,$$

$$E[X^k] = \frac{\theta^k\Gamma(k+1)\Gamma(\alpha-k)}{\Gamma(\alpha)}, \quad -1 < k < \alpha,$$

$$E[X^k] = \frac{\theta^k k!}{(\alpha-1)\cdots(\alpha-k)} \quad \text{if } k \text{ is an integer}$$

$$E[X \wedge x] = \frac{\theta}{\alpha-1}\left[1 - \left(\frac{\theta}{x+\theta}\right)^{\alpha-1}\right], \quad \alpha \neq 1,$$

$$E[X \wedge x] = -\theta\ln\left(\frac{\theta}{x+\theta}\right), \quad \alpha = 1,$$

$$E[(X \wedge x)^k] = \frac{\theta^k\Gamma(k+1)\Gamma(\alpha-k)}{\Gamma(\alpha)}\beta[k+1, \alpha-k; x/(x+\theta)]$$

$$+ x^k\left(\frac{\theta}{x+\theta}\right)^\alpha, \quad \text{all } k,$$

$$\text{Mode} = 0,$$

$$\hat{\alpha} = 2\frac{t-m^2}{t-2m^2}, \quad \hat{\theta} = \frac{mt}{t-2m^2}.$$

A.2.3.2   Inverse Pareto—τ, θ

$$f(x) = \frac{\tau\theta x^{\tau-1}}{(x+\theta)^{\tau+1}},$$

$$F(x) = \left(\frac{x}{x+\theta}\right)^\tau,$$

$$E[X^k] = \frac{\theta^k\Gamma(\tau+k)\Gamma(1-k)}{\Gamma(\tau)}, \quad -\tau < k < 1,$$

$$E[X^k] = \frac{\theta^k(-k)!}{(\tau-1)\cdots(\tau+k)} \quad \text{if } k \text{ is a negative integer,}$$

$$E[(X \wedge x)^k] = \theta^k\tau\int_0^{x/(x+\theta)} y^{\tau+k-1}(1-y)^{-k}dy$$

$$+ x^k\left[1 - \left(\frac{x}{x+\theta}\right)^\tau\right], \quad k > -\tau,$$

$$\text{Mode} = \theta\frac{\tau-1}{2}, \quad \tau > 1, \text{ else } 0.$$

A.2.3.3   Loglogistic—γ, θ (Fisk)

$$f(x) = \frac{\gamma(x/\theta)^\gamma}{x[1+(x/\theta)^\gamma]^2},$$

$$F(x) = u, \quad u = \frac{(x/\theta)^\gamma}{1+(x/\theta)^\gamma},$$

$$E[X^k] = \theta^k \Gamma(1+k/\gamma)\Gamma(1-k/\gamma), \quad -\gamma < k < \gamma,$$

$$E[(X \wedge x)^k] = \theta^k \Gamma(1+k/\gamma)\Gamma(1-k/\gamma)\beta(1+k/\gamma, 1-k/\gamma; u)$$
$$+ x^k(1-u), \quad k > -\gamma,$$

$$\text{Mode} = \theta \left(\frac{\gamma-1}{\gamma+1}\right)^{1/\gamma}, \quad \gamma > 1, \text{ else } 0,$$

$$\hat{\gamma} = \frac{2\ln(3)}{\ln(q)-\ln(p)}, \quad \hat{\theta} = \exp\left(\frac{\ln(q)+\ln(p)}{2}\right).$$

A.2.3.4   Paralogistic—α, θ This is a Burr distribution with $\gamma = \alpha$.

$$f(x) = \frac{\alpha^2(x/\theta)^\alpha}{x[1+(x/\theta)^\alpha]^{\alpha+1}},$$

$$F(x) = 1 - u^\alpha, \quad u = \frac{1}{1+(x/\theta)^\alpha},$$

$$E[X^k] = \frac{\theta^k \Gamma(1+k/\alpha)\Gamma(\alpha-k/\alpha)}{\Gamma(\alpha)}, \quad -\alpha < k < \alpha^2,$$

$$E[(X \wedge x)^k] = \frac{\theta^k \Gamma(1+k/\alpha)\Gamma(\alpha-k/\alpha)}{\Gamma(\alpha)}\beta(1+k/\alpha, \alpha-k/\alpha; 1-u)$$
$$+ x^k u^\alpha, \quad k > -\alpha,$$

$$\text{Mode} = \theta \left(\frac{\alpha-1}{\alpha^2+1}\right)^{1/\alpha}, \quad \alpha > 1, \text{ else } 0$$

Starting values can use estimates from the loglogistic (use γ for α) or Pareto (use α) distributions.

A.2.3.5   Inverse paralogistic—τ,θ   This is an inverse Burr distribution with $\gamma = \tau$.

$$
\begin{aligned}
f(x) &= \frac{\tau^2(x/\theta)^{\tau^2}}{x[1+(x/\theta)^\tau]^{\tau+1}}, \\
F(x) &= u^\tau, \quad u = \frac{(x/\theta)^\tau}{1+(x/\theta)^\tau}, \\
\mathrm{E}[X^k] &= \frac{\theta^k\Gamma(\tau+k/\tau)\Gamma(1-k/\tau)}{\Gamma(\tau)}, \quad -\tau^2 < k < \tau, \\
\mathrm{E}[(X \wedge x)^k] &= \frac{\theta^k\Gamma(\tau+k/\tau)\Gamma(1-k/\tau)}{\Gamma(\tau)}\beta(\tau+k/\tau, 1-k/\tau; u) \\
&\quad + x^k[1-u^\tau], \quad k > -\tau^2, \\
\mathrm{Mode} &= \theta\,(\tau-1)^{1/\tau}, \quad \tau > 1, \text{ else } 0.
\end{aligned}
$$

Starting values can use estimates from the loglogistic (use γ for τ) or inverse Pareto (use τ) distributions.

A.3   TRANSFORMED GAMMA FAMILY

A.3.1   Three-parameter distributions

A.3.1.1   Transformed gamma—α, θ, τ   (generalized gamma)

$$
\begin{aligned}
f(x) &= \frac{\tau u^\alpha e^{-u}}{x\Gamma(\alpha)}, \quad u = (x/\theta)^\tau, \\
F(x) &= \Gamma(\alpha; u), \\
\mathrm{E}[X^k] &= \frac{\theta^k\Gamma(\alpha+k/\tau)}{\Gamma(\alpha)}, \quad k > -\alpha\tau, \\
\mathrm{E}[(X \wedge x)^k] &= \frac{\theta^k\Gamma(\alpha+k/\tau)}{\Gamma(\alpha)}\Gamma(\alpha+k/\tau; u) \\
&\quad + x^k[1-\Gamma(\alpha; u)], \quad k > -\alpha\tau, \\
\mathrm{Mode} &= \theta\left(\frac{\alpha\tau-1}{\tau}\right)^{1/\tau}, \quad \alpha\tau > 1, \text{ else } 0.
\end{aligned}
$$

A.3.1.2 Inverse transformed gamma—α, θ, τ (inverse generalized gamma)

$$f(x) = \frac{\tau u^\alpha e^{-u}}{x\Gamma(\alpha)}, \quad u = (\theta/x)^\tau,$$

$$F(x) = 1 - \Gamma(\alpha; u),$$

$$E[X^k] = \frac{\theta^k \Gamma(\alpha - k/\tau)}{\Gamma(\alpha)}, \quad k < \alpha\tau,$$

$$E[(X \wedge x)^k] = \frac{\theta^k \Gamma(\alpha - k/\tau)}{\Gamma(\alpha)}[1 - \Gamma(\alpha - k/\tau; u)] + x^k\Gamma(\alpha; u)$$

$$= \frac{\theta^k G(\alpha - k/\tau; u)}{\Gamma(\alpha)} + x^k\Gamma(\alpha; u), \quad \text{all } k,$$

$$\text{Mode} = \theta\left(\frac{\tau}{\alpha\tau + 1}\right)^{1/\tau}.$$

A.3.2   Two-parameter distributions

A.3.2.1   Gamma—α, θ

$$f(x) = \frac{(x/\theta)^\alpha e^{-x/\theta}}{x\Gamma(\alpha)},$$

$$F(x) = \Gamma(\alpha; x/\theta),$$

$$E[X^k] = \frac{\theta^k \Gamma(\alpha + k)}{\Gamma(\alpha)}, \quad k > -\alpha,$$

$$E[X^k] = \theta^k(\alpha + k - 1)\cdots\alpha \quad \text{if } k \text{ is an integer}$$

$$E[(X \wedge x)^k] = \frac{\theta^k \Gamma(\alpha + k)}{\Gamma(\alpha)}\Gamma(\alpha + k; x/\theta) + x^k[1 - \Gamma(\alpha; x/\theta)], \quad k > -\alpha$$

$$E[(X \wedge x)^k] = \alpha(\alpha + 1)\cdots(\alpha + k - 1)\theta^k\Gamma(\alpha + k; x/\theta)$$
$$+ x^k[1 - \Gamma(\alpha; x/\theta)] \quad \text{if } k \text{ is an integer,}$$

$$M(t) = (1 - \theta t)^{-\alpha}, \quad t < 1/\theta,$$

$$\text{Mode} = \theta(\alpha - 1), \quad \alpha > 1, \text{ else } 0,$$

$$\hat{\alpha} = \frac{m^2}{t - m^2}, \quad \hat{\theta} = \frac{t - m^2}{m}.$$

A.3.2.2   Inverse gamma—α, θ (Vinci)

$$f(x) = \frac{(\theta/x)^\alpha e^{-\theta/x}}{x\Gamma(\alpha)},,$$

$$F(x) = 1 - \Gamma(\alpha; \theta/x)$$

$$\mathrm{E}[X^k] = \frac{\theta^k \Gamma(\alpha - k)}{\Gamma(\alpha)}, \quad k < \alpha,$$

$$\mathrm{E}[X^k] = \frac{\theta^k}{(\alpha - 1)\cdots(\alpha - k)} \quad \text{if } k \text{ is an integer,}$$

$$\mathrm{E}[(X \wedge x)^k] = \frac{\theta^k \Gamma(\alpha - k)}{\Gamma(\alpha)}[1 - \Gamma(\alpha - k; \theta/x)] + x^k \Gamma(\alpha; \theta/x)$$

$$= \frac{\theta^k G(\alpha - k; \theta/x)}{\Gamma(\alpha)} + x^k \Gamma(\alpha; \theta/x), \text{ all } k,$$

$$\mathrm{Mode} = \theta/(\alpha + 1),$$

$$\hat{\alpha} = \frac{2t - m^2}{t - m^2}, \quad \hat{\theta} = \frac{mt}{t - m^2}.$$

A.3.2.3   Weibull—θ, τ

$$f(x) = \frac{\tau(x/\theta)^\tau e^{-(x/\theta)^\tau}}{x},$$

$$F(x) = 1 - e^{-(x/\theta)^\tau},$$

$$\mathrm{E}[X^k] = \theta^k \Gamma(1 + k/\tau), \quad k > -\tau,$$

$$\mathrm{E}[(X \wedge x)^k] = \theta^k \Gamma(1 + k/\tau)\Gamma[1 + k/\tau; (x/\theta)^\tau] + x^k e^{-(x/\theta)^\tau}, \quad k > -\tau,$$

$$\mathrm{Mode} = \theta\left(\frac{\tau - 1}{\tau}\right)^{1/\tau}, \quad \tau > 1, \text{ else } 0,$$

$$\hat{\theta} = \exp\left(\frac{g\ln(p) - \ln(q)}{g - 1}\right), \quad g = \frac{\ln(\ln(4))}{\ln(\ln(4/3))},$$

$$\hat{\tau} = \frac{\ln(\ln(4))}{\ln(q) - \ln(\hat{\theta})}.$$

A.3.2.4   Inverse Weibull—θ, τ (log-Gompertz)

$$f(x) = \frac{\tau(\theta/x)^\tau e^{-(\theta/x)^\tau}}{x},$$

$$F(x) = e^{-(\theta/x)^\tau},$$

$$\mathrm{E}[X^k] = \theta^k \Gamma(1 - k/\tau), \quad k < \tau,$$

$$\mathrm{E}[(X \wedge x)^k] = \theta^k \Gamma(1 - k/\tau)\{1 - \Gamma[1 - k/\tau; (\theta/x)^\tau]\}$$

$$+ x^k \left[1 - e^{-(\theta/x)^\tau}\right],$$

$$= \theta^k G[1 - k/\tau; (\theta/x)^\tau] + x^k \left[1 - e^{-(\theta/x)^\tau}\right], \quad \text{all } k,$$

$$\text{Mode} = \theta \left(\frac{\tau}{\tau + 1} \right)^{1/\tau},$$

$$\hat{\theta} = \exp \left(\frac{g \ln(q) - \ln(p)}{g - 1} \right), \quad g = \frac{\ln(\ln(4))}{\ln(\ln(4/3))},$$

$$\hat{\tau} = \frac{\ln(\ln(4))}{\ln(\hat{\theta}) - \ln(p)}.$$

A.3.3   One-parameter distributions

A.3.3.1   Exponential—θ

$$\begin{aligned}
f(x) &= \frac{e^{-x/\theta}}{\theta}, \\
F(x) &= 1 - e^{-x/\theta}, \\
E[X^k] &= \theta^k \Gamma(k+1), \quad k > -1, \\
E[X^k] &= \theta^k k! \quad \text{if } k \text{ is an integer}, \\
E[X \wedge x] &= \theta(1 - e^{-x/\theta}), \\
E[(X \wedge x)^k] &= \theta^k \Gamma(k+1)\Gamma(k+1; x/\theta) + x^k e^{-x/\theta}, \quad k > -1, \\
E[(X \wedge x)^k] &= \theta^k k! \Gamma(k+1; x/\theta) + x^k e^{-x/\theta} \quad \text{if } k > -1 \text{ is an integer}, \\
M(t) &= (1 - \theta t)^{-1}, \quad t < 1/\theta, \\
\text{Mode} &= 0, \\
\hat{\theta} &= m.
\end{aligned}$$

A.3.3.2   Inverse exponential—θ

$$\begin{aligned}
f(x) &= \frac{\theta e^{-\theta/x}}{x^2}, \\
F(x) &= e^{-\theta/x}, \\
E[X^k] &= \theta^k \Gamma(1-k), \quad k < 1, \\
E[(X \wedge x)^k] &= \theta^k G(1-k; \theta/x) + x^k(1 - e^{-\theta/x}), \quad \text{all } k, \\
\text{Mode} &= \theta/2, \\
\hat{\theta} &= -q \ln(3/4).
\end{aligned}$$

A.4   OTHER DISTRIBUTIONS

A.4.1.1   Lognormal—μ,σ (μ can be negative)

$$\begin{aligned}
f(x) &= \frac{1}{x\sigma\sqrt{2\pi}} \exp(-z^2/2) = \phi(z)/(\sigma x), \quad z = \frac{\ln x - \mu}{\sigma}, \\
F(x) &= \Phi(z),
\end{aligned}$$

$$\mathrm{E}[X^k] = \exp\left(k\mu + \tfrac{1}{2}k^2\sigma^2\right),$$

$$\mathrm{E}[(X \wedge x)^k] = \exp\left(k\mu + \tfrac{1}{2}k^2\sigma^2\right)\Phi\left(\frac{\ln x - \mu - k\sigma^2}{\sigma}\right) + x^k[1 - F(x)],$$

$$\mathrm{Mode} = \exp(\mu - \sigma^2),$$

$$\hat{\sigma} = \sqrt{\ln(t) - 2\ln(m)}, \quad \hat{\mu} = \ln(m) - \tfrac{1}{2}\hat{\sigma}^2.$$

A.4.1.2 Inverse Gaussian—μ, θ

$$f(x) = \left(\frac{\theta}{2\pi x^3}\right)^{1/2}\exp\left(-\frac{\theta z^2}{2x}\right), \quad z = \frac{x - \mu}{\mu},$$

$$F(x) = \Phi\left[z\left(\frac{\theta}{x}\right)^{1/2}\right] + \exp\left(\frac{2\theta}{\mu}\right)\Phi\left[-y\left(\frac{\theta}{x}\right)^{1/2}\right], \quad y = \frac{x + \mu}{\mu},$$

$$\mathrm{E}[X] = \mu, \quad Var[X] = \mu^3/\theta,$$

$$\mathrm{E}[X \wedge x] = x - \mu z\Phi\left[z\left(\frac{\theta}{x}\right)^{1/2}\right] - \mu y\exp(2\theta/\mu)\Phi\left[-y\left(\frac{\theta}{x}\right)^{1/2}\right],$$

$$M(t) = \exp\left[\frac{\theta}{\mu}\left(1 - \sqrt{1 - \frac{2\mu^2}{\theta}t}\right)\right], \quad t < \frac{\theta}{2\mu^2},$$

$$\hat{\mu} = m, \quad \hat{\theta} = \frac{m^3}{t - m^2}.$$

A.4.1.3 log-t—r, μ, σ (μ can be negative) Let Y have a t distribution with r degrees of freedom. Then $X = \exp(\sigma Y + \mu)$ has the log-t distribution. Positive moments do not exist for this distribution. Just as the t distribution has a heavier tail than the normal distribution, this distribution has a heavier tail than the lognormal distribution.

$$f(x) = \frac{\Gamma\left(\frac{r+1}{2}\right)}{x\sigma\sqrt{\pi r}\,\Gamma\left(\frac{r}{2}\right)\left[1 + \frac{1}{r}\left(\frac{\ln x - \mu}{\sigma}\right)^2\right]^{(r+1)/2}},$$

$$F(x) = F_r\left(\frac{\ln x - \mu}{\sigma}\right) \quad \text{with } F_r(t) \text{ the cdf of a } t \text{ distribution with } r \text{ d.f.,}$$

$$F(x) = \begin{cases} \dfrac{1}{2}\beta\left[\dfrac{r}{2},\dfrac{1}{2}; \dfrac{r}{r + \left(\dfrac{\ln x - \mu}{\sigma}\right)^2}\right], & 0 < x \le e^{\mu}, \\[3em] 1 - \dfrac{1}{2}\beta\left[\dfrac{r}{2},\dfrac{1}{2}; \dfrac{r}{r + \left(\dfrac{\ln x - \mu}{\sigma}\right)^2}\right], & x \ge e^{\mu}. \end{cases}$$

A.4.1.4 Single-parameter Pareto—α, θ

$$f(x) = \frac{\alpha\theta^{\alpha}}{x^{\alpha+1}}, \quad x > \theta,$$

$$F(x) = 1 - \left(\frac{\theta}{x}\right)^{\alpha}, \quad x > \theta,$$

$$E[X^k] = \frac{\alpha\theta^k}{\alpha - k}, \quad k < \alpha,$$

$$E[(X \wedge x)^k] = \frac{\alpha\theta^k}{\alpha - k} - \frac{k\theta^{\alpha}}{(\alpha - k)x^{\alpha-k}}, \quad x \ge \theta,$$

$$\text{Mode} = \theta,$$

$$\hat{\alpha} = \frac{m}{m - \theta}.$$

Note: Although there appears to be two parameters, only α is a true parameter. The value of θ must be set in advance.

A.5 DISTRIBUTIONS WITH FINITE SUPPORT

For these two distributions, the scale parameter θ is assumed known.

A.5.1.1 Generalized beta—a, b, θ, τ

$$f(x) = \frac{\Gamma(a + b)}{\Gamma(a)\Gamma(b)}u^a(1 - u)^{b-1}\frac{\tau}{x}, \quad 0 < x < \theta, \quad u = (x/\theta)^{\tau},$$

$$F(x) = \beta(a, b; u),$$

$$E[X^k] = \frac{\theta^k\Gamma(a + b)\Gamma(a + k/\tau)}{\Gamma(a)\Gamma(a + b + k/\tau)}, \quad k > -a\tau,$$

$$E[(X \wedge x)^k] = \frac{\theta^k\Gamma(a + b)\Gamma(a + k/\tau)}{\Gamma(a)\Gamma(a + b + k/\tau)}\beta(a + k/\tau, b; u) + x^k[1 - \beta(a, b; u)].$$

A.5.1.2 beta—a, b, θ

$$f(x) = \frac{\Gamma(a+b)}{\Gamma(a)\Gamma(b)}u^a(1-u)^{b-1}\frac{1}{x}, \quad 0 < x < \theta, \quad u = x/\theta,$$

$$F(x) = \beta(a,b;u),$$

$$E[X^k] = \frac{\theta^k\Gamma(a+b)\Gamma(a+k)}{\Gamma(a)\Gamma(a+b+k)}, \quad k > -a,$$

$$E[X^k] = \frac{\theta^k a(a+1)\cdots(a+k-1)}{(a+b)(a+b+1)\cdots(a+b+k-1)} \quad \text{if } k \text{ is an integer,}$$

$$E[(X \wedge x)^k] = \frac{\theta^k a(a+1)\cdots(a+k-1)}{(a+b)(a+b+1)\cdots(a+b+k-1)}\beta(a+k,b;u)$$
$$+x^k[1-\beta(a,b;u)],$$

$$\hat{a} = \frac{\theta m^2 - mt}{\theta t - \theta m^2}, \quad \hat{b} = \frac{(\theta m - t)(\theta - m)}{\theta t - \theta m^2}.$$

Appendix B
An inventory of discrete distributions

B.1 INTRODUCTION

The 16 models fall into three classes. The divisions are based on the algorithm by which the probabilities are computed. For some of the more familiar distributions these formulas will look different from the ones you may have learned, but they produce the same probabilities. After each name, the parameters are given. All parameters are positive unless otherwise indicated. In all cases, p_k is the probability of observing k losses.

For finding moments, the most convenient form is to give the factorial moments. The jth factorial moment is $\mu_{(j)} = \mathrm{E}[N(N-1)\cdots(N-j+1)]$. We have $\mathrm{E}[N] = \mu_{(1)}$ and $\mathrm{Var}(N) = \mu_{(2)} + \mu_{(1)} - \mu_{(1)}^2$.

The estimators which are presented are not intended to be useful estimators but rather for providing starting values for maximizing the likelihood (or other) function. For determining starting values, the following quantities are

*

Loss Models: From Data to Decisions, Second Edition.
By Stuart A. Klugman, Harry H. Panjer, and Gordon E. Willmot
ISBN 0-471-21577-5   Copyright © 2004 John Wiley & Sons, Inc.

used [where n_k is the observed frequency at k (if, for the last entry, n_k represents the number of observations at k or more, assume it was at exactly k) and n is the sample size]:

$$\hat{\mu} \doteq \frac{1}{n}\sum_{k=1}^{\infty} kn_k, \quad \hat{\sigma}^2 \doteq \frac{1}{n}\sum_{k=1}^{\infty} k^2 n_k - \hat{\mu}^2.$$

When the method of moments is used to determine the starting value, a circumflex (e.g., $\hat{\lambda}$) is used. For any other method, a tilde (e.g., $\tilde{\lambda}$) is used. When the starting value formulas do not provide admissible parameter values, a truly crude guess is to set the product of all λ and β parameters equal to the sample mean and set all other parameters equal to 1. If there are two λ and/or β parameters, an easy choice is to set each to the square root of the sample mean.

The last item presented is the probability generating function,

$$P(z) = E[z^N].$$

B.2   THE $(a, b, 0)$ CLASS

The distributions in this class have support on $0, 1, \dots$. For this class, a particular distribution is specified by setting p_0 and then using $p_k = (a + b/k)p_{k-1}$. Specific members are created by setting p_0, a, and b. For any member, $\mu_{(1)} = (a+b)/(1-a)$, and for higher j, $\mu_{(j)} = (aj+b)\mu_{(j-1)}/(1-a)$. The variance is $(a + b)/(1 - a)^2$.

B.2.1.1   Poisson—λ

$$
\begin{aligned}
p_0 &= e^{-\lambda}, \quad a = 0, \quad b = \lambda, \\
p_k &= \frac{e^{-\lambda}\lambda^k}{k!}, \\
E[N] &= \lambda, \quad Var[N] = \lambda, \\
\hat{\lambda} &= \hat{\mu}, \\
P(z) &= e^{\lambda(z-1)}.
\end{aligned}
$$

B.2.1.2   Geometric—β

$$
\begin{aligned}
p_0 &= \frac{1}{1+\beta}, \quad a = \frac{\beta}{1+\beta}, \quad b = 0, \\
p_k &= \frac{\beta^k}{(1+\beta)^{k+1}}, \\
E[N] &= \beta, \quad Var[N] = \beta(1+\beta), \\
\hat{\beta} &= \hat{\mu}, \\
P(z) &= [1 - \beta(z-1)]^{-1}.
\end{aligned}
$$

This is a special case of the negative binomial with $r = 1$.

B.2.1.3 Binomial—$q, m, (0 < q < 1, m$ an integer)

$$p_0 = (1-q)^m, \quad a = -\frac{q}{1-q}, \quad b = \frac{(m+1)q}{1-q},$$

$$p_k = \binom{m}{k} q^k (1-q)^{m-k}, \quad k = 0, 1, \ldots, m,$$

$$E[N] = mq, \quad \text{Var}[N] = mq(1-q),$$

$$\hat{q} = \hat{\mu}/m,$$

$$P(z) = [1 + q(z-1)]^m.$$

B.2.1.4 Negative binomial—β, r

$$p_0 = (1+\beta)^{-r}, \quad a = \frac{\beta}{1+\beta}, \quad b = \frac{(r-1)\beta}{1+\beta},$$

$$p_k = \frac{r(r+1)\cdots(r+k-1)\beta^k}{k!(1+\beta)^{r+k}},$$

$$E[N] = r\beta, \quad \text{Var}[N] = r\beta(1+\beta),$$

$$\hat{\beta} = \frac{\hat{\sigma}^2}{\hat{\mu}} - 1, \quad \hat{r} = \frac{\hat{\mu}^2}{\hat{\sigma}^2 - \hat{\mu}},$$

$$P(z) = [1 - \beta(z-1)]^{-r}.$$

B.3 THE $(a, b, 1)$ CLASS

To distinguish this class from the $(a, b, 0)$ class, the probabilities are denoted $\Pr(N = k) = p_k^M$ or $\Pr(N = k) = p_k^T$ depending on which subclass is being represented. For this class, p_0^M is arbitrary (that is, it is a parameter) and then p_1^M or p_1^T is a specified function of the parameters a and b. Subsequent probabilities are obtained recursively as in the $(a, b, 0)$ class: $p_k^M = (a + b/k)p_{k-1}^M$, $k = 2, 3, \ldots$, with the same recursion for p_k^T There are two sub-classes of this class. When discussing their members, we often refer to the "corresponding" member of the $(a, b, 0)$ class. This refers to the member of that class with the same values for a and b. The notation p_k will continue to be used for probabilities for the corresponding $(a, b, 0)$ distribution.

B.3.1 The zero-truncated subclass

The members of this class have $p_0^T = 0$ and therefore it need not be estimated. These distributions should only be used when a value of zero is impossible. The first factorial moment is $\mu_{(1)} = (a + b)/[(1 - a)(1 - p_0)]$, where p_0 is the value for the corresponding member of the $(a, b, 0)$ class. For the logarithmic distribution (which has no corresponding member), $\mu_{(1)} = \beta/\ln(1+\beta)$. Higher factorial moments are obtained recursively with the same formula as with the $(a, b, 0)$ class. The variance is $(a + b)[1 - (a + b + 1)p_0]/[(1 - a)(1 - p_0)]^2$. For those members of the subclass which have corresponding $(a, b, 0)$ distributions, $p_k^T = p_k/(1 - p_0)$.

B.3.1.1 Zero-truncated Poisson—λ

$$
p_1^T = \frac{\lambda}{e^\lambda - 1}, \quad a = 0, \quad b = \lambda,
$$

$$
p_k^T = \frac{\lambda^k}{k!(e^\lambda - 1)},
$$

$$
E[N] = \lambda/(1 - e^{-\lambda}), \quad \mathrm{Var}[N] = \lambda[1 - (\lambda + 1)e^{-\lambda}]/(1 - e^{-\lambda})^2,
$$

$$
\tilde{\lambda} = \ln(n\hat{\mu}/n_1),
$$

$$
P(z) = \frac{e^{\lambda z} - 1}{e^\lambda - 1}.
$$

B.3.1.2 Zero-truncated geometric—β

$$
p_1^T = \frac{1}{1 + \beta}, \quad a = \frac{\beta}{1 + \beta}, \quad b = 0,
$$

$$
p_k^T = \frac{\beta^{k-1}}{(1 + \beta)^k},
$$

$$
E[N] = 1 + \beta, \quad \mathrm{Var}[N] = \beta(1 + \beta),
$$

$$
\hat{\beta} = \hat{\mu} - 1,
$$

$$
P(z) = \frac{[1 - \beta(z - 1)]^{-1} - (1 + \beta)^{-1}}{1 - (1 + \beta)^{-1}}.
$$

This is a special case of the zero-truncated negative binomial with $r = 1$.

B.3.1.3 Logarithmic—β

$$
p_1^T = \frac{\beta}{(1 + \beta)\ln(1 + \beta)}, \quad a = \frac{\beta}{1 + \beta}, \quad b = -\frac{\beta}{1 + \beta},
$$

$$
p_k^T = \frac{\beta^k}{k(1 + \beta)^k \ln(1 + \beta)},
$$

$$
E[N] = \beta/\ln(1 + \beta), \quad \mathrm{Var}[N] = \frac{\beta[1 + \beta - \beta/\ln(1 + \beta)]}{\ln(1 + \beta)},
$$

$$
\tilde{\beta} = \frac{n\hat{\mu}}{n_1} - 1 \quad \text{or} \quad \frac{2(\hat{\mu} - 1)}{\hat{\mu}},
$$

$$
P(z) = 1 - \frac{\ln[1 - \beta(z - 1)]}{\ln(1 + \beta)}.
$$

This is a limiting case of the zero-truncated negative binomial as $r \to 0$.

B.3.1.4   Zero-truncated binomial—$q, m, (0 < q < 1, m$ an integer)

$$p_1^T = \frac{m(1-q)^{m-1}q}{1-(1-q)^m}, \quad a = -\frac{q}{1-q}, \quad b = \frac{(m+1)q}{1-q},$$

$$p_k^T = \frac{\binom{m}{k}q^k(1-q)^{m-k}}{1-(1-q)^m}, \quad k = 1, 2, \ldots, m,$$

$$\mathrm{E}[N] = \frac{mq}{1-(1-q)^m},$$

$$\mathrm{Var}[N] = \frac{mq[(1-q)-(1-q+mq)(1-q)^m]}{[1-(1-q)^m]^2},$$

$$\tilde{q} = \frac{\hat{\mu}}{m},$$

$$P(z) = \frac{[1+q(z-1)]^m - (1-q)^m}{1-(1-q)^m}.$$

B.3.1.5   Zero-truncated negative binomial—$\beta, r, (r > -1, r \neq 0)$

$$p_1^T = \frac{r\beta}{(1+\beta)^{r+1} - (1+\beta)}, \quad a = \frac{\beta}{1+\beta}, \quad b = \frac{(r-1)\beta}{1+\beta},$$

$$p_k^T = \frac{r(r+1)\cdots(r+k-1)}{k![(1+\beta)^r - 1]} \left(\frac{\beta}{1+\beta}\right)^k,$$

$$\mathrm{E}[N] = \frac{r\beta}{1-(1+\beta)^{-r}},$$

$$Var[N] = \frac{r\beta[(1+\beta) - (1+\beta+r\beta)(1+\beta)^{-r}]}{[1-(1+\beta)^{-r}]^2},$$

$$\tilde{\beta} = \frac{\hat{\sigma}^2}{\hat{\mu}} - 1, \quad \tilde{r} = \frac{\hat{\mu}^2}{\hat{\sigma}^2 - \hat{\mu}},$$

$$P(z) = \frac{[1-\beta(z-1)]^{-r} - (1+\beta)^{-r}}{1-(1+\beta)^{-r}}.$$

This distribution is sometimes called the extended truncated negative binomial distribution because the parameter r can extend below 0.

B.3.2   The zero-modified subclass

A zero-modified distribution is created by starting with a truncated distribution and then placing an arbitrary amount of probability at zero. This probability, p_0^M, is a parameter. The remaining probabilities are adjusted accordingly. Values of p_k^M can be determined from the corresponding zero-truncated distribution as $p_k^M = (1-p_0^M)p_k^T$ or from the corresponding $(a, b, 0)$ distribution as $p_k^M = (1-p_0^M)p_k/(1-p_0)$. The same recursion used for the zero-truncated subclass applies.

The mean is $1 - p_0^M$ times the mean for the corresponding zero-truncated distribution. The variance is $1 - p_0^M$ times the zero-truncated variance plus $p_0^M(1-p_0^M)$ times the square of the zero-truncated mean. The probability generating function is $P^M(z) = p_0^M + (1-p_0^M)P(z)$, where $P(z)$ is the probability generating function for the corresponding zero-truncated distribution.

The maximum likelihood estimator of p_0^M is always the sample relative frequency at 0.

B.4 THE COMPOUND CLASS

Members of this class are obtained by compounding one distribution with another. That is, let N be a discrete distribution, called the **primary distribution** and let $M_1, M_2, \ldots$ be identically and independently distributed with another discrete distribution, called the **secondary distribution**. The compound distribution is $S = M_1 + \cdots + M_N$. The probabilities for the compound distributions are found from

$$p_k = \frac{1}{1 - af_0} \sum_{y=1}^{k} (a + by/k) f_y p_{k-y}$$

for $n = 1, 2, \ldots$, where a and b are the usual values for the primary distribution [which must be a member of the $(a, b, 0)$ class] and f_y is p_y for the secondary distribution. The only two primary distributions used here are Poisson (for which $p_0 = \exp[-\lambda(1 - f_0)]$) and geometric [for which $p_0 = 1/[1 + \beta - \beta f_0]$]. Because this information completely describes these distributions, only the names and starting values are given below.

The moments can be found from the moments of the individual distributions:

$$\mathrm{E}[S] = \mathrm{E}[N]\mathrm{E}[M] \quad \text{and} \quad \mathrm{Var}[S] = \mathrm{E}[N]\,\mathrm{Var}[M] + \mathrm{Var}[N]\mathrm{E}[M]^2.$$

The probability generating function is $P(z) = P_{\mathrm{primary}}[P_{\mathrm{secondary}}(z)]$.

In the following list the primary distribution is always named first. For the first, second, and fourth distributions, the secondary distribution is the $(a, b, 0)$ class member with that name. For the third and the last three distributions (the Poisson–ETNB and its two special cases) the secondary distribution is the zero-truncated version.

B.4.1 Some compound distributions

B.4.1.1 Poisson–binomial—λ, q, m ($0 < q < 1$, m an integer)

$$\hat{q} = \frac{\hat{\sigma}^2/\hat{\mu} - 1}{m - 1}, \quad \hat{\lambda} = \frac{\hat{\mu}}{m\hat{q}} \quad \text{or} \quad \tilde{q} = 0.5, \ \tilde{\lambda} = \frac{2\hat{\mu}}{m}.$$

B.4.1.2 Poisson–Poisson—λ_1, λ_2 The parameter λ_1 is for the primary Poisson distribution, and λ_2 is for the secondary Poisson distribution. This distribution is also called the **Neyman Type A**.

$$\tilde{\lambda}_1 = \tilde{\lambda}_2 = \sqrt{\hat{\mu}}.$$

B.4.1.3 Geometric–extended truncated negative binomial—$\beta_1, \beta_2, r \, (r > -1)$ The parameter β_1 is for the primary geometric distribution. The last two parameters are for the secondary distribution, noting that for $r = 0$ the secondary distribution is logarithmic. The truncated version is used so that the extension of r is available.

$$\tilde{\beta}_1 = \tilde{\beta}_2 = \sqrt{\hat{\mu}}.$$

B.4.1.4 Geometric–Poisson—β, λ

$$\tilde{\beta} = \tilde{\lambda} = \sqrt{\hat{\mu}}.$$

B.4.1.5 Poisson–extended truncated negative binomial—$\lambda, \beta, (r > -1, r \neq 0)$ When $r = 0$ the secondary distribution is logarithmic, resulting in the negative binomial distribution.

$$\tilde{r} = \frac{\hat{\mu}(K - 3\hat{\sigma}^2 + 2\hat{\mu}) - 2(\hat{\sigma}^2 - \hat{\mu})^2}{\hat{\mu}(K - 3\hat{\sigma}^2 + 2\hat{\mu}) - (\hat{\sigma}^2 - \hat{\mu})^2}, \quad \tilde{\beta} = \frac{\hat{\sigma}^2 - \hat{\mu}}{\hat{\mu}(1 + \hat{r})}, \quad \tilde{\lambda} = \frac{\hat{\mu}}{\hat{r}\hat{\beta}},$$

or,

$$\tilde{r} = \frac{\hat{\sigma}^2 n_1/n - \hat{\mu}^2 n_0/n}{(\hat{\sigma}^2 - \hat{\mu}^2)(n_0/n)\ln(n_0/n) - \hat{\mu}(\hat{\mu}n_0/n - n_1/n)},$$

$$\tilde{\beta} = \frac{\hat{\sigma}^2 - \hat{\mu}}{\hat{\mu}(1 + \hat{r})}, \quad \tilde{\lambda} = \frac{\hat{\mu}}{\hat{r}\hat{\beta}}$$

where

$$K = \frac{1}{n}\sum_{k=0}^{\infty} k^3 n_k - 3\hat{\mu}\frac{1}{n}\sum_{k=0}^{\infty} k^2 n_k + 2\hat{\mu}^3.$$

This distribution is also called the **generalized Poisson–Pascal**.

B.4.1.6 Polya–Aeppli—λ, β

$$\hat{\beta} = \frac{\hat{\sigma}^2 - \hat{\mu}}{2\hat{\mu}}, \quad \hat{\lambda} = \frac{\hat{\mu}}{1 + \hat{\beta}}.$$

This is a special case of the Poisson–extended truncated negative binomial with $r = 1$. It is actually a Poisson–truncated geometric.

B.4.1.7   Poisson–inverse Gaussian—λ, β

$$\tilde{\lambda} = -\ln(n_0/n), \ \tilde{\beta} = \frac{4(\hat{\mu} - \hat{\lambda})}{\hat{\mu}}.$$

This is a special case of the Poisson–extended truncated negative binomial with $r = -0.5$.

B.5   A HIERARCHY OF DISCRETE DISTRIBUTIONS

The following table indicates which distributions are special or limiting cases of others. For the special cases, one parameter is set equal to a constant to create the special case. For the limiting cases, two parameters go to infinity or zero in some special way.

Distribution	Is a special case of	Is a limiting case of
Poisson	ZM Poisson	Negative binomial, Poisson–binomial, Poisson–inv. Gaussian, Polya–Aeppli, Neyman–A
ZT Poisson	ZM Poisson	ZT negative binomial
ZM Poisson		ZM negative binomial
Geometric	Negative binomial ZM geometric	Geometric–Poisson
ZT geometric	ZT negative binomial	
ZM geometric	ZM negative binomial	
Logarithmic		ZT negative binomial
ZM logarithmic		ZM negative binomial
Binomial	ZM binomial	
Negative binomial	ZM negative binomial	Poisson–ETNB
Poisson–inverse Gaussian	Poisson–ETNB	
Polya–Aeppli	Poisson–ETNB	
Neyman–A		Poisson–ETNB

Appendix C
Frequency and severity relationships

Let N^L be the number of losses random variable and let X be the severity random variable. If there is a deductible of d imposed, there are two ways to modify X. One is to create Y^L, the amount paid per loss:

$$Y^L = \begin{cases} 0, & X \leq d, \\ X - d, & X > d. \end{cases}$$

In this case the appropriate frequency distribution continues to be N^L.

An alternative approach is to create Y^P, the amount paid per payment:

$$Y^P = \begin{cases} \text{undefined}, & X \leq d, \\ X - d, & X > d. \end{cases}$$

In this case the frequency random variable must be altered to reflect the

Loss Models: From Data to Decisions, Second Edition.
By Stuart A. Klugman, Harry H. Panjer, and Gordon E. Willmot
ISBN 0-471-21577-5   Copyright © 2004 John Wiley & Sons, Inc.

number of payments. Let this variable be N^P. Assume that for each loss the probability is $v = 1 - F_X(d)$ that a payment will result. Further assume that the incidence of making a payment is independent of the number of losses. Then $N^P = L_1 + L_2 + \cdots + L_N$, where L_j is 0 with probability $1 - v$ and is 1 with probability v. Probability generating functions yield the following relationships:

N^L	Parameters for N^P
Poisson	$\lambda^* = v\lambda$
ZM Poisson	$p_0^{M*} = \dfrac{p_0^M - e^{-\lambda} + e^{-v\lambda} - p_0^M e^{-v\lambda}}{1 - e^{-\lambda}}, \ \lambda^* = v\lambda$
Binomial	$q^* = vq$
ZM binomial	$p_0^{M*} = \dfrac{p_0^M - (1-q)^m + (1-vq)^m - p_0^M(1-vq)^m}{1 - (1-q)^m}$ $q^* = vq$
Negative binomial	$\beta^* = v\beta, \ r^* = r$
ZM neg. binomial	$p_0^{M*} = \dfrac{p_0^M - (1+\beta)^{-r} + (1+v\beta)^{-r} - p_0^M(1+v\beta)^{-r}}{1 - (1+\beta)^{-r}}$ $\beta^* = v\beta, \ r^* = r$
ZM logarithmic	$p_0^{M*} = 1 - (1 - p_0^M)\ln(1+v\beta)/\ln(1+\beta)$ $\beta^* = v\beta$

The geometric distribution is not presented as it is a special case of the negative binomial with $r = 1$. For zero truncated distributions, the above is still used as the distribution for N^P will now be zero modified. For compound distributions, modify only the secondary distribution. For ETNB secondary distributions the parameter for the primary distribution is multiplied by $1 - p_0^{M*}$ as obtained above while the secondary distribution remains zero truncated (however, $\beta^* = v\beta$).

There are occasions in which frequency data are collected which provide a model for N^P. There would have to have been a deductible d in place and therefore v is available. It is possible to recover the distribution for N^L, although there is no guarantee that reversing the process will produce a legitimate probability distribution. The solutions are the same as above, only now $v = 1/[1 - F_X(d)]$.

Now suppose the current frequency model is N^d, which is appropriate for a deductible of d. Now suppose the deductible is to be changed to d^*. The new frequency for payments is N^{d^*} and is of the same type. Then use the table with $v = [1 - F_X(d^*)]/[1 - F_X(d)]$.

Appendix D
The recursive formula

The recursive formula is (where the frequency distribution is a member of the $(a, b, 1)$ class),

$$f_S(x) = \frac{[p_1 - (a + b)p_0]f_X(x) + \sum_{y=1}^{x \wedge m} \left(a + \frac{by}{x}\right) f_X(y)f_S(x - y)}{1 - af_X(0)},$$

where $f_S(x) = \Pr(S = x)$, $x = 0, 1, 2, \ldots$, $f_X(x) = \Pr(X = x)$, $x = 0, 1, 2, \ldots$, $p_0 = \Pr(N = 0)$, and $p_1 = \Pr(N = 1)$. Note that the severity distribution (X) must place probability on non-negative integers. The formula must be initialized with the value of $f_S(0)$. These values are given in Table D.1. It should be noted that, if N is a member of the $(a, b, 0)$ class, $p_1 - (a+b)p_0 = 0$ and so the first term will vanish. If N is a member of the compound class, the recursion must be run twice. The first pass uses the secondary distribution for p_0, p_1, a, and b. The second pass uses the output from the first pass as $f_X(x)$ and uses the primary distribution for p_0, p_1, a, and b.

Loss Models: From Data to Decisions, Second Edition.
By Stuart A. Klugman, Harry H. Panjer, and Gordon E. Willmot
ISBN 0-471-21577-5   Copyright © 2004 John Wiley & Sons, Inc.

Table D.1   Starting values $(f_S(0))$ for recursions

Distribution	$f_S(0)$
Poisson	$\exp[\lambda(f_0 - 1)]$
Geometric	$[1 + \beta(1 - f_0)]^{-1}$
Binomial	$[1 + q(f_0 - 1)]^m$
Negative binomial	$[1 + \beta(1 - f_0)]^{-r}$
ZM Poisson	$p_0^M + (1 - p_0^M)\dfrac{\exp(\lambda f_0) - 1}{\exp(\lambda) - 1}$
ZM geometric	$p_0^M + (1 - p_0^M)\dfrac{f_0}{1 + \beta(1 - f_0)}$
ZM binomial	$p_0^M + (1 - p_0^M)\dfrac{[1 + q(f_0 - 1)]^m - (1 - q)^m}{1 - (1 - q)^m}$
ZM negative binomial	$p_0^M + (1 - p_0^M)\dfrac{[1 + \beta(1 - f_0)]^{-r} - (1 + \beta)^{-r}}{1 - (1 + \beta)^{-r}}$
ZM logarithmic	$p_0^M + (1 - p_0^M)\left\{1 - \dfrac{\ln[1 + \beta(1 - f_0)]}{\ln(1 + \beta)}\right\}$

Appendix E
Discretization of the severity distribution

There are two relatively simple ways to discretize the severity distribution. One is the method of rounding and the other is a mean-preserving method.

E.1 THE METHOD OF ROUNDING

This method has two features: All probabilities are positive, and the probabilities add to 1. Let h be the span and let Y be the discretized version of X. If there are no modifications, then

$$
\begin{aligned}
f_j &= \Pr(Y = jh) = \Pr\left[\left(j - \tfrac{1}{2}\right) h \leq X < \left(j + \tfrac{1}{2}\right) h\right] \\
&= F_X\left[\left(j + \tfrac{1}{2}\right) h\right] - F_X\left[\left(j - \tfrac{1}{2}\right) h\right].
\end{aligned}
$$

Loss Models: From Data to Decisions, Second Edition.
By Stuart A. Klugman, Harry H. Panjer, and Gordon E. Willmot
ISBN 0-471-21577-5   Copyright © 2004 John Wiley & Sons, Inc.

The recursive formula is then used with $f_X(j) = f_j$. Suppose a deductible of d, limit of u, and coinsurance of α are to be applied. If the modifications are to be applied before the discretization, then

$$g_0 = \frac{F_X(d + h/2) - F_X(d)}{1 - F_X(d)},$$

$$g_j = \frac{F_X[d + (j + 1/2)h] - F_X[d + (j - 1/2)h]}{1 - F_X(d)},$$

$$j = 1, \ldots, \frac{u - d}{h} - 1,$$

$$g_{(u-d)/h} = \frac{1 - F_X(u - h/2)}{1 - F_X(d)},$$

where $g_j = \Pr(Z = j\alpha h)$ and Z is the modified distribution. This method does not require that the limits be multiples of h but does require that $u - d$ be a multiple of h. This method gives the probabilities of payments per payment.

Finally, if there is truncation from above at u, change all denominators to $F_X(u) - F_X(d)$ and also change the numerator of $g_{(u-d)/h}$ to $F_X(u) - F_X(u - h/2)$.

E.2 MEAN PRESERVING

This method ensures that the discretized distribution has the same mean as the original severity distribution. With no modifications the discretization is

$$f_0 = 1 - \frac{E[X \wedge h]}{h},$$

$$f_j = \frac{2E[X \wedge jh] - E[X \wedge (j - 1)h] - E[X \wedge (j + 1)h]}{h}, \quad j = 1, 2, \ldots.$$

For the modified distribution,

$$g_0 = 1 - \frac{E[X \wedge d + h] - E[X \wedge d]}{h[1 - F_X(d)]},$$

$$g_j = \frac{2E[X \wedge d + jh] - E[X \wedge d + (j - 1)h] - E[X \wedge d + (j + 1)h]}{h[1 - F_X(d)]},$$

$$j = 1, \ldots, \frac{u - d}{h} - 1,$$

$$g_{(u-d)/h} = \frac{E[X \wedge u] - E[X \wedge u - h]}{h[1 - F_X(d)]}.$$

To incorporate truncation from above, change the denominators to

$$h[F_X(u) - F_X(d)]$$

and subtract $h[1 - F_X(u)]$ from the numerators of each of g_0 and $g_{(u-d)/h}$.

E.3   UNDISCRETIZATION OF A DISCRETIZED DISTRIBUTION

Assume we have $g_0 = \Pr(S = 0)$, the true probability that the random variable is zero. Let $p_j = \Pr(S^* = jh)$, where S^* is a discretized distribution and h is the span. The following are approximations for the cdf and LEV of S, the true distribution which was discretized as S^*. They are all based on the assumption that S has a uniform distribution over the interval from $(j-\frac{1}{2})h$ to $(j+\frac{1}{2})h$ for integral j. The first interval is from 0 to $h/2$, and the probability $p_0 - g_0$ is assumed to be uniformly distributed over it. Let S^{**} be the random variable with this approximate mixed distribution. (It is continuous, except for discrete probability g_0 at zero.) The approximate distribution function can be found by interpolation as follows. First, let

$$F_j = F_{S^{**}}\left[\left(j+\tfrac{1}{2}\right)h\right] = \sum_{i=0}^{j} p_i, \quad j = 0, 1, \ldots.$$

Then, for x in the interval $(j-\frac{1}{2})h$ to $(j+\frac{1}{2})h$,

$$
\begin{aligned}
F_{S^{**}}(x) &= F_{j-1} + \int_{(j-1/2)h}^{x} h^{-1} p_j \, dt = F_{j-1} + \left[x - \left(j-\tfrac{1}{2}\right)h\right] h^{-1} p_j \\
&= F_{j-1} + \left[x - \left(j-\tfrac{1}{2}\right)h\right] h^{-1}(F_j - F_{j-1}) \\
&= (1-w)F_{j-1} + wF_j, \quad w = \frac{x}{h} - j + \tfrac{1}{2}.
\end{aligned}
$$

Because the first interval is only half as wide, the formula for $0 \le x \le h/2$ is

$$F_{S^{**}}(x) = (1-w)g_0 + wp_0, \quad w = \frac{2x}{h}.$$

It is also possible to express these formulas in terms of the discrete probabilities:

$$
F_{S^{**}}(x) =
\begin{cases}
g_0 + \dfrac{2x}{h}[p_0 - g_0], & 0 < x \le \dfrac{h}{2}, \\[2ex]
\displaystyle\sum_{i=0}^{j-1} p_i + \dfrac{x - (j-1/2)h}{h} p_j, & (j-\tfrac{1}{2})h < x \le (j+\tfrac{1}{2})h.
\end{cases}
$$

With regard to the limited expected value, expressions for the first and kth LEVs are

$$
E(S^{**} \wedge x) =
\begin{cases}
x(1-g_0) - \dfrac{x^2}{h}(p_0 - g_0), & 0 < x \le \dfrac{h}{2}, \\[2ex]
\dfrac{h}{4}(p_0 - g_0) + \displaystyle\sum_{i=1}^{j-1} ihp_i + \dfrac{x^2 - [(j-1/2)h]^2}{2h} p_j \\[2ex]
\quad + x[1 - F_{S^{**}}(x)], & (j-\tfrac{1}{2})h < x \le (j+\tfrac{1}{2})h,
\end{cases}
$$

and, for $0 < x \leq \dfrac{h}{2}$,

$$E[(S^{**} \wedge x)^k] = \frac{2x^{k+1}}{h(k+1)}(p_0 - g_0) + x^k[1 - F_{S^{**}}(x)],$$

while for $(j - \frac{1}{2})h < x \leq (j + \frac{1}{2})h$,

$$
\begin{aligned}
E[(S^{**} \wedge x)^k] &= \frac{(h/2)^k(p_0 - g_0)}{k+1} + \sum_{i=1}^{j-1} \frac{h^k[(i+\frac{1}{2})^{k+1} - (i-\frac{1}{2})^{k+1}]}{k+1} p_i \\
&+ \frac{x^{k+1} - [(j-\frac{1}{2})h]^{k+1}}{h(k+1)} p_j + x^k[1 - F_{S^{**}}(x)].
\end{aligned}
$$

Appendix F
Numerical optimization and solution of systems of equations

Maximizing functions can be difficult when there are many variables. A variety of numerical methods have been developed, and most any will be sufficient for the tasks set forth in this text. Here we present two options. The first is to use the Excel® Solver add-in. It is fairly reliable, though at times it may declare a maximum has been found when there is no maximum. A second option is the simplex method. This method tends to be slower but is more reliable. The final section of this Appendix shows how the solver and goal seek routines in Excel® can be used to solve systems of equations.

Loss Models: From Data to Decisions, Second Edition.
By Stuart A. Klugman, Harry H. Panjer, and Gordon E. Willmot
ISBN 0-471-21577-5   Copyright © 2004 John Wiley & Sons, Inc.

F.1   MAXIMIZATION USING SOLVER

Solver is not automatically available when Excel® is installed. If it is available, you can tell because *Solver* will appear on Excel's Tools menu. If it does not, it must be added in. To do this, select *Add-ins* from the Tools menu, check the Solver box, and then click OK. If Solver does not appear on the add-in list, Solver was not installed when Excel® was installed on your machine. This will be the case if a typical (as opposed to full or custom) install was done. To install Solver, go to Add/Remove Programs in the Control Panel and modify your Microsoft Office® installation. You will not need to reinstall all of Office® to add the Solver.

Use of Solver is illustrated with an example in which maximum likelihood estimates for the gamma distribution are found for Data Set B right censored at 200. If you have not read far enough to appreciate this example, it is not important.

Begin by setting up a spreadsheet in which the parameters (alpha and theta) are in identifiable cells as is the objective function (lnL). In this example the parameters are in E1 and E2 and the objective function is in E3.[1]

⊠ Microsoft Excel - solver illustration.xls						
File Edit View Insert Format Tools Data Window Help						
E3 ▼ f_x =SUM(C2:C8)						
	A	B	C	D	E	F
1	x	"f(x)"	ln	alpha	1	
2	27	0.000973	-6.93476	theta	1000	
3	82	0.000921	-6.98976	lnL	-44.9125	
4	115	0.000891	-7.02276			
5	126	0.000882	-7.03376			
6	155	0.000856	-7.06276			
7	161	0.000851	-7.06876			
8	200	0.818731	-2.8			
9						
10						
11						
12						
13						

The formulas underlying this spreadsheet are given below.

---

[1] Screenshots reprinted by permission from Microsoft Corporation.

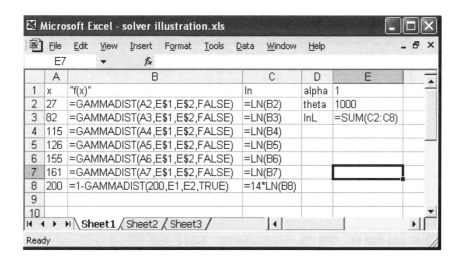

Note that trial values for alpha and theta have been entered (1 and 1,000). The better these guesses are, the higher the probability that Solver will succeed in finding the maximum. Selecting Solver from the Tools menu brings up the following dialog box:

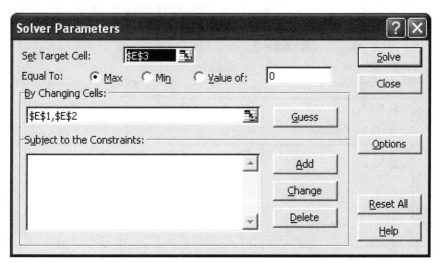

The target cell is the location of the objective function and the *By Changing Cells* box contains the location of the parameters. These cells need not be contiguous. It turns out that clicking on *Solve* will get the job done, but there are two additional items to think about. First, Solver allows for the imposition of constraints. They can be added by clicking on *Add* which brings up the following dialog box:

The constraint $\alpha \geq 0$ has been entered. Solver does not allow the constraint we really want, which is $\alpha > 0$. After entering a similar constraint for θ, the Solver dialog box looks like:

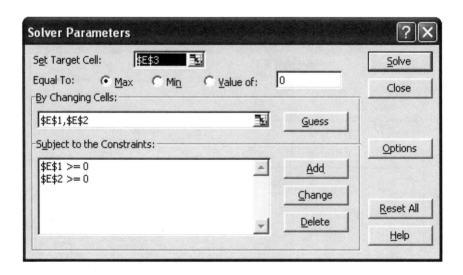

The reason adding the constraints is not needed here is that the solution Solver finds meets the constraints anyway. Clicking on *Options* brings up the following dialog box:

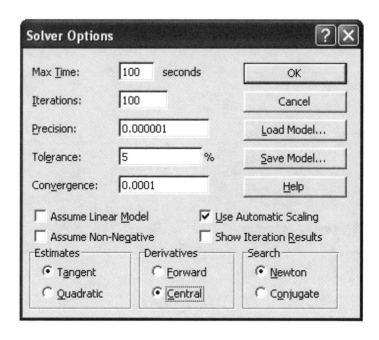

Two changes have been made from the default settings. The *Use Automatic Scaling* box has been checked. This improves performance when the parameters are on different scales (as is the case here). Also, *Central* approximate derivatives have been selected. Additional precision in the answer can be obtained by making the Precision, Tolerance, and Convergence numbers smaller. Clicking *OK* on the options box (no changes will be apparent in the Solver box) and then clicking *Solve* results in the following:

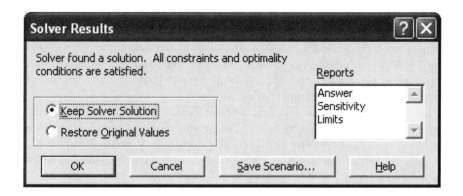

Clicking *OK* gives the answer.

	A	B	C	D	E	F	G
1	x	"f(x)"	ln	alpha	1.7022297		
2	27	0.00094832	-6.960818	theta	229.46973		
3	82	0.001627994	-6.420407	lnL	-43.648305		
4	115	0.0017879	-6.326713				
5	126	0.001817122	-6.310502				
6	155	0.001852132	-6.291418				
7	161	0.001853101	-6.290895				
8	200	0.697300093	-5.047552				
9							
10							

Microsoft Excel - solver illustration.xls

File Edit View Insert Format Tools Data Window Help

E7

Sheet1 / Sheet2 / Sheet3 /

Ready

Users of Solver (or any numerical analysis routine) should always be wary of the results. The program may announce a solution when the maximum has not been found, and it may give up when there is a maximum to be found. When the program gives up, it may be necessary to provide better starting values. To verify that an announced solution is legitimate (or at least is a local maximum), it is a good idea to check the function at nearby points to see that the values are indeed smaller.

F.2 THE SIMPLEX METHOD

The method (which is not related to the simplex method from operations research) was introduced for use with maximum likelihood estimation by Nelder and Mead in 1965 [98]. An excellent reference (and the source of the particular version presented here) is *Sequential Simplex Optimization* by Walters, Parker, Morgan, and Deming [134].

Let $\mathbf{x}$ be a $k \times 1$ vector and $f(\mathbf{x})$ be the function in question. The iterative step begins with $k+1$ vectors, $\mathbf{x}_1, \ldots, \mathbf{x}_{k+1}$, and the corresponding functional values, $f_1, \ldots, f_{k+1}$. At any iteration the points will be ordered so that $f_2 < \cdots < f_{k+1}$. When starting, also arrange for $f_1 < f_2$. Three of the points have names: $\mathbf{x}_1$ is called *worstpoint*, $\mathbf{x}_2$ is called *secondworstpoint*, and $\mathbf{x}_{k+1}$ is called *bestpoint*. It should be noted that after the first iteration these names may not perfectly describe the points. Now identify five new points. The first one, $\mathbf{y}_1$, is the center of $\mathbf{x}_2, \ldots, \mathbf{x}_{k+1}$, That is, $\mathbf{y}_1 = \sum_{j=2}^{k+1} \mathbf{x}_j / k$ and is called *midpoint*. The other four points are found as follows:

$$\begin{aligned}
\mathbf{y}_2 &= 2\mathbf{y}_1 - \mathbf{x}_1, & refpoint, \\
\mathbf{y}_3 &= 2\mathbf{y}_2 - \mathbf{x}_1, & doublepoint, \\
\mathbf{y}_4 &= (\mathbf{y}_1 + \mathbf{y}_2)/2, & halfpoint, \\
\mathbf{y}_5 &= (\mathbf{y}_1 + \mathbf{x}_1)/2, & centerpoint.
\end{aligned}$$

Then let $g_2, \ldots, g_5$ be the corresponding functional values, that is, $g_j = f(\mathbf{y}_j)$ (the value at $\mathbf{y}_1$ is never used). The key is to replace *worstpoint* ($\mathbf{x}_1$) with one of these points. The decision process proceeds as follows:

1. If $f_2 < g_2 < f_{k+1}$, then replace it with *refpoint*.

2. If $g_2 \geq f_{k+1}$ and $g_3 > f_{k+1}$, then replace it with *doublepoint*.

3. If $g_2 \geq f_{k+1}$ and $g_3 \leq f_{k+1}$, then replace it with *refpoint*.

4. If $f_1 < g_2 \leq f_2$, then replace it with *halfpoint*.

5. If $g_2 \leq f_1$, then replace it with *centerpoint*.

After the replacement has been made, the old *secondworstpoint* becomes the new *worstpoint*. The remaining k points are then ordered. The one with the smallest functional value becomes the new *secondworstpoint*, and the one with the largest functional value becomes the new *bestpoint*. In practice, there is no need to compute $\mathbf{y}_3$ and g_3 until you have reached step 2. Also note that at most one of the pairs $(\mathbf{y}_4, g_4)$ and $(\mathbf{y}_5, g_5)$ needs to be obtained, depending on which (if any) of the conditions in steps 4 and 5 hold.

Iterations continue until the set of $k + 1$ points becomes tightly packed. There are a variety of ways to measure that criterion. One example would be to calculate the standard deviations of each of the components and then average those values. Iterations can stop when a small enough value is obtained. Another option is to keep iterating until all $k + 1$ vectors agree to a specified number of significant digits.

F.3 USING EXCEL® TO SOLVE EQUATIONS

In addition to maximizing and minimizing functions of several variables, Solver can also solve equations. By choosing the *Value of:* radio button in the Solver dialog box, a value can be entered and then Solver will manipulate the *By Changing Cells* in order to set the contents of the *Target Cell* equal to that value. If there is more than one function, the constraints can be used to set them up. The following spreadsheet and Solver dialog box are set up to solve the two equations $x + y = 10$ and $x - y = 4$ with starting values $x = 8$ and $y = 5$ (to illustrate that the starting values do not have to be solutions to any of the equations).

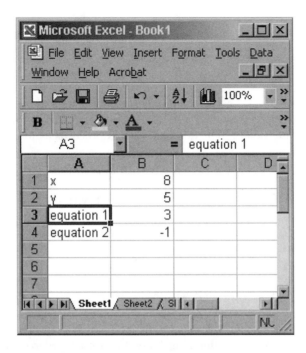

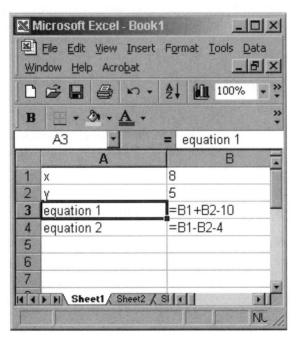

The Solver dialog box is:

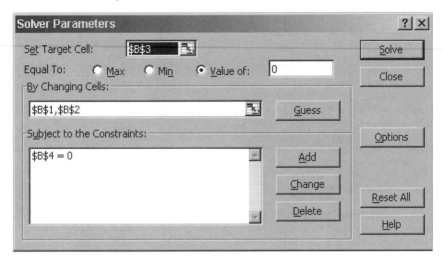

The solution is:

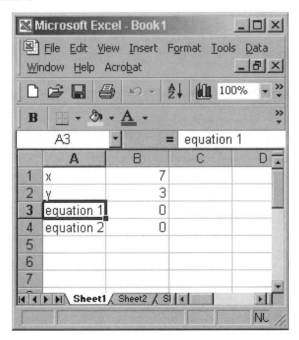

When there is only one equation with one unknown, the Goal Seek tool in Excel® is easier to use. It is on the Tools menu and is most always installed with the standard installation process. Suppose we want the solution of $xe^x = 10$. The following simple spreadsheet sets up the problem with a starting value of $x = 2$.

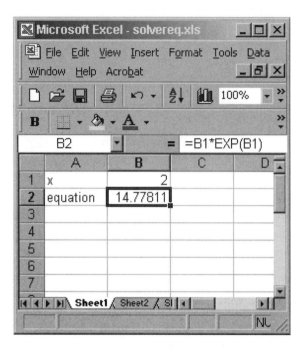

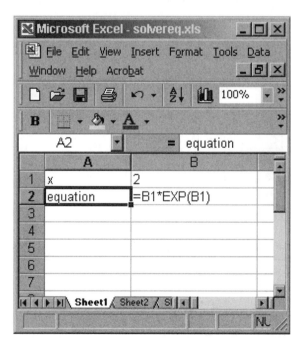

The Goal Seek dialog box is:

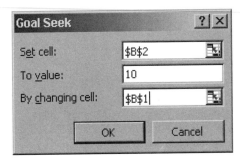

The solution is:

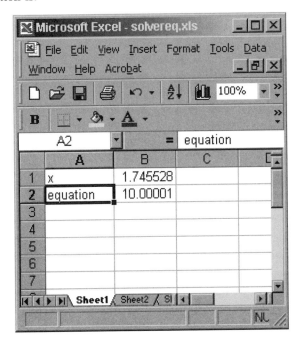

References

1. Aalen, O. (1978), "Nonparametric Inference for a Family of Counting Processes," *Annals of Statistics*, **6**, 701–726.

2. Abate, J., Choudhury, G., and Whitt, W. (2000), "An Introduction to Numerical Transform Inversion and Its Application to Probability Models," in W. Grassman, ed., *Computational Probability*, Boston: Kluwer.

3. Abramowitz, M. and Stegun, I. (1964), *Handbook of Mathematical Functions with Formulas, Graphs, and Mathematical Tables*, New York: Wiley.

4. Accomando, F. and Weissner, E. (1988), "Report Lag Distributions: Estimation and Application to IBNR Counts," in *Transcripts of the 1988 Casualty Loss Reserve Seminar*, Arlington, VA: Casualty Actuarial Society, 1038–1133.

5. Arnold, B. (1983), *Pareto Distributions (Statistical Distributions in Scientific Work)*, Vol. 5, Fairland, MD: International Co-operative Publishing House.

6. Bailey, A. (1942), "Sampling Theory in Casualty Insurance, Parts I and II," *Proceedings of the Casualty Actuarial Society*, **XXIX**, 50–95.

7. Bailey, A. (1943), "Sampling Theory in Casualty Insurance, Parts III through VII," *Proceedings of the Casualty Actuarial Society*, **XXX**, 31–65.

8. Bailey, A. (1950), "Credibility Procedures," *Proceedings of the Casualty Actuarial Society,* **XXXVII**, 7–23 and 94–115.

9. Bailey, W. (1992), "A Method for Determining Confidence Intervals for Trend," *Transactions of the Society of Actuaries,* **XLIV**, 11–54.

10. Baker, C. (1977), *The Numerical Treatment of Integral Equations,* Oxford: Clarendon Press.

11. Batten, R. (1978), *Mortality Table Construction,* Englewood Cliffs, NJ: Prentice-Hall.

12. Beard, R., Pentikainen, T., and Pesonen, E. (1984), *Risk Theory,* 3rd ed., London: Chapman & Hall.

13. Berger, J. (1985), *Bayesian Inference in Statistical Analysis,* 2nd ed., New York: Springer-Verlag.

14. Bertram, J. (1981), "Numerische Berechnumg von Gesamtschadenvertei-lungen," *Blätter der deutschen Gesellschaft Versicherungsmathematik,* B. **15.2**, 175–194.

15. Bevan, J. (1963), "Comprehensive Medical Insurance—Statistical Analysis for Ratemaking," *Proceedings of the Casualty Actuarial Society,* **L**, 111–128.

16. Bowers, N., Gerber, H., Hickman, J., Jones, D., and Nesbitt, C. (1986), *Actuarial Mathematics,* Schaumburg, IL: Society of Actuaries.

17. Brockett, P. (1991), "Information Theoretic Approach to Actuarial Science: A Unification and Extension of Relevant Theory and Applications," with discussion, *Transactions of the Society of Actuaries,* **XLIII**, 73–135.

18. Bühlmann, H. (1967), "Experience Rating and Credibility," *ASTIN Bulletin,* **4**, 199–207.

19. Bühlmann, H. (1970), *Mathematical Methods in Risk Theory,* New York: Springer-Verlag.

20. Bühlmann, H. and Straub, E. (1970), "Glaubwürdigkeit für Schadensätze (credibility for loss ratios)," *Mitteilungen der Vereinigung Schweizerischer Versicherungs-Mathematiker,* **70**, 111–133.

21. Carlin, B. and Klugman, S. (1993), "Hierarchical Bayesian Whitaker Graduation," *Scandinavian Actuarial Journal,* 183–196.

22. Carlin, B. and Louis, T. (2000), *Bayes and Empirical Bayes Methods for Data Analysis,* 2nd ed., Boca Raton, FL: CRC Press.

23. Carriere, J. (1993), "Nonparametric Estimators of a Distribution Function Based on Mixtures of Gamma Distributions," *Actuarial Research Clearing House*, **1993.3**, 1–11.

24. Casualty Actuarial Society (1990), *Foundations of Casualty Actuarial Science*, Arlington, VA: Casualty Actuarial Society.

25. deAlba, E. (2002), "Bayesian Estimation of Outstanding Claim Reserves," *North American Actuarial Journal*, **6**, 1–20.

26. DePril, N. (1986), "On the Exact Computation of the Aggregate Claims Distribution in the Individual Life Model," *ASTIN Bulletin*, **16**, 109–112.

27. DePril, N. (1988), "Improved Approximations for the Aggregate Claims Distribution of a Life Insurance Portfolio," *Scandinavian Actuarial Journal*, 61–68.

28. DePril, N. (1989), "The Aggregate Claim Distribution in the Individual Model with Arbitrary Positive Claims," *ASTIN Bulletin*, **19**, 9–24.

29. Douglas, J. (1980), *Analysis with Standard Contagious Distributions*, Fairland, MD: International Co-operative Publishing House.

30. Dropkin, L. (1959), "Some Considerations on Automobile Rating Systems Utilizing Individual Driving Records," *Proceedings of the Casualty Actuarial Society*, **XLVI**, 165–176.

31. Efron, B. (1981), "Censored Data and the Bootstrap," *Journal of the American Statistical Association*, **76**, 321–319.

32. Efron, B. (1986), "Why Isn't Everyone a Bayesian?" *The American Statistician*, **40**, 1–11 (including comments and reply).

33. Efron, B. and Tibshirani, R. (1993), *An Introduction to the Bootstrap*, New York: Chapman & Hall.

34. Ericson, W. (1969), "A Note on the Posterior Mean of a Population Mean," *Journal of the Royal Statistical Society, Series B*, **31**, 332–334.

35. Feller, W. (1968), *An Introduction to Probability Theory and Its Applications*, Vol. 1, 3rd ed. rev., New York: Wiley.

36. Feller, W. (1971), *An Introduction to Probability Theory and Its Applications*, Vol. 2, 2nd ed., New York: Wiley.

37. Fisher, A. (1915), "Note on the Application of Recent Mathematical-Statistical Methods to Coal Mine Accidents, with Special Reference to Catastrophes in Coal Mines in the United States," *Proceedings of the Casualty Actuarial Society*, **II**, 70–78.

38. Fisz, M. (1963), *Probability Theory and Mathematical Statistics*, New York: Wiley.

39. Frees, E., Carriere, J., and Valdez, E. (1996), "Annuity Valuation with Dependent Mortality," *Journal of Risk and Insurance*, **63**, 229–261.

40. Frees, E. and Valdez, E. (1998) "Understanding Relationships Using Copulas," *North American Actuarial Journal*, **2**, 1–25.

41. Genest, C. (1987), "Frank's Family of Bivariate Distributions," *Biometrika*, **74**, 549–555.

42. Genest, C. and McKay, J. (1986), "The Joy of Copulas: Bivariate Distributions with Uniform Marginals," *The American Statistician*, **40**, 280–283.

43. Gerber, H. (1982), "On the Numerical Evaluation of the Distribution of Aggregate Claims and Its Stop-Loss Premiums," *Insurance: Mathematics and Economics*, **1**, 13–18.

44. Gerber, H. and D. Jones (1976), "Some Practical Considerations in Connection with the Calculation of Stop-Loss Premiums," *Transactions of the Society of Actuaries*, **XXVIII**, 215–231.

45. Gillam, W. (1992), "Parametrizing the Workers Compensation Experience Rating Plan," *Proceedings of the Casualty Actuarial Society*, **LXXIX**, 21–56.

46. Goovaerts, M. J. and Hoogstad, W. J. (1987), *Credibility Theory, Surveys of Actuarial Studies No. 4*, Rotterdam: Nationale-Nederlanden.

47. Guiahi, F. (2001), "Fitting to Loss Distributions with Emphasis on Rating Variables," *CAS Forum*, **Winter 2001**, 133–174.

48. Hachemeister, C .A. (1975), "Credibility for Regression Models with Application to Trend," in P. Kahn, ed., *Credibility: Theory and Applications*, New York: Academic Press, 129–163.

49. Harwayne, F. (1959), "Merit Rating in Private Passenger Automobile Liability Insurance and the California Driver Record Study," *Proceedings of the Casualty Actuarial Society*, **XLVI**, 189–195.

50. Hayne, R. (1994), "Extended Service Contracts," *Proceedings of the Casualty Actuarial Society*, **LXXXI**, 243–302.

51. Heckman, P. and G. Meyers (1983), "The Calculation of Aggregate Loss Distributions from Claim Severity and Claim Count Distributions," *Proceedings of the Casualty Actuarial Society*, **LXX**, 22–61.

52. Herzog, T. (1999), *Introduction to Credibility Theory*, 3rd ed., Winsted, CT: ACTEX.

53. Herzog, T. and Lord, G. (2002), *Applications of Monte Carlo Methods to Finance and Insurance*, Winsted, CT: ACTEX.

54. Herzog, T. and Laverty, J. (1995), "Experience of Refinanced FHA Section 203(b) Single Family Mortages," *Actuarial Research Clearing House*, **1995.1**, 97–129.

55. Hewitt, C., Jr. (1967), "Loss Ratio Distributions—A Model," *Proceedings of the Casualty Actuarial Society*, **LIV**, 70–88.

56. Hewitt, C., Jr., and Lefkowitz, B. (1979), "Methods for Fitting Distributions to Insurance Loss Data," *Proceedings of the Casualty Actuarial Society*, **LXVI**, 139–160.

57. Hipp, G. (1938), "Special Funds Under the New York Workmen's Compensation Law," *Proceedings of the Casualty Actuarial Society*, **XXIV**, 247–275.

58. Hogg, R. and Craig, A. (1978), *Introduction to Mathematical Statistics*, 4th ed., New York: Macmillan.

59. Hogg, R. and Klugman, S. (1984), *Loss Distributions*, New York: Wiley.

60. Holgate, P. (1970), "The Modality of Some Compound Poisson Distributions," *Biometrika*, **57**, 666–667.

61. Holler, K., Sommer, D., and Trahair, G. (1999), "Something Old, Something New in Classification Ratemaking with a Novel Use of Generalized Linear Models for Credit Insurance," *CAS Forum*, **Winter 1999**, 31–84.

62. Hossack, I., Pollard, J., and Zehnwirth, B. (1983), *Introductory Statistics with Applications in General Insurance*, Cambridge: Cambridge University Press.

63. Hougaard, P. (2000), *Analysis of Multivariate Survival Data*, New York: Springer-Verlag.

64. Hutchinson, T. and Lai, C. (1990), *Continuous Bivariate Distributions, Emphasizing Applications*, Adelaide: Rumsby.

65. Hyndman, R. and Fan, Y. (1996), "Sample Quantiles in Statistical Packages," *The American Statistician*, **50**, 361–365.

66. Jewell, W. (1974), "Credibility Is Exact Bayesian for Exponential Families," *ASTIN Bulletin*, **8**, 77–90.

67. Johnson, N., Kotz, S., and Balakrishnan, N. (1994), *Continuous Univariate Distributions*, Vol. 1, 2nd ed., New York: Wiley.

68. Johnson, N., Kotz, S., and Balakrishnan, N. (1995), *Continuous Univariate Distributions*, Vol. 2, 2nd ed., New York: Wiley.

69. Johnson, N., Kotz, S., and Kemp, A. (1993), *Univariate Discrete Distributions*, 2nd ed., New York: Wiley.

70. Kaplan, E. and Meier, P. (1958), "Nonparametric Estimation from Incomplete Observations," *Journal of the American Statistical Association*, **53**, 457–481.

71. Karlin, S. and Taylor, H. (1975), *A First Course in Stochastic Processes*, 2nd ed., New York: Academic Press.

72. Karlin, S. and Taylor, H. (1981), *A Second Course in Stochastic Processes*, New York: Academic Press.

73. Kleiber, C. and Kotz, S. (2003), *Statistical Size Distributions in Economics and Actuarial Sciences*, New York: Wiley.

74. Klein, J. and Moeschberger, M. (1997), *Survival Analysis, Techniques for Censored and Truncated Data*, New York: Springer-Verlag.

75. Klugman, S. (1981), "On the Variance and Mean Squared Error of Decrement Estimators," *Transactions of the Society of Actuaries*, **XXXIII**, 301–311.

76. Klugman, S. (1987), "Credibility for Classification Ratemaking Via the Hierarchical Linear Model," *Proceedings of the Casualty Actuarial Society*, **LXXIV**, 272–321.

77. Klugman, S. (1992), *Bayesian Statistics in Actuarial Science with Emphasis on Credibility*, Boston: Kluwer.

78. Klugman, S. and Parsa, A. (1999), "Fitting Bivariate Distributions with Copulas," *Insurance: Mathematics and Economics*, **24**, 139–148.

79. Kornya, P. (1983), "Distribution of Aggregate Claims in the Individual Risk Model," *Transactions of the Society of Actuaries*, **XXXV**, 837–858.

80. Kotz, S., Balakrishnan, N., and Johnson, N. (2000), *Continuous Multivariate Distributions*, Vol. 1, Models and Applications, New York: Wiley.

81. Lawless, J. (2003), *Statistical Models and Methods for Lifetime Data*, 2nd ed., New York: Wiley.

82. Lemaire, J. (1995), *Automobile Insurance: Actuarial Models*, 2nd ed., Boston: Kluwer.

83. Lindley, D. (1987), "The Probability Approach to the Treatment of Uncertainty in Artificial Intelligence and Expert Systems," *Statistical Science*, **2**, 17–24 (also related articles in that issue).

84. London, D. (1985), *Graduation: The Revision of Estimates*, Winsted, CT: ACTEX.

85. London, D. (1988), *Survival Models and Their Estimation*, 3rd ed., Winsted, CT: ACTEX.

86. Longley-Cook, L. (1958), "The Employment of Property and Casualty Actuaries," *Proceedings of the Casualty Actuarial Society*, **XLV**, 9–10.

87. Longley-Cook, L. (1962), "An Introduction to Credibility Theory," *Proceeding of the Casualty Actuarial Society*, **XLIX**, 194–221.

88. Luong, A. and Doray, L. (1996), "Goodness of Fit Test Statistics for the Zeta Family," *Insurance: Mathematics and Economics*, **10**, 45–53.

89. Mardia, K. (1970), *Families of Bivariate Distributions*, London: Griffin.

90. McCullagh, P. and Nelder, J. (1989), *Generalized Linear Models*, New York: Chapman & Hall.

91. Meyers, G. (1984), "Empirical Bayesian Credibility for Workers' Compensation Classification Ratemaking," *Proceedings of the Casualty Actuarial Society*, **LXXI**, 96–121.

92. Meyers, G. (1994), "Quantifying the Uncertainty in Claim Severity Estimates for an Excess Layer When Using the Single Parameter Pareto," *Proceedings of the Casualty Actuarial Society*, **LXXXI**, 91–122 (including discussion).

93. Mildenhall, S. (1999), "A Systematic Relationship between Minimum Bias and Generalized Linear Models," *Proceedings of the Casualty Actuarial Society*, **LXXXVI**, 393–487.

94. Miller, M. (1949), *Elements of Graduation*, Philadelphia: The Actuarial Society of America and the American Institute of Actuaries.

95. Moore, D. (1986), "Tests of Chi-Squared Type," in D'Agostino, R. and Stephens, M., eds., *Goodness-of-Fit Techniques*, New York: Marcel Dekker, 63–95.

96. Mowbray, A. H. (1914), "How Extensive a Payroll Exposure Is Necessary to Give a Dependable Pure Premium?" *Proceedings of the Casualty Actuarial Society*, **I**, 24–30.

97. Murphy, K., Brockman, M., and Lee, P. (2000), "Using Generalized Linear Models to Build Dynamic Pricing Systems for Personal Lines Insurance," *CAS Forum*, **Winter 2000**, 107–140.

98. Nelder, J. and Mead, U. (1965), "A Simplex Method for Function Minimization," *The Computer Journal*, **7**, 308–313.

99. Nelson, W. (1972), "Theory and Applications of Hazard Plotting for Censored Failure Data," *Technometrics*, **14**, 945–965.

100. Norberg, R. (1979), "The Credibility Approach to Experience Rating," *Scandinavian Actuarial Journal*, 181–221.

101. Ntzoufras, I. and Dellaportas, P. (2002), "Bayesian Modeling of Oustanding Liabilities Incorporating Claim Count Uncertainty," *North American Actuarial Journal*, **6**, 113–128.

102. Patrik, G. (1980), "Estimating Casualty Insurance Loss Amount Distributions," *Proceedings of the Casualty Actuarial Society*, **LXVII**, 57–109.

103. Panjer, H. and Lutek, B. (1983), "Practical Aspects of Stop-Loss Calculations," *Insurance: Mathematics and Economics*, **2**, 159–177.

104. Panjer, H. and Wang, S. (1993), "On the Stability of Recursive Formulas," *ASTIN Bulletin*, **23**, 227–258.

105. Panjer, H. and Willmot, G. (1986), "Computational Aspects of Recursive Evaluation of Compound Distributions," *Insurance: Mathematics and Economics*, **5**, 113–116.

106. Panjer, H. and Willmot, G. (1992), *Insurance Risk Models*, Chicago: Society of Actuaries.

107. Press, W., Flannery, B., Teukolsky, S., and Vetterling, W. (1988), *Numerical Recipes in C*, Cambridge: Cambridge University Press.

108. Rao, C. (1965), *Linear Statistical Inference and Its Applications*, New York: Wiley.

109. Rioux, J. and Klugman S. (2003), "Toward a Unified Approach to Fitting Loss Models," working paper.

110. Ripley, B. (1987), *Stochastic Simulation*, New York: Wiley.

111. Robertson, J. (1992), "The Computation of Aggregate Loss Distributions," *Proceedings of the Casualty Actuarial Society*, **LXXIX**, 57–133.

112. Rohatgi, V. (1976), *An Introduction to Probability Theory and Mathematical Statistics*, New York: Wiley.

113. Rolski, T., Schmidli, H., Schmidt, V., and Teugels, J. (1999), *Stochastic Processes for Insurance and Finance*, Chichester: Wiley.

114. Ross, S. (1996), *Stochastic Processes*, 2nd ed., New York: Wiley.

115. Ross, S. (2002), *Simulation*, 3rd ed., San Diego: Academic Press.

116. Ross, S. (2003), *Introduction to Probability Models*, 8th ed., San Diego: Academic Press.

117. Schoenberg, I. (1964), "Spline Functions and the Problem of Graduation," *Proceedings of the National Academy of Science*, **52**, 947–950.

118. Scollnik, D. (2001), "Actuarial Modeling with MCMC and BUGS," *North American Actuarial Journal*, **5**, 96–124.

119. Scollnik, D. (2002), "Modeling Size-of-Loss Distributions for Exact Data in WinBUGS," *Journal of Actuarial Practice*, **10**, 193–218.

120. Self, S. and Liang, K. (1987), "Asymptotic Properties of Maximum Likelihood Estimators and Likelihood Ratio Tests Under Nonstandard Conditions," *Journal of the American Statistical Association*, **82**, 605–610.

121. Schwarz, G. (1978), "Estimating the Dimension of a Model," *Annals of Statistics*, **6**, 461–464.

122. Simon, L. (1961), "Fitting Negative Binomial Distributions by the Method of Maximum Likelihood," *Proceedings of the Casualty Actuarial Society*, **XLVIII**, 45–53.

123. Society of Actuaries Committee on Actuarial Principles (1992), "Principles of Actuarial Science," *Transactions of the Society of Actuaries*, **XLIV**, 565–628.

124. Society of Actuaries Committee on Actuarial Principles (1995), "Principles Regarding Provisions for Life Risks," *Transactions of the Society of Actuaries*, **XLVII**, 775–793.

125. Stephens, M. (1986), "Tests Based on EDF Statistics," in D'Agostino, R. and Stephens, M., eds., *Goodness-of-Fit Techniques*, New York: Marcel Dekker, 97–193.

126. Sundt, B. (1986), Special issue on credibility theory, *Insurance: Abstracts and Reviews*, **2**.

127. Sundt, B. (1999), *An Introduction to Non-Life Insurance Mathematics*, 4th ed., Mannheim: University of Mannheim Press.

128. Thyrion, P. (1961), "Contribution a l'Etude du Bonus pour non Sinstre en Assurance Automobile," *ASTIN Bulletin*, **1**, 142–162.

129. Tijms, H. (1994), *Stochastic Models—An Algorithmic Approach*, Chichester: Wiley.

130. Tröbliger, A. (1961), "Mathematische Untersuchungen zur Beitragsruckgewahr in der Kraftfahrversicherung," *Blatter der Deutsche Gesellschaft fur Versicherungsmathematik*, **5**, 327–348.

131. Tukey, J. (1962), "The future of data analysis," *Annals of Mathematical Statistics*, **33**, 1–67.

132. Venter, G. (1983), "Transformed Beta and Gamma Distributions and Aggregate Losses," *Proceedings of the Casualty Actuarial Society*, **LXX**, 156–193.

133. Verrall, R. (1990), "Bayes and Empirical Bayes Estimation for the Chain Ladder Method," *ASTIN Bulletin*, **20**, 217–243.

134. Walters, F., Parker, L., Morgan, S., and Deming, S. (1991), *Sequential Simplex Optimization*, Boca Raton, FL: CRC Press.

135. Waters, H. R. (1993), *Credibility Theory*, Edinburgh: Department of Actuarial Mathematics & Statistics, Heriot-Watt University.

136. Whitney, A.W. (1918), "The Theory of Experience Rating," *Proceedings of the Casualty Actuarial Society*, **IV**, 274–292.

137. Willmot, G. (1998), "On a Class of Approximations for Ruin and Waiting Time Probabilities," *Operations Research Letters*, **22**, 27–32.

Index

A

$(a, b, 0)$ class of distributions, 81, 644
$(a, b, 1)$ class of distributions, 83, 645
$(a, b, 1)$ class, estimation, 392
Accelerated failure time model, 414
Adjustment coefficient, 226
Aggregate loss distribution, 137
  approximating distribution, 159
  characteristic function, 142
  comparison of methods, 190
  compound geometric–exponential, 154
  compound negative
    binomial–exponential, 155
  direct calculation, 160
  distribution function, 140
  exponential severity, 154
  fast Fourier transform
    undiscretization, 178
  Heckman–Meyers, smoothing, 182
  individual risk model
    compound Poisson approximation, 201
    direct calculation, 195
    recursion, 197
  inversion method, 161, 184
    direct, 188
    fast Fourier transform, 185
    Heckman–Meyers, 188
  Laplace transform, 142

moment generating function, 142
moments, 142
probability generating function, 141
recursive formula, 161, 653
  undiscretization, 178
  compound frequency, 162
  computational issues, 165
  construction of arithmetic
    distributions, 167
  continuous severity, 166
  undiscretization, 657
recursive method, 161
severity closed under convolution, 156
simulation, 618
  smoothing, 181
Aggregate loss model, advantages, 136
Anderson–Darling test, 430
Asymptotically unbiased, 270
  maximum likelihood estimator, 352

B

Bayesian central limit theorem, 367
Bayesian estimation, 360
  Bayes estimate, 364
  Bayesian central limit theorem, 367
  credibility interval, 365
  highest posterior density (HPD)
    credibility set, 367
  improper prior distribution, 361

joint distribution, 362
loss function, 364
marginal distribution, 362
model distribution, 361
posterior distribution, 362
predictive distribution, 362, 545
prior distribution, 360
Beta distribution, 641
Beta function, incomplete, 629
Bias, 268
Binomial–beta distribution, 102
Binomial distribution, 79, 645
estimation, 389
Bivariate distribution, 402
Brownian motion, 252
relationship to ruin, 256
with drift, 253
Bühlmann credibility model, 557
Bühlmann-Straub credibility model, 560
Burr distribution, 632

C

Censoring
from above, 297
from below, 297
left, 297
right, 297
Central limit theorem, 36
Bayesian, 367
Central moment, 27
Characteristic function, 105
for aggregate loss, 142
Chi-square goodness-of-fit test, 432
Claim count random variable, 137
Closed under convolution, 156
Coefficient of variation, 27
Coinsurance, 126
Collective risk model, 135
Complete expectation of life, 29
Compound distribution
for aggregate loss, 141
frequency, 88
Compound frequency distribution, 648
estimation, 396
Compound geometric–exponential
distribution, 154
Compound Poisson frequency distribution,
95
Compound Poisson process, 225
Conditional distribution, 518
Confidence interval, 275, 309
log-transformed, 313–314
Conjugate prior distribution, 373
Consistency, 270
maximum likelihood estimator, 352
Construction of mortality tables, 322

Continuous random variable, 16
Continuous-time process, 210
Convolution, 140
numerical, 474
Copula, 403
Counting distributions, 72
Covariates
models with, 405
proportional hazards model, 406
Cox proportional hazards model, 407
Cramér's asymptotic ruin formula, 244
Credibility
Bühlmann credibility factor, 558
expected hypothetical mean, 557
expected process variance, 557
fully parametric, 590
greatest accuracy, 517, 542
Bayesian, 545
Bühlmann, 557
Bühlmann-Straub, 560
exact credibility, 566
fully parametric, 602
linear, 553
linear vs. Bayes, 569
log-credibility, 573
nonparametric, 592
semiparametric, 600
hypothetical mean, 557
limited fluctuation, 516, 530
full credibility, 532
partial credibility, 535
nonparametric, 590
partial, 535
process variance, 557
semiparametric, 590
variance of the hypothetical means, 557
Credibility factor, 535
Cubic spline, 489
Cumulative distribution function, 13
Cumulative hazard rate function, 289

D

Data-dependent distribution, 45, 284
Deductible
effect of inflation, 122
effect on frequency, 129
franchise, 118
ordinary, 116, 297
Delta method, 356
Density function, 17
Density function plot, 423
Difference plot, 424
Digamma function, 588
Discrete distribution, 72
Discrete Fourier transform, 185
Discrete random variable, 16

Discrete time process, 211, 215
Distribution
    (a, b, 0) class, 81, 644
    (a, b, 1) class, 83, 645
    aggregate loss, 137
    beta, 641
    binomial–beta, 102
    binomial, 79, 645
    bivariate, 402
    Burr, 632
    claim count, 137
    compound, 141
        moments, 142
    compound frequency, 88, 648
        recursive formula, 92
    compound Poisson frequency, 95
    conditional, 518
    conjugate prior, 373
    copula, 403
    counting distributions, 72
    data-dependent, 45, 284
    defective, 260
    discrete, 72
    empirical, 284
    exponential, 638
    exponential dispersion family, 581
    extended truncated negative binomial
        (ETNB), 87
    frailty, 62
    frequency, 137
    gamma, 48, 58, 636
    generalized beta, 640
    generalized Pareto, 631
    generalized Poisson–Pascal, 649
    generalized Waring, 103, 379
    geometric–ETNB, 649
    geometric–Poisson, 649
    geometric, 77, 644
    improper prior, 361
    individual loss, 137
    infinitely divisible, 104
    inverse Burr, 632
    inverse exponential, 638
    inverse gamma, 636
    inverse Gaussian, 48, 639
    inverse paralogistic, 635
    inverse Pareto, 633
    inverse transformed, 57
    inverse transformed gamma, 71, 635
    inverse Weibull, 58, 637
    joint, 362, 518
    k-point mixture, 43
    kernel smoothed, 284
    linear exponential family, 371
    logarithmic, 87, 646
    loglogistic, 66, 634
    lognormal, 59, 71, 638
    log-t, 639
    Makeham, 458
    marginal, 362, 518
    mixed frequency, 101
    mixture, 519
    mixture/mixing, 43, 59
    negative binomial, 76, 645
        as Poisson mixture, 78
        extended truncated, 87
    negative hypergeometric, 102
    Neyman Type A, 90, 649
    one-sided stable law, 261
    paralogistic, 634
    parametric, 41, 284
    parametric family, 42
    Pareto, 633
    Poisson–binomial, 648
    Poisson–inverse Gaussian, 650
    Poisson–Poisson, 90, 649
    Poisson–ETNB, 649
    Poisson–extended truncated negative
        binomial, 398
    Poisson–inverse Gaussian, 398
    Poisson–logarithmic, 94
    Poisson, 73, 644
    Polya–Aeppli, 649
    Polya–Eggenberger, 102
    posterior, 362
    predictive, 362, 545
    prior, 360
    scale, 41
    Sibuya, 88
    single parameter Pareto, 640
    spliced, 64
    tail weight, 48
    transformed, 57
    transformed beta, 66, 631
    transformed beta family, 69
    transformed gamma, 70, 635
    transformed gamma family, 69
    variable-component mixture, 44
    Waring, 103, 379
    Weibull, 58, 637
    Yule, 103, 379
    zero-modified, 85, 647
    zero-truncated, 85
    zero-truncated binomial, 647
    zero-truncated geometric, 646
    zero-truncated negative binomial, 647
    zero-truncated Poisson, 646
    zeta, 111, 451
Distribution function, 13
    empirical, 288
Distribution function plot, 421

E

Empirical Bayes estimation, 589
Empirical distribution, 284
Empirical distribution function, 288
Empirical model, 27
Estimate
  interval, 309
  Nelson–Aalen, 290
Estimation
  $(a, b, 1)$ class, 392
  Bayesian, 360
  binomial distribution, 389
  compound frequency distributions, 396
  credibility interval, 365
  effect of exposure, 398
  empirical Bayes, 589
  maximum likelihood, 337
  multiple decrement tables, 324
  negative binomial, 386
  point, 266
  Poisson distribution, 383
Estimator
  asymptotically unbiased, 270
  Bayes estimate, 364
  bias, 268
  confidence interval, 275
  consistency, 270
  interval, 275
  Kaplan–Meier, 299
  kernel density, 316
  mean-squared error, 271
  method of moments, 332
  percentile matching, 333
  relative efficiency, 275
  smoothed empirical percentile, 333
  unbiased, 268
  uniformly minimum variance unbiased,
    272
Exact credibility, 567
Excess loss variable, 29
Expectation, conditional, 520
Exponential distribution, 638
Exposure base, 108
Exposure, effect in estimation, 398
Extrapolation, using splines, 504

F

Failure rate, 20
Fast Fourier transform, 186
Fisher's information, 352
Force of mortality, 20
Fourier transform, 185
Frailty model, 62
Franchise deductible, 118
Frequency, 137

effect of deductible, 129
interaction with severity, 651
Frequency/severity interaction, 174
Full credibility, 532
Function
  characteristic, 105
  cumulative hazard rate, 289
  density, 17
  empirical distribution, 288
  force of mortality, 20
  gamma, 58, 630
  hazard rate, 20
  incomplete beta, 629
  incomplete gamma, 58, 627
  likelihood, 338
  loglikelihood, 339
  loss, 364
  probability, 19, 73
  probability density, 17
  probability generating, 73
  survival, 16

G

Gamma distribution, 58, 636
Gamma function, 58, 630
  incomplete, 627
Gamma kernel, 318
Generalized beta distribution, 640
Generalized linear model, 413
Generalized Pareto distribution, 631
Generalized Poisson–Pascal distribution,
    649
Generalized Waring distribution, 103, 379
Generating function
  moment, 36
  probability, 36
Geometric–ETNB distribution, 649
Geometric–Poisson distribution, 649
Geometric distribution, 77, 644
Greatest accuracy credibility, 517, 542
Greenwood's approximation, 311

H

Hazard rate, 20
  cumulative, 289
  tail weight, 50
Heckman-Meyers formula, 188
Histogram, 293
Hypothesis tests, 277, 427
  Anderson–Darling, 430
  chi-square goodness-of-fit, 432
  Kolmogorov–Smirnov, 428
  likelihood ratio test, 436, 442
  p-value, 280
  significance level, 278
  uniformly most powerful, 279

Hypothetical mean, 557

I

Incomplete beta function, 629
Incomplete gamma function, 58, 627
Independent increments, 210, 224
Individual loss distribution, 137
Individual risk model, 136, 192
  moments, 193
    direct calculation, 195
    recursion, 197
Infinitely divisible distribution, 104
Inflation
  effect of, 122
  effect of limit, 124
Information, 352
  observed, 355
Information matrix, 353
Interpolation
  modified osculatory, 505
  polynomial, 485
Interval estimator, 275
Inverse Burr distribution, 632
Inverse exponential distribution, 638
Inverse gamma distribution, 636
Inverse Gaussian distribution, 48, 639
Inverse paralogistic distribution, 635
Inverse Pareto distribution, 633
Inverse transformed distribution, 57
Inverse transformed gamma distribution,
  71, 635
Inverse Weibull distribution, 58, 637
Inversion method for aggregate loss
    calculations, 161, 184
Joint distribution, 518

K

k-point mixture distribution, 43
Kaplan–Meier estimator, 299
  large data sets, 322
  variance, 311
Kernel density estimator, 316
  gamma kernel, 318
  triangular kernel, 318
  uniform kernel, 318
Kernel smoothed distribution, 284
Kolmogorov–Smirnov test, 428
Kurtosis, 27

L

Laplace transform
  for aggregate loss, 142
Large data sets, 322
Left censored and shifted variable, 30
Left censoring, 297
Left truncated and shifted variable, 29

Left truncation, 297
Likelihood function, 338
Likelihood ratio test, 436, 442
Limit
  effect of inflation, 124
  policy, 298
Limited expected value, 30
Limited fluctuation credibility, 516, 530
  partial, 535
Limited loss variable, 30
Linear exponential family, 371
Log-t distribution, 639
Log-transformed confidence interval,
  313–314
Logarithmic distribution, 87, 646
Loglikelihood fuction, 339
Loglogistic distribution, 66, 634
Lognormal distribution, 59, 71, 638
Loss elimination ratio, 121
Loss function, 364
Lundberg's inequality, 230

M

Makeham distribution, 458
Marginal distribution, 362, 518
Markov process, 215
Maximization, 660
  simplex method, 664
Maximum aggregate loss, 239
Maximum covered loss, 126
Maximum likelihood estimation, 337
  binomial, 390
  inverse Gaussian, 350
  negative binomial, 387
  Poisson, 384
    variance, 385
  trucation and censoring, 341
Maximum likelihood estimator
  consistency, 352
  unbiased, 352
Mean, 25
Mean excess loss, 29
Mean residual life, 29
  tail weight, 50
Mean squared error, 271
Mean, conditional, 520
Median, 34
Method of moments, 332
Mixed frequency distributions, 101
Mixed random variable, 16
Mixture distribution, 519
Mixture/mixing distribution, 43, 59
Mode, 23
Model
  collective risk, 135
  empirical, 27

individual risk, 136
Model selection, 3
    graphical comparison, 421
    Schwarz Bayesian criterion, 443
Modeling, advantages, 5
Modeling process, 3
Moment, 25
Moment generating function, 36
    for aggregate loss, 142
Moment
    individual risk model, 193
    factorial, 643
    limited expected value, 30
    of aggregate loss distribution, 142
Mortality table construction, 322
Multiple decrement tables, 324

N

Negative binomial distribution, 76, 645
    as compound Poisson–logarithmic, 94
    as Poisson mixture, 78
    estimation, 386
Negative hypergeometric distribution, 102
Nelson–Aalen estimate, 290
Neyman Type A distribution, 90, 649
Noninformative prior distribution, 361

O

Observed information, 355
Ogive, 293
Ordinary deductible, 116, 297
Osculatory interpolation, 505

P

p-value, 280
Paralogistic distribution, 634
Parameter, 3
    scale, 41
Parametric distribution, 41, 284
Parametric distribution family, 42
Pareto distribution, 633
Parsimony, 440
Partial credibility, 535
Percentile, 34
Percentile matching, 333
Plot
    density function, 423
    difference, 424
    distribution funtion, 421
Point estimation, 266
Poisson–binomial distribution, 648
Poisson–ETNB distribution, 398, 649
Poisson–inverse Gaussian distribution, 398,
        650
Poisson–logarithmic distribution, 94
Poisson distribution, 73, 644

estimation, 383
Poisson process, 223
Policy limit, 124, 298
Polya–Aeppli distribution, 649
Polya–Eggenberger distribution, 102
Polynomial interpolation, 485
Polynomial, collocation, 485
Posterior distribution, 362
Predictive distribution, 362, 545
Prior distribution, noninformative or
        vague, 361
Probability density function, 17
Probability function, 19, 73
Probability generating function, 36, 73
    for aggregate loss, 141
Probability mass function, 19
Process variance, 557
Process
    Brownian motion, 252
    compound Poisson, 225
    continuous time, 210
    discrete time, 211, 215
    independent increments, 210, 224
    Markov, 215
    Poisson, 223
    stationary increments, 211, 224
    surplus, 212
    Weiner, 253
    white noise, 253
Product–limit estimator, 299
    large data sets, 322
    variance, 311
Proportional hazards model, 406
Pseudorandom variables, 612
Pure premium, 515

R

Random variable
    central moment, 27
    coefficient of variation, 27
    continuous, 16
    discrete, 16
    excess loss, 29
    kurtosis, 27
    left censored and shifted, 30
    left truncated and shifted, 29
    limited expected value, 30
    limited loss, 30
    mean, 25
    mean excess loss, 29
    mean residual life, 29
    median, 34
    mixed, 16
    mode, 23
    moment, 25
    percentile, 34

right censored, 31
skewness, 27
standard deviation, 27
support, 16
variance, 27
Recursive formula, 653
aggregate loss distribution, 161
continuous severity distribution, 655
for compound freqency, 92
Recursive method for aggregate loss
calculations, 161
Relative efficiency, 275
Relative security loading, 225
Right censored variable, 31
Right censoring, 297
Right truncation, 297
Risk model
collective, 135
individual, 136, 192
Risk set, 289, 298
Ruin
asymptotic, 244
continuous time, finite horizon, 214
continuous time, infinite horizon, 213
discrete time, finite horizon, 214
discrete time, infinite horizon, 214
evaluation by convolution, 216
evaluation by inversion, 219
Lundberg's inequality, 230
Tijms' approximation, 244–245
time to, as inverse Gaussian, 260
time to, as one-sided stable law, 261
using Brownian motion, 256
Ruin theory, 209

S

Scale distribution, 41
Scale parameter, 41
Schwarz Bayesian criterion, 443
Security loading, relative, 225
Severity, interaction with frequency, 651
Severity/frequency interaction, 174
Sibuya distribution, 88
Significance level, 278
Simplex method, 664
Simulation, 611
aggregate loss calculations, 618
Single-parameter Pareto distribution, 640
Skewness, 27
Smoothed empirical percentile estimate,
333
Smoothing splines, 505
Solver, 660
Spliced distribution, 64
Splines
cubic, 489

extraplation, 504
smoothing, 505
Standard deviation, 27
Stationary increments, 211, 224
Stop-loss insurance, 145
Support, 16
Surplus process, 212
maximum aggregate loss, 239
Survival function, 16

T

Tail weight, 48
Tijms' approximation, 244–245
Transformed beta distribution, 66, 631
Transformed beta family, 69
Transformed distribution, 57
Transformed gamma distribution, 70, 635
Transformed gamma family, 69
Triangular kernel, 318
Trigamma function, 588
Truncation
from above, 297
from below, 297
left, 297
right, 297

U

Unbiased, 4, 268
maximum likelihood estimator, 352
Uniform kernel, 318
Uniformly minimum variance unbiased
estimator (UMVUE), 272
Uniformly most powerful test, 279

V

Vague prior distribution, 361
Variable-component mixture, 44
Variance, 27, 522
conditional, 521
delta method, 356
Greenwood's approximation, 311
product-limit estimator, 311

W

Waring distribution, 103, 379
Weibull distribution, 48, 58, 637
Weiner process, 253
White noise process, 253

Y

Yule distribution, 103, 379

Z

Zero-modified distribution, 85, 647
Zero-truncated binomial distribution, 647

Zero-truncated distribution, 85

Zero-truncated geometric distribution, 646

Zero-truncated negative binomial
  distribution, 647
Zero-truncated Poisson distribution, 646
Zeta distribution, 451

WILEY SERIES IN PROBABILITY AND STATISTICS

ESTABLISHED BY WALTER A. SHEWHART AND SAMUEL S. WILKS

Editors: *David J. Balding, Noel A. C. Cressie, Nicholas I. Fisher,*
Iain M. Johnstone, J. B. Kadane, Geert Molenberghs. Louise M. Ryan,
David W. Scott, Adrian F. M. Smith, Jozef L. Teugels
Editors Emeriti: *Vic Barnett, J. Stuart Hunter, David G. Kendall*

The *Wiley Series in Probability and Statistics* is well established and authoritative. It covers many topics of current research interest in both pure and applied statistics and probability theory. Written by leading statisticians and institutions, the titles span both state-of-the-art developments in the field and classical methods.

Reflecting the wide range of current research in statistics, the series encompasses applied, methodological and theoretical statistics, ranging from applications and new techniques made possible by advances in computerized practice to rigorous treatment of theoretical approaches.

This series provides essential and invaluable reading for all statisticians, whether in academia, industry, government, or research.

ABRAHAM and LEDOLTER · Statistical Methods for Forecasting
AGRESTI · Analysis of Ordinal Categorical Data
AGRESTI · An Introduction to Categorical Data Analysis
AGRESTI · Categorical Data Analysis, *Second Edition*
ALTMAN, GILL, and McDONALD · Numerical Issues in Statistical Computing for the
    Social Scientist
AMARATUNGA and CABRERA · Exploration and Analysis of DNA Microarray and
    Protein Array Data
ANDĚL · Mathematics of Chance
ANDERSON · An Introduction to Multivariate Statistical Analysis, *Third Edition*
*ANDERSON · The Statistical Analysis of Time Series
ANDERSON, AUQUIER, HAUCK, OAKES, VANDAELE, and WEISBERG ·
    Statistical Methods for Comparative Studies
ANDERSON and LOYNES · The Teaching of Practical Statistics
ARMITAGE and DAVID (editors) · Advances in Biometry
ARNOLD, BALAKRISHNAN, and NAGARAJA · Records
*ARTHANARI and DODGE · Mathematical Programming in Statistics
*BAILEY · The Elements of Stochastic Processes with Applications to the Natural
    Sciences
BALAKRISHNAN and KOUTRAS · Runs and Scans with Applications
BARNETT · Comparative Statistical Inference, *Third Edition*
BARNETT and LEWIS · Outliers in Statistical Data, *Third Edition*
BARTOSZYNSKI and NIEWIADOMSKA-BUGAJ · Probability and Statistical Inference
BASILEVSKY · Statistical Factor Analysis and Related Methods: Theory and
    Applications
BASU and RIGDON · Statistical Methods for the Reliability of Repairable Systems
BATES and WATTS · Nonlinear Regression Analysis and Its Applications
BECHHOFER, SANTNER, and GOLDSMAN · Design and Analysis of Experiments for
    Statistical Selection, Screening, and Multiple Comparisons
BELSLEY · Conditioning Diagnostics: Collinearity and Weak Data in Regression

*Now available in a lower priced paperback edition in the Wiley Classics Library.

*BELSLEY, KUH, and WELSCH · Regression Diagnostics: Identifying Influential Data and Sources of Collinearity

BENDAT and PIERSOL · Random Data: Analysis and Measurement Procedures, *Third Edition*

BERRY, CHALONER, and GEWEKE · Bayesian Analysis in Statistics and Econometrics: Essays in Honor of Arnold Zellner

BERNARDO and SMITH · Bayesian Theory

BHAT and MILLER · Elements of Applied Stochastic Processes, *Third Edition*

BHATTACHARYA and WAYMIRE · Stochastic Processes with Applications

BILLINGSLEY · Convergence of Probability Measures, *Second Edition*

BILLINGSLEY · Probability and Measure, *Third Edition*

BIRKES and DODGE · Alternative Methods of Regression

BLISCHKE AND MURTHY (editors) · Case Studies in Reliability and Maintenance

BLISCHKE AND MURTHY · Reliability: Modeling, Prediction, and Optimization

BLOOMFIELD · Fourier Analysis of Time Series: An Introduction, *Second Edition*

BOLLEN · Structural Equations with Latent Variables

BOROVKOV · Ergodicity and Stability of Stochastic Processes

BOULEAU · Numerical Methods for Stochastic Processes

BOX · Bayesian Inference in Statistical Analysis

BOX · R. A. Fisher, the Life of a Scientist

BOX and DRAPER · Empirical Model-Building and Response Surfaces

*BOX and DRAPER · Evolutionary Operation: A Statistical Method for Process Improvement

BOX, HUNTER, and HUNTER · Statistics for Experimenters: An Introduction to Design, Data Analysis, and Model Building

BOX and LUCEÑO · Statistical Control by Monitoring and Feedback Adjustment

BRANDIMARTE · Numerical Methods in Finance: A MATLAB-Based Introduction

BROWN and HOLLANDER · Statistics: A Biomedical Introduction

BRUNNER, DOMHOF, and LANGER · Nonparametric Analysis of Longitudinal Data in Factorial Experiments

BUCKLEW · Large Deviation Techniques in Decision, Simulation, and Estimation

CAIROLI and DALANG · Sequential Stochastic Optimization

CASTILLO, HADI, BALAKRISHNAN, and SARABIA · Extreme Value and Related Models with Applications in Engineering and Science

CHAN · Time Series: Applications to Finance

CHATTERJEE and HADI · Sensitivity Analysis in Linear Regression

CHATTERJEE and PRICE · Regression Analysis by Example, *Third Edition*

CHERNICK · Bootstrap Methods: A Practitioner's Guide

CHERNICK and FRIIS · Introductory Biostatistics for the Health Sciences

CHILÈS and DELFINER · Geostatistics: Modeling Spatial Uncertainty

CHOW and LIU · Design and Analysis of Clinical Trials: Concepts and Methodologies, *Second Edition*

CLARKE and DISNEY · Probability and Random Processes: A First Course with Applications, *Second Edition*

*COCHRAN and COX · Experimental Designs, *Second Edition*

CONGDON · Applied Bayesian Modelling

CONGDON · Bayesian Statistical Modelling

CONOVER · Practical Nonparametric Statistics, *Third Edition*

COOK · Regression Graphics

COOK and WEISBERG · Applied Regression Including Computing and Graphics

COOK and WEISBERG · An Introduction to Regression Graphics

CORNELL · Experiments with Mixtures, Designs, Models, and the Analysis of Mixture Data, *Third Edition*

*Now available in a lower priced paperback edition in the Wiley Classics Library.

COVER and THOMAS · Elements of Information Theory

COX · A Handbook of Introductory Statistical Methods

*COX · Planning of Experiments

CRESSIE · Statistics for Spatial Data, *Revised Edition*

CSÖRGŐ and HORVÁTH · Limit Theorems in Change Point Analysis

DANIEL · Applications of Statistics to Industrial Experimentation

DANIEL · Biostatistics: A Foundation for Analysis in the Health Sciences, *Eighth Edition*

*DANIEL · Fitting Equations to Data: Computer Analysis of Multifactor Data,
Second Edition

DASU and JOHNSON · Exploratory Data Mining and Data Cleaning

DAVID and NAGARAJA · Order Statistics, *Third Edition*

*DEGROOT, FIENBERG, and KADANE · Statistics and the Law

DEL CASTILLO · Statistical Process Adjustment for Quality Control

DeMARIS · Regression with Social Data: Modeling Continuous and Limited Response
Variables

DEMIDENKO · Mixed Models: Theory and Applications

DENISON, HOLMES, MALLICK and SMITH · Bayesian Methods for Nonlinear
Classification and Regression

DETTE and STUDDEN · The Theory of Canonical Moments with Applications in
Statistics, Probability, and Analysis

DEY and MUKERJEE · Fractional Factorial Plans

DILLON and GOLDSTEIN · Multivariate Analysis: Methods and Applications

DODGE · Alternative Methods of Regression

*DODGE and ROMIG · Sampling Inspection Tables, *Second Edition*

*DOOB · Stochastic Processes

DOWDY, WEARDEN, and CHILKO · Statistics for Research, *Third Edition*

DRAPER and SMITH · Applied Regression Analysis, *Third Edition*

DRYDEN and MARDIA · Statistical Shape Analysis

DUDEWICZ and MISHRA · Modern Mathematical Statistics

DUNN and CLARK · Basic Statistics: A Primer for the Biomedical Sciences,
Third Edition

DUPUIS and ELLIS · A Weak Convergence Approach to the Theory of Large Deviations

*ELANDT-JOHNSON and JOHNSON · Survival Models and Data Analysis

ENDERS · Applied Econometric Time Series

ETHIER and KURTZ · Markov Processes: Characterization and Convergence

EVANS, HASTINGS, and PEACOCK · Statistical Distributions, *Third Edition*

FELLER · An Introduction to Probability Theory and Its Applications, Volume I,
Third Edition, Revised; Volume II, *Second Edition*

FISHER and VAN BELLE · Biostatistics: A Methodology for the Health Sciences

FITZMAURICE, LAIRD, and WARE · Applied Longitudinal Analysis

*FLEISS · The Design and Analysis of Clinical Experiments

FLEISS · Statistical Methods for Rates and Proportions, *Third Edition*

FLEMING and HARRINGTON · Counting Processes and Survival Analysis

FULLER · Introduction to Statistical Time Series, *Second Edition*

FULLER · Measurement Error Models

GALLANT · Nonlinear Statistical Models

GHOSH, MUKHOPADHYAY, and SEN · Sequential Estimation

GIESBRECHT and GUMPERTZ · Planning, Construction, and Statistical Analysis of
Comparative Experiments

GIFI · Nonlinear Multivariate Analysis

GLASSERMAN and YAO · Monotone Structure in Discrete-Event Systems

GNANADESIKAN · Methods for Statistical Data Analysis of Multivariate Observations,
Second Edition

*Now available in a lower priced paperback edition in the Wiley Classics Library.

GOLDSTEIN and LEWIS · Assessment: Problems, Development, and Statistical Issues

GREENWOOD and NIKULIN · A Guide to Chi-Squared Testing

GROSS and HARRIS · Fundamentals of Queueing Theory, *Third Edition*

*HAHN and SHAPIRO · Statistical Models in Engineering

HAHN and MEEKER · Statistical Intervals: A Guide for Practitioners

HALD · A History of Probability and Statistics and their Applications Before 1750

HALD · A History of Mathematical Statistics from 1750 to 1930

HAMPEL · Robust Statistics: The Approach Based on Influence Functions

HANNAN and DEISTLER · The Statistical Theory of Linear Systems

HEIBERGER · Computation for the Analysis of Designed Experiments

HEDAYAT and SINHA · Design and Inference in Finite Population Sampling

HELLER · MACSYMA for Statisticians

HINKELMAN and KEMPTHORNE: · Design and Analysis of Experiments, Volume 1: Introduction to Experimental Design

HOAGLIN, MOSTELLER, and TUKEY · Exploratory Approach to Analysis of Variance

HOAGLIN, MOSTELLER, and TUKEY · Exploring Data Tables, Trends and Shapes

*HOAGLIN, MOSTELLER, and TUKEY · Understanding Robust and Exploratory Data Analysis

HOCHBERG and TAMHANE · Multiple Comparison Procedures

HOCKING · Methods and Applications of Linear Models: Regression and the Analysis of Variance, *Second Edition*

HOEL · Introduction to Mathematical Statistics, *Fifth Edition*

HOGG and KLUGMAN · Loss Distributions

HOLLANDER and WOLFE · Nonparametric Statistical Methods, *Second Edition*

HOSMER and LEMESHOW · Applied Logistic Regression, *Second Edition*

HOSMER and LEMESHOW · Applied Survival Analysis: Regression Modeling of Time to Event Data

HUBER · Robust Statistics

HUBERTY · Applied Discriminant Analysis

HUNT and KENNEDY · Financial Derivatives in Theory and Practice

HUSKOVA, BERAN, and DUPAC · Collected Works of Jaroslav Hajek— with Commentary

HUZURBAZAR · Flowgraph Models for Multistate Time-to-Event Data

IMAN and CONOVER · A Modern Approach to Statistics

JACKSON · A User's Guide to Principle Components

JOHN · Statistical Methods in Engineering and Quality Assurance

JOHNSON · Multivariate Statistical Simulation

JOHNSON and BALAKRISHNAN · Advances in the Theory and Practice of Statistics: A Volume in Honor of Samuel Kotz

JOHNSON and BHATTACHARYYA · Statistics: Principles and Methods, *Fifth Edition*

JOHNSON and KOTZ · Distributions in Statistics

JOHNSON and KOTZ (editors) · Leading Personalities in Statistical Sciences: From the Seventeenth Century to the Present

JOHNSON, KOTZ, and BALAKRISHNAN · Continuous Univariate Distributions, Volume 1, *Second Edition*

JOHNSON, KOTZ, and BALAKRISHNAN · Continuous Univariate Distributions, Volume 2, *Second Edition*

JOHNSON, KOTZ, and BALAKRISHNAN · Discrete Multivariate Distributions

JOHNSON, KOTZ, and KEMP · Univariate Discrete Distributions, *Second Edition*

JUDGE, GRIFFITHS, HILL, LÜTKEPOHL, and LEE · The Theory and Practice of Econometrics, *Second Edition*

JUREČKOVÁ and SEN · Robust Statistical Procedures: Aymptotics and Interrelations

*Now available in a lower priced paperback edition in the Wiley Classics Library.

JUREK and MASON · Operator-Limit Distributions in Probability Theory

KADANE · Bayesian Methods and Ethics in a Clinical Trial Design

KADANE AND SCHUM · A Probabilistic Analysis of the Sacco and Vanzetti Evidence

KALBFLEISCH and PRENTICE · The Statistical Analysis of Failure Time Data, *Second Edition*

KASS and VOS · Geometrical Foundations of Asymptotic Inference

KAUFMAN and ROUSSEEUW · Finding Groups in Data: An Introduction to Cluster Analysis

KEDEM and FOKIANOS · Regression Models for Time Series Analysis

KENDALL, BARDEN, CARNE, and LE · Shape and Shape Theory

KHURI · Advanced Calculus with Applications in Statistics, *Second Edition*

KHURI, MATHEW, and SINHA · Statistical Tests for Mixed Linear Models

*KISH · Statistical Design for Research

KLEIBER and KOTZ · Statistical Size Distributions in Economics and Actuarial Sciences

KLUGMAN, PANJER, and WILLMOT · Loss Models: From Data to Decisions, *Second Edition*

KLUGMAN, PANJER, and WILLMOT · Solutions Manual to Accompany Loss Models: From Data to Decisions, *Second Edition*

KOTZ, BALAKRISHNAN, and JOHNSON · Continuous Multivariate Distributions, Volume 1, *Second Edition*

KOTZ and JOHNSON (editors) · Encyclopedia of Statistical Sciences: Volumes 1 to 9 with Index

KOTZ and JOHNSON (editors) · Encyclopedia of Statistical Sciences: Supplement Volume

KOTZ, READ, and BANKS (editors) · Encyclopedia of Statistical Sciences: Update Volume 1

KOTZ, READ, and BANKS (editors) · Encyclopedia of Statistical Sciences: Update Volume 2

KOVALENKO, KUZNETZOV, and PEGG · Mathematical Theory of Reliability of Time-Dependent Systems with Practical Applications

LACHIN · Biostatistical Methods: The Assessment of Relative Risks

LAD · Operational Subjective Statistical Methods: A Mathematical, Philosophical, and Historical Introduction

LAMPERTI · Probability: A Survey of the Mathematical Theory, *Second Edition*

LANGE, RYAN, BILLARD, BRILLINGER, CONQUEST, and GREENHOUSE · Case Studies in Biometry

LARSON · Introduction to Probability Theory and Statistical Inference, *Third Edition*

LAWLESS · Statistical Models and Methods for Lifetime Data, *Second Edition*

LAWSON · Statistical Methods in Spatial Epidemiology

LE · Applied Categorical Data Analysis

LE · Applied Survival Analysis

LEE and WANG · Statistical Methods for Survival Data Analysis, *Third Edition*

LePAGE and BILLARD · Exploring the Limits of Bootstrap

LEYLAND and GOLDSTEIN (editors) · Multilevel Modelling of Health Statistics

LIAO · Statistical Group Comparison

LINDVALL · Lectures on the Coupling Method

LINHART and ZUCCHINI · Model Selection

LITTLE and RUBIN · Statistical Analysis with Missing Data, *Second Edition*

LLOYD · The Statistical Analysis of Categorical Data

MAGNUS and NEUDECKER · Matrix Differential Calculus with Applications in Statistics and Econometrics, *Revised Edition*

MALLER and ZHOU · Survival Analysis with Long Term Survivors

MALLOWS · Design, Data, and Analysis by Some Friends of Cuthbert Daniel

MANN, SCHAFER, and SINGPURWALLA · Methods for Statistical Analysis of Reliability and Life Data

*Now available in a lower priced paperback edition in the Wiley Classics Library.

MANTON, WOODBURY, and TOLLEY · Statistical Applications Using Fuzzy Sets

MARCHETTE · Random Graphs for Statistical Pattern Recognition

MARDIA and JUPP · Directional Statistics

MASON, GUNST, and HESS · Statistical Design and Analysis of Experiments with Applications to Engineering and Science, *Second Edition*

McCULLOCH and SEARLE · Generalized, Linear, and Mixed Models

McFADDEN · Management of Data in Clinical Trials

*McLACHLAN · Discriminant Analysis and Statistical Pattern Recognition

McLACHLAN, DO, and AMBROISE · Analyzing Microarray Gene Expression Data

McLACHLAN and KRISHNAN · The EM Algorithm and Extensions

McLACHLAN and PEEL · Finite Mixture Models

McNEIL · Epidemiological Research Methods

MEEKER and ESCOBAR · Statistical Methods for Reliability Data

MEERSCHAERT and SCHEFFLER · Limit Distributions for Sums of Independent Random Vectors: Heavy Tails in Theory and Practice

MICKEY, DUNN, and CLARK · Applied Statistics: Analysis of Variance and Regression, *Third Edition*

*MILLER · Survival Analysis, *Second Edition*

MONTGOMERY, PECK, and VINING · Introduction to Linear Regression Analysis, *Third Edition*

MORGENTHALER and TUKEY · Configural Polysampling: A Route to Practical Robustness

MUIRHEAD · Aspects of Multivariate Statistical Theory

MULLER and STOYAN · Comparison Methods for Stochastic Models and Risks

MURRAY · X-STAT 2.0 Statistical Experimentation, Design Data Analysis, and Nonlinear Optimization

MURTHY, XIE, and JIANG · Weibull Models

MYERS and MONTGOMERY · Response Surface Methodology: Process and Product Optimization Using Designed Experiments, *Second Edition*

MYERS, MONTGOMERY, and VINING · Generalized Linear Models. With Applications in Engineering and the Sciences

*NELSON · Accelerated Testing, Statistical Models, Test Plans, and Data Analyses

NELSON · Applied Life Data Analysis

NEWMAN · Biostatistical Methods in Epidemiology

OCHI · Applied Probability and Stochastic Processes in Engineering and Physical Sciences

OKABE, BOOTS, SUGIHARA, and CHIU · Spatial Tesselations: Concepts and Applications of Voronoi Diagrams, *Second Edition*

OLIVER and SMITH · Influence Diagrams, Belief Nets and Decision Analysis

PALTA · Quantitative Methods in Population Health: Extensions of Ordinary Regressions

PANKRATZ · Forecasting with Dynamic Regression Models

PANKRATZ · Forecasting with Univariate Box-Jenkins Models: Concepts and Cases

*PARZEN · Modern Probability Theory and Its Applications

PEÑA, TIAO, and TSAY · A Course in Time Series Analysis

PIANTADOSI · Clinical Trials: A Methodologic Perspective

PORT · Theoretical Probability for Applications

POURAHMADI · Foundations of Time Series Analysis and Prediction Theory

PRESS · Bayesian Statistics: Principles, Models, and Applications

PRESS · Subjective and Objective Bayesian Statistics, *Second Edition*

PRESS and TANUR · The Subjectivity of Scientists and the Bayesian Approach

PUKELSHEIM · Optimal Experimental Design

PURI, VILAPLANA, and WERTZ · New Perspectives in Theoretical and Applied Statistics

PUTERMAN · Markov Decision Processes: Discrete Stochastic Dynamic Programming

*RAO · Linear Statistical Inference and Its Applications, *Second Edition*

*Now available in a lower priced paperback edition in the Wiley Classics Library.

RAUSAND and HØYLAND · System Reliability Theory: Models, Statistical Methods, and Applications, *Second Edition*

RENCHER · Linear Models in Statistics

RENCHER · Methods of Multivariate Analysis, *Second Edition*

RENCHER · Multivariate Statistical Inference with Applications

*RIPLEY · Spatial Statistics

RIPLEY · Stochastic Simulation

ROBINSON · Practical Strategies for Experimenting

ROHATGI and SALEH · An Introduction to Probability and Statistics, *Second Edition*

ROLSKI, SCHMIDLI, SCHMIDT, and TEUGELS · Stochastic Processes for Insurance and Finance

ROSENBERGER and LACHIN · Randomization in Clinical Trials: Theory and Practice

ROSS · Introduction to Probability and Statistics for Engineers and Scientists

ROUSSEEUW and LEROY · Robust Regression and Outlier Detection

RUBIN · Multiple Imputation for Nonresponse in Surveys

RUBINSTEIN · Simulation and the Monte Carlo Method

RUBINSTEIN and MELAMED · Modern Simulation and Modeling

RYAN · Modern Regression Methods

RYAN · Statistical Methods for Quality Improvement, *Second Edition*

SALTELLI, CHAN, and SCOTT (editors) · Sensitivity Analysis

*SCHEFFE · The Analysis of Variance

SCHIMEK · Smoothing and Regression: Approaches, Computation, and Application

SCHOTT · Matrix Analysis for Statistics

SCHOUTENS · Levy Processes in Finance: Pricing Financial Derivatives

SCHUSS · Theory and Applications of Stochastic Differential Equations

SCOTT · Multivariate Density Estimation: Theory, Practice, and Visualization

*SEARLE · Linear Models

SEARLE · Linear Models for Unbalanced Data

SEARLE · Matrix Algebra Useful for Statistics

SEARLE, CASELLA, and McCULLOCH · Variance Components

SEARLE and WILLETT · Matrix Algebra for Applied Economics

SEBER and LEE · Linear Regression Analysis, *Second Edition*

*SEBER · Multivariate Observations

SEBER and WILD · Nonlinear Regression

SENNOTT · Stochastic Dynamic Programming and the Control of Queueing Systems

*SERFLING · Approximation Theorems of Mathematical Statistics

SHAFER and VOVK · Probability and Finance: It's Only a Game!

SILVAPULLE and SEN · Constrained Statistical Inference: Order, Inequality and Shape Constraints

SMALL and McLEISH · Hilbert Space Methods in Probability and Statistical Inference

SRIVASTAVA · Methods of Multivariate Statistics

STAPLETON · Linear Statistical Models

STAUDTE and SHEATHER · Robust Estimation and Testing

STOYAN, KENDALL, and MECKE · Stochastic Geometry and Its Applications, *Second Edition*

STOYAN and STOYAN · Fractals, Random Shapes and Point Fields: Methods of Geometrical Statistics

STYAN · The Collected Papers of T. W. Anderson: 1943–1985

SUTTON, ABRAMS, JONES, SHELDON, and SONG · Methods for Meta-Analysis in Medical Research

TANAKA · Time Series Analysis: Nonstationary and Noninvertible Distribution Theory

THOMPSON · Empirical Model Building

THOMPSON · Sampling, *Second Edition*

THOMPSON · Simulation: A Modeler's Approach

THOMPSON and SEBER · Adaptive Sampling

THOMPSON, WILLIAMS, and FINDLAY · Models for Investors in Real World Markets

TIAO, BISGAARD, HILL, PEÑA, and STIGLER (editors) · Box on Quality and Discovery: with Design, Control, and Robustness

TIERNEY · LISP-STAT: An Object-Oriented Environment for Statistical Computing and Dynamic Graphics

TSAY · Analysis of Financial Time Series

UPTON and FINGLETON · Spatial Data Analysis by Example, Volume II: Categorical and Directional Data

VAN BELLE · Statistical Rules of Thumb

VAN BELLE, FISHER, HEAGERTY, and LUMLEY · Biostatistics: A Methodology for the Health Sciences, *Second Edition*

VESTRUP · The Theory of Measures and Integration

VIDAKOVIC · Statistical Modeling by Wavelets

VINOD and REAGLE · Preparing for the Worst: Incorporating Downside Risk in Stock Market Investments

WALLER and GOTWAY · Applied Spatial Statistics for Public Health Data

WEERAHANDI · Generalized Inference in Repeated Measures: Exact Methods in MANOVA and Mixed Models

WEISBERG · Applied Linear Regression, *Third Edition*

WELSH · Aspects of Statistical Inference

WESTFALL and YOUNG · Resampling-Based Multiple Testing: Examples and Methods for p-Value Adjustment

WHITTAKER · Graphical Models in Applied Multivariate Statistics

WINKER · Optimization Heuristics in Economics: Applications of Threshold Accepting

WONNACOTT and WONNACOTT · Econometrics, *Second Edition*

WOODING · Planning Pharmaceutical Clinical Trials: Basic Statistical Principles

WOODWORTH · Biostatistics

WOOLSON and CLARKE · Statistical Methods for the Analysis of Biomedical Data, *Second Edition*

WU and HAMADA · Experiments: Planning, Analysis, and Parameter Design Optimization

YANG · The Construction Theory of Denumerable Markov Processes

*ZELLNER · An Introduction to Bayesian Inference in Econometrics

ZHOU, OBUCHOWSKI, and McCLISH · Statistical Methods in Diagnostic Medicine

*Now available in a lower priced paperback edition in the Wiley Classics Library.